RETHINKING MIGRATIONS IN LATE PREHISTORIC EURASIA

For over 100 years the *Proceedings of the British Academy* series has provided a unique record of British scholarship in the humanities and social sciences. These themed volumes drive scholarship forward and are landmarks in their field. For more information about the series and guidance on submitting a proposal for publication, please visit www.thebritishacademy.ac.uk/proceedings.

PROCEEDINGS OF THE BRITISH ACADEMY • 254

RETHINKING MIGRATIONS IN LATE PREHISTORIC EURASIA

Edited by
MANUEL FERNÁNDEZ-GÖTZ,
COURTNEY NIMURA,
PHILIPP W. STOCKHAMMER,
AND RACHEL CARTWRIGHT

Published for THE BRITISH ACADEMY
by OXFORD UNIVERSITY PRESS

Oxford University Press, Great Clarendon Street, Oxford OX2 6DP

© The British Academy 2023

Database right The British Academy (maker)

First edition published in 2023

All rights reserved. No part of this publication may be reproduced, stored in a retrieval system, or transmitted, in any form or by any means, without the prior permission in writing of the British Academy, or as expressly permitted by law, by licence or under terms agreed with the appropriate reprographics rights organisation. Enquiries concerning reproduction outside the scope of the above should be sent to the Publications Department, The British Academy, 10–11 Carlton House Terrace London SW1Y 5AH

You must not circulate this book in any other form and you must impose this same condition on any acquirer

British Library Cataloguing in Publication Data
Data available

Library of Congress Cataloging in Publication Data
Data available

Typeset by Newgen Publishing UK
Pod

ISBN 978-0-19-726735-6
ISSN 0068-1202

Contents

List of Figures	vii
List of Tables	xi
Notes on Editors	xii
Notes on Contributors	xiii

1   Rethinking Migrations in Late Prehistoric Eurasia: An Introduction   1
MANUEL FERNÁNDEZ-GÖTZ, COURTNEY NIMURA,
PHILIPP W. STOCKHAMMER, AND RACHEL CARTWRIGHT

2   Comparing Apples and Oranges? Confronting Social Science
and Natural Science Approaches to Migration in Archaeology   21
MAJA GORI AND AYDIN ABAR

3   The Mobility and Migration Revolution in 3rd Millennium BC Europe   41
VOLKER HEYD

4   Bell Beaker Mobility: Marriage, Migration, and Mortality   63
ANDREW P. FITZPATRICK

5   Bronze Age Travellers   89
KRISTIAN KRISTIANSEN

6   Andronovo Mobility Revisited: New Research on Bronze Age
Mining and Metallurgical Communities in Central Asia   110
THOMAS STÖLLNER, HANDE ÖZYARKENT, AND ANTON GONTSCHAROV

7   Rethinking Material Culture Markers for Mobility and Migration
in the Globalising European Later Bronze Age: A Comparative
View from the Po Valley and Pannonian Plain   142
BARRY MOLLOY, CAROLINE BRUYÈRE, AND DRAGAN JOVANOVIĆ

8   Mobility at the Onset of the Bronze Age: A Bioarchaeological
Perspective   170
PHILIPP W. STOCKHAMMER AND KEN MASSY

vi *Contents*

9   Marriage, Motherhood, and Mobility in Bronze and Iron
Age Central Europe   189
KATHARINA REBAY-SALISBURY

10 Migration in Archaeological Discourse: Two Case Studies
from the Late Bronze and Early Iron Ages   209
CAROLA METZNER-NEBELSICK

11 The Scale of Population Movements: A Model for Later Prehistory   234
PETER S. WELLS

12 Alpine Connections: Iron Age Mobility in the Po Valley and the
Circum-Alpine Regions   258
VERONICA CICOLANI AND LORENZO ZAMBONI

13 Mobility and Migration in Bronze and Iron Age Britain:
The COMMIOS Project   280
IAN ARMIT

14 Migration and Ethnic Dynamics in the Lower Rhine Frontier
Zone of the Expanding Roman Empire (60 BC–AD 20):
A Historical-Anthropological Perspective   292
NICO ROYMANS AND DIEDERICK HABERMEHL

15 On the Move: Relating Past and Present Human Mobility   313
COURTNEY NIMURA, RACHEL CARTWRIGHT, PHILIPP W.
STOCKHAMMER, AND MANUEL FERNÁNDEZ-GÖTZ

Index   330

List of Figures

1.1	Participants at the Edinburgh conference	2
1.2	Fragments of Roman *militaria* from the Hoogeloon villa settlement	5
1.3	Tilly's classification of migration ideal types	6
1.4	Cover of Kossinna's book *Das Weichselland. Ein uralter Heimatboden der Germanen* ('The Vistula Land. An Ancestral Homeland of the Germans'), first published in 1919	9
1.5	Diagram of a migratory process, including some possible push and pull factors	11
2.1	Manhattan's Mulberry Street around 1900	23
2.2	Map drawn by Gimbutas to illustrate her Kurgan people invasion model	33
3.1	East to west regions of 3rd millennium BC transformations and their interrelations	42
3.2	29th/28th century BC earliest Corded Ware radiocarbon dates across Europe	46
3.3	Examples of early Corded Ware Beakers compared with Budzhak, Romanian, and Bulgarian Yamnaya Beakers	47
3.4	26th/25th-century BC early Bell Beakers in the Upper Rhine region and beyond	51
3.5	Scheme of 26th/25th-century BC early Bell Beaker transformations and their interrelations along the Rhine River	53
4.1	The extent of the Bell Beaker network and selected contemporary groups	66
4.2	Radiocarbon dates of inhumations found in the Humanejos settlement, Spain	67
4.3	Burial of the older, *c.* 8-year-old, child found at Samborzec, Poland	69
4.4	Burial of a woman found at Tišice, grave 77/99, Czech Republic, accompanied by both female and male 'gendered objects'	72
4.5	Double grave (tomb 1) with successive, not simultaneous, burials found at Humanejos	74
4.6	Collective grave of the Boscombe Bowmen, Boscombe Down, England	78
5.1	Map showing local chiefly networks and metal workshops from the Alps to Denmark during the period 1500–1300 BC	92
5.2	Model of dynamics between trade hubs, chiefly workshops/networks, and confederations	101
6.1	Andronovo phenomenon – distribution of different cultural units within Central Asia	111

viii *List of Figures*

6.2 East Kazakhstan, Delbegetey (Askaraly) Mountains: Bronze
Age sites in the surroundings of tin mines   113

6.3 East Kazakhstan, Delbegetey (Askaraly) Mountains: cemetery,
Chernogorka/Mastau Baj I, grave 2   117

6.4 Plot for the Sr isotope and Sr elemental abundance measured on the
animals from Askaraly, and human (miner/metallurgist) 87Sr/86Sr
investigation on different teeth and bones from two Andronovo grave
structures   120

6.5 Askaraly: oxygen and carbon isotope values from the cow sample
MB105 and the sheep sample MB209   122

6.6 Distribution of the isotope results performed on the bone collagen of
animals and humans   124

6.7 A combined map of oxygen isotope modelled values from
Terzer *et al.* 2013, Akhishev. Iron Age sites, nomadic pasture massifs
of 1926–30 with summer and winter camps   125

6.8 Central, south, and east Kazakhstan and its mining and metallurgical
evidence of the later Bronze Age (2nd millennium BC)   127

6.9 Nurataldy I, objects from metal deposition near grave 2   129

6.10 Lead isotope ratio of ore samples from Nurataldy I, hoard of Sejma
tradition   131

7.1 Distribution of Middle to Recent Bronze Age settlements in the
Po Valley indicating relative chronology and duration of occupation   148

7.2 Horizontal channels with hanging garland motif on vessels
from Ilandža (1 and 2) graves 10 and 1, and Casinalbo (3) grave 127   151

7.3 Urns from (1) Casinalbo, grave 29 and (2) Budjak Livade, grave 23   151

7.4 Map of currently known Tisza Site Group settlements in the south
Pannonian Plain indicating relative chronology and other
surrounding Late Bronze Age settlements   153

7.5 Photo of face motif on ceramic vessel of Dubovac-Žuto Brdo type
and sword of Sauerbrunn-Boiu type, both dated to *c.* 1500–1300 BC
and from the Carpathian Basin   156

7.6 Aerial view of A) Castel del Tartaro Terramare and B) Sakule TSG
settlement   158

7.7 Illustration of some general similarities between ceramic forms and
decoration from (1–3, 8–9) Gradište Iđoš in the Pannonian Plain
(Belegiš II) and (4–7, 10–11) Casalmoro in the Po Valley
(Final Bronze Age)   159

8.1 Relief map of the study area south of present-day Augsburg showing
cemeteries of the Final Neolithic to early Middle Bronze Age in the
Lech Valley   172

8.2 Chronology of the 3rd and early 2nd millennia BC in the Lech Valley
modelled on the basis of radiocarbon dated grave finds   174

8.3 Scatter plot of $\delta^{18}O_p$ and $^{87}Sr/^{86}Sr$ isotope ratios of subadult and
adult male individuals and adult female individuals from the
Lech Valley   177

List of Figures

ix

8.4	$^{87}Sr/^{86}Sr$ isotope ratios for individuals with multiple sampled teeth	177
8.5	Biological pedigrees reconstructed for Bell Beaker complex and Early Bronze Age	179
9.1	Burial of a 12–14-year-old girl with sheet bronze band indicating a head covering, from Franzhausen I	196
9.2	Situla from Montebelluna, grave 244	198
10.1	Distribution of the inhumation single graves and cemeteries of the pre-Scythian Mezőcsát group of mobile pastoralists, and the adjacent middle Danubian Urnfield culture	216
10.2	Pottery vessels from the cremation cemeteries of the Kyjatice group from Szajla, north-eastern Hungary and Radzovce, Slovakia, and their equivalents from inhumation graves of the Mezőcsát group	218
10.3	Examples of pottery 'imports' in Mezőcsát graves, possibly produced by non-local women	219
10.4	Inventories of Late Urnfield period cremation graves from A) the Salzburg area (Obereching, grave 21); B–C) Lower Bavaria (B: Künzing, grave 23; C: Kelheim, grave 184)	225
11.1	Map showing locations of places mentioned in the text	236
11.2	Scene in Jackson Heights, Queens, New York	241
11.3	View of the site of Marzabotto on the Reno River in the Apennine Mountains of Italy	245
11.4	Etruscan bronze jug and basin, together with an Attic Greek cup, from the rich burial at Vix in eastern France	249
12.1	Map of Iron Age north-western Italy (major sites and the three cultural regions addressed), with main Alpine passes and distribution of Golasecca-type objects north of the Alps	261
12.2	Chrono-typological scheme of the main Golasecca-type clothing items	266
12.3	Spatial analysis, quantitative and percentage distribution of Golasecca and Hallstatt ornaments across the Alps, showing the ratios of both local and foreign materials within each site	267
12.4	Shortest-path model of connectivity networks in the north-west Alpine area, including alternative connections, as shown by the quantitative analysis of contexts and distribution of Golasecca objects	269
12.5	Main settlements in Southern Piedmont and distribution of decorated coral fibulae: an example of local production and variants of Golasecca-type objects	270
13.1	Map showing distribution of sites in mainland Europe from which samples were obtained for the Patterson *et al.* 2022 study	283
13.2	Map showing distribution of sites in Britain from which samples were obtained for the Patterson *et al.* 2022 study	285
14.1	Tribal map of the Lower Germanic frontier zone in the conquest and post-conquest period, showing considerable discontinuity	297

14.2	Different variants of long houses encountered in the Batavian river area in the Early Roman period	299
14.3	Assemblage of northern-style pottery from the house ditch of a first-generation farmhouse at Tiel-Medel (*c.* 30–1 BC)	300
14.4	Distribution of bronze Nemausus I coins, widely used by the Roman army for payment of soldiers during the Germanic campaigns of Drusus (12–9 BC)	305
14.5	Model of the formation of the *Batavi* in the Lower Rhine frontier zone according to historical data and archaeological evidence. Internal political structure of the Batavian client tribe in the Augustan period	309
15.1	Swedish immigrants in Rush City, Minnesota, in 1887	318
15.2	Archaeogenetic analysis in the clean room	324

List of Tables

5.1	Different types of Bronze Age travellers, distances covered, and institutional frameworks	96
6.1	Askaraly II, Mastau Baj/Chernogorka, stone circle 2, anthropological and archaeological data	117
6.2	East Kazakhstan, Delbegetey (Askaraly) Mountains: species composition of the faunal remains found in the settlement of Mastau Baj I	118
6.3	Central Kazakhstan, hoard of Nurataldy: elemental concentrations from various copper-based alloys	130
6.4	Central Kazakhstan, hoard of Nurataldy: Pb isotope data	131
7.1	Indicators of how the movement of people may bias understanding of purpose and character towards the terms mobility or migration	144
11.1	Estimate of population figures	248
14.1	List of historically documented migrations of tribal (sub)groups in the Lower Germanic frontier	296
14.2	Overview of metal parts of 1st-century AD Roman military equipment and horse gear from (partially) excavated rural settlements in the Batavian river area	304
14.3	Specification of origin in inscriptions by Batavian individuals	307

Notes on Editors

Manuel Fernández-Götz is Abercromby Professor of Archaeology at the University of Edinburgh. His main research interests are Iron Age and Roman societies in Europe, the archaeology of identities, and conflict archaeology. He has authored over 200 publications and directed fieldwork projects in Spain, Germany, the United Kingdom, and Croatia. His research has been recognised with the award of the Philip Leverhulme Prize and the Royal Society of Edinburgh's Thomas Reid Medal. He is currently directing the Leverhulme-funded project 'Beyond Walls: Reassessing Iron Age and Roman Encounters in Northern Britain'.

Courtney Nimura is the Curator of Later European Prehistory at the Ashmolean Museum of Art and Archaeology and Research Fellow at Wolfson College, University of Oxford. She completed her PhD at the University of Reading in 2013, and since then has worked on and led several research projects on topics such as Bronze Age Northern European rock art, Iron Age art and coins, and later prehistoric rivers in Britain. Her research focuses on rock art and portable art in Europe; Bronze Age and Iron Age archaeology in Northern, Central, and Western Europe; coastal and intertidal archaeology; effects of environmental change on art production; and the intersections of archaeological and anthropological theory in prehistoric art studies.

Philipp W. Stockhammer is Professor of Prehistoric Archaeology, with a focus on the Eastern Mediterranean, at the Ludwig-Maximilians-University Munich (LMU) and Co-director of the Max Planck-Harvard Research Center for the Archaeoscience of the Ancient Mediterranean at the Max Planck Institute for Evolutionary Anthropology, Leipzig. After his PhD in Heidelberg in 2008, he worked as a Postdoctoral Researcher and Lecturer at the Universities of Heidelberg and Basel. He leads several collaborative research projects on the Bronze and Early Iron Ages in Europe and the Eastern Mediterranean, among them an ERC Starting Grant (2015) and an ERC Consolidator Grant (2020). His research focuses on intercultural encounters, social practices, bioarchaeology, mobility, food, and health.

Rachel Cartwright is a PhD candidate in the Department of Anthropology at the University of Minnesota. Previously, she studied Archaeology, History, and Classics at the University of Texas at Austin and Durham University. Her research is centred on the Viking Age migrations in the North Atlantic, with a particular focus on Iceland and northern Scotland. She has carried out fieldwork in the United States, the United Kingdom, Portugal, Spain, and Croatia.

Notes on Contributors

Aydin Abar wrote his doctoral thesis at the Ruhr University of Bochum on village life during the 3rd millennium BC in the south-east Arabian Peninsula. He is currently a Lecturer at the same institution. His primary research interest is related to approaches to prehistoric labour with traceological methods, as well as Late Iron Age rural religious practices, and the history of ideas within archaeology. His regional foci are the Italian Alps and the Iranian highlands.

Ian Armit is Chair in Archaeology at the University of York. His research centres on the cultural archaeology of the European Late Bronze and Iron Ages, the role of conflict and violence in non-state societies, funerary archaeology, and the demographic and genetic prehistory of European populations. He has directed fieldwork projects in Scotland, France, and Sicily, and has worked extensively in southeast Europe. He currently directs the European Research Council (ERC)-funded COMMIOS project examining the bioarchaeology of Iron Age Britain and the near Continent.

Caroline Bruyère is a PhD student at the School of Archaeology at University College Dublin and a Fellow on the ERC-funded 'The Fall of 1200 BC' project. She specialises in European Bronze Age archaeology with a current focus on the Balkans and the Mediterranean. Her particular interests include material culture studies, mobility, social organisation and crises, and resource management. With a background in archaeometallurgy, her current work combines pedestrian survey to evaluate settlement dynamics in Late Bronze Age settlements with archaeometry to investigate periods of social change and crisis in the Balkans and the Pannonian Plain.

Veronica Cicolani is a Researcher at the CNRS French Institute, AOrOc UMR8546 CNRS-PSL. As an archaeologist and specialist of European protohistory, her research focuses on technological and cultural interactions between the Italic and Celtic worlds and on Italic craftsmen's practices. Recent publications include the monograph *Passeurs des Alpes. La culture de Golasecca entre Méditerranée et Europe continentale à l'âge du Fer* (2017) and the edited volume *Monnaies et archéologie en Europe celtique. Mélanges en l'honneur de Katherine Gruel* (2018).

Andrew P. Fitzpatrick is an Archaeological Consultant and Honorary Research Professor at Leicester University. He has published widely on the European Iron Age, including migration, and he led the teams that excavated the Bell Beaker burials of the Amesbury Archer and the Boscombe Bowmen. The discovery that these men were migrants from the Continent helped rekindle interest in the UK in Bell Beakers and the importance of mobility in the later 3rd millennium BC.

Anton Gontscharov is a Researcher at the Deutsches Bergbau-Museum and in the Ruhr University of Bochum Institute of Archaeological Studies. His research focuses on the archaeology of Bronze Age Central Asia where he collaborated in various research projects in the Russian Federation and in Kazakhstan. In 2019 he successfully defended his PhD thesis on *Metal of Bronze Age Cultures from Central and East Kasakhstan: Production, Provenance, Distribution. An Archaeological and Archaeometrical Investigation.*

Maja Gori holds a PhD in Pre- and Protohistory and Aegean Archaeology from the University of Heidelberg in *cotutelle de thèse* with the University of Paris 1 Sorbonne Panthéon. Since 2018 she has had a permanent position as a Researcher at the Italian National Research Council. Prior to this, she worked as a Postdoctoral Researcher at the Ruhr University of Bochum, the University of Heidelberg, the University of Amsterdam, and the University of Mainz. Gori specialises in pre-historic archaeology with a focus on the Balkans and the Central Mediterranean. Her interests include large-scale mobility patterns and cultural transmission, arch-aeological theory, archaeological discourses in present-day identity building, and political uses of archaeology.

Diederick Habermehl works as a Postdoctoral Researcher, Archaeologist, and Lecturer at the Vrije Universiteit Amsterdam. He was involved in several large-scale excavation projects in the Dutch Lower Rhine area. His PhD thesis focused on the development of Roman period villa settlements in the Roman North, and was published as a book entitled *Settling in a Changing World: Villa Development in the Northern Provinces of the Roman Empire* (2013).

Volker Heyd is Professor at the University of Helsinki in Finland, where he has been working since 2018. Previously, he worked as a Heritage Manager in Germany and at the University of Bristol (UK). Volker is a prehistoric archaeologist, currently dedicating himself to topics around human mobility, migrations, identity, and eth-nicity. He also promotes scientific applications in archaeology, particularly ancient DNA, stable isotopes, and biomarker lipids. Volker has authored/edited nine books and published around 100 articles, spanning from the Early Neolithic in Anatolia to the Iron Age in Central Europe. Currently, he leads as Principal Investigator the ERC-Advanced project 'The Yamnaya Impact on Prehistoric Europe' (2019–2023).

Dragan Jovanović completed his BA in 2003 and his MA in 2009. In 2004 he was appointed as a Prehistoric Archaeologist to the City Museum in Vršac, Serbia. He has published a book on Late Bronze Age hoarding in the south-east Pannonian Plain and authored several articles and international presentations on metalwork

Notes on Contributors XV

and settlements. He is currently completing his PhD thesis on the social context of hoarding in the Late Bronze Age south Carpathian Basin at Kopar University, Slovenia. His research interests combine material culture studies and settlement archaeology of the Middle Bronze Age to Early Iron Age in the Carpathian Basin and the Balkans in order to explore long-term patterns of social change.

Kristian Kristiansen is Professor of Archaeology at the University of Gothenburg and Affiliated Professor at the University of Copenhagen. His research covers a broad spectrum of archaeological themes from heritage and the role of the past in the present, to comparative global prehistory, mainly focused on Western Eurasia during the Neolithic and Bronze Age. Throughout his career, he has collaborated with natural scientists, from pollen botanists to geneticists. He was one of the initiators of the 'mobility turn' in archaeology by developing new methodological and theoretical models for prehistoric mobility and migration, notably in his book with Thomas Larsson, *The Rise of Bronze Age Society*.

Ken Massy is Assistant Professor of Prehistoric Archaeology at the Ludwig-Maximilians-University Munich. In 2016 he earned his PhD at the LMU Munich and has continued working as a Postdoctoral Researcher in several projects on the Late Neolithic and Bronze Age at the Academy of Sciences at Heidelberg and LMU Munich. He was a mentee at the LMU Mentoring Excellence Programme of the Faculty of Cultural Studies from 2018 to 2020. His research foci are social practices visible in burial activities, communal behaviour of ritual feasting events, as well as the entanglement of archaeology and scientific data, especially radio-carbon dating, aDNA, and isotopes.

Carola Metzner-Nebelsick is Full Professor and Chair of Pre- and Protohistoric Archaeology at the Ludwig-Maximilians-University Munich. She studied Prehistory, Ancient History, and Art History in Berlin, Munich, and Oxford. She is a member of the German Archaeological Institute and the Academy of Sciences and Literature in Mainz, Germany, and a corresponding member of the Austrian Academy of Sciences. She has directed several fieldwork and interdisciplinary research projects, including sites in Romania, Bavaria, and Croatia, and was Co-speaker for the Munich Graduate School 'Distant Worlds'. Her research interests focus on the European Bronze and Iron Ages, with a wide thematic and geographical scope.

Barry Molloy is Associate Professor at the School of Archaeology, University College Dublin, Ireland. He specialises in later prehistoric archaeology in Europe and the Mediterranean, with a particular focus on the Late Bronze Age. He has published widely on the material culture and social practices surrounding pre-historic conflict and metalworking practice, using methods that encompass experimental archaeology, archaeometry, and metalwork wear analysis. Having excavated, surveyed, and conducted museum-based research throughout Greece, the Balkans, and Central and Western Europe, he is currently Principal Investigator of the ERC-funded 'The Fall of 1200 BC' project, exploring mobility, conflict, and social change in south-east Europe.

Hande Özyarkent is a Researcher at the Deutsches Bergbau-Museum and Contracted Lecturer for Archaeometry at the Ruhr University of Bochum. Her recent research focuses on archaeology/archaeometry investigations of ancient communities that are practising mining, their interactions with their landscape/ cultural space, and the investigations especially focusing on their mobility. She recently successfully defended her PhD thesis on *Economy and Mobility of Bronze Age Andronovo Culture: Investigation with Multiple Isotope Analysis on Mobility, Seasonality, and Diet.*

Katharina Rebay-Salisbury is an Archaeologist with a research focus on the European Bronze and Iron Ages. After completing her PhD in 2005, she was a Postdoctoral Researcher at the Universities of Cambridge and Leicester in the UK, where she participated in research programmes on the human body and networks. In 2015 she was awarded an ERC Starting Grant for her project 'The Value of Mothers to Society: Responses to Motherhood and Child Rearing Practices in Prehistoric Europe'. She directs the research group 'Prehistoric Identities' at the Austrian Archaeological Institute of the Austrian Academy of Sciences, and teaches at the University of Vienna.

Nico Roymans is Professor of Northwest European Archaeology at the Vrije Universiteit Amsterdam. His research interests include the social organisation of Late Iron Age societies, the archaeology of Celto-Germanic societies and their integration into the Roman world, ethnicity and ethnogenesis in the Roman Empire, and the archaeology of mass violence and genocide in antiquity. His numerous publications include the monographs *Tribal Societies in Northern Gaul: An Anthropological Perspective* (1990) and *Ethnic Identity and Imperial Power: The Batavians in the Early Roman Empire* (2004).

Thomas Stöllner holds the Chair of Pre- and Protohistory at the Ruhr University of Bochum, Germany, and is directing the Department of Research at the Deutsches Bergbau-Museum, Bochum. His main area of research is the social and economic development of mining communities throughout pre- and protohistory, with a focus on mining, the archaeometry of mining, the archaeology of technology, and social interrelation. His research spans from Old World archaeology including Central and Eastern Europe to the Caucasus, the Middle East, Central Asia, and South America. Further fields of work are the archaeology of the European Bronze and Iron Ages and methods in archaeology.

Peter S. Wells is Professor of Anthropology at the University of Minnesota. His research speciality is the Bronze and Iron Ages of temperate Europe. He has conducted excavations at three settlement sites in southern Germany. Among his books are *The Barbarians Speak: How the Conquered Peoples Shaped Roman Europe* (1999), *Beyond Celts, Germans and Scythians: Archaeology and Identity in Iron Age Europe* (2001), and *How Ancient Europeans Saw the World: Vision, Patterns, and the Shaping of the Mind in Prehistoric Times* (2012). He is co-editor of *The Oxford Handbook of the European Iron Age* (2018).

Lorenzo Zamboni is Assistant Professor in Archaeology at the University of Milan. His research covers a range of settlement, material, funerary, and theoretical aspects, mainly concerning the human presence in northern Italy between the Final Bronze Age and the Roman period. Since 2012 he has been co-director of the archaeological excavations at Iron Age Verucchio. Recent publications include the monograph *Sepolture arcaiche della pianura emiliana. Il riconoscimento di una società di frontiera* (2018) and the edited volume *Crossing the Alps: Early Urbanism between Northern Italy and Central Europe (900–400 BC)* (2020).

1

Rethinking Migrations in Late Prehistoric Eurasia: An Introduction

MANUEL FERNÁNDEZ-GÖTZ, COURTNEY NIMURA, PHILIPP W. STOCKHAMMER, AND RACHEL CARTWRIGHT

Introduction

PEOPLE MOVE. WHETHER at an individual or group level, mobility has been a constant and crucial aspect of the human journey from its very beginnings to the present (Manning 2005; Greenblatt 2010; Bellwood 2013; Fisher 2013; Hahn 2015; Cohen 2019; Daniels 2022). To paraphrase the title of an article by Demoule (1989), the journey of humankind is one of three million years of emigration and immigration. In a way, we could classify the human being as a *homo migrans* (Burmeister 2012), at least from a long-term perspective. Thus, it is not surprising that mobility in general, and migrations in particular, have been a major focus of archaeological study, although the way of conceptualising the topic has changed dramatically over time (Andresen 2004; Hakenbeck 2008; Van Dommelen 2014).

This volume focuses on mobility in late prehistoric Eurasia, from around 3000 BC to the beginning of the Common Era, a period of three millennia in which mobility ebbed and flowed. While the main geographic focus is on temperate Europe, some chapters address the connections to the wider Eurasian steppe. Furthermore, we should consider that, as expressed by Cunliffe (2008), in global terms Europe is a relatively minor peninsula attached to the large Eurasian land mass. The present volume arose from the conference 'Where Are You Going? Reconsidering Migrations in the Metal Ages', which was held on 9–10 November 2019 at the University of Edinburgh and organised within the framework of the UISPP (*Union Internationale des Sciences Préhistoriques et Protohistoriques*) Metal Ages in Europe Scientific Commission (Figure 1.1). The two-day conference was focused on rethinking mobility, migration, and movement in later prehistory – from the Chalcolithic to the end of the Iron Age.

Proceedings of the British Academy, **254**, 1–20, © The British Academy 2023.

Figure 1.1 Participants at the Edinburgh conference (image: authors)

This book includes a selection of the papers presented at the conference (Chapters 2, 5–12, and 14), as well as a number of additional contributions (Chapters 1, 3, 4, 13, and 15). Both the conference and this volume are topical for two main reasons. The first is that we are currently experiencing a 'Third Science Revolution in Archaeology' (cf. Kristiansen 2014), due to the development of new, and the improvement of existing, biomolecular scientific methods that are revolutionising our knowledge of past mobility, from ancient DNA (aDNA) to stable isotope analyses. The second is that there has been a so-called 'migration crisis' occurring across the globe, which in Europe peaked in 2015–16, leading to important public debates and heterogeneous political responses (Barlai *et al.* 2017; Squire *et al.* 2021; cf. Hamilakis 2018 for an archaeological analysis).

While stories about migrations have become a daily feature of news headlines in the media, discussions concerning the regulation of the flow of people across countries and continents represent one of the key issues in current political discourse. Due to its long-term perspective, archaeology is in an advantageous position to contribute to a deeper reflection on the topic, by counteracting isolationist narratives and showing the complexity of human mobility in the past and present and the challenges and opportunities it poses (Burmeister 2017; Garcia and Le Bras 2017; Baby-Collin *et al.* 2021). Archaeology can and should, therefore, play a role in present societal debates on population mobility, contributing to the wider field of migration studies by providing a deep-time perspective on the topic (Baker and Tsuda 2015; Altschul *et al*. 2020). This volume aims to scrutinise new and existing studies of prehistoric mobility, from large-scale population movements to the complex biographies of individuals, but equally it aims to explore the contributions that this research can make to wider discourses on the subject.

In this introductory chapter, we will outline the main aim of this volume: to go beyond simplistic narrations about human migrations on the basis of purely either archaeological or bioarchaeological datasets, integrating archaeological, anthropological, and bioarchaeological evidence in order to write new narratives on prehistoric mobility. In order to address this aim, we will briefly discuss key concepts and definitions, refer to the history of research, and review the current debates on migrations in archaeology, some of which have gained new momentum because of recent nuanced narratives produced by collaborative research initiatives. It has become clear that archaeologists have often underestimated human mobility in the deep past, and that it is also necessary to reflect on issues of scale, gender, and age, as well as on the modes, directionalities, and intentionalities of past mobilities in a novel way. In the last section of the chapter, we will entangle the lines of thought and perspectives of the different contributions to this volume, as well as raise questions that can act as inspiration for the reader about the included papers.

The diversity of migratory processes: key concepts

Definitions are always a matter of contest, but although scholars will probably never agree on a single way of understanding the terms, we think that it is important to make explicit what we mean when we speak about key concepts such as *mobility* and *migration*, as well as some of their modalities including *forced migration* and *return migration*. These terms cannot be comprehended without equal consideration of scales, both of time and space. The distance people travelled (physically or conceptually), and how long they did or did not stay, are critical factors. Our focus here is on humans, though we recognise that the movement of objects, animals, and plants is inherently tied to this topic (e.g. Milner-Gulland *et al*. 2011; Hahn and Weiss 2013; Joyce and Gillespie 2015; Meiri *et al*. 2017; Verdugo *et al*. 2019), and that humans and non-humans are intrinsically entangled (Hodder 2012).

As editors, in the introductory and concluding chapters we understand *human mobility* as an 'umbrella' term that encompasses any human movement to another place, over variable distances and times. For the case studies presented in this volume, the term *migration* is essential. Being aware of the complexity of the issue and the lack of a common understanding (Burmeister 2000; 2017; Anthony 2020), here we define *human migration* as a particular form of human mobility that involves the movement of people (either individually or as a group) to settle in another destination over a longer period of time. In that sense, we could say that all human movement to another location can be classified as mobility, but not always as migration (e.g. attending a conference can be considered as mobility – moving to settle in another region, country, or continent as migration).

The relevant factor of distance can be difficult to measure, since from an emic perspective what is relevant is the feeling of distance, of being away from home, rather than a metrical understanding. The same is true for the element of time with regard to the decision of the migrant(s) to either not return home again or only after a longer period. In addition, intention can be an important factor, since when people are involuntarily moved from their home to another place (e.g. captives, slaves) the term *forced migration* should be applied (cf. Cameron 2016; Driessen 2018). Examples of the latter are the deportation of numerous inhabitants of the Kingdom of Judah to Babylon in the 6th century BC (Stökl and Waerzeggers 2015), or the African diaspora caused by the transatlantic slave trade from the 16th to the 19th centuries (Gomez 2019). Imperial powers often imposed large-scale forced migration as a mechanism of exploitation and control. For instance, the Qin state in ancient China forcibly relocated millions of people (Barbieri-Low 2021), and in the case of the Inca Empire it is estimated that the so-called *mitma* policy resettled up to one-third of its subject population (Hu 2019). On the other hand, unintentional but voluntary migration can occur when persons move to a place with no initial intention of remaining, but end up staying for various and originally unplanned reasons (a new family, job, etc.).

As mentioned above, migrations are not uniform events, meaning one migration does not necessarily reflect another regarding either the reasons why the movement occurs or the form it takes (Kohl 2006). An important modality of migratory processes is *return migration*, which occurs when persons who have migrated to a new land return to their place of origin. As a modern-day phenomenon it has been studied since the 1960s, but it saw intense debate in the 1980s that allowed for further development of the concept in the social sciences (Cassarino 2004). The recognition of return migrations shifts our understanding of migrations from a unidirectional flow of people to multidirectional movements (Tsuda 2009). In investigating examples of this in the present day, scholars have tended to look at economic reasons for the return, in addition to the sociological ones (Abadan-Unat 1988; Dustmann and Weiss 2007; De Haas *et al.* 2015). Identifying return migration archaeologically has several challenges, especially when there is a lack of written sources. One of the primary difficulties in interpreting the material manifestations of this phenomenon is in how to differentiate between return migration and trade. However, there are some instances in which the former can be convincingly identified, for example with the evidence found for 'Celtic' mercenaries (Baray 2017) or Roman auxiliary troops who returned to their homelands, in the latter case often taking with them objects such as Roman *militaria* and military diplomas (Derks and Roymans 2006; Roymans and Derks 2017; see also Roymans and Habermehl, Chapter 14) (Figure 1.2).

Of course, multiple intersections can exist between the concepts discussed above, and many of the chapters in this volume explore their frequently interlinked nature. It is important to note that the various terms are shaped by factors such

AN INTRODUCTION 5

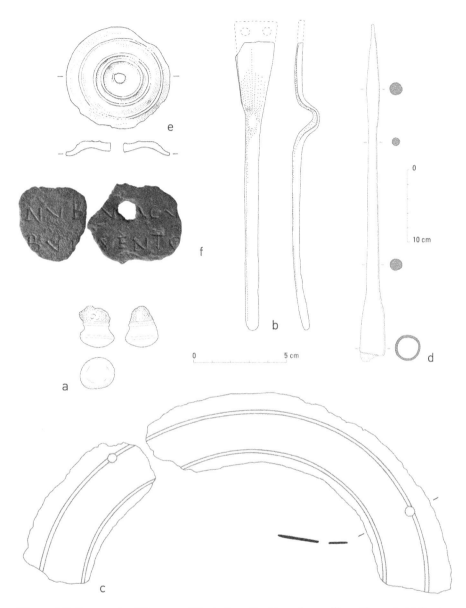

Figure 1.2 Fragments of Roman *militaria* from the Hoogeloon villa settlement. A) Bronze terminal knob from sword scabbard; B) Iron sheath fragment of sword; C) Rim of bronze *umbo*; D) Iron *pilum*; E) Bronze horse gear fitting; F) Fragments of military diploma (after Roymans and Derks 2017)

as distance, scale, time, and identity. Migratory processes can take very different forms, geographically ranging from localised movements within the same region, which we could name *short-distance* or *'local' migrations*, to, on the other extreme, relocating between different continents, which we could term *long-distance migrations*, following the terminology proposed by authors such as Tilly (1978) and Anthony (1990). In terms of scale, migrations can involve from single individuals (e.g. specialist craftspeople or tradespeople) to entire families, communities, or even polyethnic undertakings that brought together large groups of heterogeneous populations. Similarly, migration also includes the crucial factor of time: this encompasses the duration of the migratory process itself (with journeys that can take from less than a day to several years) to the time that the migrant(s) will stay at the new place of residence (temporarily for some months or years to permanently, including several generations of descendants). Finally, aspects of identity need to be taken into consideration: since societies rarely emigrate in their entirety, migrations generally imply a selection that is often based on criteria of social identity such as gender, age, or social class (Anthony 1990; Burmeister 2000; Hakenbeck 2008). These aspects can determine who emigrates and who stays at home: for example, migrant groups frequently consist mainly of young adults, who are more willing to take risks and more in need of carving out a future.

Despite the diversity of migratory movements, some attempts can be made in order to establish a certain systematisation (Figure 1.3). Thus, Anthony (1997) distinguishes between five different types of migration: local, circular, chain, career, and coerced. We can also reflect on the social unit or units that take the decision

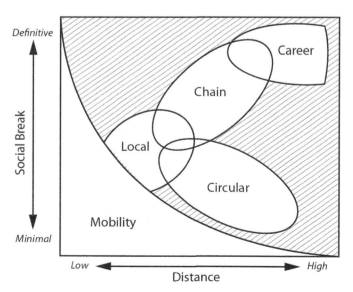

Figure 1.3 Tilly's classification of migration ideal types (redrawn after Tilly 1978)

AN INTRODUCTION

to emigrate, such as household, extended family, religious community, political group, etc. (McSparron *et al.* 2020). When doing so, as 21st-century scholars, we need to be aware of some of the biases that might affect our interpretations:

> When populations worldwide were much more sparsely distributed than they are today and communities much smaller, the circumstances under which a migrant individual or family would be welcomed into a distance community would likely have been much different from those of more recent times ... With our highly individualistic view of the world (which is exacerbated by the current emphasis on 'agency'), we must be especially cautious in attributing to people in the past the ability to make decisions about movement independent of their kin and other established social relationships.
>
> (Cameron 2000: 555–6)

There is also the issue of evidence. Human migrations do not always leave traces in the archaeological record, or sometimes the evidence is tenuous and/or open to multiple interpretations. A good example is the migration of the Galatians to Anatolia in the 3rd century BC, well attested in ancient written sources and through Hellenistic iconography, but scarcely visible archaeologically, at least not on the scale mentioned by classical authors (Darbyshire *et al.* 2000; Müller-Karpe 2006). In many cases, the 'traditional' archaeological record alone only shows us the 'tip of the iceberg' of migratory processes, as exemplified by some recent studies in which bioarchaeological methods reveal large-scale patterns of mobility that had been previously completely invisible (cf. Stockhammer and Massy, Chapter 8). Conversely, historical sources sometimes exaggerate population numbers of migrants, so they too need to be analysed cautiously and contextually (cf. Wells, Chapter 11). The temporal resolution of the archaeological data often poses additional challenges, since it frequently does not allow us to clearly locate the kind of migration on the scale between extremes like 'sudden, short-term migration of a large group of people' and 'systematic, long-term migration of individuals, for example due to marital rules'. Both extremes and everything in-between can leave similar traces in archaeological and scientific analyses, although the combination of several approaches usually enables us to narrow down the spectrum of possibilities (cf. Molloy *et al.*, Chapter 7).

While the challenges mentioned above need to serve as cautionary notes to our approaches and interpretations, archaeology has made great advances in the identification of migrations, both through 'traditional' means, such as the study of portable items (e.g. pottery, personal ornaments, coinage) and house architecture (e.g. Roymans and Habermehl, Chapter 14), and/or the application of bioarchaeological methods, such as isotopic and archaeogenetic analyses (e.g. Stockhammer and Massy, Chapter 8; Rebay-Salisbury, Chapter 9; Armit, Chapter 13; see also Gregoricka 2021). Archaeological research on migrations represents a multidisciplinary challenge (Burmeister 2016), and whenever possible we should try to incorporate different sources of evidence in order to reach plausible interpretations. The possibilities and problems associated with the identification of past mobility

Migrations in archaeology: a long and convoluted relationship

are discussed in the various contributions to this volume, and we will also come back to some of them in our concluding chapter.

The history of archaeological approaches to migrations has a long tradition, with different shifts in interpretative trends and methodologies (see also Gori and Abar, Chapter 2). Juxtapositions, such as migration versus diffusion and autochthonism versus colonisation, have defined major theoretical shifts within archaeology (Frachetti 2011), with this type of dichotomous thinking too often leading to historiographical oscillations from one extreme to the other (Fernández-Götz 2019). In the 19th and early 20th centuries, migrations were seen as the prime mover for cultural change, with the appearance of new pottery styles, house forms, or burial rites predominantly being interpreted as the result of the arrival of new peoples or 'tribes' (Andresen 2004; Trigger 2006). This conceptualisation is encapsulated in the famous expression 'pots equal people', and was part of the wider 'ethnic-cultural paradigm' *en vogue* during that time (Jones 1997; López Jiménez 2001; Fernández-Götz 2008). Montelius (1888) was one of the forerunners of this thinking, but many others across Europe and beyond adopted similar perspectives.

Interestingly, this broad interpretative framework influenced, with some nuances, scholars who were clearly nationalistic (or even racist) in their thinking, such as Kossinna (Grünert 2002) (Figure 1.4), but also others who held very different political views, for example Childe (Trigger 1980). The latter largely subscribed to the supposed direct correlation between changes in material culture and migration, stating, for example, that 'when a whole culture replaces another we are quite clearly dealing with a migration' (Childe 1950: 8). However, in his 'retrospect' he self-critically acknowledged that his early work was 'aimed at distilling from archaeological remains a preliterate substitute for the conventional politico-military history with cultures, instead of statesmen, as actors, and migrations in place of battles' (Childe 1958: 70).

While Childe clearly distanced himself from any manipulation of the past for nationalistic purposes, the first half of the 20th century saw numerous abuses that reached their peak during the Nazi regime (Legendre *et al.* 2007; Olivier 2012). The (mis)use of archaeology played an important role in supporting the ideology of the Third Reich, with military conquests often claimed to be a 'recovery' of supposed 'ancestral Germanic territories'. Distribution maps of prehistoric objects became an important argument for justifying the expansionist policy of the Nazi regime, serving as legitimation for its desire for supremacy in Europe (Arnold 1990).

In reaction to these abuses and the growing dissatisfaction with many elements of the culture-historical paradigm, Processual (New) Archaeology developed, beginning in the early 1960s, leading to an increasing critique of previous models of

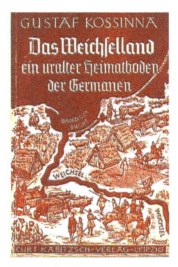

Figure 1.4 Archaeology in the service of modern politics – cover of Kossinna's book *Das Weichselland. Ein uralter Heimatboden der Germanen* ('The Vistula Land. An Ancestral Homeland of the Germans'), first published in 1919. The image of this edition shows Germanic Bronze Age settlers inhabiting the land and migrating further east (Kossinna 1940 [1919])

population movement. Thus, the topic of migrations fell out of favour among many archaeologists (see Myhre and Myhre 1972; Adams *et al*. 1978). One of the leading figures within this archaeological approach, Binford (1962), denied any causal link between cultural change and migrations. Likewise, Clark (1966: 173) criticised 'the invasion neurosis' that pervaded archaeology. However, rather than denying it any importance, Clark (1966) saw migration as essential for the spread of agriculture and metallurgy, but he considered them to be demonstrated rather than assumed. Renfrew (1969), for his part, regarded trade as the main method by which outside influence enacted cultural change, being largely against the 'invasionist model' that had been put forward by archaeologists such as Childe.

In the late 1970s some archaeologists tried to restore the study of migrations in the past (Duke *et al*. 1978; Ammerman and Cavalli-Sforza 1979), but it was not until the 1980s that it was truly revived within the field (Bettinger and Baumhoff 1982; Ammerman and Cavalli-Sforza 1984). Even Renfrew (1987) began to reconsider migrations, proposing that Indo-European languages spread following the first wave of Neolithic agriculturalists. But it was Anthony (1990) who truly reinvigorated the study of human mobility in archaeology, introducing methods for investigating migrations from a variety of other disciplines, most notably demography and geography. This seminal work by Anthony (1990) divided migrations into short- and long-distance movements and included the further subdivisions of leapfrogging, migration streams, and return migration. These divisions outlined migration as a process and thus something that archaeologists should be capable of modelling.

Burmeister (2000) further elaborated on the approaches that archaeologists can take in order to view and understand past migrations, developing a middle-range theory that could help distinguish cultural change caused by migrations as opposed to other transformative processes. The distinction between diffusion (e.g. through trade, as well as other cultural transmission and knowledge exchange activities), independent development, and migration has been a significant short-fall in archaeological research (Burmeister 2016). With the coming of the 'Third Science Revolution in Archaeology', which has introduced the usage of aDNA and isotopes in studying mobility (Kristiansen 2014), archaeology has the potential to overcome many of its methodological issues by integrating 'reliable proof of pre-historic migrations' (Burmeister 2016: 44).

Traditionally, archaeologists thought of migrations as large groups of people on the move. This was certainly influenced by the culture-historical view of 'tribes' as the main actors in (pre)history, as exemplified in Childe's 1958 quote noted above. However, this perspective has changed considerably in recent decades, and now we witness among many archaeologists an emphasis on the small-scale mobility of individuals, rather than the movement of larger groups/communities. This, again, might be reflecting current trends in archaeological thinking, being to a certain extent related to the growing importance that has been attributed to individuals as 'free agents' since the rise of post-processualism in the 1980s (for a critique, cf., for example, Bintliff 2016). Looking at the historical, archaeological, and anthropo-logical evidence, we can go beyond these dichotomies and acknowledge that both large-scale and small-scale migrations took place in the past, as they do in the present. At the risk of overgeneralising, we could state that small-scale mobility is a common and rather continuous phenomenon in most societies, while mass migra-tion occurs only occasionally but can then have a significant impact. At the same time, the complexity of possible scenarios is reflected by the fact that long-term individual mobility, e.g. in the framework of patrilocal systems, might sometimes have a comparable transformative impact on societies as the sudden migration of larger groups (cf. Stockhammer and Massy, Chapter 8) – and even produce similar archaeological evidence, which is often difficult to understand in its temporal reso-lution. Thus, the diversity of migration processes and their various causes and consequences should be acknowledged (Manning 2005; Cabana and Clark 2011).

Attempts to understand migrations in the past and present must begin by looking at the reasons behind human mobility. Anthony (2006) discusses several potential 'push' factors which might cause migrations; while these are frequently theorised to be demographic, with overpopulation and lack of resources leading to emigration, they should be viewed principally as socially driven by a desire to locate improved prospects in other lands. Any migration is always a symptom, not a primary cause, so it needs to be explained within a broader framework of socioeconomic organisation, power relations, and ideology (Kristiansen 1998). As expressed by Anthony (2007: 110): 'People do not migrate, even in today's crowded world, simply because there are too many at home. … But there are other kinds of "push" factors – war, disease, crop failure, climate change, institutionalized raiding for loot, high bride-prices, the laws of primogeniture, religious intolerance, banishment, humiliation, or simple annoyance with the neighbours'. In cases of diaspora, for example, the primary 'push' factor is often an episode of unrest or a traumatic event in the homeland (Clifford 1997; Hayes 2015). The attractive qualities of a new territory are called 'pull' factors and if found to be enticing by people who have been provided with information about them can cause immigration to the area (Anthony 2006). It goes without saying that in many cases 'push' and 'pull' factors are entangled in a complex manner (Figure 1.5). The recently proposed 'aspirations–capabilities framework' provides a further way to reconceptualise the dimensions of human mobility and in particular the relationship between agency and structural factors (De Haas 2021).

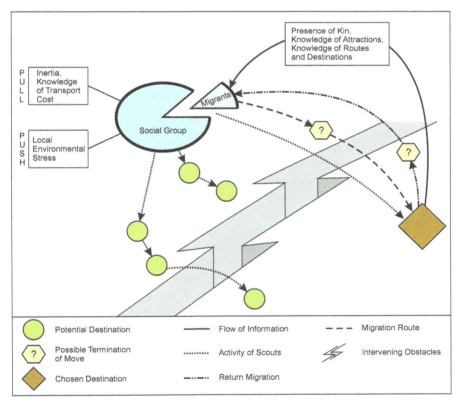

Figure 1.5 Diagram of a migratory process, including some possible push and pull factors (redrawn after Anthony 1990)

Different phases within the migratory process can also be explored and differentiated. For instance, Prien (2005) identifies four phases in any migration process: contact/exploration phase, migration phase, establishment phase, and reverse current phase. This further illustrates the complexities of migrations and human mobility. Within migration studies, it has become increasingly evident that the initial causes of a population movement, as well as the social transformations that occur throughout, can be crucial for our understanding of the process. In examining present-day migrations, Castles (2010) promotes the conceptual framing within migration studies around social transformations, as this framework aids in building understanding of the variability, complexity, contextuality, interconnecting nature, and multifaceted negotiations of migratory processes. The interdisciplinary approaches available and utilised within archaeology today are transforming our understandings of past migrations and allowing for the development of improved methodology for the interpretation of these processes.

Big questions, complex answers

As mentioned above, population movements in late prehistoric Eurasia have become a major focus of research in recent years (e.g. Frachetti 2011; Allentoft *et al*. 2015; Haak *et al*. 2015; Racimo *et al*. 2020). In light of new analytical tools and a growing corpus of archaeological data, it is now time to rethink human mobility in this crucial period by integrating all possible data, from traditional typological analysis to new aDNA approaches. Whereas human mobility – especially of elites and women – has long been assumed by archaeologists, it has been the dawn of new bioarchaeological approaches that has forced us to rethink the scales of migratory processes, their correlation with social identities, and their societal impact. What was the scale and temporality of population movements? How was travel organised? What routes did people follow and by what means did they travel? How did patterns of mobility change during later prehistory? To what extent were 'migrations' just the outcome of long-term institutionalised mobilities of individuals, e.g. due to patrilocal residence rules? How can we link global and local perspectives on mobility? And, very importantly, what can we learn from the past in order to build a better understanding of population movements in the present?

Genetic analyses in particular are revolutionising the field of later prehistory (Reich 2018), and will continue to do so through the ongoing development of new methods such as the so-called Identity by Descent (IBD) (cf. Nimura *et al.*, Chapter 15). New publications are continuously creating big headlines, with influential studies published within the last few years addressing aspects such as the spread of the Bell Beaker phenomenon (Olalde *et al*. 2018) and the migration of populations from the Eurasian steppe belt to Central/Northern Europe in the 3rd millennium BC (Allentoft *et al*. 2015; Haak *et al*. 2015). However, caution is needed when interpreting the new data (e.g. Vander Linden 2016; Eisenmann *et al*.

2018; Furholt 2018; 2021). In addition to the ever-evolving nature of the technical side of the analysis and the still rather small – although rapidly growing – number of samples, which includes considerable gaps both geographically and chronologically, there is a temptation to provide quick, simple answers to complex questions (Callaway 2018). Even more concerning, in some cases we can observe a return to simplistic equations between population mobility, culture, ethnicity, and even language, which resonate with old culture-historical approaches of the early 20th century (Heyd 2017; Frieman and Hofmann 2019). In this sense, we should keep in mind the cautionary words expressed by Collis: 'Genetics must not be confused with language groups, ethnic groups, social structures, or material culture; these are all separate categories which can be fruitfully compared, but they cannot be equated with one another' (Collis 2009: 42). Connecting empirical studies with social theory is necessary when studying migrations of the past and present (Castles 2010).

Contents of the volume

In this book, we aim to present a middle-ground approach that combines new data from natural science analyses, a careful and contextual study of the archaeological evidence, and theoretical and methodological perspectives that consider the complexity and diversity of population mobility. We identify important case studies in European later prehistory where an interdisciplinary focus on traces and impacts of mobility allows us to gain a deep historical perspective on the scale and gender-, status-, and age-related issues of this phenomenon. Whereas we are hardly able to grasp the long-term impact of present-day mobilities, the past enables such long-term views. How often did migrations happen? What were the main reasons/triggers? How were groups of migrants (trans)formed on their way and how did they interact with other communities? What was the long-term impact of institutions of mobility (e.g. patrilocality) as well as mobile groups on local economies, subsistence strategies, settlement patterns, etc.?

The diversity of realisations of human mobility requests manifold histories and narratives, zooming in and out of case studies and integrations that do not simplify, but rather entangle, the complexities. This volume approaches this task through a group of scholars who all agree on: first, the importance of human mobility for past societies; second, the relevance of integrating archaeology and anthropology with cutting-edge scientific analyses; and third, the need for building a bridge from the past into the present in order to contribute to ongoing public discourses.

The chapters are organised roughly chronologically, starting with this introduction. Chapter 2 by Maja Gori and Aydin Abar delves into the history of migration studies and its relationship to archaeology, providing an introduction to many of the arguments presented in the chapters of this volume. It calls for a more integrated, interdisciplinary approach to be employed by archaeologists regarding mobility and migration. In Chapter 3, Volker Heyd examines four movements of people associated with the archaeological phenomena of so-called Yamnaya, Early Corded Ware, Late Corded Ware, and Bell Beaker. He uses a combination of genetic evidence and archaeological data in order to provide an overview of these migrations, putting forward several paradigms through which these movements should be viewed. Chapter 4 by Andrew Fitzpatrick provides an up-to-date overview of the late 3rd millennium BC mobility and migration of the Bell Beaker network across Central and Western Europe. He presents recent work from different evidence types at varying spatial scales, from large-scale aDNA studies to smaller-scale isotopic analyses. Interpreting the available data, Fitzpatrick focuses on the aspect of shared worldviews as opposed to genetic relatedness. Movement is a process, and safe movement from one place to another might have required an extensive political infrastructure. This is partly also the topic of Chapter 5 by Kristian Kristiansen, who moves us further into the Bronze Age. He explores the evidence for political economies, using case studies from Denmark *c.* 1500–1100 BC and drawing on ideas of fosterage, kinship, and guest-friendship.

Moving to Central Asia in Chapter 6, Thomas Stöllner, Hande Özyarkent, and Anton Gontscharov discuss the research carried out on the Andronovo culture. They explore this group's mobility through an analysis of metallurgical activities and animal husbandry. In Chapter 7 discussion of the Bronze Age continues with a contribution by Barry Molloy, Caroline Bruyère, and Dragan Jovanović, who compare the emergence of complex settlement networks in the South Pannonian Plain and the Po Valley. By examining the life- and deathways of these two regions, they show sustained mobility between them with episodes of more intense interaction around 1600 and 1200 BC. Philipp Stockhammer and Ken Massy give an overview of the comprehensive, interdisciplinary work undertaken in the Lech Valley (southern Germany) in Chapter 8. Bringing together the results from multiple studies on Late Neolithic to Middle Bronze Age burials, they show through archaeogenetics and isotope analyses the complex lives of people residing in a group of farmsteads. In addition, they discuss the evidence and potential impact of an infectious disease on the existing population. This chapter has much to say about women and their social role, which leads neatly into a discussion on female mobility/gendered migration by Katharina Rebay-Salisbury in Chapter 9. She explores the specifics of marriage and motherhood in the European Bronze and Iron Ages, from parenting practices to childbearing age and breastfeeding, tying these aspects of women's lives to their patterns of mobility.

In the following Chapter 10, Carola Metzner-Nebelsick presents two case studies of migration. The first focuses on the interaction of mobile pastoralists from the Eastern European steppe and sedentary Carpathian and Central European communities in the 9th–8th centuries BC. The second presents the results of a six-year interdisciplinary research project that examined Late Bronze Age Urnfield transalpine mobility. In both case studies, Metzner-Nebelsick thinks critically about the intersections of biomolecular analyses and humanistic approaches. In Chapter 11, Peter Wells proposes a model for examining the scale of migrations, using three case studies that have both archaeological and textual evidence available. Using this model, he reflects on the likely number of people involved in the 5th–4th-century BC Gallic migrations to the Italian Peninsula, described by Livy, among others. Continuing with Italy, in Chapter 12 Veronica Cicolani and Lorenzo Zamboni discuss Iron Age mobility in the Po Valley and Circum-Alpine regions. Through the re-evaluation of small finds and clothing elements and the use of spatial analysis, they attempt to reconstruct the social complexities and interactions of the Iron Age groups of these areas.

In Chapter 13, Ian Armit introduces readers to the European Research Council (ERC)-funded COMMIOS project, the results of which should have a major impact on our understanding of Iron Age society. Although this chapter is an introduction to an ongoing project, it provides a helpful example of an interdisciplinary framework and also presents some preliminary results. In the latest time period covered in this book, Nico Roymans and Diederick Habermehl take us on a tour of Roman military expansion in North-West Europe in Chapter 14. They tackle changing power relations and emerging communities that occurred along the Roman frontiers, focusing particularly on the evidence from the Lower Rhine. The consequences of fusion, fission, and migration on the edge of the Empire are shown through material culture and written sources. Finally, the concluding Chapter 15 by the editors summarises the key threads that tie together the chapters included in the volume, and looks ahead in order to highlight the potential of archaeology for contributing to our understanding of migrations in the past, present, and future.

New scientific and archaeological approaches have forced us to radically rethink mobility in the prehistoric past and develop new pathways of integrating all available evidence to move beyond simplistic narratives of human migration. By considering the complexity of anthropological and archaeological evidence, the chapters in this volume comprise one of the first large-scale archaeological reactions to these new lines of evidence. It is our goal that the volume will be of interest not only to archaeologists specialised in late prehistoric Eurasia, but also to a wider audience interested in the ever-developing field of migration studies.

Acknowledgements

We would like to thank the British Academy for accepting this volume within their publication series, and all the reviewers for their useful comments that have helped to improve the quality of the contributions. Further thanks go to Dr Dirk Brandherm (Belfast) for his support and advice as President of the UISPP Metal Ages in Europe Scientific Commission, and to Dr Janine Fries-Knoblach (Munich) for her assistance in the production of the volume. Finally, we would like to thank Portia Taylor for her invaluable guidance as Production Editor for the *Proceedings of the British Academy*.

References

Abadan-Unat, N. (1988), 'The socio-economic aspects of return migration in Turkey', *Migration*, 3: 29–59.

Adams, W.Y., Van Gerven, D.P., and Levy, R.S. (1978), 'The retreat from migrationism', *Annual Review of Anthropology*, 7: 483–532.

Allentoft, M.E., Sikora, M., Sjögren, K.-G., Rasmussen, S., Rasmussen, M., *et al.* (2015), 'Population genomics of Bronze Age Eurasia', *Nature*, 522: 167–72.

Altschul, J.H., Kintigh, K.W., Aldenderfer, M., Alonzi, E., Armit, I., *et al.* (2020), 'Opinion: to understand how migrations affect human securities, look to the past', *Proceedings of the National Academy of Sciences of the United States of America*, 117(34): 20342–5.

Ammerman, A.J. and Cavalli-Sforza, L.L. (1979), 'The wave of advance model for the spread of agriculture in Europe', in C. Renfrew and K.L. Cooke (eds), *Transformations: Mathematical Approaches to Culture Change* (New York, Academic Press), 275–94.

Ammerman, A.J. and Cavalli-Sforza, L.L. (1984), *The Neolithic Transition and Genetics of Populations in Europe* (Princeton, Princeton University Press).

Andresen, M. (2004), *Studien zur Geschichte und Methodik der archäologischen Migrationsforschung* (Münster, Waxmann Verlag).

Anthony, D.W. (1990), 'Migration in archeology: the baby and the bathwater', *American Anthropologist*, 92(4): 895–914.

Anthony, D.W. (1997), 'Prehistoric migration as social process', in J. Chapman and H. Hamerow (eds), *Migrations and Invasions in Archaeological Explanation* (Oxford, Archaeopress), 21–32.

Anthony, D.W. (2006), 'Three deadly sins in steppe archaeology: culture, migration and Aryans', in D.L. Peterson, L.M. Popova, and A.T. Smith (eds), *Beyond the Steppe and the Sown: Proceedings of the 2002 University of Chicago Conference on Eurasian Archaeology* (Leiden and Boston, Brill), 40–62.

Anthony, D.W. (2007), *The Horse, the Wheel, and Language: How Bronze-Age Riders from the Eurasian Steppes Shaped the Modern World* (Princeton, Princeton University Press).

Anthony, D.W. (2020), 'Ancient DNA, mating networks, and the Anatolian split', in M. Serangeli and T. Olander (eds), *Dispersals and Diversification: Linguistic and Archaeological Perspectives on the Early Stages of Indo-European* (Leiden, Brill), 21–53.

Arnold, B. (1990), 'The past as propaganda: totalitarian archaeology in Nazi Germany', *Antiquity*, 64(244): 464–78.

Baby-Collin, V., Collin-Bouffier, S., Mourlane, S., and Pentsch, P. (2021), *Atlas des migrations en Méditerranée: De l'Antiquité à nos jours* (Paris, Actes Sud).

Baker, B. and Tsuda, T. (eds) (2015), *Migration and Disruptions: Toward a Unifying Theory of Ancient and Contemporary Migrations* (Gainesville, University Press of Florida).

Baray, L. (2017), *De Carthage à Jéricho: Mythes et réalités du mercenariat celtique (Ve–Ier siècle a.C.)* (Bordeaux, Ausonius Éditions).

Barbieri-Low, A. (2021), 'Coerced migration and resettlement in the Qin imperial expansion', *Journal of Chinese History*, 5(2): 181–202.

Barlai, M., Faehnrich, B., Griessler, C., and Rhomberg, M. (eds) (2017), *The Migrant Crisis: European Perspectives and National Discourses* (Münster, LIT Verlag).

Bellwood, P. (2013), *First Migrants: Ancient Migration in Global Perspective* (Chichester, Wiley-Blackwell).

Bettinger, R.L. and Baumhoff, M.A. (1982), 'The Numic spread: Great Basin cultures in competition', *American Antiquity*, 47: 485–503.

Binford, L.R. (1962), 'Archaeology as anthropology', *American Antiquity*, 28: 217–25.

Bintliff, J. (2016), 'Agency, structure and the unconscious in the *longue durée*', in M. Fernández-Götz and D. Krausse (eds), *Eurasia at the Dawn of History: Urbanization and Social Change* (New York, Cambridge University Press), 243–53.

Burmeister, S. (2000), 'Archaeology and migration: approaches to an archaeological proof of migration', *Current Anthropology*, 41(4): 539–67.

Burmeister, S. (2012), '*Homo migrans*: Migration und die plurale Gesellschaft, eine Herausforderung für die archäologischen Museen', *Museumskunde*, 77(2): 30–7.

Burmeister, S. (2016), 'Archaeological research on migration as a multidisciplinary challenge', *Medieval Worlds*, 4: 42–64.

Burmeister, S. (2017), 'The archaeology of migration: what can and should it accomplish?', in H. Meller, F. Daim, J. Krause, and R. Risch (eds), *Migration und Integration von der Urgeschichte bis zum Mittelalter* (Halle/Saale, Landesmuseum für Vorgeschichte), 57–68.

Cabana, G. and Clark, J. (eds) (2011), *Rethinking Anthropological Perspectives on Migration* (Gainesville, University Press of Florida).

Callaway, E. (2018), 'Divided by DNA: the uneasy relationship between archaeology and ancient genomics', *Nature*, 555: 573–6.

Cameron, C.M. (2000), 'Comment to S. Burmeister "Archaeology and migration: approaches to an archaeological proof of migration"', *Current Anthropology*, 41(4): 555–6.

Cameron, C.M. (2016), *Captives: How Stolen People Changed the World* (Lincoln and London, University of Nebraska Press).

Cassarino, J.-P. (2004), 'Theorising return migration: the conceptual approach to return migrants revisited', *International Journal on Multicultural Societies*, 6(2): 253–79.

Castles, S. (2010), 'Understanding global migration: a social transformation perspective', *Journal of Ethnic and Migration Studies*, 36(10): 1565–86.

Childe, V.G. (1950), *Prehistoric Migrations in Europe* (Oslo, Instituttet for Sammenlignende Kulturforskning).

Childe, V.G. (1958), 'Retrospect', *Antiquity*, 32(126): 69–74.

Clark, G. (1966), 'The invasion hypothesis in British archaeology', *Antiquity*, 40(159): 172–89.

Clifford, J. (1997), *Routes: Travel and Translation in the Late Twentieth Century* (Cambridge, Harvard University Press).

Cohen, R. (2019), *Migration: The Movement of Humankind from Prehistory to the Present* (London, Welbeck Publishing Group).

Collis, J. (2009), 'Celts and Indo-Europeans: linguistic determinism?', in M. Vander Linden and K. Jones-Bley (eds), *Departure from the Homeland: Indo-Europeans and Archaeology* (Washington, Institute for the Study of Man), 29–45.

Cunliffe, B. (2008), *Europe between the Oceans: 9000 BC to AD 1000* (New Haven, Yale University Press).

Daniels, M. (ed) (2022), *Homo Migrans: Modeling Mobility and Migration in Human History* (Albany, SUNY Press).

Darbyshire, G., Mitchell, S., and Vardar, L. (2000), 'The Galatian settlement in Asia Minor', *Anatolian Studies*, 50: 75–97.

De Haas, H. (2021), 'A theory of migration: the aspirations–capabilities framework', *Comparative Migration Studies*, 9, DOI: 10.1186/s40878-020-00210-4.

De Haas, H., Fokkema, T., and Fihri, M.F. (2015), 'Return migration as failure or success?', *Journal of International Migration and Integration*, 16(2): 415–29.

Demoule, J.-P. (1989), 'Trois millions d'années d'immigration', *Le Genre Humain*, 19: 19–37.

Derks, T. and Roymans, N. (2006), 'Returning auxiliary veterans: some methodological considerations', *Journal of Roman Archaeology*, 19: 121–35.

Driessen, J. (ed) (2018), *An Archaeology of Forced Migration: Crisis-Induced Mobility and the Collapse of the 13th c. BCE Eastern Mediterranean* (Louvain-la-Neuve, Presses Universitaires de Louvain).

Duke, P.G., Egbert, J., Langemann, G., and Buchner, A.P. (eds) (1978), *Diffusion and Migration: Their Roles in Cultural Development* (Calgary, University of Calgary Archaeological Association).

Dustmann, C. and Weiss, Y. (2007), 'Return migration: theory and empirical evidence from the UK', *British Journal of Industrial Relations*, 45(2): 236–56.

Eisenmann, S., Bánffy, E., Van Dommelen, P., Hofmann, K.P., Maran, J., *et al.* (2018), 'Reconciling material cultures in archaeology with genetic data: the nomenclature of clusters emerging from archaeogenomic research', *Scientific Reports*, 8: 13003, DOI: 10.1038/s41598-018-31123-z.

Fernández-Götz, M. (2008), *La construcción arqueológica de la etnicidad* (Noia, Editorial Toxosoutos).

Fernández-Götz, M. (2019), 'Migrations in Iron Age Europe: a comparative view', in P. Halkon (ed), *The Arras Culture of Eastern Yorkshire: Celebrating the Iron Age* (Oxford, Oxbow), 179–99.

Fisher, M.H. (2013), *Migration: A World History* (Oxford, Oxford University Press).

Frachetti, M.D. (2011), 'Migration concepts in Central Eurasian archaeology', *Annual Review of Anthropology*, 40: 195–212.

Frieman, C.J. and Hofmann, D. (2019), 'Present pasts in the archaeology of genetics, identity, and migration in Europe: a critical essay', *World Archaeology*, 51(4): 528–45.

Furholt, M. (2018), 'Massive migrations? The impact of recent aDNA studies on our view of third millennium Europe', *European Journal of Archaeology*, 21(2): 159–91.

Furholt, M. (2021), 'Mobility and social change: understanding the European Neolithic period after the archaeogenetic revolution', *Journal of Archaeological Research*, 29: 481–535.

Garcia, D. and Le Bras, H. (eds) (2017), *Archéologie des migrations* (Paris, Éditions La Découverte).

Gomez, M.A. (2019), *Reversing Sail: A History of the African Diaspora* (New York, Cambridge University Press).

Greenblatt, S. (ed) (2010), *Cultural Mobility: A Manifesto* (Cambridge, Cambridge University Press).

Gregoricka, L.A. (2021), 'Moving forward: a bioarchaeology of mobility and migration', *Journal of Archaeological Research*, 29: 581–635.

Grünert, H. (2002), *Gustaf Kossinna (1858–1931) – Vom Germanisten zum Prähistoriker: Ein Wissenschaftler im Kaiserreich und in der Weimarer Republik* (Rahden/Westf., Verlag Marie Leidorf).

Haak, W., Lazaridis, I., Patterson, N., Rohland, N., Mallick, S., *et al.* (2015), 'Massive migration from the steppe was a source for Indo-European languages in Europe', *Nature*, 522: 207–11.

Hahn, H.-P. (2015), 'Migration, Mobilität und kultureller Wandel als Grundlage menschlicher Gesellschaften', in T. Otten, J. Kunow, M.M. Rind, and M. Trier (eds), *Revolution Jungsteinzeit: Archäologische Landesausstellung Nordrhein-Westfalen* (Darmstadt, Theiss Verlag), 103–9.

Hahn, H.-P. and Weis, H. (eds) (2013), *Mobility, Meaning and Transformations of Things: Shifting Contexts of Material Culture Through Time and Space* (Oxford, Oxbow).

Hakenbeck, S. (2008), 'Migration in archaeology: are we nearly there yet?', *Archaeological Review from Cambridge*, 23(2): 9–26.

Hamilakis, Y. (ed) (2018), *The New Nomadic Age: Archaeologies of Forced and Undocumented Migration* (Bristol, Equinox Publishing).

Hayes, K.H. (2015), 'Indigeneity and diaspora: colonialism and the classification of displacement', in C.N. Cipolla and K.H. Hayes (eds), *Rethinking Colonialism: Comparative Archaeological Approaches* (Gainesville, University Press of Florida), 54–75.

Heyd, V. (2017), 'Kossinna's smile', *Antiquity* 91(356): 348–59.

Hodder, I. (2012), *Entangled: An Archaeology of the Relationships between Humans and Things* (Chichester, Wiley-Blackwell).

Hu, D. (2019), 'Making space under the Inca: a space syntax analysis of a mitmaq settlement in Vilcas Huamán Province, Peru', *Antiquity*, 93(370): 990–1008.

Jones, S. (1997), *The Archaeology of Ethnicity: Constructing Identities in the Past and Present* (London, Routledge).

Joyce, R.A. and Gillespie, S.D. (eds) (2015), *Things in Motion: Object Itineraries in Anthropological Practice* (Santa Fe, School for Advanced Research Press).

Kohl, P. (2006), 'The early integration of the Eurasian steppes with the Ancient Near East: movements and transformations in the Caucasus and Central Asia', in D.L. Peterson, L.M. Popova, and A.T. Smith (eds), *Beyond the Steppe and the Sown: Proceedings of the 2002 University of Chicago Conference on Eurasian Archaeology* (Leiden and Boston, Brill), 3–39.

Kossinna, G. (1940 [1919]), *Das Weichselland: Ein uralter Heimatboden der Germanen* (Leipzig, Curt Kabitzsch Verlag).

Kristiansen, K. (1998), *Europe before History* (Cambridge, Cambridge University Press).

Kristiansen, K. (2014), 'Towards a new paradigm: the Third Science Revolution and its possible consequences in archaeology', *Current Swedish Archaeology*, 22: 11–34.

Legendre, J.-P., Olivier, L., and Schnitzler, B. (eds) (2007), *L'archéologie nazie en Europe de l'Ouest* (Paris, Infolio).

López Jiménez, O. (2001), 'Europa y la creación de los modelos "célticos": El origen del paradigma étnico-cultural', *Trabajos de Prehistoria*, 58: 69–88.

Manning, P. (2005), *Migration in World History* (London and New York, Routledge).

McSparron, C., Donnelly, C., Murphy, E., and Geber, J. (2020), 'Migration, group agency, and archaeology: a new theoretical model', *International Journal of Historical Archaeology*, 24: 219–32.

Meiri, M., Stockhammer, P.W., Marom, N., Bar-Oz, G., Sapir-Hen, L., *et al.* (2017), 'Eastern Mediterranean mobility in the Bronze and Early Iron Ages: inferences from ancient DNA of pigs and cattle', *Scientific Reports*, 7: 701, DOI: 10.1038/s41598-017-00701-y.

Milner-Gulland, E.J., Fryxell, J.M., and Sinclair, A.R.E. (eds) (2011), *Animal Migration: A Synthesis* (Oxford, Oxford University Press).

Montelius, O. (1888), 'Über die Einwanderung unserer Vorfahren in den Norden', *Archiv für Anthropologie*, 17: 151–60.

Müller-Karpe, A. (2006), 'Zur historischen Deutung von Funden keltischer Trachtelemente in Anatolien', in M. Szabó (ed), *Celtes et Gaulois, l'archéologie face à l'histoire 3: Les civilisés et les barbares du Ve au IIe siècle avant J.-C.* (Glux-en-Glenne, Centre Archéologique Européen), 119–23.

Myhre, B.M. and Myhre, B. (1972), 'The concept "immigration" in archaeological contexts illustrated by examples from West Norwegian and North Norwegian Early Iron Age', *Norwegian Archaeological Review*, 5(1): 45–61.

Olalde, I., Brace, S., Allentoft, M.E., Armit, I., Kristiansen, K., *et al.* (2018), 'The Beaker phenomenon and the genomic transformation of northwest Europe', *Nature*, 555: 190–6.

Olivier, L. (2012), *Nos ancêtres les Germains: Les archéologues au service des Nazis* (Paris, Tallandier).

Prien, R. (2005), *Archäologie und Migration: Vergleichende Studien zur archäologischen Nachweisbarkeit von Wanderungsbewegungen* (Bonn, Habelt).

Racimo, F., Woodbridge, J., Fyfe, R.M., Sikora, M., Sjögren, K.-G., *et al.* (2020), 'The spatio-temporal spread of human migrations during the European Holocene', *Proceedings of the National Academy of Sciences of the United States of America*, 117(16): 8989–9000.

Reich, D. (2018), *Who We Are and How We Got Here: Ancient DNA and the New Science of the Human Past* (Oxford, Oxford University Press).

Renfrew, C. (1969), 'Trade and culture process in European prehistory', *Current Anthropology*, 10(2/3): 151–69.

Renfrew, C. (1987), *Archaeology and Language: The Puzzle of Indo-European Origins* (London, Jonathan Cape).

Roymans, N. and Derks, T. (2017), 'Rural habitation in the area of the Texuandri (southern Netherlands/northern Belgium)', in M. Reddé (ed), *Gallia Rustica 1: Les campagnes du nord-est de la Gaule, de la fin de l'Âge du Fer à l'Antiquité tardive* (Bordeaux, Ausonius Éditions), 97–123.

Squire, V., Perkowski, N., Stevens, D., and Vaughan-Williams, N. (2021), *Reclaiming Migration: Voices from Europe's 'Migrant Crisis'* (Manchester, Manchester University Press).

Stökl, J. and Waerzeggers, C. (eds) (2015), *Exile and Return: The Babylonian Context* (Berlin and Boston, Walter de Gruyter).

Tilly, C. (1978), 'Migration in modern European history', in W. McNeill and R. Adams (eds), *Human Migration: Patterns and Policies* (Bloomington: Indiana University Press), 48–74.

Trigger, B.G. (1980), *Gordon Childe: Revolutions in Archaeology* (London, Thames & Hudson).

Trigger, B.G. (2006), *A History of Archaeological Thought* (Cambridge, Cambridge University Press).

Tsuda, T. (ed) (2009), *Diasporic Homecomings: Ethnic Return Migration in Comparative Perspective* (Stanford, Stanford University Press).

Vander Linden, M. (2016), 'Population history in third-millennium BC Europe: assessing the contribution of genetics', *World Archaeology*, 48(5): 714–28.

Van Dommelen, P. (2014), 'Moving on: archaeological perspectives on mobility and migration', *World Archaeology*, 46(4): 477–83.

Verdugo, M.P., Mullin, V.E., Scheu, A., Mattiangeli, V., Daly, K.G., *et al.* (2019), 'Ancient cattle genomics, origins, and rapid turnover in the Fertile Crescent', *Science*, 365(6449): 173–6.

2

Comparing Apples and Oranges?
Confronting Social Science and Natural
Science Approaches to Migration
in Archaeology

MAJA GORI AND AYDIN ABAR

Introduction

IN THIS CHAPTER we will discuss the 'tension' between natural science- and social science-driven approaches to human migration in late prehistory by outlining the most relevant issues and trends that characterise current research on migration in prehistoric archaeology, especially as it relates to the 3rd millennium BC, which we use as our case study. The following questions are at the core of what follows:

1) What differentiates natural science- and social science-driven approaches to migration as concerns interpretative paradigms?
2) Is it possible to reconcile palaeogenetic and ethnographic anthropological research streams in archaeological investigations of migration, with the aim of drafting synthetic paradigms on the subject?
3) Is archaeology actually able to contribute to research on present migration?
4) What are the roles of well-established research fields, such as migration studies or human geography, within archaeological research?

A thorough review of the literature on prehistoric migrations in archaeology and an exhaustive analysis of all the trends in migration studies are far beyond the scope of the present chapter. Therefore, in order to establish what we understand to be relevant issues at the core of these tensions, we discuss as a case study some of the most-quoted papers published in the last few years (roughly 2015 to present) that address 3rd millennium BC migration and are based on data derived from ancient genomes.

Proceedings of the British Academy, **254**, 21–40, © The British Academy 2023.

The European Continent was subject to two major migrations during the Holocene that changed the genetic composition of its inhabitants. The first occurred during the Neolithic and the second during the Bronze Age, when westward movement of the so-called Yamnaya steppe population occurred in association with extensive ideologically motivated interactive networks. Recent aDNA-based research focusing on the 3rd millennium BC has revived archaeological debates on migration, primarily due to the huge advances in bioarchaeological research targeting this period which do not correspond with developments in archaeological concepts on mobility, social relationship, kinship, and group composition (Furholt 2019a; 2019b; 2021). We discuss the approaches to human migration presented in these works by comparing them with relevant contemporary publications (2015–2020), adopting an archaeological approach to the study of present-day migration, and interpretative paradigms deriving from social sciences that have been profitably used to understand archaeological migrations. We conclude by outlining some issues which, in our understanding of the problem, could be addressed so as to facilitate possible new pathways in research on migrations in prehistoric archaeology.

Migration strikes back

'Migration theories of archaeologists, like most other archaeologists' theories, have a pragmatic quality ... [and for] ... the most part they are simply ad hoc and somewhat mechanical explanations for anomalous site or trait distributions' (Adams *et al.* 1978: 487).

Over 40 years ago Adams, Van Gerven, and Levy (1978) published a detailed critique of theories regarding migration as a concept in archaeology, showing that such narratives are as old as the discipline itself. They began as reflections on migration narratives known from the Old Testament to the mid-19th century, and onwards in the fields of *Altertumswissenschaften* and of history as conceived by the prominent German historian Leopold von Ranke. In many cases migrations formed an element of narratives based on the three-phased concept of 'beginning' – 'heyday' – 'decay', serving as disruptive features and as such often marking the end of an epoch or phase (Wiedemann 2017: 139–41, 154). A good example is presented in the lively discussions about the origin and migration routes of the allegedly physically and mentally superior Indo-Germanic warriors: the movement of a clearly defined ethnic group was taken for granted, and the fierce, sometimes polemic debate raged with regard to the start and end points of this movement – the first usually defined as the *Urheimat* – between disciples of the two concepts of *ex oriente lux* versus *ex septentrione lux* (Wiwjorra 2002).

Wiedemann (2017: 146) points out that the intensification of debate on past migrations at the end of the 19th century was influenced by the migratory movements of groups within the framework of industrialisation and imperialism.

The industrialisation of the 19th century, indeed, produced an urban society and high migration rates that subsequently abated in the 20th century. The iconic Mulberry Street in Lower Manhattan (Figure 2.1) is an example of the effects of such a phenomenon, as it was home to a large number of Italians who had migrated to New York, giving life to the characteristic Italian-American culture. Thus, it does not come as a surprise that European prehistory between the 1930s and 1950s was dominated by research on migration, which was sometimes aligned, and at other times in conflict, with concepts of cultural and technological diffusion (Adams *et al.* 1978). As Van Dommelen (2014: 477) reminds us, 'Gordon Childe's *Prehistoric Migrations in Europe* (1950) is as much a towering landmark as it is a defining benchmark of that era and perspective'.

One of the harshest criticisms of culture-historical approaches to migration by proponents of processualism and post-processualism alike has always been the lack of explication of the mechanics of the models intended to explain the changes in material culture supposedly caused by the movement of people from one region to another, usually referred to as migration, or often even as 'invasion'. These models are defined as 'migrationist/invasion paradigms' (Parker Pearson *et al.* 2019; see also Crellin 2020).

Starting in the 1960s, processual and ecological perspectives framed 'migration' as a destination- and task-oriented universal pattern. Aiming at elucidating

Figure 2.1 Manhattan's Mulberry Street around 1900 (public domain)

universal processes that explained both stasis and change, the neo-evolutionary paradigm focused on internal factors at the expense of external ones. Migration was regarded as an external, unique historical event that was unpredictable and thus a phenomenon with which one could not come to terms. From the 1980s – in the framework of post-processualism – migration was perceived as an old-fashioned, ad hoc explanatory paradigm for spatial distribution patterns and change in material culture. These trends are evident in the dominant Anglophone archaeological circles, while in other areas of Europe, such as Central Europe (Jung 2017) or the Balkans, migration never really disappeared from archaeological interpretation (Gori and Ivanova 2017). In the Balkans, for example, German scholarship from the 1960s and '70s played an important role in shaping and propagating an approach to later prehistory that focused on chronology, cultural history, and the diffusion of culture, laying greater emphasis on pottery than on other types of finds. Within this framework, change was naturally perceived as coming from the outside through migration, war, or environmental disasters, and the transformative power of agency and the heterogeneity of any given society's social space were not taken into consideration (Maran 2017). To explain the reason behind the difficulties of challenging well-established archaeological paradigms, Babić (2002: 315) pointed to the retreat of Serbian archaeology into an atheoretical refuge of chronological sequences and pottery typologies, thus moving beyond the scope of interest of nationalist ideologies that exploded during the 1990s conflict.

Today, migration is fully back on the mainstream archaeological agenda. This renewed interest is related to two concurrent factors, which have experienced significant visibility in the last decade. The first is a rapid advance in genomic and isotopic research, targeting past human and animal movements. Bioarchaeological research was, until recently, primarily concerned with examining the genetics of the Mesolithic–Neolithic transition in Europe and whether there was a demic expansion from West Asia that contributed to the spread of agriculture and domestic animals. Ideally paired with biogeoarchaeology, ancient DNA research has become consistently present in archaeological research on later periods as well as the 3rd millennium BC. In his introduction to *Who We Are and How We Got Here: Ancient DNA and the New Science of the Human Past*, David Reich refers to Luigi Cavalli-Sforza as having been convinced that the field of genetics would soon be able to solve many questions related to migrations and make it possible to reconstruct migrations on the basis of genetic differences among modern humans (Reich 2019: XIV). Though advancements in this field have undoubtedly contributed significantly to research, those who believed in the self-explanatory potential of aDNA data to understand migrations remained disappointed.

While information provided by isotope analysis performed on human remains traces the movement of individuals during their lifetimes, the data derived from aDNA provides genetic evidence for spatial and temporal large-scale movements of people. Results arising from the latter have made clear that, over the course of human history, moving and mating have been more the rule than the exception, and that past mobilities were 'the currents of life that make up human existence' (Leary 2014: 2).

The resulting migration models produced for the movement of 'Yamnaya people' from the Eurasian steppe to Central Europe in the 3rd millennium BC were, however, often criticised. In particular, those emerging out of aDNA research have been described as too simplistic (Vander Linden 2016; Furholt 2018; 2021), being heavily influenced by the culture-historical approach and even reminiscent of an ethnic identification with archaeological culture (Heyd 2017; Heyd, Chapter 3). An example of the latter is the paper 'Genetic origins of the Minoans and Mycenaeans', in which it is argued that 'Modern Greeks resemble the Mycenaeans, but with some additional dilution of the Early Neolithic ancestry' and that the 'results support the idea of continuity but not isolation in the history of populations of the Aegean, before and after the time of its earliest civilizations' (Lazaridis *et al*. 2017: 214). The paper was then featured on the homepage of the neo-fascist political group 'Golden Dawn' in support of a 'Blood and Soil'-based racial continuity between the ancient inhabitants of the Greek peninsula and those of present-day Greece (Hamilakis 2017; Frieman and Hofmann 2019). The link to the Golden Dawn web page featuring this study is not available anymore; however, the announcement appears also on other far-right, racist, and anti-immigrant online magazines, for example *Defendevropa*. The utilisation of such models in nationalist narratives by far-right groups provoked fervent critique and heated debate within the archaeological community (Hakenbeck 2019), leading to questions about how migration is framed and conceptualised within the discipline, as well as the way in which archaeology enters into contemporary discourses on migration and identity (e.g. Hamilakis 2017).

The second factor which has stimulated the resurgence of archaeological interest in migration is present-day migration into Europe – this has attracted the attention of scholars in all of the social sciences. The remarkable flow of people from the Global South to the Global North known as the 'migration crisis', caused by a combination of climate change, conflict, dislocation/forced migration, economic issues, and food insecurity, has inspired archaeological research encompassing past and present migrations alike (Driessen 2018). Present migration flows are researched and understood by adopting an archaeological approach to their material traces, and at the same time, archaeological migrations were conceived of as a nuanced and multidimensional phenomenon. The 'migration crisis' has also provoked some archaeologists to openly engage with ethical and political issues, challenging the way in which past and present migrations are understood, and the way in which they are represented in current narratives (De León 2015; Driessen 2018; Hamilakis 2018a; 2018b; Hicks and Mallett 2019).

The individual interests of archaeologists tend to lie in one of the following two research streams: natural science-driven and rooted in processualism, or archaeo-anthropology-driven and rooted in post-processualism. This, combined with their belonging to different epistemological traditions, has influenced the ways in which archaeology frames migration as an academic subject, creating ground for theoretically and methodologically informed discussion, as is evident from the large number of workshops and conferences organised in the last few years, including the one from which this volume originates. Of course, this binary division is simplistic, but it suits the heuristic function of framing the different arguments presented in the archaeological debate on migration and can help us to understand how and in which fruitful directions we can proceed with research on archaeological migrations. Both perspectives have provoked controversies, prompting heated debate between practitioners following one approach or the other.

The use of the verb 'reconcile' in the titles of recent research papers (e.g. Eisenmann *et al.* 2018; Riede *et al.* 2019) concerned with this topic, or those suggesting an uneasy relationship between archaeology and ancient genomics (e.g. Callaway 2018), openly indicates the existence of such tensions. The use of the prefix 're-' in titles such as 'Re-integrating archaeology: a contribution to aDNA studies and the migration discourse on the 3rd millennium BC in Europe' (Furholt 2019a) and 'Re-theorising mobility and the formation of culture and language among the Corded Ware culture in Europe' (Kristiansen *et al.* 2017) suggests the widely shared perception that migration's return to the research agenda is anything but unproblematic, especially as concerns the difficulty archaeology faces in keeping pace with bioarchaeology. This problem is not new and was addressed by Brown and Pluciennik (2001: 101) 20 years ago: 'Typically, humanities-based archaeologists may be perceived as Luddite in their anti-science rhetoric, while scientists may be accused of ignorance of cultural and interpretative process'. This issue was neatly summarised by Eisenmann and her colleagues, who pointed out that the task in the coming years is to develop a proper conjunction between archaeogenomic studies and archaeology (Eisenmann *et al.* 2018), since as Furholt (2018: 2) notes, 'migration as an explanatory model for cultural change in pre-history is dealt with by the mainstream of prehistoric archaeologists working in Europe [...] largely sticking to units of classification that are conceptualised as monothetic blocks'.

The reappearance of migration in mainstream archaeology has, however, not only unveiled problems raised by archaeogenomic studies but has also revealed a worrying lack of understanding of present-day migration as it is approached by some other fields, particularly sociology and migration studies. Insights from these disciplines are often absent from most lines of argument, and their researchers are seldom found at relevant archaeological conferences on migration, as research on present human behaviour is often perceived by mainstream archaeology as irrelevant to understanding past ones. In this way, a vast amount of scholarship focusing on theoretical and methodological approaches to understand human migrations and the mechanisms behind their multiple causes – conflict, climate change, crisis, etc. – is disregarded. Similarly, Leary (2014: 16) states that archaeologists ignore the New Mobilities Paradigm (hereafter NMP) formed within the social sciences to their peril. By the same token, social scientists operating within mobility studies should not ignore archaeology and the temporal richness the discipline involves. The NMP 'challenges the ways in which much social science research has been a-mobile' (i.e. not considering mobility as a relevant factor) by putting social relations into travel and by connecting different forms of transport with complex patterns of social experience conducted through communications at a distance (Sheller and Urry 2006: 208). Its importance for archaeology lies in the criticism of sedentarist theories, as 'sedentarism treats as normal stability, meaning, and place, and treats as abnormal distance, change, and placelessness' (Sheller and Urry 2006: 208). Following Sheller and Urry (2006: 211), the NMP 'delineates the context in which both sedentary and nomadic accounts of the social world operate, and it questions how that context is itself mobilised, or performed, through ongoing sociotechnical practices, of intermittently mobile material worlds'. Within several recent archaeological projects addressing migration, the NMP has been well received and applied to archaeological enquiry. The NMP can be best described as a mode to understand the world in which movement plays an important role in shaping social relations between individuals as well as groups: 'It serves to legitimize questions about the practical, discursive, technological, and organizational ways in which societies deal with distance and the appropriate methods for their study' (Caletrío 2016).

According to Urry's classification (2008), migration is one of the four general modes of mobility. It is defined as a semi-permanent geographical movement, a 'horizontal sense of being "on the move," that refers to traveling between countries or continents often in search of a "better life" or to escape from drought, persecution, war, starvation, and so on' (Urry 2008: 480). Although Urry's (2008: 480) interest lies in present mobilities, in addressing migration, he clearly acknowledges its key role for previous cultures which also presupposed considerable movement. By addressing the processes of migration, dislocation, and displacement, and their multiple, overlapping, and turbulent dimensions, Urry (2008: 488) acknowledges that the analyses of migration and diasporas are central to critiques of the bounded and static categories of nation, ethnicity, community, and state present in many social sciences (Urry 2008: 487). Unsurprisingly, the critique that Urry offers of sociology can be moved close to those in archaeology regarding the use of units of classification that are conceptualised as monothetic blocks (i.e. archaeological cultures). These are indeed seen as highly problematic and unsatisfactory for the understanding of migrations and for a fruitful junction of outcomes from aDNA analyses and archaeological knowledge (for different aspects of this problem concerning archaeological cultures and units of classification, see Roberts and Vander Linden 2011; Gori and Ivanova 2017; Furholt 2018: 2; Riede *et al.* 2019).

The NMP is at the core of Leary's work (2014) on archaeological approaches to mobility. By adopting a relational approach, Leary explores the wider concept of mobility at different scales. In Leary's edited volume from 2014, migration is never specifically discussed as a category of mobility, but it is dealt with within the larger category of movement. Indeed, the term migration appears only 13 times in the entire book and not always associated with human movement. Leary argues that archaeology needs to discuss mobility, but also go beyond the fact of the journey in order to discuss the rhythms, meanings, complexities, performance, and social relations of mobility, as well as how different forms of mobility affect people and groups. This work is also a call for an archaeology of movement rather than an archaeology of stasis and advocates for the development of a distinctive archaeological approach to mobility. This would entail privileging movement over place, and explicitly accepting that movement and mobility are and always have been sources of meaning and knowledge for all humans. Notably, the volume comprises contributions written by scholars with different backgrounds, among them an essay by Brown (2014) specifically addressing the DNA evidence for female mobility and exogamy in prehistory.

A recently published opinion paper underlines the fact that we struggle to understand contemporary migrations and how they affect human securities because we have so little knowledge about past ones (Altschul *et al.* 2020). The deep-time perspective offered by comparative, synthetic archaeological research is indeed crucial. For example, exploring in a systematic way the interaction of social and ecological factors within contexts of climate-related migration is enriched by using the deep-time perspective offered by comparative, synthetic archaeological research.

Together with migration, topics such as climate change, social inequality, demography, and infectious diseases are widely researched within the discipline of archaeology (Kintigh *et al.* 2014) and are thus able to provide large, complex datasets that can be utilised to obtain deeper knowledge of present human behaviour. From this succinct overview, it appears clear that an aspect on which the scholars dealing with prehistoric migrations agree is the lack of understanding of past migrations, and thus the need for developing this field of research further within archaeology and establishing truly interdisciplinary cooperation.

Archaeology of migration between past and present

The so-called refugee crisis of 2015–16 exposed how displacement of people has – again – become an urgent issue in the Global North, as migrants from the Global South entered the European Union's Mediterranean borders. Images of refugees from Lampedusa, Lesbos, and Calais and of the bodies floating over the Mediterranean have provoked a strong emotional response from archaeologists (Gori and Revello Lami 2018; Gori *et al.* 2018: with references). As a consequence, these years witnessed an upsurge of archaeological research on both past and present migration that combines scholarly work with other forms of expression, in some cases paired with political activism. Examples are the works by Hamilakis (2018b) in Lesbos and of De León (2015) at the Mexico–US border. The latter is the founder of the 'Undocumented Migration Project' (www.undocumentedm igrationproject.org), a non-profit, research-art-education-media collective that started 'Hostile Terrain 94'. This is an itinerant, participatory, political art project consisting of a 4–6 m-long map of the border between Arizona and Mexico with more than 3,400 handwritten toe tags representing the recovered bodies of people who have died between the mid-1990s and 2020 while crossing the border dividing the US and Mexico in the Sonoran Desert.

Archaeological ethnographies of contemporary migration are openly engaging with politics; one example is *Lende: The Calais 'Jungle' and Beyond*, edited by Hicks and Mallett (2019). In this work, approaches from anthropological archaeology are applied to the most recent past and the undocumented present by addressing material culture, the built environment, and landscapes and ecologies. In *Lende*, the border regime is criticised together with the outlining of 'forms of resistance in the shape of visual politics and of materiality, seen as memory work, providing the temporal space, in museums and elsewhere, for reflection and critique' (Hamilakis 2019: 1372).

Migration and refugee studies is a growing and diverse transdisciplinary field of scholarship and activism that is quickly developing within archaeology, based on cultural anthropology and ethnography. In her illuminating essay, Heath Cabot (2019) addresses interest in – if not a *fascination* with – refugees, and the trend of research on migration within the discipline of anthropology. By focusing mainly on the United States, Cabot addresses this increasing attention by scholars, presenting examples of several major scientific events organised after 2015 that featured research on migration. The American Anthropological Association (AAA) annual meeting in 2017, in which 293 papers included the word 'refugee' or 'refugees' in the title or the abstract, compared with 70 in 2015. The public education project 'World on the Move: 100,000 Years of Human Migration' was initiated in 2016 by the same association and was meant to push public understandings of mobility beyond 'ideology and rhetoric' (Cabot 2019: 263). The 2017 theme of the Society for Cultural Anthropology's first virtual meeting – 'Displacements' – showed how the imagery of the refugee crisis permeated diverse arenas of anthropological investigation. The theme of the 2018 meeting of the European Association for Social Anthropologists – 'Staying, Moving, Settling' – saw organisers and hosts repeatedly emphasise the urgency for addressing these themes. Drawing from her expertise in the field and thus on her engagement as grant reviewer for projects based on ethnography of refugees, Cabot clearly points out that recent anthropological scholarship on and of the 'refugee crisis' can be highly problematic due to the risk of replicating logics of apartheid and marginalisation. Such logics become particularly egregious when the business of academic work intersects with other industries that (like many brands of current anthropology) may also appear benign, helpful, or even liberational in their framing (Cabot 2019: 262).

A similar interest in migration can be observed at other European meetings as well, where migrations have been debated at several interdisciplinary conferences. The first large conference on the topic was 'The Archaeology of Migrations', an international colloquium organised by Inrap in 2015, in partnership with the National Museum of Immigration History in France. The symposium, 'by confronting archaeological, historical, geographic and demographic data from different periods and places', was aimed at moving 'beyond a simple observation of large-scale population movements, by looking at the points of contact between migrants and their host societies' (Inrap 2017).

Archaeologists' engagement with contemporary migrations still needs to fully explore its potential in the understanding of past migrations by offering novel insights not gained from other approaches and methods. However, the engagement of archaeology with present migrations has two remarkable merits: the first is that it has shown to fellow archaeologists that human migration is a complex and nuanced phenomenon that cannot be understood as a simple *from–to* equation with starting and arrival points drawn on a map, or by using bounded concepts such as archaeological cultures as a principal unity of enquiry (Furholt 2019b). The archaeology of present migration has also stimulated a more profound engagement of archaeologists with anthropology, ethnography, human geography, and other disciplines that specifically address migration (Leary 2014). Secondly, it has reminded practitioners that archaeology as a discipline – as every other field of knowledge – cannot be detached from the historical, political, and cultural environment in which archaeologists live and work (Trigger 1989).

Ways to move forward

In this concluding section, we summarise the most relevant issues regarding different approaches to the study of prehistoric migrations as outlined in the examples discussed above. If correctly addressed, these points could favour synergies between different approaches and improve archaeological understanding of migration.

Adopting explicit working definitions

There are several works in which detailed classifications for types of archaeological migration are presented (e.g. Burmeister 2000; Prien 2005; Barnard and Wendrich 2008). It is not our intention to provide here a further definition for migration or to choose a single and more effective one from among those already provided. The reason is that there is no single and final definition for migration that can embrace all the aspects of this complex and multifaceted phenomenon. Instead, we advocate for the adoption of working definitions for migrations in our research and – most importantly – we suggest making these working definitions explicit within our writing. As editors of *Rethinking Anthropological Perspectives on Migration*

(2011), Cabana and Clark devoted a large part of the introduction to putting forward the need for a minimal definition of migration – 'one-way residential relocation to a different "environment" by at least one individual' (Cabana and Clark 2011: 5) – as a foundation on which to build research in this field. Migration 'is movement between two "places" that are conceived of as different because some sort of real and perceived boundary has been traversed' (Cabana and Clark 2011: 6).

The choice of adopting a minimal definition derived from the fact that the participants in the workshop on which Cabana and Clark's book was based were indeed not able to agree on a common and final definition for migration, and thus they opted for a fluid working one. It is interesting to underline that in the International Union of Prehistoric and Protohistoric Sciences conference – the basis of the present volume – there was disagreement on migration as well, since the concept of migration was understood in various ways by different scholars, provoking circular arguments in the discussion and many misunderstandings. This difficulty is also rooted in the current boom in aDNA studies, in which a specific model of migration – the single-event mass migration – appears to be dominant, as is exemplified in the phrase 'massive migration' chosen for the title of the paper by Haak and his colleagues (Haak *et al*. 2015). By explicitly defining in our works what we understand in our use of the term migration – whether using our own definition or an already existing one – the models that we will propose will be more solid and clear, and a constructive debate will undoubtedly be facilitated.

Adopting different scales

The existence of different space and timescales, and the way in which we approach them, is a central problem in archaeology. Gosden and Kirsanow (2006: 27) have reminded us how temporal scales are less intuitively grasped and trouble humans much more than the questions of spatial ones: time in archaeological interpretation is not straightforward as it involves dealing with different measurements, timescales, spans, and durations. An example of this problem in the case of Haak and his colleagues' (Haak *et al*. 2015) mass migration model is pointed out by Furholt (2018: 165), as he discusses discrepancies between the proposed model of a sudden event – based on the conceptualisation of Corded Ware as a single and bounded culture – and the timescale utilised, which encompasses about 700 years, calculated as the time between the latest Middle Neolithic individual without the Eastern European genetic component (3300 and 3100 cal BC) and the earliest Corded Ware individual (around 2560 cal BC to 2470 cal BC). The traditional idea of time in archaeology is conceived as a linear progression. This concept is influenced by the predominance of technological advancements as chrono-cultural markers and is used in the construction of archaeological phases. Such notions of duration equated with unity account for the mistaken equation of the passage of time with change, which is one of the most prominent misconceptions in the study of archaeological time (Bailey 1983).

Also crucial is the combination and interpretation of data reflecting different timescales, such as those deriving from isotope analyses and those provided by aDNA. The first give information on movement within an individual lifetime, while the second provide information based on different generations. Complexity is neither to be separated nor dissolved into simpler forms (Gosden and Kirsanow 2006: 36). We should rather acknowledge the possibilities and limitations that working with different scales presents by choosing the right proxies for the proper questions (Riede *et al.* 2019). While large-scale aggregate phenomena such as the 3rd millennium BC migrations are undoubtedly fascinating, research on the topic should also make efforts to understand the medium and small geographic scales of migration. Likewise, working on different and meaningful timescales can help us to understand migration dynamics through time in a better way, thus allowing for the proposal of better migration models.

Changing visual representations

When comparing old maps depicting human migration in prehistory with many of those recently published, one can observe that the ways of representing movement have changed little. Archaeological sites are usually represented as small dots on a map showing geographic features, while the distribution of material culture is often represented as a bounded whole. Long-distance movements of humans – or rather of objects taken as proxies for mobility – are represented in the shape of a variety of different arrows. An example of such maps is the one drawn by Gimbutas (1963: 826) to illustrate her Kurgan invasion model of warlike male pastoralist groups from the north Pontic region of the then USSR (Figure 2.2). This map is an example of Gimbutas' work, which was first proposed in 1956 and subsequently developed over a period of three decades, representing a milestone in research on the Yamnaya migrations (e.g. Anthony 1990), although also widely criticised (e.g. Kristiansen 1989). In a widely quoted article, Harley (1989) questioned the view of maps as objective and accurate representations of the world, which obfuscates how they are instead part of mapping traditions, the ways maps are influenced by the preconditions of the mapper, and their authoritative role in social construction. Recently, Van Houtum and Bueno Lacy (2020: 196) have elaborated on the role of maps as artefacts of power, not only conveying descriptive information but narrating complex models in a simplified manner, due to their 'deceptive iconographic simplicity'. This matter has been seldom discussed in archaeology (Smith 2005; Grunwald 2016; 2017; Gosselain 2017), even as maps are an essential device to transfer knowledge in archaeological publications.

Following Van Leeuwen's social semiotic approach (2004), we understand most maps as multimodal phenomena combining a large scale of different drawn and written signs, which play different roles in the creation of information. Maps used to illustrate migrations are for the most part composed of two main elements, one being the polygons indicating the limits of certain technological features or

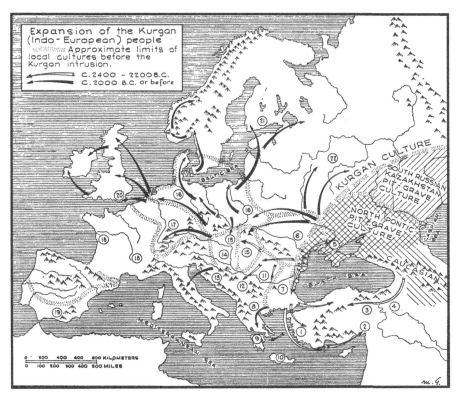

Figure 2.2 Map drawn by Gimbutas (1963: 826) to illustrate her Kurgan people invasion model (reproduced by permission of the American Anthropological Association from *American Anthropologist*, 65(4), 815–36, 1963. Not for sale or further reproduction)

the spread of material culture (i.e. archaeological cultures), and the other being the arrows, which we understand as vectors creating information regarding the movement under discussion. In most cases, start and end points are defined on the basis of a specific type of evidence (e.g. most ancient and most recent dates for an archaeological feature), while the line segments themselves are frequently of a more intuitive nature. Arrows are little more than a tentative interpolation of data and are not able to give any information about the routes and paths taken by past humans. Well-crafted, thoughtful visualisations of data could indeed help us to explore new ways of transmitting information in illustrations. A growing body of research targeting data visualisation techniques in academic research shows that cross-sector collaboration, as well as sharing data with others so that they can produce visualisations, are the most effective means for overcoming the lack of effectiveness in scientific visualisations (Gatto 2015). In archaeology, the 'maps and arrows visual narratives' could also cede place to more thoughtful ways of visualising data, for example by promoting a more intensive collaboration with scholars from other fields, especially those working within migrations studies, a discipline in which these issues are the object of lively debate (Van Houtum and Bueno Lacy 2020: 208–12). The representations of present migration flows via circular plots used by Abel and Sander (2014) illustrate this point. Visual representation of numeric and non-numeric data does not replace narrative, and it should be used in combination with it to improve understanding and reduce knowledge gaps. Data visualisation should thus be used by academics because it enhances the understanding of information for both research producers (i.e. scientists) and research consumers (i.e. society).

Acknowledging the role of politics

Since Trigger's seminal book (1989), a large amount of scholarly work has been devoted to exploring the role of politics in shaping archaeology and the manifold ways we choose our research topics, as well as the way our social and cultural environments influence our interpretation of the past (Díaz-Andreu and Champion 1996; Graves-Brown *et al.* 1996; Kohl and Fawcett 1996; Meskell 1998; Hamilakis 2007; Karamanolakis 2008). On the other hand, archaeologists have the ability to impact societal and political discourses in one way or another (Bernbeck and Pollock 2007; for an example see Abar 2020). It is therefore too easy to withdraw to a position that their discipline is irrelevant to society in comparison with other research fields.

By analysing how publications on the genetic impact of the populations making and using the Yamnaya material culture were picked up enthusiastically by the media, Hakenbeck (2019: 5–6) has clearly shown that scholars working on genomic population histories have thus far not engaged enough with their sociopolitical impact and the wider social context in which their work is received, frequently passively feeding these narratives. Headlines focusing on narratives of migrations and the origins of Europeans have been used to feed into far-right and white supremacist narratives rooted in the 19th century. There is little surprise in observing tension between scholars working on genomic population histories and scholars working in anthropological and ethnographic research, as the latter are often engaged with present-day migrations and thus with the people that the far-right groups promoting aDNA-based narratives are discriminating against.

Discussions involving politics and worldviews are always delicate and problematic; however, we are convinced that the study of migration will improve if archaeologists are willing to engage in debate, refraining from hiding themselves behind claims of the supposed neutrality of science. The role of ethics in research has been increasing when it comes to questions of how samples are being taken and how consent is communicated between the scientists and the individuals providing genetic samples. Ethical concerns are not new to biology, as Tauber (1999), more than 20 years ago, reminded us that science is too significant to be left to scientists alone. By contrast, why are ethical aspects not explicitly involved or sometimes disregarded as concerns the societal and political implications of the archaeological narratives that we produce? As already clearly shown in dedicated research on the topic, acknowledging the role of politics in our work and the role of our work in politics does not mean that we are allowing political agendas into our research. On the contrary, discussing prehistoric migration with this awareness will facilitate a resolution of 'tensions' within the discipline and scientific progress.

Actually being interdisciplinary

Research by geneticists has left many archaeologists doubtful of the reliability of genetic data, especially since they seem to contradict other types of evidence, as discussed, for example, by Hofmann (2015) in dealing with the Neolithic *Linearbandkeramik*. She stresses how genetic information provides no answers regarding an individual's experienced sense of belonging and calls for a true collaboration. This would require archaeologists to observe the necessary protocols when retrieving human remains, and geneticists to publish information that allows their data to be linked back to the graves they sampled, ideally with archaeological advice (Hofmann 2015). 'In this way' – argues Hofmann (2015: 469) – 'archaeologists and geneticists can make the most of the opportunities of interdisciplinary collaboration and fully exploit the potential of aDNA analyses to change our understandings of the Neolithic'.

Furholt (2018; 2021) has clearly addressed the tension between the social processes as visible in archaeological data and the molecular biological data as concerns research on 3rd millennium BC migrations. He shows that the renewed emphasis on migration as an explanatory framework in European prehistory, as it is expressed in the publications of aDNA studies discussed here (Brandt *et al.* 2013; Lazaridis *et al.* 2014; Allentoft *et al.* 2015; Haak *et al.* 2015; Mathieson *et al.* 2015), promotes an approach to archaeological material that neglects two central achievements within archaeology. The first of these is the deconstruction of the assumption that shared material culture can be equated with a single, socially homogenous culture in a simple manner. The second is the 'realization that the variability and multiplicity of social phenomena and agencies that constructed those seemingly homogenous material cultural groups were in fact underscored by diverse approaches to subsistence, settlement patterns, social practices, and ritual expressions' (Furholt 2018: 160).

If we look at some of the most relevant and discussed publications of aDNA studies (e.g. Brandt *et al.* 2013; Lazaridis *et al.* 2014; Allentoft *et al.* 2015; Haak *et al.* 2015; Mathieson *et al.* 2015), we note a strong imbalance in the disciplinary orientation of scholars involved in favour of researchers with a biomolecular background. None of the researchers involved – at least to our knowledge – has worked extensively in the field of migration studies or human geography. Human geographers have developed a variety of approaches and methods to study present mobility, focusing on flows and networks of connections and on hybrid geographies of human–non-human interactions (Whatmore 2002). Cresswell (2010: 19, 21) pointed out that mobility 'involves a fragile entanglement of movement, representations, and practices' and is the result of physically getting from one place to another, but also of the different meanings that all sorts of movements take on, and the experienced and embodied practice of movement. Certainly, all these components are not easy to untangle in prehistoric migrations, but it is also true that movement is just one aspect of mobility (Hakenbeck 2008).

We are convinced that social and natural scientific approaches to understanding past migrations only appear irreconcilable as they both focus on the same phenomenon: human migration. A genuinely interdisciplinary research strategy, bringing together scholars from all fields including migration studies, may help in overcoming entrenched positions and fostering knowledge advancement in archaeological migration.

Acknowledgements

The authors are grateful to the University of Bochum for the financial support provided for attending the UISPP Metal Ages in Europe Scientific Commission Conference 'Where Are You Going? Reconsidering Migrations in the Metal Ages' in Edinburgh. We are also grateful to the reviewers for carefully reading our chapter and providing useful comments and remarks that contributed to improving the quality of our work. Maja Gori would like to thank Michael Allan Patton, Trevor Roy Dunn, and Preston Lea Spruance III for being a constant source of inspiration in these difficult times.

References

Abar, A. (2020), 'Legacy of Teispian and Achaemenian materiality: reassessing the history and role of monuments in 19th–21st century Iranian nationalism', *EX NOVO Journal of Archaeology*, 5: 93–118.

Abel, G.J. and Sander, N. (2014), 'Quantifying global international migration flows', *Science*, 343(6178): 1520–2.

Adams, W.Y., Van Gerven, D.P., and Levy, R.S. (1978), 'The retreat from migrationism', *Annual Review of Anthropology*, 7: 483–532.

Allentoft, M.E., Sikora, M., Sjögren, K.-G., Rasmussen, S., Rasmussen, M., *et al.* (2015), 'Population genomics of Bronze Age Eurasia', *Nature*, 522(7555): 167–72.

Altschul, J.H., Kintigh, K.W., Aldenderfer, M., Alonzi, E., Armit, I., *et al.* (2020), 'To understand how migrations affect human securities, look to the past', *Proceedings of the National Academy of Sciences of the United States of America*, 117(34): 20342–5.

Anthony, D.W. (1990), 'Migration in archeology: the baby and the bathwater', *American Anthropologist*, 92(4): 895–914.

Babić, S. (2002), 'Still innocent after all these years? Sketches for a social history of archaeology in Serbia', in P. Biehl, A. Gramsch, and A. Marciniak (eds), *Archäologien Europas/Archaeologies of Europe. Geschichte Methoden und Theorien/History, Methods and Theory* (Münster, Waxmann Verlag), 309–21.

Bailey, G.N. (1983), 'Concepts of time in Quaternary prehistory', *Annual Review of Anthropology*, 12: 165–92.

Barnard, H. and Wendrich, W. (2008), *The Archaeology of Mobility: Old World and New World Nomadism* (Los Angeles, Cotsen Institute of Archaeology Press).

Bernbeck, R. and Pollock, S. (2007), '"Grabe wo Du stehst!": an archaeology of perpetrators', in Y. Hamilakis and P. Duke (eds), *Archaeology and Capitalism: From Ethics to Politics* (Walnut Creek, Left Coast Press), 217–33.

Brandt, G., Haak, W., Adler, C.J., Roth, C., Szécsényi-Nagy, A., *et al.* (2013), 'Ancient DNA reveals key stages in the formation of Central European mitochondrial genetic diversity', *Science*, 342(6155): 257–61.

Brown, K.A. (2014), 'Women on the move: the DNA evidence for female mobility and exogamy in prehistory', in J.P. Leary (ed), *Past Mobilities: Archaeological Approaches to Movement and Mobility* (Farnham, Ashgate), 155–73.

Brown, K.A. and Pluciennik, M. (2001), 'Archaeology and human genetics: lessons for both', *Antiquity*, 75(287): 101–6.

Burmeister, S. (2000), 'Archaeology and migration: approaches to an archaeological proof of migration', *Current Anthropology*, 41(4): 539–67.

Cabana, G.S. and Clark, J.L. (2011), 'Introduction. Migration in anthropology: where we stand', in G.S. Cabana and J.L. Clark (eds), *Rethinking Anthropological Perspectives on Migration* (Gainesville, University Press of Florida), 3–15.

Cabot, H. (2019), 'The business of anthropology and the European refugee regime', *American Ethnologist*, 46(3): 261–75.

Caletrío, J. (2016), 'Mobilities paradigm', accessed 1 December 2020, https://en.forumvies mobiles.org/marks/mobilities-paradigm-3293.

Callaway, E. (2018), 'Divided by DNA: the uneasy relationship between archaeology and ancient genomics', *Nature*, 555(7698): 573–6.

Childe, V.G. (1950), *Prehistoric Migrations in Europe* (Oslo, H. Aschehoug & Co).

Crellin, R.J. (2020), *Change and Archaeology* (Abingdon, Routledge).

Cresswell, T. (2010), 'Towards a politics of mobility', *Environment and Planning D: Society and Space*, 28(1): 17–31.

De León, J. (2015), *The Land of Open Graves: Living and Dying on the Migrant Trail* (Oakland, University of California Press).

Díaz-Andreu García, M. and Champion, T.C. (eds) (1996), *Nationalism and Archaeology in Europe* (London, Routledge).

Driessen, J. (ed) (2018), *An Archaeology of Forced Migration: Crisis-Induced Mobility and the Collapse of the 13th c. BCE Eastern Mediterranean* (Louvain, Presses Universitaires de Louvain).

Eisenmann, S., Bánffy, E., Van Dommelen, P., Hofmann, K.P., Maran, J., *et al.* (2018), 'Reconciling material cultures in archaeology with genetic data: the nomenclature of clusters emerging from archaeogenomic analysis', *Scientific Reports*, 8(1): 13003, DOI: 10.1038/s41598-018-31123-z.

Frieman, C.J. and Hofmann, D. (2019), 'Present pasts in the archaeology of genetics, identity, and migration in Europe: a critical essay', *World Archaeology*, 51(4): 528–45.

Furholt, M. (2018), 'Massive migrations? The impact of recent aDNA studies on our view of third millennium Europe', *European Journal of Archaeology*, 21(2): 159–91.

Furholt, M. (2019a), 'Re-integrating archaeology: a contribution to aDNA studies and the migration discourse on the 3rd millennium BC in Europe', *Proceedings of the Prehistoric Society*, 85: 115–29.

Furholt, M. (2019b), 'De-contaminating the aDNA – archaeology dialogue on mobility and migration: discussing the culture-historical legacy', *Current Swedish Archaeology*, 27: 53–68.

Furholt, M. (2021), 'Mobility and social change: understanding the European Neolithic period after the archaeogenetic revolution', *Journal of Archaeological Research*, 29: 481–535.

Gatto, M.A. (2015), *Making Research Useful: Current Challenges and Good Practices in Data Visualisation* (Oxford, Reuters Institute for the Study of Journalism).

Gimbutas, M. (1963), 'The Indo-Europeans: archeological problems', *American Anthropologist*, 65: 815–36.

Gori, M. and Ivanova, M. (eds) (2017), *Balkan Dialogues: Negotiating Identity between Prehistory and the Present* (London, Routledge).

Gori, M. and Revello Lami, M. (2018), 'From Lampedusa to Trieste: tracing forced migrations to understand identity patterns', in J. Driessen (ed), *An Archaeology of Forced Migration: Crisis-Induced Mobility and the Collapse of the 13th c. BCE Eastern Mediterranean* (Louvain, Presses Universitaires de Louvain), 31–53.

Gori, M., Revello Lami, M., and Pintucci, A. (2018), 'Editorial: practices, representations and meanings of human mobility in archaeology', *Ex Novo Journal of Archaeology*, 3: 1–6.

Gosden, C. and Kirsanow, K. (2006), 'Timescales', in G. Lock and B. Molyneaux (eds), *Confronting Scale in Archaeology: Issues of Theory and Practice* (Boston, Springer), 27–37.

Gosselain, O. (2017), 'A tradition in nine maps: un-layering Niger River polychrome water jars', in M. Gori and M. Ivanova (eds), *Balkan Dialogues: Negotiating Identity between Prehistory and the Present* (London, Routledge), 85–105.

Graves-Brown, P., Gamble, C.S., and Jones, S. (eds) (1996), *Cultural Identity and Archaeology* (Hoboken, Taylor & Francis).

Grunwald, S. (2016), 'Archäologischer Raum ist politischer Raum: Neue Perspektiven auf die archäologische Kartographie', *Forum Kritische Archäologie*, 5: 50–75.

Grunwald, S. (2017), 'Metaphern – Punkte – Linien: Zur sprachlichen und kartographischen Semantik ur- und frühgeschichtlicher Wanderungsnarrative bei Gustaf Kossinna', in F. Wiedemann, K.P. Hofmann, and H.-J. Gehrke (eds), *Vom Wandern der Völker: Migrationserzählungen in den Altertumswissenschaften* (Berlin, Edition Topoi), 285–323.

Haak, W., Lazaridis, I., Patterson, N., Rohland, N., Mallick, S., *et al.* (2015), 'Massive migration from the steppe was a source for Indo-European languages in Europe', *Nature*, 522(7555): 207–11.

Hakenbeck, S.E. (2008), 'Migration in archaeology: are we nearly there yet?', *Archaeological Review from Cambridge*, 23(2): 9–26.

Hakenbeck, S.E. (2019), 'Genetics, archaeology and the far right: an unholy trinity', *World Archaeology*, 9(3): 1–11.

Hamilakis, Y. (2007), *The Nation and Its Ruins: Antiquity, Archaeology, and National Imagination in Greece* (Oxford, Oxford University Press).

Hamilakis, Y. (2017), 'Who are you calling Mycenaean?', *London Review of Books*, 10 August 2017, accessed 1 December 2020, www.lrb.co.uk/blog/2017/august/who-are-you-calling-mycenaean.

COMPARING APPLES AND ORANGES? 39

Hamilakis, Y. (2018a), 'Decolonial archaeology as social justice', *Antiquity*, 92(362): 518–20.

Hamilakis, Y. (ed) (2018b), *The New Nomadic Age: Archaeologies of Forced and Undocumented Migration* (London, Equinox Publishing).

Hamilakis, Y. (2019), 'Planet of camps: border assemblages and their challenges', *Antiquity*, 93(371): 1371–7.

Harley, J.B. (1989), 'Deconstructing the map', *Cartographica*, 26(2): 1–20.

Heyd, V. (2017), 'Kossinna's smile', *Antiquity*, 91(356): 348–59.

Hicks, D. and Mallet, S. (2019), *Lande: The Calais 'Jungle' and Beyond* (Bristol, Bristol University Press).

Hofmann, D. (2015), 'What have genetics ever done for us? The implications of aDNA data for interpreting identity in Early Neolithic Central Europe', *European Journal of Archaeology*, 18(3): 454–76.

Inrap (2017), 'Archaeology of migrations', accessed 30 November 2020, www.inrap.fr/en/archaeology-migrations-11965.

Jung, M. (2017), 'Wanderungsnarrative in der Ur- und Frühgeschichtsforschung', in F. Wiedemann, K.P. Hofmann, and H.-J. Gehrke (eds), *Vom Wandern der Völker: Migrationserzählungen in den Altertumswissenschaften* (Berlin, Edition Topoi), 161–87.

Karamanolakis, V. (2008), 'University of Athens and archaeological studies: the contribution of archaeology to the creation of a national past (1911–32)', in D. Damaskos and D. Plantzos (eds), *A Singular Antiquity: Archaeology and Hellenic Identity in Twentieth-Century Greece* (Athen, Mouseio Benaki), 185–95.

Kintigh, K.W., Altschul, J.H., Beaudry, M.C., Drennan, R.D., Kinzig, A.P., *et al.* (2014), 'Grand challenges for archaeology', *Proceedings of the National Academy of Sciences of the United States of America*, 111(3): 879–80.

Kohl P.L. and Fawcett, C. (eds) (1996), *Nationalism, Politics, and the Practice of Archaeology* (New York, Cambridge University Press).

Kristiansen, K. (1989), 'Prehistoric migrations: the case of the Single Grave and Corded Ware cultures', *Journal of Danish Archaeology*, 8(1): 211–25.

Kristiansen, K., Allentoft, M., Frei, K., Iversen, R., Johannsen, N., *et al.* (2017), 'Re-theorising mobility and the formation of culture and language among the Corded Ware culture in Europe', *Antiquity*, 91(356): 334–47.

Lazaridis, I., Patterson, N., Mittnik, A., Renaud, G., Mallick, S., *et al.* (2014), 'Ancient human genomes suggest three ancestral populations for present-day Europeans', *Nature*, 513(7518): 409–13.

Lazaridis, I., Mittnik, A., Patterson, N., Mallick, S., Rohland, N., *et al.* (2017), 'Genetic origins of the Minoans and Mycenaeans', *Nature*, 548(7666): 214–18.

Leary, J.P. (2014), 'Past mobility: an introduction', in J.P. Leary (ed), *Past Mobilities: Archaeological Approaches to Movement and Mobility* (Farnham, Ashgate), 1–19.

Maran, J. (2017), 'Later Balkan prehistory: a transcultural perspective', in M. Gori and M. Ivanova (eds), *Balkan Dialogues: Negotiating Identity between Prehistory and the Present* (London, Routledge), 17–37.

Mathieson, I., Lazaridis, I., Rohland, N., Mallick, S., Patterson, N., *et al.* (2015), 'Genome-wide patterns of selection in 230 ancient Eurasians', *Nature*, 528(7583): 499–503.

Meskell, L. (ed) (1998), *Archaeology under Fire: Nationalism, Politics and Heritage in the Eastern Mediterranean and Middle East* (London and New York, Routledge).

Parker Pearson, M., Sheridan, A., Jay, M., Chamberlain, A., Richards, M.P., *et al.* (2019), *The Beaker People: Isotopes, Mobility and Diet in Prehistoric Britain* (Oxford, Oxbow).

40   *Maja Gori and Aydin Abar*

Prien, R. (2005), *Archäologie und Migration: Vergleichende Studien zur archäologischen Nachweisbarkeit von Wanderungsbewegungen* (Bonn, Habelt).

Reich, D. (2019), *Who We Are and How We Got there: Ancient DNA and the New Science of the Human Past* (Oxford, Oxford University Press).

Riede, F., Hoggard, C., and Shennan, S. (2019), 'Reconciling material cultures in archaeology with genetic data requires robust cultural evolutionary taxonomies', *Palgrave Communications*, 5: 1, DOI: 10.1057/s41599-019-0260-7.

Roberts, B.W. and Vander Linden, M. (2011), 'Investigating archaeological cultures: material culture, variability and transmission', in B.W. Roberts and M. Vander Linden (eds), *Investigating Archaeological Cultures: Material Culture, Variability, and Transmission* (New York, Springer Science & Business Media), 1–21.

Sheller, M. and Urry, J. (2006), 'The new mobilities paradigm', *Environment and Planning A: Economy and Space*, 38(2): 207–26.

Smith, M.L. (2005), 'Networks, territories, and the cartography of ancient states', *Annals of the Association of American Geographers*, 95(4): 832–49.

Tauber, A.I. (1999), 'Is biology a political science?', *BioScience*, 49(6): 479–86.

Trigger, B.G. (1989), *A History of Archaeological Thought* (Cambridge, Cambridge University Press).

Urry, J. (2008), 'Mobilities and social theory', in B.S. Turner (ed), *The New Blackwell Companion to Social Theory* (Oxford, Wiley-Blackwell), 475–95.

Van Dommelen, P. (2014), 'Moving on: archaeological perspectives on mobility and migration', *World Archaeology*, 46(4): 477–83.

Van Houtum, H. and Bueno Lacy, R. (2020), 'The migration map trap: on the invasion arrows in the cartography of migration', *Mobilities*, 15(2): 196–219.

Van Leeuwen, T. (2004), *Introducing Social Semiotics* (Abingdon, Routledge).

Vander Linden, M. (2016), 'Population history in third-millennium-BC Europe: assessing the contribution of genetics', *World Archaeology*, 48(5): 714–28.

Whatmore, S. (2002), *Hybrid Geographies: Natures, Cultures, Spaces* (London, Sage).

Wiedemann, F. (2017), 'Zirkuläre Verknüpfungen: Völkerwanderungen und das Motiv der Wiederkehr in den Wissenschaften vom Alten Orient um 1900', in F. Wiedemann, K.P. Hofmann, and H.-J. Gehrke (eds), *Vom Wandern der Völker: Migrationserzählungen in den Altertumswissenschaften* (Berlin, Edition Topoi), 137–60.

Wiwjorra, I. (2002), '"Ex oriente lux" – "Ex septentrione lux": über den Widerstreit zweier Identitätsmythen', in A. Leube and M. Hegewisch (eds), *Prähistorie und Nationalsozialismus: Die mittel- und osteuropäische Ur- und Frühgeschichtsforschung in den Jahren 1933–1945* (Heidelberg, Synchron), 73–106.

3

The Mobility and Migration Revolution in 3rd Millennium BC Europe

VOLKER HEYD

Introduction

SINCE THE THREE ancient DNA papers published in *Nature* in 2015 (Allentoft *et al.* 2015; Haak *et al.* 2015) and 2018 (Olalde *et al.* 2018), virtually every prehistorian is aware of the importance of the sequence Yamnaya – Corded Ware – Bell Beaker as a dynamic upheaval covering much of Europe in the 3rd millennium BC.[1] While there can be no doubt that this millennium saw people on the move, there is no consensus on the scale, size, extent, directions, or speed of the events. Uncertainty over the term 'mass migrations' is an example, without explaining the demographics and defining from which moment the term 'mass' is really applicable (Furholt 2018). More speculation rather than proper modelling also refers to the triggers, mechanisms, and ideologies that facilitated these events. What is clear is a complex interplay of three novel international complexes – Yamnaya, Corded Ware, and Bell Beaker – against the background of a set of 'indigenous' societies, genetically descended from 'Early Neolithic farmers' and people of 'western hunter-gatherer' ancestry. Culturally, these related populations figure prominently east of the Rhine River. To simplify, this contribution aims to:

1) Bring together the latest archaeological and (published) genetic evidence;
2) Highlight the regional geography and frontiers;
3) Evaluate potential mechanisms and ideologies;
4) Assess the overall role of migration and mobility.

---

[1] All dates given in the text are cal BC, based on the 2-sigma range of calibrated radiocarbon dates, with the exception of the dendrochronological dates of the Wädenswil site in Switzerland, which are absolute dates.

Proceedings of the British Academy, **254**, 41–62, © The British Academy 2023.

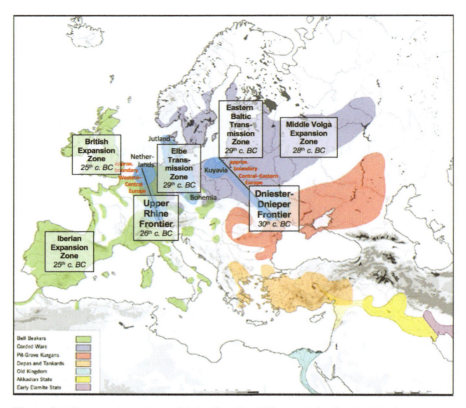

Figure 3.1 East to west regions of 3rd millennium BC transformations and their interrelations: 1) the Dnieper-Dniester interfluvial frontier; 2) the Elbe River and Eastern Baltic transmission zones; 3) the Upper Rhine River frontier; 4) the British, Iberian, and Middle Volga expansion zones (background map after Risch *et al.* 2015)

The events are split into three stages, linked with three different geographical zones (Figure 3.1).

Terminology and its proper application are confusing these days. Since the advent of aDNA studies, it is becoming harder to explain the most recent aDNA results in the 3rd millennium BC and draw a line between 'pots' and 'people'. For the time being, researchers look out more for the exceptions, i.e. when Yamnaya or Corded Ware graves and individuals without steppe ancestry become known. Nevertheless, I would like to continue to differentiate between archaeological cultures and biological populations, in the same way that one can distinguish between identity and ethnicity. For clarity, I will speak about international Yamnaya, Corded Ware, and Bell Beaker complexes with their regional cultural groups but also about users of Corded Ware or Bell Beaker pottery, in the hope of finding an acceptable compromise.

Yamnaya expanding westwards (from 3100–3050 BC)

The formation of Yamnaya proper (nota bene: not Repin of the Volga-Don region as a potential forerunner) happens in a short period around 3300–3200 BC. Within a few generations, we see the earliest Yamnaya kurgans being erected and graves placed in the plains north-west of the Black Sea. Besides occupying the steppe immediately along the Black Sea coast and eventually forming the Budzhak group (Ivanova 2014; 2015), we see their users moving north-west and northwards along the Prut and Dniester Valleys into a forest steppe environment. Research from a recent Ukrainian-Polish expedition shows Yamnaya burials dating to around 3000 BC near Yampil (Włodarczak 2017), while their northernmost extent reached to near the town of Chernivtsi in the region of Bukovina. The same encroachment is visible around the Dnieper River as far north as Kiev (Merpert 1974: Figure 1; Kaiser 2019).

Afterwards, Yamnaya people entered the steppe west of the Black Sea and South-East Europe. The beginnings of Yamnaya in Romania (Diaconescu 2020; Preda-Bălănică et al. 2020) and Bulgaria (Alexandrov 2020) are indistinguishable from those in Hungary (Dani 2020) and Serbia (Koledin et al. 2020), at approximately 3010/3050 BC. Apparently, they moved in one go to the end of the Eurasian steppe belt at the Tisza River. Being well adapted to the steppe, it consequently became orthodoxy (including for myself) that their burials could only be found within the limitations of the steppe corridor. However, more recently, we have data on Yamnaya-related graves in eastern Thrace (Turkey) and southern Serbia, Kosovo, and Albania. A similar scenario could exist for regions further to the west, north-west, and north, across the Tisza, where local interaction occurred and the same components of burial customs are visible in the records.

Possible triggers and mechanisms for this Yamnaya westward migration (and a contemporary eastward migration to the Altai Mountains in the form of the Afanasievo culture) were expressed in Frînculeasa et al. (2015: 84–6, Figure 18) and Heyd (2019: 127–8). In a nutshell, it is a socioeconomic model based on the introduction of a key innovation, 'wheel and wagon', against the background of climatic change towards increasing aridity. This led a newly formed but rapidly expanding society to become cattle herders and pastoralists, if not eventually the first true nomads. Their constant search for pastures for their animals, as their major source of subsistence, subsequently drew them westwards. That climate and environmental change played a key role in events is shown by a series of similar cultural changes and population movements across Europe, the most important of them being the expansion of Globular Amphora culture to both the east and west (Woidich 2014; Szmyt 2018; 2021). A strange Y chromosome bottleneck effect, not yet fully explained, also seems to have occurred globally around the same time (Poznik et al. 2016; Zeng et al. 2018). Besides our socioeconomic model, the idea that chiefs direct migrations of societal segments during times of crises with rising levels of conflict is plausible too (Anthony 2020). Pastoralist societies might even be particularly prone to this, as written history indicates repeatedly. The idea of an 'ideology of travellers' in 3rd millennium BC Europe (see Wentink 2020: 239–47) might have added another trigger.

The first regional transmission: the Dniester–Dnieper River frontier and the emergence of the Corded Ware cultural complex (2950–2750 BC)

All recent Corded Ware aDNA/archaeology publications (Juras *et al.* 2018; Malmström *et al.* 2019; Furtwängler *et al.* 2020; Linderholm *et al.* 2020; Saag *et al.* 2020; Egfjord *et al.* 2021; Papac *et al.* 2021; Haak *et al.* 2022) point to a paradox. While Corded Ware graves, particularly those dating to 2900–2700 BC, always display a high degree of steppe ancestry (with a few of them nearly 100 per cent), only two of them have the typical Y chromosome of Yamnaya, R1b-Z2103. The majority of Y chromosomes are of the distinct R1a type (almost all of M417 and Z282), while R1b is also well represented, albeit with L51 and U106. Q1b and I2a play only minor roles, with I2a burials mostly being rather late and geographically peripheral. This can only mean that the vast majority of Corded Ware users were *not* direct descendants of Yamnaya people, but rather of other steppe populations, rich in steppe ancestry but with divergent Y chromosome signatures. Yamnaya burial customs are nevertheless the best inspiration for some of the key features of early Corded Ware graves, i.e. mounds, the idea of the individual, east–west orientation, and supine upper body (Furholt 2019: legend of Figure 1). The same is true for their supposed pastoralism. However, other important features do not really fit, such as gender differentiation, grave goods customs, and weapon display. Also, Corded Ware users never took over the peculiar Yamnaya hair fashion with the silver hair rings, so widely distributed (Kaiser 2019: Figure 125). So, Yamnaya does not completely stand aside when it comes to the formation of early Corded Ware. However, if Yamnaya was not in the driving seat, who was?

The answer is probably a mixture of various peoples with different regional backgrounds, as both the variety of Y chromosomes and cultural aspects imply. But let us pinpoint the geography.

Firstly, it is not the steppe proper, as by 3000 BC the process of Yamnaya homogenisation is well underway, including brotherhood-like uniformity of what becomes the typical Yamnaya Y chromosome. This development leads to a different trajectory. There is the facet of the cord-decorated Beaker vessels (Figure 3.3), widely distributed among child burials in the Budzhak group and Romania, with examples reaching as far south as Bulgaria. While Ivanova sees them as genuine Corded Ware vessels, and their appearance in the Budzhak group as a result of contacts with Corded Ware users (Ivanova 2019), they seem to appear as early as 2900 BC (Frînculeasa *et al.* 2015), making this direction of the link questionable. More research and better dating may clarify their role in the Corded Ware formation.

THE MOBILITY AND MIGRATION REVOLUTION   45

Secondly, the steppe ancestry and Yamnaya contacts refer to the more northerly forest steppe zone with its greater heterogenity. The preference for forest steppe might be justified when looking into the distribution of typical Corded Ware jewellery, like bone toggles, bone/shell discs, and perforated tooth chains (i.e. Mansfeld 2003; Kaiser 2019: Figure 145). Indeed, they might point to a wider catchment.

Thirdly, a few 'Early Neolithic farmer' and 'western hunter-gatherer' ancestries in Corded Ware users, seemingly from the beginnings, can help in limiting their range, as only the forest steppe regions possessed settlements of these farmers around 3000 BC (Nordqvist and Heyd 2020: Figure 9). Regions further to the east, between the Dnieper and Don and in the immediate Black Sea hinterland, do not have this substrate.

It is the multicultural boundary between the Dniester and Dnieper, with three different farming societies (i.e. the local late TRB, Tripolye C2, and Globular Amphora cultures) arriving from the north-west. In the last third of the 4th millennium BC, this zone was also inhabited by several highly differentiated steppe groups labelled as 'post-Stog' or 'late post-Stog' (Rassamakin 2013) from which the graves of the super-regional Zhivotilovka-Volchansk group (Rassamakin 1999; more recently Demchenko 2016; Manzura 2016) stand out. These are defined as individual burials with side-crouched body position on both the left and right side, with arms bent and hands in front of the face/chest, while other components of their burial customs can vary, e.g. pit form, cover, orientation, ochre straying, and grave goods. This 'cultural horizon' might well become the missing link. Particularly intriguing is the equal number of left- and right-sided individuals, so that left-sided skeletons have their heads in the north-east and east, and right-sided ones have them in the south and south-east (Manzura 2016: 61). Although there is no confirmation from the bio-anthropological side, it reminds everyone familiar with 3rd millennium BC archaeology of the gender-differentiated Corded Ware burial customs.

Nonetheless, this all makes the Dniester–Dnieper frontier a perfect transmission zone. The arrival of Globular Amphora users is particularly noted, being themselves on an expansionist drive both to the west and east around 3000 BC, and taking over territory previously settled by late TRB and Tripolye C2 groups. This might have triggered reflexes in local steppe populations, facilitating the emergence of Corded Ware as a belligerent response. This case of Globular Amphora culture in the east is of great interest anyway. Their male users mostly belong to Y chromosome I2a, a haplogroup which after 2800 BC no longer had a great future: it disappeared almost completely from the aDNA records in Central and Eastern Europe in favour of the steppe signatures R1a and R1b. Obviously, we see two contrasting expansions here, between the Dniester and Dnieper, one directed from north-west to south-east and based on the Globular Amphora culture, and an opposite one connected to Yamnaya–Corded Ware and steppe ancestry that eventually was to gain the upper hand. Such a clash across Eastern Europe may have determined the later course of events in Europe.

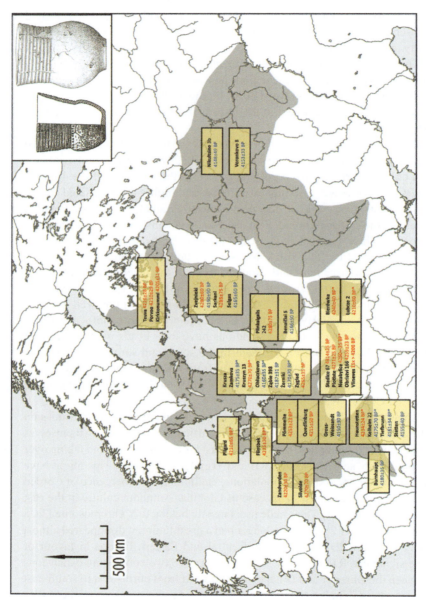

Figure 3.2 29th/28th century BC earliest Corded Ware radiocarbon dates across Europe (image: author; background map after Nordqvist and Heyd 2020; site name; in red dates >4200 BP, in blue dates >4150 BP; *=several dates from same grave, in which case the oldest is taken; W=possible old-wood-effect; R=possible reservoir effect; settlement sites are Burnhaupt, Kirkkonummi, Porvoo, Teuva, and Zandverden).

Additionally, there are surprisingly few early Corded Ware graves (Figure 3.2) in south-eastern Poland, Silesia, and Moravia (Czech Republic). This does not speak for any crossing of the Carpathian Mountains as a source for Yamnaya–Corded Ware transmissions (Anthony 2022; or see the arrow in Allentoft *et al.* 2015: 168, Figure 1). This minimises the potential impact of the Danubian branch of Yamnaya on Corded Ware. Some early Corded Ware graves were found in Greater Poland (Pospiezny 2015; Pospiezny *et al.* 2015). Likewise, several graves and settlement sites prove the Eastern Baltic region was the target of an early Corded Ware trajectory from *c.* 2900 BC (Piličiauskas *et al.* 2018; Pesonen *et al.* 2019), although some reservoir effects likely apply here. Another landscape with early Corded Ware graves surrounds the course of the Elbe River linking Jutland and Bohemia. A radiocarbon dating programme has recently increased the number of Bohemian early Corded Ware graves, some dating as early as 2900 BC, making it a true centre for further dispersal (Dobeš and Limburský 2013; Papac *et al.* 2021; Dobeš *et al.* 2021). Many of these early graves have no or only minimal equipment (i.e. flint knifes) and, without radiocarbon dating, would be unrecognisable. They fit perfectly, however, within the definition of the so-called Kalbsrieth graves (Furholt 2003) known

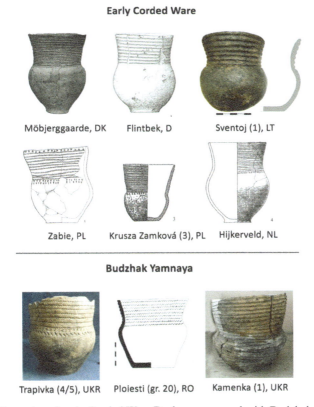

Figure 3.3 Examples of early Corded Ware Beakers compared with Budzhak, Romanian, and Bulgarian Yamnaya Beakers (image: author; not scaled)

from the Mittelelbe-Saale region, down the course of the Elbe River. Further north, graves belonging to the 29th century BC were recognised at Flintbeck, Schleswig-Holstein (Brozio 2018) and in Danish Jutland (Iversen 2019). Early Corded Ware graves of roughly the same century are known from the Netherlands (Beckerman 2015) and Bavaria. Here, the graves from the sites of Augsburg-Haunstetten, Kelheim, Moosham (all Heyd 2000), and Wartenberg are good examples, with some fitting the Kalbsrieth criterion. The Rhine River is the western boundary of any early Corded Ware expression. For the Upper Rhine, this impact is genetically recognisable in the megalithic dolmen of Aesch (Switzerland) where one individual (no. 25), dated to 2864–2501 cal BC at 2 sigma, displays a high degree of steppe ancestry and Y chromosome R1b-L51 (Furtwängler *et al.* 2020).

Overall, we see nothing short of a true prehistoric revolution in Europe: from the arrival of Yamnaya north-west of the Black Sea to Corded Ware in Bohemia and the transmission of steppe ancestry from the Dniester/Dnieper to the Rhine, it took around 150 years (*c.* 3050–2900 BC), or perhaps five to six generations (with 25–30 years per generation). Within these few generations, people on the move were adapting to completely new environments and also changing culture, forming what we understand as Corded Ware. No matter whether or not pronouncedly more males than females were moving (Goldberg *et al.* 2017; Scorrano *et al.* 2021), current figures speak for leapfrog rather than wave-of-advance migrations. This becomes quite clear when comparing these facts to the Early Neolithic farming colonisation of Europe which, for the same distance of 1500 km from the Aegean to the Rhine River, took no less than a thousand years (*c.* 6500 to 5500 BC). Thus, completely different mechanisms seem to have been at work for these two migration events.

Another Corded Ware mobility event (from 2700/2600 BC)?

From *c.* 2700/2600 BC, regional Corded Ware networks dominated between the Volga and Rhine Rivers. At least in Central Europe, this was the period of the Craców-Sandomierz group in Małopolska, the so-called Lokalgruppe III in Bohemia and Moravia, the Mansfeld group in the Mittelelbe-Saale region, or the Geiselgasteig type (Schnurkeramik C) in Bavaria. Everywhere we see homogenisations of burial customs and deposition rules, as well as the foundation of larger Corded Ware flat cemeteries, such as Zerniki Górne, Vikletice, Bergrheinfeld, and Lauda-Königshofen. Only a few sites, such as the hillfort of Burgerroth in Lower Franconia (Bavaria; Link 2016; 2018), indicate the survival of descendants of Early Neolithic farmer ancestry in core Corded Ware territory, albeit heavily impacted by their Corded Ware neighbours, as an isotope study from the same region demonstrated (Sjögren *et al.* 2016). It is only at the western boundary of the overall Corded Ware distribution, on the Upper Rhine River, that non-R1 Y chromosomes were recently recorded with a higher frequency (Furtwängler *et al.* 2020). Similar results probably also apply to the southern boundary of the Corded Ware distribution, i.e. the Alps (indirectly Mittnik *et al.* 2019), Upper and Lower Austria, and Moravia. No doubt, there was a good deal of internal Corded Ware mobility, as highlighted by the wide exchange of stone battle axes and raw materials (e.g. Müller *et al.* 2009).

Additionally, there might have been an even more dramatic case of Corded Ware migrations, only recognised due to recent aDNA discoveries. The first hint is linked to the Esperstedt Corded Ware graves of the Mittelelbe-Saale region in eastern Germany (Haak *et al.* 2015). Although never fully published, they are very rich in steppe ancestry but date late within Corded Ware (*c.* 2500–2300 BC), at a time when their percentage of steppe ancestry should have been diluted by local people rich in Early Neolithic farmer ancestries (Malmström *et al.* 2019). The Y chromosome of its best-preserved individual (I1014; grave 11) is R1a-M417; the others seem identical. The second piece of evidence refers to Bohemia where, after initial Y chromosome diversity, a bottleneck situation occurred in which only men with R1a-M417 prevailed after *c.* 2600 BC (Papac *et al.* 2021). The third indication comes from a regional aDNA study of Małopolska Corded Ware, dated to 2500–2300 BC and thus contemporary with Esperstedt (Linderholm *et al.* 2020). These graves are relatively rich in steppe ancestry and closer to Samara, Yamnaya, and Afanasievo than is typical for Corded Ware burials. Most display here a significant change in their Y chromosomes from earlier Corded Ware to the unusual R1b-M269.

So, was there a second major Corded Ware demic diffusion event? A migration that happened within the – at the time – widely established, nearly pan-European Corded Ware cultural complex? The answer is unclear. However, Piotr Włodarczak (2018; 2021; Kośko and Włodarczak 2018) advocates for a western push of people linked with the Ukrainian/Belarus Middle-Dnieper culture of the wider Corded Ware family, ultimately linked with the expansion of Katacombnaya in the steppes. While this has some credibility, other archaeologists favour links, based on pottery similarities, with the late Budzhak group (e.g. Ivanova 2019). Włodarczak's archaeological arguments mainly refer to connections in pottery, but for Małopolska he also highlights changes in burial customs such as the emergence of catacombs and of richer grave goods. He also emphasises the enhanced role of the craftsman or warrior in the grave, the latter furnished with sets of new flint arrowheads, originally in quivers. While these seem to be novelties in regions further west, too, there is no indication that a kind of peopling cascade was set in motion, although it would be a nice hypothesis that some Corded Ware mass graves were due to intra-Corded Ware conflicts linked with such migrations. A second major Corded Ware demic diffusion might also help explain the strange distribution of craftsmen's graves in the 3rd millennium BC. As a reminder, craftsmen's graves were rare in Yamnaya contexts, with none known west of the Black Sea. They were, however, popular with Katacombnaya. In Corded Ware they were unknown except for a few,

50 *Volker Heyd*

seemingly late graves, perhaps contemporary with early/middle Bell Beakers from *c.* 2500 BC (Harrison and Heyd 2007).

The second regional transmission: the Rhine River frontier (2600–2450 BC) and the emergence of the 'steppe' Bell Beaker component

The importance of the Rhine as a major watershed in Europe cannot be highlighted enough. Not only do the Rhine and its tributaries form the geographical boundary between Western and Central Europe, the region has also been a cultural boundary for millennia in prehistory. For the early 3rd millennium BC, it formed the approximate western border of the pan-European Corded Ware distribution (Toussaint 2009; Denaire *et al.* 2014; Blouet *et al.* 2019; Wentink 2020: 36), and before that the same for the Globular Amphora culture (Woidich 2014). Like the Dniester–Dnieper Rivers, boundary zones can be geographical opportunities for innovations. This was exactly the case when it came to the Bell Beaker phenomenon, which was clearly a blend of west and east. West, in terms of the origins of the Maritime Beaker vessel, a proto-package, long-distance exchange, and some of the earliest radiocarbon dates from the very west of the Iberian Peninsula. East, as there are obviously links with Corded Ware when it comes to the All-Over-Corded (AOC) and All-Over-Ornamented (AOO) Beakers, individualisation, gender differentiation, and warrior display (Lemercier 2018).

The same east–west dichotomy was also highlighted recently in aDNA (Olalde *et al.* 2018). No wonder in such a constellation that the Lower Rhine River was once, in the so-called Dutch Model (Lanting and Van der Waals 1976), regarded as a possible cradle for the emergence of the whole Bell Beaker phenomenon. However, the Lower Rhine appears, in this respect, problematic since Sandra Beckerman (2015) and Karsten Wentink (2020) showed that Maritime Beakers did not start before 2500/2450 BC. They are clearly later than the AOC and AOO Beakers, which can be either culturally Corded Ware (or Single Graves culture as it is called here) or Bell Beaker, or even something in-between. Individual graves with AOC/AOO Beakers in northern and west-central France initiated, probably throughout the 26th century BC, the first steps towards individualisation. This contrasts with the 'Beakerisation' spreading from the south-west and ultimately from Iberia, along the maritime routes of the Atlantic façade (Salanova 2016).

There is, however, another region along the Rhine which recently provided a series of early radiocarbon dates for Bell Beaker contexts, namely Alsace (eastern France), south-western Germany, and northern Switzerland (Figure 3.4). Two of these early radiocarbon dates come from female graves in Alsace at Achenheim (Dép. Bas-Rhin; GrA-15976: 4045 ± 40 BP; Ulrich 1942) and Hégenheim (Dép. Haut-Rhin; MAMS-25935: 4047 ± 29 BP; Billoin *et al.* 2010; Olalde *et al.* 2018). A third grave, recently excavated and not yet dated, from Kolbsheim belongs to a >40 year-old woman equipped with six amber beads and a similar but slimmer,

THE MOBILITY AND MIGRATION REVOLUTION   51

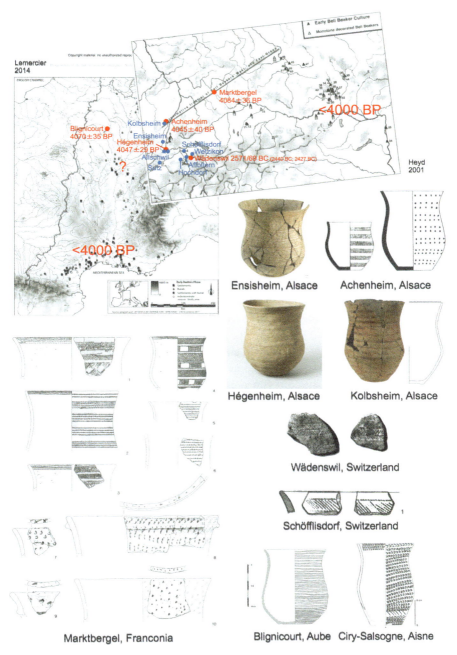

Figure 3.4 26th/25th-century BC early Bell Beakers in the Upper Rhine region and beyond (image: author; background maps after Lemercier 2014 and Heyd 2001; Beaker examples from Achenheim, Hégenheim, Kolbsheim, Wädenswil, Schöfflisdorf, and Marktbergel; Blignicourt and Ciry-Salsogne added for comparison; not scaled)

cord-zoned Maritime Beaker (Dép. Bas-Rhin; Schneikert 2019: 39–40). Further Maritime Beakers were discovered at Allschwil (Basel; Heyd 2001). While the completeness of the cord-zoned *Sandweg* Beaker, discovered in 1938, speaks for a destroyed grave, another Maritime, yet broader, vessel comes from a group of three graves of the *Friedhof* site, two women and a child. Besides these graves, there is the early Bell Beaker site of Marktbergel in Central Franconia (Bavaria), east of the Rhine. Although still awaiting full publication (Nadler 1997), the lowest levels of this *dolina* fill yielded the earliest Bell Beaker vessels, i.e. cord-zoned Maritime and AOC Beakers with frequent inner-rim decoration and red paint cover. One of the lowest levels, number 7, produced a radiocarbon date of 4084 ± 36 BP (Hd-19574), which is slightly earlier than those mentioned before. Two further well-preserved Maritime Beakers are recorded from the Swiss lake sites of Hochdorf-Baldegg (Lucerne; Bill 1983) and Sutz-Lattrigen (Bern; Nielsen and Bacher 1984), where they are regarded as intrusive in late Corded Ware dwellings. However, their contexts are not well known so they do not add much to the chronology. This is, luckily, the case for two Maritime Beaker sherds from Wädenswil-Vorderau found in late Corded Ware settlement layers, dendro-dated to 2571/2569 BC, 2440 BC, and 2427 BC (Zürich; Eberschweiler 1999). While all authors since their first publication, including myself (Heyd 2000: 469), favoured the dendro-dates falling into the 25th century BC, it is only now, with these recent early radiocarbon dates in mind, that the dendro-date of 2571/2569 BC has gained credibility. It may even be preferable, as it fits better with Corded Ware pottery development and chronology in eastern Switzerland.

One could now add slim Maritime Beakers which, albeit not radiocarbon dated, are seemingly early, cord-zoned, and sometimes decorated on the inner rim. Specimens come from the Middle Rhine (e.g. Altlussheim, Ilvesheim, Huttenheim; Grossmann 2017), along the Moselle River (e.g. Beaufrement, Marly-sur-Seille, Perl-Borg; Blouet *et al.* 2019) as one of the most important western tributaries of the Rhine, and north-eastern French graves with AOC beakers from Blignicourt-'Rotrate' (Dép. Aube; Chauvin *et al.* 2018) and Ciry-Salsogne 'La Bouche à Vesle' (Dép. Aisne; Hachem *et al.* 2011). These latter two have another early radiocarbon date (Poz-94880: 4070 ± 35 BP, for a female burial) or a stunning near 100 per cent steppe ancestry (Brunel *et al.* 2020), respectively. More important are the following conclusions at this point: the Upper Rhine region yields the largest collection of Maritime Beakers in Central Europe. This fact might support a longer duration of the Maritime tradition here, pinpointing earlier beginnings than anywhere else, already in the first half of the 26th century BC, which would fit well with the 2571/2569 BC dendro-date from Wädenswil. As such, this region might be a replication of the situation in Bohemia, having been a hotspot for the earliest Corded Ware leapfrog dispersal 300 years earlier.

Graves with Maritime Beakers exclusively contained women above the age of 40, but we cannot explain this pattern. Nevertheless, they already display the orientations, gender differentiation, and body position typical of the burial custom of the Bell Beaker's East Group (Heyd 2007). With that in mind, there can be no doubt that the 'Beakerisation' of the East Group started from here (Figure 3.5) and

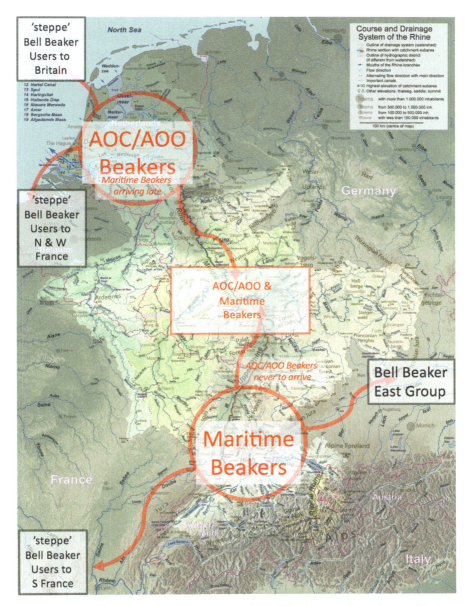

Figure 3.5 Scheme of 26th/25th-century BC early Bell Beaker transformations and their interrelations along the Rhine River (image: author; background map: https://upload.wikimedia.org/wikipedia/commons/d/dc/Flusssystemkarte_Rhein_04.jpg)

54 *Volker Heyd*

then jumped the short distance to the Danube River catchment (Heyd 2001). This is also confirmed by hundreds of radiocarbon dates for the Bell Beaker's East Group from Bavaria, Austria, Hungary, the Czech Republic, Poland, and eastern Germany, falling into the period after 4000 BP. However, the spread of Maritime Beakers along the Rhine could also have started here when considering that the earliest Bell Beaker context with true Maritime Beakers from the Netherlands (Lanting's 2Ia beakers: see Lanting and Van der Waals 1976) only dates to after 4000 BP (Beckerman 2012). The Middle Rhine region might also reflect this well, taking an intermediate position with AOC/AOO Beakers arriving from the Lower and Maritime Beakers from the Upper Rhine.

Interestingly, there is another part of Europe which has, so far, not delivered that many Bell Beaker radiocarbon dates older than 4000 BP, namely east-central and southern France (Lemercier 2014; Lemercier *et al.* 2014). The few specimens published certainly do not match our early dates from the Upper Rhine. A scenario in which the Upper Rhine region also radiated to the west and south-west is therefore not entirely out of the question but would contradict the orthodoxy that French Bell Beakers ultimately arrived from Iberia via Mediterranean routes (Lemercier 2012). In fact, recent time-depth genetic calculations on the beginnings of steppe ancestry in southern France confirm the very early arrival of 'steppe' Bell Beaker users (Seguin-Orlando *et al.* 2021; however, perhaps not as early as claimed), while one might imagine the Iberian 'pioneers', bringing over the novel Beaker idea, to be rather invisible archaeologically and genetically, as they may not have been large in numbers.

In the scenario proposed here, some of these pioneers may have arrived in the Upper Rhine region from the Mediterranean via the Rhône–Saône River system and, in doing so, created a first Central European 'Maritime' hotspot for further Bell Beaker radiation. The same may have happened in the Lower Rhine region via the Atlantic and North Sea networks but materialised differently, i.e. via the AOC/AOO Beakers. With this in mind, it is not surprising to realise that Y chromosome differences between Bell Beaker men of the Lower Rhine and Central European regions were recognised recently (Papac *et al.* 2021). Within a few generations, at some point around 2500 BC, this radiation turned into a proper demic event which brought Bell Beaker users, as descendants of local Single Grave culture/Corded Ware users rich in steppe ancestry, on the move to regions further to the west, triggering the 'Beakerisation' of Britain, Ireland, France, and finally Iberia. But it remains to be seen whether it is the initial Upper Rhine or the population reservoir of the Middle Danube where the East Group (Heyd 2001; 2007) and subsequently the Western European Y chromosome of R1b-P312 type really originated.

Conclusions: Europe moving and shaking

Between 3100 and 2450 BC, from the Black Sea to Britain and Iberia, migrants moved through Europe and shook it profoundly. Three distinct migration events, directed from east to west, were identified. The first was linked with Yamnaya, the second with the Corded Ware complex, and the third with Central European Bell Beakers. A fourth, awaiting confirmation, might have happened within established Corded Ware. These are 600 years in which, following our archaeological records, every 150 to 200 years a major migration event culturally transformed parts of Europe. Only those spreading westwards have been described here. Afanasievo people and Globular Amphora users, as was briefly mentioned above, went the opposite direction to the east, and so the Fatyanovo culture of the wider Corded Ware family appeared (Nordqvist and Heyd 2020). A few centuries later, the formation of the Russian Babyno culture of the Dnieper-Don region was bound in a similar long-distance migration. This one, dated to *c.* 2100–1800 BC, was formed out of an input from Central European Early Bronze Age cultures and subsequent local amalgamation (Lytvynenko 2013; Mimokhod 2018; Grigoriev 2019).

Taking into consideration our well-known chronological problems with the 3rd millennium BC in the form of broad standard deviations and radiocarbon plateaus, the picture can only mean that we are confronted with a process of constant mobility. What we grasp are only oscillating peaks, i.e. recognisable changes of material culture and of burial customs in a given region. It might well justify the term 'large scale' and dwarf – in relative terms due to the different demographic scale – the historical Migration Period (AD 375–568). Taking into account the endemic distribution of the Plague (*Yersinia pestis*: e.g. Rascovan *et al.* 2019) and other dreadful diseases presumably to be added when more aDNA samples have been tested, it is but a short step to likewise assuming that violence and warfare played their inglorious roles, too. It comes as no surprise that weapons, warriors, and heroes find their ostentatious display in graves and as anthropomorphic stone stelae on mounds. Add subsistence shortcomings – famine – and it seems the *Four Horsemen of the Apocalypse* were never far away in the 3rd millennium BC.

However, the models of a near complete replacement of populations that were proposed in the aDNA papers of 2015/18 need adjustment. At least, they only roughly fit to regions north of the Carpathians and the Alps and to southern Scandinavia. A middle corridor along the course of the Danube River only seems to be halfway affected, with local populations still recognisable in both whole genome and Y chromosome even after the middle of the millennium. Along the northern shores of the Mediterranean, cultures were only periodically touched by events. But overall, the westward spread wanes, so that Iberia faces only 40 per cent replacements, despite being in the northern 'corridor'. That is why geography is so important for understanding the scale, size, and extent of these migrations. Equally, one can envisage three distinct geographical zones in Europe: 1) the forest steppe between Dnieper and Dniester, 2) the Upper Rhine, and 3) the Elbe River catchment.

This raises the question why were people moving so much? I like the idea of the traveller and the migrant (Wentink 2020), with the overtones of cultural wanderlust or missionary vocation. This may be ultimately responsible for the core of Yamnaya burial ideology, seen in the footprint/sandal images on their anthropomorphic stelae and the supine body position with flexed upright legs so that feet still stand on the ground. However, there must be more: more than just enhanced mobility facilitated by wagons, horses, and a pastoral economy with a protein-rich diet (Frachetti 2012; Wentink 2020: 34). Therefore, human aspects, repeated many times in history, should not be ruled out either: seeking social promotion and personal satisfaction, receiving recognition and searching for fame, gaining wealth and sexual partners, and following charismatic leaders, perhaps combined with a persuasive religious element, could all be enticing motives for migration and travel. Excitement and novelty were doubtlessly as seductive 5,000 years ago as they are today.

Acknowledgements

I am grateful for the comments of the two reviewers with which they drew my attention to the weaknesses in my argumentation and my linguistic deficits. The possibility that the latter were resolved I owe to Professor Emeritus Richard J. Harrison. Thank you, Richard.

References

Alexandrov, S. (2020), 'Bronze Age barrow graves in Upper Thrace: old and new questions', in S. Hansen (ed), *Repräsentationen der Macht. Beiträge des Festkolloquiums zu Ehren des 65. Geburtstags von Blagoje Govedarica* (Berlin, Deutsches Archäologisches Institut – Eurasien-Abteilung & Wiesbaden, Harrasowitz), 147–70.

Allentoft, M.E., Sikora, M., Sjögren, K.-G., Rasmussen, S., Rasmussen, M., *et al.* (2015), 'Population genomics of Bronze Age Eurasia', *Nature*, 522: 167–72.

Anthony, D.W. (2020), 'Nomads in the closet: the hidden history of nomad-farmer relations in Europe and Anatolia. Review of: Neumann, I.B. & Wigen, E. (2020), The Steppe Tradition in International Relations: Russians, Turks and European State Building 4000 BCE–2017 CE (Cambridge, Cambridge University Press)', *Cambridge Review of International Affairs*, 33(6): 937–43.

Anthony, D.W. (2022), 'Migration, ancient DNA, and Bronze Age pastoralists from the Eurasian steppes', in M. Daniels (ed), *Homo Migrans: Modeling Mobility and Migration in Human History* (Albany NY, SUNY Press), page numbers to be confirmed.

Beckerman, S.M. (2012), 'Dutch beaker chronology re-examined', *Palaeohistoria*, 53/ 54: 25–64.

Beckerman, S.M. (2015), *Corded Ware Coastal Communities: Using Ceramic Analysis to Reconstruct Third Millennium BC Societies in the Netherlands* (Leiden, Sidestone Press).

Bill, J. (1983), 'Der Glockenbecher aus Hochdorf-Baldegg', *Helvetia Archaeologica*, 55/ 56: 167–72.

Billoin, D., Denaire, A., Jeunesse, C., and Thiol, S. (2010), 'Une nouvelle sépulture campaniforme à Hégenheim (F-Haut-Rhin)', in C. Jeunesse and A. Denaire (eds), *Du Néolithique final au Bronze ancien dans le Nord-Est de la France. Actualité de la recherche* (Strasbourg, Maison Interuniversitaire des Sciences de l'Homme /Alsace & Zimmersheim, Association pour la Promotion de la Recherche Archéologique en Alsace), 31–42.

Blouet, V., Brénon, J.-C., Franck, J., Klag, T., Koenig, M.-P., *et al.* (2019), 'Le troisième millénaire entre la Sarre et la Meuse Française', in C. Montoya, J.-P. Fagnart, and J.-L. Locht (eds), *Préhistoire de l'Europe du Nord-Ouest: Mobilités, climats et identités culturelles. XXVIIIe congrès préhistorique de France, Amiens, 30 Mai–4 Juin 2016* (Paris, Société Préhistorique française), 321–43.

Brozio, J.P. (2018), 'Zur absoluten Chronologie der Einzelgrabkultur in Norddeutschland und Nordjütland', *Germania*, 96: 45–92.

Brunel, S., Bennett, E.A., Cardin, L., Garraud, D., Barrand-Emam, H., *et al.* (2020), 'Ancient genomes from present-day France unveil 7,000 years of its demographic history', *Proceedings of the National Academy of Sciences of the United States of America*, 117(23): 12791–8.

Chauvin, S., Allard, P., Fronteau, G., Garnier, N., Hachem, L., *et al.* (2018), 'Une sépulture campaniforme en plaine du briennois (Blignicourt, Aube)', *Internéo*, 12: 149–58.

Dani, J. (2020), 'Kurgans and their builders: the Great Hungarian Plain at the dawn of the Bronze Age', *Hungarian Archaeology*, 9(2): 1–20.

Demchenko, T.I. (2016), 'К вопросу о выделении культурной группы Бурсучень в рамках гординештско-позднемайкопского феномена/On the issue of the Bursuchenskaia cultural group identification within Gordineşti-Maykopsk village phenomenon', in L. Sîrbu, N. Telnov, L. Ciobanu, Gh. Sîrbu, and M. Kaşuba (eds), *Culturi, Procese şi Contexte în Arheologie. Volum Omagial Oleg Leviţki la 60 de Ani* (Chişinău, IPC AŞM), 84–99.

Denaire, A., Vergnaud, L., Mauvilly, M., Barrand-Emam, H., Boury, L., *et al.* (2014), 'Geispolsheim "Schlossgarten", un nouveau site de la culture à Céramique cordée en Alsace', in P. Lefranc, A. Denaire, and C. Jeunesse (eds), *Données récentes sur les pratiques funéraires néolithiques de la Plaine du Rhin supérieur* (Oxford, Archaeopress), 155–72.

Diaconescu, D. (2020), 'Step by steppe: Yamnaya culture in Transylvania', *Prähistorische Zeitschrift*, 95(1): 17–47.

Dobeš, M. and Limburský, P. (eds) (2013), *Pohřebiště staršího eneolitu a Šňůrové keramiky ve Vliněvsi* (Praha, Vydání Archeologický ústav AV ČR).

Dobeš, M., Pecinovská, M., and Ernée, M. (2021), 'On the earliest Corded Ware in Bohemia', in V. Heyd, G. Kulcsár, and B. Preda-Bălănică (eds), *Yamnaya Interactions: International Workshop, University of Helsinki, 25–26 April 2019* (Budapest, Archaeolingua), 487–512.

Eberschweiler, B. (1999), 'Die jüngsten endneolithischen Ufersiedlungen am Zürichsee. Mit einem Exkurs von E. Gross-Klee, Glockenbecher: Ihre Chronologie und ihr zeitliches Verhältnis zur Schnurkeramik aufgrund von 14C-Daten', *Jahrbuch der Schweizerischen Gesellschaft für Ur- und Frühgeschichte*, 82: 39–64.

Egfjord, A.F.-H., Margaryan, A., Fischer, A., Sjögren, K.-G., Price, T.D., *et al.* (2021), 'Genomic steppe ancestry in skeletons from the Neolithic Single Grave culture in Denmark', *PLoS ONE*, 16(1): e0244872, DOI: 10.1371/journal.pone.0244872.

Frachetti, M.D. (2012), 'Multiregional emergence of mobile pastoralism and nonuniform institutional complexity across Eurasia', *Current Anthropology*, 53(1): 2–38.

Frînculeasa, A., Preda, B., and Heyd, V. (2015), 'Pit-Graves, Yamnaya and Kurgans along the Lower Danube: disentangling IVth and IIIrd millennium BC burial customs, equipment and chronology', *Prähistorische Zeitschrift*, 90(1–2): 45–113.

Furholt, M. (2003), *Die absolutchronologische Datierung der Schnurkeramik in Mitteleuropa und Südskandinavien* (Bonn, Habelt).

Furholt, M. (2018), 'Massive migrations? The impact of recent aDNA studies on our view of third millennium Europe', *European Journal of Archaeology*, 21(2): 159–91.

Furholt, M. (2019), 'Re-integrating archaeology. A contribution to aDNA studies and the migration discourse on the 3rd millennium BC in Europe', *Proceedings of the Prehistoric Society*, 85: 115–29.

Furtwängler, A., Rohrlach, A.B., Lamnidis, T.C., Papac, L., Neumann, G.U., *et al.* (2020), 'Ancient genomes reveal social and genetic structure of Late Neolithic Switzerland', *Nature Communications*, 11: 1915, DOI: 10.1038/s41467-020-15560-x.

Goldberg, A., Günther, T., Rosenberg, N.A., and Jakobsson, M. (2017), 'Ancient X chromosomes reveal contrasting sex bias in Neolithic and Bronze Age Eurasian migrations', *Proceedings of the National Academy of Sciences of the United States of America*, 114(10): 2657–62.

Grigoriev, S. (2019), 'Central European impulses in Eastern Europe in the early second millennium BC', *Slovenská Archeológia*, 67(2): 225–39.

Grossmann, R. (2017), *Das dialektische Verhältnis von Schnurkeramik und Glockenbecher zwischen Rhein und Saale* (Bonn, Habelt).

Haak, W., Lazaridis, I., Patterson, N., Rohland, N., Mallick, S., *et al.* (2015), 'Massive migration from the steppe was a source for Indo-European languages in Europe', *Nature*, 522: 207–11.

Haak, W., Furholt, M., Sikora, M., Rohrlach, A.B., Papac, L., *et al.* (2022), 'The Corded Ware complex in Europe in the light of current archaeogenetic and environmental evidence', in K. Kristiansen (ed), *When Archaeology Meets Linguistics and Genetics: Proceedings of the International Conference, Department of Historical Studies, University of Gothenburg, Sweden* (Cambridge, Cambridge University Press).

Hachem, L., Allard, P., Convertini, F., Robert, B., Salanova, L., *et al.* (2011), 'La sépulture campaniforme de Ciry-Salogne "La Bouche à Vesle" (Aisne)', in L. Salanova and Y. Tcheremissinoff (eds), *Les sépultures individuelles campaniformes en France* (Paris, CNRS Éditions), 21–35.

Harrison, R.J. and Heyd, V. (2007), 'The transformation of Europe in the third millennium BC: the example of "Le Petit Chasseur I+III" (Sion, Valais, Switzerland)', *Prähistorische Zeitschrift*, 82(2): 129–214.

Heyd, V. (2000), *Die Spätkupferzeit in Süddeutschland: Untersuchungen zur Chronologie von der ausgehenden Mittelkupferzeit bis zum Beginn der Frühbronzezeit im süddeutschen Donaueinzugsgebiet und den benachbarten Regionen bei besonderer Berücksichtigung der keramischen Funde* (Bonn, Habelt).

Heyd, V. (2001), 'On the earliest Bell Beakers along the Danube', in F. Nicolis (ed), *Bell Beakers Today: Pottery, People, Culture and Symbols in Prehistoric Europe* (Trento, Ufficio Beni Culturali), 387–409.

Heyd, V. (2007), 'Families, prestige goods, warriors and complex societies: Beaker Groups of the 3rd millennium cal BC along the Upper and Middle Danube', *Proceedings of the Prehistoric Society*, 73: 321–70.

Heyd, V. (2019), 'Yamnaya – Corded Wares – Bell Beakers, or how to conceptualize events of 5000 years ago that shaped modern Europe', in T. Vulchev (ed), *Studia in Honorem Iliae Iliev. A Jubilee Collection Dedicated to the 70th Anniversary of Ilia Iliev* (Yambol, Regional Historical Museum), 125–36.

Ivanova, S.V. (2014), 'Балкано-карпатский вариант ямной культурно-исторической области/Balkan-Carpathian version of the Yamnaya cultural-historical region', *Российская археология*, 2: 5–20.

Ivanova, S.V. (2015), '"Протобуджакский горизонт" Северо-Западного Причерноморья/ "Proto-Budzhak horizon" of the north-western Black Sea region', *Stratum plus*, 2: 275–94.

Ivanova, S.V. (2019), 'буджацька культура північно-західного причорномор'я: Контакти і зв'я зки з кулЬтурами шнурової кераміки/Budzhak culture of the north-west Pontic region: contacts and connections with Corded Ware culture', *Археологія і давня історія України*, 33(4): 32–59.

Iversen, R. (2019), 'On the emergence of Corded Ware societies in Northern Europe: reconsidering the migration hypothesis', in B.A. Olsen, T. Olander, and K. Kristiansen (eds), *Tracing the Indo-Europeans: New Evidence from Archaeology and Historical Linguistics* (Oxford, Oxbow), 73–95.

Juras, A., Chyleński, M., Ehler, E., Malmström, H., Żurkiewicz, D., *et al.* (2018), 'Mitochondrial genomes reveal an east to west cline of steppe ancestry in Corded Ware populations', *Scientific Reports*, 8: 11603, DOI: 10.1038/s41598-018-29914-5.

Kaiser, E. (2019), *Das dritte Jahrtausend im osteuropäischen Steppenraum* (Berlin, Edition Topoi).

Koledin, J., Bugaj, U., Jarosz, P., Novak, M., Przybyła, M., *et al.* (2020), 'First archaeological investigation of barrows in the Bačka region and the question of the Eneolithic/ Early Bronze Age barrows in Vojvodina', *Prähistorische Zeitschrift*, 95(2): 350–75.

Kośko, A. and Włodarczak, P. (2018), 'A Final Eneolithic research inspirations: Subcarpathia borderlands between Eastern and Western Europe', *Baltic-Pontic Studies*, 23: 259–90.

Lanting, J.N. and Van der Waals, J.D. (1976), 'Beaker culture relations in the Lower Rhine Basin', in J.N. Lanting and J.D. Van der Waals (eds), *Glockenbechersymposion Oberried, 18.–23. März 1974* (Bussum/Haarlem, Fibula), 1–80.

Lemercier, O. (2012), 'Interpreting the Beaker phenomenon in Mediterranean France: an Iron Age analogy', *Antiquity*, 86(311): 131–43.

Lemercier, O. (2014), 'Bell Beakers in Eastern France and the Rhone-Saone-Rhine axis question', in M. Besse (ed), *Around the Petit-Chasseur Site in Sion (Valais, Switzerland) and New Approaches to the Bell Beaker Culture* (Oxford, Archaeopress), 181–204.

Lemercier, O. (2018), 'Think and act. Local data and global perspectives in Bell Beaker archaeology', *Journal of Neolithic Archaeology*, 20: 77–96.

Lemercier, O., Furestier, R., Gadbois-Langevin, R., and Schulz Paulsson, B. (2014), 'Chronologie et périodisation des campaniformes en France méditerranéenne', in I. Senepart, F. Leandri, J. Cauliez, T. Perrin, and E. Thirault (eds), *Chronologie de la Préhistoire récente dans le sud de la France: Acquis 1992–2012. Actualité de la rechercheééhistorique*, 175–95.

Linderholm, A., Kılınç, G.M., Szczepanek, A., Włodarczak, P., Jarosz, P., *et al.* (2020), 'Corded Ware cultural complexity uncovered using genomic and isotopic analysis from south-eastern Poland', *Scientific Reports*, 10: 6885, DOI: 10.1038/s41598-020-63138-w.

Link, T. (2016), 'Zwei endneolithische Grubenhäuser auf dem "Alten Berg" bei Burgerroth (Lkr. Würzburg, Unterfranken)', in J. Pechtl, T. Link, and L. Husty (eds), *Neue Materialien des Bayerischen Neolithikums: Tagung im Kloster Windberg vom 21. bis 23. November 2014* (Würzburg, University Press), 99–126.

Link, T. (2018), 'Eine mehrphasige Grabenanlage des 3. Jahrtausends v. Chr. in Burgerroth, Lkr. Würzburg', in L. Husty, T. Link, and J. Pechtl (eds), *Neue Materialien des Bayerischen Neolithikums 2: Tagung im Kloster Windberg vom 18. bis 20. November 2016* (Würzburg, University Press), 179–98.

Lytvynenko, R.O. (2013), 'Central European parallels to the Dnieper-Don center of Babyno culture', *Baltic-Pontic Studies*, 18: 121–38.

Malmström, H., Günther, T., Svensson, E.M., Juras, A., Fraser, M., *et al.* (2019), 'The genomic ancestry of the Scandinavian Battle Axe culture people and their relation to the broader Corded Ware horizon', *Proceedings of the Royal Society B*, 286: 20191528, DOI: 10.1098/rspb.2019.1528.

Mansfeld, G. (2003), 'Das frühbronzezeitliche Grab von Korinto/Achalgori und seine weitreichenden Beziehungen: Überlegungen zum Phänomen der Hammerkopfnadeln', *Metalla*, 12: 23–68.

Manzura, I. (2016), 'North Pontic steppes at the end of the 4th millennium BC: the epoch of broken borders', in A. Zanoci, E. Kaiser, M. Kashuba, E. Izbitser, and M. Băţ (eds), *Mensch, Kultur und Gesellschaft von der Kupferzeit bis zur frühen Eisenzeit im Nördlichen Eurasien. Contributions in Honour of the 60th Anniversary of Eugen Sava* (Berlin, Freie Universität & Chişinău, National Museum of History of Moldova), 53–75.

Merpert, N.Y. (1974), *Древнейшие скотоводы Волжск-Уральского междуречья/The Most Ancient Pastoralists of the Volzhsk-Ural Interfluve* (Москва, Наука).

Mimokhod, R.A. (2018), 'Палеоклимат и культурогенез в Восточной Европе в конце III тыс. до н.э./Paleoclimate and cultural genesis in Eastern Europe at the end of the 3rd millennium BC', *Российская археология*, 2: 33–48.

Mittnik, A., Massy, K., Knipper, C., Wittenborn, F., Pfrengle, S., *et al.* (2019), 'Kinship-based social inequality in Bronze Age Europe', *Science*, 366(6466): 731–4.

Müller, J., Seregély, T., Becker, C., Christensen, A.-M., Fuchs, M., *et al.* (2009), 'A revision of Corded Ware settlement pattern: new results from the Central European low mountain range', *Proceedings of the Prehistoric Society*, 75: 125–42.

Nadler, M. (1997), 'Kein "reisig Volk von Bogenschützen"! Der Siedlungskomplex der Glockenbecherkultur aus Marktbergel, Lkr. Neustadt a.d. Aisch-Bad Windsheim, Mittelfranken', *Das Archäologische Jahr in Bayern*, 61–4.

Nielsen, E.H. and Bacher, R.L.A. (1984), 'Der Glockenbecher von Sutz, eine Neurekonstruktion', *Archäologie der Schweiz*, 7(3): 118–9.

Nordqvist, K. and Heyd, V. (2020), 'The forgotten child of the wider Corded Ware family: Russian Fatyanovo culture in context', *Proceedings of the Prehistoric Society*, 86: 65–93.

Olalde, I., Brace, S., Allentoft, M., Armit, I., Kristiansen, K., *et al.* (2018), 'The Beaker phenomenon and the genomic transformation of Northwest Europe', *Nature*, 555(7695): 190–6.

Papac, L., Ernée, M., Dobeš, M., Langová, M., Rohrlach, A.B., *et al.* (2021), 'Dynamic changes in genomic and social structures in third millennium BCE Central Europe', *Science Advances*, 7(35), 1–17.

Pesonen, P., Larsson, Å.M., and Holmqvist, E. (2019), 'The chronology of Corded Ware culture in Finland – reviewing new data', *Fennoscandia Archaeologica*, 36: 130–41.

Piličiauskas, G., Asheichyk, V., Osipowicz, G., Skipitytė, R., Varul, L., *et al.* (2018), 'The Corded Ware culture in the Eastern Baltic: new evidence on chronology, diet, beaker, bone and flint tool function', *Journal of Archaeological Science: Reports*, 21: 538–52.

Pospieszny, Ł. (2015), 'Freshwater reservoir effect and the radiocarbon chronology of the cemetery in Ząbie, Poland', *Journal of Archaeological Science*, 53: 264–76.

Pospieszny, Ł., Sobkowiak-Tabaka, I., Price, T.D., Frei, K.M., Hildebrandt-Radke, I., *et al.* (2015), 'Remains of a Late Neolithic barrow at Kruszyn. A glimpse of ritual and everyday life in early Corded Ware societies of the Polish Lowland', *Prähistorische Zeitschrift*, 90(1–2): 185–213.

Poznik, G.D., Xue, Y., Mendez, F.L., Willems, T.F., Massaia, A., *et al.* (2016), 'Punctuated bursts in human male demography inferred from 1,244 worldwide Y-chromosome sequences', *Nature Genetics*, 48: 593–9.

Preda-Bălănică, B., Frînculeasa, A., and Heyd, V. (2020), 'The Yamnaya impact north of the Lower Danube: a tale of newcomers and locals', *Bulletin de la Société Préhistorique Française*, 117(1): 85–101.

Rascovan, N., Sjögren, K.-G., Kristiansen, K., Nielsen, R., Willerslev, E., *et al.* (2019), 'Emergence and spread of basal lineages of *Yersinia pestis* during the Neolithic decline', *Cell*, 176: 1–11.

Rassamakin, Y.Y. (1999), 'The Eneolithic of the Black Sea steppe: dynamics of cultural and economic development 4500–2300 BC', in M. Levine, Y.Y. Rassamakin, A. Kislenko, and N. Tatarintseva (eds), *Late Prehistoric Exploitation of the Eurasian Steppes* (Cambridge, Cambridge University Press), 59–182.

Rassamakin, Y.Y. (2013), 'From the Late Eneolithic period to the Early Bronze Age in the Black Sea steppe: what is the Pit Grave culture (late fourth to mid- third millennium BC)?', in V. Heyd, G. Kulcsár, and V. Szeverényi (eds), *Transitions to the Bronze Age* (Budapest, Archaeolingua), 113–38.

Risch R., Meller H., Arz, H.W., and Jung, R. (2015), 'Vorwort der Herausgeber / Preface of editors', in H. Meller *et al.* (eds), *2200 BC – Ein Klimasturz als Ursache für den Zerfall der Alten Welt? 2200 BC – A climatic breakdown as a cause for the collapse of the old world?* (Halle, Landesamt für Denkmalpflege und Archäologie Sachsen-Anhalt, Landesmuseum für Vorgeschichte), 9–22.

Saag, L., Vasilyev, S.V., Varul, L., Kosorukova, N.V., Gerasimov, D.V., *et al.* (2020), 'Genetic ancestry changes in Stone to Bronze Age transition in the East European plain', *Science Advances*, 7(4), eabd6535, DOI: 10.1126/sciadv.abd6535.

Salanova, L. (2016), 'Behind the Warriors: Bell Beakers and identities in Atlantic Europe (3rd millennium BC)', in J.T. Koch and B. Cunliffe (eds), *Celtic from the West 3: Atlantic Europe in the Metal Ages — Questions of Shared Language* (Oxford, Oxbow), 13–34.

Schneikert, F. (2019), 'Kolbsheim, Bas-Rhin. A355 – Contournement Ouest de Strasbourg – troncon 2B: Rapport de diagnostic préventif, no. 016713, Archéologie Alsace', accessed 18 December 2020, https://en.calameo.com/read/0037250380ed5c04a6ce8.

Scorrano, G., Yediay, F.E., Pinotti, T., Feizabadifarahani, M., and Kristiansen, K. (2021), 'The genetic and cultural impact of the steppe migration into Europe', *Annals of Human Biology*, 48(3): 223–33.

Seguin-Orlando, A., Donat, R., Der Sarkissian, C., Southon, J., Thèves, C., *et al.* (2021), 'Heterogeneous hunter-gatherer and steppe-related ancestries in Late Neolithic and Bell Beaker genomes from present-day France', *Current Biology*, 31: 1–12.

Sjögren, K.-G., Price, T.D., and Kristiansen, K. (2016), 'Diet and mobility in the Corded Ware of Central Europe', *PLoS ONE*, 11(5): e0155083, DOI: 10.1371/journal.pone.0155083.

Szmyt, M. (2018), 'Between the seas: Baltic–Pontic contact space in the 3rd millennium BC', *Vita Antiqua*, 10: 155–64.

Szmyt, M. (2021), 'Yamnaya and Globular Amphora culture relationships: Facts and gaps', in V. Heyd, G. Kulcsár, and B. Preda-Bălănică (eds), *Yamnaya Interactions: International Workshop, University of Helsinki, 25–26 April 2019* (Budapest, Archaeolingua), 415–34.

Toussaint, M. (2009), 'Les sépultures néolithiques du bassin mosan wallon et leurs relations avec les bassins de la Seine et du Rhin', in F. Le Brun-Ricalens, F. Valotteau, and A. Hauzeur (eds), *Relations interrégionales au Néolithique entre Bassin parisien et Bassin rhénan* (Luxembourg, Musée National d'Histoire et d'Art), 507–49.

Ulrich, H. (1942), 'Ein Zonenbechergrab von Achenheim im Elsass', *Germania*, 26: 175–7.

Wentink, K. (2020), *Stereotype. The Role of Grave Sets in Corded Ware and Bell Beaker Funerary Practices* (Leiden, Sidestone Press).

Włodarczak, P. (2017), 'Kurgan rites in the Eneolithic and Early Bronze Age Podolia in light of materials from the funerary-ceremonial centre at Yampil', *Baltic-Pontic Studies*, 22: 246–83.

Włodarczak, P. (2018), 'Chronometry of the Final Eneolithic cemeteries at Święte in the perspective of cultural relation between Lesser Poland, Podolia and north-western Black Sea region', *Baltic-Pontic Studies*, 23: 178–212.

Włodarczak, P. (2021), 'Eastern impulses in cultural and demographic change during the end of the southeastern Polish Eneolithic', in V. Heyd, G. Kulcsár, and B. Preda-Bălănică (eds), *Yamnaya Interactions: International Workshop, University of Helsinki, 25–26 April 2019* (Budapest, Archaeolingua), 435–62.

Woidich, M. (2014), *Die westliche Kugelamphorenkultur. Untersuchungen zu ihrer raumzeitlichen Differenzierung, kulturellen und anthropologischen Identität* (Berlin, Walter de Gruyter).

Zeng, T.C., Aw, A.J., and Feldman, M.W. (2018), 'Cultural hitchhiking and competition between patrilineal kin groups explain the post-Neolithic Y chromosome bottleneck', *Nature Communications*, 9: 2077, DOI: 10.1038/s41467-018-04375-6.

4

Bell Beaker Mobility: Marriage, Migration, and Mortality

ANDREW P. FITZPATRICK

Introduction

As DEFINED BY Strahm (2004), the Bell Beaker network is a fundamental building block of the later prehistory of Europe in the 3rd millennium BC. Migration has been fundamental to its interpretation for over a century and has been brought into renewed and sharpened focus by the application of new scientific techniques, notably aDNA, which have placed considerable emphasis on mobility and migration as explanatory factors. Those methods do not in themselves make interpretations any more accurate, and they can also reinforce long-standing archaeological assumptions. In the case of the Bell Beaker network, those assumptions include ones concerning social statuses and the composition of both social and residential groups, the evidence for which is based primarily on funerary evidence. It is timely, therefore, to review existing interpretations of Bell Beaker groups, which are based largely on studies of social status from across Europe, against the results of the first generation of aDNA studies and the suggestion (Olalde *et al.* 2018) that there was large-scale migration to Britain.

People and pots: the Bell Beaker network

It is important at the outset to understand the importance of the Beaker pot to the definition of the Bell Beaker network. In the 19th century AD archaeologists recognised that the same type of small, decorated, fine ware pot was found in graves in many regions in Central and Western Europe, even though the burial rites varied. In Iberia and western France many graves are collective graves to which inhumation burials were added successively. In North-West and Central Europe burials are usually single inhumation graves, while in Hungary cremation

Proceedings of the British Academy, **254**, 63–88, © The British Academy 2023.

burial was practised alongside inhumation. The pots were thought to be bell-shaped drinking cups – or Beakers. Some graves contained other objects such as buttons made of precious materials, and this allowed a set, or group, of grave goods to be defined. The occasional presence of objects made of copper allowed the burials to be dated to an early stage in the Metal Ages. The widespread distribution of graves accompanied by Beakers was explained initially as the result of trade, but this was soon superseded by the idea of them representing the migration of a 'Beaker folk'. Where these 'folk' originally came from and where the Beaker pot developed has been debated for over a century. The definition of peoples through their physical anthropology, most frequently their skulls, and the way in which the concept of an archaeological culture became enmeshed with this have been well reviewed elsewhere (e.g. Lemercier 2020). Although migration as an explanation for change passed out of academic fashion in some parts of Europe in the later 20th century AD, the Bell Beaker network was regarded as an exception and partly because of this, many assumptions about social identities, genetics, and material culture remained unchallenged. That there was significant mobility was eventually confirmed by early studies of stable isotopes such as that by Price and colleagues (2004) of the strontium isotope of individuals in Central Europe, which indicated that a high proportion of them (over 60 per cent; 51/81) had changed residences over their lifetimes and that females and males did so in equal numbers, as children and adults alike.

Most discussions have been based on evidence from graves because, until recently, settlements were poorly understood – this is an important constraint on interpreting the funerary evidence. In many parts of Europe settlements are often represented by only a few pits, some postholes, and scatters of domestic debris (Gibson 2019; Kleinje 2019). While this was often interpreted as indicating a pastoralist, semi-nomadic lifestyle, a priori it may only indicate that in some regions most buildings did not leave substantial archaeological features and that settlements were only occupied for a few generations. Even where there is good evidence for buildings found in open-area excavations, for example in western Switzerland or the Budapest region (cf. Gibson 2019), the composition of the residential groups is not yet established. Lithic assemblages and bone and antler tools point to a wide range of crafts being practised, while pottery assemblages comprise coarse wares, whose forms are normally a mixture of local and interregional ones (Besse 2003). Evidence for the types of crops grown is emerging across Europe but the relative significance of cereal cultivation is yet to be determined. In Britain stable isotope analyses indicate that animal protein products were consumed at a relatively high level in some regions (Parker Pearson *et al.* 2019: 303–39) and if pastoralism was important, it may have led to residence being multi-local. Annual cycles of residence are hinted at by the isotope evidence from Britain, and this has been considered to be largely compatible with journeys made as part of an annual round, such as herding animals or travelling to religious gatherings (Parker Pearson *et al.* 2019: 436–59).

If settlements were short-lived, associated cemeteries (where they exist) may contain the graves of only some of the residents. Such mobility might also lead to seasonal fluctuations in the composition and size of residential groups, but despite the often ephemeral nature of the settlement evidence, it is frequently assumed that they represent farms that were occupied by families with patriarchal, patrilinear, and patrilocal residency lines (e.g. Heyd 2007: 338; Sjögren *et al.* 2020).

Today, the Bell Beaker network is recognised to have included regions from Morocco to Norway over the centuries of its existence (Figure 4.1) and its variability in settlement, material culture, farming practices, and burial rites has been well expressed as 'similar but different' (Czebreszuk 2004). As currently understood, the distribution of the regions in which Bell Beaker groups lived remains uneven, over space and time, with marked differences existing between regions in the number of finds from them. Some areas still have very few or no Beaker finds. For this reason, the distribution has been characterised as a series of 'islands' of regional groups which together comprise the network. The precise chronology of this network is still being refined but radiocarbon dating is steadily making it clear that in much of Europe it developed in the 26th century BC and lasted into the 22nd century BC, varying in extent over these centuries. This is a shorter period than has often been argued and the strongest similarities in material culture between regions occur in the three centuries between *c.* 2500 and 2200 BC (cf. Lemercier 2018). This floruit can be obscured by where Beaker pots are placed in different regional chronologies and the different lengths of sub-phases within the period of Beaker usage (Lemercier 2018). In some regions, Beakers are assigned to a Copper Age, in others they are assigned to the Late Neolithic, and sometimes to a metal-using Neolithic or 'Aeneolithic'. In Britain they were used to define a 'Beaker period' which, confusingly, continues well into the Early Bronze Age and the 2nd millennium BC (Allen *et al.* 2012).

Despite the prominence of Beakers in graves and the central place they occupy in archaeological interpretation, in some regions such as central Spain, the decorated Beakers found in graves comprise only a small proportion of domestic assemblages, leading to the suggestion that these vessels were used only in certain ceremonies or rituals (e.g. Garrido-Pena *et al.* 2011). Here, Ciempozuelos-style pots comprise a set of three vessels: a large open bowl, a small serving bowl, and the decorated Beaker, which is suggested to have been used specifically for libations (Guerra Doce and Delibes 2019). Like the placing of Beakers as grave goods, this interpretation emphasises the ritual uses of Beakers and suggests that the Bell Beaker network represents one of more widely shared religious beliefs, which Strahm (2004) characterised as the 'Bell Beaker phenomenon'.

The importance that archaeologists ascribe to the adoption of these beliefs varies. In Central Europe the adoption of the new funerary rite is sometimes seen as a new and striking contrast to Corded Ware rites (Heyd 2007) and sometimes as an adaptation of them that amounted to little more than a change in the orientation of burials and the swapping of the battle axe for a bow and arrow (e.g. Sjögren

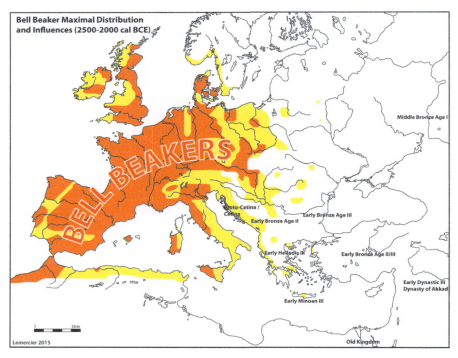

Figure 4.1 The extent of the Bell Beaker network and selected contemporary groups. The yellow indicates regions in which there is comparatively little evidence for Bell Beaker groups (after Lemercier 2018: Figure 1)

et al. 2020). Little emphasis is placed on the way that the region was now part of a new and extensive network. This view contrasts markedly with current research in Iberia that emphasises expansive exchange networks and the control exercised over commodities such as salt and metals by Bell Beaker groups (e.g. Delibes and Guerra 2019). In Spain it has been established that Bell Beaker groups lived alongside ones who did not share their beliefs. Here, graves were often placed within settlements and in the Madrid region, radiocarbon dating has demonstrated that some graves that contain Beakers are contemporary with others that do not (Blasco and Liesau 2019; Garrido-Pena *et al.* 2019: 25) (Figure 4.2). At the Camino de la Yeseras settlement the graves without Beakers were simpler and contained fewer grave goods than the ones with Beakers. These graves were larger, with individual chambers often containing a wider range of grave goods, including ones made from exotic materials. This evidence has been interpreted as showing two distinct social or religious groups. Comparable religious differences must also have existed in those regions, such as Poland, where there is clear evidence that the earliest Bell Beaker groups were migrants who introduced their religious beliefs.

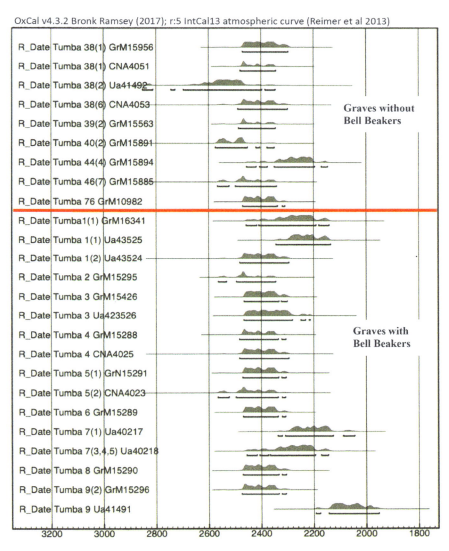

Figure 4.2 Radiocarbon dates of inhumations found in the Humanejos settlement, Spain, indicating that burials that were not (above the red line) and were (below) accompanied by Bell Beakers were contemporaneous (after Garrido-Pena *et al.* 2019: Figure 11)

Social statuses

Most interpretations of Bell Beaker societies have been based on studies of grave goods and they have usually sought to identify social ranking and the status of individuals (e.g. Makarowicz 2015), often using the extensive evidence from Central

Europe. Here, females were usually buried with their heads to the south and males with their heads to the north, and these gendered body positions are often used as a proxy for the sex of the deceased where it cannot be determined osteologically. It is more difficult to undertake similar analyses based on grave goods for the collective graves of Iberia and north-west France but the range of grave goods, as well as the smaller number of individual graves, suggest that similar practices were followed in these regions.

Studies have usually been based on the number and types of grave goods (e.g. Makarowicz 2015; Salanova 2016) and they consistently suggest that in all Bell Beaker groups, males were in general buried with more grave goods than females, but the burials of some women were very well furnished. In addition to one or more Beakers, copper awls were often buried with females, and their animal skin or textile costumes were often decorated with conical, v-bored buttons made of precious materials such as amber, jet, or ivory. The awls could have been used for working animal hide and flint, as well as other materials, and this suggests that in death women were often characterised as makers. Precious metal ornaments such as tress rings, earrings, and diadems were buried with both women and men.

Where several grave goods were buried with men, the status of a hunter or warrior was often portrayed, usually by flint or chert arrowheads that were sometimes accompanied by an archer's wristguard or bracer. Wooden bows may also have been placed in the grave. Less frequently, copper knives, usually called daggers despite their small size – often less than 10 cm – were also offered as grave goods. Across much of Central and Western Europe copper remained a rare and valuable material. Perhaps because of this and their ability to access copper and precious metals as much as an ability to work them, metalworkers appear to have been ascribed very high social status. This status was given almost exclusively to males and it was also often marked by the over-provision of grave goods. Some metalworkers also had flint flakes, often for arrowheads, and antler pressure flakers buried with them, emphasising their role as makers, although here it may allude to hunting or fighting as much as flint working (Fitzpatrick 2011: 222–9). While it has been argued that only a small range of idealised social identities were portrayed in burial rites (e.g. Fokkens *et al.* 2008; Fitzpatrick 2011: 208–29; Wentink 2020), it is increasingly clear, as shown below, that there was some fluidity in the ways in which gender and social status were ascribed.

Graves from across Europe indicate that an individual's status changed through their lifetime. Burials of children below the age of 6 are rare in general, particularly in relation to the high rates of infant mortality that might be anticipated. Where the remains of babies, infants, and young children have been found, it is often alongside those of adults. This has been interpreted as indicating that in burial, at least, they were defined in relation to their parents (e.g. Turek 2000; Herrero-Corral *et al.* 2019). When children reached middle childhood, as defined by physical anthropology (*c.* 6–12 years), individual status appears to have been conferred (Figure 4.3). The timing of this change may have been determined by when milk

BELL BEAKER MOBILITY 69

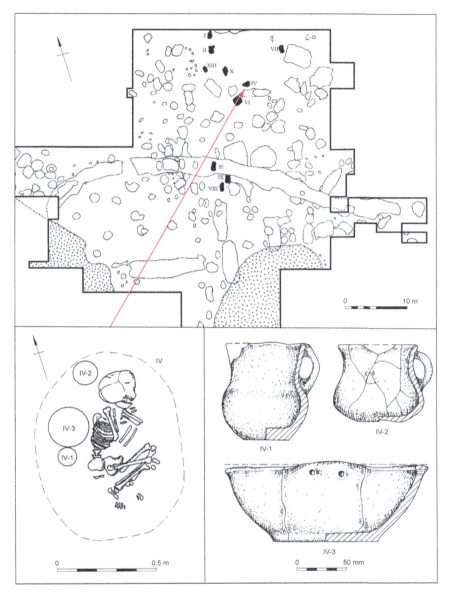

Figure 4.3 Burial of the older, *c.* 8-year-old, child found at Samborzec, Poland. As is usual in Poland the Beakers have handles (after Budzisewski and Włodarczak 2010: Plate xvi)

or baby teeth started to fall out in order to make way for adult teeth around the age of 5 or 6.

Even in middle childhood, it is unclear if all children, particularly girls, were buried in cemeteries. Turek (2000) observed that in Moravia only 26 per cent of children were in the female position. The recent aDNA analyses of the Irlbach and

Alburg cemeteries in Bavaria (Sjögren *et al*. 2020) have confirmed that there are fewer burials of girls than boys. Turek (2000) also considered how gender was ascribed and drew attention to the aDNA results from the Hoštice-I cemetery. Only one of the seven children and adolescents buried in the female position was biologically female and she was old enough – 15–20 years old – to have been regarded as an adult. In addition, two of the 14 burials in the male position were adolescents determined as biologically female. Turek suggested that the two may have been brought up as boys (Turek 2019: 213–14). Even if some males were raised as females, perhaps because male gender was not ascribed until a certain age or status had been achieved, the imbalance between the sexes remains, and the wider implication is that at least some Bell Beaker cemeteries did not contain all the members of a residential group.

From middle childhood, females could have copper awls buried with them, and Koch has suggested that during the Early Bronze Age in Central Europe this symbolised that the girl had been integrated into the working community (Koch 2014). Across Europe, the Bell Beaker females given well-furnished burials were adolescents or adults, suggesting that this status, even if ascribed, was not achieved until puberty. In contrast, some boys were ascribed the status of a hunter or warrior in middle childhood, suggesting that this status was inherited. Thus, a 5-year-old buried in the Humanejos settlement near Madrid was accompanied by an adult-sized wristguard that had been reduced in size; a small Beaker was also present (Herrero-Corral *et al*. 2019). In Central Europe wristguards have been found in the graves of several children (Nicolas 2020: 46–7, Table 8). Most well-furnished male burials are of adolescents or adults, suggesting that this status was also age-related. Thus, although the 17-year-old given an exceptionally well-furnished burial at Fuente-Olmedo, Spain would still have been growing, he was almost certainly regarded as an adult.

Turek (2002; 2011: 55–6; 2019: 214–16) has also drawn attention to a small number of women in Central Europe who had had copper knives/daggers buried with them. Most of their graves were well furnished, but as some of the weapons are relatively small, he suggested that they were primarily symbolic. Moreover, as some of the women were older, he argued that they represented age-related changes in which women could assume some statuses usually attributed to the men. However, the grave goods placed with a woman buried at Tišice, Bohemia, included an awl, a knife/dagger, and not one, but two wristguards (Figure 4.4). As noted above, the over-provision of objects is characteristic of well-furnished burials and this hints that certain attributes could be passed through the female line; and so their presence in graves was not necessarily dependent on the age of the woman. There is comparable evidence in Spain where several younger women, including an adolescent found in the La Magdalena settlement near Madrid, were buried with awls and copper knives/daggers (Blasco *et al*. 2019: 268–70; Garrido-Pena *et al*. 2019: 226; Herrero-Corral *et al*. 2019: 69–70).

Some of the collective tombs at Humanejos appear to have been for elite groups (Figure 4.5), and what appears to be a group of exceptionally well-furnished burials of women has been found in the Hulín-'Pravčice' 2 cemetery in Moravia. Unfortunately, the skeletal remains did not survive there, but a remarkable row of nine well-furnished burials all contained items associated with archery and six contained copper knives/daggers. In one grave (number 63) the location of the golden hair ornaments at the south of the grave suggests that the burial was of a woman; the other grave goods included a copper knife/dagger and a wristguard. Grave 54 could have contained two individuals, although if this was the case, it was the only such grave in the cemetery. If it was a single burial, the location of the silver hair ornaments in the south of the grave would suggest it was also of a female; the other grave goods included a copper knife/dagger, a wristguard, 16 arrowheads, and two stone tools for metalworking (Peška 2016: 9–10, Figure 12). This row of well-furnished burials suggests that they were those of an elite group in which some females were buried with objects usually associated with males, including metalworkers' tools. The relationship between them and the others buried in the cemetery is not known.

Family groups?

The possibility that there were elite groups suggests that the social organisation of Bell Beaker groups may have been more complex than interpretations based on binary oppositions of sex and gender, and which emphasise male – and particularly warrior – status (e.g. Heyd 2007), might suggest. It has often been assumed that the basic residential unit was similar to many modern Western perceptions of a nuclear family, that is to say they were normative, patriarchal, and monogamous. While this tells us as much about recent Western thought as it does about the past, aDNA has opened new possibilities for exploring family relationships and kinship: the two are not necessarily the same. Questions of scale are important (Vander Linden 2016) and the results clearly depend on both the preservation of aDNA and the number of individuals sampled. The size of sample suitable for studying population biology is often too small to be useful for studying archaeological questions about social groups, and most Bell Beaker cemeteries in Central and Western Europe are relatively small. In Bavaria, Heyd (2007) demonstrated that the earliest cemeteries (his phase A1–2a; 25th–24th centuries BC) contained 10 or fewer graves and were not used in later phases. In contrast, cemeteries established later (in phase A2b) did continue in use and were also larger, though none contained more than 30 graves (Heyd 2007: 335–8, Figure 7). Of these cemeteries, only the one at Landau can be shown to lie close to a contemporary settlement. A few much larger cemeteries are known in Moravia such as Šlapanice (60 graves), while the Hoštice-I cemetery contained over 150 graves organised in linear groups (Matějíčková and Dvořák 2012). What are interpreted as communal cemeteries are found in the even larger burial grounds of the Csepel Group around Budapest, particularly at Budakalász and Szigetszentmiklós. It may not be coincidental that this region has not only the best evidence for houses but also the largest number of them.

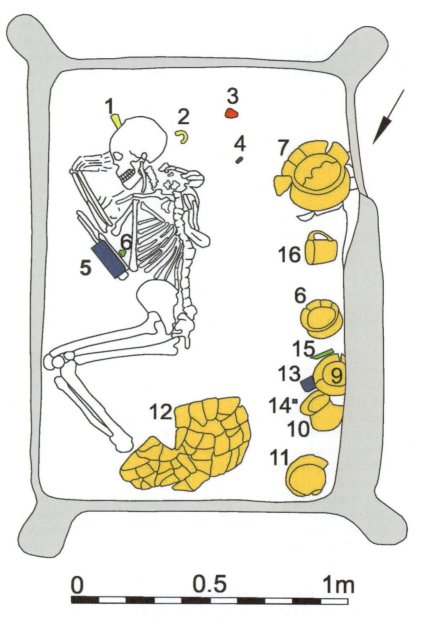

Figure 4.4 Burial of a woman found at Tišice, grave 77/99, Czech Republic, accompanied by both female and male 'gendered objects'; 1–2: gold diadem plates; 3: flint flake; 4: possible bone object; 5: wristguard; 6: copper knife/dagger; 7–11: Bell Beakers; 12: pottery jar; 13: wristguard; 14: amber v-bored button; 15: copper awl; 16: handled Beaker. Phosphate analyses indicate that an organic object or a foodstuff was placed behind the woman's back (left after Turek 2006: Figure 87; right after Turek 2019: Figure 6; photograph: Petr Berounský)

BELL BEAKER MOBILITY 73

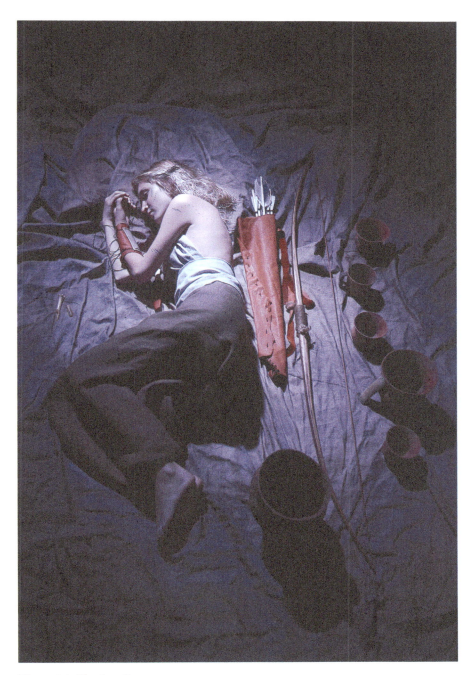

Figure 4.4 (Continued)

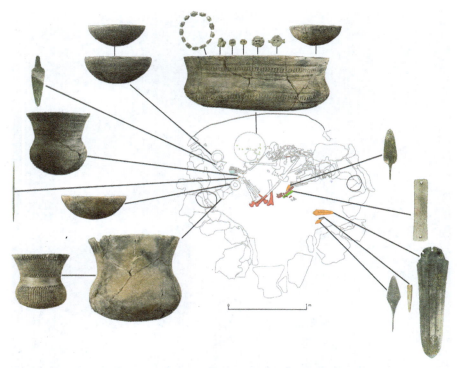

Figure 4.5 Double grave (tomb 1) with successive, not simultaneous, burials found at Humanejos. A 25-year-old woman and a 45-year-old or older man were accompanied by a copper awl, a copper halberd – a large weapon rarely found in graves – a copper knife/dagger, two copper Palmela points, a wristguard, and a bone cone. The necklace and v-bored buttons are made of ivory and the pots are all Ciempozuelos style. Traces of cinnabar on the skeletons are coloured red (after Garrido-Pena et al. 2019: Figure 24)

An aDNA study of fundamental importance by Iñigo Olalde and colleagues examined 226 individuals from across Central and Western Europe who were buried with Beakers or other objects from the Bell Beaker Set as well as earlier and later burials (Olalde et al. 2018). Few of the cemeteries can be associated with a settlement with certainty and only a sample of the individuals in most of them was analysed. Further individuals have since been analysed from a small number of the cemeteries included in the 2018 study. These cemeteries are all in Bavaria, in the Lech Valley south of Augsburg (Knipper et al. 2017; Mittnik et al. 2019), and c. 150 km to the north-east at Alburg and Irlbach, which are some 17 km apart (Sjögren et al. 2020). The latter two sites were included in the pioneering studies that used stable isotopes to examine migration (e.g. Price et al. 2004). In Spain the relationships between the individuals found at Humanejos who were included in the study by Olalde and colleagues (2018) were examined further in the excavation report (Garrido-Pena et al. 2019), and the genetic ancestry of several individuals found in the Stonehenge region of southern England has also been explored,

BELL BEAKER MOBILITY

although most of them are from small groups of graves – typically one to two – not larger cemeteries, and most date to after 2200 BC (Booth *et al.* 2021).

Discussion of these studies, particularly that by Olalde and colleagues (2018), has concentrated largely on the concepts underlying them (e.g. Heyd 2017; Carlin 2018: 197–200; 2020; Furholt 2018; Frieman and Hofmann 2019; Blakey 2020 and comments; Crellin and Harris 2020). These critiques have emphasised how bio-determininistic models of identity, sex, and gender can be projected on to the past, because scientific methods are often assumed to be value-free; this can exacerbate the difficulties caused by prior archaeological assumptions. With the notable exception of a thoughtful study of the evidence from Britain by Booth and colleagues (2021), these critiques have paid little attention to the information that aDNA can provide about the social composition of Bell Beaker groups. Although relatively few genetic relationships were identified in the Continental cemeteries in the 2018 study, they still provide useful information that has not been discussed previously, which complements that from the site-specific studies.

Those relationships included one example of a family. A 20–25-year-old woman (individual I6582) was buried in a settlement at Kornice in southern Poland (Olalde *et al.* 2018; see also Furmanek *et al.* 2015, where four of the eight Bell Beaker individuals were analysed). Her father and a brother whose graves were close to each other were also buried in the settlement. It is noteworthy that she was afforded a more well-furnished burial than either of them, with her grave goods including silver ornaments. At Haunstetten-Unterer Talweg 58, a woman buried with a man in a double burial shared the same MtDNA haplotype as the man in the adjacent grave, and it was suggested that the graves are of a nuclear family of mother, father, and son (Massy *et al.* 2017). In the more extensive study of Irlbach, both parents of an older child were found, as was the father of an 11–12-year-old male, in addition to a great aunt and great uncle of the young adolescent. The aDNA evidence from Irlbach (18/24 individuals analysed) and Alburg (15/17 inhumations analysed) shows that lines of descent could span four to six generations, but neither cemetery contained all the burials of a nuclear family (Sjögren *et al.* 2020). Instead, most individuals were not related, though this does not necessarily mean that they were not regarded as kin.

Five individuals buried at Irlbach shared a non-metric trait – the incomplete fusion of the distal joint surface of the humerus – and although some non-metric traits are relatively common and there is, as yet, no systematic study of them, this offers encouragement to the view that, in the absence of aDNA analyses, individuals sharing less common non-metric traits may be related. For example, the Königsbrunn-Ampack cemetery (Phase A2) in the Lech Valley contained five individuals, four of whom were male and three of whom shared a non-metric trait, a persisting metopic suture in their skulls (Heyd 2007: 337).

Young children buried in the same cemetery as their mothers were also identified (e.g. Landau graves 3–5: Olalde *et al.* 2018), as were older children buried in the same cemetery as their parents (e.g. Alburg graves 9–12). Some adults were buried in the same cemetery as their mothers (e.g. Alburg graves 4–6: Sjögren *et al.* 2020). No certain examples of adult sisters were identified, though an adult sister and brother were identified at Radovesice where the 50-year-old woman and her 30–40-year-old brother were buried in nearby graves that were the only two found in this location (Olalde *et al.* 2018: I7283 and 7282; 2/2). Their graves were both well furnished: the woman is one of those accompanied by a copper knife/dagger, and the man also had a knife and a wristguard. Pairs of adult brothers were identified more frequently: at Alburg (graves 2–13) (with a possible third brother in grave 1 who died when an adolescent); at Brandysek in Bohemia (9/23 individuals analysed) where both men were aged 30–50 (Olalde *et al.* 2018, I2728 and I7271); and at Sierentz in eastern France (2/4 individuals analysed). At Sierentz the brothers, who shared an (unspecified) non-metric trait, were buried in adjacent graves with the status of hunters or warriors (Olalde *et al.* 2018, I1389 and 90; Vergnaud 2014). Second- and third-degree relationships were identified less frequently, mostly in the larger samples from Irlbach and Alburg, but second-degree relatives were identified at Mondelage in eastern France (2/8 individuals analysed). Here, large open-area excavations found eight widely dispersed Bell Beaker graves, but the only two close together were those of a man and a 10–11-year-old who were second-degree relatives (Olalde *et al.* 2018, I1381–2).

This emphasis on male lineage is also seen in the cemeteries analysed more fully, where there are many mitochondrial haplotypes but only a small number of Y chromosome haplotypes, usually of the lineage R1b-M269 – the dominant subtype among Bell Beaker males. In the Lech Valley, 19 individuals found in small groups and single burials shared 16 different mitochondrial haplotypes (Mittnik *et al.* 2019); at Irlbach, 18 individuals shared 14; and at Alburg, 16 shared nine. Where the subtypes of the males from the latter two cemeteries could be determined, all of them had the R1b-S116/P312 polymorphism. Even allowing for the risk of death during childbirth, why there is so little variation in the Y chromosomes both here and at larger scale remains to be explained satisfactorily. The stable isotope analyses from the Lech Valley indicate that many more adolescent and adult females than males had moved to the area (Knipper *et al.* 2017), whereas the study by Price *et al.* (2004) had previously indicated that across Bavaria the ratio of 'movers' between the sexes was equal. These results have been interpreted as indicating an exogamous marriage system with patrilocal residence and, if so, the rules for marriage must have been extensive and complex (cf. Stockhammer and Massy, Chapter 8).

At both Irlbach and Alburg only a relatively small number of first-degree (parent) or second-degree (grandparents or aunts and uncles) relationships were identified and more widely, as noted above, most cemeteries do not contain the number of children or juveniles that might be anticipated in pre-industrial societies, with fewer girls than boys being found. It does not seem likely that this pattern can be explained by the incomplete excavation of cemeteries, the poor survival of the remains of these young individuals, or the subsequent destruction of some graves by cultivation. The reasons why only some young people were buried in these cemeteries also remain to be explored critically, and this is one of many challenges raised by the genetic evidence. Among the most important of these are the types of residential group. Were they, as often assumed, nuclear families or extended families, or were there different types of kinship group? Genetic relatedness, particularly in the male line, clearly was important, but some households may have been more complex due to social ranking. The existence of some elite groups is suggested, for example, by the siblings found at Radovesice and graves such as those in the Hulín-'Pravčice' 2 cemetery or the Humanejos collective tomb 1. In addition to the possibility of multi-local residence associated with annual cycles, individuals might also have spent defined periods of residence (not necessarily fosterage) in other households. This has previously been suggested as one mechanism that could help explain the similarities in material culture between the apparently discrete 'islands' with the Bell Beaker network (e.g. Fitzpatrick 2013). Examples of this include the man buried in the double grave Haunstetten-Unterer Talweg 58 (see above), who appears to have been raised locally before moving away for a period that included his young adolescence and finally returning. The woman he was buried alongside was raised locally (Massy *et al.* 2017). The 11–12-year-old male found at Irlbach mentioned above was an isotopic outlier, with possible explanations for this including residence in another household, being orphaned and raised by relatives who lived elsewhere before returning to his birthplace, or being born while his parents did not live at Irlbach. This evidence raises the possibility that it was intended that some older children identified as migrants should return to their birthplaces.

Large-scale migration?

The difficulties in determining residence and relatedness are also evident in the examples of the earliest Bell Beaker migrants to Britain. The Boscombe Bowmen, the Amesbury Archer, and the Companion were buried within a kilometre of each other on Boscombe Down in Wessex (Fitzpatrick 2011). The collective grave of the Boscombe Bowmen (Figure 4.6) contained remains from seven, possibly eight, Bell Beaker individuals. Bayesian modelling of the radiocarbon dates from them indicates that the first of them to die did so between 2500 and 2340 cal BC. Where their sex could be determined, all were male and at least three shared the common non-metric trait of ossicles in the lambdoid sutures of their skulls. The two whose aDNA was analysed (I2416 and 17) were paternal cousins or half-brothers. The dentition of only three individuals (including I2416 and 17) was complete enough to allow stable isotope analysis, but this revealed that they had been resident in two different locations when aged *c.* 5 to 7 and 11 to 13, neither of which was in Wessex. This suggests they all followed the same migratory path at a similar age, though whether they made their journeys at the same time is not known. The early date of the grave and their collective burial rite suggests that the men had travelled from the Continent. The last of the Boscombe Bowmen to be buried (25004; I2416) has the lowest level of steppe-related ancestry of the Bell Beaker and Bronze Age

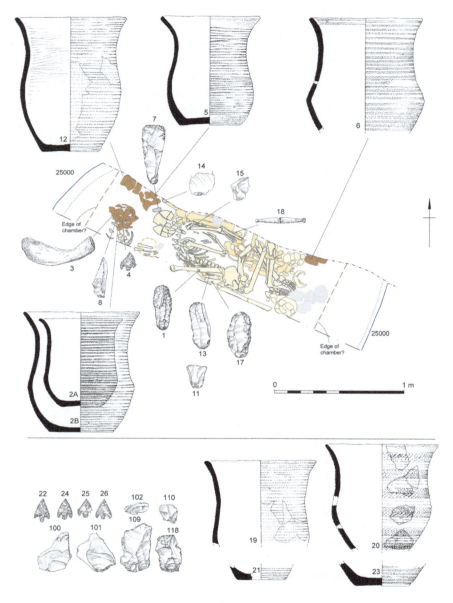

Figure 4.6 Collective grave of the Boscombe Bowmen, Boscombe Down, England. At least seven individuals, five adults, one adolescent, and one or possibly two children, all of whom were male, were buried in the grave, which is one of the earliest yet found in Britain. Because of the disarticulated state of the burials, it was only possible to analyse three individuals by stable isotope analyses. All three were shown to be migrants including the last, still articulated, burial (25004), who has the lowest proportion of steppe-related ancestry of Bell Beaker individuals in Britain. Apart from one Cord Zone Maritime Beaker (no. 20), the Beakers are all 'All Over Cord' (after Fitzpatrick 2011: Figure 7)

individuals from Britain, suggesting that the genetic ancestry of one parent, probably his mother, was like that of the population of Neolithic Britain. This admixture may have occurred on the Continent – Brittany has been suggested on the basis that part of the Neolithic ancestry of Britain was derived from migrants from the Atlantic façade (Parker Pearson *et al*. 2019) – but it is also possible that the man's mother had travelled from Britain to the Continent. Or, if the admixture occurred in Britain, in order for the man to have followed the same migratory path as the other two, he would have had to move away, probably to the Continent, prior to the age of about 5 years before starting the journeys that are documented by stable isotope analysis.

The Amesbury Archer (I14200), whose burial is dated to 2380–2290 cal BC and who probably lived at the same time as the last Bowman to die (I2416), and the Companion (I2565), who was buried next to him, dated to 2350–2260 cal BC, were buried half a kilometre away. Both were buried with rare gold ornaments of the same type, and they shared a rare non-metric trait in their feet (coalition of the navicular), which suggests they were genetically related. However, their radiocarbon determinations could be consistent with a generation gap, such as great-grandfather and great-grandson or further removed, i.e. third degree or greater; their aDNA is consistent with this (Patterson *et al*. 2022). Isotopic evidence indicates that the Amesbury Archer was a first-generation immigrant, probably from the Alpine forelands – his comparatively high level of Neolithic ancestry recalling results from eastern France (see below) – and in view of his likely birthplace, he may have made several shorter journeys before arriving in Wessex, rather than a single long one. He did not travel alone. His mourners buried him following rites, notably the over-provision of grave goods, which are best known in Central Europe. These people may have travelled with him, burying him according to these continental rites. In contrast, the Companion lived in Wessex as a young child before moving away and then returning. That journey may have been to the same region where the Archer grew up, where he may have lived in the household of a member of a wider kinship group there. As the Companion was an older child when the long journey was made, he probably travelled in the company of adults.

This fine-grained detail of genetic relations and complex journeys is at odds with one of the major conclusions of the study by Olalde and colleagues (2018) – namely that 'the arrival of people associated with the Beaker complex precipitated a demographic transformation in Britain, exemplified by the presence of individuals with large amounts of steppe-related ancestry after 2450 BC' and that 'in other parts of Europe, the expansion of the Beaker complex was driven to a substantial extent by migration. This genomic transformation is clearest in Britain' (Olalde *et al*. 2018: 194). By 1500 BC the genetic ancestry of the indigenous Neolithic populations had been almost entirely displaced and it has been argued that the new arrivals comprised 'large numbers of men from the continent' and that 'there appears to be a very strong case, therefore, that the Beaker phenomenon in Britain was introduced by large-scale movement of people from the continent' (Armit and Reich 2018: 17–18).

80   *Andrew P. Fitzpatrick*

Olalde and colleagues observed that:

> the genetic profile of British Beaker-complex-associated individuals (n=37) shows strong similarities to that of Central European Beaker-complex-associated individuals. This observation is not restricted to British individuals associated with the "All Over Cord" Beaker pottery style that is shared between Britain and Central Europe: we also find this genetic signal in British individuals associated with Beaker pottery styles derived from the "Maritime" forms, which were predominant earlier in Iberia.
>
> (Olalde *et al.* 2018: 193)

However, the evidence is both more complex and slight. In Britain, as in France, Bell Beaker groups do not appear to have settled in some regions in any numbers, if at all, for example north-west England, meaning that the burial rite cannot be taken as a normative one that was followed across the island. In fact, 'All Over Cord' Beakers were found in only two, possibly three, of the graves analysed in Britain, one of which (the Boscombe Bowmen) also contained the only Cord Zone Maritime Beaker in the sample. The radiocarbon dates show that almost three times as many individuals of Early Bronze Age date were analysed than earlier ones and, correspondingly, most of the Beakers are later types. In other words, the 'British Beaker-complex' considered by Olalde and colleagues (2018) lasted for over 500 years. Clearly, many factors other than large-scale movement could have contributed to genetic change during this time (Booth *et al.* 2021).

Olalde and colleagues (2018) remarked that their interpretation was notable, given that a large-scale study of stable isotopes in mainland Britain individuals, some of whom were also included in their own study (Parker Pearson *et al.* 2016; 2019), did not provide evidence for extensive migration from Continental Europe. They suggested that 'isotope data are only sensitive to first-generation migrants and do not rule out movements from regions such as the lower Rhine area or from other geologically similar regions for which aDNA sampling is still sparse' (Olalde *et al.* 2018: 194). While the difference between the results of the two techniques might indeed be explained in this way, stable isotope analyses provide direct, individual evidence for migration and it is difficult to reconcile the large-scale movement of people with the evidence from across Northern Europe for small and short-lived settlements.

Olalde and colleagues (2018: 194) also remarked that the data for British Late Neolithic individuals was limited and that 'the exact [genetic] turnover rate and its geographic pattern await refinement with more ancient samples'. The characterisation of indigenous populations was based largely on Early Neolithic individuals and just four individuals of Late Neolithic date were analysed, only one of whom was found in southern England (I5374). It was not possible to compare the Bell Beaker data from Britain with the near Continent because no individuals from central or western France or Belgium, where Bell Beaker single burials are rare, were included in the study. The continental individuals whose genome-wide data is closest to the British ones and who were used as a surrogate for Continental Europe were found in the Lower Rhine region, in the Early Bronze Age barrow at Oostwould, the Netherlands. However, these individuals lived at least 200, and up to 500, years after the earliest Bell Beaker migrants arrived in Britain so the relevance of their genetic ancestry to the early migrants is uncertain. None of the individuals buried at Oostwould was accompanied by a Beaker or other pot, and the unaccompanied inhumation that predates the barrow has been interpreted as a Bell Beaker individual solely on the basis of the radiocarbon date. In contrast, many Bell Beaker individuals found in Germany, Poland, and Hungary who lived at the same time as the earliest Bell Beaker migrants to Britain display less steppe-related ancestry than them (cf. Olalde *et al.* 2018: 191–2, Figure 2a). If there had been large-scale movement to Britain, particularly from Central Europe, the continental individuals might be expected to display similar proportions of steppe-related ancestry as on the Continent. In contrast, a woman buried at Hégenheim (Dép. Haut-Rhin) in central eastern France (I1392) had predominantly Neolithic ancestry and while, as Olalde and colleagues (2018) noted, the associated radiocarbon date is early, a slightly later variety of the type of Beaker was found at Forcalquier-La Fare (Dép. Alpes-de-Haute-Provence) further to the south buried with a man (I2575) who has also been shown to have predominantly Neolithic ancestry (Brunel *et al.* 2020, Figure 1c).

These comments about the scale and chronology of the movement of Bell Beaker groups to Britain do not diminish the fundamental contribution of the 2018 study. The earliest Bell Beaker migrants in Britain, the Boscombe Bowmen and the Amesbury Archer, do have steppe-related ancestry and so too do the slightly later graves of men born in Britain: the Companion (I2565), the man (I5379) buried in south-west England at Canada Farm accompanied by a Wessex/Middle Rhine-type Beaker, and the man (I6776) buried at Wick Barrow accompanied by one related to Cord Zone Maritime types (Patterson *et al.* 2022). The earliest Bell Beaker female burial in Britain was found at Sorisdale in the Inner Hebrides off mainland Scotland (I5367). This woman was a first-generation immigrant who has a high level of steppe-related ancestry, and she is the only other person analysed who was certainly accompanied by an 'All Over Cord' Beaker. The woman buried slightly later at Abingdon in the Midlands of England, who was buried without a Beaker but with an awl (I2450), also has steppe-related ancestry. The ancestries of these women suggest that the earliest migrant groups comprised both women and men. This is supported by the later appearance of new mitochondrial haplogroups and the wider absence of the admixture of Neolithic ancestry that might be anticipated if early migrant groups comprised only males, marrying local women. Instead of indicating the large-scale movement of people, and men in particular, the aDNA evidence is compatible with previous interpretations of small migrant groups, perhaps households or kinship groups who initially intermarried (e.g. Needham 2007; cf. Carlin 2018: 198), and so their children had high levels of steppe-related ancestry. Shortly before 2000 BC, the proportions of British Neolithic ancestry began to rise, suggesting that marriage with indigenous groups became more common in the Early Bronze Age (cf. Booth *et al.* 2021).

82   Andrew P. Fitzpatrick

The Bell Beaker Set may also have been introduced into some other northern regions by small groups of migrants, though the evidence for this takes different forms. In Małopolska, the physical anthropology of the people buried in cemeteries such as Szamborzec has been shown to be different from those of the Corded Ware communities (Haduch 2015; Makarowicz 2015), while the aDNA evidence from Kornice in Upper Silesia (see above) shows that several of the Bell Beaker individuals were genetically related. In Ireland, there is sufficient circumstantial evidence, such as that from the mine at Ross Island, to infer the arrival of migrant groups, perhaps from different regions of the Continent (e.g. Fitzpatrick 2013; O'Brien 2014). Similarly, the first Bell Beaker groups in Denmark, and perhaps also Norway (Prescott and Glørstad 2015), may have been migrants.

Subsequent longitudinal aDNA studies of individuals buried in France (Brunel *et al.* 2020) and Iberia (Olalde *et al.* 2019) have provided important perspectives on the results from Britain. The study of France did not include many Bell Beaker individuals, but one was the man buried at Ciry-Salsogne (Dép. Aisne) in northern France (individual CBV95; Hachem *et al.* 2011). He had steppe-related ancestry (R1b haplogroup), and Salanova (e.g. 2011) has previously argued that the 'All Over Cord' Beaker buried with him falls between the Single Grave types found in the Netherlands and 'true' Bell Beakers. She also highlighted the knife of Grand-Pressigny flint buried with him. Such knives are found widely in the Netherlands and the adjacent regions of north-west Germany (Ihuel *et al.* 2015: 114–15, Figure 10.1), and this pairing of 'All Over Cord' Beaker and knife of Grand-Pressigny flint is also found in northern France at Jablines (Dép. Seine-et-Marne), and to the south-west at La Folie near Poitiers (Dép. Vienne), *c.* 50 km south-west of Grand-Pressigny. These individuals are all radiocarbon dated to early in the 24th century BC, and Salanova (e.g. 2016: 27, Figure 1.9) interprets them as migrants or traders buried according to Corded Ware rites who facilitated the networks through which Grand-Pressigny flint reached the Netherlands and beyond. In the PCA analysis by Brunel and colleagues, the man buried at Ciry-Salsogne (Dép. Aisne) falls genetically between the Corded Ware and Bell Beaker groups (Brunel *et al.* 2020, Figure 1). This indicates that steppe-related ancestry was present in northern and western France shortly before the Bell Beaker Set was adopted in these regions, but when it first arrived remains to be determined.

In contrast, steppe-related ancestry did not appear in central Spain until about the 23rd century BC when it is documented in males buried at two cemeteries in the Madrid region: La Magdalena (I6471–2) and Humanejos (I6539, 6588–9; Olalde *et al.* 2018, SI 147; Garrido-Pena *et al.* 2019). At Humanejos all the individuals were found in tomb 7. Two were 25–35-year-olds whose disarticulated remains were present in the upper fill of the tomb and who were second-degree relatives, probably in the male line. The third was a *c.* 15-year-old whose burial was one of the last three to be made and was articulated. Although no relationship between the adolescent and the men was established, it seems likely they were genetically related. Cinnabar was found on the bones of the men buried at La Magdalena and all of the last three burials at Humanejos. This treatment was reserved for individuals of the highest status (Garrido-Pena *et al.* 2019). A subsequent longitudinal genetic study of Iberia showed that after 2200 BC, steppe-related ancestry became increasingly common, to the extent that by *c.* 2000 BC it comprised *c.* 40 per cent, and the Y chromosomes typical of the Copper Age were almost completely replaced by the R1b-269 lineage. Unlike the situation in Britain, this genetic turnover was not interpreted as being caused by large-scale migration – Bell Beaker burial rites having already been practised for centuries in Spain – but as the result of incoming groups of males who lived alongside the local peoples (Olalde *et al.* 2019: 1231).

Conclusion

The boundaries between moving and migrating are porous, and why first-generation migrants made their journeys is a matter of continuing debate. It has been suggested that primogeniture, in which only the first-born male in a family inherits certain rights or properties, and according to which in order to achieve similar statuses younger brothers had to move away, was intrinsic to Bell Beaker groups (Sjögren *et al.* 2020). While some of the earliest known migrants in Britain are males, as are the individuals with the earliest steppe-related ancestry in Spain, the aDNA evidence for pairs of brothers elsewhere, and the suggestion that groups of migrants included females, point to a more complex pattern. Population pressure, in combination with the opportunity to move to less densely settled areas, has also been proposed (Vander Linden 2011). In Britain, for example, it has been claimed that summed, calibrated, radiocarbon date probability distributions can be interpreted as indicating an increase in population in the later 3rd millennium BC after a decline in the Middle Neolithic that may be related to a decrease in cereal yields due to worsening climatic conditions (Woodbridge *et al.* 2014; Vander Linden 2016; Colledge *et al.* 2019).

It is, of course, improbable that there was a single reason why groups decided to migrate and the heterogeneous nature of the evidence currently available cautions against following normative models uncritically. Here, attention has been drawn to the fluidity of social statuses, the complex relationships evident in small cemeteries in which many individuals were not genetically related, and the complexity of individual journeys. This should encourage the rethinking of several points that have been central to recent work. These include the suggestion that only a range of prescribed social identities were represented in Bell Beaker burials; the similarities and differences between biological relatedness and kinship; and the composition of the groups who lived on Bell Beaker settlements. Finally, attention should be drawn to a point that is central to understanding the Bell Beaker network but which has been omitted almost entirely from recent studies: religion. Arguably, the most important result of the 2018 study by Olalde and colleagues was to show that although Bell Beaker groups in both Iberia and Central Europe shared similar

84 Andrew P. Fitzpatrick

religious beliefs as signified by their burial rites, their genetic make-up was initially quite different. Their shared cultural, and probably religious, identities were not the same as genetic identity (cf. Vander Linden 2016; 2019: 85; Carlin 2018: 197–200; 2020) and this supports the idea that, at a high level, the Bell Beaker network, which displays great similarities in material culture, was connected by ideas and beliefs. Migration and mobility were among the mechanisms by which ideas were transferred, and it is time to reintegrate those beliefs into research on Bell Beaker mobility.

Acknowledgements

I am grateful to the editors for inviting me to contribute to this book and to them, and Philipp Stockhammer in particular, for their comments on an earlier draft of this chapter which Alison Sheridan also kindly read. Tom Booth provided guidance on working with aDNA results and Iñigo Olalde and David Reich discussed the aDNA of the burials from Boscombe Down. Olivier Lemercier, Rafael Garrido-Pena, and Jan Turek kindly supplied the original files of their illustrations and I thank them and many other friends and colleagues in the 'Archéologie et Gobelets' association for their spirit of collegiality in researching the Bell Beaker network. Rob Goller of Wessex Archaeology prepared the artwork.

References

Allen, M.J., Gardiner, J., and Sheridan, A. (eds) (2012), *Is there a British Chalcolithic? People, Place and Polity in the Late Third Millennium* (Oxford, Oxbow).

Armit, I. and Reich, D. (2018), 'Beakers. How ancient DNA is changing the way we think about prehistoric Britain', *British Archaeology*, May/June 2018: 14–19.

Besse, M. (2003), *L'Europe du 3ᵉ millénaire avant notre ère. Les céramiques communes du Campaniforme* (Lausanne, Musée cantonal d'archéologie et d'histoire).

Blakey, M.L. (2020), 'On the biodeterministic imagination', *Archaeological Dialogues*, 27: 1–16.

Blasco, C. and Liesau, C., (2019), 'Mundos paralelos: La convivencia de otras prácticas funerarias con los rituales campaniformes', in G. Delibes and E. Guerra (eds), *¡Un brindis por el príncipe! El vaso campaniforme en el interior de la península Ibérica (2500–2000 a.C.)* (Madrid, Museo Arqueológico Regional), 341–63.

Blasco, C., Liesau, C., and Ríos, P. (2019), 'El registro funerario campaniforme de la Región de Madrid reflejo de una sociedad plural y compleja', in G. Delibes and E. Guerra (eds), *¡Un brindis por el príncipe! El vaso campaniforme en el interior de la península Ibérica (2500–2000 a.C.)* (Madrid, Museo Arqueológico Regional), 247–77.

Booth, T.J., Brück, J., Brace, S., and Barnes, I. (2021), 'Tales from the supplementary information: ancestral change in Chalcolithic and Early Bronze Age Britain was gradual with varied kinship organization', *Cambridge Archaeological Journal*, 31(3): 379–400.

Brunel, S., Bennett, E.A., Cardin, L., Garraud, D., Barrand-Emam, H., *et al.* (2020), 'Ancient genomes from present-day France unveil 7,000 years of its demographic history',

Proceedings of the National Academy of Sciences of the United States of America, 117(23): 12791–8.

Budziszewski, J. and Włodarczak, P. (2010), *Kultura pucharów dzwonowatych na Wyżynie Małopolskiej* (Kraków, Instytut Archeologii I Etnologii PAN).

Carlin, N. (2018), *The Beaker Phenomenon: Understanding the Character and Context of Social Practices in Ireland 2500–2000 BC* (Leiden, Sidestone Press).

Carlin, N. (2020), 'Haunted by the ghost of the Beaker folk?', *Biochemist*, 42(1): 30–3.

Colledge, S., Conolly, J., Crema, E., and Shennan, S. (2019), 'Neolithic population crash in northwest Europe associated with agricultural crisis', *Quaternary Research*, 92: 686–707.

Crellin, R.J. and Harris, O.J.T. (2020), 'Beyond binaries: interrogating ancient DNA', *Archaeological Dialogues*, 27: 37–56.

Czebreszuk, J. (ed) (2004), *Similar but Different: Bell Beakers in Europe* (Poznań, Adam Mickiewicz University).

Fitzpatrick, A.P. (2011), *The Amesbury Archer and the Boscombe Bowmen: Bell Beaker Burials at Boscombe Down, Amesbury, Wiltshire* (Salisbury, Wessex Archaeology).

Fitzpatrick, A.P. (2013), 'The arrival of the Bell Beaker Set in Britain and Ireland', in J.T. Koch and B. Cunliffe (eds), *Celtic from the West 2: Rethinking the Bronze Age and the Arrival of Indo-European in Atlantic Europe* (Oxford, Oxbow), 41–70.

Fokkens, H., Achterkamp, Y. and Kuijpers, M. (2008), 'Bracers or bracelets? About the functionality and meaning of Bell Beaker wrist-guards', *Proceedings of the Prehistoric Society*, 74: 109–40.

Frieman, C.J. and Hofmann, D. (2019), 'Present pasts in the archaeology of genetics, identity, and migration in Europe: a critical essay', *World Archaeology*, 58: 528–45.

Furholt, M. (2018), 'Massive migrations? The impact of recent aDNA studies on our view of third millennium Europe', *European Journal of Archaeology*, 21: 159–91.

Furmanek, M., Hałuszko, A., Mackiewicz, M., and Myślecki, B. (2015), 'New data for research on the Bell Beaker culture in Upper Silesia, Poland', in H. Meller, H.W. Arz, R. Jung, and R. Risch (eds), *2200 BC. Ein Klimasturz als Ursache für den Zerfall der Alten Welt?/2200 BC. A Climatic Breakdown as a Cause for the Collapse of the Old World?* (Halle, Landesmuseum für Vorgeschichte), 525–38.

Garrido-Pena, R., Rojo Guerra, M.Á., Garciá-Martínez de Lagrán, Í., and Tejeor-Rodriguez, C. (2011), 'Drinking and eating together: the social and symbolic context of commensality rituals in the Bell Beakers of the interior of Iberia (2500–2000 cal BC)', in G. Aranda Jiménez, S. Montan-Subías, and M. Sánchez Romero (eds), *Guess Who's Coming to Dinner: Feasting Rituals in the Prehistoric Societies of Europe and the Near East* (Oxford, Oxbow), 109–29.

Garrido-Pena, R., Flores Fernández, R., and Herrero-Corral, A.M. (2019), *Las sepulturas campaniformes de Humanejos (Parla, Madrid)* (Madrid, Comunidas de Madrid).

Gibson, A.M. (ed) (2019), *Bell Beaker Settlement in Europe: The Bell Beaker Phenomenon from a Domestic Perspective* (Oxford, Oxbow).

Guerra Doce, E. and Delibes de Castro, G. (2019), 'La ceramica campaniforme Ciempozuelos, una vajilla al servicio de una liturgia', in G. Delibes and E. Guerra (eds), *¡Un brindis por el príncipe! El vaso campaniforme en el interior de la península Ibérica (2500–2000 a.C.)* (Madrid, Museo Arqueológico Regional), 223–41.

Hachem, L., Allard, P., Convertini, F., Robert, B., Salanova, L., *et al.* (2011), 'La sépulture campaniforme de Ciry-Salsogne "La Buche à Vesle" (Aisne)', in L. Salanova and Y. Tchérémissinoff (eds), *Les sépultures individuelles campaniformes en France* (Paris, CNRS Éd.), 21–35.

Haduch, E. (2015), 'Bell Beakers and Corded Ware people in the Little Poland upland: An anthropological point of view', in M.P. Prieto Martínez and L. Salanova (eds), *The Bell Beaker Transition in Europe: Mobility and Local Evolution during the 3rd Millennium BC* (Oxford, Oxbow), 8–14.

Herrero-Corral, A.-M., Garrido-Pena, R., and Flores Fernández, R. (2019), 'The inheritors: Bell Beaker children's tombs in Iberia and their social context (2500–2000 cal BC)', *Journal of Mediterranean Archaeology*, 32: 63–87.

Heyd, V. (2007), 'Families, prestige goods, warriors & complex societies: Beaker groups of the 3rd millennium cal BC along the Upper & Middle Danube', *Proceedings of the Prehistoric Society*, 73: 327–79.

Heyd, V. (2017), 'Kossina's smile', *Antiquity*, 91: 348–59.

Ihuel, E., Malet, N., Pegegrin, J., and Verjux, C. (2015), 'The dagger phenomenon: circulation from the Grand-Pressigny region (France, Indre-et-Loire) in Western Europe', in M.P. Prieto Martínez and L. Salanova (eds), *The Bell Beaker Transition in Europe: Mobility and Local Evolution during the 3rd Millennium BC* (Oxford, Oxbow), 113–26.

Kleijne, J. (2019), *Embracing Bell Beaker: Adopting New Ideas and Objects across Europe during the Later 3rd Millennium BC (c. 2600–2000 BC)* (Leiden, Sidestone Press).

Knipper, C., Mittnik, A., Massy, K., Kociumaka, C., Kucukkalipci, I., *et al.* (2017), 'Female exogamy and gene pool diversification at the transition from the Final Neolithic to the Early Bronze Age in Central Europe', *Proceedings of the National Academy of Sciences of the United States of America*, 114: 10083–8.

Koch, J.K. (2014), 'Von Geburt an Frau? Mädchen in der westdanubischen Frühbronzezeit', in S. Moraw and A. Kieburg (eds), *Mädchen im Altertum/Girls in Antiquity* (Münster, Waxmann Verlag), 41–59.

Lemercier, O. (2018), 'Think and act: local data and global perspectives in Bell Beaker archaeology', *Journal of Neolithic Archaeology*, 20: 77–96.

Lemercier, O. (2020), 'The Bell Beaker question: from historical-cultural approaches to aDNA analyses', in T. Lachenal, R. Roure, and O. Lemercier (eds), *Demography and Migration: Population Trajectories from the Neolithic to the Iron Age* (Oxford, Archaeopress Archaeology), 116–40.

Makarowicz, P. (2015), 'Personal identity and social structure of Bell Beakers: the Upper Basins of the Oder and Vistula Rivers', in M.P. Prieto Martínez and L. Salanova (eds), *The Bell Beaker Transition in Europe: Mobility and Local Evolution during the 3rd Millennium BC* (Oxford, Oxbow), 15–27.

Massy, K., Knipper, C., Mittnik, A., Kraus, S., Pernicka, E., *et al.* (2017), 'Patterns of transformation from the Final Neolithic to the Early Bronze Age: a case study from the Lech Valley south of Augsburg', in P.W. Stockhammer and J. Maran (eds), *Appropriating Innovations: Entangled knowledge in Eurasia, 5000–1500 BCE* (Oxford, Oxbow), 241–61.

Matějíčková, A. and Dvořák, P. (eds) (2012), *Pohřebiště z období zvoncovitých pohárů na trase dálnice D1 Vyškov–Mořice/Funerary Areas of the Bell Beaker Period on the D1 Vyškov–Mořice motorway* (Brno, Ústav Archeologické Památkové Péče).

Mittnik, A., Massy, K., Knipper, C., Wittenborn, F., Friedrich, R., *et al.* (2019), 'Kinship-based social inequality in Bronze Age Europe', *Science*, 366: 731–4.

Needham, S. (2007), 'Isotopic aliens: Beaker movement and cultural transmissions', in M. Larsson and M. Parker Pearson (eds), *From Stonehenge to the Baltic: Living with Cultural Diversity in the Third Millennium BC* (Oxford, Archaeopress), 41–6.

Nicolas, C. (2020), 'Bracer ornaments! An investigation of Bell Beaker stone "wrist-guards" from Central Europe', *Journal of Neolithic Archaeology*, 22: 15–108.

O'Brien, W. (2014), *Prehistoric Copper Mining in Europe: 5500–500 BC* (Oxford, Oxford University Press).

Olalde, I., Brace, S., Allentoft, M.E., Armit, I., Kristiansen, K., *et al.* (2018), 'The Beaker phenomenon and the genomic transformation of northwest Europe', *Nature*, 555: 190–6.

Olalde, I., Mallick, S., Patterson, N., Rohland, N., Villalba-Mouco, V., *et al.* (2019), 'The genomic history of the Iberian Peninsula over the past 8000 years', *Science*, 363(6432): 1230–4.

Parker Pearson, M., Chamberlain, A., Jay, M., Richards, M., Sheridan, A., *et al.* (2016), 'Beaker People in Britain: migration, mobility and diet', *Antiquity*, 90: 620–37.

Parker Pearson, M., Sheridan, A., Jay, M., Chamberlain, A., Richards, M.P., *et al.* (2019), *The Beaker People: Isotopes, Mobility and Diet in Prehistoric Britain* (Oxford, Oxbow).

Patterson, N., Isakov, M., Booth, T., Büster, L., Fischer, C.-E., *et al.* (2022) 'Large-scale migration into southern Britain at the end of the Bronze Age', *Nature*, 601: 588–94.

Peška, J. (2016), 'Graves of metallurgists in the Moravian Beaker cultures', in E. Guerra Doce and C. Liesau von Lettow-Vorbeck (eds), *Analysis of the Economic Foundations Supporting the Social Supremacy of the Beaker Groups* (Oxford, Archaeopress), 1–18.

Prescott, C. and Glørstad, H. (2015), 'Expanding 3rd millennium transformations: Norway', in M.P. Prieto Martínez and L. Salanova (eds), *The Bell Beaker Transition in Europe: Mobility and Local Evolution during the 3rd Millennium BC* (Oxford, Oxbow), 77–87.

Price, T.D., Knipper, C., Grupe, G., and Smrcka, V. (2004), 'Strontium isotopes and prehistoric human migration: the Bell Beaker period in Central Europe', *European Journal of Archaeology*, 7: 9–40.

Salanova, L. (2011), 'Chronologie et facteurs d'évolution des sépultures individuelles campaniformes dans le nord de la France', in L. Salanova and Y. Tchérémissinoff (eds), *Les sépultures individuelles campaniformes en France* (Paris, CNRS Éd.), 125–42.

Salanova, L. (2016), 'Behind the warriors: Bell Beakers and identities in Atlantic Europe (3rd millennium BC)', in J.T. Koch and B. Cunliffe (eds), *Celtic from the West 3: Atlantic Europe in the Metal Ages – Questions of Shared Language* (Oxford, Oxbow), 13–39.

Sjögren, K.-G., Olalde, O., Carver, S., Allentoft, M.E., Knowles, T., *et al.* (2020), 'Kinship and social organization in Copper Age Europe: a cross-disciplinary analysis of archaeology, DNA, isotopes, and anthropology from two Bell Beaker cemeteries', *PLoS ONE*, 15(11): e0241278, DOI: 10.1371/journal.pone.0241278.

Strahm, C. (2004), 'Das Glockenbecher-Phänomen aus der Sicht der Komplementär-Keramik', in J. Czebreszuk (ed), *Similar but Different: Bell Beakers in Europe* (Poznań, Adam Mickiewicz University), 101–26.

Turek, J. (2000), 'Being a Beaker child: The position of children in Late Eneolithic Society/ Děti v Období Snůrové Keramiky a Zvoncovitých Pohárů: Postavení Dětí ve Společnosti Pozdního Eneolitu', in I. Pavlů (ed), *In Memoriam Jan Rulf* (Praha, Archeologický Ústav AV ČR), 424–38.

Turek, J. (2002), 'Cherche la femme! Archeologie zenského světa a chybějící doklady zenských pohřbů z období zvoncovitých pohárů v Čechách/Cherche la femme! The archaeology of woman's world and the missing evidence of female burials in the Bell Beaker period in Bohemia', in E. Neustupný (ed), *Archeologie Nenalézaného: Sborník přátel, kolegů a žáků k životnímu jubileu Slavomila Vencla* (Prague and Pilzen, Aleš Čeněk), 217–40.

Turek, J. (2006), 'Období zvoncovitých pohárů v Evropě', *Archeologie ve středních Čechách*, 10(1): 275–368.

Turek, J. (2011), 'Age and gender identities and the social differentiation in the Central European Copper Age', in L. Amundsen-Meyer, N. Engel, and S. Pickering (eds), *Identity Crisis: Archaeological Perspectives on Social Identity. Proceedings of the 42nd (2009) Annual Chacmool Archaeology Conference* (Calgary, Chacmool Archaeological Association and University of Calgary), 49–61.

Turek, J. (2019), 'Copper Age transformations and gender identities: an essay', in J.K. Koch and W. Kirleis (eds), *Gender Transformations in Prehistoric and Archaic Societies* (Leiden, Sidestone Press), 205–20.

Vander Linden, M. (2011), 'Demography and mobility in northwestern Europe during the 3rd millennium cal BC', in C. Prescott and H. Glørstad (eds), *Becoming European: The Transformation of 3rd Millennium Europe and the Trajectory into the Second Millennium BC* (Oxford, Oxbow), 19–29.

Vander Linden, M. (2016), 'Population history in third millennium Europe: assessing the contribution of genetics', *World Archaeology*, 48: 714–28.

Vander Linden, M. (2019), 'Teorías sobre el fenómeno campaniforme', in G. Delibes and E. Guerra (eds), *¡Un brindis por el príncipe! El vaso campaniforme en el interior de la península Ibérica (2500–2000 a.C.)* (Madrid, Museo Arqueológico Regional), 77–89.

Vergnaud, L. (2014), 'Les sépultures campaniforme de Sierentz "Les Villas d'Aurèle" (Haut-Rhin)', in P. Lefranc, A. Denaire, and C. Jeunesse (eds), *Données récentes sur les pratiques funéraires néolithiques de la Plaine du Rhin supérieur* (Oxford, Archaeopress), 173–210.

Wentink, K. (2020), *Stereotype: The Role of Grave Sets in Corded Ware and Bell Beaker Funerary Practices* (Leiden, Sidestone Press).

Woodbridge, J., Fyfe, R.M., Roberts, N., Downey, S., Edinborough, K., *et al.* (2014), 'The impact of the Neolithic agricultural transition in Britain: a comparison of pollen-based land-cover and archaeological 14C date-inferred population change', *Journal of Archaeological Science*, 51: 216–24.

5

Bronze Age Travellers

KRISTIAN KRISTIANSEN

Introduction

WHEN BRONZE WAS introduced as the main source of technology for tools, weapons, and ornaments after 2000 BC in Europe, a new trading economy came to dominate in order to distribute metal to all farmsteads. New political alliances had to be established that linked areas of copper and tin production to areas of consumption throughout Europe (O'Brien 2015). Warriors with efficient bronze weapons emerged to both protect and control trade, which represented a new form of wealth. This, in turn, invited attempts to raid trade caravans and ultimately to take control over important hubs in the trade network through conquest. Power was from now on rooted in a new political economy where local economies could no longer remain economically independent of larger political power structures (Earle *et al*. 2015). It represented a new form of pre-modern globalisation, or 'bronzization' (Vandkilde 2016).

The implications of this new situation would be that more people travelled longer distances and that political alliances could now encompass larger geographical regions in the form of confederations (Kristiansen and Suchowska-Ducke 2015). However, local travels would also speed up as part of the metal distribution to consumers. We should expect to see this reflected in strontium values for human mobility, in lead isotope values for copper, and in long-distance exchange of prestige goods between chiefly polities.

In the following, I shall therefore take a closer look at recent results in these fields of research to help answer the following questions. Who travelled and how far? Which institutions supported travellers along the route? What were the quantities of goods traded? I shall then look into some specific cases of travelling individuals during the period 1500–1100 BC in Denmark that may serve to illuminate how a variety of institutions that represented different social groups made it possible to integrate local and global economies during the Bronze Age, sometimes referred to as 'glocalism' (Galaty 2018). This is followed by a discussion of how

Proceedings of the British Academy, **254**, 89–109, © The British Academy 2023.

90 *Kristian Kristiansen*

written sources on kinship, fosterage, and guest-friendship may inform archaeological evidence on travellers. Based on this, I synthesise Bronze Age political economies during this period.

New evidence for the mobility of goods and people

In the last five years we have witnessed an explosion of new evidence from the Danish and south Scandinavian Early and Middle Bronze Age (1600–1100 BC) in the fields of archaeometallurgy, especially lead isotope analyses (Ling *et al.* 2018; Melheim *et al.* 2018), ornament production through extensive and detailed analyses of technical traditions of metal workshop traditions in Denmark and northern Germany (Nørgaard 2018), and lastly in the field of strontium isotopic analyses of humans and woollen textiles (Frei *et al.* 2015; 2017a; 2017b). In the following, I therefore present an overview of this evidence with respect to its implications for mobility of people and goods.

Archaeometallurgy

Systematic analyses of both lead isotopes and chemical composition have now been carried out on several hundred objects from south Scandinavia by a Scandinavian team led by Johan Ling (Ling *et al.* 2018) and Lene Melheim (Melheim *et al.* 2018). These were recently supplemented with results from Heide Nørgaard's project for the earliest Bronze Age (Nørgaard *et al.* 2019). The use of lead isotope analysis for the first time allows the precise location of the origins of copper, even if we may still be missing some data from yet undiscovered Bronze Age mines. Results obtained so far demonstrate conclusively that most copper was extracted from a few dominant mines that supplied large parts of Europe; mining operations had become highly organised, and mining itself became a profession (Stöllner 2018). Before 1600/1500 BC, most of the metal came in the form of finished products, mostly axes and ring ingots from the Unetice culture, who controlled most of the flow of copper to Denmark after 2000 BC. Ingots may represent the introduction of fixed values needed in a new age of commodity trade in metals (Kuijpers and Popa 2021). There were two main sources – a western source from the British Isles and an eastern source mostly from the Slovak Ore Mountains, but also including the eastern Alps. During the time period between 2000 and 1600 BC, the first long-distance trade networks emerged, and they seem to have been organised from a few central hubs in south Scandinavia, as demonstrated by Helle Vandkilde (2016) in her masterful analysis of the period. She proposes the dominance of maritime trade, even if some land-based networks were necessary to reach the eastern Alps and Slovakia.

In south Scandinavia, the formation of long-distance maritime metal trade coincides with the first appearance of rock art along coastal hubs, and here we also find depictions of the early axe types from the period (Skoglund 2017). However, ships soon became the dominant motif, especially after 1700 BC (Ling 2008). Thus, we witness the emergence of an institutionalised maritime transport economy with its own ritual expression, evidenced in rock art and coastal cairns that continued to be in operation during the whole Bronze Age (Ling *et al.* 2018).

After 1600 BC, new trade networks were established between Carpathian tell cultures and south Scandinavia (Vandkilde 2016), which is reflected in copper sources originating in Slovakia and Mitterberg in the Austrian Alps (Pernicka *et al.* 2016). We also witness the first emergence of copper from the Italian Alps, which came to dominate during the following centuries (Ling *et al.* 2018; Melheim *et al.* 2018). It coincided with the formation of a new trade network between the south German Tumulus culture and Denmark (Figure 5.1). Thus, copper from the Italian Alps dominated throughout the Tumulus culture and the Nordic culture, and it also reached the British Isles. Slovakian copper was rather linked to trade along the Elbe River (Ling *et al.* 2019: Figure 21).

It has been conclusively demonstrated that finished bronze objects were produced from raw copper and tin extracted on a large scale from a few dominant mining areas. This in turn would have demanded the operation of regular and safe transportation networks throughout Europe to secure the distribution of metal to consumers. However, there also emerged local and regional workshop traditions where professional craft specialists produced tools, weapons, and ornaments in local styles, thereby transforming neutral copper into objects signalling cultural identity. I shall therefore take a closer look at how such local workshop traditions operated and interacted in south Scandinavia.

Metalworking traditions

We now have at our disposal a most extensive in-depth analysis defining craft techniques for specialist workshop traditions during the period 1500–1100 BC in Denmark and adjacent regions (Nørgaard 2018). This study of the production and distribution of female ornaments is based on incredibly detailed analyses of individual tool traces, use of stamps, small mistakes, and other traits that sometimes allow the definition of single individuals (Nørgaard 2018: Map 35). Leading workshops of extremely high-quality decorated belt plates and neck collars were located on Zealand during the Nordic Bronze Age Period II (Nørgaard 2018: Figure 4.053), and their products were distributed to surrounding areas, where they had a profound effect. Several workshops are identified also in Jutland and northern Germany, and it can be demonstrated how they interacted (Nørgaard 2018: Figure 4.047). Some of this interaction must have taken place in the form of learning and practice, and Nørgaard (2018: Maps 25–6) is able to demonstrate products made by novices, who had not yet reached full mastery, or those produced by lower-ranking smiths; she also demonstrates that high-quality work could exhibit small mistakes due to haste (Nørgaard 2018: Map 41). All of this implies that copper and tin were at hand

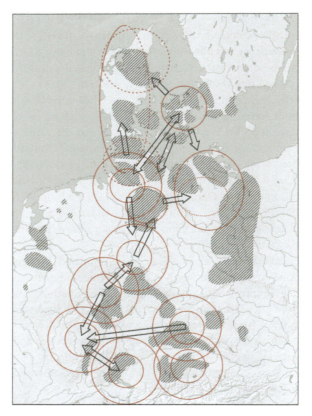

Figure 5.1 Map showing local chiefly networks and metal workshops from the Alps to Denmark during the period 1500–1300 BC. Circles indicate suggested chiefly territories, arrows indicate the movement of ornaments and possibly women taking part in marriage alliances, while hatched areas suggest local culture groups (image: author, based on Wels-Weyrauch 1989: Figure 11–12; Kristiansen and Larsson 2005: Figure 107; Nørgaard 2018: Figure 4.007)

in quantities large enough to keep groups of craft specialists continuously busy – sometimes too busy!

Products from the high-quality workshops could have been distributed by travelling smiths or as gifts, but some must clearly have been distributed by the women who carried them, like in the rich burial of a 20-year-old woman from Hverrehus, Gjedsted in northern Jutland (Aner *et al.* 2008: number 6201A, plate 123–5; Figure 150).[1] Nørgaard's work makes it possible to integrate local traditions in

---

[1] Unfortunately, her teeth could not be found. She combines high-status Nordic jewellery with two pairs of Tumulus type arm-rings with spiral ends. She could thus have been an encultured foreign woman like the Egtved woman, but much richer. There were several burials at this location, and in one of them of a little girl her teeth were preserved; she was local (Frei *et al.* 2019a).

ornament style with workshop traditions and the interaction between them, in much the same way as previously done for the Tumulus culture by Jockenhövel (1991). It suggests that strong chiefdoms in Zealand with superior ornament-producing workshops were able to make alliances with groups on Funen, and even in Jutland and northern Germany. The results thus mirror the situation in the Tumulus culture, where a more extended map was published in Kristiansen and Larsson's book *The Rise of Bronze Age Society* (2005: Figure 107), based on the work of Wels-Weyrauch (1989: Figures 11–12). With the new results from Nørgaard (2018: Figure 4.007), we can join together the evidence of chiefly polities in Denmark and Germany during the period 1500–1300 BC into a single map (Figure 5.1).

Figure 5.1 shows how chiefdoms, or rather chiefly polities, based on culture group identities and workshop traditions interacted from the Italian Alps to Denmark during this period and made it possible to distribute metal and other goods between them. It would allow traders and warriors safe passage as well as guest-friendship when they travelled with their goods – copper, cloth, and perhaps slaves – which presupposes stable political relations between all participating chiefdoms. We must therefore envisage political confederacies as the glue between the groups in Figure 5.1 (Kristiansen and Suchowska-Ducke 2015; Ling *et al.* 2018). The map also demonstrates that exchange and possible marriage alliances assumed from the movement of high-status female ornaments were mostly between neighbouring chiefdoms, at distances from 50 to 150 km, which was the size of local cultural groups/chiefdoms. It raises another question: who travelled and how far? Were trade caravans based on shifting groups of people, or did some people make the entire journey from Central Europe to Denmark and back? To answer these questions, we must turn to strontium isotope analyses.

Strontium isotopes

In recent years, results from strontium isotopic tracing opened a new window to Bronze Age mobility. Even if the question of how to establish reliable baselines is still being debated,[2] we can still with some probability demonstrate who is local or non-local. We can also compare non-local origins and, with the support of archaeology and supplementary diet studies, sometimes pinpoint probable origins. This

---

[2] There has been a debate about the role of agricultural lime on strontium signals in western Jutland (Thomsen and Andreasen 2019). However, a very recent study of a soil profile and the respective pore waters from farmland in the glaciogenic outwash plain of western Jutland shows that strontium from agricultural lime is effectively retained near the surface (Frei *et al.* 2019b). Hence, agricultural liming does not appear to contaminate the groundwater-supported surface waters in western Jutland, making the previous baseline maps based on such waters (Frei and Frei 2011) relevant to provenance studies. Finally, a study by Douglas Price (2021) supports the notion that areas with higher strontium are small and thus without real significance for the interpretation of strontium isotopes. He concludes: 'There is good reason to suspect that these "hotspots" are generally small and do not have a major impact on human $^{87}Sr/^{86}Sr$ values in southern Scandinavia' (Price 2021).

94   *Kristian Kristiansen*

has opened a door to reconstruct kinship, rules of marriage, and fosterage during the 3rd and early 2nd millennia BC (Sjögren *et al.* 2016; 2020; Knipper *et al.* 2017; Mittnik *et al.* 2019). These papers demonstrate that the dominant kinship system was based on patrilocal and patrilineal households where women married in from the outside through female exogamy, often from many different locations, with distances from local to supra-local. This can be supported with evidence from south Scandinavia.

A recent paper summarising mobility in Denmark during the 3rd and 2nd millennia BC was able to demonstrate that from 1600 BC onwards strontium signatures of non-locals had multiple origins, in opposition to the preceding period where non-locals had their origin in a few regions (Frei *et al.* 2019a), which could have been the Unetice regions, based on metalwork (Vandkilde 2017). However, after 1600 BC, new lines of trade opened up both between Eastern Central Europe/ the Carpathians and Western Central Europe and the Tumulus culture, which also represented new origins for the supply of copper (Melheim *et al.* 2018; Pernicka *et al.* 2016). The change in strontium isotopic signals around 1600 BC thus corresponds rather closely with changes and diversification of trade routes. The social identity of the buried populations mostly belonged to the status group of free farmers, often with rich grave goods, and always in a barrow. However, people of lower rank or even unfree were also buried. This was demonstrated both in central Germany for the Early Bronze Age (Mittnik *et al.* 2019) and in Scania, southern Sweden. Here, individuals of non-elite status (commoners/unfree) were buried outside the normal Bronze Age chiefly barrows in flat graves, mostly without grave goods. Among them we also find some non-locals (Bergerbrant *et al.* 2017), perhaps brought in from raids as captives (Cameron 2016). In Denmark, however, most of the 'commoner' burials were local individuals (Frei *et al.* 2019a: 14). Furthermore, it has become possible in some areas with distinct geological strontium baseline variations to distinguish between short- and long-distance mobility. Such small-scale patterns of mobility have also been demonstrated for northern Italy (Cavazzuti *et al.* 2019; Cavazzuti and Arena 2020) and western Sweden (Blank *et al.* 2018: Figure 15). In western Sweden, the evidence suggests that mobility was high (up to 70 per cent) in the period 2000–1500 BC, much of which was short distance.

In areas such as Denmark, baseline variation is limited, and therefore non-locals originated outside the region, eliminating the possibility of tracing small-scale mobility inside Denmark. We see evidence of long-distance movements of young women such as Egtved and Skrydstrup. They were buried in uniquely conserved oak coffins which preserved not only textiles and organic material, but also hair and nails (Frei *et al.* 2015; 2017a). Based on tight measurements of preserved hair, mobility could be traced in monthly detail within the last years of their life. It demonstrated that the Egtved woman had travelled twice between her birthplace and Denmark/Egtved during the last two years of her life, before she died at the age of 18. She was locally acculturated with a Nordic belt plate but had retained a worn bracelet with broken-off spirals of Tumulus culture origin, which points to her birthplace. In the case of the Skrydstrup woman, she arrived in southern Jutland when she was around 14 years old and stayed there until she died at the age of 18. The habit with the gold wire that she presumably wore around her ears has parallels mostly in Bohemia and Slovakia, which would fit with many other signs of cultural and economic connections to Eastern Central Europe during this time.

However, there are also clear signs of males moving long distances and then settling in Denmark. One such case is a warrior burial from Thy, northwest Jutland. This male buried in a stone cist in a barrow at Jestrup, dated to the Nordic Bronze Age period III, is indicative of the community's and perhaps individuals' trade relations of the time.[3] He was buried with a Nordic bow-fibula, bronze double button, and a most likely imported grip-plate sword (Aner *et al.* 2001: 33–4, plate 19, Figure 16a–b). The sword belongs to the Rixheim type, which has an assumed origin in present-day Switzerland (Schauer 1971: plate 115). The metal of the Jestrup sword is quite typical for the period, not just in Thy but from all over Northern and Western Central Europe (Ling *et al.* 2019: Figures 16–17): arsenic and nickel are the main impurities, but otherwise it contains only minor traces of other elements (although Pb is at 0.21 per cent). The tin content of the sword is quite high, at 13.10 per cent, which is not unusual for this period in the Nordic realm, although tin contents decrease slightly from period II to III (Bunnefeld 2016). Similarly, high tin contents are present among other period III swords from Thy (Kristiansen *et al.* 2020).

South Tyrol is pinpointed as the most likely source of the copper, and the sword type originates just north of the Italian Alps, suggesting a close geographical match between copper sources and sword type. While period II in the Thisted region is characterised by a wider range of potential source areas, period III is completely dominated by copper coming from one source area, matching ore bodies in south Tyrol in the Italian Alps. The Jestrup sword fits neatly into this picture, being cast with the dominant copper type from Italy to south Scandinavia (Ling *et al.* 2019). Most likely, he travelled north as a warrior protecting one of the copper transports, and unlike most of his contemporaries decided to settle in the distant north rather than return. This individual thus travelled a long distance from the Alps to Thy in Denmark, north-west Jutland.

If we assume that this case is also characteristic of other imported or rather 'foreign'-type swords (Bech and Rasmussen 2018: 76–7; Felding *et al.* 2020), then we can start calculating the number of foreign warriors/traders who decided to settle in Denmark as a result of intense trade connections, and perhaps even some conquest migrations, one of which ended in the Battle of the Tollense Valley around 1250 BC (Terberger *et al.* 2018). I take the relationship between Nordic full-hilted swords

---

[3] A previous investigation by Van der Sluis (2017) yielded a radiocarbon date for this individual (sample from the femur) Lim-hb-143, UBA-31283 BP, 3114 ± 40, C13-19.9, 1455–1269 cal BC, which seems to be in concordance with the typological date that places the burial to the beginning of period III, even if a bit older than expected (period III starts around 1300 BC or a little earlier in some regions).

96 *Kristian Kristiansen*

and flange-hilted swords as a starting point for defining Nordic versus foreign, since they display different origins and distributions (Kristiansen and Suchowska-Ducke 2015). This does not imply that all flange-hilted swords were produced outside Denmark, even if some specific types had a Central European origin. Most flange-hilted swords were probably produced locally (Molloy 2016). However, they define warrior groups who were in constant connection with each other, sharing an identical sword type and fighting style from Central Europe to Denmark. In short, they were travellers, taking service at chiefly courts as war leaders and employed to protect trade caravans and for other duties. Among the foreign types are also octagonally hilted swords that were produced both in south Germany and Denmark, but by foreign smiths, as they used a non-Nordic casting technique. However, their peculiar octagonally formed hilt carried a symbolic meaning, as the eight sides of the hilt refers to the number of young warrior bands mentioned in Indo-European sources, but possibly also depicted on petroglyphs, such as at Kivik (Brown and Anthony 2019). This sword could then symbolise a specific warrior/trader sodality. In opposition to these 'foreign' sword types, Nordic full-hilted swords remained the dominant sword type in high-status burials in the Nordic realm throughout the period 1500–1100 BC, indicating their ritual and political role as local leaders of free farmers (Bunnefeld 2018). They would host travellers, but once in office they would stay at home.

I shall now take a look at the social institutions needed to support travellers, as evidenced in written and linguistic sources, and their support in archaeological evidence. In Table 5.1 I have summarised these groups, their institutional framework, and the proposed distances covered based on Figure 5.1. After this, I shall consider evidence from later written sources on institutions supporting mobility and how they can be demonstrated in the archaeological record.

Table 5.1 Different types of Bronze Age travellers, distances covered, and institutional frameworks (table: author, based on Figure 5.1)

Bronze Age travellers			
Who	Warriors	Traders	Kin Groups
Why	raiding and protection	goods and services	marriage and fosterage
How	caravans (land and sea)	caravans (land and sea)	caravans (land and sea)
Social institution	warriors sodalites / retinues	trade partners guest-friendship	marriage alliances/ guest-friendships
Political institution	confederations	confederations	confederations
Distances	150–500 km	150–500 km	50–150 km (in confederations ≤ 500 km)

Alliances and the flow of people: brides, foster children, traders, and warriors

Alliances allow for people to travel; that is indeed their rationality: to forge social and economic links between chiefdoms. Such alliances, however, had to be 'secured' in more earthly and concrete ways: marriage would only be a first step. The bride price would be received for giving away a daughter, but such economic bonds would soon be followed by further social bonds: male offspring resulting from the alliance would then be placed as foster sons with the family of the mother's brother, to further strengthen bonds. Upon his return as a grown-up, if he returned, the foster son would have forged a foster brother relationship with one or several of the sons of his maternal uncle, and such bonds were indeed strong and would last throughout life (Karl 2005 for Celtic sources; Olsen 2019 for earlier Indo-European sources). Classic foster brothers were, of course, Achilles and Patroclus.

Even if fosterage may be considered a kind of hostage, to secure a marriage contract or other forms of contracts linked to trade alliances (Karl 2005), it nonetheless represented a socially integrating mechanism between two parties, which for more opportunistic (often economic) reasons had decided to join forces. Fosterage could include both young boys and girls and is well described in Celtic written sources (Karl 2005), but also in older Indo-European linguistic sources (Olsen 2019). Boys would typically be placed with socially superior groups, where they would be brought up and taught the skills of the foster family, whether as a warrior, craftsperson, or learned person (druid, bard). Girls would typically be married away to lower-standing groups, already at a young age, so that fosterage and marriage would be part of the same deal. Recent research has demonstrated that the practice of fosterage had ancient roots in the Bronze Age, and even further back into the 3rd millennium BC (Knipper *et al.* 2017; Mittnik *et al.* 2019; Sjögren *et al.* 2020; see also Stockhammer and Massy, Chapter 8). Among the many non-local individuals in stone cists from western Sweden dated mainly to the period 2200–1700 BC, several were children, and thus potential examples of fosterage (Blank *et al.* 2018). We can therefore also consider it an established institution during the 2nd millennium BC, even if the number of proven cases remains low so far (see Bergerbrant 2019 for Sweden). For Denmark, the Egtved woman was buried with the cremated bones of a 5-year-old child with the same non-local origin as hers, in all probability a foster child, which perhaps died on the way north to Egtved and was cremated to allow the bones to be carried on to a final resting place. Interestingly, a rich double male burial from Karlstrup on Zealand with rich Nordic grave goods, including Nordic swords, exhibited high non-local strontium values (Frei *et al.* 2019a: 15). These two Nordic chiefs must have had their upbringing outside Denmark, possibly in south Sweden, on Bornholm or in Central Europe, where we find similar strontium values. Given their Nordic affiliation, I am tempted to consider them as returned foster brothers from high-status alliance partners, in one of the aforementioned regions.

Such social bonds could then be further strengthened by contracts of guest-friendship, often linked to trading partners, well known also from ethnographic/historical sources (Gell 1998; Oka and Kusimba 2008; Ling *et al*. 2022). Hospitality, or guest-friendship especially, is well known from later Indo-European sources (Karl 2006: 281–2, 371–2) and represented an extremely valued relationship among the chiefly stratum, sometimes more than other forms of kinship. It could be transmitted through generations in the same families. In ancient Greece it was termed *Xenia*, and it was considered sacred, being instituted by the gods (Kaul 2018). Kaul states that '*Xenia* was seen as a moral and religious obligation of hospitality securing food and accommodation to travellers. *Xenia* was instituted by the gods, Zeus being the protector of the traveller, and those who did not obey the rules of guest-friendship would call down divine wrath'. Thus, the institution of guest-friendship would bind together for several generations a political confederacy, which is precisely what we see unfolded in Figure 5.1. It also explains the distribution of prestige goods between *Xenia* members of these chiefly policies, as their relationship was among other things kept alive through gift giving. Among top ranking gifts were women, cattle, and finished objects of metal (Morris 1986).[4]

This form of hospitality and generosity thus demanded resources that could only be provided for among the chiefly elites, and it therefore formed a vital ingredient in their political strategies, which also included clients of dependent groups that could provide a steady influx of human labour and food provisions in the form of tribute (Kristiansen 2013: Figure 13.1, 13.6; Nakassis *et al*. 2016). Warriors and traders would be the typical groups to enjoy the fruits of such hospitality, and the international distribution of warrior swords during our period, cross-cutting regional cultural groups, is a testimony to this institution. It also supports the notion that these groups shared a more independent position in society and could travel more freely between different chiefdoms (Oka and Kusimba 2008: 357–8). This is supported by a number of strontium case studies, both in Denmark and northern Italy (Cavazzuti *et al*. 2019; Frei *et al*. 2019a). Indeed, travelling and exploring had the potential of making heroes, as revealed in epics (Miller 2000; Lane Fox 2008), material culture (Anderson 2018), Scandinavian rock art (Ling and Toreld 2018), bronze figurative art (Zaghetto 2017), and rich burial inventories with foreign imports, testifying to long-distance connections (Kristiansen and Larsson 2005). The centre of such activities, including guest-friendship, were chiefly halls of large size (Dollar and Poulsen 2015; Mikkelsen and Kristiansen 2018), which are often found in areas of rich settlements and burial monuments, and which may have represented the hubs between which trading caravans would have moved, whether over land or across the sea.

While some forms of power were inheritable through primogeniture, especially those linked to the household and its possessions, such as land, cattle, and clients

---

[4] Most recently, Karsten Wentink (2020: Chapter 10) has applied this institution to the Bell Beaker culture of the 3rd millennium BC.

(Holst *et al.* 2013; Olsen 2019), those without inheritance had to achieve prestige and wealth by personal prowess, through trading expeditions, warrior service, or colonising ventures. Such activities formed an important outlet for creating alternative career strategies in Bronze Age society.

Forces of expansion: Bronze Age career strategies

Now that we have reconstructed the institutional networks of Bronze Age mobility, and the social groups peopling them, we still need to answer the question: what were the forces of expansion, beyond economic motifs? The immediate answer is demographic surplus. After 2000 BC, the new Bronze Age economies led to a rapid population growth throughout Europe, as demonstrated by Johannes Müller (2015: Figure 17.9). Between 2000 and 1500 BC, European populations rose from *c.* 8 million to 13 million people. We can document this European trend also in local studies of high resolution, such as at Falbygden in Sweden (Blank *et al.* 2020: Figure 17). We have reasons to believe that the trend continued after 1500 BC, as demonstrated in Thy and south-west Norway (Bech and Rasmussen 2018: Figure 2.11; Olsen and Kanstrup 2018: Figure 2c). Many factors were responsible for this demographic growth, among them improved health conditions due to warmer woollen dress and better preservation of food through salting. However, after 2000 BC, better housing conditions are evidenced in larger farmhouses with bole-constructed walls of solid planks and the stalling of cattle, which might have improved interior climate (Fokkens 2019; Nielsen 2019).

Surplus populations challenge existing power structures if too many male warriors have to compete for the rather limited number of chiefly positions. Therefore, chiefly strategies also included explorations into new territories in search for alliances and wealth, and this would represent a way of sending off surplus populations to colonise new lands, sometimes through conquest migrations. Historically, this was a major motivation behind Celtic and Viking expansions (Kristiansen 1998: 320–1). A well-documented Bronze Age case is represented by the Thy region in north-west Jutland, which during a few hundred years between 1500 and 1100 BC became a chiefly hub for maritime trade and explorations from North-West Europe to south Norway and beyond. Through its central position, it was able to amass a remarkable concentration of wealth, as well as rich warrior burials (Kristiansen *et al.* 2020). However, it can also be demonstrated that men and women migrated to Thy from the south (Bech and Rasmussen 2018). But people from Thy likewise travelled north towards south-west Norway and Jæren, where we find burials with clear Danish parallels and a similar environmental history (Prøsch-Danielsen *et al.* 2018). Thus, during a few hundred years between 1500 and 1100 BC, but especially between 1300 and 1100 BC, Thy emerged as a centre of political alliances, trade, and small-scale population movements between North-West Europe and south-west Scandinavia (Ling *et al.* 2018). Such colonising ventures in all probability also included the taking of captives, much needed for labour at the chiefly farms and a global feature of pre-state societies (Cameron 2016). This can be further supported by strontium isotopic analyses of non-elite burials from this period in Scania (Bergerbrant *et al.* 2017). We may assume that they were housed within the known settlements and farms, as demonstrated by Mikkelsen (2020). Thus, all members of society from free farmers to commoners and unfree lived closely together, even if divided by the quality of housing, lifestyle, and burial rituals.

I have now presented the institutional and organisational framework for the operation of Bronze Age mobility and the built-in demographic and social forces of expansion. Next to consider is how this system was set into motion by economic forces of trade.

Trade and the political economy

Volumes of trade are decisive for understanding economic motivations, as well as the organisation of trade. For Denmark, it has been possible to calculate volumes of annual imports of copper and textiles based on the number of farms in Denmark and the size of households (Kristiansen and Sørensen 2020; Kristiansen 2022). For the period in question, annual copper imports would have been in the order of 1–2 tons, and imports of large pieces of cloth in the order of 5,000 pieces. If these figures from Denmark are added up on to a European scale, we are probably talking about more than 1,000 tons of copper that had to be distributed annually throughout Europe. In addition to this, one can imagine other products being traded along with metal and textiles, such as salt, humans, and animals.

These figures for yearly quantities of imported copper and textiles have obvious implications for the organisation of trade. Thus, it becomes increasingly clear that safe, regular journeys for trade purposes along networks of interlinked trails and spanning several hundred kilometres would have been impossible without the existence of large chiefdoms or confederacies of chiefdoms who secured safe passage, guest-friendship for overnight accommodation, and a range of other necessary services. Long linear confederacies are typical of the nomadic and maritime societies that also characterise Bronze Age societies (Gibson 2011; Ling *et al.* 2018). The homes of such confederacies could very well have been associated with the bottlenecks or hubs of large, richly furnished barrows and the largest chiefly halls/ farmsteads, which could offer guest-friendship and protection (Kaul 2018). Such farmsteads were already in existence from around 2000 BC, when the copper trade took off, and they can be up to 400–500 m², like later royal Viking halls (Dollar and Poulsen 2015). Central hubs or bottlenecks existed in the system where greater riches accumulated, such as in Thy. The system needed such regular meeting places or hubs for the negotiation of all kinds of deals – from the trading of goods to the reinforcement of alliances. The relation between trade hubs, chiefly networks, and confederations are summarised in a single model in Figure 5.2.

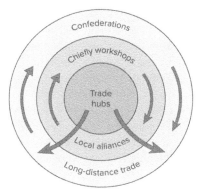

Figure 5.2 Model of dynamics between trade hubs, chiefly workshops/networks, and confederations (image: author)

According to Holst and Rasmussen (2013), we should envisage the long lines of barrows in Jutland, which connected northern and southern Jutland, and western and central Jutland, as cattle trails for herdsmen driving cattle to shifting grazing grounds in a horizontal system of transhumance. Perhaps we should envisage farms with twin living quarters, such as that at Legaard (Mikkelsen and Kristiansen 2018), as being geared to accommodating these groups of herders during the grazing season. The barrow lines stretching hundreds of kilometres indicate trading and travel routes that connected northern and southern Jutland (Rasmussen 2017: Figure 1A), and ultimately led further south along the Elbe and Weser Rivers or land routes to the south of the river. We should envisage groups of warriors/traders on the move, sometimes driving small herds of cattle along with them for trade, and perhaps as bride wealth payments to cement alliances with partners along this long north–south route (Bergerbrant 2007; Holst and Rasmussen 2013). In Figure 5.2 I propose a model for the dynamic interaction of hubs of trade between which caravans would be protected along lines of local chiefdoms, linked by alliances.

Quantities and distances involved presuppose small- to medium-sized groups or caravans in order also to secure protection between stops. Warriors would have to accompany the journeys, and sometimes they would stay and not return to their homeland, taking service in the local chief's retinue. This would explain the occurrence of many foreign swords – octagonally-hilted and flange-hilted warrior swords – during this period in Denmark (Bergerbrant 2007: 124–5). It also explains the non-local values of groups of warriors in cemeteries such as Neckarsulm (Wahl and Price 2013) and the multiple origins of warriors in the Tollense Battle (Price *et al.* 2017). The semi-professional warrior was part of the new political economy of the Middle Bronze Age in Europe (Kristiansen 2018; Felding *et al.* 2020). Their numbers must have been substantial, even if local retinues were small, and the provision of weapons, especially swords and lances, likewise an important goal. The Thy project (Bech *et al.* 2018) offers a glimpse of the organisation of retinues, as there are more warrior burials there than anywhere else in Europe.

102 *Kristian Kristiansen*

In eastern Thy around the local Aas area, Mikkelsen (2018) was able to calculate the number of settlements to around 60, each with one or two barrows. He could further show that from the barrows there was information of 26 swords mainly from period III, which means that at least 30 per cent of all settlements had a sword-bearing warrior. Perhaps there were more, as not all barrows have been excavated. It therefore seems reasonable to suggest that every farm had at least one warrior, further that all warriors would have one or two lances, which was common in the few burials with lances in Europe at the time. Lances were weapons for close combat, not for throwing, as demonstrated by extensive use–wear studies by Horn (2013; 2018, Figure 21.3). In Denmark lances were not considered grave goods, but rather functional weapons, and most are therefore found in hoards.

Thus, if we assume that all household heads provided one warrior with two lances, this equates to *c.* 44,000 lances in circulation in Denmark. If we reduce the number of lance-bearing warriors to half, the figures are still high enough to heavily impact annual needs for new supplies of bronze. If we estimate one sword-bearing leader for 10 farms, that makes 4,000 swords in use at any time (cf. Bunnefeld 2018: 206–7). If we were to apply the higher figure from eastern Thy of one for every three farms, then the figure would be 12,000 swords in circulation. If these figures are applied to Europe, we would be talking about several hundred thousand warriors and lances at any time. Even if we assume that not all warriors were carrying lances, but also bows and arrows were much used as in Tollense (Lidge *et al.* 2018), we would still be talking about substantial numbers that should be added to the demand for copper and tin.

In a decentralised political economy, horizontal networks provided social security and supplies for travelling trading parties, which allowed annual movements of thousands of woollen textiles and hundreds of kilos of copper between Central and Northern Europe. But these very same networks were also able to mobilise substantial numbers of warriors from their wide geographical range in case of regional conflicts or threats, as witnessed in the Tollense Battle, where the strontium evidence demonstrated diverse geographical origins (Price *et al.* 2017). An apparently small-scale economy at the local level had, in the contexts of hundreds of connected settlements, the capacity to operate occasionally at a much larger and more powerful scale.

The horizon of the Bronze Age traveller: from the Alps to Denmark and back

Our journey into Bronze Age travellers has come to an end, and the conclusion is that we cannot understand the various forms of Bronze Age mobility unless we are able to identify different types of travellers, their social roles, and their institutional framework (Harding 2021). This in turn demands an ability to combine different types of evidence, from science and archaeology, and from historical linguistics and texts to comparative anthropology. In this chapter, it has been possible to reconstruct the geographical and social horizons of some typical Bronze Age travellers and wanderers, the institutions that supported them, and distances covered. From this, we may deduce that they travelled along well-trodden paths in familiar landscapes (Løvschal 2013) and with familiar destinations of social peers along the route. The same was true of maritime journeys, where destinations were marked by coastal cairns along the route and safe natural harbours for resting. In their vicinity, we often find rock art panels whose motifs point to ceremonies when meeting your peers and celebrating guest-friendship (Ling 2008). These peers all belonged to the chiefly elites of free farmers, whether warriors, traders, craft specialists, learned persons, whether male or female, children, teenagers, or grown-ups. However, we cannot understand their deeds and manifestations in the land-scape without also understanding the daily life of those who stayed home and toiled on with their duties; they represented a backbone to those rather few who traded, raided, and had monuments built for their afterlife. But history is often shaped by the extraordinary deeds of a small elite, upheld by a less privileged majority of the population (Earle 1997). By the Middle Bronze Age, Nordic and Central European Bronze Age societies were already heavily stratified, with a minority group of free household-owning farmers and warriors dominating a majority of commoners and unfree labour. Even if we assume that social dynamics were oper-ating allowing some of those less privileged the possibility of making an alternative career and thus raising their social position by accompanying traders and warriors, or becoming raiders and colonisers, there still remained a substantial group of the Bronze Age population that were rendered archaeologically invisible or less vis-ible, as unfree or dependent clients (Bergerbrant *et al.* 2017).

This social differentiation was ritually sanctified, as exemplified in different types of burials for elites and commoners. However, it allowed for an efficient organisation of trade systems, including political confederacies, which was supported by mobile warriors to protect caravans and to provide paddlers for sea journeys. The formation of a maritime economy had already begun in 2000 BC, as documented by Helle Vandkilde (2017: Figure 27), and the interaction between cattle-owning farmers and maritime specialists along coastal hubs in Scandinavia materialised in coastal cairns and rock art from 1600/1500 BC onwards (Ling *et al.* 2018: Figure 1; Austvoll 2020). In this respect, Bronze Age society and Viking Age society are very similar, only geographical scale expanded with more advanced Viking Age ship technologies. History does not repeat itself, but similar forces of change may produce related outcomes in the form of historical regularities. This in turn is the foundation for comparative studies in the social sciences to which archaeology and history belong.

References

Anderson, K. (2018), 'Becoming the warrior: constructed identity or functional identity', in C. Horn and K. Kristiansen (eds), *Warfare in Bronze Age Society* (Cambridge, Cambridge University Press), 213–28.

104 *Kristian Kristiansen*

Aner, E., Kersten, K., Koch, E., and Willroth, K.-H. (2001), *Die Funde der älteren Bronzezeit des nordischen Kreises in Dänemark, Schleswig-Holstein und Niedersachsen. 11: Thisted Amt* (Neumünster, Wachholtz).

Aner, E., Kersten, K., Koch, E., and Willroth, K.-H. (2008), *Die Funde der älteren Bronzezeit des nordischen Kreises in Dänemark, Schleswig-Holstein und Niedersachsen. 12: Viborg Amt* (Neumünster, Wachholtz).

Austvoll, K.I. (2020), *Seaways to Complexity: A Study of Sociopolitical Organisation along the Coast of Northwestern Scandinavia in the Late Neolithic and Early Bronze Age* (Sheffield and Bristol, Equinox Publishing).

Bech, J.-H. and Rasmussen, M. (2018), 'Thy and the outside world: regional variations in a North Sea perspective', in J.-H. Bech, B.V. Eriksen, and K. Kristiansen (eds), *Bronze Age Settlement and Land Use in Thy, Northwest Denmark, Vol. I–II* (Højbjerg, Jutland Archaeological Society/Aarhus University Press), 25–106.

Bech, J.-H., Eriksen, B.V., and Kristiansen, K. (eds) (2018), *Bronze Age Settlement and Land Use in Thy, Northwest Denmark, Vol. I–II* (Højbjerg, Jutland Archaeological Society/ Aarhus University Press).

Bergerbrant, S. (2007), *Bronze Age Identities: Costume, Conflict, and Contact in Northern Europe, 1600–1300 BC* (Lindome, Bricoleur Press).

Bergerbrant, S. (2019), 'Transcultural fostering in the Bronze Age? A case study of grave 4/2 in mound II at Abbekås, Sweden', in C. Ljung, A. Andreasson Sjögren, I. Berg, E. Engström, A.-M. Hållans Stenholm, *et al.* (eds), *Tidens Landskap: En vänbok til Anders Andren* (Stockholm, Nordic Academic Press), 62–4.

Bergerbrant, S., Kristiansen, K., Allentoft, M.E., Frei, K.M., Price, T.D., *et al.* (2017), 'Identifying commoners in the Early Bronze Age: burials outside barrows', in S. Bergerbrant and A. Wessman (eds), *New Perspectives on the Bronze Age* (Oxford, Archaeopress), 37–64.

Blank, M., Tornberg, A., and Knipper, C. (2018), 'New perspectives on the Late Neolithic of southwestern Sweden: an interdisciplinary investigation of the gallery grave Falköping Stad 5', *Open Archaeology*, 4: 1–35.

Blank, M., Sjögren, K.-G., and Storå, J. (2020), 'Old bones or early graves? Megalithic burial sequences in southern Sweden based on 14C datings', *Archaeological and Anthropological Sciences*, 12: 89, DOI: 10.1007/s12520-020-01039-9.

Brown, D. and Anthony, D. (2019), 'Late Bronze Age midwinter dog sacrifices and warrior initiations at Krasnosamarskoe, Russia', in B.A. Olsen, T. Olander, and K. Kristiansen (eds), *Tracing the Indo-Europeans: New Evidence from Archaeology and Historical Linguistics* (Oxford, Oxbow), 97–122.

Bunnefeld, J.-H. (2016), *Älterbronzezeitliche Vollgriffschwerter in Dänemark und Schleswig-Holstein. Studien zu Form, Verzierung, Technik und Funktion, Vol. I–II* (Kiel, Wachholtz & Murmann Publishers).

Bunnefeld, J.-H. (2018), 'The Chief and his sword? Some thoughts on the swordbearer's rank in the early Nordic Bronze Age', in C. Horn and K. Kristiansen (eds), *Warfare in Bronze Age Society* (Cambridge, Cambridge University Press), 198–212.

Cameron, C.M. (2016), *Captives: How Stolen People Changed the World* (Lincoln, NB, University of Nebraska Press).

Cavazzuti, C., Cardarelli, A., Quondam, F., Salzani, L., Ferrante, M., *et al.* (2019), 'Mobile elites at Frattesina: flows of people in Late Bronze Age "port of trade" in northern Italy', *Antiquity*, 93(369): 624–44.

Cavazzuti, C. and Arena, A. (2020), 'The bioarchaeology of social stratification in Bronze Age Italy', *Arheo*, 37: 69–105.

Dollar, S.R. and Poulsen, M.E. (2015), 'Early Bronze Age settlements at Vejen in southern Jutland, Denmark: new perspectives on the three-aisled longhouses from Period II', in P. Suchowska-Ducke, S. Scott Reiter, and H. Vandkilde (eds), *Forging Identities: The Mobility of Culture in Bronze Age Europe* (Oxford, British Archaeological Reports), 175–81.

Earle, T. (1997), *How Chiefs Come to Power: The Political Economy in Prehistory* (Stanford CA, Stanford University Press).

Earle, T., Ling, J., Uhnér, C.O., Stos-Gale, Z., and Melheim, L. (2015), 'The political economy and metal trade in Bronze Age Europe: understanding regional variability in terms of comparative advantages and articulations', *European Journal of Archaeology*, 18(4): 633–57.

Felding, L., Reiter, S.S., Frei, K.M., and Vandkilde, H. (2020), 'Male social roles and mobility in the Early Bronze Age: a perspective from SE Jutland', *Danish Journal of Archaeology*, 9: 1–167.

Fokkens, H. (2019), 'The structure of Late Neolithic and Early Bronze Age settlements and houses in the Netherlands', in H. Meller, S. Friederich, M. Küssner, H. Stäuble, and R. Risch (eds), *Siedlungsarchäologie des Endneolithikums und der frühen Bronzezeit* (Halle, Landesamt für Denkmalpflege und Archäologie Sachsen-Anhalt and Landesmuseum für Vorgeschichte), 915–36.

Frei, K.M. and Frei, R. (2011), 'The geographic distribution of strontium isotopes in Danish surface waters: a base for provenance studies in archaeology, hydrology and agriculture', *Applied Geochemistry*, 26: 326–40.

Frei, K.M., Mannering, U., Kristiansen, K., Allentoft, M.E., Wilson, A.S., *et al.* (2015), 'Tracing the life story of a Bronze Age girl with high societal status', *Nature Scientific Reports*, 5: 10431.

Frei, K.M., Villa, C., Jørkov, M.-L., Allentoft, M.E., Kaul, F., *et al.* (2017a), 'A matter of months: high precision migration chronology of a Bronze Age female', *PLoS ONE*, 12(6): e0178834, DOI: 10.1371/journal.pone.0178834.

Frei, K.M., Mannering, U., Berghe, I.V., and Kristiansen, K. (2017b), 'Bronze Age wool: provenance and dye investigations of Danish textiles', *Antiquity*, 91(357): 640–54.

Frei, K.M., Bergerbrant, S., Sjögren, K.-G., Jørkov, M.L., Lynnerup, N., *et al.* (2019a), 'Mapping human mobility during the third and second millennia BC in present-day Denmark', *PLoS ONE*, 14(8): e0219850, DOI: 10.1371/journal.pone.0219850.

Frei, R., Frei, K.M., and Jessen, S. (2019b), 'Shallow retardation of the strontium isotope signal of agricultural liming: implications for isoscapes used in provenance studies', *Science of The Total Environment*, 706: 135710, DOI: 10.1016/j.scitotenv.2019.135710.

Galaty, M.L. (2018), 'Mycenaean glocalism: Greek political economies and international trade', in K. Kristiansen, T. Lindkvist, and J. Myrdal (eds), *Trade and Civilisation: Economic Networks and Cultural Ties, from Prehistory to the Early Modern Era* (Cambridge, Cambridge University Press), 143–71.

Gell, A. (1998), *Art and Agency: An Anthropological Theory* (Oxford, Oxford University Press).

Gibson, B.D. (2011), 'Chiefdom confederacies and state origins', *Social Evolution & History*, 10(1): 215–33.

Harding, A. (2021), *Bronze Age Lives* (Berlin & Boston, Walter de Gruyter).

Holst, M.K. and Rasmussen, M. (2013), 'Herder communities: longhouses, cattle and landscape organization in the Nordic Early and Middle Bronze Age', in S. Bergerbrant and S. Sabatini (eds), *Counterpoint: Essays in Archaeology and Heritage Studies in Honour of Professor Kristian Kristiansen* (Oxford, Archaeopress), 99–110.

Holst, M.K., Rasmussen, M., Kristiansen, K., and Bech, J.-H. (2013), 'Bronze Age "Herostrats": ritual, political and domestic economies in Early Bronze Age Denmark', *Proceedings of the Prehistoric Society*, 79: 265–96.

Horn, C. (2013), 'Weapons, fighters, and combat: spears and swords in Early Bronze Age Scandinavia', *Danish Journal of Archaeology*, 2(1): 20–44.

Horn, C. (2018), 'Warfare vs. exchange? Thoughts on an integrative approach', in C. Horn and K. Kristiansen (eds), *Warfare in Bronze Age Society* (Cambridge, Cambridge University Press), 47–60.

Jockenhövel, A. (1991), 'Räumliche Mobilität von Personen in der mittleren Bronzezeit des westlichen Mitteleuropa', *Germania*, 69: 49–62.

Karl, R. (2005), 'Neighbourhood, hospitality, fosterage and contracts: Late Hallstatt and Early La Tène complex social interaction north of the Alps', accessed 4 March 2014, www.academia.edu/520419/Neighbourhood_Hospitality_Fosterage_and_Contracts.

Karl, R. (2006), *Altkeltische Sozialstrukturen* (Budapest, Archaeolingua).

Kaul, F. (2018), 'Middle Bronze Age long distance exchange: early glass, amber and guest-friendship, xenia', in B. Nessel, D. Neubaum, and M. Bartelheim (eds), *Bronzezeitlicher Transport. Akteure, Mittel und Wege* (Tübingen, Tübingen University Press), 189–211.

Knipper, C., Mittnik, A., Massy, K., Kociumaka, C., Kucukkalipci, I., *et al.* (2017), 'Female exogamy and gene pool diversification at the transition from the Final Neolithic to the Early Bronze Age in Central Europe', *Proceedings of the National Academy of Sciences of the United States of America*, 114(38): 10083–8.

Kristiansen, K. (1998), *Europe before History* (Cambridge, Cambridge University Press).

Kristiansen, K. (2013), 'Households in context: cosmology, economy, and long-term change in the Bronze Age of Northern Europe', in M. Madella, G. Kovacs, B. Berzsenyi, and Godino, I.B. (eds), *The Archaeology of Household* (Oxford, Oxbow), 235–68.

Kristiansen, K. (2018), 'Warfare and the political economy: Europe 1500–1100 BC', in C. Horn and K. Kristiansen (eds), *Warfare in Bronze Age Society* (Cambridge, Cambridge University Press), 23–46.

Kristiansen, K. (2022), 'Towards a new prehistory: re-theorizing genes, culture, and migratory expansions', in M. Daniels (ed), *Homo Migrans: Modeling Mobility and Migration in Human History* (Albany, SUNY Press), 1–33.

Kristiansen, K. and Larsson, T.B. (2005), *The Rise of Bronze Age Society: Travels, Transmission and Transformations* (Cambridge, Cambridge University Press).

Kristiansen, K. and Suchowska-Ducke, P. (2015), 'Connected histories: the dynamics of Bronze Age interaction and trade 1500–1100 BC', *Proceedings of the Prehistoric Society*, 81: 361–92.

Kristiansen, K. and Sørensen, M.L.S. (2020), 'Wool in the Bronze Age: concluding reflections', in S. Sabatini and S. Bergerbrant (eds), *The Textile Revolution in Bronze Age Europe: Production, Consumption and Specialisation* (Cambridge, Cambridge University Press), 317–32.

Kristiansen, K., Melheim, L., Bech, J.-H., Mortensen, M.F., and Frei, K.M. (2020), 'Thy at the crossroads: a local Bronze Age community's role in a macro-economic system', in K.I. Austvoll, M.H. Eriksen, P.D. Fredriksen, L. Melheim, L. Skogstrand, *et al.* (eds), *Contrasts of the Nordic Bronze Age: Essays in Honour of Christopher Prescott* (Turnhout, Brepols), 269–82.

Kuijpers, M.H.G. and Popa, C.N. (2021), 'The origins of money: calculation of similarity indexes demonstrates the earliest development of commodity money in prehistoric Central Europe', *PLoS ONE*, 16(1): e0240462, DOI: 10.1371/journal.pone.0240462.

BRONZE AGE TRAVELLERS 107

Lane Fox, R. (2008), *Travelling Heroes: Greeks and their Myths in the Epic Age of Homer* (New York, Vintage Books & Random House).

Lidge, G., Brinker, U., Jantzen, D., Dombrowsky, A., Dräger, J., *et al.* (2018), 'Warfare or sacrifice? Archaeological research on the Bronze Age site in the Tollense Valley, northeast Germany', in C. Horn and K. Kristiansen (eds), *Warfare in Bronze Age Society* (Cambridge, Cambridge University Press), 153–67.

Ling, J. (2008), *Elevated Rock Art: Towards a Maritime Understanding of Bronze Age Rock Art in Northern Bohuslän, Sweden* (Gothenburg, University of Gothenburg).

Ling, J. and Toreld, A. (2018), 'Maritime warfare in Scandinavian rock art', in C. Horn and K. Kristiansen (eds), *Warfare in Bronze Age Society* (Cambridge, Cambridge University Press), 61–80.

Ling, J., Earle, T., and Kristiansen, K. (2018), 'Maritime mode of production: raiding and trading in seafaring chiefdoms', *Current Anthropology*, 59(5): 488–524.

Ling, J., Hjärthner-Holdar, E., Grandin, L., Stos-Gale, Z., Kristiansen, K., *et al.* (2019), 'Moving metals IV: swords, metal sources and trade networks in Bronze Age Europe', *Journal of Archaeological Science: Reports*, 26: 1–34.

Ling, J., Chacon, R., and Kristiansen, K. (eds) (2022), *Trade before Civilization* (Cambridge, Cambridge University Press).

Løvschal, M. (2013), 'Ways of wandering in the Late Bronze Age barrow landscape of the Himmerland-area, Denmark', in D. Fontijn, A.J. Louwen, S. van der Vaart, and K. Wentink (eds), *Beyond Barrows: Current Research on the Structuration and Perception of the Prehistoric Landscape through Monuments* (Leiden, Sidestone Press), 225–50.

Melheim, L., Gradin, L., Persson, P.-O., Billström, K., Stos-Gale, Z., *et al.* (2018), 'Moving metals III: oossible origins for copper in Bronze Age Denmark based on lead isotopes and geochemistry', *Journal of Archaeological Science*, 96: 85–105.

Mikkelsen, M. (2018), 'The Bronze Age Settlement at Aas, eastern Thy, Denmark', in J.-H. Bech, B.V. Eriksen, and K. Kristiansen (eds), *Bronze Age Settlement and Land Use in Thy, Northwest Denmark, Vol. I–II* (Højbjerg, Jutland Archaeological Society/ Aarhus University Press), 477–504.

Mikkelsen, M. (2020), 'Slaves in Bronze Age Southern Scandinavia?', *Acta Archaeologica (København)*, 91(1): 147–90.

Mikkelsen, M. and Kristiansen, K. (2018), 'Legaard (with contributions from Bente Draiby and Timothy Earle)', in J.-H. Bech, B.V. Eriksen, and K. Kristiansen (eds), *Bronze Age Settlement and Land Use in Thy, Northwest Denmark, Vol. I–II* (Højbjerg, Jutland Archaeological Society/Aarhus University Press), 505–38.

Miller, D.A. (2000), *The Epic Hero* (Baltimore MD, Johns Hopkins University Press).

Mittnik, A., Massy, K., Knipper, C., Wittenborn, F., Friedrich, R., *et al.* (2019), 'Kinship-based social inequality in Bronze Age Europe', *Science*, 366(6466): 731–34.

Molloy, B.P.C. (2016), 'Nought may endure but mutability: eclectic encounters and material change in the 13th to 11th centuries BC Aegean', in B. Molloy (ed), *Of Odysseus and Oddities: Scales and Modes of Interaction between Prehistoric Aegean Societies and their Neighbours* (Oxford, Oxbow), 343–84.

Morris, I. (1986), 'Gift and commodity in Archaic Greece', *Man*, 21(1): 1–17.

Müller, J. (2015), 'Eight million Neolithic Europeans: social demography and social archaeology on the scope of change – from the Near East to Scandinavia', in K. Kristiansen, L. Smedja, and J. Turek (eds), *Paradigm Found: Archaeological Theory Present, Past and Future. Essays in Honour of Evzen Neustupny* (Oxford, Oxbow), 200–15.

Nakassis, D., Galaty, M.L., and Parkinson, W. (eds) (2016), 'Discussion and debate: reciprocity in Aegean palatial societies. Gifts, debt, and the foundations of economic exchange', *Journal of Mediterranean Archaeology*, 29(1): 61–132.

Nielsen, P.O. (2019), 'The development of the two-aisled longhouse in the Neolithic and Early Bronze Age', in L.R. Sparrevohn, O.T. Kastholm, and P.O. Nielsen (eds), *Houses for the Living: Two-Aisled Houses from the Neolithic and Early Bronze Age in Denmark, Vol. 1* (Copenhagen, The Royal Society of Northern Antiquities and University Press of Southern Denmark), 9–50.

Nørgaard, H.W. (2018), *Bronze Age Metalwork: Techniques and Traditions in the Nordic Bronze Age 1500–1100 BC* (Oxford, Archaeopress).

Nørgaard, H.W., Pernicka, E., and Vandkilde, H. (2019), 'On the trail of Scandinavia's early metallurgy: provenance, transfer and mixing', *PLoS ONE*, 14(7): e0219574, DOI: 10.1371/journal.pone.0219574.

O'Brien, W. (2015), *Prehistoric Copper Mining in Europe, 5500-500 BC* (Oxford, Oxford University Press).

Oka, R. and Kusimba, C.M. (2008), 'The archaeology of trading systems, part 1: towards a new trade synthesis', *Journal of Archaeological Research*, 16: 339–95.

Olsen, B.A. (2019), 'Aspects of family structure among the Indo-Europeans', in B.A. Olsen, T. Olander, and K. Kristiansen (eds), *Tracing the Indo-Europeans: New Evidence from Archaeology and Historical Linguistics* (Oxford, Oxbow), 145–64.

Olsen, J. and Kanstrup, M. (2018), 'Cumulative probability distributions. What can they tell us?', in J.-H. Bech, B.V. Eriksen, and K. Kristiansen (eds), *Bronze Age Settlement and Land Use in Thy, Northwest Denmark, Vol. I–II* (Højbjerg, Jutland Archaeological Society/Aarhus University Press), 90–106.

Pernicka, E., Nessel, B., Mehofer, M., and Safta, E. (2016), 'Lead isotope analyses of metal objects from the Apa Hoard and other Early and Middle Bronze Age items from Romania', *Archaeologia Austriaca*, 100: 57–86.

Price, D. (2021), 'Problems with strontium isotopic proveniencing in Denmark?', *Danish Journal of Archaeology*, 10: 1–12.

Price, T.D., Frei, R., Brinker, U., Lidke, G., Terberger, T., *et al.* (2017), 'Multi-isotope proveniencing of human remains from a Bronze Age battlefield in the Tollense Valley in northeast Germany', *Archaeological and Anthropological Sciences*, 11(1): 33–49.

Prøsch-Danielsen, L., Prescott, C., and Holst, M.K. (2018), 'Economic and social zones during the Late Neolithic/Early Bronze Age in Jæren, southwest Norway: reconstructing large-scale land-use patterns', *Prähistorische Zeitschrift*, 93(1): 48–88.

Rasmussen, M. (2017), 'Time warps and long-term structures: images of Early Bronze Age landscape organisation in south-west Denmark', in S. Bergerbrant and A. Wessman (eds), *New Perspectives on the Bronze Age* (Oxford: Archaeopress), 177–86.

Schauer, P. (1971), *Die Schwerter in Süddeutschland, Österreich und der Schweiz I (Griffplatten-, Griffangel- und Griffzungenschwerter)* (Munich, C.H. Beck Verlag).

Sjögren, K.-G., Price, T.D., and Kristiansen, K. (2016), 'Diet and mobility in the Corded Ware of Central Europe', *PLoS ONE*, 11(5): e0155083, DOI: 10.1371/journal.pone.0155083.

Sjögren, K.-G., Olalde, I., Carver, S., Allentoft, M.E., Knowles, T., *et al.* (2020), 'Kinship and social organization in Copper Age Europe: a cross-disciplinary analysis of archaeology, DNA, isotopes, and anthropology from two Bell Beaker cemeteries', *PLoS ONE*, 15(11): e0241278, DOI: 10.1371/journal.pone.0241278.

Skoglund, P. (2017), 'Axes and long distance trade: Scania and Wessex in the early second millennium BC', in P. Skoglund, J. Ling, and U. Bertilsson (eds), *North Meets South: Theoretical Aspects on the Northern and Southern Rock Art Traditions in Scandinavia* (Oxford: Oxbow), 199–213.

Stöllner, T. (2018), 'Mining as a profession in prehistoric Europe', in S. Alexandrov, Y. Dimitrova, H. Popov, B. Horejs, and K. Chukalev (eds), *Злато & Бронз. Gold & Bronze. Metals, Technologies and Interregional Contacts in the Eastern Balkans during the Bronze Age* (Sofia, National Archaeological Institute with Museum and Bulgarian Academy of Sciences), 71–85.

Terberger, T., Jantzen, D., Krüger, J., and Lidge, G. (2018), 'Das bronzezeitliche Kampfgeschehen im Tollensetal – ein Großereignis oder wiederholte Konflikte?', in S. Hansen and R. Krause (eds), *Bronzezeitliche Burgen zwischen Taunus und Karpaten* (Bonn, Habelt), 103–24.

Thomsen, E. and Andreasen, R. (2019), 'Agricultural lime disturbs natural strontium isotope variations: implications for provenance and migration studies', *Science Advances*, 5(3): eaav8083, DOI: 10.1126/sciadv.aav8083.

Van der Sluis, L.G. (2017), *Investigating Palaeodietary Changes from the Mesolithic to the Viking Age in the Limfjord Area in Northern Denmark*, Unpublished PhD thesis (Belfast, Queen's University).

Vandkilde, H. (2016), 'Bronzization: the Bronze Age as pre-modern globalization', *Prähistorische Zeitschrift*, 91(1): 103–23.

Vandkilde, H. (2017), *The Metal Hoard from Pile in Scania, Sweden: Place, Things, Time, Metals, and Worlds around 2000 BCE* (Aarhus, Aarhus University Press).

Wahl, J. and Price, T.D. (2013), 'Local and foreign males in a Late Bronze Age cemetery at Neckarsulm, southwestern Germany: strontium isotope investigations', *Anthropologischer Anzeiger*, 70(3): 289–307.

Wels-Weyrauch, U. (1989), 'Mittelbronzezeitliche Frauentrachten in Süddeutschland: Beziehungen zur Hagenauer Gruppierung', in Ministère de l'Éducation Nationale, de la Jeunesse et des Sports – Comité des Travaux Historiques et Scientifiques (ed), *Dynamique du bronze moyen Europe occidentale* (Paris, CTHS), 117–34.

Wentink, K. (2020), *Stereotype: The Role of Grave Sets in Corded Ware and Bell Beaker Funerary Practices* (Leiden, Sidestone Press).

Zaghetto, L. (2017), *La situla Benvenuti di Este. Il poema figurato degli antichi Veneti* (Bologna, Ante Quem).

6

Andronovo Mobility Revisited: New Research on Bronze Age Mining and Metallurgical Communities in Central Asia

THOMAS STÖLLNER, HANDE ÖZYARKENT,
AND ANTON GONTSCHAROV

Introduction: aspects of mobility and migrations in the Central Asian steppe region during the Andronovo period and beyond

RECENTLY, MODERN GENOME studies have provided insights into population relationships between the Eastern European plains and the Central Asian forest steppe and steppe zone since the late 4th and early 3rd millennia BC (Allentoft *et al.* 2015; Haak *et al.* 2015; Mathieson *et al.* 2015; Narasimhan *et al.* 2019). These relationships were explained by expected early pastoral economic cycles of the Pit Grave or Yamnaya culture or the Corded Ware groups integrated into the dynamics since the early 3rd millennium BC (e.g. Czebreszuk 2004; for a more differentiated argumentation see Kaiser 2010; 2016; also Frachetti 2011). According to this line of interpretation, Eastern European and Caucasian-European populations and their genomes spread to Central Asia and there partly replaced other more Central Siberian-Asian populations, whose specific genetic pattern remained clearly determinable until the end of the 3rd millennium BC (e.g. Afanasievo: Mathieson *et al.* 2015; Narasimhan *et al.* 2019).

From a bird's-eye view, this gene flow with supposedly light-pigmented European-Caucasian populations looked like a great wave of migration that finally spread to Central Asia by the end of the 3rd millennium BC, and a little later to the Tarim Basin, the southern areas of Central Asia, and the Minussinsk Basin (Kuzmina 1994; Mallory and Mair 2008; Narasimhan *et al.* 2019). This is where the older conceptions of a dispersal of Indo-European-speaking people met with ideas of the formation of the so-called Andronovo culture in the 2nd millennium

Proceedings of the British Academy, **254**, 110–141, © The British Academy 2023.

BC (e.g. Gimbutas 1970; Mallory 1989; Anthony 2007) (Figure 6.1). The use of wagons and certain elements of riding by a militarily dominant elite were ultimately viewed as an element of identity and ideology that would have connected the Indo-European societies within wider Central and Western Asia. Kuzmina (1994; 2007) also spoke of the spread of elements of material culture to the south and east, mainly based on archaeological evidence. She linked this with the implementation of metallurgy and an intensification of metal extraction as a whole (Kuzmina 1991).

In Central Asia, the Bactria-Margiana-Archaeological Complex (BMAC) developed in the middle of the 3rd millennium BC and was often viewed as a transformation area (overviews: Masson and Sarianidi 1972; Kohl 2007; Vidale 2017). This would have passed cultural (including possible linguistic) traditions to the Indus and Ganges valleys, as well as to the Iranian central plateau on the southern side of the Kopet Dagh Mountains. Mallory even developed a 'culture bullet' (*Kulturkugel*) theory of cultural diffusion in order to be able to connect the clearly different cultural elements of these areas with the steppe nomads (Mallory and Adams 1997: 73). Such leaps are problematic, especially when we consider that the North Indian and Iranian Iron Ages (and also the Yaz cultural phenomenon)

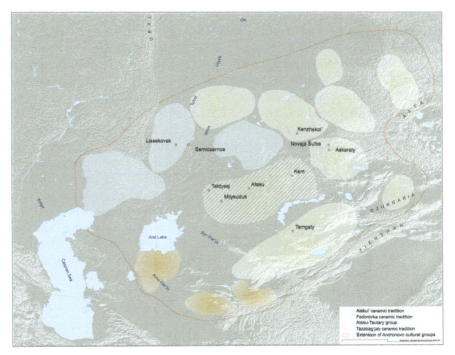

Figure 6.1 Andronovo phenomenon – distribution of different cultural units within Central Asia (after Parzinger 2006; Kuzmina 2007; mapping: DBM, A. Hornschuch, J. Garner, and T. Stöllner)

are at least 300 to 500 years younger (see Narasimhan *et al.* 2019 for the genetic ancestry of North Indian populations). Additionally, genetic sequences showed a different genetic ancestry for the BMAC communities as compared with Yamnaya populations, and gene flow towards the steppe regions (Narasimhan *et al.* 2019).

Even against the background of genetic relationships, such conclusions have to be doubted. Current genetic data from the regions concerned are not linked as closely as desired, e.g. from graves of the Hindustan/Swat culture dating to the late 2nd and early 1st millennia BC (Narasimhan *et al.* 2019). Nor do sufficient genomic data exist from the Iranian central plateau for the late 2nd millennium BC, which earlier researchers saw as the destination of Iranian-speaking immigrants from the north (Ghirshman 1964; 1977; Young 1967; for a recent summary see Potts 2016). Those who saw the Indo-Aryan ancestry in the Andronovo complex (Kuzmina 2007) connected these ideas on a conceptual level.

Research of the Bronze Age archaeological cultures has long pursued fundamental problems of the chronological classification and geographical delimitation of the various regional forms of 'Andronovo' (e.g. Kuzmina 1994; Parzinger 2006, 356–441; Varfolomeev and Evdokimov 2013). The main focus of observation was the Bronze Age pottery of the steppe, its ceramic technology, and its variegated decorative systems. Researchers termed them Fedorovka, Alakul', or Atasu-Tautary tradition and determined their spatially different distribution areas. Some concepts followed a chronological sequence of individual ceramic styles (e.g. for the temporal priority of Alakul' ceramic tradition in the west) or assumed that these styles were spread through migration events. The traditional view that migration can be recorded by the spread of characteristics of material culture (e.g. ceramics), however, has recently been contradicted in the sense of a 'pots as people' concept (for arguments see Frachetti 2011: 201–3). Such interpretations are paired with the idea that particular regional and group-specific characteristics and identities are reflected in the ceramic decoration in particular, but this is by no means certain (Varfolomeev and Evdokimov 2013). Kuzmina (1991) regarded the metallurgical and mining activities closely connected with the Andronovo cultures as an interpretative background. In the search for metal ores, individual groups would have moved, e.g. to Central Asia (Tazabag'jab variant of the Andronovo complex), into the Minussinsk Basin (Fedorovka variant), or even to Xinjiang via the Tien Shan Mountains and the Dzungarian Gate (Kuzmina 1991; 1994; see also Tkacheva and Tkachev 2008). If we consider the significant intensification of metallurgical activities or the fact that certain metal forms are found widely spread throughout Central Asia at the time (see Chernykh 1992), this interpretation may have its value.

One important aspect is the widespread Sejma-Turbino phenomenon (Černych 2013) (Figure 6.2) and the introduction of tin bronzes into the forest steppe regions and, to a minor extent, also to the steppe regions. Tin ores from east Kazakhstan may have played an important role within this exchange, as the recent lead isotope investigation of a bronze object, found in the tin-bronze free Sintashta complex of Konopljanka in the Central Urals, has demonstrated (Krause 2013). Tin bronzes themselves were introduced from the late 3rd millennium BC Minussinsk Basin and were common across the Altai Mountains in eastern Kazakhstan (Okunev, Krotovo, Samus', Elunino, and Kanaj Group: Chernikov 1960; Parzinger 2002; 2006: 324) to the middle Urals. In the west, there was also a possible connection between the Black Sea region and Troy, which can be seen best by the metalwork in the famous Borodino Hoard (Shishlina and Loboda 2019) that also displays connections to the metalwork of the Sejma-Turbino phenomenon. The lead isotope similarities between the early tin bronzes from Troy and the East Kazakh tin bronzes and their regional origin (Pernicka *et al.* 2003; Stöllner *et al.* 2011: 247–9) might possibly raise the question of whether the steppe itself was the connective background for exchange relations. The early use of tin bronze, especially in the regions between the upper Irtysh River, the Altai Mountains, and the Minussinsk Basin, provides good arguments for seeing one possible origin of this technology in these regions. The Sejma-Turbino phenomenon makes it more than clear that tin ore extraction and alloying were already developed before the start of the Andronovo phenomenon (for a new radiocarbon chronology: Marchenko *et al.* 2017).

Figure 6.2 East Kazakhstan, Delbegetey (Askaraly) Mountains: Bronze Age sites in the surroundings of tin mines (pick/hammer symbols): rhomboids=graves; dots=settlements (mapping: DBM, Hornschuch and Stöllner)

114   *Thomas Stöllner et al.*

This also becomes clear when looking at the Early Bronze Age steppe connections that ran towards the later Tazabag'jab group at the fringe of the BMAC in Middle Asia. Avanesova (2013) and Parzinger (2006: 329–35) referred to the importance of metal processing and the relations to the steppe regions further north in the late 3rd millennium BC, but also for earlier time horizons, e.g. the Zaman-Baba culture in Bukhara, which has not yet been well researched. The site of Tugaj near Samarkand, Uzbekistan, however, demonstrates already for the period of the late 3rd millennium BC close ties to the northern Kazakh Petrovka culture (Avanesova 1996; 2015). Like the later communities of the Tazabag'jab culture, these groups might have visited the higher summer pastures and mining areas (e.g. those of Mushiston: Parzinger and Boroffka 2003; for early dates: Garner 2014) of the western Tien Shan and Pamir Mountains (for the Inner Asian Mountain Corridor see Frachetti 2012; Spengler *et al.* 2014). Ore deposits in low mountain ranges at the foot of the high mountains were probably seasonally exploited, as illustrated by the Andronovo settlement of Sichkonchi near the Karnab tin deposit in Uzbekistan (Parzinger and Boroffka 2003).

From an archaeological point of view, interpretation must be focused on the social and economic practices in the steppe region, especially the different levels of the cultural sphere (language, material culture, ideology) involved in the formation of ethnic identities. Biomolecular archaeology can direct our attention to new questions, but a detailed archaeological analysis must follow. Mobility in its various forms (up to larger migration events) is an important factor here. One can ask what caused this increasing mobility. Metals and their exchange probably only represented an economic background for the increasing patterns of movement in Central Asia. In the Eurasian forest steppe and steppe zone, semi-mobile or mobile herding can form an important background. However, it is still not fully clear how the pasture management systems ultimately took shape (Ventresca Miller *et al.* 2019; 2020). Numerous research contributions assume that Bronze Age societies still persisted in smaller-scale pastoral systems and that an extensive nomadisation of societies would only have been a phenomenon of the subsequent Iron Ages (Frachetti 2008; 2012). Therefore, another aspect must also be considered: Central Asia is essentially characterised by east–west-oriented environmental corridors, which in turn have contributed to extensive exchange networks. Apart from the actual grass steppes, the northern forest steppes, and the southern zones each have their own ecosystem, e.g. the desert steppe areas (Pott 2005: 521–38; Boroffka 2013).

The progressive aridisation southwards towards the Central Asian desert areas led, especially in the southern zones, to important connecting corridors along the major rivers, as well as along the mountainous areas. The river valleys (similar to the climatically favourable mountain valleys of the large mountain ranges) could have served as winter quarters, while the spring and summer pastures were also associated with mining and metallurgical activities. Ethnographic evidence for pastoral transhumance from the early 20th century shows that distances of many hundreds of kilometres are not unusual in the context of seasonal pasture movements (Khazanov 1994; Stasevič 2013). It is therefore obvious that material goods could also spread widely as a result. Therefore, it is ultimately impossible to clearly separate goods that were spread by a single migration from those distributed through permanent pasture-related mobility. So, the main point in this chapter will be to find arguments for the different kinds of mobility patterns required for understanding the Andronovo complex as a network of mobility rather than the result of unidirectional migration events.

The Bochum Kazakhstan project: goals and methods

By the early 2nd millennium BC, metal practice was already established in Central Asia, a process that began well before the actual Andronovo culture (e.g. Chernykh 1992; Grigoriev 2015). Bronze played a central role in this, e.g. in the Sejma-Turbino phenomenon. While copper is available in many places within the deposit zones of the Central Asian Tethyan-Eurasian Metallogenic Belt (TEMB) and north of it (e.g. Seltmann 2013), tin deposits are much rarer (see the overview in Garner 2014). Bronze occurs in numerous and sometimes large metal associations, such as large deposits in southern and eastern Kazakhstan (Chernykh 1992; Černych 2013; Stöllner et al. 2013a; Grigoriev 2015; Stöllner and Gontscharov 2021). It was therefore rewarding to investigate the question of mobility and migration on the basis of evidence for tin extraction and the distribution of the oldest tin bronzes.

In 2003 a long-term cooperation project with the Archaeological Institute A.Ch. Margulan of the Republic of Kazakhstan began, which continued with field research until 2010 and resulted in an exhibition (Stöllner and Samašev 2013) and other projects that processed part of the collected data in dissertations (Naumann 2016; Gontscharov 2019; Özyarkent 2019).[1] The central question of

---

[1] The project was generously supported by the Gerda Henkel Foundation in three successive projects between 2003 and 2008; I have to express my gratitude to the foundation's officials and boards for the uncomplicated and effective collaboration, especially to Dr A.-M. Lauter (special programme Central Asia), Dr A. Kühnen, and the chairman, Dr M. Hansler. The project itself was initiated by Sergej Berdenov†, Jan Cierny†, Dr Zeinolla Samaschev, and Dr Thomas Stöllner during a first field trip in 2003. The programme was supported by many Kazakh and German colleagues: A. Gorelik took over many of the responsibilities and supported the project with his expertise. We would like to thank M. Doll, J. Garner, A. Gorelik, A. Hauptmann, R. Herd, G.A. Kushtch, V. Merz, T. Riese, A. Kuczminski, B. Song, and B. Zickgraf, but also G. Suvorova, A. 'Sascha' Kolmogorov, J. Digon, and Director Djusupov of the Kraevedcheskij Museum in Ust-Kamenogorsk. Also former students I. Merz, J. Kazizov, A. Tschotbajev, A. Alpamys Zhalgasuly, and O. Balyk, as well as K. Malek, M. Rabe, A. Kramer, N. Löwen, P. Thomas, and B. Sikorski from Bochum. For this article the authors were provided access to the fascinating metals of Nurataldy; we especially thank Dr V. Loman and Dr I. Kukushikin (Karaganda).

the projects funded by the Gerda Henkel Foundation and the Leibniz Association (RITaK project) ultimately aimed at researching the economic foundations of the metal-producing Bronze Age communities of the Andronovo culture, their predecessors, and successors in central and eastern Kazakhstan. In the course of the project, surveys and excavations were carried out on Bronze Age tin- and copper-producing communities in north-east and eastern Kazakhstan. The excavations in the Delbegetey Massif (Askaraly) in the Kalba-Narym zone of eastern Kazakhstan identified a Bronze Age landscape with mining evidence, settlements, grave finds, and ritual sites (Stöllner *et al.* 2011; 2013a). The mineralisation in Askaraly is of cassiterite-tourmaline type. It is known that producing bronze from cassiterite is easier and can be sufficiently co-melted in a crucible. Therefore, this ore has the potential to be used within rather simple metallurgical techniques. Indeed, there are hints (i.e. Elunino-type sherds) that indicate the Askaraly tin ore might have been used already during the Early Bronze Age (Naumann 2016: 42, plate 20). By being rich in valuable tin deposits and situated on the transition zone between the true steppes and the semi-desert steppes and between central and eastern Kazakhstan, Askaraly had the potential to be used as a major tin source during the Bronze Age.

The archaeological site of Askaraly II is of great importance in this context because a community of the Andronovo culture engaged in tin mining can be examined here through a settlement site, a burial ground, and a tin mine, which is unique for the steppe and forest steppe regions. The burials at Mastau Baj/ Chernogorka, many of which contained hammerstones as grave goods, were seemingly directly related to the mining and possibly represent part of the mining community (Stöllner *et al.* 2010) (Figure 6.3; Table 6.1). A settlement, partly excavated nearby at Mastau Baj, allowed insight into daily pastoral and metallurgical practices and subsistence activities. Besides meat consumption and pastoral activities (Doll 2013; Özyarkent 2019) (Table 6.2), there is also indication of some crop planting activities (Stöllner *et al.* 2011: 245, Figure 14).

A second subject of investigation included the question of the exchange of metals and metal objects. The German-Kazakh project has been able to investigate numerous Bronze Age metals from different parts of Kazakhstan since 2006. Among other things, the focus was on exchange processes between different Bronze Age groups and the question of whether and how the tin deposits of eastern Kazakhstan contributed to the bronze supply of Bronze Age steppe communities. This question will be discussed here on the basis of findings from the Nurataldy cemetery. The study is based on nearly 400 metal analyses, of which only a small selection will be discussed here. Gontscharov will present those results in full in the planned printed version of his dissertation (Gontscharov 2019; for the methods see Stöllner and Gontscharov 2021).

ANDRONOVO MOBILITY REVISITED

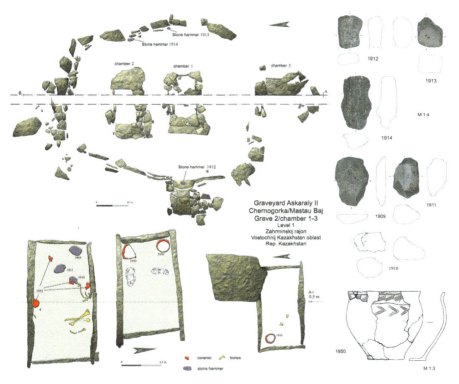

Figure 6.3 East Kazakhstan, Delbegetey (Askaraly) Mountains: cemetery, Chernogorka/Mastau Baj I, grave 2 (mapping/photos/drawings: Institut Margulan/Vostochnij Kazakhstan Museum/DBM, Garner, Cierny, and Digon)

Table 6.1 Askaraly II, Mastau Baj/Chernogorka, stone circle 2, anthropological and archaeological data (source DBM/RUB)

Askaraly II, Mastau Baj/Chernogorka, stone circle 2, elliptic, 6.8 x 5.5 m							
Cist	Orientation	Robbed/ reopened	Burial rites	Sex	Ceramic	Metal finds	Stone artefacts
							6 hammers deposited in stone circle
1	E-W	X	inhumation	male, mature	fragments	ring fragments	3 stone hammers
2	E-W	X	cremation	female (?)	1 pot, 1 bowl		
3	E-W	X	inhumation	unclear	1 vessel in NW-corner		

Table 6.2 East Kazakhstan, Delbegetey (Askaraly) Mountains: species composition of the faunal remains found in the settlement of Mastau Baj I (after Doll 2013)

Species	NISP	NISP (%)	Weight	Weight (%)
Unidentified fragments of middle-sized species	1022	68.6 %	1285.4 g	44.7 %
Unidentified fragments of large-sized species	466	31.3 %	1590.7 g	55.3 %
Total of unidentified species	1488	100.0 %	2876.1 g	100.0 %
Cattle (*Bos taurus*)	1062	50.0 %	20937.7 g	70.8 %
Sheep (*Ovis aries*)	90	4.2 %	2077.9 g	7.0 %
Goat (*Capra hircus*)	10	0.5 %	295.0 g	1.0 %
Sheep or goat (*Ovis / Capra*)	890	41.9 %	4858.5 g	16.4 %
Dog (*Canis familiaris*)	2	0.1 %	7.4 g	0.0 %
Wild or domestic horse	69	3.2 %	1405.7 g	4.8 %
Unidentified bird	1	0.1 %	0.8 g	0.0 %
Total of identified specimens	2124	100.0 %	29570.0 g	100.0 %
Total share of identified specimens	2124	58.8 %	29570.0 g	92.4 %
Total share of unidentified specimens	1488	41.2 %	2876.1 g	7.6 %
Total of specimens	3612	100.0 %	32446.1 g	100.0 %

Multiple isotope analysis at Askaraly: a tin-mining community and its mobility

The goal of the research was to investigate movements on the landscape, especially regarding the provenance, diet, and climatic signals. The method of investigation developed for this research can be labelled as multiple isotope analysis cross-validation. Multiple isotope studies in our case meant the combination $^{86}Sr/^{87}Sr$ in order to detect the geological background of human and animal samples, as well as $\delta^{13}C/^{15}N$ to discuss the background of predominant nutrition patterns, and this in combination with $\delta^{18}O$ isotope ranges to get a climate signal involved. Here, we only present some results selected from a larger sample series that was collected and investigated within the context of a PhD study (Özyarkent 2019). Similar studies have already been performed for western Siberia and northern Kazakhstan (Motuzaite Matuzeviciute *et al.* 2015; Ventresca Miller *et al.* 2018; 2020) and for southern Kazakhstan and the Inner Asian Mountain Corridor (Spengler *et al.* 2014; Hermes *et al.* 2019; Wang *et al.* 2020), but not for central and eastern Kazakhstan.

The main sample group consisted of herd animals since they would be the main resource for a moving pastoral community. In Central Asia, changing pastures according to the climatic and ecological conditions during the seasons and moving to nurture the herd in better pastures is a characteristic subsistence strategy and lifestyle. Moreover, from a methodological point of view, the incrementally mineralising enamel of the hypsodont tooth of herbivores is a better medium for observing temporal isotopic changes, given the current state of isotope research and the results from laboratory experiments based on controlled feeding. Since the aim of the investigation was the entire community, the dataset was enlarged by two human samples in the first step. These two individuals were miners, as suggested by their grave goods (see above). The cemetery in total represents a household occupation consisting of variously aged adult men, women, and infants (Kunter 2009).

One part of the study is based on the results of strontium isotope analysis. The investigation of strontium isotopes from the hydroxyapatite of the bone/tooth of animals and humans for examining their provenance is an established method and has proved itself in the last decades with numerous archaeometry studies, first, by Ericson (1985) and followed by Sealy *et al.* (1991), Sillen and LeGeros (1991), Price *et al.* (1994), Ezzo (1997), Grupe *et al.* (1997), Sillen *et al.* (1998), and recently, Knipper (2017). Strontium is an alkaline earth element that incorporates into crystal structures of bone and teeth, as well as other materials (i.e. shell, antler, hair, etc.) in the place of calcium due to the similarity in the atomic valence of both elements. Strontium isotope ratios show variation in nature, and to a great extent this is related to the age and origin of the rocks. The strontium element then travels into the habitat by the weathering of rocks and other processes (i.e. meteoric water, soil formation, etc.). The observed variations in the ratio of two strontium isotopes, a less-occurring radiogenic isotope (^{87}Sr) and a more common stable isotope (^{86}Sr), provide a tool for investigation within the landscape. By comparing the isotope ratios, it is possible to connect the organism or the organic material to the bedrock where the organism took its food.

The Askaraly archaeological sites (including Askaraly II) are situated on a granitic hill (Delbegetey), and the lowland around the hill is a carboniferous oceanic sea basin which continues southwards (Chara Basin). This geological setting, with higher radiogenic values on the hill (due to the granitic rocks) and lower values in the lowland (due to substrates of carbonate and shale), provides a suitable isotopic background for investigating the mobility in question with strontium isotope analysis (see below). According to the results of the strontium isotope analysis, it was possible to distinguish a foreign signal among the herd animals from Askaraly (Figure 6.4). The local strontium isotope value range is determined by calculating the confidence interval from the local non-migrating animals, used for comparison (Özyarkent 2019: 220–2). Outliers such as most of the cows and some sheep/goats are outside this designated local range and, in this case, mainly have low radiogenic values.

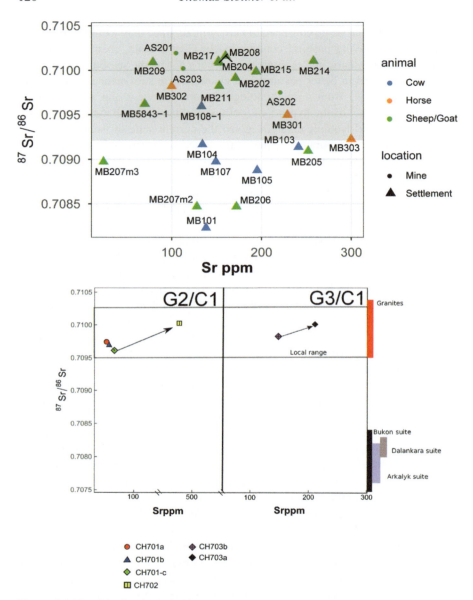

Figure 6.4 Top: Plot for the Sr isotope and Sr elemental abundance measured on the animals from Askaraly. Grey area indicates the value range between upper and lower limits of the 95 per cent CI from the local range calculated using the non-migrating local animals. Bottom: Human (miner/metallurgist) 87Sr/86Sr investigation on different teeth and bones from two Andronovo grave structures. The samples of two human individuals show regional mobility during their lifetime: CH701a: M1; CH701b: canine; CH701c: M3; CH702: tibia of the same individual; CH703a/b: teeth; note the higher elemental abundance of Sr in bone regarding the teeth (after Özyarkent 2019)

Another method used in this research is oxygen isotope analysis, which is used to indicate seasonal temperature changes. Variation of $\delta^{18}O$ in the food cycle is biased towards the oxygen isotopic values of meteoric water, which is determined by various factors but to a large extent by seasonal temperature changes (Dansgaard 1964; Sponheimer and Lee-Thorp 1999: 723–4; Gat 2001). These variations can be correlated to the meteoric water in other food sources (i.e. tree leaves, plants, fish, etc.), and when an organism consumes these while its bone and tooth enamel apatite is formed, the $\delta^{18}O$ of CO_3 in the matrix of their hard tissues would be biased towards the value of these food and water sources (Longinelli 1984; Luz *et al.* 1984; Iacumin *et al.* 1996; Koch 2007). With this premise, it is possible to detect temperature changes based on the oxygen ratios derived from food and water (e.g. summer–winter). In the case of herbivores, the water from plant consumption is the most determinant factor for the $\delta^{18}O$ values, and to a lesser extent (despite obligatory drinking) the meteoric drinking water affects the overall oxygen isotope value (Bryant and Froelich 1995: 4527–8). Carbon isotope $\delta^{13}C$ values were measured and calculated together with the $\delta^{18}O$ values in order to compare different plant sets typical of specific habitations (e.g. C3 and C4 plants) and climatic zones, on the same sample and in accordance with the growth structure of the enamel, from the tip to the cement enamel junction (for the method see Balasse 2002; Balasse *et al.* 2012). Using these means, it was possible to examine both diet and climatic conditions from the same sample in a temporal resolution.

Humans are omnivores, and the dietary isotope values from the human samples reflect the mixture of plants, meat, and other dietary components (e.g. fish, dairy products). There are two main sources for obtaining dietary values. One is from the carbonate phase of the hydroxyapatite of humans and other mammals that originates from the blood carbonate pool and thus reflects the carbon isotope values of the whole diet (Lee-Thorp *et al.* 1989; Jim *et al.* 2004). A second analysis on collagen/gelatine extracted from bones reflects only the protein part of the diet (DeNiro and Epstein 1978; 1981; Ambrose and DeNiro 1986). Carbon isotope ratios measured and calculated from the collagen/gelatine extraction from bone indicate variations related to the components of the diet derived from dietary organic compounds (e.g. amino acids in the case of meat and cellulose in the case of plants, etc.). Nitrogen isotope ratios, which are also measured on the same extracted collagen samples, demonstrate the trophic level of the organism by enrichment in every step of the trophic level (Peterson and Fry 1987). Nitrogen isotopes also indicate the aridity and salinity conditions indirectly related to the degree of intensity of bacterial activity in the soil where the plants originated (DeNiro and Epstein 1981; Ambrose and DeNiro 1989; Ambrose 1991; Koch 1998).

As an example of the combination of methods applied, we will discuss the cow tooth MB105, an M3 tooth, which is mineralised when animals are 9–22 months old (Hillson 2005: Table 3.3) (Figure 6.5 left). According to its Sr isotope ratio, the cow likely came from abroad, as the mineralisation of the tooth certainly had occurred long before it was slaughtered (Figure 6.5 top). The animal was slaughtered at

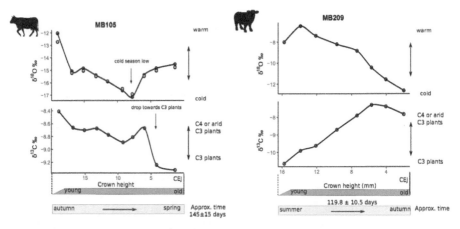

Figure 6.5 Askaraly: oxygen and carbon isotope values from the cow sample MB105 (left) and the sheep sample MB209 (right); oxygen isotope values are calculated to show the meteoric water values using equations from D'Angela and Longinelli (after Özyarkent 2019)

approximately 3.5–6 years old according to the tooth wear stage approximation (beginning of stage G with the cement enamel junction in q position after the scheme by Grant 1982; Jones and Sadler 2012). The slaughter age of the animal suggests that it was used for dairy production, rather than meat (see below and Doll 2013). The results show values from a time interval beginning at the end of the warm season (autumn, October/November) and continuing to the next one (spring, March/April) (see also Hermes *et al.* 2019: 3). According to the mineralisation pace calculation, this period equals approximately 145±15 days (Zazzo *et al.* 2010; Kierdorf *et al.* 2013). The $\delta^{13}C$ values are in negative correlation with the $\delta^{18}O$ values. At the end of winter, the values from carbon isotopes show increased C4 plant diet (e.g. dried grass), and in spring more C3 plants in the diet (e.g. herbs and leaves). The Sr isotope ratio of this sample is outside of the local range (0.70888).

Another sample from the site comes from sheep enamel (MB 209), sampled using the same method as the previous one (Figure 6.5 right). Based on the mineralisation pace of sheep enamel, this M2 tooth reflects a time period of approximately 119.8±10.5 days, and thus the first-year isotopic history of the animal. The Sr isotope level of this tooth indicates that the sheep lived in the region during this time (cf. Figure 6.4 above). The mineralisation period shows a warm season/summer peak and cold season, with the beginning of autumn. In the case of the diet, the results of $\delta^{18}O$ and $\delta^{13}C$ indicate a pattern similar to the previous one (cow) with regards to seasonality and nutrition differences. The summer months show negative $\delta^{13}C$ values, which indicate more C3 plants. Towards the winter months, especially in autumn, C4 plants increased in the diet of the animal.

Among the human samples, the foreign signal was less easily determined than it was in the herd animals. This is a known issue, as in humans the enamel formation has a slower pace when compared with herbivores. This extended mineralisation period and the yet undetermined mineralisation direction lead to a masking effect in the enamel samples of humans (Hillson 2005; Simmer *et al.* 2010). Therefore, the temporality cannot be ascertained at this state of research, and it should be further investigated and interpreted. On the other hand, human Sr isotope results have shown a pattern similar to the animals, even though the analysed samples are within the designated local range. An analysed tibia from one of the miners (grave 2, chamber 1, 40–60-year-old) has a higher radiogenic isotope ratio when compared with the analysed teeth of the same individual. The miner's teeth values show a variation from his early to later years, manifested in the M1 (sample CH701a), canine (sample CH701b), and M3 (sample CH701c) (cf. Figure 6.4 bottom). Since human teeth mineralise in time spans of approximately four years, with M1 spanning 0–4 years, C 4 months–6 years, and M3 8–14 years (White and Folkens 2005: Figure 19.2), the $^{87}Sr/^{86}Sr$ values represent these time intervals for the individual's isotope accumulation in the apatite of bone and teeth. The early years of this individual have a higher isotope value than found in the M3, which is formed in later childhood. The canine tooth, on the other hand, has a lower radiogenic value as compared with M1. This difference might be due to the two-year period (from the 4th to the 6th year of the individual) between the mineralisation of M1 and M3. In contrast, the tibia sample (CH702) exhibits a higher radiogenic isotope accumulation than that from later childhood. The second individual (grave 3, chamber 1) was sampled by an incisor CH703b (crown formation *c.* 3.5–8 years) and a molar CH703a. This individual showed a similar variation pattern within the local range as did the first individual. These variations observed among different periods of life in both individuals will be investigated in more detail.

The diet investigation results from the carbon and nitrogen analyses show that the first miner (grave 2, chamber 1) did not directly consume C4 plants (Figure 6.6). For later periods, studies have shown a C4 plant diet for both humans and animals. However, a slight inclination towards lower $\delta^{13}C$ values can occur indirectly via animals that have consumed C4 plants, since the human collagen values are in line with the mixture of the animals represented in the sample dataset. Likewise, the $\delta^{15}N$ values are in line with the offset of the trophic level, as it is known that, in the trophic chain, every step up equals + 3 to +5 per mille or ‰ enrichment (Peterson and Fry 1987). Another interesting result was the difference between apatite–collagen spacing (Lee-Thorp *et al.* 1989). These spacings are related to the trophic level of mammals, and in the case of the miner, the values are close to observations from carnivores (Lee-Thorp *et al.* 1989). Therefore, with these results from the miner sample from the Askaraly mining complex, it is possible to infer that the human diet was based mostly on meat consumption, and most likely a higher amount of sheep meat was consumed as opposed to beef. Moreover, an archaeozoological study on the animal remains from the site suggests that cows were kept especially for dairy production, and sheep/goats for meat, because of the age/slaughter pattern (Doll 2013). This will be further investigated by amino acid and stable isotope analyses on residues from ceramics in the near future.

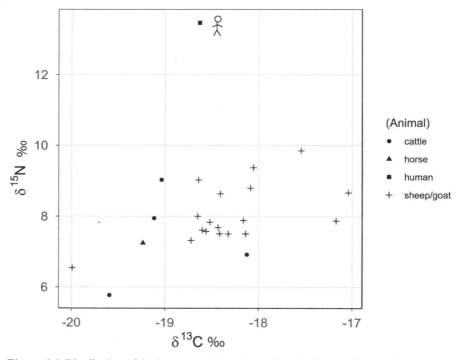

Figure 6.6 Distribution of the isotope results performed on the bone collagen of animals and humans. Error bars in both axis directions represent the reproducibility of the samples. The clustered samples are also from the animals that are in the local range with Sr isotope ratios. The outliers on the right with higher carbon isotope ratios and generally higher nitrogen isotope ratios indicate aridity and a high proportion of C4 plants in their diet. The sample on the left of the plot (MB201) is a goat and its position reflects its diet based on grazing, which was mostly C3 plants (after Özyarkent 2019)

Askaraly is situated in the transition zone from grass steppes to the dry steppes, but it is in a location with close connections to the Irtysh River and its tributaries (Figure 6.7). In modern times, people in the Askaraly region practise village-based animal husbandry, collect hay for winter, and practise rain-fed agriculture. However, there are debates on ethnographical sources for the Semei region, as to whether rain-fed agriculture was possible in historical times. The adoption of agriculture, under the influence of Russia, especially since the 19th century AD, led to a gradual immobilisation and a semi-mobile lifestyle, keeping animals in stalls (see more in Tairov 2017). Agriculture is not unusual, even for the pastoral nomad lifestyle, but its solutions are more eclectic. This is a characteristic of steppe pastoral nomadic communities, because flexibility is an important strategy to cope with possible subsistence catastrophes (like *dzhud*=the great famine) that could deplete the herds upon which people are dependent (Khazanov 1994). It is possible, however, to use the wild progenitors of cereals, which are abundant in the grass steppe zone. Even with the inclusion of plants, the pastoral routes, and especially

Figure 6.7 A combined map of oxygen isotope modelled values from Terzer *et al.* 2013, Akhishev. Iron Age sites, nomadic pasture massifs of 1926–30 with summer and winter camps (after Tairov 2017: Figure 37, after Federovich; prepared by Özyarkent)

the summer and winter camps, were chosen for specific ecological features (warm winter habitations with nutritious pastures and water; cool summer habitations with grass steppe ecology) (Asanov *et al.* 1992).

In the case of Askaraly (and other sites, in preparation), the results have shown that there is mobility towards southern latitudes for arid climate 'winter' pasturing. The cow presented as an example here plots outside the local range of Sr isotope values and is considered to have a foreign signal. The climate and temperature indications from oxygen isotope results also show that the lowest signal from this cow is higher than the modelled value for Askaraly, which is -23.5 per mille or ‰ for February (modelled after Terzer *et al.* 2013) (cf. Figure 6.7). These warm winter temperatures are accompanied by the increased C4 plant consumption in the animals' diets. Similarly, the isotope values obtained from the sheep sample is in line with the results for the cow, but the image that could be obtained from the enamel piece is limited and also belongs to the summer values. This is due to the difference in the birthing time of cows and sheep. As a result, it seems the cow was born in autumn while the sheep was born in spring. Thus, the data reflects different parts of the year. The representation in the enamel is also restricted by the ablation of the hypsodont tooth. Since the teeth of herbivores mineralise from the use surface towards the cement enamel junction, the ablation in time erases the earliest mineralisation phases. In the summer peak the diet was high in C3 plants, and towards the cold months, at the beginning of autumn, an increase in C4 plants can be observed in the diet.

126 *Thomas Stöllner et al.*

The low winter values for oxygen isotopes obtained from the cow point to southern latitudes. The closest location with similar oxygen isotope ratios and C4 plants in meadows is the Ayaguz region, and this landscape continues towards Taldy Kurgan and its surroundings. The Semirechye region, which is located between Lake Balkhash and the Tien Shan Mountains, is thought to have been a preferred winter camp location for nomads of later periods (Saka-Iron Age, 1st millennium BC), due to the intensity of evidence for kurgans and petroglyphs (Parzinger 2006; Gass 2014; Tairov 2017; cf. also the Akhishev map). Therefore, it is possible to connect the regions through aspects of material culture. The Andronovo-Semirechye type has similarities to central Kazakhstan and east Kazakhstan Andronovo, as can be seen by rectangular and oval grave constructions with a cist in the centre or with soil burials, both as inhumations and cremations (Parzinger 2006; Bendezu-Sarmiento 2007; Gass 2014; for a later occupation by Mukri people with elements similar to central Kazakhstan see Frachetti *et al.* 2010). Askaraly also has similar grave types and other cultural finds in comparison with the central Kazakh Atasu group. This indicates connections between regions north of the Kazakh borderlands and the winter pastures in the south.

'Mobile metals': tin bronzes and the Nurataldy case

Chemical and lead isotope data from approximately 400 metal objects, metallurgical educts (i.e. slag), and ores from eastern and north-east Kazakhstan were collected between 2006 and 2014 (Stöllner *et al.* 2013a; Gonts32harov 2019; Stöllner and Gontscharov 2021: Figure 8) (Figure 6.8). Lead isotope data from the Tien Shan, Ural, and Altai Mountains, as well as central Kazakhstan, were gathered from the literature (Syusyura *et al.* 1987; Chiaradia *et al.* 2006; Box *et al.* 2012). Chemical analyses have been performed in the laboratories of the Deutsches Bergbau-Museum Bochum (DBM) with Inductively Coupled Plasma Optical Emission Spectrometry (ICP-OES) until 2008 (cf. Prange 2001: 98, Figures 83–4 for procedure) (laboratory numbers /06), and from 2009 onwards with ICP-Mass Spectrometry (ICP-MS) (cf. Kiderlen *et al.* 2016: 305 for procedure). Detection limits of both methods are shown in Prange (2001: 24, Table 4). Lead isotope analyses from 2006–9 were done with Thermal Ionisation Mass Spectrometry (TIMS) in the Institut für Mineralogie, Zentrallabor für Geochronologie in Münster (cf. Bode *et al.* 2009: 186–8 for procedure) (laboratory numbers /06), and from 2009 onwards with Multi-Collector-ICP-MS (MC-ICP-MS) at the Institut für Geowissenschaften in Frankfurt am Main (see Klein *et al.* 2009: 62–4).

Concerning the analytical interpretation of such data, there are limitations related to methodological aspects in general, as well as the way of sampling and developing the database. In Central Asia there is a generally high variation of deposits from different geological ages (cf. Seltmann 2013). There are the Ural Mountains and the comparatively old Altai Mountains in the east, as well as the

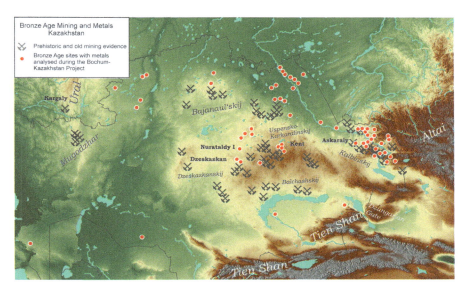

Figure 6.8 Central, south, and east Kazakhstan and its mining and metallurgical evidence of the later Bronze Age (2nd millennium BC) (source: DBM/RUB, Stöllner based on Stöllner and Samashev 2013; Garner 2014, after Stöllner and Gontscharov 2021)

aforementioned TEMB-girdle in the south including the Tien Shan and Pamir Mountains (Seltmann *et al.* 2011); here we find a great variety of Proterozoic and Palaeozoic cratons that were mobilised during the Variscan orogeny. Such geological basements stretch from the Southern Urals to central and east Kazakhstan, such as the Kalba-Narym zone in the north-east, the Valerianov zone in the west, the Altai-Sayan Uplands in the east, and the central Kazakhstan/Karakum zone in the centre (Zonenshain *et al.* 1990; Nikichenko 2002).

Various preconditions make it difficult to unambiguously interpret geochemical patterns. Lead isotopes, for instance, provide only negative evidence, while positive matching is a mere indication of the possibility but not proof. As the geology is complex and shows remobilisation of host rocks and ores, it is important to know the exact location of a sample within a deposit (Stöllner and Gontscharov 2021: Figure 4). Unfortunately, not all the mining districts were sampled with a comparative level of detail. According to work carried out so far by Russian and Kazakh colleagues, as well as American and German scholars (e.g. Degtjareva 1985; Chernykh 1992; Hanks and Doonan 2009; Černych 2013; Krause 2013; Stöllner *et al.* 2013b; Grigoriev 2015), there is a reasonable amount of data available that we are able to discuss.

The bronzes of the so-called Sejma-Turbino phenomenon are a perfect example of exploring a large sphere of exchange and mobility (Chernykh and Kuzminych 1989; Parzinger 2002; 2006; Schwarzberg 2009; Serikov *et al.* 2009; Černych

2013; Chernykh *et al.* 2017). After decades of discussion, it is now widely accepted that most of the artefacts belong to a period from the end of the 3rd to the first half of the 2nd millennium BC (Marchenko *et al.* 2017). As Chernykh and Kuzminykh (1989) already stated, they seldom occur in graves, but instead in hoards and ritual contexts where the depositional character can be observed, particularly by putting them to the ground or burying them at selected topographical sites. It has been further stated that they display delicate casting technologies and often a high amount of tin, which is outstanding in itself, especially for the typologically earliest examples.

Considering the Sejma-Turbino 'mode of deposition' (weapons plunged vertically into the soil), it has to be mentioned that the hoard of Nurataldy is the first case in which such a deposition mode is combined with Eurasian types (Kukushkin and Loman 2014: 584–7). Two spearheads and three daggers were stuck into the ground together with an arrowhead, three pieces of metal, a wrapped metal sheet, a casting piece, and a broken metal fragment (Figure 6.9). The hoarded items of Nurataldy I are the best contexts for understanding the social dimension of an artefact assemblage in early Andronovo culture. The graveyard consisted of four slab cists, three of which were disturbed, but one remained untouched. Two horse burials were discovered nearby. The complex, which remains unpublished so far, has been dated by the excavators Kukushkin and Loman (2014) to the early phases of the Andronovo/Alakul' culture. The burial of two horses can be understood as a reference to the wagon symbolism, characteristic of the Nurtaj group in central Kazakhstan that was in close chronological relation with the Petrovka group (Tkachev 2002: 147 [part 2]; Kukushkin 2013). What stresses this cultural classification is the mode of deposition of the bronzes that were stuck into the earth near the north-western corner of slab cist 2. Although the deposition mode clearly relates the Nurataldy I deposition to the Sejma-Turbino phenomenon, there are no Sejma-Turbino objects sensu strictu but rather objects that belong to the Eurasian component of the phenomenon (Chernykh and Kuzminykh 1989: Table 17).

All daggers (KZ 651–3) contained a high percentage of tin (Table 6.3), but when looking more carefully at their Lead Isotope Analysis (LIA) ratios, it is clear that two daggers, the rolled metal sheet, and one spearhead did not come from central Kazakhstan (KZ 651–652, 680, 694) (for the chemical/isotope data see Stöllner and Gontscharov 2021: Table 2, 4) (Figure 6.10; Table 6.3–4). One spearhead and one dagger are very close to each other (KZ 652, 694) and were made using east Kazakh copper. The metal was most likely alloyed with tin from there as well. This fits also with the elevated Bi and Pb contents that are known from east Kazakh ores and metals (Stöllner *et al.* 2013b: 388–9, Figure 5). On the other hand, there are objects whose LIA ratios and trace elements would instead fit the LIA reference data from the 'Kent' field of central Kazakhstan (KZ 653, 682, 695, 731): dagger, spearhead, arrowhead, and metal cast.

The metal cast, maybe a small ingot, perhaps best resembles regional copper. It is a relatively pure copper with very low impurities and contains nearly no tin, as it is unalloyed (cf. Table 6.3). It is different from the spearhead with the short socket, which had a low tin level and some antimony and lead that do not really

Figure 6.9 Nurataldy I, objects from metal deposition near grave 2 (source: DBM/RUB, photo A. Gontsharov, by courtesy of Loman and Kukushkin, Karaganda)

match levels found in the east, but perhaps rather in central Kazakhstan. Two other striking facts can be mentioned: the arrowhead KZ 731 has a rather high lead content and was thus likely alloyed. It is therefore impossible to make clear statements as to its origin on the basis of the LIA ratios. The opposite is the case for the metal fragment KZ 681. The LIA ratios indicate a composition that must be from completely outside central Kazakhstan. They would perhaps better correlate with Uralian and north Kazakh deposits: Ag, Co, and especially As are represented in higher values (for the ores, especially type 4, see Tkačev *et al.* 2013: 475–7).

The differentiation between a central Kazakh and an east Kazakh group within the deposit can also be supported by typological considerations. If looking at the typological and chronological investigations by Avanesova (1991: 23–4, Figure 22), it becomes clear that the daggers are part of a larger typology, in which not all objects date to the same time period: whether the east Kazakh dagger and spearhead were synchronous is difficult to assess. The dagger, KZ 652, can be identified as a rather 'eastern' Andronovo-Fedorovka dagger type (type 3/4 after Avanesova 1991), while the spearhead belongs to the Sejma-Turbino phenomenon sensu lato. On the other hand, the second 'outsider' (KZ 651) and the central Kazakh tin bronze dagger KZ 653 show the rather early feature of long lateral indentions (central Kazakh Nurtaj group: Tkachev 2002: 158–287). With this information combined, there is reason to believe that the deposit was a roughly synchronous assemblage with objects of varying origins. If so, one could assume that this was the case not only for the objects, but also for the bearers. Is it possible that one dagger/spearhead

Table 6.3 Central Kazakhstan, hoard of Nurataldy: elemental concentrations from various copper-based alloys (source: DBM/RUB, M. Bode; analytical data have been normalised to 100 per cent: see Stöllner and Gontscharov 2021)

Lab.-Nr.	Inv.-Nr.	Site	Artefact	Sn	As	Pb	Fe	Zn	Ag	Au	Sb	Bi	P	S	Co	Ni	Se	Te	Hg	Cu	sum
Nurataldy 1, hoard, early Andronovo period (beginning of 2nd millennium BC)																					
4395_14	KZ-651	Nurataldy 1	dagger	8.48	0.03	0.36	0.004	0.003	0.019	0.0001	0.009	0.013	0.00005	0.016	0.0002	0.004	0.0004	0.002	0.0001	91.11	100
4396_14	KZ-652	Nurataldy 1	dagger	11.5	0.17	0.16	0.005	0.005	0.039	0.0002	0.017	0.018	0.00005	0.041	0.001	0.01	0.0023	0.003	0.0001	88.16	100
4397_14	KZ-653	Nurataldy 1	dagger	10.03	1.57	0.03	0.228	0.016	0.05	0.0001	0.004	0.027	0.00005	0.067	0.005	0.014	0.0004	0.004	0.0001	88.14	100
4399_14	KZ-680	Nurataldy 1	sheet metal/ ingot	17.83	0.26	0.22	0.002	0.003	0.165	0.0002	0.005	0.034	0.033		0.219	0.001	0.005	0.0004	0.003	0.0001	81.68	100
4400_14	KZ-681	Nurataldy 1	ingot	0.2	1.01	0.004	0.503	0.011	0.047	0.0002	0.004	0.013	0.00005	0.112	0.011	0.039	0.0004	0.005	0.0001	98.28	100
4401_14	KZ-682	Nurataldy 1	ingot	0.01	0.1	0.05	0.026	0.025	0.022	0.0002	0.003	0.001	0.001		0.112	0.004	0.006	0.0008	0.004	0.0001	99.82	100
4393_14	KZ-694	Nurataldy 1	spearhead	15.19	0.02	0.1	0.02	0.045	0.026	0.00004	0.006	0.003	0.002		0.049	0.001	0.003	0.0011	0.003	0.0001	84.67	100
4394_14	KZ-695	Nurataldy 1	spearhead	1.62	0.01	0.16	0.002	0.003	0.077	0.00004	0.75	0.003	0.00005	0.009	0.0001	0.007	0.0011	0.002	0.0001	97.45	100
4398_14	KZ-731	Nurataldy 1	awl	10.47	0.07	1.54	0.007	0.005	0.017	0.0005	0.017	0.014	0.00005	0.006	0.0001	0.004	0.0008	0.003	0.0001	87.9	100

Table 6.4 Central Kazakhstan, hoard of Nurataldy: Pb isotope data (source: DBM/RUB, M. Bode; see Stöllner and Gontscharov 2021)

Lab-Nr.	Inv.-Nr.	Site	artefact	$^{206}Pb/^{204}Pb$	$^{207}Pb/^{206}Pb$	$^{208}Pb/^{206}Pb$
Nurataldy, early Andronovo period, around 2000 BC							
4400_14	KZ-681	Nurataldy 1	ingot	18.59021	0.84166	2.08558
4401_14	KZ-682	Nurataldy 1	ingot	18.06612	0.86206	2.10580
4395_14	KZ-651	Nurataldy 1	dagger	17.86462	0.87120	2.12577
4396_14	KZ-652	Nurataldy 1	dagger	17.79648	0.87212	2.11867
4397_14	KZ-653	Nurataldy 1	dagger	18.04660	0.86176	2.10413
4399_14	KZ-680	Nurataldy 1	tin/ingot	17.95412	0.86733	2.11326
4393_14	KZ-694	Nurataldy 1	spearhead	17.80066	0.87169	2.11741
4394_14	KZ-695	Nurataldy 1	spearhead	18.16330	0.85949	2.10007
4398_14	KZ-731	Nurataldy 1	awl	18.04366	0.86333	2.10994

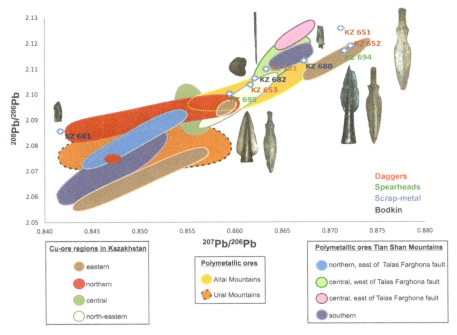

Figure 6.10 Lead isotope ratio of ore samples from Nurataldy I, hoard of Sejma tradition (source: DBM/RUB, Bode and Stöllner)

132   *Thomas Stöllner et al.*

assemblage (KZ 652, 694) came with a person from east Kazakhstan while another assemblage (KZ 653, 695, 731) might have been fabricated with copper from central Kazakhstan and perhaps tin from east Kazakhstan?

The Nurataldy I deposit thus also displays social realities during the earlier 2nd millennium BC in the steppe and forest steppe zone of Central Asia: metal objects and their origins were of importance within social interactions. It can only be assumed that the foreignness of materials (tin) and objects helped to memorise the actions and people involved when the Nurataldy I deposit was buried, most likely until the end of the ritual activity in the Nurataldy I graveyard. If following these ideas, we may certainly find traditions of handling artefacts in a memory context over a longer time, thus bridging the centuries from the end of the 3rd to the middle of the 2nd millennium BC (which is possibly characteristic of the Sejma-Turbino phenomenon). Therefore, it was informative to look at other artefact groups of the Andronovo culture (for instance 'Srubnaya daggers') in more detail (see Gontscharov 2019; Stöllner and Gontscharov 2021).

The example of the early Andronovo complex of Nurataldy I and other widespread artefact groups (such as daggers of the Srubnaya type) show that metals were distributed in the early 2nd millennium BC by means of individual exchange processes. One possibility is that mobile communities obtained the necessary metals from different locations – the other that mobile craftspeople moved from place to place with their moulds (e.g. Minasjan 2013). These artisans might have been involved in pastoral groups and moved with them to rich summer pastures. Of course, entire prestige outfits with their porters could have travelled between the individual areas. If we compare this mobility pattern with the one caused by animals (e.g. demonstrated mobility in Askaraly), then this movement could have occurred over long distances between the winter locations and the summer pastures. Groups from different regions may have met and negotiated pasture and usable areas (e.g. for raw material extraction), especially during the major changes in weather and temperature in spring and autumn. Celebrations and the exchange of gifts could have been important social forms of negotiation. It is certainly worthwhile to analyse the pasture quality of individual mining areas in more detail. The gentle mountain range of the Delbegetey with its valleys of the Chara and Kyzylzu Rivers can be described in any case as a favourable grazing zone (cf. Figure 6.3). It would be conceivable that many objects were manufactured in the winter pasture season, while raw materials were procured and products were exchanged during pastoral activities in the warm season.

The wider context of our datasets: mobility or migrations of 2nd millennium BC communities and their consequences for the Andronovo concept

It is possibly too early to judge all the variants of mobility of steppe communities during the Bronze Age. While the research team of Frachetti discussed seasonal herding patterns within the Inner Asian Mountain Corridor down to the south Kazakh plains (for a general discussion see Frachetti 2012; Hermes *et al.* 2019), the results of our research support further mobility patterns. The examples discussed in this chapter make clear that herding activities included longer-distance movements between summer and winter pastures crossing the Kazakh borderlands. For Askaraly and its mountainous landscape, it is likely that communities used the region as summer pastures, while also taking part in mining and metallurgical activities. This would also include single animals that were coming to the summer pastures from their winter pastures (such as cattle), as well as others (such as sheep) that were born in the spring and possibly killed after the colder season already had begun. The pattern is complex as winter pastures could have been situated either in protected valley grounds in the nearby Altai or in the climatically favourable plains south of the Kazakh borderlands (Tairov 2017: Figure 7). As for Askaraly, but most likely also for other mining districts, it may be supposed that areas which provided favourable grazing and mining potential were visited by different groups, possibly from different winter camp origins.

Complex enterprises like mining and metallurgy – even when carried out only by smaller communities – would probably have required assembling larger cooperative groups. In the settlement of Mastau Baj (Askaraly II) we can follow such different regional traditions in the pottery styles. Naumann (2016) was able to analyse these pottery styles and their making. Her stylistic analysis identified regional Marinka and Kyzyltas pottery styles as well as styles from abroad, such as the central Kazakh Nurtaj and Atasu type wares. The pottery production partly took place regionally, as is demonstrated, for example, by the use of regional temper. One should also mention that the settlement was presumably reused several times, as indicated by the chronologically different ceramic record in the half-pit house.

The house itself was rebuilt at least once (Stöllner *et al.* 2013a: 373; Naumann 2016: 78). There is also clear evidence of a later Bronze Age phase to which a piece of wheel-thrown pottery most likely belongs. Pieces of foreign wheel-thrown ceramics of a Southern Central Asian pottery tradition indicate that groups also carried whole vessels to Askaraly, possibly from regions where such prestigious vessels were used to a larger extent, e.g. the Altai steppe zones, Kyrgyzstan, and central Kazakhstan (Kuzmina 2007: 365, 418; Varfolomeev 2013: 486, Figure 5). Taking other pieces of evidence into account, e.g. a rock art depiction of a Sejma-style horse (Stöllner *et al.* 2011: 247, Figure 16), it may be a surmisable conclusion that the Delbegetej/Askaraly region was used as a seasonal meeting place to which various groups came in order to use the pastures and the tin deposits during warmer seasons.

This reconstruction largely differs from older concepts that were favoured for over a century. In this chapter, we are not looking at the migrations of Andronovo groups through the pottery tradition (e.g. the Alakul or Fedorovka types). It is not yet possible to observe a mass migration event just before or during the Bronze Age. According to the archaeological record, we rather observe a gradual development of technological innovations and a pastoralism-based subsistence strategy with diverse mobility solutions. It is even possible to assume that this kind of mobility as well as the rise of metallurgical traditions (such as the tin bronze technology) was a connecter for the groups in Central Asia before some kind of Andronovo 'unity' ever occurred after 2000 BC.

As the Nurataldy I case showed in a nutshell, there was a high range of social interrelation and hybrid social practices connecting Sejma-Turbino groups of the forest steppe with steppe communities of early Andronovo. Sets of prestigious goods were exchanged using jointly understood social practices, which certainly created, in cases like Nurataldy I, a shared memory and identity (Gontscharov 2019). This would explain metals more as a means of social interrelation and an expression of connectedness between those vast areas. The foreignness of objects from different origins was certainly considered and even valued (such as at Nurataldy I) as an expression of social prestige and connectedness between the groups involved (see Stöllner and Gontscharov 2021). Therefore, the cultural system of the Andronovo groups can likely be understood as enabling this kind of interconnectivity between different groups that were active in metallurgy and pastoralism. In light of this interpretative concept, it becomes more understandable how the vast cultural and economic networks called Andronovo could evolve. Constant mobility was part of the everyday life of these communities, and the spread of such a lifestyle is what one would possibly call a larger unit like Andronovo. It is therefore important to understand their extended mobility as a whole and not only to use selected search for single migration events either by genetic, isotopic, or typological argumentation.

References

Allentoft, M.E., Sikora, M., Sjögren, K.-G., Rasmussen, S., Rasmussen, M., *et al.* (2015), 'Population genomics of Bronze Age Eurasia', *Nature*, 522: 167–72.

Ambrose, S.H. (1991), 'Effects of diet, climate and physiology on nitrogen isotope abundances in terrestrial foodwebs', *Journal of Archaeological Science*, 18(3): 293–317.

Ambrose, S.H. and DeNiro, M.J. (1986), 'The isotopic ecology of East African mammals', *Oecologia*, 69(3): 395–406.

Ambrose, S.H. and DeNiro, M.J. (1989), 'Climate and habitat reconstruction using stable carbon and nitrogen isotope ratios of collagen in prehistoric herbivore teeth from Kenya', *Quaternary Research*, 31(3): 407–22.

Anthony, D.W. (2007), *The Horse, the Wheel, and Language: How Bronze Age Riders from the Eurasian Steppes Shaped the Modern World* (Princeton, Princeton University Press).

Asanov, K.A., Shakh, B., Alimayev, I.I., and Prayanishnikov, S.N. (1992), *Pasture Farming in Kazakhstan* (Tsukuba, Japan International Research Center for Agricultural Sciences).

Avanesova, N.A. (1991), *Культура пастушеских племён эпохи бронзы азиатской части СССР (по металлическим изделиям)* (Tashkent, Academy of Sciences of the Uzbek SSR & Institute of Archeology).

Avanesova, N.A. (1996), 'Pasteurs et agriculteurs de la vallée du Zeravshan (Ouzbékistan) au début de l'age du Bronze: Relations et influences mutuelles', in B. Lyonnet (ed),

Sarazm (Tadjikistan). Céramique. Chalcolithique et Bronze Ancien (Paris, De Boccard), 117–31.

Avanesova, N.A. (2013), 'Zhukov, un "sanctuaire" énéolithique d'anciens nomades dans la vallée du Zeravshan (Ouzbékistan)', *Paléorient*, 39(2): 85–108.

Avanesova, N.A. (2015), 'Керамика поселения горняков-металлургов Зарафшана', in А.Э. Бердимурадова (ed), *История материальной культуры Узбекистана* (Самарканд, Academy of Sciences of the Republic of Uzbekistan and Institute of Archaeology), 47–62.

Balasse, M. (2002), 'Reconstructing dietary and environmental history from enamel isotopic analysis: time resolution of intra-tooth sequential sampling', *International Journal of Osteoarchaeology*, 12(3): 155–65.

Balasse, M., Boury, L., Ughetto-Monfrin, J., and Tresset, A. (2012), 'Stable isotope insights ($\delta^{18}O$, $\delta^{13}C$) into cattle and sheep husbandry at Bercy (Paris, France, 4th millennium BC): birth seasonality and winter leaf foddering', *Environmental Archaeology*, 17(1): 29–44.

Bendezu-Sarmiento, J. (2007), *De l'âge du bronze à l'âge du fer au Kazakhstan, gestes funéraires et paramètres biologiques. Identités culturelles des populations Andronovo et Saka* (Paris, De Boccard).

Bode, M., Hauptmann, A., and Mezger, K. (2009), 'Tracing Roman lead sources using lead isotope analyses in conjunction with archaeological and epigraphic evidence: a case study from Augustan/Tiberian Germania', *Archaeological and Anthropological Science*, 1: 177–94.

Boroffka, N. (2013), 'Klimatische Schwankungen und Siedlungsgeschehen in der frühen Geschichte Kasachstans', in T. Stöllner and Z. Samašev (eds), *Unbekanntes Kasachstan: Archäologie im Herzen Asiens* (Bochum, Deutsches Bergbau-Museum), 55–66.

Box, S.E., Syusura, B., Seltmann, R., Creaser, R.A., Dolgopolova, A., and Zientek, M.L. (2012), 'Dzhezkazgan and associated sandstone copper deposits of the Chu-Sarysu Basin, central Kazakhstan', in J.W. Hedenquist, M. Harris, and F. Camus (eds), *Geology and Genesis of Major Copper Deposits and Districts of the World: A Tribute to Richard H. Sillitoe* (Littleton, Society of Economic Geologists), DOI: 10.5382/SP.16.13.

Bryant, D.J. and Froelich, P.N. (1995), 'A model of oxygen isotope fractionation in body water of large mammals', *Geochimica et Cosmochimica Acta*, 59(21): 4523–37.

Černych, E. (2013), 'Die Eurasische (westasiatische) metallurgische Provinz der Spätbronzezeit: Aufstieg – Blüte – Niedergang', in T. Stöllner and Z. Samašev (eds), *Unbekanntes Kasachstan: Archäologie im Herzen Asiens* (Bochum, Deutsches Bergbau-Museum), 185–200.

Chernikov, S.S. (1960), *Vostotshnyj Kazachstan v epochu bronzy* (Moskow and Leningrad, Nauka).

Chernykh, E.N. (1992). *Ancient Metallurgy in the USSR: The Early Metal Age* (Cambridge, Cambridge University Press).

Chernykh, E.N. and Kuzminykh, S.V. (1989), *Древняя металлургия Северной Евразии (сеймо-турбинский феномен)* (Moskow, Nauka).

Chernykh, E.N., Korochkova, O.N., and Orlovskaya, L. (2017), 'Проблемы календарной хронологии сейминско-турбинского транскультурного феномена', *Archaeology, Ethnology and Anthropology of Eurasia*, 45(2): 45–55.

Chiaradia, M., Konopelko, D., Seltmann, R., and Cliff, R.A. (2006), 'Lead isotope variations across terrane boundaries of the Tien Shan and Chinese Altay', *Miners Deposita*, 41: 411–28.

136 *Thomas Stöllner et al.*

Czebreszuk, J. (2004), 'Corded Ware from east to west', in P. Bogucki and P.J. Crabtree (eds), *Ancient Europe 8000 BC–AD 1000: Encyclopedia of the Barbarian World* (New York, Charles Scribner's Sons), 431–5.

Dansgaard, W. (1964), 'Stable isotopes in precipitation', *Tellus*, 16: 436–68.

Degtjareva, A.D. (1985), *Металлообрабатывающее производство Казахстана и Киргизии в эпоху поздней бронзы (XII–IX вв. до н.э.): Автореф. дис. канд. ист. наук/The Metalworking Industry of Kazakhstan and Kyrgyzstan during the 12th to the 9th century BCE*, Unpublished PhD thesis (Moskva).

DeNiro, M.J. and Epstein, S. (1978), 'Influence of diet on the distribution of carbon isotopes in animals', *Geochimica et Cosmochimica Acta*, 42: 495–506.

DeNiro, M.J. and Epstein, S. (1981), 'Influence of diet on the distribution of nitrogen isotopes in animals', *Geochimica et Cosmochimica Acta*, 45: 314–51.

Doll, M. (2013), *Guarding Livestock and Rolling Dices in Bronze Age Kazakhstan*, Unpublished report.

Ericson, J.E. (1985), 'Strontium isotope characterization in the study of prehistoric human ecology', *Journal of Human Evolution*, 14: 503–14.

Ezzo, J. (1997), 'Analytical perspectives on prehistoric migration: a case study from east-central Arizona', *Journal of Archaeological Science*, 24(5): 447–66.

Frachetti, M. (2008), *Pastoralist Landscapes and Social Interaction in Bronze Age Eurasia* (Berkeley, University of California Press).

Frachetti M. (2011), 'Migration concepts in Central Eurasian archaeology', *Annual Review of Anthropology*, 40: 195–212.

Frachetti, M. (2012), 'Multiregional emergence of mobile pastoralism and non-uniform institutional complexity across Eurasia', *Current Anthropology*, 53(1): 2–21.

Frachetti, M.D., Benecke, N., Maryashev, A., and Doumani, P.N. (2010), 'Eurasian pastoralists and their shifting regional interactions at the steppe margin: settlement history at Mukri, Kazakhstan', *World Archaeology*, 42(4): 622–46.

Garner, J. (2014), *Das Zinn der Bronzezeit in Mittelasien, Vol. 2: Die montanarchäologischen Forschungen an den Zinnlagerstätten* (Mainz, Verlag Philipp von Zabern).

Gass, A. (2014), *Das Land der sieben Flüsse im 2. bis 1. Jahrtausend v. Chr.* (Berlin, Edition Topoi, Walter De Gruyter).

Gat, J.R. (2001), *Environmental Isotopes in the Hydrological Cycle, Vol. 2: Principles and Applications – Atmospheric Water* (Vienna/Paris, International Atomic Energy Agency and United Nations Educational, Scientific, and Cultural Organization).

Ghirshman, R. (1964), 'Invasions des nomades sur le Plateau Iranien aux premiers siècles du Ier millénaire avant J.-C.', in R. Ghirshman, E. Porada, R.H. Dyson Jr, J. Tembach, R.S. Young, *et al.* (eds), *Dark Ages and Nomads c. 1000 BC: Studies in Iranian and Anatolian Archaeology* (Istanbul, Nederlands Historisch-Archaeologisch Instituut in het Nabije Oosten), 3–8.

Ghirshman, R. (1977), *L'Iran et la migration des Indo-Aryens et des Iraniens* (Leiden, Brill).

Gimbutas, M. (1970), 'Proto-Indo-European Culture: the Kurgan culture during the fifth, fourth, and third millennia BC', in G. Cardona, H.-M. Hoenigswald, and A. Senn (eds), *Indo-European and Indo-Europeans* (Philadelphia, University of Pennsylvania Press), 155–97.

Gontscharov, A. (2019), *Metall der bronzezeitlichen Kulturen aus Zentral- und Ostkasachstan*, Unpublished PhD thesis (Bochum, Ruhr-Universität Bochum).

Grant, A. (1982), 'The use of tooth wear as a guide to the age of domestic ungulates', in R. Wilson (ed), *Ageing and Sexing Animal Bones from Archaeological Sites* (Oxford, British Archaeological Reports), 91–108.

Grigoriev, S. (2015), *Metallurgical Production in Northern Eurasia in the Bronze Age* (Oxford, Archaeopress).

Grupe, G., Price, T.D., Schröter, P., Söllner, F., Johnson, C.M., *et al.* (1997), 'Mobility of Bell Beaker people revealed by strontium isotope ratios of tooth and bone: a study of southern Bavarian skeletal remains', *Applied Geochemistry*, 12(4): 517–25.

Haak, W., Lazaridis, I., Patterson, N., Rohland, N., Mallick, S., *et al.* (2015), 'Massive migration from the steppe was a source for Indo-European languages in Europe', *Nature*, 522: 207–11.

Hanks, B. and Doonan, R. (2009), 'From scale to practice: a new agenda for the study of early metallurgy on the Eurasian Steppe', *World Prehistory*, 22: 329–56.

Hermes, T.R., Frachetti, M.D., Doumani Dupuy, P.N., Maryashev, A., Nebel, A., *et al.* (2019), 'Early integration of pastoralism and millet cultivation in Bronze Age Eurasia', *Proceedings of the Royal Society B*, 286: 20191273, DOI: 10.1098/rspb.2019.1273.

Hillson, S. (2005), *Teeth: Cambridge Manuals in Archaeology* (Cambridge and New York, Cambridge University Press).

Iacumin, P., Bocherens, H., Mariotti, A., and Longinelli, A. (1996), 'Oxygen isotope analyses of co-existing carbonate and phosphate in biogenic apatite: a way to monitor diagenetic alteration of bone phosphate?', *Earth and Planetary Science Letters*, 142(1/2): 1–6.

Jim, S., Ambrose, S.H., and Evershed, R.P. (2004), 'Stable carbon isotopic evidence for differences in the dietary origin of bone cholesterol, collagen, and apatite: implications for their use in palaeodietary reconstruction', *Geochimica et Cosmochimica Acta*, 68(1): 61–72.

Jones, G.G. and Sadler, P. (2012), 'Age at death in cattle: methods, older cattle, and known-age reference material', *Environmental Archaeology*, 17(1): 11–28.

Kaiser, E. (2010), 'Migrationen in der Vorgeschichte am Beispiel der Jamnaja-Kultur im nordpontischen Steppenraum', *Mitteilungen der Berliner Gesellschaft für Anthropologie, Ethnologie und Urgeschichte*, 31: 191–202.

Kaiser, E. (2016), 'Migrationen von Ost nach West. Die Archäologie von Wanderungsbewegungen im 3. Jahrtausend v. Chr.', *Mitteilungen der Berliner Gesellschaft für Anthropologie, Ethnologie und Urgeschichte*, 37: 31–44.

Khazanov, A.M. (1994), *Nomads and the Outside World*, 2nd edn (Madison, University of Wisconsin Press).

Kiderlen, M., Bode, M., Hauptmann, A., and Bassiakos, Y. (2016), 'Tripod cauldrons produced at Olympia give evidence for trade with copper from Faynan (Jordan) to southwest Greece, *c.* 950–750 BC', *Journal of Archaeological Science: Reports*, 8: 303–13.

Kierdorf, H., Kierdorf, U., Frölich, K., and Witzel, C. (2013), 'Lines of evidence: incremental markings in molar enamel of Soay Sheep as revealed by a fluorochrome labeling and backscattered electron imaging study', *PLoS ONE*, 8(9): e74597, DOI: 10.1371/journal.pone.0074597.

Klein, S., Domergue, C., Lahaye, Y., Brey, G.P., and von Kaenel, H.-M. (2009), 'The lead and copper isotopic composition of copper ores from the Sierra Morena (Spain)', *Journal of Iberian Geology*, 35: 59–68.

Knipper, C. (2017), 'Isotopenanalysen zum Nachweis von Mobilität in der Ur- und Frühgeschichte: Rückblick und Ausblick', in H. Meller, F. Daim, J. Krause, and R. Risch (eds), *Migration und Integration von der Urgeschichte bis zum Mittelalter* (Halle/Saale, Landesamt für Denkmalpflege und Archäologie Sachsen-Anhalt), 39–56.

138   *Thomas Stöllner et al.*

Koch, P.L. (1998), 'Isotopic reconstruction of the past continental environments', *Annual Review of Earth and Planetary Sciences*, 26(1): 573–613.

Koch, P.L. (2007), 'Isotopic study of the biology of modern and fossil vertebrate', in R. Michener and K. Lajtha (eds), *Stable Isotopes in Ecology and Environmental Science* (Malden, Blackwell), 99–154.

Kohl, P. (2007), *The Making of Bronze Age Eurasia* (Cambridge, Cambridge University Press).

Krause, R. (2013), 'The metallurgy of Kamennyi Ambar: Settlement and cemetery', in R. Krause and L.N. Koryakova (eds), *Multidisciplinary Investigations of the Bronze Age Settlements in the Southern Trans-Urals (Russia)* (Bonn, Habelt), 203–25.

Kukushkin, I. (2013), 'Streitwagen in Kasachstan und in den angrenzenden Gebieten', in T. Stöllner and Z. Samašev (eds), *Unbekanntes Kasachstan: Archäologie im Herzen Asiens* (Bochum, Deutsches Bergbau-Museum), 221–30.

Kukushkin, I.A. and Loman, V.G. (2014), 'Краткие итоги исследования элитных курганов эпохи бронзы Центрального Казахстана/Brief results of the study of the elite mounds of the Bronze Age in Central Kazakhstan', in *Труды IV (XX) Всероссийского Археологического съезда/Proceedings of the IV (XX) All-Russian Archaeological Congress* (Kazan, Otechestvo Publishing), 584–7.

Kunter, M. (2009), *Menschliche Skelettreste aus dem Gräberfeld Askaraly II: Černogorka*, Unpublished report.

Kuzmina, E.E. (1991), 'Die urgeschichtliche Metallurgie der Andronovo-Kultur. Bergbau, Metallurgie und Metallbearbeitung', *Zeitschrift für Archäologie*, 25: 29–48.

Kuzmina, E.E. (1994), *Откуда пришли индоарии?/Where Did the Indo-Aryans Come from?* (Moscow, Российская академия наук).

Kuzmina, E.E. (2007), *The Origin of the Indo-Iranians* (Leiden, Brill).

Lee-Thorp, J.A., Sealy, J.C., and Van der Merwe, N.J. (1989), 'Stable carbon isotope ratio differences between bone collagen and bone apatite, and their relationship to diet', *Journal of Archaeological Science*, 16(6): 585–99.

Longinelli, A. (1984), 'Oxygen isotopes in mammal bone phosphate: a new tool for paleo-hydrological and paleo-climatological research?', *Geochimica et Cosmochimica Acta*, 48(2): 385–90.

Luz, B., Kolodny, Y., and Horowitz, M. (1984), 'Fractionation of oxygen isotopes between mammalian bone-phosphate and environmental drinking water', *Geochimica et Cosmochimica Acta*, 48(8): 1689–93.

Mallory, J.P. (1989), *In Search of the Indo-Europeans: Language, Archaeology, and Myth* (London, Thames & Hudson).

Mallory, J.P. and Adams, D.Q. (1997), *Encyclopedia of Indo-European Culture* (London, Taylor & Francis).

Mallory, J P. and Mair, V.H. (2008), *The Tarim Mummies: Ancient China and the Mystery of the Earliest Peoples from the West* (London, Thames & Hudson).

Marchenko, Z.V., Svyatko, S.V., Molodin, V.I., Grishin, A-E., and Rykun, M.P. (2017), 'Radiocarbon chronology of complexes with Seima-Turbino type objects (Bronze Age) in Southwestern Siberia', *Radiocarbon*, 59(5): 1–17.

Masson, V.M. and Sarianidi, V.I. (1972), *Central Asia: Turkmenia before the Achaemenids* (London, Thames & Hudson).

Mathieson, I., Lazaridis, I., Rohland, N., Mallick, S., Patterson, N., *et al.* (2015), 'Genome-wide patterns of selection in 230 ancient Eurasians', *Nature*, 528(7583): 499–503.

Minasjan, R. (2013), 'Die Steingussform aus Mynčunkur', in T. Stöllner and Z. Samašev (eds), *Unbekanntes Kasachstan: Archäologie im Herzen Asiens* (Bochum, Deutsches Bergbau-Museum), 399–402.

Motuzaite Matuzeviciute, G., Kiryushin, Y.F., Rakhimzhanova, S.Z., Svyatko, S., Tishkin, A.A., *et al.* (2015), 'Climatic or dietary change? Stable isotope analysis of Neolithic–Bronze Age populations from the Upper Ob and Tobol River basins', *Holocene*, 26: 1711–21.

Narasimhan, V.M., Patterson, N., Moorjani, P., Rohland, N., Bernardos, R., *et al.* (2019), 'The formation of human populations in South and Central Asia', *Science*, 365(6457): 1–15.

Naumann, L. (2016), *Die Keramik von Mastau Baj (Ostkasachstan): Typologie, Chaîne Operatoire und ethnische Interpretatons(un-)möglichkeiten bronzezeitlicher Keramikfunde*, Unpublished masters thesis (Bochum, Ruhr-Universität Bochum).

Nikichenko, I.I. (2002), *Explanatory Note of the Map of the Mineral Resources of the Republic of Kazakhstan: 1:1,000,000 Scale* (Kokchetav).

Özyarkent, H. (2019), *Economy and Mobility of Bronze Age Andronovo Culture in Central and Eastern Kazakhstan: Multiple Isotope Analysis Approach to Questions of Provenance, Diet and Mobility*, Unpublished PhD thesis (Bochum, Ruhr-Universität Bochum).

Parzinger, H. (2002), 'Das Zinn in der Bronzezeit Eurasiens', in Ü. Yalçin (ed), *Anatolian Metal II* (Bochum, Deutsches Bergbau-Museum), 159–77.

Parzinger, H. (2006), *Die frühen Völker Eurasiens: Vom Neolithikum bis zum Mittelalter* (Munich, C.H. Beck Verlag).

Parzinger, H. and Boroffka, N. (2003), *Das Zinn der Bronzezeit in Mittelasien I: Die siedlungsarchäologischen Forschungen im Umfeld der Zinnlagerstätten* (Mainz, Verlag Philipp von Zabern).

Pernicka, E., Eibner, C., Öztunalı, Ö., and Wagner, G.A. (2003), 'Early Bronze Age Metallurgy in the Northeast Aegean', in G.A. Wagner, E. Pernicka, and H.P. Uerpmann (eds), *Troia and the Troad* (New York, Springer), 143–72.

Peterson, B.J. and Fry, B. (1987), 'Stable isotopes in ecosystem studies', *Annual Review of Ecology and Systematics*, 18(1): 293–320.

Pott, R. (2005), *Allgemeine Geobotanik: Biogeosysteme und Biodiversität* (Berlin and Heidelberg, Springer).

Potts, D. (2016), *Nomadism in Iran: From Antiquity to the Modern Era* (Oxford, Oxford University Press).

Prange, M. (2001), '5000 Jahre Kupfer im Oman: Vergleichende Untersuchungen zur Charakterisierung des omanischen Kupfers mittels chemischer und isotopischer Analysenmethoden', *Metalla*, 8(1/2): 1–126.

Price, T.D., Johnson, C.M., Ezzo, J.A., Ericson, J., and Burton, J.H. (1994), 'Residential mobility in the prehistoric southwest United States: a preliminary study using strontium isotope analysis', *Journal of Archaeological Science*, 21: 315–30.

Schwarzberg, H. (2009), 'Sejma-Turbino-Formenkreise frühbronzezeitlichen Prestigegutes in Eurasien', in J. Bagley, C. Eggl, D. Neumann, and M. Schefzik (eds), *Alpen, Kult und Eisenzeit: Festschrift für Amei Lang zum 65. Geburtstag* (Rahden/Westf., Verlag Marie Leidorf), 83–96.

Sealy, J.C., Van der Merwe, N.J., Sillen, A., Kruger, F.J., and Krueger, H.W. (1991), '87Sr/86Sr as a dietary indicator in modern and archaeological bone', *Journal of Archaeological Science*, 18(3): 399–416.

Seltmann, R. (2013), 'Erzreichtum Kasachstans', in T. Stöllner and Z. Samašev (eds), *Unbekanntes Kasachstan: Archäologie im Herzen Asiens* (Bochum, Deutsches Bergbau-Museum), 67–76.

Seltmann, R., Konopelko, D., Biske, G., Divaev, F., and Sergeev, S. (2011), 'Hercynian postcollisional magmatism in the context of Paleozoic magmatic evolution of the Tien Shan orogenic belt', *Journal of Asian Earth Sciences*, 43(5): 821–38.

Serikov, Y.B., Korochkova, O.N., Kuzminykh, S.V., and Stefanov, V.I. (2009), 'Shaitanskoye Ozero II: new aspects of the Uralian Bronze Age', *Archaeology, Ethnology and Anthropology of Eurasia*, 37(2): 67–78.

Shishlina, N. and Loboda, A. (2019), 'Metalworking techniques on the Eurasian steppes in the Late Bronze Age: technical analyses of the Borodino Treasure spearheads', *Oxford Journal of Archaeology*, 38(4): 420–42.

Sillen, A. and LeGeros, R. (1991), 'Solubility profiles of synthetic apatites and of modern and fossil bones', *Journal of Archaeological Science*, 18(3): 385–97.

Sillen, A., Hall, G., Richardson, S., and Armstrong, R. (1998), '87Sr/86Sr ratios in modern and fossil food-webs of the Sterkfontein Valley: implications for early hominid habitat preference', *Geochimica et Cosmochimica Acta*, 62(14): 2463–73.

Simmer, J.P., Papagerakis, P., Smith, C.E., Fisher, D.C., Rountrey, A.N., *et al.* (2010), 'Regulation of dental enamel shape and hardness', *Journal of Dental Research*, 89(10): 1024–38.

Spengler, R., Frachetti, M., Doumani, P., Rouse, L., Cerasetti, B., *et al.* (2014), 'Early agriculture and crop transmission among Bronze Age mobile pastoralists of Central Eurasia', *Proceedings Royal Society B*, 281: 20133382, DOI: 10.1098/rspb.2013.3382.

Sponheimer, M. and Lee-Thorp, J.A. (1999), 'Isotopic evidence for the diet of an early hominid, *Australopithecus africanus*', *Science*, 283: 368–70.

Stasevič, I. (2013), 'Die sozio-ökonomischen Modelle der Viehzüchter Kasachstans. Ein historischer Abriss', in T. Stöllner and Z. Samašev (eds), *Unbekanntes Kasachstan: Archäologie im Herzen Asiens* (Bochum, Deutsches Bergbau-Museum), 19–26.

Stöllner, T. and Gontscharov, A. (2021), 'Social practice and the exchange of metals and metallurgical knowledge in 2nd millennium Central Asia', *Metalla*, 25(2): 45–76.

Stöllner, T. and Samašev, Z. (eds) (2013), *Unbekanntes Kasachstan: Archäologie im Herzen Asiens* (Bochum, Deutsches Bergbau-Museum).

Stöllner, T., Samašev, Z., Berdenov, S., Cierny, J., Garner, J., *et al.* (2010), 'Bergmannsgräber im bronzezeitlichen Zinnrevier von Askaraly, Ostkasachstan', *Anschnitt*, 62(3): 86–99.

Stöllner, T., Samašev, Z., Berdenov, S., Cierny, J., Doll, M., *et al.* (2011), 'Tin from Kazakhstan: steppe tin for the west', in Ü. Yalçın (ed), *Anatolian Metal V* (Bochum, Deutsches Bergbau-Museum), 231–51.

Stöllner, T., Samašev, Z., Berdenov, S., Cierny, J., Doll, M. *et al.* (2013a), 'Zinn und Kupfer aus dem Osten Kasachstans: Ergebnisse eines deutsch-kasachischen Projektes 2003–8', in T. Stöllner and Z. Samašev (eds), *Unbekanntes Kasachstan: Archäologie im Herzen Asiens* (Bochum, Deutsches Bergbau-Museum), 357–82.

Stöllner, T., Bode, M., Gontscharov, A., Gorelik, A., Hauptmann, A. *et al.* (2013b), 'Metall und Metallgewinnung der Bronze- und Früheisenzeit, in T. Stöllner and Z. Samašev (eds), *Unbekanntes Kasachstan: Archäologie im Herzen Asiens* (Bochum, Deutsches Bergbau-Museum), 383–97.

Syusyura, B.B., Glybovskiy, V.O., Khalilov, V.A., Yurgens, A.V., and Sal'kov, S.A. (1987), 'Participation of sulfur in the genesis of copper sandstone ores of the Dzhezkazgan-Sarysuysk region' (in Russian), *Izvestiya Akademii Nauk Kazakhskoy SSR, Seriya Geologicheskaya=Khabarlary Kazakh SSR, Fylym Akademiyasynyn*, 1987(3): 31–41.

Tairov, A. (2017), 'Early nomads of the Zhaiyk-Irtyhs interfluve in VIII–VII cc BC', in Z. Samašev (ed), *Cultural Heritage: Materials and Researches, Vol. 3* (Astana, Kazakh Research Institute of Culture).

Terzer, S., Wassenaar, L.I., Araguás-Araguás, L.J., and Aggarwal, P.K. (2013), 'Global isoscapes for δ18O and δ2H in precipitation: improved prediction using regionalized climatic regression models', *Hydrology and Earth System Sciences*, 17(11): 4713–28.

Tkačev, V., Zajkov, V., and Juminov, A. (2013), 'Das spätbronzezeitliche Bergbau-metallurgische Zentrum von Mugodžary im Sytem der eurasischen metallurgischen Provinz: Geoarchäologische Untersuchungen in Mugodžary', in T. Stöllner and Z. Samašev (eds), *Unbekanntes Kasachstan: Archäologie im Herzen Asiens* (Bochum, Deutsches Bergbau-Museum), 471–82.

Tkachev, A.A. (2002), *Центральный Казахстан в эпоху бронзы, Ч I/.II/Central Kazakhstan in the Bronze Age, Part 1/2* (Tiumen, Institute of Northern Development, Siberian Branch of the Russian Academy of Sciences).

Tkacheva, N.A. and Tkachev, A.A. (2008), 'The role of migration in the evolution of the Andronov community', *Archaeology, Anthropology and Ethnology of Eurasia*, 35(3): 88–96.

Varfolomeev, V. (2013), 'Die Begazy-Dandybaj-Kultur', in T. Stöllner and Z. Samašev (eds), *Unbekanntes Kasachstan: Archäologie im Herzen Asiens* (Bochum, Deutsches Bergbau-Museum), 483–98.

Varfolomeev, V. and Evdokimov, V. (2013), 'Die Andronovo-Kulturen', in T. Stöllner and Z. Samašev (eds), *Unbekanntes Kasachstan: Archäologie im Herzen Asiens* (Bochum, Deutsches Bergbau-Museum), 289–305.

Ventresca Miller, A.R., Winter-Schuh, C., Usmanova, E.R., Logvin, A., Shevnina, I., and Makarewicz, C.A. (2018), 'Pastoralist mobility in Bronze Age landscapes of Northern Kazakhstan: 87Sr/86Sr and δ18O analyses of human dentition from Bestamak and Lisakovsk', *Environmental Archaeology*, 23(40): 352–66.

Ventresca Miller, A.R., Bragina, T.M., Abil, Y.A., Rulyova, M.M., and Makarewicz, C.A. (2019), 'Pasture usage by ancient pastoralists in the northern Kazakh steppe informed by carbon and nitrogen isoscapes of contemporary floral biomes', *Archaeological and Anthropological Sciences*, 11: 2151–66.

Ventresca Miller, A.R., Haruda, A., Varfolomeev, V., Goryachev, A., and Makarewicz, C.A. (2020), 'Close management of sheep in ancient Central Asia: evidence for foddering, transhumance, and extended lambing seasons during the Bronze and Iron Ages', *STAR: Science & Technology of Archaeological Research*, 6(1): 41–60.

Vidale, M. (2017), *Treasures from the Oxus: The Art and Civilization of Central Asia* (London and New York, L.B. Tauris & Co).

Wang, W., Liu, Y., Duan, F., Zhang, J., *et al.* (2020), 'A comprehensive investigation of Bronze Age human dietary strategies from different altitudinal environments in the Inner Asian Mountain Corridor', *Journal of Archaeological Science*, 121: 105201, DOI: 10.1016/j.jas.2020.105201.

White, T.D. and Folkens, P.A. (2005), *The Human Bone Manual* (Leiden, Elsevier).

Young, T.C. Jr (1967), 'The Iranian migration into the Zagros', *Iran*, 5: 11–34.

Zazzo, A., Balasse, M., Passey, B.H., Moloney, A.P., Monahan, F.J., *et al.* (2010), 'The isotope record of short- and long-term dietary changes in sheep tooth enamel: implications for quantitative reconstruction of paleodiets', *Geochimica et Cosmochimica Acta*, 74(12): 3571–86.

Zonenshain, L.P., Kuzmin, M.I., and Natapov, L.M. (1990), *Geology of USSR: A Plate-Tectonic Synthesis* (Washington D.C., American Geophysical Union).

7

Rethinking Material Culture Markers for Mobility and Migration in the Globalising European Later Bronze Age: A Comparative View from the Po Valley and Pannonian Plain

BARRY MOLLOY, CAROLINE BRUYÈRE, AND DRAGAN JOVANOVIĆ

Introduction

UNTIL THE MIDDLE of the 20th century AD, migration and invasion were commonly used as an interpretative framework for archaeological explanations of culture change (Clark 1966; Gregoricka 2021). The core premise was that groups moving from one area into another brought with them their material culture traditions and continued making these in a new setting, usually displacing a preceding material tradition. The movement of people was conceived as being at a near whole-community level, directional, short in duration, and its impact was regarded as rapid and transformative on established communities. The reasons why such invasion models are long out of vogue have been discussed in recent papers (Heyd 2017; Kristiansen *et al.* 2017; Frieman and Hofmann 2019; cf. Gori and Abar, Chapter 2).

Here, we revisit a case study of two interrelated regions for which migration models retain influence in ongoing discussions of culture change: the Po Valley and the Pannonian Plain in the period between 1600 and 1150 BC. These were two interlocking hubs – one bounded by the Alps and looking into the Mediterranean region and the other linked into the river networks of Europe. Together, they influenced large regions of Europe – visible, for example, through the spread of Urnfield mortuary practices or metalwork styles – from the far north to the Aegean palatial world (Fischl *et al.* 2013; Molloy 2016a; Vandkilde 2016; Iacono *et al.* 2021; Cavazzuti *et al.* 2022). How these areas related to each other has important implications for understanding Mediterranean Europe networks of the later Bronze Age and is the focus of this chapter. We discuss the movement of people between these two hubs and consider how this is reflected in the material record, particularly

Proceedings of the British Academy, **254**, 142–169, © The British Academy 2023.

in light of advances in the study of past human mobility more broadly (Hahn and Weiss 2013; Knappett 2013; Kristiansen 2014; Knappett and Kiriatzi 2017; Dawson and Iacono 2021; Gregoricka 2021).

It has been argued that the second half of the 2nd millennium BC was a period of intensified interaction across Europe – lauded by some as an early globalising trend – which linked many far-flung corners of the Continent in political, economic, and ideological networks (Sherratt 1993; Kristiansen and Larsson 2005; Sherratt 2010). Such networks are believed to reflect the movement of people, things, and ideas and are commonly defined through the lens of material culture, though how we disaggregate those three manifestations of mobility is limited by the archaeological record itself.

Developments in biomolecular and stable isotope research in the past decade have called on us to revisit the movement of people in prehistory with a renewed vigour, if not always rigour (Heyd 2017; Frieman and Hofmann 2019). As a field, we have rightly shifted away from 'invasion models' of old, yet multi-centennial 'waves' of change linked to the movement of people in large numbers and operating at a continental scale, which have been identified in the 3rd millennium BC in particular, are engendering debate (Vander Linden 2016; Furholt 2018; cf. Heyd, Chapter 3). The situation in Europe appears quite different by the later Bronze Age of the 2nd millennium BC because such spatially extensive models for the movement of people are absent. In this context, mobility is commonly modelled as involving small groups, being commonplace and covering short to very long distances in otherwise quite stable societies (Kristiansen and Larsson 2005). As a consequence, our perspectives on mobility and migration will inevitably be different because networks binding a myriad of distinct communities are expected. Friend or foe, linkages were comprehensive whether by inclusion or exclusion, trade or war. Such relations would expand and invert, contract and exaggerate, depending on short-term political currents within the longer-term macrocultural infrastructures through which intergenerational knowledge was reinforced and reproduced.

We are commonly confronted with the terms mobility and migration to explain the movement of people in the Bronze Age, though there is considerable ambiguity in how we identify or differentiate material traces specific to either term. Migration in particular has long been a bone of contention within the discipline and has been subject to intense debate following the surge in papers using genetic data to identify the movement of people (for an up-to-date overview, see Fernández-Götz *et al.*, Chapter 1; Gori and Abar, Chapter 2). At the same time, the increased interest in mobility has seen that term used commonly in recent literature, though when it is more appropriate to use this than migration is less clear (Knappett and Kiriatzi 2017). Recognising the risk of getting bogged down in semantics because the nature of our evidence may not allow differentiation and terms may even justifiably be interchangeable, Table 7.1 proposes some broad criteria that may justify the choice of one word over the other, even if this should be context-dependent.

Table 7.1 Indicators of how the movement of people may bias understanding of purpose and character towards the terms mobility or migration. In practice, these are not mutually exclusive (table: authors)

Mobility	Migration
• Predictable intended outcomes	• Greater possibility of unpredictable outcomes. Socially exploratory component
• Within established networks/well-known communities	• Moving beyond core networks, long distance and/or engaging with communities with social "otherness"
• Embedded in or requiring a form of social stability	• May arise from or relate to social instability
• Peaceful in principle	• Potential to be intrusive by choice (even invasive) or forced by others
• Expected return to base(s)	• Reception at destination to be negotiated
• Usually a fraction of a given social group moving at any one time	• May range from individual to whole social group level

Historical turning points, such as the abandonment of tells in the Carpathian Basin, may have been drivers of directional migration by elements within a society such as disenfranchised elites. These people must have served as anchors that encouraged continued mobility between the origin and destination thereafter. Alternatively, strong economic and ideological networks could have forged the conduit through which people could move into relatively familiar settings and be integrated there. More models could be offered, but this in itself demonstrates the exceptional difficulty or subjectivity of using material culture to differentiate forms of movement between closely linked yet distinct communities that were components of the same networks. In practice, neither mobility nor migration should be considered as implicitly meaningful and they require contextualisation in any given discussion.

To better understand routine interactions between societies of the Po Valley and Pannonian Plain, we will look beyond elites and exceptional objects or contexts to the realm of routine practices that characterise lifeways. Through material culture, in this chapter we attempt to explore some 'what ifs' of multigenerational demic entanglements between distinct societies in the European later Bronze Age. In such a scenario, our challenge is to identify the scale, frequency, duration, and nature of the movement of people within networks and through this to aim to characterise the links between communities across a large geographic scale (Molloy 2016b). The exchange of resources, metals in particular, lend themselves well to identifying macro-scale networks, though the focus is largely on economic links and this tells us little about migration of people between communities (Radivojević *et al.* 2019).

The very concept of a globalising world should integrate the flow of people as well as things.

When we look to the macrocultural traditions – that is, the underlying knowledge base, conventions/manners, ideologies, and even styles of a community inherited across centuries – how these articulate between regions has the potential to inform us about shared experiences arising from deeper social engagements. Migrations in recent literature have tended to be contextualised within disjunctures, though our aim in this chapter is to focus on those types of migration occurring alongside regular mobility, which were linked to stability and predictable conditions. In Anthony's still influential modelling of modes of migration, this may fall under his 'chain migration', or at times of disruption even his 'coerced migration' (Anthony 1997: 25–7). The former is founded upon first-group migrants establishing a link between two distant areas after which following generations may move, leap-frogging less-connected areas in-between (Anthony 1997: 26). This encourages *homophily*, or 'preferential relationships among similar entities' which facilitate continued interaction over decades or centuries between mutually receptive groups (Cavazzuti *et al.* 2022: 2).

We approach this cultural sharing by exploring the coalescences of habitus that emerge through repeated shared experiences as visible in material, settlement, and mortuary datasets. If a regular feature, chain migration should have served to encourage macrocultural coalescence or cross-fertilisation that developed simultaneously in distinct areas across multiple fields of activity, thereby shaping the material record. At the same time, the disconnects and resistances to sameness are also important to recognise, since these are perhaps more prevalent in these two societies. Our argument is that demic flow was a two-way street between these communities and was particularly strong, but not exclusive of other areas. This allowed each to thrive and the network they were central nodes of to be influential at a pan-regional scale.

Notions of ancient communities occupying defined spaces in landscapes as hermetically sealed, self-reproducing units might be regarded as an implicit position in some culture-historical frameworks, even if such a static view is rarely explicated. Accepting that we need not fully depend on the movement of people to explain culture change, we recognise that it occurred. In many ways, our challenge is to better understand the extent and nature of the permeability of past societies in which ideas could be introduced and gain traction as strands within local trajectories. The very concept of 'foreign' is a construct which we cannot impose on past ideologies or materialities (Panagiotopoulos 2012). By the same token, the very notion of 'local' may be a misnomer, whether we are referring to material culture or people, because it depends on a binary relationship with 'non-local', with little grey area in-between.

It is increasingly evident that we need to account for the social impacts of personal mobility as a norm rather than an exception in the later Bronze Age and that the constitution of communities was dynamic over generations. In the Po Valley, strontium isotope analyses indicate that mobility between relatively distant settlements was clearly identifiable (Cavazzuti 2019b). Arguably, to circumvent the growth of narrow-lineage powerful families/factions, a social strategy of inter-settlement mobility may itself serve to underpin a particular ideological framework which resists hierarchisation – such masking of differentiation has been argued for the Po Valley (Cardarelli 2020). Motivations for women and men to move may have been similar or distinct, dependent on what networks or opportunities were being exploited (Brück 2021). The tools of the 'third science revolution' are doubtless increasing our capacity to identify what in prehistory was moving and when it was doing so, but explaining how or why requires engagement with societal scale perspectives that cut across multiple fields of social discourse – routine life- and deathways in particular.

Switching now to our case studies, our starting point is that in early archaeological discourse migration from the Carpathian Basin, or more specifically the Pannonian Plain in the centre of the basin, to the Po Valley was said to have been a major catalyst for the emergence of the Terramare system in the second half of the 2nd millennium BC (Pigorini 1909; Vanzetti 2013: 274; Cardarelli 2020: 56; Cardarelli *et al.* 2020: 231–2). Despite archaeology's retreat from migrationism, this mobility has not been disproven and indeed remains a matter of ongoing debate (Cardarelli 2009: 35–7; Vanzetti 2013: 274; Danckers 2017; Dalla Longa 2019; Cardarelli *et al.* 2020: 233 with citations; Pau 2020). Recent work shifts the emphasis to inward migration from various areas on the periphery of the Po Valley itself (Cardarelli 2018: 362). A different trend is also promoted, which emphasises the importance of incremental growth at a local level in the development of the Terramare system (Vanzetti 2013; Dalla Longa 2019). Importantly, recent palaeogenetic research indicates the occurrence of steppe ancestry in northern Italy from *c.* 2000 BC, increasing proportionally in the following centuries (Saupe *et al.* 2021). Though larger datasets are needed to model the nature of this flow, current data suggest increasing levels of external contacts or inward migration from the Italian Middle Bronze Age onwards (Saupe *et al.* 2021: 2586).

Cavazzuti *et al.* (2022: 2) argue that homophily – 'preferential relationships among similar entities' – means that communication is increasingly effective when groups 'share common meanings, attitudes and beliefs'. They make the case that centuries of interaction, even in periods of lower intensity, between our two areas of interest created a long-term knowledge network through which the very concept of sharing ideas became part of their respective worldviews. As this knowledge is not just the superficial features of objects but the routines of how they were appropriately used and contextualised, we must speak of people interacting and not just their objects or styles diffusing through down-the-line networks. This is particularly the case when we are looking to social arenas where a degree of conservatism may be predicted, such as religion or mortuary practices (Cavazzuti *et al.* 2022).

In the Pannonian Plain, a prevailing model has been that Middle Bronze Age systems collapsed around 1600 BC alongside the inward migration of Tumulus culture groups (Fischl *et al.* 2013; Kienlin *et al.* 2017). Depopulation of the Pannonian Plain due to a collapse therefore coincided directly in time with an increase in

CULTURE MARKERS FOR MOBILITY AND MIGRATION 147

population in the Po Valley, providing a simple solution. Of course, such a neat model struggles under scrutiny because the collapse extended over as much as a century and, as argued below, there was no such depopulation in the former area. Furthermore, in the Po Valley there was no sudden explosion of new settlements in the 16th century BC or new material culture introduced en masse (Dalla Longa 2019; Duffy *et al.* 2019). However, with our growing knowledge of a newly discovered Late Bronze Age settlement network in the Pannonian Plain contemporary to that of the Terramare network, the need for a sudden and crisis-driven change is reduced and the opportunity to explore longer-term patterns of mobility is called for.

The Po Valley in the Middle to Late Bronze Age

Settlement

In Italian chronology, 1600 to 1150 BC covers the later Middle and Recent Bronze Age (Cavazzuti and Arena 2020: Table 1). The plain of the Po Valley in northern Italy is bounded by mountains to the north and south and the Adriatic Sea to the east. The Po River and its tributaries run from the west to the east in a flat to gently undulating landscape. The density, and complexity, of settlement in the Po Valley (Figure 7.1) between 1500 and 1150 BC was unprecedented in that region (Cardarelli 2020). Settlement is characterised by Terramare sites, which are defined as 'quadrangular settlements surrounded by an artificial embankment and ditch into which the waters of a nearby river or natural canal were re-routed', and a smaller number of Palafitte sites, which are defined as waterside pile dwellings, and small, often shorter lived, open settlements (De Marinis 2009; Blake 2014; Cavazzuti *et al.* 2019a: 625).

From 1500 BC, settlement numbers increased, though the earliest sites were less than 2 ha in area (Cardarelli 2009: 456; Vanzetti 2013; Dalla Longa *et al.* 2019: 7; Cardarelli *et al.* 2020: 233). From the 14th century BC, settlements came to occupy increasingly diverse topographies, including more low-lying sites. They were consistently close to rivers or other 'damp locations', characterising a trend in location choice towards a 'systematic wetland-oriented strategy' (De Marinis 2009: 535; Dalla Longa 2019: 101–2). During the 13th century BC, settlement numbers appear to have increased in parts of the plain north of the Po River (Cupitò and Leonardi 2015; Dalla Longa 2019). At this same time, site size increased in many cases both north and south of the Po River, with sites such as Fondo Paviani (16 ha), Case del Lago (22.5 ha), and Case Cocconi (up to 60 ha) being developed (Blake 2014: 117).

Within Po Valley settlements, houses were densely packed and generally laid out in loosely ordered rows (Vanzetti 2013: 271; Cardarelli 2020: 56). Domestic and craft activities, including weaving and metalworking, are attested within the sites (Iaia 2015). The settlements were densely spaced and there were as many as 220 constructed during the Bronze Age, though not all were occupied at the same time (Cardarelli 2009; Blake 2014; Cavazzuti *et al.* 2019a: 625).

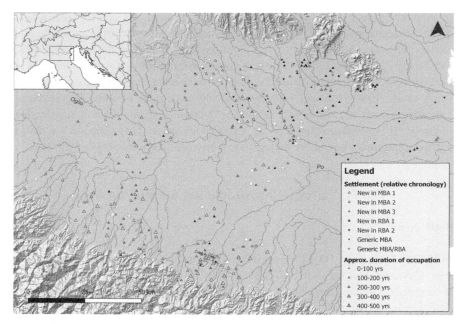

Figure 7.1 Distribution of Middle to Recent Bronze Age settlements in the Po Valley indicating relative chronology and duration of occupation.

Note: duration of occupation is approximated by association with relative chronology period, e.g. associated with Middle Bronze Age 3 and Recent Bronze Age 1=100–200 years duration (map by authors, data after Dalla Longa 2019; Cardarelli 2009). Base layer EU CLSM 2017 (© European Union, Copernicus Land Monitoring Service 2017, European Environment Agency EEA)

There is a dramatic change in the 12th century BC, with site numbers falling to less than a quarter of their previous total north of the Po and most settlements south of the river being abandoned entirely (Cardarelli 2009; Blake 2014: 118; Dalla Longa et al. 2019: Figure 5). This trajectory of intense growth and then population collapse is in contrast with other areas of Italy which show more gradual growth punctuated by modest upswings and declines throughout the Bronze Age (Blake 2014; Capuzzo et al. 2018; Cardarelli 2018; Ialongo 2018; Iacono 2019; Roberts et al. 2019). It is notable that of the few investigated sites which survived or were established after 1200 BC, most are greater in extent than the Terramare. The settlement(s) at Casalmoro extends over some 700 ha – the kind of massive settlement only found before this date in the Pannonian Plain (Pau 2020).

Cardarelli (2020: 55) argues that the Terramare are too populous and densely spaced for society to be defined strictly by kinship and that the relative homogeneity of house size indicates limited hierarchy within communities. In his view, society was ordered on a territorial basis with multiple sites constituting the same political entity, with hierarchical relations existing between sites (Cardarelli 2018: 363; 2020: 56). He further argues that identity-based, rather than wealth-based, social differentiation was paramount and that Terramare society was defined by an 'inherent contradiction between a highly developed economic and political order and a social structure which is apparently little differentiated in terms of inequality' (Cardarelli 2020: 56). It remains plausible that migrants within early communities were from many different areas and that the very distinctive structure of the Terramare system was a vehicle which gradually integrated these diverse elements.

Mortuary

Mortuary practices are another useful source for understanding the life- and deathways of the residents of the Po Valley. In the Middle Bronze Age, inhumation burial was virtually exclusive (though cemeteries are rare) and a transition to bi-ritual cemeteries with cremation began in the 15th century BC (Cardarelli *et al.* 2020: 238). By the 14th century BC, cremation had taken over as the (almost) exclusive mortuary rite throughout the entire Po Valley, as had flat cemeteries where possible family group clusters emerged (Cardarelli 2014). Cremations are partial, whereby a token amount of a few hundred grams of bone was recovered and placed in upright urns usually lacking a lid (Cardarelli 2014: 109–433). Notably, there is a substantial reduction in the inclusion of valuable metal objects in burials relative to those of the Middle Bronze Age and few ancillary ceramic vessels are typically included as this shift to flat cemeteries emerged. In the late 13th and into the 12th century BC, it became common for a bowl to be inverted and used as a lid for cremation urns (Bianco Peroni *et al.* 2010). This is a small but important development for exploring relationships with the Pannonian Plain, as we will discuss. Together with the undifferentiated house sizes within settlements, the mortuary record demonstrates an active resistance to hierarchies or even identity symbolism. This ideological 'flatness' is a fundamental characteristic of Terramare culture and is a striking contrast with the other well-investigated complex society of Bronze Age Mediterranean Europe – the Mycenaeans – that exhibits clear signs of social differentiation.

Strontium isotope analysis of individuals has recently been conducted for the cemeteries of the Early Bronze Age site of Sant'Eurosia, the Terramare sites of Casinalbo and Scalvinetto/Fondo Paviani, and the Final Bronze Age site of Frattesina (Cavazzuti *et al.* 2019a: 633; 2019b: 36). These studies demonstrate that, at the height of the Terramare, communities included people who had been raised in the immediate hinterlands and others who had spent their childhood outside a radius of 50 km, especially apparent in the important centre of Fondo Paviani. Indeed, some of these had dwelt beyond the Po Plain for extensive periods. Conceivably, on the basis of the documented strontium isotope values, extended periods of their life could have been spent in the Pannonian Plain because the bioavailable strontium signatures are so similar (Cavazzuti *et al.* 2019b: 31–2; Giblin 2020: 113–6). Most cases exhibiting this distinct pattern of mobility in the Po Plain are said to be women, which has been taken to suggest a patrilocal society in which women were mobile, potentially through networks for marriage alliances (Cavazzuti *et al.* 2019a; 2019b). It remains unclear how relationships were negotiated or power exercised through this mobility; with women being more mobile than men, this may well relate to choices by women to aggrandise their position within society (Brück 2021). After the collapse of the Terramare system, strontium isotopes show that those buried in the cemetery at the new and well-networked settlement of Frattesina predominantly grew up and spent much of their lives in the immediate locale (on the basis of strontium levels at least), indicating a contraction of the networks through which personal mobility had previously taken place. Cardarelli (2020: 59) argues that because multiple groups coalesced to form the Terramare societies, they had previously been defined by a heritage of permeability and integration since initial colonisation, reflected in ongoing mobility patterns, which appear to change after 1150 BC.

Material culture

The ceramic vessels of the Po Valley are characteristic of the area and are variants of *impasto* style. Indeed, between the Middle and Recent Bronze Age, an original diversity of ceramic forms gives way to more regionally cohesive norms, some even rendered in wood rather than ceramic. For the present study, developments in the 13th century BC are particularly notable. Biconical urns, cups, and smaller vases are common (Cupito *et al.* 2012: Figures 2, 8, 10). In the Recent Bronze Age, channel decoration becomes increasingly common and is concentrated on prominent morphological features of vessels, such as the carination, neck, or rim. On vases of Cardarelli's (2014) type E, stylised hanging garlands curving down from horizontal channels are particularly common (Figure 7.2). Biconical urns with four protomes on the carination are found, decorated with channels banded around a vertical neck and a sharply everted rim with decoration on its horizontal surface (Figure 7.3). Other vessels such as carinated cups with single low- or high-looped handles and channel decoration on the carination occur by the 13th century BC. By the 12th century BC, bowls with in-turned rims and channelled and incised decoration are also commonplace.

Similarities in metalwork have long been recognised between the Po Valley and the Pannonian Plain. The focus has primarily been on a handful of Middle Bronze Age metalwork forms, but it is clear that from 1600 to at least 1100 BC, both the style and function of metalwork in both areas evolved closely in tandem. In the beginning, specific object types such as the Sauerbrunn-Boiu swords were placed in graves and these stand out as being not only common to each area, but also only rarely found outside of them (Neumann 2009; Pearce 2013). The swords themselves are characterised by a long and thin blade with incised decoration around the shoulders. This often takes the appearance of a stylised face, which led Cowen to attribute an element of animism or personality to these objects (Cowen 1966; Pearce 2013). Using these swords in both societies was thus not a craft convenience; it relates to shared technological and martial practices, as well as beliefs

CULTURE MARKERS FOR MOBILITY AND MIGRATION 151

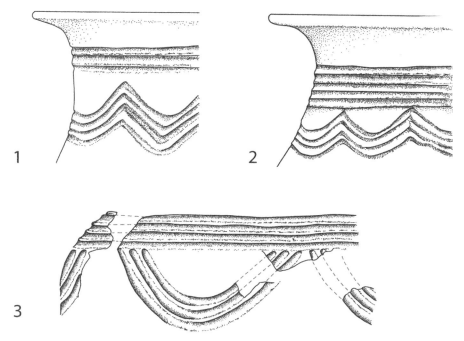

Figure 7.2 Horizontal channels with hanging garland motif on vessels from Ilandža (1 and 2) graves 10 and 1, and Casinalbo (3) grave 127 (after Bukvić 2000: Table 10; Cardarelli 2014: Figure 185; redrawn by Sara Nylund).

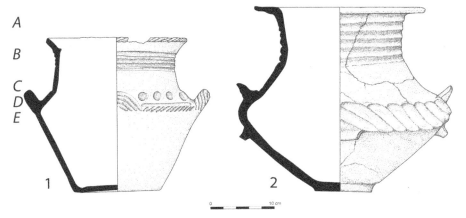

Figure 7.3 Urns from (1) Casinalbo, grave 29 and (2) Budjak Livade, grave 23 (1 redrawn after Cardarelli 2014: Figure 227 by Sara Nylund, 2 drawn by Rena Maguire and Sara Nylund). A) Strongly everted rim; B) horizontal channelling on cylindrical neck; C) four symmetrically located handles/protomes above belly-shoulder transition; D) oblique channels on belly-shoulder transition; E) biconical shape with cylindrical neck

around swords in society. Though these are the most striking objects from the Middle Bronze Age, bronze pins with perforations through the shank below the head or specific types of bronze horse tack are indicative of shared craft and equitation practices, for example (Sofaer *et al.* 2013; cf. Cardarelli *et al.* 2020: 233).

From the 13th century BC, the range of shared metalwork styles increased. While the intricacies of typology may be debated, highly similar fibulae, pins, swords, spears, axes, palstaves, razors, and bodily ornaments were in use in both areas. Comparing, for example, weapons in the hoards from Pila del Brancon in the Po Valley with those from around Slavonski Brod along the Sava River, there are striking similarities, even if sockets on Italian spearheads are usually shorter (Vinski-Gasparini 1973; Salzani 1994). Situlas – sheet bronze vessels for storage and/or cooking – from 13th century BC contexts in the Po Valley find clear parallels in the Pannonian Plain, again suggesting aspects of style and function common to both areas surrounding commensality (Jankovits 2017). We lack sufficient chronological resolution to indicate directionality in the spread of forms, but given how comprehensive this was, it is probable that this diffusion occurred within a well-connected and bilateral milieu.

The Pannonian Plain in the Late Bronze Age

Settlement

We focus on settlement networks of the south-eastern part of the Pannonian Plain, because we have both robust data and a high density of settlement contemporary to the Terramare. In the chronology of the region, while subdivisions are contested, we adhere to a three-tier system of Late Bronze Age 1 as 1600–1400 BC, Late Bronze Age 2 as 1400–1200 BC, and Late Bronze Age 3 as 1200–1000/900 BC, broadly speaking (Molloy *et al.* 2020; Gogâltan and Stavilă 2021). This is a flat landscape with many large and small rivers, and the area we focus on is defined by the Maros (N), Tisza (W), and Danube Rivers (S), and the Transylvanian Plateau (E). The settlement history of the Pannonian Plain was fundamentally different to the Po Valley because the Late Bronze Age networks were preceded by complex and hierarchical settlement networks of the Early to Middle Bronze Age. These had existed since the turn of the millennium and tell sites may have occupied the centre of polities (Earle and Kristiansen 2010; Németi and Molnár 2012; though see Kienlin *et al.* 2017; Dani *et al.* 2019; Kienlin 2020).

The collapse of this network is increasingly seen as a demographic decline and a simplification of social structures rather than outright depopulation (Gogâltan *et al.* 2014; Duffy *et al.* 2019; Nicodemus and O'Shea 2019). As with the Po Valley, the next phase has been traditionally argued to begin with inward migration, in this case by Tumulus culture groups (Mozsolics 1957; Bóna 1958; Fischl *et al.* 2013). It is probable that the previous Middle Bronze Age political order was challenged by new ideologies, driven in part by inward migration from the fringes of the basin. This arguably provides a push factor for some of the local population – such as disenfranchised elites – to depart along well-established networks to places, including the Po Valley (Cardarelli *et al.* 2020). In such a scenario, this is not a mass exodus of the base population, but certain members of society moving under particular conditions.

However it unfolded, it is clear that the political systems and the existing centres of power of the Middle Bronze Age came to a rapid end and that a new system emerged between 1600 and 1500 BC which had clear-cut differences. Contrary to long-standing models of decline and simplification, in the fertile south Pannonian Plain, our recent work reveals that settlement numbers actually increased significantly, both in number and hectares occupied (Figure 7.4). Furthermore, these sites are clustered with unprecedented density in a very flat landscape dissected by frequent large and small watercourses. We see this particularly in the complex network of sites extending along the Tisza River in Serbia, the first of which were established by the 16th century BC (Molloy *et al.* 2020; Grosman, pers. comm.).

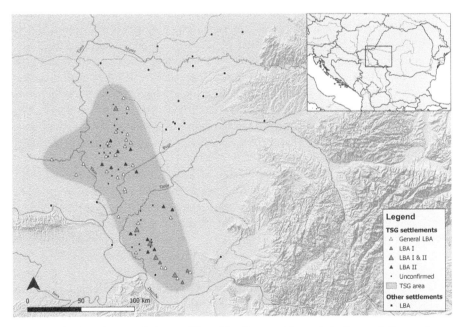

Figure 7.4 Map of currently known Tisza Site Group settlements in the south Pannonian Plain indicating relative chronology and other surrounding Late Bronze Age settlements.

Note: the dating of TSG sites is preliminary based on small surface pottery samples from ground truthing and may not represent all periods of occupation – this data is pending full systematic pedestrian survey (map by authors). Base layer EU CLSM 2017 (© European Union, Copernicus Land Monitoring Service 2017, European Environment Agency EEA)

154 *Barry Molloy et al.*

This network of sites is termed the Tisza Site Group (TSG), and settlements range from less than 10 to up to 200 ha. Most are defined by having one or several enclosure ditches and contain characteristic pale spots which were loci of domestic activity. In most cases, there are between 15 and 30 of these activity areas within each TSG settlement and they are evenly spaced. Finds representing craft and domestic activity are found within these enclosures. Settlements are commonly within 5–10 km of each other and set in two broad clusters north and south of the Tamiš River.

The presence of local-scale site clusters, where sites are lying within the carrying capacity hinterlands of each other, indicates that these were not all independent autonomous communities. As with the Terramare sites, there is also a clear relationship with both major and minor watercourses, including the Tisza, Danube, Maros, Begej, and Tamiš Rivers. A hierarchy of complexity is noted both on the basis of size and the number and nature of enclosure ditches (Molloy *et al.* 2020).

Highly similar material culture to that of the TSG is found at other massive and fortified sites to the east. These include the 1750 ha megasite of Cornesti Iarcuri and just outside of this catchment area, the fortified sites of Csanádpalota and Santana (Heeb *et al.* 2017; Szeverényi *et al.* 2017; Sava *et al.* 2019). As with sites of the TSG, these are complexes of multiple enclosures. The site of Santana has exceptionally broad ramparts surrounded by ditches, reminiscent in dimensions to the Terramare enclosures, even if these are more extensive enclosing over 100 ha (Sava *et al.* 2019).

Where we have absolute dates, the Late Bronze Age phases of all of the above sites were founded in the 15th century BC and abandoned between 1300 and 1200 BC. Surface finds, however, suggest that a 16th century BC foundation date is probable for several sites in this network. The abandonment phase is also noted in the relative chronology of ceramics recovered through surface survey at sites. It is clear that there was a major horizon of change in the 13th century BC that led to widespread abandonment of the large settlements, which had formed the centre of local and regional networks.

At the local level, this new knowledge of Late Bronze Age settlements is a game changer for our understanding of long-term sociopolitical trajectories, while at a regional level this complex system helps us make better sense of the obvious links with the Terramare network. In light of this new evidence, the traditional model of a single horizon of collapse in one place triggering directional movement of people to a new location, which in turn led to growth there, appears increasingly problematic. Yet movement was important, as it is clear there was organisational capacity in both areas to support continuous flows of people, materials, and ideas over several centuries, not just during a brief window.

Mortuary

Cremation had a long history in the Pannonian Plain as a part of the Vatya and Transdanubian Encrusted Pottery traditions (Stig Sørensen and Rebay-Salisbury 2008). In the Füzesabony tradition in the east Pannonian Plain and in the area south of the Maros and east of the Tisza Rivers, however, inhumation remained dominant at Maros tradition cemeteries like Mokrin and Ostojićevo in the Middle Bronze Age. Few human remains have been documented in the southern area of the TSG where Vatin pottery was used (Milleker 1905: 62, Figure XVI; Medović 2007).

In the surroundings of the TSG there is a continual and gradual emergence of the classic Urnfield model for treating the dead in individual cemeteries – cremation placed in an upright urn buried in a flat cemetery with few grave goods and with no surviving surface markers of graves (Tasić 2004; Ložnjak Dizdar 2014; Cardarelli *et al.* 2020: 235). The cemetery of Budžak-Livade is associated with the megafort of Gradište Iđoš, and absolute dates from burials show that in the late 17th to 15th/14th century BC transition, inhumation was practised side-by-side with cremation. The form of the cremation burials, however, was in upright urns with a handful of cremated bone and often with a second vessel serving as a lid. This is characteristic of the earliest Belegiš I tradition, which begins between 1600 and 1500 cal BC (Todorović 1977; Szentmiklosi 2009; Sava 2020).

At Budžak-Livade, deposition of small pieces of metalwork in burials was comparatively frequent before 1400 BC, a feature common to other contemporary cemeteries. After this point, inhumation ceased and cremations were placed in urns with very few grave goods. The striking similarity in timelines and all aspects of mortuary practice between the Po Valley and along the Danube and Sava Rivers has been discussed recently by Cardarelli *et al.* (2020) and Cavazzuti *et al.* (2022). Communities living within the TSG settlements were instrumental in the social relations which enabled this coeval development of mortuary practices.

Similar to the Po Valley, strontium isotopes provide possible evidence for a limited level of exogamy in the Vatya tradition, as well as the general presence of people born beyond the area they were interred during the Middle Bronze Age at some sites (Cavazzuti *et al.* 2021). While there are currently no relevant biomolecular or stable isotope studies of mobility published in the Pannonian Plain for the later 2nd millennium BC, current research as part of 'The Fall of 1200 BC' project (led by Molloy) and other projects (e.g. Giblin *et al.* 2019) will be completed in the near future.

Material culture

The development of pottery in the Pannonian Plain is much debated, though concisely stated, the high diversity and local trends which characterised the Middle Bronze Age gave way to more unified traditions over the course of the Late Bronze Age. There is also increased standardisation of surface treatment and decorative techniques across a broad area of the Pannonian Plain after 1400 BC (Coxon 2018). We read this as part of a social strategy by community leaders to stimulate cultural cohesion across the territories of the south Pannonian Plain megaforts, including sites of the TSG. This is not simply a matter of aesthetics, but the ceramic forms in question can be seen to structure practice and the performance of identity. Acknowledging the risk of falling foul of pots=people equations, it is clear that ceramic vessels in the Middle Bronze Age had formed part of strategies to articulate cultural boundaries in discrete parts of the Pannonian Plain. And so we read the reduction in ceramic diversity in the south Pannonian Plain over the Late Bronze Age as signifying a mechanism to draw together groups who had previously materially expressed differences through ceramics (Dietrich 2015). Such a strategy for integration may have been manifested through systemic mobility of people between sites, similar to the model suggested by Cavazzuti for the Po Valley (Cavazzuti *et al.* 2019a; 2019b).

Beginning *c.* 1600 BC, biconical urns with four protomes and flaring necks were introduced, and by 1400 BC new elements included channels around the neck below the rim and oblique channels on the carination/junction of the upper and lower cone of the vessel (cf. Figure 7.3). Bowls with inverted rims with channel decoration either parallel or oblique to the rim were also introduced around 1400 BC and became widespread by 1300 BC (Molloy *et al.* 2020: Figure 10; Sava 2020). Single-handled carinated cups, some with oblique channelled decoration, were also contemporary and recalled those mentioned above from the Po Valley. Hanging garlands executed in channel decoration were derived from incised motifs of the various encrusted pottery traditions of the Middle Bronze Age, and these were often attached to horizontal channelled ornaments. They occurred mainly on bowls and urns. On bowls, this same motif combines to form a multi-pointed star if viewing the vessel from its base and this combination is particularly characteristic of the Belegiš II ceramic horizon. A partial skeuomorph of this combination may be contemporary with embossed bronze plates (and helmets) of broadly similar diameter.

Along with actual swords of Sauerbrunn-Boiu type cited above, the characteristic stylised face motif was occasionally translated to contemporary pottery in the Pannonian Plain, demonstrating it was used beyond weaponry. This in turn indicates it was part of a broader shared symbology spanning both regions (Figure 7.5).

 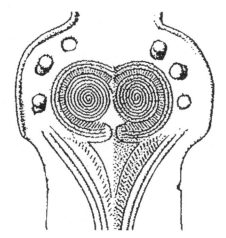

Figure 7.5 Photo of face motif on ceramic vessel of Dubovac-Žuto Brdo type and sword of Sauerbrunn-Boiu type, both dated to *c.* 1500–1300 BC and from the Carpathian Basin (motif on ceramic vessel from Banatska Palanka-Rudine, Inv. N. 11372, original photograph with kind permission of the City Museum Vršac), motif on sword from Tass, Hungary (after Kemenczi 1988: plate 15, 168; redrawn by Barry Molloy)

CULTURE MARKERS FOR MOBILITY AND MIGRATION 157

Absolute dating of contexts with diagnostic Late Bronze Age pottery has shifted the dating of ceramic wares considered to be 12th century BC back into the early 14th century BC, notably at Gradište Iđoš and Santana (Sava *et al.* 2019; Sava 2020; Molloy *et al.* 2020). It appears probable that many metalwork forms dated by hoard associations to the 13th to 12th centuries BC developed before 1300 BC. It is clear that material represented in hoards first emerged during the lifetime of the TSG and related sites. The forms of metalwork common to both the Po Valley and Pannonian Plain may be seen to constitute a cultural as well as technological *koiné* that was endogenous simultaneously to the Po and Pannonian zones.

Discussion

We can observe the following key similarities between the Po Valley and Pannonian Plain, particularly between 1500 and 1200 BC:

1) Communities occupied a relatively flat plain with an extensive drainage network which enabled wetland-oriented occupation strategies.
2) Site placement strategies were closely related to both local watercourses and major river routeways.
3) Settlements with internal and external spaces were routinely defined through the use of large enclosures (Figure 7.6).
4) An ideology of large-scale, coordinated group efforts for building and maintaining monumental features of small to large settlements prevailed.
5) Settlements were exceptionally densely spaced relative to their size, indicating shared landscape resources.
6) Clear hierarchies of settlement size and complexity can be defined, which relate to social centrality.
7) Flat cemeteries with token cremations in upright urns accompanied by few grave goods are the norm when settlement numbers and density reach their maximum after 1400 BC.
8) Clear similarities in the shape, decoration, and function of a range of ceramics and metalwork indicate parity in domestic and craft activities, personal appearance, and specialised practices, such as combat arts.

The coeval evolution of flat cemeteries with cremations placed in upright urns in both areas suggests that the 'urnfield model' of cremation cemeteries was 'embraced quite radically' in these areas at the same time, but not yet in surrounding areas (Cardarelli *et al.* 2020: 238). From settlements to cemeteries, a person moving between these regions would thus not be entering into an utterly foreign and strange world – as they may experience in Mycenaean Greece or the Nordic Chiefdoms – but would find their habitus and lifeway replicated closely. This is similarity, not sameness, because there were of course local conventions for each of these shared features of life- and deathways. The important thing for addressing mobility is that

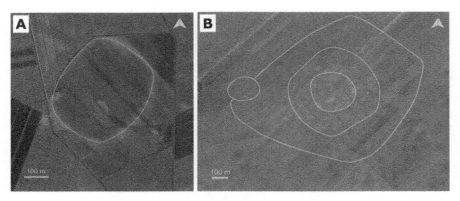

Figure 7.6 Aerial view of A) Castel del Tartaro Terramare and B) Sakule TSG settlement (base images: Google Earth, Maxar Technologies)

these similarities are found across so many different strands of society, including the household level, and so they are clearly not the product of high-level economic or political forms of interaction alone. They appear in the routine conditions of life and ways of knowing the world for many in society (Barrett and Boyd 2019: 9, 41, 60). Domestic pottery, while clearly not the same and falling into very distinct typological categories, nonetheless commonly shared stylistic and functional similarities during the 14th to 12th centuries BC. This included, for example, biconical urns, bowls with in-turned rims, or carinated cups with high-looping handles (Figure 7.7).

Previous work focused on the earliest Terramare, which coincided with the latest tell settlements, thereby constituting a brief window to explore interactions around 1600 to 1550 BC. This has been recognised as a brief window of changes in societies and the networks that bound them affecting many parts of Europe (Vandkilde 2014; 2016; Risch and Meller 2015). In our case, the material culture has long told another story, revealing continuing parity or coalescences between 1500 and 1150 BC. If we consider interaction to have been systematic, regular, and socially embedded, then this may help us better explain the material record. This could arguably be simply considered mobility or a form of chain migration. In either case, in our view, people moving between these regions was predictable and normal in this linked-up social world and it included people settling in communities that were distant from those into which they were born.

It is important that we do not identify dependency relationships in any of the material evidence; thus, concepts of core-periphery relationships do not appear appropriate (Sherratt 1993; Harding 2013). As a working concept, peer groups with mutually beneficial interlinkages might have connected communities from domestic to political units. In this way, similarity in material culture and social practices goes beyond aesthetic choices and may reveal ideologies reflecting mutually intelligible

CULTURE MARKERS FOR MOBILITY AND MIGRATION 159

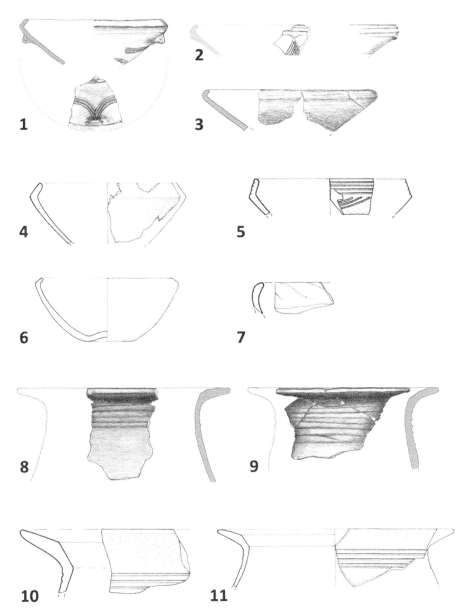

Figure 7.7 Illustration of some general similarities between ceramic forms and decoration from (1–3, 8–9) Gradište Iđoš in the Pannonian Plain (Belegiš II) and (4–7, 10–11) Casalmoro in the Po Valley (Final Bronze Age) (drawings by Dragan Jovanović and Laura Pau, with permissions)

worldviews and lifeways. The study of how interactions between these two regions related to cultural change in both of them has ranged from rare to absent since the 1960s until very recently (Mozsolics 1957; 1967; Bóna 1958; Basler *et al.* 1983; Cardarelli *et al.* 2020; Cavazzuti *et al.* 2022). This contrasts with a continuing fascination with hunting the transient and ephemeral Aegean links in recent works, making the dearth of research exploring the substantially more intense and formative links between the Pannonian Plain and Po Valley striking.

While our focus has been on these two regions, it is important to be clear that in neither case are we suggesting exclusive relationships – each was networked with other neighbours near and far also. It is nonetheless salient that the similarities discussed do not occur to the same extent in societies lying beyond the two plains. Along the Sava River – forming a conduit between the regions – settlements are smaller and ceramics generally undecorated (Karavanić 2009). Metalwork, on the other hand, is closely similar and flat cremation cemeteries are common, in urns set in both upright and inverted positions (Ložnjak Dizdar and Rajić Šikanjić 2016). In Istria, there is a dense distribution of stone-built fortifications, many of which are contemporary, though they are smaller in size. Flat cremation cemeteries are rare there and pottery is predominantly of local styles (Hänsel *et al.* 2015).

We would argue that the collapse of Middle Bronze Age systems in the Pannonian Plain and subsequent reconfiguration of Late Bronze Age societies represents the toppling of elite systems. People and macrocultural traditions continued, new ideas were introduced, and substantial changes to lifeways unfolded over the course of a century. This follows the framework of recent theoretical discourse on collapse that views such change unfolding over a multi-decadal scale (e.g. Johnson 2017; Middleton 2017). Lineages and even communities which had benefited from the Middle Bronze Age system appear to have been gradually disenfranchised by a new order which integrated existing and recently arrived groups. While some were integrated, others sought their fortunes elsewhere, and one place was the Po Valley following 'pre-existing corridors' (Cardarelli 2020: 233, 234). The genetic data available to date are too few to demonstrate this, though they certainly fit with such a scenario (Saupe *et al.* 2021). The Middle Bronze Age groups of the Pannonian Plain had lived in riverine networks and we find a similar context in the Po Valley – what Vanzetti (2013: 279) called the introduction of 'a settling strategy highly suited to the alluvial plain management'. In such a model, immigrant groups would have formed a minority component in communities, while they also retained social links with the Pannonian Plain. Over time and generations, this relationship continued and developed promoting the *homophily* recognised by Cavazzuti *et al.* (2022). We might even see in such a network that regular mobility of people can become a fundamental component of the functioning of each society, whether that be marriage or fostering of children, for example (Kristiansen and Larsson 2005: 236–40).

We therefore consider a variety of social venues for interaction driving these similarities. This would include the exchange of Alpine metals into the river networks of the Balkan-Carpathian zone (Gavranović *et al.* 2022), mobility for marriage, mobility of craftworkers (even as 'objects' of exchange or patronage), and the maintenance of family and community bonds. We also recognise that warriors – fundamental elements of Bronze Age societies – were mobile, as visible in the co-evolution of the hardware and associated martial art traditions of combat (Kristiansen and Suchowska-Ducke 2015). It remains plausible that intimate connections across multiple aspects of society continued over centuries without personal mobility, but given how much of society is implicated and that the materials in question are not restricted to high-value commodities, this is a less attractive scenario to us.

Despite similarities, the differences are generally sufficient to rule out mobility of craftworkers as explaining this confluence (for example, following Anthony's [1997: 26] model of 'career migration'). The mechanism underlying this transcultural spread, we would argue, was people moving with knowledge of the forms and aesthetics of vessels which craftworkers interpreted, giving rise to similarities but not sameness. Particular social worlds were being constructed through this use of material culture which were relevant in both distinct regions in their own ways. The dearth of identified imported ceramic vessels is certainly relevant, because any argument for emulation of frequently seen imports would lack material support. It is also crucial to note the transmission of intangible ideologies conveyed through the material culture, settlement design, and mortuary practice we have discussed.

We tentatively identify two points in time when interactions may have intensified. The first is the much-discussed 1600 BC horizon (Meller *et al.* 2015). The second is around 1200 BC – a potential end point for the TSG sites and the beginning of the period of crisis which engulfed the Po Valley (Molloy 2022). After 1600 BC, there was increased influence from pottery styles and mortuary practices, and some metalwork forms, from the Pannonian Plain visible in the Po Valley. It is also a time of substantial settlement growth in both areas. A similar expansion of influences from Pannonian Plain traditions in this post-collapse period after 1200 BC is seen in other regions. This includes the introduction of idiosyncratic elements of pottery styles to settlements in the Morava and Vardar/Axios Valleys and northern Greece at this time, as well as into the fringes of the Eastern Alps and even into Poland to the north (Bulatović 2007; Przybyła 2010; Ruppenstein 2020; Bulatović *et al.* 2021).

We are confronted with the need, on the one hand, to explain depopulation of the Pannonian Plain and its megasites during the 1200 BC horizon, and on the other, the spread of material culture indicative of the area's influence after this collapse had happened. As Cardarelli *et al.* (2020) argued for the 1600 BC horizon, there is a strong case to be made for directional movement of people through existing networks following established diplomatic relations and using buffering mechanisms of political relationships to deal with crises. The abandonment of megasites and cemeteries around 1200 BC must be regarded as just that – a human crisis – and while we suggest people moved along established networks, we have no idea about the reception or the local impacts of such movements. It certainly would seem appropriate to view such movements as disruptive. Whether the Po Valley was a further target of these outward migrations from the Pannonian Plain *c*. 1250–1200 BC, and prior to the crises engulfing the Po Valley *c*. 1200–1150 BC, remains to be seen and may even be accessible through genetic research.

We have out of necessity prioritised discussion of Pannonian Plain influences in the Po Valley due to the state of current research. In this brief overview, the general trends in ceramics and mortuary practices which were shared appeared first in the Pannonian Plain. On the other hand, it is clear that metalwork styles, and indeed metal as a raw material, coming from and through the Po Valley, were brought to the Pannonian Plain. The developments in settlement systems, on current evidence, are virtually synchronous. As more refined chronologies and new excavations begin to change our knowledge of the Late Bronze Age settlement in the Pannonian Plain, revisiting themes touched on in this chapter will no doubt be required.

Conclusion

It has long been clear that similarities in pottery styles and metalwork connected the Po Valley and Pannonian Plain around the 16th century BC. Similarities in mortuary practices have recently been elaborated upon by Cardarelli *et al.* (2020) and Cavazzuti *et al.* (2022), and further observations have been made above. The important contribution that settlement archaeology can make to investigating societal similarities in the Po Valley and Pannonian Plain between 1600 and 1150 BC has been reviewed for the first time in this chapter. This has enabled an expansion in how we compare social conditions, and in so doing, the role of mobility within and between the two areas. We have argued that there was sustained mobility through regularised and predictable networks. This allowed cultural ideas to flow unimpeded across multiple centuries, so that the societies of the Po Valley and Pannonian Plain, particularly the south-east, continually influenced each other. There were punctuations between 1600 and 1500 BC and between 1250 and 1150 BC which demonstrate that mobility, even when regularised, was also shaped by larger historical forces. Even when it appears regular, the ebbs and flows reveal the particularly historical circumstances of each society at any given time.

As we conclude, it is clear that further palaeogenetic research is needed to better explore the balance between the mobility of people, things, and ideas. This will no doubt enhance the kind of comparative regional analyses explored in this chapter. With regard to stable isotope research into mobility, it is unfortunate that baseline strontium isotopes values for each area are so similar because this all but excludes this means to assess mobility between these areas (Cavazzuti *et al.* 2019b; Giblin *et al.* 2019). Our hope in better understanding personal mobility lies with aDNA studies currently under way on the few available and relevant inhumations. It will be fundamental for such palaeogenetic work to draw upon bioarchaeological, contextual, and material culture

CULTURE MARKERS FOR MOBILITY AND MIGRATION

data to best explore how particular signatures of individual mobility articulate with societal norms or ideologies (Furholt 2018; Gregoricka 2021).

The clear challenge for future research is to disaggregate modes of mobility and/ or migration as we seek to define the intensity, tempo, and phasing of relationships which clearly linked the people of the Pannonian Plain and Po Valley in the 2nd millennium BC. Indeed, it is a particularly relevant case study for assessing the relative value of mobility and migration as terms for explaining cultural and demic entanglements. Our new knowledge of settlement archaeology has enabled a more holistic comparison of the societal norms and beliefs in both areas that complements what we have learned through material culture studies. Whether new genetic evidence points towards brief migration events, systemic mobility, or neither of these, the interpretative doors those new data open or shut will undoubtedly be instrumental for better understanding why these two societies shared so much in common despite their distance apart.

Acknowledgements

This research is being conducted as part of 'The Fall of 1200 BC' project funded through an ERC Consolidator Grant (GA #772753). We are grateful to Miroslav Birclin, Lidija Milašinović, Aleksandar Šalamon, Neda Mirković Marić, and Miroslav Marić for advice and assistance during fieldwork related to this chapter. We thank Francesco Iacono and Laura Pau for comments on the text. Our thanks to the anonymous reviewers and to the editors for suggestions to help improve our manuscript. Thanks also to Sara Nylund for her illustration contributions and for permission from Laura Pau and Andrea Cardarelli to reproduce images.

References

Anthony, D.W. (1997), 'Prehistoric migration as social process', in J. Chapman and H. Hamerow (eds), *Migrations and Invasions in Archaeological Explanation* (Oxford, Archaeopress), 21–32.

Barrett, J.C. and Boyd, M.J. (2019), *From Stonehenge to Mycenae: The Challenges of Archaeological Interpretation* (London, Bloomsbury Publishing).

Basler, D., Alojz, B., Gabrovec, S., Garašanin, M., Tasić, N., *et al.* (1983), *Praistorija Jugoslavenskih Zemalja IV: Bronzana Doba*, *Vol. IV* (Sarajevo, Svjetlost OOUR Izdavačka djelatnost).

Bianco Peroni, V., Peroni, R., and Vanzetti, A. (2010), *La necropoli del Bronzo finale di Pianello di Genga* (Firenze, All'Insegna del Giglio).

Blake, E. (2014), *Social Networks and Regional Identity in Bronze Age Italy* (Cambridge, Cambridge University Press).

Bóna, I. (1958), 'Die Chronologie der Hortfunde vom Koszider Typus', *Acta Archaeologica Academiae Scientiarum Hungaricae*, 9: 213–43.

Brück, J. (2021), 'Ancient DNA, kinship and relational identities in Bronze Age Britain', *Antiquity*, 95(379): 228–37.

Bukvić, L. (2000), *Kanelovana keramika Gava kompleksa u Banatu* (Novi Sad, Serbian Academy of Sciences and Arts).

Bulatović, A. (2007), 'South Morava Basin in the transitional period from the Bronze to the Iron Age', *Starinar*, 57: 57–82.

Bulatović, A., Molloy, B., and Filipović, V. (2021), 'The Balkan-Aegean migrations revisited: changes in material culture and settlement patterns in the Late Bronze Age Central Balkans in the light of new data', *Starinar*, 71: 61–105.

Capuzzo, G., Zanon, M., Corso, M.D., Kirleis, W., and Barceló, J.A. (2018), 'Highly diverse Bronze Age population dynamics in Central-Southern Europe and their response to regional climatic patterns', *PLoS ONE*, 13(8): e0200709, DOI: 10.1371/journal. pone.0200709.

Cardarelli, A. (2009), 'The collapse of the Terramare culture and growth of new economic and social system during the Late Bronze Age in Italy', in A. Cardarelli, A. Cazella, M. Frangipane, and R. Peroni (eds), *Atti del convegno internazionale 'Le ragioni del cambiamento/Reasons for Change'*, Roma, 15–17 Giugno 2006 (Rome, Quasar), 449–519.

Cardarelli, A. (2014), *La necropoli della terramara di Casinalbo* (Sesto Fiorentino, All'Insegna del Giglio).

Cardarelli, A. (2018), 'Before the city: the last villages and proto-urban centres between the Po and Tiber Rivers', in M. Frangipane and L. Manzanilla (eds), *Rethinking Urbanization and its Living Landscapes from the Inspiring Perspective of a Great 'Maestro'* (Rome, Gangemi Editore), 359–82.

Cardarelli, A. (2020), 'The horizontal and vertical egalitarian systems in the vision of Marcella Frangipane: a comparison with the Terramare society of the Po valley (Italy)', in F. Balossi Restelli, A. Cardarelli, G. Di Nocera, L. Manzanilla, L. Mori, *et al.* (eds), *Pathways through Arslantepe: Essays in Honour of Marcella Frangipane* (Viterbo, Edizioni Sette Città), 53–62.

Cardarelli, A., Cavazzuti, C., Fritzl, M., Gavranović, M., Hajdu, T., *et al.* (2020), 'The connections between the plains of the Po and the Danube during the Bronze Age seen through the spread of the "urnfield model"', *Rivista di Scienze Preistoriche*, 70(21): 231–43.

Cavazzuti, C. and Arena, A. (2020), 'Bioarchaeology of social stratification in Bronze Age Italy', *Arheo*, 37: 68–105.

Cavazzuti, C., Cardarelli, A., Quondam, F., Salzani, L., Ferrante, M., *et al.* (2019a), 'Mobile elites at Frattesina: flows of people in a Late Bronze Age "port of trade" in northern Italy', *Antiquity*, 93(369): 624–44.

Cavazzuti, C., Skeates, R., Millard, A.R., Nowell, G., Peterkin, J., *et al.* (2019b), 'Flows of people in villages and large centres in Bronze Age Italy through strontium and oxygen isotopes', *PLoS ONE*, 14(1): e0209693, DOI: 10.1371/journal.pone.0209693.

Cavazzuti, C., Hajdu, T., Lugli, F., Sperduti, A., Vicze, M., *et al.* (2021), 'Human mobility in a Bronze Age Vatya "urnfield" and the life history of a high-status woman', *PLoS ONE*, 16(7): e0254360, DOI: 10.1371/journal.pone.0254360.

Cavazzuti, C., Arena, A., Cardarelli, A., Fritzl, M., Gavranović, M., *et al.* (2022), 'The First 'Urnfields' in the Plains of the Danube and the Po', *Journal of World Prehistory*, 35: 45–86.

Clark, G. (1966), 'The invasion hypothesis in British archaeology', *Antiquity*, 11: 172–89.

Cowen, J.D. (1966), 'The origins of the flange-hilted sword of Bronze in continental Europe', *Proceedings of the Prehistoric Society*, 32: 362–412.

Coxon, S. (2018), 'Variability in the *chaîne opératoire*: the case of Belegiš cremation vessels', in L. Jørgensen, J. Sofaer, and M. Sørensen (eds), *Creativity in the Bronze Age: Understanding Innovation in Pottery, Textile, and Metalwork Production* (Cambridge, Cambridge University Press), 107–14.

Cupitò, M. and Leonardi, G. (2015), 'Il Veneto tra Bronzo antico e Bronzo recente', in G. Leonardi and V. Tinè (eds), *Preistoria e protostoria del Veneto* (Firenze, Istituto Italiano di Preistoria e Protostoria), 201–39.

Cupitò, M., Dalla Longa, E., Donadel, V., and Leonardi, G. (2012), 'Resistances to the 12th century BC crisis in the Veneto region: the case studies of Fondo Paviani and Montebello Vicentino', in J. Kneisel, W. Kirleis, M. Dal Corso, N. Taylor, and V. Tiedtke (eds), *Collapse and Continuity? Environment and Development of Bronze Age Human Landscapes* (Bonn, Habelt), 55–70.

Dalla Longa, E. (2019), 'Settlement dynamics and territorial organization in the Middle and Low Veneto Plain south of the ancient Adige River in the Bronze Age', *Preihstoria Alpina*, 49: 95–121.

Dalla Longa, E., Dal Corso, M., Vicenzutto, D., Nicosia, C., and Cupitò, M. (2019), 'The Bronze Age settlement of Fondo Paviani (Italy) in its territory. Hydrography, settlement distribution, environment and in-site analysis', *Journal of Archaeological Science: Reports*, 28: 102018, DOI: 10.1016/j.jasrep.2019.102018.

Danckers, J. (2017), 'Back to epistemological basics: a critical historiography of the origins of the Terramare', *World Archaeology*, 49(2): 211–25.

Dani, J., Fischl, K.P., Kulcsár, G., Szeverényi, V., and Kiss, V. (2019), 'Dividing space, dividing society: fortified settlements in the Carpathian Basin (*c.* 2300–1500 BC)', in H. Meller, S. Friedrich, M. Küßner, H. Stäuble, and R. Risch (eds), *Late Neolithic and Early Bronze Age Settlement Archaeology* (Halle/Saale, Landesmuseums für Vorgeschichte), 851–68.

Dawson, H. and Iacono, F. (eds) (2021), *Bridging Social and Geographical Space Through Networks* (Leiden, Sidestone Press).

De Marinis, G. (2009). 'Continuity and discontinuity in northern Italy from the Recent to the Final Bronze Age: a view from north-western Italy', in A. Cardarelli, A. Cazella, M. Frangipane, and R. Peroni (eds), *Atti del convegno internazionale 'Le ragioni del cambiamento/Reasons for Change'*, Roma, 15–17 Giugno 2006 (Rome, Quasar), 535–45.

Dietrich, L. (2015), 'A new world order: the spread of channelled ware in Late Bronze Age and Early Iron Age Transylvannia', in P. Suchowska-Ducke, S. Scott Reiter, and H. Vandkilde (eds), *Forging Identities: The Mobility of Culture in Bronze Age Europe* (Oxford, BAR Publishing), 165–73.

Duffy, P.R., Parditka, G.M., Giblin, J.I., and Paja, L. (2019), 'The problem with tells: lessons learned from absolute dating of Bronze Age mortuary ceramics in Hungary', *Antiquity*, 93(367): 63–79.

Earle, T. and Kristiansen, K. (eds) (2010), *Organizing Bronze Age Societies: The Mediterranean, Central Europe, and Scandinavia Compared* (Cambridge, Cambridge University Press).

Fischl, K., Kiss, V., Kulcsár, G., and Szeverényi, V. (2013), 'Transformations in the Carpathian Basin around 1600 BC', in H. Meller, F. Bertemes, H.-R. Bork, and R. Risch (eds), *1600 – Kultureller Umbruch im Schatten des Thera-Ausbruchs?* (Halle/Saale, Landesamt für Denkmalpflege und Archäologie Sachsen-Anhalt), 355–71.

Frieman, C.J. and Hofmann, D. (2019), 'Present pasts in the archaeology of genetics, identity, and migration in Europe: a critical essay', *World Archaeology*, 51(4): 528–45.

Furholt, M. (2018), 'Massive migrations? The impact of recent aDNA studies on our view of third millennium Europe', *European Journal of Archaeology*, 21(2): 159–91.

Gavranović, M., Mehofer, M., Kapuran, A., Koledin, J., Mitrović, J., *et al.* (2022), 'Emergence of monopoly – copper exchange networks during the Late Bronze Age in the western and central Balkans', *PLoS ONE*, 17(3): e0263823.

Giblin, J. (2020), *Isotope Analysis on the Great Hungarian Plain: An Exploration of Mobility and Subsistence Strategies from the Neolithic to the Copper Age* (Budapest, Archaeolingua).

Giblin, J., Ayala, D., Czene, A., Csányi, M., Dani, J., *et al.* (2019), 'Bronze Age burials from the Carpathian Basin: New isotope results', Society for American Archaeology, 84th Annual Meeting, Albuquerque, New Mexico, 10–14 April, 2019 (unpublished poster).

Gogâltan, F. and Stavilă, A. (2021), 'The Late Bronze Age settlement from Giroc (Timiş County): the 1992–3 archaeological excavations', *Ziridava Studia Archaeologica*, 34: 189–242.

Gogâltan, F., Cordoş, C., and Ignat, A. (2014), *Bronze Age Tell, Tell-like and Mound-Like Settlements on the Eastern Frontier of the Carpathian Basin: History of Research* (Cluj-Napoca, Editura MEGA).

Gregoricka, L.A. (2021), 'Moving forward: a bioarchaeology of mobility and migration', *Journal of Archaeological Research*, 29: 581–635.

Hänsel, B., Mihovilić, K., and Teržan, B. (2015), *Monkodonja 1: Forschungen zu einer protourbanen Siedlung der Bronzezeit Istriens* (Pula, Arheološki Muzej Istre).

Hahn, H. and Weiss, H. (2013), 'Introduction: biographies, travels and itineraries of things', in H. Hahn and H. Weiss (eds), *Mobility, Meaning and the Transformations of Things: Shifting Contexts of Material Culture through Time and Space* (Oxford, Oxbow), 1–14.

Harding, A. (2013), 'World systems, cores and peripheries in prehistoric Europe', *European Journal of Archaeology*, 16(3): 378–400.

Heeb, B.S., Szentmiklosi, A., Bălărie, A., Lehmpuhl, R., and Krause, R. (2017), 'Corneşti-Iarcuri – 10 years of research (2007–2016): some important preliminary results', in B.S. Heeb, A. Szentmiklosi, R. Krause, and M. Wemhoff (eds), *Fortifications: Rise and Fall of Defended Sites in the Late Bronze and Early Iron Age of South-East Europe* (Berlin, Staatliche Museen zu Berlin), 217–28.

Heyd, V. (2017), 'Kossinna's smile', *Antiquity*, 91(356): 348–59.

Hofmann, D. (2019), 'Commentary: archaeology, archaeogenetics and theory – challenges and convergences', *Current Swedish Archaeology*, 27(1): 133–40.

Iacono, F. (2019), *The Archaeology of Late Bronze Age Interaction and Mobility at the Gates of Europe: People, Things and Networks around the Southern Adriatic Sea* (London, Bloomsbury Publishing).

Iacono, F., Borgna, E., Cattani, M., Cavazzuti, C., Dawson, H., *et al.* (2021), 'Establishing the Middle Sea: the Late Bronze Age of Mediterranean Europe (1700–900 BC)', *Journal of Archaeological Research*, DOI:10.1007/s10814-021-09165-1.

Iaia, C. (2015), 'Ricerche sugli strumenti da metallurgo nella protostoria dell'Italia settentrionale: Gli utensili a percussione', *Padusa*, 50: 69–109.

Ialongo, N. (2018), 'Crisis and recovery: the cost of sustainable development in Nuragic Sardinia', *European Journal of Archaeology*, 21(1): 18–38.

Jankovits, K. (2017), 'Kurd-type situlas: evidence for Late Bronze Age connections between the Carpathian Basin and northern Italy', in G. Kulcsár and G.V. Szabó (eds), *State of the Hungarian Bronze Age Research* (Budapest, Hungarian Academy of Sciences), 447–62.

Johnson, S.A. (2017), *Why Did Ancient Civilizations Fail?* (New York, Routledge).

Karavanić, S. (2009), *The Urnfield Culture in Continental Croatia* (Oxford, Archaeopress).

Kienlin, T. (2020), *Bronze Age Tell Communities in Context – An Exploration into Culture, Society, and the Study of European Prehistory. Part 2: Practice. The Social, Space, and Materiality.* (Oxford, Archaeopress).

Kienlin, T., Fischl, K., and Marta, L. (2017), 'Exploring divergent trajectories in Bronze Age landscapes: tell settlement in the Hungarian Borsod Plain and the Romanian Ier Valley', *Ziridava Studia Archaeologica*, 31: 93–129.

Knappett, C. (2013), 'Introduction: why networks', in C. Knappett (ed), *Network Analysis in Archaeology: New Approaches to Regional Interaction* (Oxford, Oxford University Press), 3–16.

Knappett, C. and Kiriatzi, E. (2017), 'Technological mobilities: perspectives from the Eastern Mediterranean – an introduction', in E. Kiriatzi and C. Knappett (eds) *Human Mobility and Technological Transfer in the Prehistoric Mediterranean* (Cambridge, Cambridge University Press), 1–17.

Kristiansen, K. (2014), 'Towards a new paradigm? The Third Science Revolution and its possible consequences in archaeology', *Current Swedish Archaeology*, 22: 11–34.

Kristiansen, K. and Larsson, T.B. (2005), *The Rise of Bronze Age Society: Travels, Transmissions and Transformations* (Cambridge, Cambridge University Press).

Kristiansen, K. and Suchowska-Ducke, P. (2015), 'Connected histories: the dynamics of Bronze Age interaction and trade 1500–1100 BC', *Proceedings of the Prehistoric Society*, 81: 361–92.

Kristiansen, K., Allentoft, M.E., Frei, K.M., Iversen, R., Johannsen, N.N., *et al.* (2017), 'Re-theorising mobility and the formation of culture and language among the Corded Ware culture in Europe', *Antiquity*, 91(356): 334–47.

Ložnjak Dizdar, D. (2014), 'South-eastern periphery of the Urnfield culture? The Croatian perspective', in D. Ložnjak Dizdar and M. Dizdar (eds), *The Beginning of the Late Bronze Age between the Eastern Alps and the Danube* (Zagreb, Institut za arheologiju), 235–48.

Ložnjak Dizdar, D. and Rajić Šikanjić, P. (2016), 'Funerary practices at the end of the Late Bronze Age in the southern Middle Danube Region', in V. Sîrbu, M. Jevtić, K. Dmitrović, and M. Ljuština (eds), *Funerary Practices during the Bronze and Iron Ages in Central and Southeast Europe* (Belgrade/Čačak, University of Belgrade Faculty of Philosophy and National Museum Čačak), 109–26.

Medović, P. (2007), *Stubarlija – nekropola naselja Feudvar* (Novi Sad, Muzej Vojvodine).

Middleton, G.D. (2017), *Understanding Collapse: Ancient History and Modern Myths* (Cambridge, Cambridge University Press).

Milleker, B. (1905), 'A Vattinai östelep', *Történelmi és régészeti értesitö*, XXI: 1–75.

Molloy, B. (2016a), 'Nought may endure but mutability: intercultural encounters and material transformations in the thirteenth to eleventh century BC Southeast Europe', in B. Molloy (ed), *Of Odysseys and Oddities: Scales and Modes of Interaction in the Prehistoric Aegean* (Oxford, Oxbow), 343–84.

Molloy, B. (2016b), 'Introduction: thinking of scales and modes of interaction in prehistory', in B. Molloy (ed), *Of Odysseys and Oddities: Scales and Modes of Interaction in the Prehistoric Aegean* (Oxford, Oxbow), 1–24.

Molloy, B. (2022), 'Was there a 3.2 ka crisis in Europe? A Critical comparison of climatic, environmental, and archaeological evidence for radical change during the Bronze Age–Iron Age transition', *Journal of Archaeological Research*, DOI: 10.1007/s10814-022-09176-6.

Molloy, B., Jovanović, D., Bruyère, C., Marić, M., Bulatović, J., *et al.* (2020), 'A new Bronze Age mega-fort in southeastern Europe: recent archaeological investigations at Gradište Iđoš and their regional significance', *Journal of Field Archaeology*, 45(4): 293–314.

Mozsolics, A. (1957), 'Archäologische Beiträge zur Geschichte der großen Wanderung', *Acta Archaeologica Academiae Scientiarum Hungaricae*, 8: 119–56.

Mozsolics, A. (1967), *Bronzefunde des Karpatenbeckens: Depotfundhorizonte von Hajdúsámson und Kosziderpadlás* (Budapest, Akadémiai kiadó).

Németi, J. and Molnár, Z. (2012), *Bronzkori hatalmi központok Északnyugat-Erdélyben: A Nagykároly-Bobáld* (Szeged, Szegedi Tudományegyetem Régészeti Tanszék).

Neumann, D. (2009), 'Bemerkungen zu den Schwertern der Typenfamilie Sauerbrunn-Boiu-Keszthely', in J.M. Bagley, C. Eggl, D. Neumann, and M. Schefzik (eds), *Alpen, Kult und Eisenzeit: Festschrift für Amei Lang zum 65. Geburtstag* (Rahden/Westf., Verlag Marie Leidorf), 97–114.

Nicodemus, A. and O'Shea, J. (2019), '"the nearest run thing...": the genesis and collapse of a Bronze Age polity in the Maros Valley of southeastern Europe', in A. Gyucha (ed), *Coming Together: Comparative Approaches to Population Aggregation and Early Urbanization* (New York, SUNY Press), 61–80.

Panagiotopoulos, D. (2012), 'Encountering the foreign: (de-)constructing alterity in the archaeologies of the Bronze Age Mediterranean', in J. Maran and P.W. Stockhammer (eds), *Materiality and Social Practice: The Transformative Capacities of Intercultural Encounters* (Oxford, Oxbow), 51–61.

Pau, L. (2020), *The Final Bronze Age Settlement of Casalmoro (Mantua, Italy): Finds and Chronology* (Oxford, BAR Publishing).

Pearce, M. (2013), 'The spirit of the sword and spear', *Cambridge Archaeological Journal*, 23(1): 55–67.

Pigorini, L. (1909), 'I primi abitatori dell'Italia', *Nuova Antologia*, 144: 277–97.

Przybyła, M. (2010), 'Pottery analyses as the basis for studying migrations: the case of Danubian Pottery groups from the end of 2nd millennium BC', in K. Dzięgielewski, M.S. Przybyła, and A. Gawlik (eds), *Migration in Bronze and Early Iron Age Europe* (Kraków, Księgarnia Akademicka), 87–104.

Radivojević, M., Roberts, B.W., Pernicka, E., Stos-Gale, Z., Martinón-Torres, M., *et al.* (2019), 'The provenance, use, and circulation of metals in the European Bronze Age: the state of debate', *Journal of Archaeological Research*, 27: 131–85.

Risch, R. and Meller, H. (2015), 'Change and continuity in Europe and the Mediterranean around 1600 BC', *Proceedings of the Prehistoric Society*, 81: 239–64.

Roberts, C.N., Woodbridge, J., Palmisano, A., Bevan, A., Fyfe, R., *et al.* (2019), 'Mediterranean landscape change during the Holocene: synthesis, comparison and regional trends in population, land cover and climate', *Holocene*, 29(5): 923–37.

Ruppenstein, F. (2020), 'Migration events in Greece at the end of the second millennium BC and their possible Balkanic background', in J. Maran, R. Băjenaru, S.-C. Ailincăi, A.-D. Popescu, and S. Hansen (eds), *Objects, Ideas and Travelers: Contacts between the Balkans, the Aegean and Western Anatolia during the Bronze and Early Iron Age* (Bonn, Habelt), 107–22.

Salzani, L. (1994), 'Nogara. Rinvenimento di un ripostiglio di bronzi in località "Pila del Brancón"', *Quaderni di Archeologia del Veneto*, 10: 83–94.

Saupe, T., Montinaro, F., Scaggion, C., Carrara, N., Kivisild, T., *et al.* (2021), 'Ancient genomes reveal structural shifts after the arrival of steppe-related ancestry in the Italian Peninsula', *Current Biology*, 31(12): 2576–91.

Sava, V. (2020), 'The Late Bronze Age pottery in the South-Eastern Carpathian Basin', *Slovenská archeológia*, 68(2): 253–96.

Sava, V., Gogâltan, F., and Krause, R. (2019), 'First steps in the dating of the Bronze Age mega-fort in Sântana-Cetatea Veche (southwestern Romania)', in R. Krause and S. Hansen (eds), *Bronze Age Fortresses in Europe* (Bonn, Habelt), 161–77.

Sherratt, A. (1993), 'What would a Bronze Age world system look like? Relations between temperate Europe and the Mediterranean in later prehistory', *Journal of European Archaeology*, 1(2): 1–57.

Sherratt, S. (2010), 'The Aegean and the wider world: some thoughts on a world systems perspective', in W.A. Parkinson and M.L. Galaty (eds), *Archaic State Interaction: The Eastern Mediterranean in the Bronze Age* (Santa Fe, SAR Press), 81–197.

Sofaer, J., Bender Jorgensen, L., and Choyke, A. (2013), 'Craft production: ceramics, textiles, and bone', in A. Harding and H. Fokkens (eds), *The Oxford Handbook of the European Bronze Age* (Oxford, Oxford University Press), 469–91.

Stig Sørensen, M.L. and Rebay-Salisbury, K. (2008), 'Landscapes of the body: burials of the Middle Bronze Age in Hungary', *European Journal of Archaeology*, 11(1): 49–74.

Szentmiklosi, A. (2009), *Settlements of the Cruceni-Belegiš Culture in the Romanian Banat*, Unpublished PhD thesis (Alba Iulia, University of Alba Iulia).

Szeverényi, V., Czukor, P., Priskin, A., and Szalontai, C. (2017), 'Recent work on Late Bronze Age fortified settlements in south-east Hungary', in B.S. Heeb, A. Szentmiklosi, R. Krause, and M. Wemhoff (eds), *Fortifications: Rise and Fall of Defended Sites in the Late Bronze and Early Iron Age of South-East Europe* (Berlin, Staatliche Museen zu Berlin), 135–48.

Tasić, N. (2004), 'Historical development of Bronze Age cultures in Vojvodina', *Starinar*, 53/54: 23–34.

Todorović, J. (1977), *The Prehistoric Karaburma II* (Belgrade, City of Belgrade Museum).

Vander Linden, M. (2016), 'Population history in third-millennium-BC Europe: assessing the contribution of genetics', *World Archaeology*, 48: 714–28.

Vandkilde, H. (2014), 'Breakthrough of the Nordic Bronze Age: transcultural warriorhood and a Carpathian crossroad in the sixteenth century BC', *European Journal of Archaeology*, 17: 602–33.

Vandkilde, H. (2016), 'Bronzization: the Bronze Age as pre-modern globalization', *Praehistorische Zeitschrift*, 91: 103–23.

Vanzetti, A. (2013), '1600? The rise of the Terramara system (northern Italy)', in H. Meller, F. Bertemes, H.-R. Bork, and R. Risch (eds), *1600 – Kultureller Umbruch im Schatten des Thera-Ausbruchs?* (Halle/Saale, Landesamt für Denkmalpflege und Archäologie Sachsen-Anhalt), 267–82.

Vinski-Gasparini, K. (1973), *Kultura polja sa žarama u sjevernoj Hrvatskoj* (Zagreb, Filozofski fakultet).

8

Mobility at the Onset of the Bronze Age: A Bioarchaeological Perspective

PHILIPP W. STOCKHAMMER AND KEN MASSY

Introduction

WHEN JOHANNES KRAUSE and the first author of this chapter applied for their collaborative WIN programme[1] research project 'Times of Upheaval: Changes of Society and Landscape at the Beginning of the Bronze Age', neither the genetic transformations of the 3rd millennium BC were known nor was the possibility to generate large-scale full-genomic evidence foreseeable. Back then, the aim of our project was to add complexity to our understanding of the Late Neolithic to Early Bronze Age transition by zooming in to micro-regional developments. For many decades, researchers have proposed the transition from the Neolithic to the Bronze Age in Central Europe during the 3rd and early 2nd millennia BC as a linear process following the basic notion of Paul Reinecke's chronology (1902; 1924). It was often assumed that the novel bronze technology was initially adopted in different regions at around the same time and then increasingly mastered, whereby hammered metal objects with a low content of tin were subsequently replaced by cast metal objects with higher amounts of tin. Whereas this linear and evolutionist understanding of technological development has raised criticism for decades (Pare 2000; Kienlin 2008; 2010; Strahm 2009), we were convinced that only large series of radiocarbon datasets for the 3rd and 2nd millennium BC combined with a micro-regional perspective would enable us to clarify some of these issues.

The main region we chose for our study was a small section of the Lech Valley south of Augsburg (Bavaria) (Figure 8.1) with its rich, recently excavated but by then still unpublished corpus of 33 cemeteries with altogether *c.* 450 individuals from the Corded Ware complex to the early Middle Bronze Age. Ten years later,

---

[1] Junior staff development: www.hadw-bw.de/en/young-academy/win-kolleg (accessed 6 October 2022).

Proceedings of the British Academy, **254**, 170–188, © The British Academy 2023.

MOBILITY AT THE ONSET OF THE BRONZE AGE 171

our project has turned the Lech Valley into one of the most intensively and comprehensively studied prehistoric landscapes in Europe, and our study has become a pioneer with regard to the integration of archaeological and bioarchaeological datasets. Meanwhile, most of our project results have been published in articles focusing on different aspects of chronology, mobility, social structure, and health (Krause and Stockhammer 2014; 2015; Stockhammer *et al.* 2015a; 2015b; 2018; Mittnik and Stockhammer 2016; 2017; Andrades Valtueña *et al.* 2017; Knipper *et al.* 2017; Massy *et al.* 2017; Olalde *et al.* 2018; Massy and Stockhammer 2019; Mittnik *et al.* 2019; Stockhammer in press). Based on the project, the computer game BRONZEON was created in 2019 to communicate our results to a young audience and has been integrated into high school teaching in Bavaria (Stockhammer 2020). Moreover, all Early Bronze Age and early Middle Bronze Age burials were published in a detailed monograph presenting the archaeological and anthropological analyses (Massy 2018). Only our extensive metal analyses, as well as datasets on stable carbon and nitrogen isotopes, remain unpublished. However, the nature of article-based, subsequent publications has prevented us from fully integrating all these studies into a comprehensive picture which entangles the different methodological approaches. We will fill this gap in this chapter by integrating previously published individual results, but without repeating all the state-of-the-art, methodological issues, and discussions that we have presented in our aforementioned publications. Moreover, we want to go beyond our previous conclusions by proposing further interpretations for the (bio)archaeological evidence, which, due to their more hypothetical nature, have not been introduced in our previous publications.

In this chapter, we will first give an overview of the geographical and temporal frame and the correlation of archaeological phenomena and radiocarbon dates. We will then present our insights into human mobility and social structures in the Lech Valley during this time period and discuss issues of health. Finally, we will reflect upon the end of the Lech Valley Early Bronze Age society around 1550 cal BC.

Geographical frame and settlement structure

The region under study is situated in the territory, and south of the present-day city, of Augsburg in the Lech Valley in Bavaria, southern Germany. It roughly measures 20 km by 6 km. The Lech River originates in Vorarlberg in the Northern Alps and runs from south to north through southern Bavaria until it flows into the Danube River. The Lech Valley south of Augsburg is characterised by a broad and extremely fertile loess terrace in the centre of the valley. The Lech River runs to its east, the Wertach River to its west, and the latter joins the Lech just a few kilometres to the north of Augsburg city centre. The fertility of the loess terrace resulted in its agricultural use until the present day, whereas the accompanying settlements have always been situated at the terrace's border on the gravel plain between the rivers

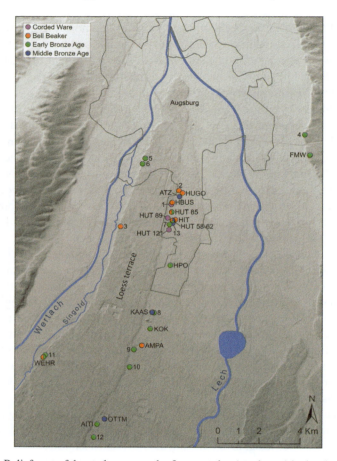

Figure 8.1 Relief map of the study area south of present-day Augsburg (city borders marked by black line) showing cemeteries of the Final Neolithic to early Middle Bronze Age in the Lech Valley (© Ken Massy).

Note: sites labelled with abbreviations were sampled (at least for radiocarbon dating) within the WIN project. **Corded Ware complex**: HUT 89=Haunstetten-Unterer Talweg 89, HUT 121= Haunstetten-Unterer Talweg 121. **Bell Beaker complex**: HUGO=Augsburg-Hugo-Eckener-Straße, HBUS=Haunstetten-Bürgermeister-Ulrich-Straße, HUT 85=Haunstetten-Unterer Talweg 85, HIT= Haunstetten-Im Tal 6, HUT 58–62=Haunstetten-Unterer Talweg 58–62, AMPA=Königsbrunn-Ampack, WEHR=Wehringen-Hochfeld. **Early Bronze Age**: FMW=Friedberg-Metzgerwäldchen, HUT 85=Haunstetten-Unterer Talweg 85, HUT 58–62=Haunstetten-Unterer Talweg 58–62, HPO= Haunstetten-Postillionstraße, KOK=Königsbrunn-Obere Kreuzstraße, WEHR=Wehringen-Hochfeld, AITI=Kleinaitingen-Gewerbegebiet Nord. **Middle Bronze Age**: ATZ=Augsburg-Technologiezentrum, HUT 58–62=Haunstetten-Unterer Talweg 58–62, KAAS=Königsbrunn-Afra- und Augustusstraße, OTTM=Oberottmarshausen-Kiesgrube Lauter. **Sites not sampled in the project**: 1=Haunstetten-Bürgermeister-Ulrich-Strasse 100 (Siemens), 2=Augsburg-Universität, 3=Inningen-Libellenweg, 4= Friedberg-Rathaus, 5=Göggingen-Richard-Wagner-Straße, 6=Göggingen-Gerhard-Hauptmann-Straße, 7=Haunstetten-Unterer Talweg 109–113, 8=Königsbrunn-Simpertstrasse, 9=Königsbrunn-Oberes Feld, 10=Königsbrunn-Kiesgrube Burkhart, 11=Wehringen-Mittelunterfeld, 12=Kleinaitingen-Herbst- and Friedenstrasse, 13=Haunstetten-Im Tal 14 and the terrace. In prehistory, settlement activity was concentrated on the narrow space between the loess terrace and the floodplain of the rivers. This narrow space has been the focus of urban development in recent decades, and related building activities were accompanied by large-scale rescue excavations which produced an impressive corpus of archaeological evidence, not only from the Early Bronze Age. From this body of evidence, we chose the burials of the 3rd and first half of the 2nd millennia BC for our project.

The comprehensive fieldwork also enabled us to understand the structure of human habitation within space. Although we are lacking settlement evidence of the Late and Final Neolithic, which is extremely rare in all of southern Germany, the situation of the Early Bronze Age is clear: farmsteads were placed like pearls on a necklace on both sides of the loess terrace with only a distance of a few hundred metres between them. There is no evidence for agglomerated farmsteads, some kind of villages, or even settlements with a 'central site' character. Contemporaneous neighbouring farmsteads were within view of each other, and communication between the farmsteads was an easy task. East of every farmstead, a cemetery was placed and obviously associated with the deceased inhabitants of the respective farmstead. In several cemeteries, rows of posts were placed running eastwards from specific burials, and cattle teeth were regularly placed below these posts (Massy 2018: 106–13). At several places (e.g. Haunstetten-Unterer Talweg 58–62), Bell Beaker, Early Bronze Age, and early Middle Bronze Age cemeteries were placed close to each other (Massy *et al.* 2017: 248, Figure 20.5). This indicates that Bell Beaker and Middle Bronze Age farmsteads must have also been situated similarly to Early Bronze Age farmsteads. The sequence of radiocarbon dates for the cemeteries and the time gap between successive dates at a certain place point to a regular system, with a farmstead existing for *c.* 100–150 years, followed by *c.* 100–150 years remaining fallow, and finally the existence of a new farmstead at the same place for a similar range of time, and so on (Massy *et al.* 2017).

With regard to the structuring of space, it seems that the community living in the Lech Valley had a common understanding about, and maybe even rules for, how and where to build a farmstead and the related cemetery that persisted from 2500–1500 cal BC.

Temporal frame

So far, evidence for any kind of local Late Neolithic (Figure 8.2) settlement activity in the Lech Valley is missing. The earliest radiocarbon dates for the 3rd millennium derive from the small number (n=2) of Corded Ware complex burials which fall between the 29th and 27th centuries BC (Stockhammer *et al.* 2015b). Although earliest radiocarbon ranges of Bell Beaker complex graves (n=28) all start in the mid-26th century BC, we assume continuous settlement activity during the 3rd millennium BC. Since the beginning of our research, the Bell Beaker complex–Early

Bronze Age transition has been of major significance to us, as we were interested in the diversity of decisions of local actors to appropriate the novel technology of bronze metalworking (Stockhammer and Maran 2017). In this context, the double burial Wehringen-Hochfeld, grave 14, was of particular interest (Massy 2018: 611–12): it contained the burial of a typical Bell Beaker complex male individual with a wristguard, flint arrowhead, and pottery. On the right arm of this man, an adult female individual was placed, who was equipped with a typical Early Bronze Age metal spiral tutulus. At first glance, it seemed that this was a bi-epochal double burial, where a traditional male and his new-fashioned female partner were buried together. However, it became evident that there was a gap of c. 300 years (i.e. between 2200–1900 cal BC) between the radiocarbon ranges of both individuals (Stockhammer et al. 2015b). Thus, several hundred years after the adult male individual had been buried in the pit, the grave was reopened in a careful manner without disturbing the old skeleton, and the recently deceased woman was placed on his arm indicating the construction of ancestry and social belonging, at least in the moment of deposition.

Our modelling of the latest Bell Beaker complex and earliest Early Bronze Age radiocarbon ranges indicated that all farmsteads in the Lech Valley shifted from Bell Beaker complex to Early Bronze Age material culture (at least with regard to the selection of grave goods) within very few decades around 2150 BC and that there was no coexistence of Bell Beaker complex and Early Bronze Age cemeteries/farmsteads at all (Stockhammer et al. 2015b; Massy 2018). With regard to the subsequent Early Bronze Age, one of our major findings based on the large number of radiocarbon dates (n=96) was that the traditional and strict chronological sequence from Bz A1 to Bz A2 does not fit for the Lech Valley, as Bz A1-type fossils were still in use when Bz A2 objects were introduced and appropriated into the burial practices of the Lech Valley population. Thus, a quick change within one or two decades from hammered copper to cast bronze artefacts is not plausible in our view (Stockhammer et al. 2015b; Massy 2018; Massy and Stockhammer 2019). The necessity to replace the still dominating relative-chronological orders with a radiocarbon-based chronology has also become clear for other areas of Central

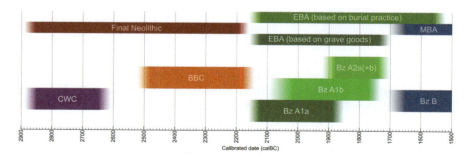

Figure 8.2 Chronology of the 3rd and early 2nd millennia BC in the Lech Valley modelled on the basis of radiocarbon dated grave finds (© Ken Massy)

Europe, where new radiocarbon series have demonstrated the insufficiency of type fossil-based dating (Schwarz 2016; Massy *et al.* 2018; Massy and Stockhammer 2019; Šabatová and Parma 2019). Moreover, attempts to re-establish a single supra-regional relative-chronological system have not been convincingly argued (Brunner *et al.* 2020).[2] In contrast to the transition from Bell Beaker complex to Early Bronze Age, the transition from Early Bronze Age to Middle Bronze Age is characterised by a surprisingly long coexistence of farmsteads adhering to Early Bronze Age or Middle Bronze Age material culture. This is most visible in the two cemeteries of Kleinaitingen (Early Bronze Age, 34 radiocarbon dates) and Oberottmarshausen (Middle Bronze Age, 21 radiocarbon dates), which are only 600 m away from each other. Our previous modelling of the radiocarbon dates points to a coexist-ence of both cemetery-related farmsteads for at least 100–150 years between 1700 and 1550 cal BC. It is, however, interesting to note that none of the burials after 1700 cal BC at Kleinaitingen contained any Early Bronze Age metal-type fossils – although strictly observing all other Early Bronze Age burial customs until 1550 cal BC (Massy 2018: 75–85). In contrast, the earliest Middle Bronze Age-type fossils from Oberottmarshausen and other Middle Bronze Age cemeteries of the Lech Valley (Massy and Stockhammer 2019) date to 1700/1650 cal BC but remain rare in numbers until 1600/1550 cal BC. Therefore, if we associate the end of the Early Bronze Age with the latest radiocarbon date for a grave with Early Bronze Age-type fossils, the Early Bronze Age in the Lech Valley ends already around 1700 cal BC. To sum up (Figure 8.2), depending on the archaeologists' decision, the Early Bronze Age in the Lech Valley either ends *c.* 1700 cal BC (with the latest Early Bronze Age-type fossils) or *c.* 1550 cal BC (with the last burials in Early Bronze Age tradition in an Early Bronze Age cemetery).

Human mobility and societal organisation

On the basis of the settlement structure and the radiocarbon dates, a continuous development from the Bell Beaker complex to the Early Bronze Age could be assumed – in contrast to the complex Early Bronze Age–Middle Bronze Age tran-sition. We aimed to better understand human mobility and societal organisation during the 3rd and early 2nd millennia BC by integrating large-scale analyses of strontium isotopes, archaeogenetics, archaeology, and physical anthropology (Knipper *et al.* 2017; Massy *et al.* 2017; Massy 2018; Mittnik *et al.* 2019;

---

[2] Taking the recently proposed chronology by Brunner *et al.* (2020) seriously would mean that the most emblematic Bronze Age (Bz) A2 burial, i.e. the princely grave of Leubingen, would be dated within the absolute range of Bronze Age A1, as the authors propose the transition from Bronze Age A1 to A2 to have happened sometime during 1875–1820 BC. As Leubingen is clearly dated to 1942 +/- 10 BC on the basis of dendrochronology, this new attempt to save the traditional chronology over a vast geographical and cultural range is not convincing.

Stockhammer in press). We decided to undertake bioarchaeological analyses in a most comprehensive way for all individuals buried within selected cemeteries and chose as representative as possible a set of samples for the larger cemeteries (e.g. Kleinaitingen, Haunstetten-Postillionstraße, Oberottmarshausen). Altogether, we produced strontium isotope data for 147 individuals and sampled 118 individuals for genetic analyses. The extraordinary DNA preservation in the region enabled us to achieve sufficient genetic resolution for 104 individuals to be used for analyses of biological relatedness. With regard to strontium isotope analyses, we were in the fortunate situation to base our results on a very good understanding of bioavailable strontium in southern Germany. This enabled us to identify an astonishing share of adult female individuals of non-local origin at each of the cemeteries (Figure 8.3). On the basis of strontium and oxygen isotope data, these women could be further separated into three subgroups. One subgroup shows exceptionally high strontium isotope ratios in their second molars (i.e. 2nd–6th/7th year of life) and third molars (i.e. 6th/7th–16th/17th year of life) (Figure 8.3; Figure 8.4). These women must have spent their time before adulthood outside of southern Bavaria, most probably either in central Germany or in Bohemia, i.e. in areas of the Únětice culture, where those strontium isotope signatures are found in fertile soils. Moreover, archaeological evidence also points to strong interactions between these regions. These female individuals therefore entered the Lech Valley after their 17th year of life. The second subgroup (Figure 8.3) also shows elevated strontium isotope ratios in their second and third molars, but not as high as the first group. Based on the strontium isotope data alone, a southern Bavarian origin cannot be completely excluded for this subgroup. On the basis of archaeological provenance analysis of the grave goods, none of these non-local or probably non-local women would have been recognised as such, as they were all buried with typically local metal and non-metal objects (Massy 2018). Only 50 per cent (23 out of 46) of the women (Figure 8.3) showed a strontium isotope ratio consistent with the local bioavailable strontium in the Lech Valley.

In contrast with the adult female individuals, male and subadult individuals predominantly showed strontium isotope ratios consistent with the local bioavailable strontium (Figure 8.3), and non-local signatures of male and subadult individuals were only detected in 3 per cent and 2 per cent of the cases, respectively. However, by comparing the values for the second and third molar, we were able to identify a small group of male individuals whose second molar was consistent with the local range, whereas the third molar clearly exhibited a non-local signature. We interpreted this evidence as indication of mobility during childhood where boys at the age of 6 or 7 years were sent out to live with another family at a distant place only to return as adults – probably together with a partner – and were finally buried in the Lech Valley probably at the farmstead from which they originated. Such systems of fosterage are well known for prehistoric and historic societies (Parkes 2004; 2006; Lallemand 2007; Müller-Scheeßel et al. 2015; O'Donnell 2020). In many cases, fosterage was linked with marked differences in power and/or wealth between

MOBILITY AT THE ONSET OF THE BRONZE AGE

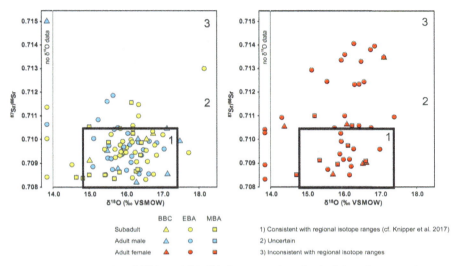

Figure 8.3 Scatter plot of $\delta^{18}O_p$ and $^{87}Sr/^{86}Sr$ isotope ratios of subadult and adult male individuals (left) and adult female individuals (right) from the Lech Valley. The grey boxes (no. 1) indicate the local ranges of both isotope ratios. Samples plotted on the y axis lack $\delta^{18}O_p$ data. VSMOW=Vienna standard mean ocean water (© Corina Knipper; Knipper *et al.* 2017: Figure 3)

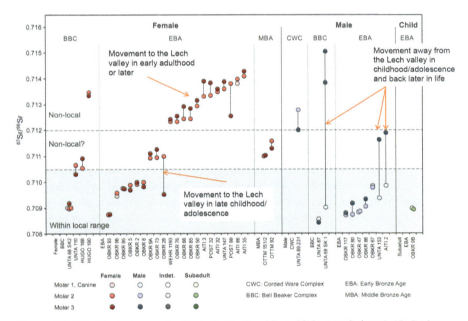

Figure 8.4 $^{87}Sr/^{86}Sr$ isotope ratios for individuals with multiple sampled teeth (© Corina Knipper; cf. Mittnik *et al.* 2019: Figure S12)

communities. Pressed by, for example, political and/or economic circumstances, parents were forced to send their children abroad to be educated and/or exploited in another household (Zimmermann *et al.* 2012). Interestingly, there is no evidence that such political and/or economic forces might have played a role in the system of fosterage visible in the Lech Valley evidence. As our current evidence indicates that this practice was confined to male subadults, the network-and-bride option combined with the creation and maintenance of transregional networks is the most probable explanation of this system.

Complementary with the results of the strontium isotope data, mtDNA analysis pointed to a stable exogamous social practice over a significant amount of time (Knipper *et al.* 2017). Our full-genomic evidence is in accordance with the appearance of the so-called steppe signature in most parts of Europe in the 3rd millennium, as the Bell Beaker complex individuals in the Lech Valley all show this characteristic admixture of this signature with previously local genetic patterns (Mittnik *et al.* 2019). The appearance of the steppe signature has been interpreted as evidence for the movement of larger groups of people from east to west throughout Europe, leading to complex coexistences and entanglements of mobile individuals or groups with previously existing societies, and has even been associated by some authors with the spread of Indo-European languages (Allentoft *et al.* 2015; Haak *et al.* 2015; Olalde *et al.* 2018; 2019; Mittnik *et al.* 2019; Fernandes *et al.* 2020; Furtwängler *et al.* 2020). From a genetic perspective, the Bell Beaker complex individuals from the Lech Valley show a great diversity of admixture proportions – ranging from close to previous Neolithic signatures to high shares of steppe ancestry typical for genetic patterns of individuals associated with the Corded Ware complex (Olalde *et al.* 2018; Mittnik *et al.* 2019). We are not able to determine if this obviously recent admixture also took place in the Lech Valley and/or southern Germany, as evidence for Late Neolithic societies coexisting with Corded Ware complex, and even Bell Beaker complex individuals, is almost completely missing. The extraordinary preservation of ancient DNA in the Lech Valley also allowed us to transform the cemeteries into biological pedigrees (Figure 8.5), thereby confirming that at least some of the individuals living together in the individual farmsteads were also biologically related and part of a core family.

However, the evidence showed much more complexity indicating the existence of complex households in the Early Bronze Age, which comprised both biologically related and unrelated individuals. For several cemeteries, we were able to reconstruct pedigrees over four to five generations, whereby we could not detect biological ancestors of any adult female individual anywhere in the Lech Valley. The only female individuals with biological ancestors buried in the cemeteries died already at a subadult age. As a result of this, maternal lineages do not exceed a parent–child level – in accordance with the aforementioned mtDNA evidence. This indicates a strictly patrilocal system with systematic exogamy for the Early Bronze Age which already existed for the Bell Beaker complex in the broader region (Sjögren *et al.* 2020). Interestingly, all male offspring were buried in the respective cemetery, and the importance of the patrilineal line was further emphasised by material culture – e.g. by the concentration of triangular metal daggers in the burials of the male line. For all male individuals equipped with daggers and/or other weapons, where aDNA analysis gave sufficient results, at least a 3rd–5th-degree relationship to another individual from the cemetery could be detected, most of them even being 1st- or 2nd-degree relatives. The importance of the family pedigrees also materialised in the positioning of the graves: a couple were always buried close to each other, and their offspring, who died at a subadult age, were buried close to them. When their son died after reaching adulthood and starting a partnership, a new burial group was opened inside the cemetery – often close to his parents – with his wife and untimely deceased children again buried close to him. Similar to the overall structure of the geographical space, the space inside the cemeteries was also structured according to clear and very stable rules of practice.

It came as a surprise that none of the women from afar (i.e. probably from an Únětice background) had any offspring who were buried in the valley. This indicates that, even if they reached the Lech Valley as marriage partners, their role

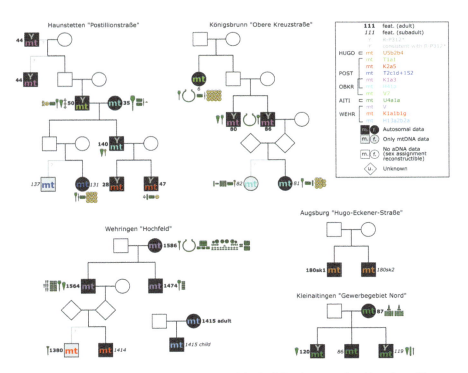

Figure 8.5 Biological pedigrees reconstructed for Bell Beaker complex (Augsburg-Hugo-Eckener-Straße) and Early Bronze Age (Haunstetten-Postillonstraße, Königsbrunn-Obere Kreuzstraße, Wehringen-Hochfeld, Kleinaitingen-Gewerbegebiet Nord) (© Ken Massy; cf. Mittnik et al. 2019)

was either not to produce offspring or their offspring left the Lech Valley and/or had no right to be buried in the Valley. This was even more surprising, as in the double burial of Königsbrunn-Obere Kreuzstraße, grave 33 (feature 8.9), a possibly non-local adult woman was buried together with a subadult individual with strontium isotope values within the local range. Archaeogenetic analyses showed that there was no biological relationship between them, because both had different mtDNA haplogroups. The double burial, therefore, expressed notions of social belonging which were not based on mere biological factors.

Besides the individuals belonging to the family pedigree and the non-local women, we identified adult male and female individuals with strontium values consistent with the local bioavailable strontium, who at the same time were all biologically unrelated to any other individual and – in contrast with the members of the family pedigree and the non-local women – also characterised by small numbers and poor quality of grave goods. Therefore, we interpret this group of individuals as menial staff (or maybe even slaves) who were part of the individual household of every farmstead, which thus integrated biologically related and unrelated, local and non-local, rich and poor, high- and low-status individuals in one community of practice (Mittnik *et al.* 2019). Whereas sex and age do not seem to have been relevant for these differences in status, it remains unknown whether religion or other kinds of worldviews, or even the existence of social institutions like 'classes' or 'castes', could have played a role in the determination and stabilisation of the status differences evidenced in the Lech Valley farmsteads.

Integrating and summing up the isotopic and archaeogenetic evidence creates the following picture. The most astonishing result is the high degree of mobility among women and possibly also children and the stability of this system over *c.* 700 years from the Bell Beaker complex to the Early Bronze Age: at least two-thirds of all adult females were of non-local origin and came from beyond the Lech Valley – several of them even from beyond the northern Alpine foreland – and arrived in the Valley in late adolescence or adulthood. None of these women could have been identified as non-local on the basis of the associated material culture – e.g. 'exotic' or non-local elements of costumes and accessories as postulated for '*Fremde Frauen*' ('foreign women') by Jockenhövel (1991: 51). According to this previous understanding of 'foreign women', these women always remained foreigners in their new communities, and it was even important to emphasise their foreignness in the burial process. Now, bioarchaeological results unravel the complexity in the representation of 'foreign women' in burials and go beyond what was suggested for marriage partners from neighbouring regions (Wels-Weyrauch 1989; Jockenhövel 1991: 60). The evidence from the Lech Valley society clearly indicates a successful integration of the non-local women, for whom 'non-local' specifies their place of origin, but not their perception within the Lech Valley. Therefore, calling them 'foreign' seems inappropriate, as their participation in the local community was clearly emphasised in their burials. Even a large proportion of the females associated with the menial staff were probably non-local, as they had

MOBILITY AT THE ONSET OF THE BRONZE AGE   181

no ancestors anywhere in the valley. Therefore, we have evidence for a strict and stable patrilocal residential rule.

However, although the bulk of adult women buried in the Lech Valley were not born there, their individual societal background, origin, and the geographical distance of their place of birth determined their role within the local society: women from far away – most probably from an Únětice background – never had offspring or at least no offspring which were buried in the Lech Valley region. In one case, two half-sisters had moved into the Lech Valley from afar, but lived in two different farmsteads, as one of them was buried in Haunstetten–Postillionstraße, grave 32 (feature 99), and the other one in Königsbrunn-Obere Kreuzstraße, grave 31 (feature 76). We interpreted the role of these women from abroad as mediators of knowledge, probably even bringing the advanced knowledge of metal technology of the Únětice culture into the Lech Valley (Stockhammer *et al.* 2015b). They were also crucial in the constitution and maintenance of stable and continuous long-distance relations which facilitated the transfer of further knowledge, goods, and people. Moreover, the first author has proposed that these women had an additional role as wet nurses – indicated by the aforementioned double burial and the success with which Bell Beaker complex and Early Bronze Age communities raised offspring (Stockhammer in press). If this was the case, these women became pregnant in their place of origin but had to leave their first child there, or they became pregnant in the Lech Valley, but their offspring was either not buried in the valley or sent to another place, e.g. back to the woman's place of origin. If the woman gave birth to her child before moving to the Lech Valley, she needed to continue producing milk with manual practices in order to keep lactation ongoing also during the two to three months of travel. Moreover, it is possible to initiate breast milk production without having given birth before and only with the help of manual practices. The women in the pedigree probably came from neighbouring regions, as their strontium signatures are consistent with southern Bavaria, and females born in the Lech Valley and reaching adulthood probably moved to these neighbouring regions as part of a supra-regional marital network. How the low-status/economically lesswealthy women reached the Lech Valley remains unclear, as does whether or not their status was inherited or created and if they came voluntarily (like menial staff) or involuntarily (e.g. as slaves or captives). Recently, the importance of captives in prehistoric societies has been emphasised (Cameron 2011; 2020; Kristiansen 2020), but if these women (and men) can be identified accordingly needs to remain open on the basis of the available data. However, the data leaves no doubt that every farmstead was characterised by the diversity of its inhabitants with regard to kinship, status, societal roles, freedom, and origin.

The astonishing mobility of female individuals (and partly children) also raised the question about how long-distance travel was organised, as the stability of the system clearly indicates that a significant share of the women and children must have reached their final destination successfully. Such travel – sometimes over several hundred kilometres and accordingly over several weeks – required the existence of specialists and institutions like caravans, guest houses, guarded travel, etc., of which we have hardly found any evidence in the archaeological record so far. Moreover, the finding of partners was probably organised during communal meetings, where families/parents with their children met and arranged marriages or the fostering for their boys at distant places. Again, the long stability of the system leaves no doubt that there was hardly any freedom of individual action on either side. Societies over larger regions of Central Europe obviously followed this social practice and were willing to arrange marriages and exchange children, marital partners, and female specialists.

The absence of cross-marriages between the different farmsteads of the valley indicates that the different farmsteads – in spite of not forming an agglomerated settlement – understood themselves as belonging to the same community inside which marital partners were seemingly not exchanged. It was also interesting to see that there was no evidence for offspring from parents buried at different farmsteads. This may point to a strictly monogamous system and the existence of strict rules of sexual behaviour and associated taboos. However, this might also indicate that only children from specific partnerships had the right to stay and be buried in the Lech Valley, whereas offspring from intercourse between partners from different farmsteads, between local men and non-local women from afar, as well as all off-spring from the supposed menial staff, did not have the right to be buried in the farmsteads' cemeteries and possibly even had to leave the Lech Valley at some time.

As sons stayed at the farmstead of their parents, it is plausible that they jointly inherited their parents' land and livestock. The richness of the fertile soils probably enabled such a system, where splitting up farmland still left enough resources. While the farmstead and associated wealth was obviously inherited via the male line, it is interesting to note that the richest burials were usually associated with the women from far away, who had neither biological ancestors nor visible offspring in the valley. This again indicates that their wealth was an expression of their social importance and status which was not based on biological relationships, whereas in the case of the adult man it was exactly their biological relationship which shaped the selection of burial goods by the burying community. It was the coexistence of different, but always stable, strict, and individual-related, rules and practices which determined status positions and enabled successful cohabitation within regularly diverse and complex households.

Health

The extraordinary DNA preservation and the selection of teeth for the extraction of aDNA also enabled us to trace remains of infectious diseases as part of our standard screening for bacterial DNA in the DNA extracts. Although we are now able to identify a broad range of infectious diseases (e.g. plague, leprosy, typhoid fever, etc.), we were only able to identify evidence for *Yersinia pestis*, i.e. the causative agent of the plague, in several individuals from the Lech Valley. Two of these (from Haunstetten-Postillonstraße and Haunstetten-Unterer Talweg 85) have already been published (Andrades Valtueña *et al.* 2017), and three more (from Kleinaitingen and Oberottmarshausen) will follow soon (Andrades Valtueña *et al.* 2022); thus, they span the complete Early Bronze Age and the early Middle Bronze Age. It needs to be kept in mind that evidence for infectious diseases is nothing but the tip of an iceberg, namely those individuals who actually died from or during the disease and had extraordinarily good DNA preservation. With, for example, one out of 20 screened individuals in Oberottmarshausen and two out of 28 screened individuals in Kleinaitingen, the Lech Valley presents one of the highest concentrations of plague-positive individuals in Europe, which can best be explained by the excellent DNA preservation in the region. From a cultural point of view, it is important to note that none of the individuals who died from the plague was buried in a strikingly different way – neither with regard to grave goods nor the positioning of the grave. This cause of death obviously did not question the local worldviews to such an extent that new ways of managing the death needed to be created. This goes hand in hand with the observation that the 3rd and early 2nd millennia variant of the *Yersinia pestis* bacterium was lacking those genes which enabled the bacterium to use rodent fleas, especially the rat flea, as the perfect host (Rasmussen *et al.* 2015; Andrades Valtueña *et al.* 2017; Rascovan *et al.* 2019). How *Yersinia pestis* spread during the Bell Beaker complex and Early Bronze Age, the speed of the course of disease, and its lethality are still unclear. Most likely, the illness was not transmitted by infected humans over large distances. It is also clear that the rat flea could not have played a role, as both the relevant pathogen mutation and rats were missing in Central Europe at the time. The first author believes that birds might have played a crucial role as animal vectors, most likely species such as ravens or migratory birds who were usually hunted and eaten. They could then have transmitted the disease, for example, via the respective avian fleas or blood splashed during the slaughter and plucking of the bird.

The continuity of the farmsteads as well as the social institutions and practices in the Lech Valley through the centuries indicates that there was no major interruption or collapse due to the emergence of some kind of epidemic. It rather seems that the plague struck the valley repeatedly every few decades, killing several individuals but never all the inhabitants of a particular farmstead. This shows that the character of these outbreaks must have been completely different from, for example, the Medieval Black Death, which annihilated complete families and significant parts of local communities within a short time. Whereas the *Yersinia pestis* of the Bell Beaker complex and Early Bronze Age Lech Valley was definitely lethal, it still did not have the potential to develop into an epidemic – be it due to a lack of virulence and/or social practices of isolating diseased individuals from the rest of the farmstead's inhabitants. It seems that the social institutions in the Bell Beaker complex and Early Bronze Age were stable enough to build up a resilience against small-scale outbreaks of a disease.

The end of the Bell Beaker and Early Bronze Age community continuum

In spite of its overall stability, the number of farmsteads rapidly decreased during the 18th century BC, with only a few Early Bronze Age farmsteads, most prominently Kleinaitingen, continuing after 1700 BC. This decrease of farmsteads still requires explanation. It is theoretically possible that several farmsteads moved together in the place of Kleinaitingen. Whereas the farmstead(s) of Kleinaitingen have not been excavated so far, the large cemetery with its 61 burials might possibly indicate some kind of *synoikismos* – maybe in accordance with processes of settlement concentration visible in the emergence of hilltop settlements at the Early Bronze Age to Middle Bronze Age transition in southern Bavaria (Koschik 1981; Bankus 2004). It is also possible that individuals or families left the Lech Valley due to different reasons. However, it is interesting to note that, from 1650 BC onwards, farmsteads and associated cemeteries with Middle Bronze Age material culture were founded at those places where Early Bronze Age farmsteads had formerly been placed (e.g. Haunstetten-Unterer Talweg 58–62: Massy *et al.* 2017; Augsburg-Technologiezentrum: Massy and Schnetz 2016). As we have argued before, the appearance of Middle Bronze Age material culture and related social practices and worldviews are hard to explain out of local continuities and changes, especially with Kleinaitingen and Oberottmarshausen showing the aforementioned coexistence of two completely different ways of living and burial practices close by. The Middle Bronze Age farmsteads in the Lech Valley show no evidence of female mobility similar to the Early Bronze Age, and the strict sex differentiation of the Bell Beaker complex and Early Bronze Age burials was replaced by a unisex, stretched, supine burial position (Mittnik *et al.* 2019). Moreover, the changes observed in the Lech Valley are not limited to this specific region. In most areas of Central Europe, the end of the Early Bronze Age marks a major turning point in the Bronze Age along with different settlement patterns, burial customs, and hoarding practices, even resulting in systemic collapse of previously long-lasting, stable communities and networks. Especially the disruptive end of the Únětice culture, which was certainly one of the main partners of the interregional network and a possible origin of the non-local females in the Lech Valley, had severe consequences on life in southern Germany (cf. Ernée 2013, 464–5). It seems that not only material culture, but more importantly also notions of sex and gender, structured mobility, and social structure in the Middle Bronze Age farmsteads in the Lech Valley were completely different and incompatible with those of the previous Early Bronze Age. The apparent continuity of genetic patterns with no large turnovers or shifts cannot be taken as an argument against the arrival of non-local groups at the beginning of the Middle Bronze Age, as there was no significant difference of genetic signatures in Central Europe during this time which would allow us to differentiate newcomers from other regions in Central Europe (Mittnik *et al.* 2019). During the 16th century BC, the last Early Bronze Age farmsteads and their accompanying cemeteries faded out – together with almost all traditions, rules, and practices which had shaped the Lech Valley for *c.* 700 years. The future belonged to the Middle Bronze Age communities.

References

Allentoft, M., Sikora, E., Sjögren, M., Rasmussen, S., Rasmussen, M., *et al.* (2015), 'Population genomics of Bronze Age Eurasia', *Nature*, 522: 167–72.

Andrades Valtueña, A., Mittnik, A., Key, A., Haak, F.M., Allmäe, S., *et al.* (2017), 'The Stone Age plague and its persistence in Eurasia', *Current Biology*, 27(23): 3683–91.

Andrades Valtueña, A., Neumann, G.U., Spyrou M.A., Musralina, L., Aron, F., *et al.* (2022), 'Stone Age *Yersinia pestis* genomes shed light on the early evolution, diversity and transmission ecology of plague', *Proceedings of the National Academy of Sciences of the United States of America*, 119(17): e2116722119, DOI: 10.1073/pnas.2116722119.

Bankus, M. (2004), *Der Freisinger Domberg und sein Umland: Untersuchungen zur prähistorischen Besiedlung* (Rahden/Westf., Verlag Marie Leidorf).

Brunner, M., Von Felten, J., Hinz, M., and Hafner, A. (2020), 'Central European Early Bronze Age chronology revisited: a Bayesian examination of large-scale radiocarbon dating', *PLoS ONE*, 15(12): e0243719, DOI: 10.1371/journal.pone.0243719.

Cameron, C.M. (2011), 'Captives and culture change: implications for archaeology', *Current Anthropology*, 52(2): 169–209.

Cameron, C.M. (2020), *Captives: How Stolen People Changed the World* (Lincoln NE and London, University of Nebraska Press).

Ernée, M. (2013), 'Bernstein und der Zusammenbruch der klassischen Aunjetitzer Kultur in Böhmen', in H. Meller, F. Bertemes, H.-R. Bork, and R. Risch (eds), *1600 – Kultureller Umbruch im Schatten des Thera-Ausbruchs?* (Halle/Saale, Landesamt für Denkmalpflege und Archäologie Sachsen-Anhalt), 453–67.

Fernandes, D.M., Mittnik, A., Olalde, I., Lazaridis, I., Cheronet, O., *et al.* (2020), 'The spread of steppe and Iranian-related ancestry in the islands of the Western Mediterranean', *Nature Ecology & Evolution*, 4(3): 334–45.

Furtwängler, A., Rohrlach, A.B., Lamnidis, T.C., Papac, L., Neumann, G.U., *et al.* (2020), 'Ancient genomes reveal social and genetic structure of Late Neolithic Switzerland', *Nature Communications*, 11(1): 1915, DOI: 10.1038/s41467-020-15560-x.

Haak, W., Lazaridis, I., Patterson, N., Rohland, N., Mallick, S., *et al.* (2015), 'Massive migration from the steppe was a source for Indo-European languages in Europe', *Nature*, 522: 207–11.

Jockenhövel, A. (1991), 'Räumliche Mobilität von Personen in der mittleren Bronzezeit des westlichen Mitteleuropa', *Germania*, 69: 49–62.

Kienlin, T.L. (2008), *Frühes Metall im nordalpinen Raum: Eine Untersuchung zu technologischen und kognitiven Aspekten früher Metallurgie anhand der Gefüge frühbronzezeitlicher Beile* (Bonn, Habelt).

Kienlin, T.L. (2010), *Traditions and Transformations: Approaches to Eneolithic (Copper Age) and Bronze Age Metalworking and Society in Eastern Central Europe and the Carpathian Basin* (Oxford, Archaeopress).

Knipper, C., Mittnik, A., Massy, K., Kociumaka, C., Kucukkalipci, I., *et al.* (2017), 'Female exogamy and gene pool diversification at the transition from the Final Neolithic to the Early Bronze Age in Central Europe', *Proceedings of the National Academy of Sciences of the United States of America*, 114(38): 10083–8.

Koschik, H. (1981). *Die Bronzezeit im südwestlichen Oberbayern* (Kallmünz/Opf., Verlag Michael Lassleben).

Krause, J. and Stockhammer, P.W. (2014), 'Zeiten des Umbruchs? Gesellschaftlicher und naturräumlicher Wandel am Beginn der Bronzezeit', *Jahrbuch der Heidelberger Akademie der Wissenschaften*: 239–45.

Krause, J. and Stockhammer, P.W. (2015), 'Zeiten des Umbruchs? Gesellschaftlicher und naturräumlicher Wandel am Beginn der Bronzezeit', *Jahrbuch der Heidelberger Akademie der Wissenschaften*: 256–61.

Kristiansen, K. (2020), 'Review of: Cameron, C.M. (2016), Captives: how stolen people changed the world (Lincoln NE and London: University of Nebraska Press)', *European Journal of Archaeology*, 23(2): 312–14.

Lallemand, S. (2007), *La circulation des enfants en société traditionnelle: Prêt, don, échange* (Paris, Editions L'Harmattan).

Massy, K. (2018), *Die Gräber der Frühbronzezeit im südlichen Bayern: Untersuchungen zu den Bestattungs- und Beigabensitten sowie gräberfeldimmanenten Strukturen* (Kallmünz/Opf., Verlag Michael Lassleben).

Massy, K. and Schnetz, M. (2016), 'Vielfalt in der Mittelbronzezeit: Ein selten vollständiges Gräberfeld in Augsburg-Göggingen, Schwaben', *Das Archäologische Jahr in Bayern*: 38–41.

Massy, K. and Stockhammer, P.W. (2019), 'Testing Reinecke's chronology of the Early Bronze Age with radiocarbon dating: new evidence from southern Bavaria', *Studia Hercynia*, 23(2): 22–35.

Massy, K., Knipper, C., Mittnik, A., Kraus, S., Pernicka, E., *et al.* (2017), 'Patterns of transformation from the Final Neolithic to the Early Bronze Age: a case study from the Lech Valley south of Augsburg', in P.W. Stockhammer and J. Maran (eds), *Appropriating Innovations: Entangled Knowledge in Eurasia, 5000–1500 BCE* (Oxford, Oxbow), 241–61.

Massy, K., Hanöffner, S., Carlichi-Witjes, N., and Stockhammer, P.W. (2018), 'Früh- und ältermittelbronzezeitliche Gräber und Siedlungsreste aus Altenmarkt, Stadt Oster-hofen, Lkr. Deggendorf', in L. Husty and K. Schmotz (eds), *Vorträge des 36. Niederbayerischen Archäologentages* (Rahden/Westf, Verlag Marie Leidorf), 123–74.

Mittnik, A. and Stockhammer, P.W. (2016), 'Zeiten des Umbruchs? Gesellschaftlicher und naturräumlicher Wandel am Beginn der Bronzezeit', *Jahrbuch der Heidelberger Akademie der Wissenschaften*: 219–25.

Mittnik, A. and Stockhammer, P.W. (2017), 'Zeiten des Umbruchs? Gesellschaftlicher und naturräumlicher Wandel am Beginn der Bronzezeit', *Jahrbuch der Heidelberger Akademie der Wissenschaften*: 289–95.

Mittnik, A., Massy, K., Knipper, C., Wittenborn, F., Pfrengle, S., *et al.* (2019), 'Kinship-based social inequality in Bronze Age Europe', *Science*, 366(6466): 731–4.

Müller-Scheeßel, N., Grupe, G., Tütken, T. (2015), 'In der Obhut von Verwandten? Die Zirkulation von Kindern und Jugendlichen in der Eisenzeit Mitteleuropas', in R. Karl and J. Leskovar (eds), *Interpretierte Eisenzeiten: Fallstudien, Methoden, Theorie, Tagungsbeiträge der 6. Linzer Gespräche zur interpretativen Eisenzeitarchäologie* (Linz, Oberösterreichisches Landesmuseum), 9–23.

O'Donnell, T.C. (ed) (2020), *Fosterage in Medieval Ireland: An Emotional History* (Amsterdam, Amsterdam University Press).

Olalde, I., Brace, S., Allentoft, M.E., Armit, I., Kristiansen, K., *et al.* (2018), 'The Beaker phenomenon and the genomic transformation of northwest Europe', *Nature*, 555: 190–6.

Olalde, I., Mallick, S., Patterson, N., Rohland, N., Villalba-Mouco, V., *et al.* (2019), 'The genomic history of the Iberian Peninsula over the past 8000 years', *Science*, 363(6432): 1230–4.

Pare, C.F.E. (2000), 'Bronze and the Bronze Age', in C.F.E. Pare (ed), *Metals Make the World Go Round: The Supply and Circulation of Metals in Bronze Age Europe* (Oxford, Oxbow), 1–38.

Parkes, P. (2004), 'Fosterage, kinship, and legend: when milk was thicker than blood?', *Comparative Studies in Society and History*, 46(3): 587–615.

Parkes, P. (2006), 'Celtic fosterage: adoptive kinship and clientage in northwest Europe', *Comparative Studies in Society and History*, 48(2): 359–95.

Rascovan, N., Sjögren, K.-G., Kristiansen, K., Nielsen, R., Willerslev, E., *et al.* (2019), 'Emergence and spread of basal lineages of *Yersinia pestis* during the Neolithic decline', *Cell*, 176(1–2): 295–305.

Rasmussen, S., Allentoft, M.E., Nielsen, K., Orlando, L., Sikora, M., *et al.* (2015), 'Early divergent strains of *Yersinia pestis* in Eurasia 5,000 years ago', *Cell*, 163(3): 571–82.

Reinecke, P. (1902), 'Beiträge zur Kenntnis der frühen Bronzezeit Mitteleuropas', *Mitteilungen der Anthropologischen Gesellschaft in Wien*, 32: 104–54.

Reinecke, P. (1924), 'Zur chronologischen Gliederung der süddeutschen Bronzezeit', *Germania*, 8: 43–4.

Šabatová, K. and Parma, D. (2019), 'The Early to Middle Bronze Age transition as exemplified by Moravia', *Studia Hercynia*, 24: 124–39.

Schwarz, R. (2016), 'Rezension: P.W. Stockhammer *et al.* (2015), Rewriting the Central European Early Bronze Age chronology: evidence from large-scale radiocarbon dating (2015)', *Jahresschrift für mitteldeutsche Vorgeschichte*, 95: 473–88.

Sjögren, K.-G., Olalde, I., Carver, S., Allentoft, M.E., Knowles, T., *et al.* (2020), 'Kinship and social organization in Copper Age Europe: a cross-disciplinary analysis of archaeology, DNA, isotopes, and anthropology from two Bell Beaker cemeteries', *PLoS ONE*, 15(11): e0241278, DOI: 10.1371/journal.pone.0241278.

Stockhammer, P.W. (2020), 'Bronzeon: learning by gaming', *Archaeologist*, 110: 24–5.

Stockhammer, P.W. (in press), 'Fostering women and mobile children in Final Neolithic and Early Bronze Age Central Europe', in K. Kristiansen, G. Kroonen, and E. Willerslev (eds), *Archaeology, Genetics and Linguistics: Towards a New Synthesis* (Cambridge, Cambridge University Press).

Stockhammer, P.W. and Maran, J. (eds) (2017), *Appropriating Innovations: Entangled Knowledge in Eurasia, 5000–1500 BCE* (Oxford, Oxbow).

Stockhammer, P.W., Massy, K., Knipper, C., Friedrich, R., Kromer, B., *et al.* (2015a), 'Kontinuität und Wandel vom Endneolithikum zur frühen Bronzezeit in der Region Augsburg', in H. Meller, H.W. Arz, R. Jung, and R. Risch (eds), *2200 BC. Ein Klimasturz als Ursache für den Zerfall der alten Welt?* (Halle/Saale, Landesamt für Denkmalpflege und Archäologie Sachsen-Anhalt), 617–41.

Stockhammer, P.W., Massy, K., Knipper, C., Friedrich, R., Kromer, B., *et al.* (2015b), 'Rewriting the Central European Early Bronze Age chronology: evidence from large-scale radiocarbon dating', *PLoS ONE*, 10(10): e0139705, DOI: 10.1371/journal.pone.0139705.

Stockhammer, P.W., Mittnik, A., Massy, K., and Knipper, C. (2018), 'Mobilität: Die wissenden Frauen vom Lechtal', *Spektrum der Wissenschaft: Spezial*, 4: 38–41.

Strahm, C. (2009), 'Prestige versus Ingenium: Die Beweggründe für die Entwicklung der Metallurgie', in S. Grunwald, J.K. Koch, D. Mölders, U. Sommer, and S. Wolfram (eds), *ArteFact: Festschrift für Sabine Rieckhoff zum 65. Geburtstag* (Bonn, Habelt), 343–53.

Wels-Weyrauch, U. (1989), 'Mittelbronzezeitliche Frauentrachten in Süddeutschland (Beziehungen zur Hagenauer Gruppierung)', in Ministère de l'Éducation Nationale, de la Jeunesse et des Sports – Comité des Travaux Historiques et Scientifiques (ed), *Dynamique du Bronze moyen en Europe occidentale* (Paris, CTHS), 117–34.

Zimmermann, S., Brugger, C., and Bereuter, E. (eds) (2012), *Die Schwabenkinder: Arbeit in der Fremde vom 17. bis 20. Jahrhundert* (Ostfildern, Jan Thorbecke Verlag).

9

Marriage, Motherhood, and Mobility in Bronze and Iron Age Central Europe

KATHARINA REBAY-SALISBURY

Introduction

MOBILITY AND MIGRATION shaped the European Bronze and Iron Ages. An increase in connectivity between people and communities led to innovations, knowledge exchange, and resource acquisition that we have been able to trace archaeologically throughout the Continent for decades. At the same time, gender is an important factor in all movements of people, from personal mobility to large-scale migrations involving whole communities. Gender shapes every part of a person's migration experience, from causes to consequences – gender influences who migrates and how the decision is made, how migration affects migrants, and how migration impacts sending and receiving areas. Migration influences gender relations, by either entrenching inequalities and traditional roles, or challenging and changing them.

Only in recent years, bioarchaeological approaches have made it possible to link mobility to the remains of specific gendered persons. Gendered aspects of mobility have emerged as a topic of renewed interest since it has become feasible to trace individuals' residence changes during adolescence and early adulthood via genetic and isotopic analyses (Oelze *et al.* 2012a; 2012b; Knipper *et al.* 2017; Monroy Kuhn *et al.* 2018; Mittnik *et al.* 2019; Furtwängler *et al.* 2020). Genetic studies of kinship, however, by their focus on the mother's and father's contribution to sexual reproduction, give limited information on the social composition of families and on how they operated. Whereas male mobility tends to be explained by explorations, travels, craftsmanship, trade, and warfare, female mobility is frequently linked to marriage and motherhood. Women reproduce societies – both biologically and socially.

This contributon takes a closer look at what marriage and motherhood entail, at their implications for prehistoric personal identities, and discusses archaeological

Proceedings of the British Academy, **254**, 189–208, © The British Academy 2023.

evidence that may provide insights into how these social institutions may have been conceptualised and operated in the past. Drawing on theories of evolutionary origins and cross-cultural observations, the analogies used ultimately have no probative value for later European prehistory, but enable informed interpretations.

Bronze Age scholars have long understood marriage as a universal principle of all human societies (e.g. Brodie 1997; Vander Linden 2007; Brück 2019), but recently began to question it as heteronormative, timeless, and gender-fixing, calling for proper definitions and reimagination (Crellin 2020). Marriage is mentioned only five times in the *Oxford Handbook of the European Bronze Age* (Fokkens and Harding 2013), while it appears as often as 42 times in the *Oxford Handbook of the European Iron Age* (Haselgrove *et al.* 2018). In part, this may be due to the publication date, because genetic and isotopic studies became more widely available in the course of the second decade of the 21st century. Another reason may be that Bronze Age communities in Europe tend to be imagined as unbounded communities in loose contact with each other, whereas the concept of political organisations such as tribes is much more at the forefront in Iron Age Europe, particularly in the later phases vis-à-vis the expanding Roman Empire. In addition, the Medieval and pre-modern feudal system of land tenure, in which serfs were not free to move and relocate, overshadows interpretations of institutionalised mobility in the Metal Ages (Walvin 1983; Rio 2017).

Since they so prominently serve as explanatory models for female mobility, a discussion of the meaning of marriage and motherhood in prehistory is long overdue. Rather than providing concise definitions of marriage and motherhood that may prove unsustainable for individual archaeological contexts, this chapter presents the deep evolutionary history of marriage, discusses definitions from cross-cultural studies, and investigates evidence based on which we may identify some of the characteristics of Bronze and Iron Age marriage and motherhood.

The deep history of marriage

Although we do not normally attribute marital status to our closest primate relatives, an evolutionary perspective may shed light on the origins of marriage, how it evolved, and developed. From a sociobiological point of view, male and female mammals have different mating strategies. While female reproduction is time-, energy-, and labour-consuming, and its capacity is limited by long gestation and lactation periods, male reproduction requires little effort and is limited only by access to fertile females. Females are careful in selecting the qualitatively best partner. Males maximise their fitness by quantity – mating with as many females as possible – and may optimise their reproductive strategy by offering females food, protection, and help with childrearing, or conversely, taking the shortcut of sexual coercion (Smuts 1995). In humans, women across cultures tend to be attracted to signs of wealth and power, whereas men prefer youth and health as signs of fertility (Buss 2006).

Today's living hominids – the great apes including humans – exhibit some variation in how groups live together, how males and females pair up, and how individuals relocate upon adolescence. Orangutans, as our farthest removed relatives, live semi-solitary lives (Galdikas 1985). Males as well as females with offspring live largely alone, although adolescent females spend some time in groups, and individuals form groups travelling between food sources. Non-dominant males frequently force copulation on females, which females aim to avoid by protection through dominant males; females use facultative association as a mechanism of exercising some choice of mates (Delgado Jr and Van Schaik 2000; Knott *et al.* 2010). Orangutans are territorial, and while females settle close to their mothers, males range more widely (Singleton and Van Schaik 2002).

Gorillas tend to live in troops of 5–30 individuals, composed of one adult male, multiple females, and their offspring. Females and males leave their natal groups as they mature, with females joining other groups and males living alone or forming all-male groups until it is time to challenge a dominant male. Some variation in group composition has recently been observed (Robbins *et al.* 2004).

Chimpanzee communities encompass 20–150 individuals. Males and females operate relatively independently and form smaller fission–fusion units of any sex and age, including all-male hunting groups and nursery groups of a few females with their young (Matsumoto-Oda 1999). Within the group, the unstable dominance hierarchy of males leads to frequent building of coalitions and conflicts. Females are promiscuous and mate with several males within and outside the community; dominant males, however, may try to control females' sexuality and practise infanticide (Lowe *et al.* 2019; Mitani *et al.* 2002).

Bonobos, who live in close proximity and in a comparable environment to chimpanzees, similarly live in groups of *c.* 40–120 individuals that form smaller fission–fusion groups. Bonobos are best known for their sexual behaviour fostering social relationships (de Waal 2006), including sexual behaviour directed to the same sex (Monk *et al.* 2019). The groups are matriarchal and consist of several females and their young. Both sexes establish a dominance hierarchy, and the status of males is often inherited from the mother. Males stay in the natal group upon adolescence, whereas females join other groups in which they aim to establish alliances with mature females.

There is a clear link between the degree of sexual dimorphism in great apes and the way in which males and females interact, giving rise to inferences about how kinship was construed in the past (Foley and Gamble 2009). In contrast with other living hominins, who either exhibit stable breeding bonds or rudimentary descent patterns, but not both (Fox 1967), it is thought that our ancestors combined pair bonding with shifting from matri-focal groups to bi-focal families no longer exclusively centred on mothers, but also on fathers, soon after the Pan–Homo split around 6 million years ago (Lovejoy 1981). Pair bonding included reduced female mobility, food sharing, and continual female sexual receptivity. The recognition of relatives through mothers and fathers led to strong networks of affinity and human kinship. Pair bonding may also have led, albeit not directly, to both parents investing in provisioning and thus sharing the costs of raising children, which is unusually high in humans (Chapais 2008: 168).

Earliest hominids most likely lived in promiscuous multi-male, multi-female groups and first evolved towards polygynous groups, with some males monopolising several females, while other males remained unmated. With the development of the upright gait and the use of tools and weapons, excessive competition between males became too costly. This is why our species evolved towards the multi-family groups that compose 80 per cent of today's societies, in which most families are monogamous and a small proportion polygynous (Chapais 2008: 171). Marriage thus developed as a binding mechanism between groups. Primarily women, not men, moved between the groups (Chapais 2008: 103). Until recently, women had been understood as subjects of exchange between men, but today, exogamy is viewed as a peace-making mechanism between groups that contributed to the development of larger, tribal units.

Barbara Smuts formulated six hypotheses of how gender inequality developed over the course of human evolution: patriarchy developed through a reduction in female allies, the elaboration of male–male alliances, increased male control over resources, increased hierarchy formation among men, female strategies that reinforced male control over females, and the evolution of language and its power to create ideology (Smuts 1995). The female Venus figurines of the Upper Palaeolithic may represent a tangible material expression of such a shared ideology. Shared properties of this type of mobile art indicate contact between groups over a wide Eurasian territory (White *et al.* 1982). One interpretation sees the figurines as tokens representing brides (Taylor 1996: 125), suggesting a starting point of marriage in the Upper Palaeolithic. However, their wide variability includes young and old, thin and obese, as well as pregnant representations, which makes a single and simple explanation of their meaning and function unlikely (Rice 1981; Nelson 2008).

Marriage as a cultural universal

Concepts of marriage differ enormously across cultures, and there is little consensus on the definition of marriage and what exactly it entails. Furthermore, definitions and circumscriptions developed in tandem with societal changes from the beginning of anthropology as a discipline until today. The traditional definition of 'marriage is a union between a man and a woman such that children born to the woman are recognised legitimate offspring of both parents' (Royal Anthropological Institute of Great Britain and Ireland 1951: 111) remains at the heart of most attempts to describe the common denominators of marriage; legitimacy of children, mutual access to sexuality, labour, and property rights, as well as establishing bonds between social groups are listed among the many functions most marriages may entail (Leach 1955: 183).

MARRIAGE, MOTHERHOOD, AND MOBILITY 193

In recent decades, a fierce debate has developed in social and cultural anthropology about what kinship is and is not. On the one hand, the debate centres on the question of to what degree observations and interpretations of Western ethnographers are products of their own (patriarchal) worldviews and imaginations, or discovered real-world social structures; on the other hand, it considers to what extent social kinship is based on genetic relations (Schneider 1984; Carsten 2003; Sahlins 2011a; 2011b; Shapiro 2018).

These are both important concerns for the interpretation of archaeological data, for which traditional ethnographies were frequently employed as analogies. Most cultural anthropologists acknowledge that marriage is found in all societies across the globe (Stone 2009: 18). Importantly, marriage does not imply a wedding; the transition to marital status may be marked by a wedding ceremony as an important rite of passage (Van Gennep 1960 [1909]), but does not necessitate it. Marriage may simply begin informally, by matchmaking or the start of a new relationship.

Alliance theory stresses the bonds created between groups through marriage. Claude Lévi-Strauss, drawing on gift-giving (Mauss 1954), identified reciprocal exogamy as an (almost) universal principle, in that women – sisters and daughters – are exchanged between groups as the most precious commodities, the 'supreme gift' (Lévi-Strauss 1969: 62). In this line of thinking, the significance of marriage lies in the creation of in-laws, who are instrumental in establishing and maintaining peaceful relationships between families and groups. Widespread female exogamy has been put forward as an explanation of why, cross-culturally, there are so few women warriors: not because of a lack of aggressiveness or strength, but because of competing loyalties to husbands and brothers/fathers in case conflicts arise within the marriage network (Adams 1983).

Marriage takes many forms and may include more than two persons, who do not necessarily have to be male and female, or even human. Gough speaks of marriage as 'a relationship established between a woman and one or more other persons, which provides that a child born to the woman under circumstances not prohibited by the rules of the relationship, is accorded full birth-status rights common to normal members of his society or social stratum' (Gough 1959: 32).

Not all definitions of marriage necessitate a link to children's legitimacy. Duran Bell, for instance, sought a definition that acknowledges the common distinction between spouse and lover. In his view, a key concern of marriage is regulating sexual access and moderating the violence of competition through the production of social order. Neither the men nor the women need to be biologically male or female in this definition. Thus, 'marriage is a relationship between one or more men (male or female) in severalty to one or more women that provides those men with a demand-right of sexual access within a domestic group and identifies women who bear the obligation of yielding to the demands of those specific men' (Bell 1997: 241). Legitimacy implies a social order with unequal access to benefits and/ or wealth, to which access may be restricted based on parenthood. 'Both marriage and legitimacy are institutions that relate to the appropriation of scarce resources' (Bell 1997: 244). Nevertheless, the social affiliation of children remains a key

194 *Katharina Rebay-Salisbury*

component of the purpose of marriage. Differentiating the affiliation of children from legitimacy reaches a compromise in this regard, defining marriage as 'one social institution that links rules of sexual access with rules for affiliation of children' (Burton 1997).

Modern definitions expand the concept of marriage to apply to two or more individuals of any sex, aiming to avoid heteronormative notions. As an institution with rights and responsibilities, marriage is a socially or ritually recognised union between spouses, encompassing intimate relations and an intent of permanency (Stone 2009). Since the advent of genetic tests, a biological definition of paternity is gradually replacing the social and legal framework that marriage provided. A child born within marriage was, until recently, understood to be the mother's husband's in many Western societies. Within a marital union, adoption and surrogacy are less problematic if links are socially rather than biologically defined.

Marriage and motherhood in Bronze and Iron Age Europe

Direct archaeological evidence for marriage in the archaeological record is elusive, as it is not possible to excavate social conventions and legal frameworks in prehistoric societies. We can nevertheless perhaps safely assume that forms of marriage existed, and aim to discover some of their properties through inferences from archaeological contexts and pictorial sources. Several studies allow insights into different aspects in different regions and times, but a coherent picture of the development during the last three millennia BC is yet to emerge.

Motherhood does not automatically follow marriage, but as social institutions, the concepts overlap, even if they do not map exactly on to each other. This warrants investigating marriage and motherhood together. Like marriage, motherhood can be understood as both a personal experience and social institution. Adrienne Rich argued that motherhood has two meanings, 'one superimposed on the other: the potential relationship of any woman to her powers of reproduction and to children; and the institution, which aims at ensuring that that potential – and all women – shall remain under male control' (Rich 1997 [1976]: 13). Motherhood has recently become a subject of exploration by anthropologists, archaeologists, and historians, who are contributing knowledge about both aspects of motherhood in past and present (e.g. Liamputtong 2007; Hackworth Petersen and Salzman-Mitchell 2012; O'Reilly 2014; Cooper and Phelan 2017; Myers 2017; Romero and López 2018).

Taking both marriage and motherhood as contributing to female identity, formation results in four possibilities:

1) women who married, but did not have children;
2) women who married and had children;
3) women who did not marry, but still had children;
4) women who did not marry and did not have children.

MARRIAGE, MOTHERHOOD, AND MOBILITY

In this crude categorisation, the specifics of what constitutes motherhood are not addressed, for example if mothering (potentially genetically unrelated) children or biological parturition defines becoming a mother, or whether and for how long the offspring would have had to survive. It also does not imply that marriage and motherhood are the most important aspects of identity, as there are many others that may be more significant, such as age, status, family membership, or personal achievements.

Not all women that were expected to become mothers would have been able to. Infertility affects around 15 per cent of couples worldwide today (Sun *et al.* 2019), and certainly affected women in the past, but it is completely unclear how people of the Bronze and Iron Age dealt with it, if it constituted a problem. Possible fields of action may have included trying to conceive from a lover, commissioning a surrogate mother, or procuring another wife, in addition to/or divorcing the first one.

Some individuals may have had the choice to remain unmarried and/or childless and control their own fertility. Only about half of all women between 15 and 50 years of age were married before industrialisation in Western Europe; the others were spinsters, nuns, or widowed early (Hajnal 1965). Census data from 19th-century Austria suggests a link between micro-regional socioeconomic structures and marriage rates, which ranged between 30 and 60 per cent (Teibenbacher 2012). Marriage was linked to the ownership of land and property, and a limit of resources limits the number of marriages that can take place – a mechanism that has also been assumed for the Celtic Iron Age (Karl 2006).

If a certain amount of wealth and/or property were indeed a precondition of marriage, this may result in several effects. It would have excluded the less well-off from (legitimate) reproduction, and it may have raised the age at marriage, as spouses would have had to wait until sufficient resources were accumulated or inherited. The age of first motherhood has profound implications on maternal mortality, the total number of children a woman will have, and on gender relations. Women who start reproduction at a young age, when their pelvis is not yet mature, carry medical risks for themselves and their babies (Ganchimeg *et al.* 2014). Socially, however, girls as young as 12–14 appear to have been adorned with jewellery and costume elements like adult women in Early Bronze Age cemeteries such as Franzhausen I (Figure 9.1) (Neugebauer and Neugebauer 1997) or Gemeinlebarn F (Neugebauer 1991) in Lower Austria.

That a young age for marriage and motherhood is not just a burial custom, but was reality at least for some, is demonstrated by several instances of teenage pregnant women in Early Bronze Age cemeteries (Rebay-Salisbury 2017b; Rebay-Salisbury *et al.* 2018). Adolescent women tend to be married younger during conflicts and war and in unstable political systems, often to much older partners that promise protection the birth family can no longer provide. Child marriage among Syrian refugees has been recently documented (United Nations Population Fund 2017) and is addressed as a gender-specific challenge for female migrants.

Figure 9.1 Burial of a 12–14-year-old girl with sheet bronze band indicating a head covering, from Franzhausen I (Verf. 334) (© Bundesdenkmalamt Austria)

A shift towards a higher marital age may indicate more peaceful times and explain why, in comparison with the Early Bronze Age, there are fewer pregnant women under 20 in the Iron Age (Rebay-Salisbury 2018b). However, there are many other factors at play. Women in Late Iron Age Northern Europe married significantly later than Roman women in the south, with those marrying later having fewer offspring overall (Burmeister and Gebühr 2018).

Unequal access to wealth and resources among men may enable some men to have multiple wives. Direct evidence for polygyny may be expected from advancement in kinship studies through ancient DNA. While serial monogamy cannot be differentiated from polygyny, the ratio of men and women reproducing can be estimated. Neolithisation is thought to coincide with a bottleneck in Y chromosome diversity (Karmin *et al.* 2015), with as many as 17 women reproducing for each man, rather than the global average of four–five. In addition, a male bias in admixture events such as the Late Neolithic/Early Bronze Age Pontic–Caspian Steppe migration has been suspected (Irrgeher *et al.* 2012; Goldberg *et al.* 2017; cf. Lazaridis and Reich 2017). In the Graeco-Roman, and later Christian, tradition, it was not an option to be married to more than one wife at any one time, despite the possibilities of divorce and remarriage. This contrasts with ancient Germanic, Near Eastern, and Judaic traditions, in which polygyny is a distinct possibility (Scheidel 2009). Polygamy, particularly in the form of polygyny, remains a likely form of marriage for prehistoric communities with differential access to wealth.

Unequal access to wealth and resources between the sexes may lead to age differences between the man and woman of a couple. In Bronze Age cemeteries, the combination of a man with a woman who is a decade or more his junior is common. At Early Bronze Age Unterhautzenthal in Lower Austria, for example, a 35–40-year-old male was buried with a 17–20-year-old woman and the remains of an infant in one of the largest and best-equipped graves of the group (Rebay-Salisbury *et al.* 2018). The exceptional cremation grave with a sword from Late Bronze Age Brno-Horní Heršpice in Moravia (Fojtík and Parma 2018; Kala 2018), to present a second example, contained a similar combination of an old, young, and foetal individual.

Social groups for which reproduction was discouraged might have existed; the depiction of sexless persons in Iron Age art may allude to a group of people for which gender and reproduction were not the primary concern (Rebay-Salisbury 2016). Wedding scenes on Early Iron Age situlae from the Circum-Alpine region depict sex between a man and a woman, always witnessed by a bystander, who ensures biological relatedness of the father in the absence of paternity tests. From this concern about the legitimisation of children through marriage, it follows that there was socially sanctioned and supported reproduction, as well as children that were born out of wedlock, who did not have the same status and access to resources. A closer look at diet, health, and status among children from prehistoric cemeteries may reveal differences that may be explained – among others – by their different legal status.

Figure 9.2 Situla from Montebelluna, grave 244 (drawing by Stefano Buson and Leonardo Di Simone after Serafini and Zaghetto 2019: 69, Figure 1; CC BY 4.0 International Public Licence)

On situlae, the depiction of movement is frequently paired with marital scenes. The situla from Pieve d'Alpago, prov. Belluno (Gangemi 2013) shows a procession of travellers in the first two friezes, while the last frieze centres on courtship, sex in a variety of positions, and a birth, the result of the marital union. The situla from Montebelluna, prov. Treviso (Figure 9.2) embeds the crucial marital scene in the full repertoire of travelling and feasting imagery, and perhaps shows its result in the form of a pregnant woman spinning wool (Serafini and Zaghetto 2019). The woman travelling as a passenger on a two-wheeled cart in the first frieze may allude to her residence change upon marriage.

The image fits the exogamous marriage and patrilocal residence patterns inferred among the Early Iron Age elite in south-west Germany through similarities in material culture and genetic analyses (Arnold 2012). Women changed their appearance at the onset of adulthood by covering their head with a veil; since a significant proportion of, but not all, women are buried with pins that fit the head cover, a connection to marriage rather than age alone has been suggested (Lenerz-de Wilde 1989). The recent discovery of an exceptionally rich grave of a 2–3-year-old girl with jewellery pointing to Etruscan connections, and an equally well-equipped grave of a 30–40-year-old woman in a double grave at Herbertingen-Bettelbühl near the Heunburg (Krausse and Ebinger-Rist 2018) underline that prestige through far-reaching connections may be heritable, if it was not also children themselves that travelled.

Marriage mobility and gendered migration

Marriage is often the cause of individuals' residence change, as couples settle together, either founding a new household, or moving in with or near to the father's (patrilocality) or the mother's family (matrilocality). A cross-cultural comparison of house sizes revealed that in agricultural societies, large dwellings tend to be associated with matrilocality, whereas smaller dwellings point to patrilocality (Hrnčíř *et al.* 2020). Whether this applies to European prehistory, with the longhouses of the Central European Linear Pottery Culture or the Northern European Bronze and Iron Ages, remains to be further explored.

Inferences about matrilocality and patrilocality have been attempted predominantly through the analysis of strontium isotope analysis in human dental enamel and cremated bone (e.g. Oelze *et al.* 2012a; 2012b; Knipper *et al.* 2018; Cavazzuti *et al.* 2019). The geochemical signatures of the geology from which an individual's diet was sourced are incorporated into body tissues during the life course (Bentley 2006; Montgomery 2010). Most of the strontium isotope signals are incorporated during tissue growth, and remain affected from bone turnover. Testing specific bones and teeth for which the age at formation is understood allows for a detailed mobility reconstruction. First, second, and third molars cover a time span from birth to skeletal maturity, even if the exact age ranges are hard to pinpoint, particularly for the third molar (Knipper 2011: 132). Strontium isotope ratios in the cremated otic capsule of the petrous portion of the inner ear have been shown to correspond to those of premolar enamel (Harvig *et al.* 2014; Snoeck *et al.* 2015).

The identification of non-local individuals is based on discrepancies of the 87Sr/86Sr ratio measured in individuals' dental enamel or cremated bone, and the expected range of the local geology. This approach is of limited use if the geology exhibits too little or too much variation, and if the food sources are not well understood. In terms of interpreting movement as taking place before or after marriage, the formation age of the third molar is of critical importance. Women may enter marital age well before physical maturity, and transition to social adulthood before the biological cut-off age at around 20 years (Rebay-Salisbury and Pany-Kucera 2020).

With bioarchaeological studies alone, it is often impossible to differentiate local interactions from migrations (Kolář 2020). It is here where we need to turn to classic modes of investigation in archaeology such as the distribution patterns of material culture. Residence change may be local, i.e. within the same village, or farther afield – from neighbouring villages to crossing territorial boundaries. The term 'mobility', as used in archaeology, conveys a short-term change of residency, not being rooted in one place, but perhaps in multiple places (Wood *et al.* 2015). It is more often used for individuals, short distances, and movement within known territory. 'Migration' is more often seen as permanent, implying a fixed change of residence, long-distance movement, the crossing of boundaries, and is applied to groups.

High levels of mobility have been found connected to the Corded Ware and Bell Beaker groups in the 3rd millennium BC, in particular the discovery of the introduction of steppe ancestry throughout Europe with its initial male bias (Allentoft *et al.* 2015; Haak *et al.* 2015; Furholt 2017). The patchy distribution of the Bell Beaker

200   *Katharina Rebay-Salisbury*

phenomenon over much of Western Europe may be explained by generalised, open exogamy (Vander Linden 2007), without necessarily being exclusively female. Isotopic studies from Central Europe, Austria, Bavaria, and Hungary identified high levels of mobility for males and females (Price *et al.* 2004; Irrgeher *et al.* 2012). Similarly, male and female migration histories of Beaker people were found to be comparable in Britain (Parker Pearson *et al.* 2016).

Genomic and isotopic data from 104 individuals of the Late Neolithic to Middle Bronze Age brought detailed insights into kinship patterns across the multi-generational farmsteads of the Lech Valley in Bavaria (Massy *et al.* 2017; Mittnik *et al.* 2019). The results imply patrilocality and female exogamy, and more specifically a high-status core family, a number of wealthy, but unrelated, non-local women with no identified offspring, as well as local, low-status individuals.

That women changed residence upon marriage in the Bronze Age has been suspected on the basis of foreign dress elements for a long time (Wels-Weyrauch 1989; Jockenhövel 1991; Kristiansen 1998). The distance between elite women's original and receiving communities is often around three days of travelling, and it would be interesting to know how such travels were organised. Travelling long distances, overcoming exotic and unknown territories, has been largely attributed to male explorers in the Bronze Age (Kristiansen and Larsson 2005), but at least for some Scandinavian Bronze Age women (and children, e.g. the cremated child from Egtved, southern Denmark region), travels of similar magnitude have been suspected (Frei *et al.* 2015; Persson 2017; Bergerbrant 2019; cf. Thomsen and Andreasen 2019).

As marriage has the key function of building alliances between groups of people, it is perhaps useful to consider that individuals may be rooted in more than one place, and move back and forth between the native and marital community to strengthen the networks. It is the bride and groom's families, and often the older female generations, who are most invested in negotiating the terms of marriage. Agency and power may not be in the hands of the younger generation, whose lives were most affected by the actions of the brokers (Frieman *et al.* 2019). It further needs to be considered that marriages might break down, alliances change and rupture, and the pawns of the game return to the field of origin, be they wives or other persons entangled in the building of networks, such as foster children and apprentices (Karl 2005). Marriage might thus be the cause of more than single, uni-directional movements (Reiter and Frei 2019: 462).

In how far women had any say in this process, were allowed to choose their partners, and were involved in decision making about where to relocate is an open question. There are reasons to assume that women's agency was limited. Middle Bronze Age dress and costume, for example, appear heavy and impractical at best, and limit women's scope of action (Sørensen 2013). Use–wear suggests that the items were worn in life, and not just produced for funerary use. The most drastic example is perhaps the woman from Zwiefalten-Upflamör, distr. Reutlingen (Wels-Weyrauch 1989), whose feet were tied together by connecting the leg rings with

MARRIAGE, MOTHERHOOD, AND MOBILITY

a short chain. In addition, it has been cross-culturally observed that during war and conflicts, women may be captured and integrated into a foreign community as wives or slaves (Cameron 2016).

In societies where exogamy combined with patrilocal residence is the norm, maternal grandparents generally do not live in the same economic group as the new family. Women who came from communities farther away might not have had adequate help from their own mothers and maternal relatives when they gave birth, although local support networks might have been in place. Practical help and economic support from maternal grandmothers has a beneficial effect on the survival of children, while the paternal grandparents have little or adverse effects (Hawkes 2004); patrilocal forms of residence might therefore have contributed to high maternal and infant mortality in the past. The longer the distance from the birth family, the less likely maternal grandparents could have been involved (Appleby 2018). Conversely, birth assistance as well as the care for new mothers and young babies may have been one of the mechanisms though which long-distance, return mobility of female relatives may have operated.

Women assuming the role of midwives might have routinely moved between communities. Although breastfeeding (Fulminante 2015) most likely accounted for most of infant feeding, the feeding vessels found in Late Bronze and Iron Age Central Europe show that persons other than the mother were involved in childcare (Rebay-Salisbury 2017a; Dunne *et al.* 2019).

Finally, it is important to note that marriage and post-marital residence change will unlikely suffice to explain all patterns of women's movements. Routine mobility may have included fetching water and tending fields. Longer travels, for example to look after animals on pastures away from the residence, may have been undertaken by one or the other gender preferentially. Transhumance in the high pastures of the Alps is an interesting case in point: due to diverging economic embedding, early modern dairy production was strongly associated with men in the Swiss Alps, but with women in the Austrian Alps (Fath and Fath 2007).

Conclusion

Mobility is – like all experiences – gendered. The motivations for personal mobility, such as finding a partner, work, better conditions to raise a family, or responding to crisis, war, or climate change, are closely bound to gender roles and expectations. Female exogamy and patrilocal residence patterns provide a universal explanation for the increasing wealth of bioarchaeological evidence from Bronze and Iron Age Europe that points to women rather than men changing their residence in adolescence and early adulthood (see also Stockhammer and Massy, Chapter 8). Marriage and the transition to motherhood are the most significant identity changes women may experience. The intersection between gender-specific mobility, marriage, and motherhood, however, needs to be further explored. Studies of mobility

202 *Katharina Rebay-Salisbury*

and migration will benefit from a better understanding of how motherhood was organised, including the age at which women had their first children, the possible marriage and kinship constellations, the distance to the birth family after marriage, and the consequences for continued interaction. When considering women's reproductive roles – both biologically and socially – we can investigate in more detail the role of female movement in shaping societies.

Acknowledgements

Michaela Fritzl has contributed the now omitted case study of Late Bronze Age Inzersdorf in our co-authored presentation in Edinburgh. I would like to thank her for discussions on the topic of female movement and mobility. Rachel J. Crellin, Catherine J. Frieman, and Daniela Hofmann provided very helpful critical comments on previous versions of the manuscript. The project 'The Value of Mothers to Society: Responses to Motherhood and Child Rearing Practices in Prehistoric Europe' has received funding from the ERC under the European Union's Horizon 2020 research and innovation programme (grant agreement no. 676828).

References

Adams, D. (1983), 'Why there are so few women warriors', *Behavior Science Research*, 18(3): 196–212.

Allentoft, M., Sikora, E., Sjögren, M., Rasmussen, S., Rasmussen, M., *et al.* (2015), 'Population genomics of Bronze Age Eurasia', *Nature*, 522: 167–72.

Appleby, J. (2018), 'Grandparents in the Bronze Age?', in G. Lillehammer and E. Murphy (eds), *Across the Generations: The Old and the Young in Past Societies* (Stavanger, Museum of Archaeology and University of Stavanger), 49–60.

Arnold, B. (2012), 'Gender, temporalities, and periodization in Early Iron Age West-Central Europe', *Social Science History*, 36(1): 85–112.

Bell, D. (1997), 'Defining marriage and legitimacy', *Current Anthropology*, 38(2): 237–53.

Bentley, A.R. (2006), 'Strontium isotopes from the Earth to the archaeological skeleton: a review', *Journal of Archaeological Method and Theory*, 13(3): 135–87.

Bergerbrant, S. (2019), 'Revisiting "the Egtved girl"', in R. Berge and M.M. Henriksen (eds), *Arkeologi og kulturhistorie fra norskekysten til Østersjøen: Festskrift til professor Birgitta Berglund* (Trondheim, NTNU Vitenskapsmuseet), 18–39.

Brodie, N. (1997), 'New perspectives on the Bell Beaker culture', *Oxford Journal of Archaeology*, 16(3): 297–314.

Brück, J. (2019), *Personifying Prehistory: Relational Ontologies in Bronze Age Britain and Ireland* (Oxford, Oxford University Press).

Burmeister, S. and Gebühr, M. (2018), 'Demographic aspects of Iron Age societies', in C. Haselgrove, K. Rebay-Salisbury, and P.S. Wells (eds) (2018), *The Oxford Handbook of the European Iron Age* (Oxford, Oxford University Press), DOI: 10.1093/oxfordhb/9780199696826.013.9.

Burton, M.L. (1997), 'Comments on "Defining marriage and legitimacy" by Duran Bell', *Current Anthropology*, 38(2): 244–6.

Buss, D.M. (2006), 'Strategies of human mating', *Psihologijske Teme*, 15(2): 239–60.

Cameron, C.M. (2016), *Captives: How Stolen People Changed the World* (Lincoln NE and London, University of Nebraska Press).

Carsten, J. (2003), *After Kinship: New Departures in Anthropology* (Cambridge, Cambridge University Press).

Cavazzuti, C., Skeates, R., Millard, A.R., Nowell, G., Peterkin, J., *et al.* (2019), 'Flows of people in villages and large centres in Bronze Age Italy through strontium and oxygen isotopes', *PLoS ONE*, 14(1): e0209693, DOI: 10.1371/journal.pone.0209693.

Chapais, B. (2008), *Primeval Kinship: How Pair-Bonding Gave Birth to Human Society* (Cambridge MA, Harvard University Press).

Cooper, D. and Phelan, C. (eds) (2017), *Motherhood in Antiquity* (New York NY, Palgrave Macmillan).

Crellin, R.J. (2020), 'Review of: Brück, J. (2019), Personifying prehistory: relational ontologies in Bronze Age Britain and Ireland (Oxford: Oxford University Press)', *Cambridge Archaeological Journal*, 30(2): 360–1.

De Waal, F.B.M. (2006), 'Bonobo sex and society', *Scientific American Special Editions*, 16(3): 14–21.

Delgado Jr, R.A. and Van Schaik, C.P. (2000), 'The behavioral ecology and conservation of the orangutan (*Pongo pygmaeus*): a tale of two islands', *Evolutionary Anthropology: Issues, News, and Reviews*, 9(5): 201–18.

Dunne, J., Rebay-Salisbury, K., Salisbury, R.B., Frisch, A., Walton-Doyle, C., *et al.* (2019), 'Milk of ruminants in ceramic baby bottles from prehistoric child graves', *Nature*, 574: 246–8.

Fath, T. and Fath, W. (2007), *Frauenleben in alter Zeit: Mütter und Töchter erzählen* (Wien, Böhlau Verlag).

Fojtík, P. and Parma, D. (2018), 'Doba bronzová / Bronzezeit', in K. Geislerová and D. Parma (eds), Výzkumy: Ausgrabungen 2011–16 (Brno, Ústav Archeologické Památkové Péče), 53–68.

Fokkens, H. and Harding, A. (eds) (2013), *The Oxford Handbook of the European Bronze Age* (Oxford, Oxford University Press), DOI: 10.1093/oxfordhb/9780199572861.001.0001.

Foley, R. and Gamble, C. (2009), 'The ecology of social transitions in human evolution', *Philosophical Transactions of the Royal Society of London B*, 364: 3267–79.

Fox, R. (1967), *Kinship and Marriage: An anthropological perspective* (Baltimore MD, Penguin Books).

Frei, K.M., Mannering, U., Kristiansen, K., Allentoft, M.E., Wilson, A.S., *et al.* (2015), 'Tracing the dynamic life story of a Bronze Age female', *Scientific Reports*, 5: 10431, DOI: 10.1038/srep10431.

Frieman, C.J., Teather, A., and Morgan, C. (2019), 'Bodies in motion: narratives and counter narratives of gendered mobility in European later prehistory', *Norwegian Archaeological Review*, 52(2): 148–69.

Fulminante, F. (2015), 'Infant feeding practices in Europe and the Mediterranean from prehistory to the Middle Ages: a comparison between the historical sources and bioarchaeology', *Childhood in the Past*, 8(1): 24–47.

Furholt, M. (2017), 'Massive migrations? The impact of recent aDNA studies on our view of third millennium Europe', *European Journal of Archaeology*, 21(2): 159–91.

Furtwängler, A., Rohrlach, A.B., Lamnidis, T.C., Papac, L., Neumann, G.U., *et al.* (2020), 'Ancient genomes reveal social and genetic structure of Late Neolithic Switzerland', *Nature Communications*, 11(1): 1915, DOI: 10.1038/s41467-020-15560-x.

Galdikas, B.M.F. (1985), 'Orangutan sociality at Tanjung Putting', *American Journal of Primatology*, 9(2): 101–19.

Ganchimeg, T., Ota, E., Morisaki, N., Laopaiboon, M., Lumbiganon, P., *et al.* (2014), 'Pregnancy and childbirth outcomes among adolescent mothers: a World Health Organization multicountry study', *BJOG: An International Journal of Obstetrics and Gynaecology*, 121: 40–8.

Gangemi, G. (2013), 'La situla della tomba I di Pieve d'Alpago', in M. Gamba (ed), *Venetkens: Viaggio nella terra dei Veneti antichi, Padova, Palazzo della Ragione, 6 Aprile–17 Novembre 2013* (Venezia, Marsilio), 283–7.

Goldberg, A., Günther, T., Rosenberg, N.A., and Jakobsson, M. (2017), 'Ancient X chromosomes reveal contrasting sex bias in Neolithic and Bronze Age Eurasian migrations', *Proceedings of the National Academy of Sciences of the United States of America*, 114(10): 2657–62.

Gough, E.K. (1959), 'The Nayars and the definition of marriage', *Journal of the Royal Anthropological Institute of Great Britain and Ireland*, 89(1): 23–34.

Haak, W., Lazaridis, I., Patterson, N., Rohland, N., Mallick, S., *et al.* (2015), 'Massive migration from the steppe was a source for Indo-European languages in Europe', *Nature*, 522: 207–11.

Hackworth Petersen, L. and Salzman-Mitchell, P. (eds) (2012), *Mothering and Motherhood in Ancient Greece and Rome* (Austin TX, University of Texas Press).

Hajnal, J. (1965), 'European marriage patterns in perspective', in D.V. Glass and D.E.C. Eversley (eds), *Population in History* (Chicago IL, Aldine), 101–43.

Harvig, L., Frei, K.M., Price, T.D., and Lynnerup, N. (2014), 'Strontium isotope signals in cremated petrous portions as indicator for childhood origin', *PLoS ONE*, 9(7): e101603, DOI: 10.1371/journal.pone.0101603.

Haselgrove, C., Rebay-Salisbury, K., and Wells, P.S. (eds) (2018), *The Oxford Handbook of the European Iron Age* (Oxford, Oxford University Press), DOI: 10.1093/oxfordhb/9780199696826.001.0001.

Hawkes, K. (2004), 'Human longevity: the grandmother effect', *Nature*, 428: 128–9.

Hrnčíř, V., Duda, P., Šaffa, G., Květina, P., and Zrzavý, J. (2020), 'Identifying post-marital residence patterns in prehistory: a phylogenetic comparative analysis of dwelling size', *PLoS ONE*, 15(2): e0229363, DOI: 10.1371/journal.pone.0229363.

Irrgeher, J., Teschler-Nicola, M., Leutgeb, K., Weiß, C., Kern, D., *et al.* (2012), 'Migration and mobility in the Latest Neolithic of the Traisen Valley, Lower Austria: Sr isotope analysis', in E. Kaiser, J. Burger, and W. Schier (eds), *Population Dynamics in Prehistory and Early History: New Approaches by Using Stable Isotopes and Genetics* (Berlin and Boston, Walter de Gruyter), 199–211.

Jockenhövel, A. (1991), 'Räumliche Mobilität von Personen in der mittleren Bronzezeit des westlichen Mitteleuropas', *Germania*, 69: 49–62.

Kala, J. (2018), 'Antropologie / Anthropologie', in K. Geislerová and D. Parma (eds), *Výzkumy: Ausgrabungen 2011–16* (Brno, Ústav Archeologické Památkové Péče), 155–80.

Karl, R. (2005), 'Master and apprentice, knight and squire: education in the "Celtic" Iron Age', *Oxford Journal of Archaeology*, 24(3): 255–71.

Karl, R. (2006), *Altkeltische Sozialstrukturen* (Budapest, Archaeolingua).

Karmin, M., Saag, L., Vicente, M., Wilson Sayres, M.A., Järve, M., *et al.* (2015), 'A recent bottleneck of Y chromosome diversity coincides with a global change in culture', *Genome Research*, 25(4): 459–66.

Knipper, C. (2011), *Die räumliche Organisation der linearbandkeramischen Rinderhaltung: Naturwissenschaftliche und archäologische Untersuchungen* (Oxford, Archaeopress).

MARRIAGE, MOTHERHOOD, AND MOBILITY 205

Knipper, C., Mittnik, A., Massy, K., Kociumaka, C., Kucukkalipci, I., *et al.* (2017), 'Female exogamy and gene pool diversification at the transition from the Final Neolithic to the Early Bronze Age in Central Europe', *Proceedings of the National Academy of Sciences of the United States of America*, 114(38): 10083–8.

Knipper, C., Pichler, S.L., Brönnimann, D., Rissanen, H., Rosner, M., *et al.* (2018), 'A knot in a network: residential mobility at the Late Iron Age proto-urban centre of Basel-Gasfabrik (Switzerland) revealed by isotope analyses', *Journal of Archaeological Science: Reports*, 17: 735–53.

Knott, C.D., Emery Thompson, M., Stumpf, R.M., and McIntyre, M.H. (2010), 'Female reproductive strategies in orangutans, evidence for female choice and counterstrategies to infanticide in a species with frequent sexual coercion', *Proceedings of the Royal Society B*, 277(1678): 105–13.

Kolář, J. (2020), 'Migrations or local interactions? Spheres of interaction in third-millennium BC Central Europe', *Antiquity*, 94(377): 1168–85.

Krausse, D. and Ebinger-Rist, N. (eds) (2018), *Das Geheimnis der Keltenfürstin: Der sensationelle Fund von der Heuneburg* (Darmstadt, Theiss Verlag).

Kristiansen, K. (1998), *Europe Before History* (Cambridge, Cambridge University Press).

Kristiansen, K. and Larsson, T.B. (2005), *The Rise of Bronze Age Society: Travels, Transmissions and Transformations* (Cambridge, Cambridge University Press).

Lazaridis, I. and Reich, D. (2017), 'Failure to replicate a genetic signal for sex bias in the steppe migration into Central Europe', *Proceedings of the National Academy of Sciences of the United States of America*, 114(20): e3873–4, DOI: 10.1073/pnas.1704308114.

Leach, E. (1955), 'Polyandry, inheritance and the definition of marriage', *Man*, 55: 182–6.

Lenerz-de Wilde, M. (1989), 'Überlegungen zur Frauentracht der Späthallstattzeit an der oberen Donau', *Fundberichte aus Baden-Württemberg*, 14: 251–72.

Lévi-Strauss, C. (1969), *The Elementary Structures of Kinship/Les Structures élémentaires de la parenté*, 1949 translation, J. Harle Bell, J. Richard von Sturmer, and R. Needham (eds) (Boston MA, Beacon Press).

Liamputtong, P. (ed) (2007), *Reproduction, Childbearing and Motherhood: A Cross-Cultural Perspective* (New York NY, Nova Science).

Lovejoy, O. (1981), 'The origin of man', *Science*, 211(4480): 341–50.

Lowe, A.E., Hobaiter, C., and Newton-Fisher, N.E. (2019), 'Countering infanticide: chimpanzee mothers are sensitive to the relative risks posed by males on differing rank trajectories', *American Journal of Physical Anthropology*, 168(1): 3–9.

Massy, K., Knipper, C., Mittnik, A., Kraus, S., Pernicka, E., *et al.* (2017), 'Patterns of transformation from the Final Neolithic to the Early Bronze Age: a case study from the Lech Valley south of Augsburg', in P.W. Stockhammer and J. Maran (eds), *Appropriating Innovations: Entangled Knowledge in Eurasia 5000–1500 BCE* (Oxford, Oxbow), 241–61.

Matsumoto-Oda, A. (1999), 'Mahale chimpanzees: grouping patterns and cycling females', *American Journal of Primatology*, 47(3): 197–207.

Mauss, M. (1954), *The Gift: Forms and Functions of Exchange in Archaic Societies* (London, Cohen & West).

Mitani, J.C., Watts, D.P., and Muller, M.N. (2002), 'Recent developments in the study of wild chimpanzee behavior', *Evolutionary Anthropology: Issues, News, and Reviews*, 11(1): 9–25.

Mittnik, A., Massy, K., Knipper, C., Wittenborn, F., Pfrengle, S., *et al.* (2019), 'Kinship-based social inequality in Bronze Age Europe', *Science*, 366(6466): 731–4.

Monk, J.D., Giglio, E., Kamath, A., Lambert, M.R., and McDonough, C.E. (2019), 'An alternative hypothesis for the evolution of same-sex sexual behaviour in animals', *Nature Ecology & Evolution*, 3(12): 1622–31.

Monroy Kuhn, J.M., Jakobsson, M., and Günther, T. (2018), 'Estimating genetic kin relationships in prehistoric populations', *PLoS ONE*, 13(4): e0195491, DOI: 10.1371/journal.pone.0195491.

Montgomery, J. (2010), 'Passports from the past: investigating human dispersals using strontium isotope analysis of tooth enamel', *Annals of Human Biology*, 37(3): 325–46.

Myers, A.D. (2017), *Blessed Among Women? Mothers and Motherhood in the New Testament* (Oxford, Oxford University Press).

Nelson, S.M. (2008), 'Diversity of the Upper Paleolithic "Venus" figurines and archeological mythology', *Archeological Papers of the American Anthropological Association*, 2(1): 11–22.

Neugebauer, J.-W. (1991), *Die Nekropole F von Gemeinlebarn, Niederösterreich: Untersuchungen zu den Bestattungssitten und zum Grabraub in der ausgehenden Frühbronzezeit in Niederösterreich südlich der Donau zwischen Enns und Wienerwald* (Mainz, Verlag Philipp von Zabern).

Neugebauer, C. and Neugebauer, J.-W. (1997), *Franzhausen: Das frühbronzezeitliche Gräberfeld I* (Horn, Ferdinand Berger & Söhne).

Oelze, V.M., Koch, J.K., Kupke, K., Nehlich, O., Zauner, S., *et al.* (2012a), 'Multi-isotopic analysis reveals individual mobility and diet at the Early Iron Age monumental tumulus of Magdalenenberg, Germany', *American Journal of Physical Anthropology*, 148(3): 406–21.

Oelze, V.M., Nehlich, O., and Richards, M.P. (2012b), '"There's no place like home": no isotopic evidence for mobility at the Early Bronze Age cemetery of Singen, Germany', *Archaeometry*, 54(4): 752–78.

O'Reilly, A. (ed) (2014), *Mothers, Mothering and Motherhood across Cultural Difference: A Reader* (Toronto, Demeter Press).

Parker Pearson, M., Chamberlain, A., Jay, M., Richards, M., Sheridan, A., *et al.* (2016), 'Beaker people in Britain: migration, mobility and diet', *Antiquity*, 90(351): 620–37.

Persson, C.P. (2017), 'Another female Bronze Age icon is now known to have travelled across Europe', accessed 11 April 2017, http://sciencenordic.com/another-female-bronze-age-icon-now-known-have-travelled-across-europe.

Price, T.D., Knipper, C., Grupe, G., and Smrcka, V. (2004), 'Strontium isotopes and prehistoric human migration: the Bell Beaker period in Central Europe', *European Journal of Archaeology*, 7(1): 9–40.

Rebay-Salisbury, K. (2016), 'Male, female and sexless figures of the Hallstatt Culture: indicators of social order and reproductive control?', *Expression*, 11: 58–63.

Rebay-Salisbury, K. (2017a), 'Breast is best – and are there alternatives? Feeding babies and young children in prehistoric Europe', *Mitteilungen der Anthropologischen Gesellschaft in Wien*, 147: 13–29.

Rebay-Salisbury, K. (2017b), 'Bronze Age beginnings: the conceptualisation of motherhood in prehistoric Europe', in D. Cooper and C. Phelan (eds), *Motherhood in Antiquity* (New York NY, Palgrave Macmillan), 169–96.

Rebay-Salisbury, K. (2018a), 'Personal relationships between co-buried individuals in the Central European Early Bronze Age', in G. Lillehammer and E. Murphy (eds), *Across the Generations: The Old and the Young in Past Societies* (Stavanger, Museum of Archaeology and University of Stavanger), 35–48.

Rebay-Salisbury, K. (2018b), 'Tod während Schwangerschaft und Geburt in der Eisenzeit', in H. Wendling, M. Augstein, J. Fries-Knoblach, K. Ludwig, R. Schumann, *et al.* (eds),

MARRIAGE, MOTHERHOOD, AND MOBILITY   207

Übergangswelten – Todesriten: Forschungen zur Bestattungskultur der europäischen Eisenzeit (Langenweissbach, Verlag Beier & Beran), 91–107.

Rebay-Salisbury, K. and Pany-Kucera, D. (2020), 'Introduction: children's developmental stages from biological, anthropological and archaeological perspectives', in K. Rebay-Salisbury and D. Pany-Kucera (eds), *Ages and Abilities: The Stages of Childhood and their Social Recognition in Prehistoric Europe and Beyond* (Oxford: Archaeopress), 1–9.

Rebay-Salisbury, K., Pany-Kucera, D., Spannagl-Steiner, M., Kanz, F., Galeta, P., *et al.* (2018), 'Motherhood at Early Bronze Age Unterhautzenthal, Lower Austria', *Archaeologia Austriaca*, 102: 71–134.

Rebay-Salisbury, K., Pany-Kucera, D., Spannagl-Steiner, M., Strobl, C., and Parson, W. (in prep), 'Tracing maternal relatedness in the Bronze Age through mitochondrial DNA'.

Reiter, S.S. and Frei, K.M. (2019), 'Interpreting past human mobility patterns: a model', *European Journal of Archaeology*, 22(4): 454–69.

Rice, P.C. (1981), 'Prehistoric Venuses: symbols of motherhood or womanhood?', *Journal of Anthropological Research*, 37(4): 402–14.

Rich, A.C. (1997 [1976]), *Of Woman Born: Motherhood as Experience and Institution* (London, Virago).

Rio, A. (2017), *Slavery after Rome, 500–1100* (Oxford, Oxford University Press).

Robbins, M.M., Bermejo, M., Cipolletta, C., Magliocca, F., Parnell, R.J., *et al.* (2004), 'Social structure and life-history patterns in western gorillas (gorilla gorilla gorilla)', *American Journal of Primatology*, 64(2): 145–59.

Romero, M.S. and López, R.C. (eds) (2018), *Motherhood and Infancies in the Mediterranean in Antiquity* (Oxford, Oxbow).

Royal Anthropological Institute of Great Britain and Ireland (1951), *Notes and Queries on Anthropology* (London, Routledge and Kegan Paul).

Sahlins, M. (2011a), 'What kinship is (part one)', *Journal of the Royal Anthropological Institute*, 17(1): 2–19.

Sahlins, M. (2011b), 'What kinship is (part two)', *Journal of the Royal Anthropological Institute*, 17(2): 227–42.

Scheidel, W. (2009), 'A peculiar institution? Greco-Roman monogamy in global context', *History of the Family*, 14: 280–91.

Schneider, D. (1984), *A Critique of the Study of Kinship* (Ann Arbor MI, University of Michigan Press).

Serafini, A.R. and Zaghetto, L. (2019), 'L'attesa della signora: Le filatrici sulla situla della tomba 244 di Montebelluna', in G.C. Marrone, G. Gambacurta, and A. Marinetti (eds), *Il dono di Altino: Scritti di archeologia in onore di Margherita Tirellia* (Venezia, Ca' Foscari), 57–72.

Shapiro, W.L. (2018), 'Fifteen complaints against the new kinship studies', *Anthropos*, 113: 21–38.

Singleton, I. and Van Schaik, C.P. (2002), 'The social organisation of a population of Sumatran orang-utans', *Folia Primatologica*, 73(1): 1–20.

Smuts, B. (1995), 'The evolutionary origins of patriarchy', *Human Nature*, 6(1): 1–32.

Snoeck, C., Lee-Thorp, J., Schulting, R., de Jong, J., Debouge, W., *et al.* (2015), 'Calcined bone provides a reliable substrate for strontium isotope ratios as shown by an enrichment experiment', *Rapid Communications in Mass Spectrometry*, 29(1): 107–14.

Sørensen, M.L.S. (2013), 'Identity, gender, and dress in the European Bronze Age', in H. Fokkens and A. Harding (eds), *The Oxford Handbook of the European Bronze Age* (Oxford, Oxford University Press), 216–33.

Stone, L. (2009), *Kinship and Gender: An Introduction* (Boulder CO, Westview).

Sun, H., Gong, T.-T., Jiang, Y.-T., Zhang, S., Zhao, Y.-H., *et al.* (2019), 'Global, regional, and national prevalence and disability-adjusted life-years for infertility in 195 countries and territories, 1990–2017: results from a global burden of disease study, 2017', *Aging*, 11(23): 10952–91.

Taylor, T. (1996), *The Prehistory of Sex: Four Million Years of Human Sexual Culture* (London, Fourth Estate).

Teibenbacher, P. (2012), 'Fertility decline in the southeastern Austrian Crown lands: was there a Hajnal line or a transitional zone?', *Max Planck Institute for Demographic Research Working Paper WP-2012-020*, DOI: 10.4054/MPIDR-WP-2012-020.

Thomsen, E. and Andreasen, R. (2019), 'Agricultural lime disturbs natural strontium isotope variations: implications for provenance and migration studies', *Science Advances*, 5(3): eaav8083, DOI: 10.1126/sciadv.aav8083.

United Nations Population Fund (2017), 'New study finds child marriage rising among most vulnerable Syrian refugees', accessed 15 October 2020, www.unfpa.org/news/new-study-finds-child-marriage-rising-among-most-vulnerable-syrian-refugees.

Van Gennep, A. (1960 [1909]), *The Rites of Passage/Les rites de passage*, translation, M.B. Vizedom and G.L. Caffee (London, Routledge).

Vander Linden, M. (2007), 'What linked the Bell Beakers in third millennium BC Europe?', *Antiquity*, 81: 343–52.

Walvin, J. (1983), 'Slaves and Serfs', in J. Walvin (ed), *Slavery and the Slave Trade: A Short Illustrated History* (London, Macmillan Education UK), 13–24.

Wels-Weyrauch, U. (1989), 'Mittelbronzezeitliche Frauentrachten in Süddeutschland: Beziehungen zur Hagenauer Gruppierung', in Ministère de l'Éducation Nationale, de la Jeunesse et des Sports – Comité des Travaux Historiques et Scientifiques (ed), *Dynamique du Bronze moyen en Europe occidentale* (Paris, CTHS), 117–34.

White, R., Arts, N., Bahn, P.G., Binford, L.R., Dewez, M., *et al.* (1982), 'Rethinking the Middle/Upper Paleolithic transition [and comments and replies]', *Current Anthropology*, 23(2): 169–92.

Wood, G., Hilti, N., Kramer, C., and Schier, M. (2015), 'A residential perspective on multi-locality', *Tijdschrift voor Economische en Sociale Geografie*, 106(4): 363–77.

10

Migration in Archaeological Discourse: Two Case Studies from the Late Bronze and Early Iron Ages

CAROLA METZNER-NEBELSICK*

Introduction: perspectives on migration in past discourses

MIGRATION IS CURRENTLY one of the most hotly debated topics in archaeological discourse. This volume pays tribute to that. As Stefan Burmeister (2017) recently stated with reference to the German historian Klaus J. Bade (2002), migration is a *conditio humana*.

The amount of literature dealing with migration, especially in archaeology, is vast. Today, this may not seem surprising at all. When we open our daily newspaper or check the news online, we are confronted with often tragic reports of millions of people on the move on a global scale.[1] They migrate because they were forced to leave their homes due to various life-threatening events like wars and conflicts, or the effects of the current climate crisis. The hundreds of reported deaths of people who drown every year in their fatal attempts to cross the Mediterranean in pursuit of personal safety or better living conditions in Europe are just one example of the cruel realities of migration in the 21st century.

Before I present my two case studies, I would like to compare this current situation with that in the early 1990s when I started to work as an archaeologist. At that time, two iconic papers triggered a still ongoing debate. These were 'Migration in archeology: the baby and the bathwater' by David Anthony (1990) and the slightly earlier article by Kristian Kristiansen on the Danish Single Grave and continental

---

* Dedicated to the memory of my friend Eva Hübner, a leading authority on the Single Grave Culture.
[1] The International Organization of Migration (IOM) of the United Nations (UN) state in their World Migration Report 2020 that in 2019, 272 million people or 3.5 per cent of the world's population were migrants: www.un.org/sites/un2.un.org/files/wmr_2020.pdf (accessed 22 February 2021). This estimate combines various kinds of migrants including, for instance, labour migration.

Proceedings of the British Academy, **254**, 209–233, © The British Academy 2023.

210   *Carola Metzner-Nebelsick*

Corded Ware cultures (Kristiansen 1989), in which he strongly argued in favour of the immigration of the latter into Late Neolithic Denmark.[2] This is not the place for a detailed account of the ensuing discourse on migration in archaeology (e.g. Chapman and Hamerow 1997; Härke 1998; Burmeister 2000). However, an important argument within this discourse needs to be reconsidered, since it is significant for my first case study in the second part of this chapter. Namely, the question put forward by Burmeister (2000: 539–40; 2017: 4–5) about why the topic of migrations was not significant in archaeology from the 1960s to the 1980s, which contrasts with debates taking place in different disciplines, such as in politics or other social sciences. Kristiansen suggested that from a Central or Western European perspective, this could be explained by the then peaceful political situation, or as Heinrich Härke (1998) pointed out, the interest in or the avoidance of migration as a topic was/is very much dependent on the political environment in general. However, Burmeister (2000) remarked that if the latter was true, we must explain why our discipline took a different turn and only integrated migration into the debate with a substantial delay compared with other disciplines such as social sciences or political studies. He suggested that the reasons for this reluctance to engage with the topic of migration lie within the discipline itself.

In my opinion, at least in Germany, the neglect or rather a certain reluctance to deal with migration phenomena as we understand them today can be directly explained by the troubled history of research in the Nazi period.[3] In addition, during the last quarter of the 20th century, theoretical and mostly terminological differentiation was, bar a few exceptions, not part of the overall archaeological discourse (Chapman and Hamerow 1997; Burmeister 2000; Prien 2005). The missing epistemological debate[4] about different forms of migration and mobility tended to limit the concept of migration to its aggressive form (i.e. invasion). For some young researchers like myself, writing in the last quarter of the 20th century, invasionist narratives instrumentalised and misused by lethal Nazi ideology made migration a tainted or at best an unattractive topic.

The processual archaeology prevailing in the 1970s and early 1980s negated migration as an explanatory factor for cultural change and featured a relatively static understanding of culture. Together with the increasing awareness and greater receptivity towards critical assessments of archaeological theories in general, this approach had then the attractive appeal of modernity. Moreover, before the fall of the Iron Curtain, the seemingly unchangeable political world order created a general, perhaps unconsciously sensed, feeling of stasis. The absence of the internet, which today offers what were then unthinkable forms of mass communication

---

[2] For a thorough discussion up to the 1990s of the debate on the origin or emergence of the Single Grave culture in Denmark see Hübner 2005: 39–56, 708–19.

[3] See Anthony 1996: 83 on how archaeological interpretation is influenced by or contingent on local history.

[4] This applies to prehistoric archaeology in particular; for the debate concerning the Migration Period and the Early Middle Ages see Prien 2005; Burmeister 2013; Wiedmann *et al.* 2017.

and information, certainly supported this static perception. Besides, the overall social and political environment in the saturated 'Western World' did not create an atmosphere in which migration was seen as a prominent or inherent phenomenon affecting cultural theory.[5]

The current situation

As we all know, the recent groundbreaking leaps forward in biomolecular methodology and its applications to archaeology, which include isotope analyses and ancient DNA studies, combined with the vast potential of next-generation sequencing (NGS) and advanced computational developments allowing modelling of more complex and big data, resulted in a paradigm shift (Kuhn 1970) in archaeological science and archaeology in general. Kristiansen (2014) referred to this development as the 'Third Science Revolution in Archaeology'. With the advancements in ancient DNA analyses, migration was back on the agenda with a big bang and is undoubtedly proving to have been a major impact factor in cultural change in prehistory. The first papers (Brandt *et al.* 2013; Allentoft *et al.* 2015; Haak *et al.* 2015)[6] which proposed significant changes in the European gene pool in the 3rd millennium BC as the result of a large-scale migration or rather immigration from Eastern Europe, however, met well-grounded criticism concerning the cultural interpretations connected with their genetic findings (Heyd 2017; Furholt 2018; 2019).

Ontological approaches

(Pre)history describes complex interactions of individuals or groups of individuals who act within specific networks of social and/or religious norms and beliefs, who share practices, habits, traditions, and likely also language, and who adhere to temporal and spatially determined aesthetic concepts of self-expression. This complex composite vision of prehistoric realities would be much more limited if we only referred to the physical traits of individuals, like genetic markers or other biological indicators. This applies especially to the question of migration. When considering migration, we can address the phenomenon from two different angles or by using different ontological concepts. One is a culture-historical approach rooted in the humanities. The other is a scientific, biological, and positivistic approach. Ideally,

---

[5] Burmeister (2000; 2017) dismissed the argument that the political environment influenced the migration debate because other humanities such as political and social sciences did not neglect migration as a topic. However, one needs to consider that these disciplines were exposed to a significantly higher pressure to be innovative or predictive than those dealing with the past.

[6] For a summary of the history of the recent discussions in archaeogenetics see Harding 2021: 11–17.

to achieve a complete picture, one should combine these approaches to correlate cultural developments with individual life histories.

The importance of defining the distinction between migration and movement/mobility has been pointed out by various scholars over the past few decades (Chapman and Hamerow 1997; Burmeister 2000; Prien 2005). Mobility involves living beings and things. Being mobile entails various modes of movement in a physical space. Mobility can also take place in a social context, as mobility between social groups, ranks, and classes, as well as within gender- or age-related groups, to name just a few examples. Furthermore, the agency of objects can also involve aspects of mobility, although object biographies (Kopytoff 1986; Fontijn 2002; Harding 2021: 40–50) are inevitably tied to the actions of the people using them. This may seem banal, but this fact is often neglected when dealing with distribution patterns of objects, which archaeologists – including myself – map to illustrate complex forms of interaction.

Mobility involves various kinds of temporary and repeated movements. The reasons for different types of mobility are manifold, and they may include seasonal perambulations of pastoralists, as well as travelling traders, crafts specialists, miners, or warriors. Exogamy (Jockenhövel 1991; Arnold 2004; Knipper *et al.* 2017) represents a specific form of mobility. For the mobile woman, it entails a final act of moving from her birth family's home to that of her husband's. In a slight modification of the aforementioned notion that migration is part of the *conditio humana*, I would argue that *mobility* is a basic human trait. If not restricted by force, people are mobile.

In contrast with mobility, migration has a destination. It entails a more final act of moving from a starting point to another place. This connotation of finality marks the difference to mobility. Migration with its aspect of finality is often a reaction to force. People migrate from one location to another to stay there for a longer period, if not forever. Often the trigger for modern migrations involves disrupting events like war, famine, or other hardships of various kinds, which force people to leave their homes to seek a better life. The pursuit of happiness or wealth can also be a vehement pull factor for human migration events. In many cases, migrations involve selection; the exodus of an entire population is rather rare, and such whole-scale migrations are difficult to prove archaeologically. Finally, we need to bear in mind that, while migration is often a process that is intended to be irrevocable, individuals can and sometimes do return, transmitting information to the remaining members of their social unit and thus potentially stimulating additional migration processes (see discussion in Fernández-Götz *et al.*, Chapter 1). In such cases the sudden and absolute character often attributed to migration is somewhat mitigated.

In the second part of this chapter, I would like to consider two examples of migration and mobility in more detail. I hope that they will support my argument that in discussing migration in archaeology, we are at least to a certain extent shaped by the sociopolitical and intellectual environment of our own time. I also chose the following case studies to show how our interpretation of the archaeological record can profit from the advances in scientific methodologies. The first case study stands in the context of the discourses of the end of the 20th century. The second example is contextualised in the current debate surrounding the 'Third Science Revolution in Archaeology' (Kristiansen 2014).

The case of pre-Scythian pastoralists in the Carpathian Basin

The Mezőcsát group

In my first case study, I will focus on the topic of the impact of the mobile pastoralists of the Eastern European steppe on sedentary Carpathian and Central European communities at the end of the Bronze Age in the 9th–8th centuries BC. Traditionally, this eastern impact has been connected with a so-called 'Cimmerian' migration or invasion into the Carpathian lands and further to the west. I have studied this topic for some time (cf. Metzner-Nebelsick 1998; 2000; 2002: 32–45; 2010; 2020). It serves as a good example to illustrate how the archaeological record has been interpreted in different periods. Moreover, it shows in which direction future research may move, or rather how the recent developments in bioarchaeological methods may offer deeper insights into historical contexts in the future.

Paul Reinecke coined the term 'Thraco-Cimmerian finds' in 1925 to describe a group of gold hoards found in Circum-Carpathian lands (Reinecke 1925; Metzner-Nebelsick 2020). In the 1930s the term was applied to a group of horse gear types, but also weapons, ceremonial items, and some other finds which represented novel forms of Late Bronze Age artefacts in the western Carpathian Basin and southern Central Europe. It was assumed that the appearance of these finds occurred as a very short-term event, connected with the arrival of mounted warriors from the Eastern European steppes. At the very beginning of the 20th century, the Berlin prehistorian Hubert Schmidt – who made his name with the excavations at the eponymous Copper Age site of Cucuteni in Romania and publications of material from Troy – was the first to suggest a westward migration of ethnic Cimmerians into the area of modern Hungary (Schmidt 1902). In 1934 the Romanian Prehistorian Ion Nestor proposed that Cimmerians – who according to Herodotus (*Hist.* 4,11) were expelled from their homeland at the north Pontic steppes by the invading Scythians from Asia and subsequently attacked the kingdom of Urartu, the northern neighbour of Assyria, and various locations in Anatolia – had also moved westward into the Carpathian Basin. There, the Cimmerians mingled with local Thracians (Nestor 1934). Similar arguments were put forward by the Hungarian researchers Sándor Gallus and Tibor Horváth (1939). The German archaeologist Friedrich Holste (1940) identified 'Thraco-Cimmerian' horse gear items of Eastern European style, distributed as far as Bavaria, as potential remnants of an eastern influx. Although no historical record about a westward migration of so-called Cimmerians exists, Holste postulated a short-term migration event into areas west of the Carpathians and dated it to the

214   *Carola Metzner-Nebelsick*

last quarter of the 8th century BC. He based this on Assyrian annals reporting a Cimmerian onslaught on the kingdoms of Urartu in 714 BC (Metzner-Nebelsick 2000; Sauter 2000). For him, this event was the main reason for the transition of the Late Bronze to the Early Iron Age or Hallstatt C (Ha C) period in Central Europe. In 1950 Gordon Childe concluded in his monograph on migrations in prehistory: 'But I admit that the whole case for a nomad invasion of Central Europe at the beginning of the Hallstatt period remains speculative. ... if such an invasion occurred, it was pre-Scythian' (Childe 1950: 228). The notion of a short-term character of the event – a so-called Thraco-Cimmerian horizon – remained the prevailing narrative of central European prehistory until the 1980s. The construct of a migration based on an almost total absence of archaeological material or findings was considered as the prime agent for cultural change. In Eastern Central European countries, the migrationist approach to interpreting archaeological records remained en vogue until the late 1990s.

In the 1930s the prevailing interpretation that change came about through violence and disruption reflected the then current volatile political situation. Although migration was not a topic of interest in post-World War II Germany, the culture-historical approach championing migration as an explanation for cultural change in the Late Bronze Age was not questioned. I was the first to challenge the model of a short-term aggressive 'Cimmerian' migration event as an explanation of the complex archaeological record of Late Bronze and Iron Age data in the Carpathian Basin and southern Central Europe. I cannot rehearse my arguments again in detail in this chapter, and would instead refer to previous publications (Metzner-Nebelsick 1998; 2000; 2002; 2010). Violence or the conquest of communities in the eastern Carpathian Basin and beyond to the west was not the picture I perceived.

My main argument was as follows. I was able to show that we are not dealing with a short-term immigration or invasion but rather a 150- to 200-year-long process of complex interaction between East European steppe populations of mobile pastoralists, with communities west of the Carpathian Mountains, and especially with sedentary groups of the Late Urnfield period west of the Danube Bend. Although I did not exclude the possibility of personal contacts with north Pontic or north Caucasian communities of steppe-bound warrior elites, my main emphasis was different. I proposed a multifactorial model of interaction and mobility between different regions, involving different communities and different lifestyles (Metzner-Nebelsick 2010: 125, Figure 1). I still regard this model unrefuted in principle, although today I see that my first idea of a mainly peaceful character of the process of change with only minor incidents of immigrations of specialists or smaller groups of people may have been the result of the then reigning Zeitgeist. But what does the archaeological record tell us?

It can be demonstrated that mainly north Caucasian prototypes of new bronze bridle types were incorporated into characteristic Carpathian assemblages as hoard finds. They stood for a new bridling technique and were originally developed among communities in the Northern Caucasus or the Eurasian steppe belt. Intensive contacts between pastoral communities on both sides of the Carpathians led to the creation of specifically Carpathian hybrids of bridles and horse trappings (Metzner-Nebelsick 2002: 207–362). The success of the new forms of horse bridles and possibly associated imports of horses and grooms can best be explained by assuming that these new horse bridles made horseback warfare more effective. The threat of mounted warriors led to a reaction by sedentary communities, which also incorporated the new role model of the rider into the traditional way of status representation within graves.[7]

How can this transmission of knowledge and specific practices be envisaged? How did East European steppe ideology and military advantages affect Central European communities? Why did they have such a lasting impact on the emergence of the Early Iron Age bridling style?[8] In my opinion, these people can be identified with the Mezőcsát group (also referred to as the Füzesabony-Mezőcsát group), first described in the 1980s by the Hungarian archaeologist Erzsébet Patek (1989–90; 1993) as a distinct group of inhumation burials in the eastern Hungarian plain.[9] Their burial ritual marked a significant shift away from the traditional cremation rite practised by Late Bronze Age communities in the Carpathian and the Urnfield cultures of the middle Danube region (Figure 10.1). Smaller grave groups or single inhumation graves replaced the earlier large cremation cemeteries. Traits of ritual behaviour in graves that have close parallels in the north Pontic steppes, the absence of traditional Urnfield period metal grave goods, and the lack of a specific pottery style mark the otherness of this group within the cultural setting of the Carpathian Basin in the 9th–8th centuries BC. Summing up all traits and the absence of contemporary settlements, I identified this group with mobile pastoralists originating at least in part from areas beyond the Carpathian range. However, even with this seemingly clear evidence, I was reluctant to support the model of a large-scale 'Cimmerian' invasion.

In my opinion, these pastoralists filled a gap that occurred after a system collapse in the Late Bronze Age in the eastern Carpathian Basin because of over-exploitation of resources due to extensive copper mining and metalworking processes, household fires, and building activities between the 14th and 10th centuries BC.[10] The suggested emerging resource crisis of regional wood shortages had, according to my model, challenged and finally undermined existing power

---

[7] For the role of horses within Iron Age communities in the Dolenjsko region, Slovenia, see also Frie 2018; for the significant symbolic meaning of horses in Iron Age communities in general see Kmetová 2018.

[8] For the distribution of Hallstatt period burials with horse gear for a single horse instead of the traditional harness for two horses for a four-wheeled wagon see Parc 1992: 346–56.

[9] For Slovakian examples see Romsauer 1999; for more recent finds see Mogyorós 2018 including a map with some debatable finds.

[10] Large-scale metal production is, among other things, indicated by the large number of bronze hoards of this period (e.g. Hansen 1994). They represent those items which did not re-enter the recycling process.

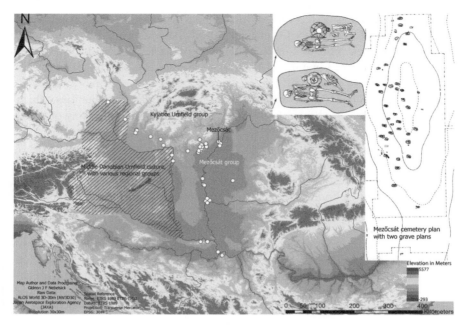

Figure 10.1 Distribution of the inhumation single graves and cemeteries of the pre-Scythian Mezőcsát group of mobile pastoralists (white dots), and the adjacent middle Danubian Urnfield culture (hatched) (illustration design: author; map © Gideon J.F. Nebelsick; cemetery plan after Patek 1993)

structures. Perhaps a brief climate deterioration after 1159 BC (Baillie 1995) might have played an additional role (see also Harding 1982; Metzner-Nebelsick 1998: 404). Supported by the re-emerging open landscapes including forest steppe formations, which is a natural vegetation form in the eastern Carpathian Basin (Breu 1970–89), the proposed internal crisis offered perfect conditions for the establishment of a subsistence economy largely based on husbandry (Gyulai 1993: 30) and a partly mobile lifestyle (Metzner-Nebelsick 1998: 408). Subsequent seasonal movements of mobile pastoralists created exchange networks on both sides of the Carpathian Mountains.

The recent discovery of a series of mega-forts (Harding 2017) of the Late Bronze Age in western Romania dating to 1500–1000 BC (Kienlin *et al.* 2012: Figure 16; Heeb *et al.* 2017a; Sava *et al.* 2019) underscores my previous argument of intensive land use by settlement activity during the Late Bronze Age. However, ^{14}C-dates (Sava 2020: 260–8) indicate that none of the complex settlements lasted longer than the 12th century BC, leading Victor Sava (2020: 290) to propose a system collapse at this time. Again, this cannot be commented on in detail here. There are evident changes at this time, but hoarding practices as well as settlement activities continued, so that a fundamental system collapse before 1000 BC is unlikely.

In my first major article on the topic (Metzner-Nebelsick 1998), I even played with the idea that the formerly sedentary local groups within the Great Hungarian Plain may have adopted a mobile pastoral lifestyle to better cope with changing environmental conditions. Although indications for a modified subsistence strategy after *c.* 1100 BC are evident, I later championed another interpretation as the better explanation for the apparent changes of the cultural setting within the eastern Carpathian Basin. The practice of intermarrying between incoming pastoralists and local women from sedentary communities offered a more convincing interpretation for the similarities of pottery styles between the Late Urnfield period or Late Bronze Age groups on the one hand, and the ceramic repertoire in Mezőcsát graves on the other (Figure 10.2) (Metzner-Nebelsick 2000; 2010).

Although I never excluded immigration, I was at first reluctant to accept the former invasion model and instead favoured internal transformation processes and more complex ways of interaction as equally relevant explanations for cultural change. I was led to this approach by several observations of which I will provide one example. Within the Late Urnfield culture in Central Europe and the middle Danube region, i.e. the time between roughly 1350 and 800 BC, horse bridles were deposited in graves as pairs (Pare 1987; 1992). They either accompanied a wagon or, in case of the absence of the actual vehicle, symbolised a wagon harness. In southern Central Europe, four-wheeled wagons and accompanying horse gear appeared for the first time in the context of elite graves in the 13th century BC (Pare 1987). The funeral tradition associated with this kind of status representation survived the introduction of new forms of horse gear and rein ornaments of Pontic or Caucasian origin and their Carpathian hybrids in the 9th century BC. In an act of appropriation, Late Urnfield and Early Hallstatt period – i.e. Late Bronze and Early Iron Age – elites adopted these new types of horse gear. Simultaneously, however, they used them as the traditional two-horse wagon harness. In the eastern Carpathian Basin, home of the Mezőcsát group, horse gear is a rare grave good and there is a complete absence of any weapons (Patek 1993; Metzner-Nebelsick 1998). This stands in contrast with both north Caucasian warrior burials and princely tombs of pre-Scythian date from the north Pontic steppes which regularly contain horse gear and/or weapons (Machortych 1993; 1994; Metzner-Nebelsick 2002; Reinhold 2003; 2007). Other characteristics of the Mezőcsát group, which cannot be described in this chapter in detail (cf. Metzner-Nebelsick 1998), also mark these communities as different from those located east of the Carpathian Mountains and account for their peculiarity as a cultural group. At the same time, however, the Mezőcsát group was distinct from neighbouring communities due to its inhumation burial rite, the absence of larger pottery sets in graves, and different dress accessories.

In addition, we can observe varying degrees of interaction between the Late Bronze Age/Early Iron Age sedentary agrarian communities in the Alpine fringes and the middle Danube region with the pastoralists of the eastern Carpathian Basin. This is best shown by similar pottery types or imports (Figure 10.3). Whereas in

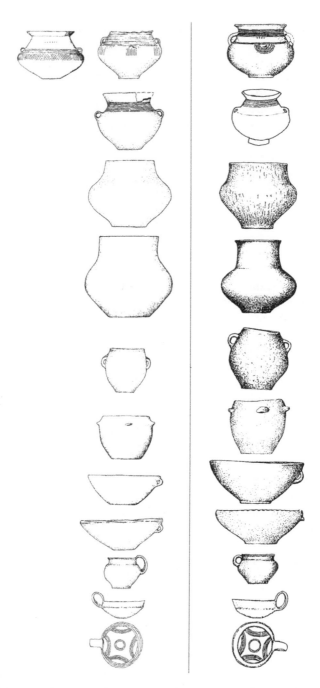

Figure 10.2 Pottery vessels from the cremation cemeteries of the Kyjatice group from Szajla, north-eastern Hungary and Radzovce, Slovakia (left), and their equivalents from inhumation graves of the Mezőcsát group (right) (image: author, based on images by Kemenczei 1984; Patek 1989–90; Furmánek 1990)

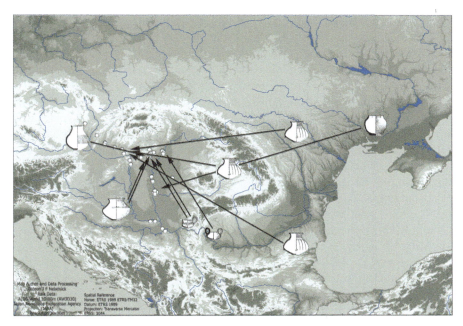

Figure 10.3 Examples of pottery 'imports' in Mezőcsát graves, possibly produced by non-local women. The icons symbolise the areas in which these pottery types usually occur; the arrows point at the Mezőcsát sites where they were found (illustration design: author; map © Gideon J.F. Nebelsick).

Bavaria, Pontic-Caucasian bridles and harness ornaments were the only eastern-style artefacts present in elite graves, the integration of dress accessories as well as eastern types of swords/daggers in the communities of the middle Danubian Urnfield culture in north-east Croatia, Lower Austria, and Moravia reflect a higher degree of interaction with eastern Carpathian pastoralists (Metzner-Nebelsick 2017). Earrings/lockrings in women's graves hint at the appropriation of eastern fashion style(s), whereas western pots in Mezőcsát graves can be read as traces of exogamy and western women producing their traditional craft in their new home. Exogamy is a term that has a positive undertone. However, we cannot exclude the possibility that the women who produced those pots had actually been robbed from neighbouring sedentary communities. The possibility of exogamy could be resolved by systematic isotope analysis of the Mezőcsát individuals.

Other players in a game of multiple contacts

It is likewise unclear whether the iconic warrior from tumulus 1 in the Pécs-Jakabhegy cemetery in south-west Hungary was a local man or a foreigner, with his north Caucasian weapon set – often called 'Cimmerian' (Kossack 1980; 1994) – including a bi-metallic dagger, an iron axe and spear, and a horse

220 *Carola Metzner-Nebelsick*

bridle (Metzner-Nebelsick 2002: 276, Figure 129, plate 121A). Previously, I have argued for a local origin of this man, who belonged to the founders of the barrow necropolis in front of the impressive Iron Age hillfort of Péc-Jakabhegy (Maráz 1996; Bertók and Gáti 2014: 123–37). I based this assumption on various observations, mainly the presence of local characteristics of his grave, such as the traditional cremation rite, local-style pottery, and a burial chamber and barrow of local design. I saw these features as indicators of his status as a member of a new but local elite. The 'Cimmerian'-style weapon set is structurally comparable to the Late Urnfield/Early Iron Age combination of a sword, a socketed axe, and a spear, but with items en vogue at the time, it also offered a new form of elite status representation for a – as I saw it – *homo novus* among his community.[11]

The other possibility, which is to view him as an invader from the Northern Caucasus, must remain speculative until isotope analysis of his cremated bones is available to provide conclusive evidence. Another way to explain the unusual weapon set of the Pécs-Jakabhegy warrior is to imagine that he had travelled to the Northern Caucasus as a young man and brought the Caucasian weapons back home.

One of the important intermediaries between east and west was the Basarabi group, located around the Iron Gate in southern Romania and Serbia.[12] This group can be identified with sedentary pastoralists with cattle as the main species (Boroffka 2005: 128) who practised the rite of inhumation and are further characterised by a specific pottery style and female dress accessories (Popović and Vukmanović 1998). During the Middle Iron Age period in Romanian terminology (late 8th–7th centuries BC) a 'diffusion' of Basarabi-style pottery into inner Transylvania (Ursuţiu 2002: 166–7) can be observed. It happens at the same time as settlement activity plummets around the site of Feudvar-Mošorin in northern Serbia, which Frank Falkenstein (1998: 276) attributes to a (regional) crisis. There may have been small-scale migrations of bearers of the Basarabi group into Transylvania and also into north-east Croatia. Here, in the Urnfield culture cemetery of Vukovar-Lijeva bara, inhumations with Basarabi equipment are attested among the traditional cremation graves (Vinski-Gasparini 1973: 222, plate 121–5; Ložnjak Dizdar 2004). Basarabi pottery also occurs as far east as the lower Don River area in southern Russia (Metzner-Nebelsick 2010: 138, Figure 4; see Daragan 2011 for west–east contacts), accounting for movements of pastoralists and warriors in both directions from east to west and vice versa. The Basarabi sedentary pastoralists around the Iron Gate were part of a network

---

[11] That the eastern weapons were made of iron may also have played a significant part in their attractiveness; for early iron see Pare (2017).

[12] This specific group should not be equated with the distribution of the ostentatious stamped and incised Basarabi-style pottery (Vulpe 1986; Metzner-Nebelsick 1992; Gumă 1993; Ursuţiu 2002).

of polities producing different pottery styles of incised and stamped ceramics referred to as cultural groups, which were distributed as far east as the Dnieper/Dnipro River (Kašuba 2007). This network included sedentary communities and pastoralists in the Ukrainian forest steppe zone (Daragan 2011). In addition, members of an elite group of mounted warriors are visible in the archaeological record. They were active between the piedmont zone of the northern Caucasus and the eastern Carpathian Basin (Metzner-Nebelsick 2020). Judging from the archaeological record, it is impossible to determine if these elite warriors belonged to a larger group of people.

What I wanted to stress with these examples is that a thorough investigation of the archaeological record is necessary to produce a 'thick description' (Geertz 1973) of the cultural record at hand, thus helping us to better reconstruct and at best to understand the past.

In the case of the 'Cimmerian' finds from areas west of the Danube Bend or the distribution of the Mezőscát group, interpretative modelling has been impacted by the Zeitgeist. To further elucidate the character of this cultural group, the new scientific methodologies in biomolecular analysis, like isotope and aDNA analyses, will offer opportunities to test models based on a broader cultural analysis.

Mobility patterns and foodscapes of humans and animals can be tested by stable isotope analysis and offer promising new trajectories of research.[13] In the case of ancient DNA studies, however, I only see biased additional information potential. Because the preceding cultural units of the middle Danubian Urnfield culture (Metzner-Nebelsick 2010, 139, Figure 5a; 140 Figure 5b) or the Gáva culture in the eastern Carpathian Basin all practised cremation or did not bury their dead systematically (Király et al. 2013), genetic differences between local communities and potential newcomers would be difficult to evaluate.

However, another strand of genetic analysis might help us to better understand the above-mentioned deeper reasons for the fundamental change of the 9th–8th centuries BC in the eastern Carpathian Basin. Perhaps more intensive contacts with the Eastern European steppe populations resulted in the transmission of new forms of diseases like the plague (Rasmussen et al. 2015) or other zoonoses. Scenarios championing diseases as an explanation for the apparent decrease in settlement activity and the scarce burial record as signs of a putative population decline will, however, be a question for future research. At the same time, the disease hypothesis is another reflection of the dependence of our theory building on the Zeitgeist, during a time when pandemics like the recent COVID-19 crisis make us realise that diseases are a potent factor in culture change.

---

[13] For isotopic analyses of Iron Age individuals from the north Pontic steppe zone and the Kuban region in the Scythian period see Gerling 2015.

Transalpine mobility in the Late Bronze Age Urnfield period

In my second case study, I would like to briefly introduce an example of the significant potential of biomolecular analyses in archaeology for assessing migration while simultaneously revealing its limitations. This research was part of the six-year interdisciplinary research project 'Transalpine Mobility and Cultural Transfer' at the ArchaeoBioCenter of LMU Munich, which was conducted from 2015–20 by a team of physical anthropologists, geologists, mineralogists, zooarchaeologists, archaeologists, and computer scientists, under the direction of anthropologist Gisela Grupe (Grupe *et al.* 2015; 2017a). In contrast with other projects that have emphasised population history using genetics, the Munich research group focused on the analysis of stable isotopes for determining migratory activity in combination with the identification of possible types of mobility leading to different forms of cultural transfer and appropriation.

The research unit's goal was the development of an isotope fingerprint for bioarchaeological findings with special regard to cremated bones and its application to archaeological and culture-historical questions. The isotopic fingerprints tested in our group were five stable isotopic ratios for uncremated skeletal finds, namely $^{87}Sr/^{86}Sr$, $^{206}Pb/^{204}Pb$, $^{207}Pb/^{204}Pb$, $^{208}Pb/^{204}Pb$, and $\delta^{18}O$. The fingerprint was quantified using modern data mining methods. For cremated finds, the fingerprint consisted only of stable strontium and lead isotopic ratios, since delta^{18}O is thermally instable (Grupe *et al.* 2017a; 2017b; 2017c; Mauder *et al.* 2017; Toncala *et al.* 2017; Lengfelder *et al.* 2019). Both fingerprints were compared by methods of similarity search (Tschetsch *et al.* 2020). The expectation-maximisation (EM) algorithm is based on a mixture model of continuous distributions, like a Gaussian Mixture Model (Mauder *et al.* 2017). Our catchment area comprised sites both north and south of the Alps (Grupe *et al.* 2017a). We concentrated on periods in which cremation was the prevailing burial custom. Our catchment area of the Central Eastern Alps was particularly suitable for the relatively new method of isotope analysis of cremated bones in order to detect mobility. In this region, cremation was the predominantly or exclusively practised burial rite in most of the later prehistoric periods and Roman times. As a result, models proposing migration or mobility could not be tested via natural science methods for a long time, since isotopic analyses of cremated bones represent a relatively recent advance in isotope studies (Snoeck *et al.* 2015). In addition to the interdisciplinary approach of combining natural sciences and archaeology, our projects also incorporated computational science to apply data mining and similarity search among big data series.

The transit route via the Inn–Isarco–Adige corridor has long been identified as an essential passageway across the Central Eastern Alps, beginning in the Mesolithic (Lang 2002; Metzner-Nebelsick *et al.* 2017). Passes connecting the Italian Peninsula with Central Europe and beyond belong to the most crucial long-distance contact routes in Europe (Nebelsick and Metzner-Nebelsick 2020). They are thus well suited for assessing the role of migration or mobility in prehistoric communities.

My research project within the group, the Urnfield Period of the 13th to 9th centuries BC in Tyrol, provided an ideal study area (Reuß and Metzner-Nebelsick 2017). One of the most important fahlore copper deposits in Europe and one of the major copper-producing regions of Early Bronze Age Europe (Goldenberg 2015) are located in the Tyrolean Inn Valley. Due to the replacement of tennantite copper ore (fahlore copper) by the new copper source sulphidic chalcopyrite (Kupferkies), which began to be exploited in the Mitterberg region south of Salzburg *c.* 1700 BC (Stöllner 2015: 102, Figure 9), the north Tyrolean Inn Valley temporarily lost its interregional significance. During the Urnfield Period, the Inn valley regained its importance as a mining and metal-producing area, as a research project based at Innsbruck University has shown (Goldenberg 2015; Stöllner 2015). During the 13th and 12th centuries BC this coincided with a significant increase in burials in the region, since new cemeteries were founded that contained significantly more graves than the ones of the Middle Bronze Age. What is equally important is the fact that grave constructions displayed a new design with well-equipped urn burials (Reuß and Metzner-Nebelsick 2017). Furthermore, certain artefact types in these new cemeteries mirror a spectrum that is alien to the local Middle Bronze Age Alpine cultural environment but match perfectly with grave inventories in southern Bavaria (Grupe *et al.* 2017c: 235, Figure 2).

While the emergence of the Late Bronze Age Urnfield culture in the 13th century BC in southern Bavaria can be derived from a local substrate, burials of the Middle Bronze Age are rare and ephemeral in north Tyrol. Thus, the numerous graves dating to the 13th and 12th centuries BC, which feature Bavarian traits, mark a significant change. Immigration of people from the north Alpine piedmont zones is a likely explanation for this phenomenon. These similarities were interpreted by Lothar Sperber as evidence for a north Alpine migration of elite families from present-day Bavaria to Tyrol in order to exploit the rich copper deposits (Sperber 1997; 2004).

New studies focusing on archaeometallurgy, mining activities, and settlement structure even speak of colonisation by newcomers (Stöllner and Oeggl 2015). It was presumed that the reason for the proposed influx of people from present-day Bavaria was to exploit the copper ore deposits of the Inn Valley and to control the trade of copper ore or raw copper to the north (Sperber 2003). The fact that north Tyrolean copper was used north of the Alps not only in the Early Bronze Age but also in the Urnfield period was confirmed by metallurgical analyses (Sperber 2004; Möslein and Pernicka 2019).

The analysis of the archaeological record of the Tyrolean grave inventories by Simone Reuß (Reuß and Metzner-Nebelsick 2017) has shown that we do not find grave assemblages exclusively equipped with regionally specific objects. An example is the cemetery of Kitzbühel-Lebensberg located in the north-east of Tyrol, in the greywacke zone, which is rich in copper ore. Only six cremations of the 40 recorded graves could be subjected to isotopic analysis. Among those cremations, the deceased female in grave 20 does not appear to be clearly local. In comparison with the other graves, her strontium ratio is lower and would fit into the Upper Bavarian cluster. Yet, the lead ratio could be local. Looking at the archaeological evidence, an even more complex picture evolves. The rich female from grave 20 contained local and a variety of foreign grave goods (Reuß and Metzner-Nebelsick 2017: 201, Figure 17; Metzner-Nebelsick *et al.* 2020), including items with parallels in southern Bavaria and northern Franconia, and ceramics in local style. Her Bavarian-style dress pin was manufactured from local copper ore, while her knife was made of copper from the Mitterberg deposit.

When the isotope ratios of all analysed cremated bones are examined, we observe a clear differentiation of a cluster in south Tyrol, while a north Alpine cluster, the Tyrolean Inn Valley, shows mixed signatures. The final publication of the results is still in preparation. However, it can already be said that the percentage of non-local individuals tested within our project is significant,[14] indicating a high level of mobility.

While only 14 out of 149 individuals (9.4 per cent) could be recognised as non-local based on the strontium isotope ratio alone, the combination of strontium and lead resulted in 25 non-local individuals and a significantly higher rate of 16.8 per cent. In the demographic comparison of normal immigration rates of prehistoric communities, the percentage of non-locals is high and seems to confirm the immigration hypothesis. Since only a limited number of individuals from the north Tyrolean Inn Valley could be analysed, the possible colonisation of the area by northern immigrants remains a question for future research. The exact comparison with the archaeological markers will also produce further interesting results. In any case, it was shown that a single isotope system has only limited interpretative potential for the detection of migration.

A limiting factor was the fact that the cremation graves we analysed did not provide evidence for the reconstruction of the individual's life history. In contrast to inhumations with good tooth preservation, in the Late Bronze Age cremated bones were only selectively deposited in the graves, and teeth were rarely included. Therefore, we are unable to say where an individual was born or spent his/her youth. That certainly limits our ability to determine movements of people within their lifetimes. Allochthonous individuals can only be detected if they moved to a new area within roughly ten years before their death; this is the time of bone remodelling, i.e. the turnover rate of bone collagen in long bones or ribs of an adult.[15]

After *c.* 1000 BC, burial activity in the north Tyrolean Inn Valley and the Munich Plain shows a significant decline in comparison with the previous three centuries. This was likely due to a decreasing population. At the same time, further to the north in the

---

[14] I am grateful to Gisela Grupe, Pia Schellerer, and Dominika Klaut for this information.
[15] Turnover or remodelling rates differ in various skeletal elements and influence isotopic signals. Femoral bones have a slower turnover rate than ribs (Hedges *et al.* 2007; see also Fahdy *et al.* 2017 on diet).

Danube area between the Ingolstadt Basin and Lower Bavaria, a noticeable increase in cemeteries with sometimes hundreds of cremation graves can be ascertained. Whether these changes in burial activity can be explained by migrating communities still needs further research. However, other indications hint at more fundamental changes in the economic and political situation after 1000 BC in southern Bavaria and adjacent areas. During the Late Urnfield period or the 9th century BC, cemeteries like Obereching and Bischofshofen (Höglinger 1993; Lippert 2009) were founded in the Salzach Valley. Some of the grave inventories (Figure 10.4) closely resemble graves dating to the 9th century BC from Lower Bavaria and the Upper Palatinate. As an explanation, the exploitation of the copper deposits in the Mitterberg-Pongau region may be the reason for this possible immigration of northern settlers. A minor test series of isotope analyses of strontium and lead isotope ratios from 46 individuals from Obereching and Bischofshofen in the Austrian Salzach Valley and the cemeteries from Künzing and Kelheim in Lower Bavaria was undertaken within our project (Schellerer 2020). Six individuals (13 per cent) in both regions showed a non-local signature. The results of the isotopic analysis, however, are more complicated than the archaeological evidence suggested. Migration did occur, but not in a single direction from north to south as expected due to the biased selection of seemingly non-local, i.e. 'Lower Bavarian'-type, grave inventories. Some individuals possessed

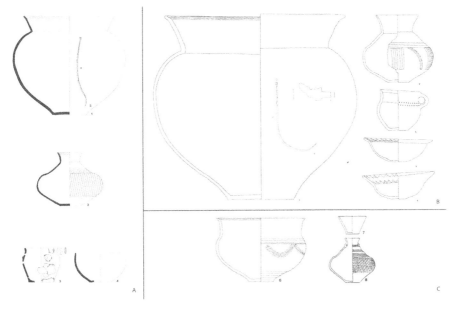

Figure 10.4 Inventories of Late Urnfield period cremation graves from A) the Salzburg area (Obereching, grave 21); B–C) Lower Bavaria (B: Künzing, grave 23; C: Kelheim, grave 184). Typological similarities of the ceramic vessels are seen as hints for the presence of putative migrants from Lower Bavaria into the Salzburg area (image: author, based on Höglinger 1993; Schopper 1995; Pfauth 1998)

isotopic signals of geographical regions which neither matched the Bavarian nor the inner Alpine catchment areas. Unfortunately, we were unable to differentiate between individual mobility and migration, and the interplay of the two on the basis of the isotopic structure of the cremated bone material. Because of the turnover rates of long bones or ribs (see above) – and in the absence of teeth – we could not exclude that in reality a higher percentage of originally non-local individuals was present in the sampled community. If non-local individuals migrated to the community of their resting place at a certain time prior to their death, their isotopic signals would classify them as locals. In addition, putative mobility patterns such as single or repeated visits to their childhood communities would likewise not be detectable. In view of the comparatively small number of analysed individuals, however, migratory events still seemed to have played a role among Late Bronze and Early Iron Age communities in this part of Europe. Despite the limits of the current analytical tools, these examples show the vast potential of isotope studies for provenance analysis, even for cremated bones.

Conclusion

Scientific methods offer immense potential for providing detailed information on the life history of individuals, their kinship, and ancestry. This includes individual mobility as well as nutrition and thus, to a certain degree, offers insights into geographical environments, cultural networks, and food webs. These techniques allow different models of mobility and migration to be tested against what can be seen in the material culture record. As I have tried to show, these analyses need to be accompanied by a thorough cultural, or if one prefers humanistic, approach, in this case, in the form of archaeological analysis in order to reveal a complex history of the past and help to avoid oversimplified approaches of broad-stroke narratives. This holistic approach is especially important in times of growing nationalism, including a rise in white supremacy movements. As cultural historians, we should be aware that humans possess different levels and varied forms of identity, which are determined by a plethora of cultural settings of social norms, beliefs, and traditions or, at best, by choice but not by physical disposition. The positivistic methodology of the biomolecular approaches must be augmented with the hermeneutical skills of the cultural historians.

References

Allentoft, M.E., Sikora, E., Sjögren, M., Rasmussen, S., Rasmussen, M., *et al.* (2015), 'Population genomics of Bronze Age Eurasia', *Nature*, 522: 167–72.
Anthony, D.W. (1990), 'Migration in archeology: the baby and the bathwater', *American Anthropologist*, 92(4): 895–914.

MIGRATION IN ARCHAEOLOGICAL DISCOURSE

Anthony, D.W. (1996), 'Nazi and eco-feminist prehistories: ideology and empiricism in Indo-European archaeology', in P. Kohl and C. Fawcett (eds), *Nationalism, Politics and the Practice of Archaeology* (Cambridge, Cambridge University Press), 82–96.

Arnold, B. (2004), 'Mobile men, sedentary women? Material culture as a marker of regional and supra-regional interaction in Iron Age Europe', in H. Dobrzańska, V. Megaw, and P. Poleska (eds), *Celts on the Margin: Studies in European Cultural Interaction 7th Century BC–1st Century AD Dedicated to Zenon Woźniak* (Kraków, Institute of Archaeology and Ethnology of the Polish Academy of Sciences), 17–26.

Bade, K. (2002), 'Historische Migrationsforschung', in K. Bade (ed), *Migration in der europäischen Geschichte seit dem späten Mittelalter* (Osnabrück, Institut für Migrationsforschung und Interkulturelle Studien), 21–44.

Baillie, M.G.L. (1995), *A Slice through Time* (London, Batsford).

Bertók, G. and Gáti, C. (2014). 'IV. Mounds in the forest, cropmarks in the field: remains of the Iron Age in Baranya county, the Pécs-Jakabhegy Hillfort', in G. Bertók (ed), *Old Times – New Methods: Non-invasive Archaeology in Baranya County (Hungary) 2005–13* (Budapest, Archaeolingua), 123–37.

Boroffka, N. (2005), 'Siedlungsmuster im bronzezeitlichen Siebenbürgen: Am Beispiel des Gebiets um Aiud, jud. Alba', in B. Horejs, R. Jung, E. Kaiser, and B. Teržan (eds), *Interpretationsraum Bronzezeit: Bernhard Hänsel von seinen Schülern gewidmet* (Bonn, Habelt), 126–42.

Brandt, G., Haak, W., Adler, C.J., Roth, C., Szécsényi-Nagy, A., *et al.* (2013), 'Ancient DNA reveals key stages in the formation of Central European mitochondrial genetic diversity', *Science*, 342(6155): 257–61.

Breu, J. (ed) (1970–89), *Atlas der Donauländer/Atlas of the Danubian Countries/Atlas des pays Danubiens* (Wien, Österreichisches Ost- und Südosteuropa Institut).

Burmeister, S. (2000), 'Archaeology and migration', *Current Anthropology*, 41(4): 539–67.

Burmeister, S. (2013), 'Migration und Ethnizität: Zur Konzeptualisierung von Mobilität und Identität', in M.K.H. Eggert and U. Veit (eds), *Theorie in der Archäologie: Zur jüngeren Diskussion in Deutschland* (Münster, Waxmann Verlag), 229–67.

Burmeister, S. (2017), 'One step beyond: migration als kulturelle Praxis', *Distant Worlds Journal*, 3: 3–16.

Chapman, J. and Hamerow, H. (eds) (1997), 'On the move again: migrations and invasions in archaeological explanation', in J. Chapman and H. Hamerow (eds), *Migration and Invasions in Archaeological Explanation* (Oxford, Archaeopress), 1–10.

Childe, V.G. (1950), *Prehistoric Migrations in Europe* (Oslo and Cambridge, Harvard University Press).

Daragan, M.N. (2011), *Načalo rannego železnogo veka v dneprovskoj pravoberežnoj lesostepi* (Kiev, KHT).

Fahdy, G.E., Deter, C., Pitfield, R., Miszkiewicz, J.J., and Mahoney, P. (2017), 'Bone deep: variation in stable isotope ratios and histomorphometric measurements of bone remodeling within adult humans', *Journal of Archaeological Science*, 87: 10–16.

Falkenstein, F. (1998), *Feudvar 2: Die Siedlungsgeschichte des Titeler Plateaus* (Kiel, Oetker-Voges).

Fontijn, D.R. (2002), *Sacrificial Landscapes: Cultural Biographies of Persons, Objects and 'Natural' Places in the Bronze Age of the Southern Netherlands, c. 2300–600 BC* (Leiden, University of Leiden).

Frie, A.C. (2018), 'Horses and the embodiment of elite masculinity in the Dolenjska Hallstatt culture', *Oxford Journal of Archaeology*, 31(1): 25–44.

228   *Carola Metzner-Nebelsick*

Furholt, M. (2018), 'Massive migrations? The impact of recent aDNA studies on our view of third millennium Europe', *European Journal of Archaeology*, 21(2): 159–91.

Furholt, M. (2019), 'Re-integrating archaeology: a contribution to aDNA studies and the migration discourse on the 3rd millennium BC in Europe', *Proceedings of the Prehistoric Society*, 85: 115–29.

Furmánek, V. (1990), *Radzovce osada l'udu popolnicových polí* (Bratislava, Veda).

Gallus, S. and Horváth, T. (1939), *Un peuple cavalier préscythique en Hongrie* (Leipzig, Harrassowitz Verlag).

Geertz, C. (1973), 'Thick description: toward an interpretive theory of culture', in C. Geertz, *The Interpretation of Cultures: Selected Essays* (New York, Basic Books), 3–30.

Gerling, C. (2015), *Prehistoric Mobility and Diet in the West Eurasian Steppes 3500 to 300 BC* (Berlin and Boston, Walter de Gruyter).

Goldenberg, G. (2015), 'Prähistorische Kupfergewinnung aus Fahlerzen der Lagerstätte Schwaz-Brixlegg im Unterinntal, Nordtirol', in T. Stöllner and K. Oeggl (eds), *Bergauf, Bergab: 10.000 Jahre Bergbau in den Ostalpen* (Bochum and Rahden/Westf., Deutsches Bergbau-Museum and Verlag Marie Leidorf), 151–63.

Grupe, G., Grünewald, M., Gschwind, M., Hölzl, S., Balazs, K., *et al.* (2015), 'Networking in bioarchaeology: the example of the DFG Research Group FOR 1670 "Transalpine Mobility and Cultural Transfer"', in G. Grupe, G. McGlynn, and J. Peters (eds), *Bioarchaeology beyond Osteology* (Rahden/Westf., Verlag Marie Leidorf), 13–51.

Grupe, G., Grigat, A., and McGlynn, G. (eds) (2017a), *Across the Alps in Prehistory: Isotopic Mapping of the Brenner Passage by Bioarchaeology* (Cham, Springer Nature).

Grupe, G., Hölzl, S., Mayr, C., and Söllner, F. (2017b), 'The concept of isotopic landscapes: modern ecogeochemistry versus bioarchaeology', in G. Grupe, A. Grigat, and G. McGlynn (eds), *Across the Alps in Prehistory: Isotopic Mapping of the Brenner Passage by Bioarchaeology* (Cham, Springer Nature), 27–48.

Grupe, G., Grünewald, M., Gschwind, M., Hölzl, S., Kröger, P., *et al.* (2017c), 'Current synthesis and future options', in G. Grupe, A. Grigat, and G. McGlynn (eds), *Across the Alps in Prehistory: Isotopic Mapping of the Brenner Passage by Bioarchaeology* (Cham, Springer Nature), 229–50.

Gumă, M. (1993), *Civilizaţia primei epoci a fierului în sud-vestul României* (Bucureşti, Institutul Român de Tracologie).

Gyulai, F. (1993), *Environment and Agriculture in Bronze Age Hungary* (Budapest, Archaeolingua).

Haak, W., Lazaridis, I., Patterson, N., Rohland, N., Mallick, S., *et al.* (2015), 'Massive migration from the steppe was a source for Indo-European languages in Europe', *Nature*, 522: 207–11.

Härke, H. (1998), 'Archaeologists and migrations: a problem of attitude?', *Current Anthropology*, 39: 19–45.

Hansen, S. (1994), *Studien zu den Metalldeponierungen während der älteren Urnenfelderzeit zwischen Rhônetal und Karpatenbecken* (Bonn, Habelt).

Harding, A. (1982), *Climate Change in Later Prehistory* (Edinburgh, Edinburgh University Press).

Harding, A. (2017), 'Corneşti-Iarcuri and the rise of mega-forts in Bronze Age Europe', in B.S. Heeb, A. Szentmiklosi, R. Krause, and M. Wemhoff (eds), *Fortifications: Rise and Fall of Defended Sites in the Late Bronze and Early Iron Age of South-East Europe* (Berlin, Staatliche Museen zu Berlin), 9–14.

Harding, A. (2021), *Bronze Age Lives* (Berlin and Boston, Walter de Gruyter).

Hedges, R.E.M., Clement, J.G., Thomas, C.D.L., and O'Connell, T.C. (2007), 'Collagen turnover in the adult femoral mid-shaft: modelled from anthropogenic radiocarbon tracer measurements', *Amercian Journal of Physical Anthropology*, 133(2): 808–16.

Heeb, B.S., Szentmiklosi, A., Bălărie, A., Lehmpuhl, R., and Krause, R. (2017), 'Corneşti-Iarcuri – 10 years of research (2007–16): some important preliminary results', in B.S. Heeb, A. Szentmiklosi, R. Krause, and M. Wemhoff (eds), *Fortifications: Rise and Fall of Defended Sites in the Late Bronze and Early Iron Age of South-East Europe* (Berlin, Staatliche Museen zu Berlin), 217–28.

Heyd, V. (2017), 'Kossinna's smile', *Antiquity*, 91(356): 348–59.

Höglinger, P. (1993), *Das urnenfelderzeitliche Gräberfeld von Obereching, Land Salzburg* (Salzburg, Amt der Salzburger Landesregierung).

Holste, F. (1940), 'Zur Bedeutung und Zeitstellung der sogenannten "thrako-kimmerischen" Pferdegeschirrbronzen: Ein Urnengrab von Steinkirchen, Landkreis Deggendorf', *Wiener Prähistorische Zeitschrift*, 27: 7–32.

Hübner, E. (2005), *Jungneolithische Gräber auf der Jütischen Halbinsel: Typologische und chronologische Studien zur Einzelgrabkultur* (København, Det Kongelige Nordiske Oldskriftselskab).

Jockenhövel, A. (1991), 'Räumliche Mobilität von Personen in der mittleren Bronzezeit des westlichen Mitteleuropa', *Germania*, 69: 49–62.

Kašuba, M. (2007), 'Zur Entstehung der Basarabi-Kultur in Osteuropa', in M. Blečić, M. Črešnár, B. Hänsel, A. Hellmuth, E. Kaiser, *et al.* (eds), *Scripta Praehistorica in Honorem Biba Teržan* (Ljubljana, Narodni Muzej Slovenije), 369–80.

Kemenczei, T. (1984), *Die Spätbronzezeit Nordostungarns* (Budapest, Akadémiai Kiadó).

Kienlin, T., Marta, L., Schramm, P., and Rung, E. (2012), 'Results of the geophysical survey in the swamp fortification of the Gáva culture at Căuaş-Sighetu in the Ier valley, north-western Romania', *Satu Mare Studii şi Comunicări*, 28: 83–99.

Király, A., Sebők, K., Zoffmann, Z.K., and Kovács, G. (2013), 'Early Iron Age "mass graves" in the middle Tisza region: investigation and interpretation', in N. Müller-Scheeßel (ed) (2013), *'Irreguläre' Bestattungen in der Urgeschichte: Norm, Ritual, Strafe ...?* (Bonn, Habelt), 307–26.

Kmetová, P. (2018), '"And four strong-necked horses he threw swiftly on the pyre ...": on human-horse relationship in the Early Iron Age Central Europe from the perspective of interregional contacts', in P. Pavúk, V. Klontza-Jaklová, and A. Harding (eds), *ΕΥΔΑΙΜΩΝ: Studies in Honour of Jan Bouzek* (Prague and Brno, Charles University, Faculty of Arts and Masaryk University), 267–89.

Knipper, C., Mittnik, A., Massy, K., Kociumaka, C., Kucukkalipci, I., *et al.* (2017), 'Female exogamy and gene pool diversification at the transition from the Final Neolithic to the Early Bronze Age in Central Europe', *Proceedings of the National Academy of Sciences of the United States of America*, 114(38): 10083–8.

Kopytoff, I. (1986), 'The cultural biography of things: commoditization as process', in A. Appaduri, *The Social Life of Things: Commodities in Cultural Perspective* (Cambridge, Cambridge University Press), 64–91.

Kossack, G. (1980), '"Kimmerische" Bronzen: Bemerkungen zur Zeitstellung in Ost- und Mitteleuropa', *Situla*, 20/21: 109–43.

Kossack, G. (1994), 'Neufunde aus dem Novočerkassker Formenkreis und ihre Bedeutung für die Geschichte steppenbezogener Reitervölker der späten Bronzezeit', *Il Mar Nero*, 1: 19–54.

Kristiansen, K. (1989), 'Prehistoric migrations: the case of the Single Grave and Corded Ware cultures', *Journal of Danish Archaeology*, 8: 211–25.

230 *Carola Metzner-Nebelsick*

Kristiansen, K. (2014), 'Towards a new paradigm? The Third Science Revolution and its possible consequences in archaeology', *Current Swedish Archaeology*, 22: 11–34.

Kuhn, T. (1970), *The Structure of Scientific Revolution* (Chicago, University of Chicago Press).

Lang, A. (2002), 'Das Inntal als Route für Verkehr und Handel in der Eisenzeit', in G. Schnekenburger, *Über die Alpen: Menschen – Wege – Waren* (Stuttgart, Landesmuseum Baden-Württemberg), 49–57.

Lengfelder, F., Grupe, G., Stallauer, A., Huth, R., and Söllner, F. (2019), 'Modelling strontium isotopes in past biospheres: assessment of bioavailable $^{87}Sr/^{86}Sr$ ratios in local archaeological vertebrates based on environmental signatures', *Science of the Total Environment*, 648: 236–52.

Lippert, A. (2009), *Das spätbronze- und früheisenzeitliche Gräberfeld von Bischofshofen-Pestfriedhof* (Bonn, Habelt).

Ložnjak Dizdar, D. (2004), 'Odnos daljske i bosutske grupe na prostoru hrvatskog Podunavlja početkom starijeg željeznog doba/Das Verhältnis der Dalj- und Bosut-Gruppe auf dem Gebiet des kroatischen Donauraums am Anfang der älteren Eisenzeit', *Prilozi Instituta za arheologiju u Zagrebu*, 21: 19–35.

Machortych, S.V. (1993), *Rannie končevniki Severnogo Pričornomor'ja i okružajuščja sreda* (Kiiv, Nauka Dumka).

Machortych, S.V. (1994), *Kimmerijcy na Severnom Kavkaze* (Kiiv, Nauka dumka).

Maráz, B. (1996), 'Pécs-Jakabhegy: Ausgrabungsergebnisse und die Fragen der Frühhallstattkultur in Südostpannonien', in E. Jerem and A. Lippert, *Die Osthallstattkultur* (Budapest, Archaeolingua), 255–65.

Mauder, M., Ntoutsi, E., Kröger, P., and Kriegel, H.-P. (2017), 'The isotopic fingerprint: new methods of data mining and similarity search', in G. Grupe, A. Grigat, and G. McGlynn (eds), *Across the Alps in Prehistory: Isotopic Mapping of the Brenner Passage by Bioarchaeology* (Cham, Springer Nature), 105–25.

Metzner-Nebelsick, C. (1992), 'Gefäße mit basaraboider Ornamentik aus Frög', in A. Lippert and K. Spindler (eds), *Festschrift zum 50jährigen Bestehen des Instituts für Ur- und Frühgeschichte der Leopold-Franzens-Universität Innsbruck* (Bonn, Habelt), 349–83.

Metzner-Nebelsick, C. (1998), 'Abschied von den "Thrako-Kimmeriern"? Neue Aspekte der Interaktion zwischen karpatenländischen Kulturgruppen der späten Bronze- und frühen Eisenzeit mit der osteuropäischen Steppenkoine', in B. Hänsel and J. Machnik (eds), *Das Karpatenbecken und die osteuropäische Steppe. Nomadenbewegungen und Kulturaustausch in den vorchristlichen Metallzeiten (4000–500 v. Chr.)* (Rahden/Westf., Verlag Marie Leidorf), 361–422.

Metzner-Nebelsick, C. (2000), 'Early Iron Age nomadism in the Great Hungarian Plain – migration or assimilation? The Thraco-Cimmerian problem revisited', in J. Davis-Kimball, E. Murphy, L. Koryakova, and L.T. Yablonsky (eds), *Kurgans, Ritual Sites, and Settlements: Eurasian Bronze and Iron Age* (Oxford, Archaeopress), 160–84.

Metzner-Nebelsick, C. (2002), *Der 'thrako-kimmerische' Formenkreis aus der Sicht der Urnenfelder- und Hallstattzeit im südöstlichen Pannonien* (Rahden/Westf., Verlag Marie Leidorf).

Metzner-Nebelsick, C. (2010), 'Aspects of mobility and migration in the Eastern Carpathian Basin and adjacent areas in the Early Iron Age (10th–7th centuries BC)', in K. Dzięgielewski, M.S. Przybyła, and A. Gawlik (eds), *Migration in Bronze and Early Iron Age Europe* (Kraków, Księgarnia Akademicka), 121–51.

Metzner-Nebelsick, C. (2017), 'At the crossroads of the Hallstatt East', in R. Schumann and S. Van der Vaart-Verschoof (eds), *Connecting Elites and Regions: Perspectives on*

MIGRATION IN ARCHAEOLOGICAL DISCOURSE   231

Contacts, Relations and Differentiation during the Early Iron Age Hallstatt C Period in Northwest and Central Europe (Leiden, Sidestone Press), 349–79.

Metzner-Nebelsick, C. (2020), 'Золотой клад из Даля/Der Goldfund von Dalj', in A.J. Alekseev, M. Nawroth, A. Gass, and J.J. Piotrovskij (eds), *Eisenzeit – Europa ohne Grenzen: 1. Jahrtausend v. Chr.* (Sankt Petersburg, Moskow, and Berlin, Tabula Rasa Publishing House), 108–16.

Metzner-Nebelsick, C., Lang, A., Sommer, C.S., and Steidl, B. (2017), 'Transalpine mobility and trade since the Mesolithic', in G. Grupe, A. Grigat, and G. McGlynn (eds), *Across the Alps in Prehistory: Isotopic Mapping of the Brenner Passage by Bioarchaeology* (Cham, Springer Nature), 1–26.

Metzner-Nebelsick, C., Reuss, S., and Klaut, D. (2020), 'Zwischen Bayern und Tirol: Mobilität in der späten Bronzezeit', *Archäologie in Deutschland*, 1: 24–7.

Möslein, S. and Pernicka, E. (2019), 'The metal analyses of the SSN-project (with catalogue)', in R. Turck, T. Stöllner, and G. Goldenberg (eds), *Alpine Copper II/Alpenkupfer II/Rame delle Alpi II/Cuivre des Alpes II: New Results and Perspectives on Prehistoric Copper Production* (Bochum, Deutsches Bergbau-Museum and Verlag Marie Leidorf), 399–454.

Mogyorós, P. (2018), 'Pre-Scythian burial in Tiszakürt', in D. Bartus (ed), *Dissertationes Archaeologicae ex Instituto Archaeologico Universitatis de Rolando Eötvös Nominatae 3.6* (Budapest, Eötvös Loránd University, Institute of Archaeological Sciences), 361–70.

Nebelsick, L. and Metzner-Nebelsick, C. (2020), 'From Genoa to Günzburg: new trajectories of urbanisation and acculturation between the Mediterranean and South-Central Europe', in L. Zamboni, M. Fernández-Götz, and C. Metzner-Nebelsick (eds), *Crossing the Alps: Early Urbanism between Northern Italy and Central Europe (900–400 BC)* (Leiden, Sidestone Press), 43–67.

Nestor, I. (1934), 'Zu den Pferdegeschirrbronzen aus Stillfried a.d. March, N.-Ö.', *Wiener Prähistorische Zeitschrift*, 21: 108–30.

Pare, C.E.F. (1987), 'Der Zeremonialwagen der Hallstattzeit: Untersuchungen zu Konstruktion, Typologie und Kulturbeziehungen', in F.E. Barth, J. Biel, M. Egg, A. France-Lanord, H.-E. Joachim, *et al.*, *Vierrädrige Wagen der Hallstattzeit: Untersuchungen zu Geschichte und Technik* (Mainz, Römisch-Germanisches Zentralmuseum), 189–248.

Pare, C.E.F. (1992), *Wagons and Wagon-Graves of the Early Iron Age in Central Europe* (Oxford, Oxford University Committee for Archaeology).

Pare, C.E.F. (2017), 'Frühes Eisen in Südeuropa: Die Ausbreitung einer technologischen Innovation vom 2. zum 1. Jahrtausend v. Chr.', in E. Miroššayová, C. Pare, and S. Stegmann-Rajtár (eds), *Das nördliche Karpatenbecken in der Hallstattzeit: Wirtschaft, Handel und Kommunikation in früheisenzeitlichen Gesellschaften zwischen Ostalpen und Westpannonien* (Budapest, Archaeolingua), 1–116.

Patek, E. (1989–90), 'A Szabó János Győző által feltárt "preskíta" síranyag: A Füzesabony-Mezőcsát típusú temetkezések újabb emlékei Heves megyében', *Egri Múzeum Évkönyve / Annales Musei Agriensis*, 25/26: 61–118.

Patek, E. (1993), *Westungarn in der Hallstattzeit* (Weinheim, VCH Acta Humaniora).

Pfauth, U. (1998), *Beiträge zur Urnenfelderzeit in Niederbayern* (Regensburg, Universitätsverlag Regensburg).

Popović, P. and Vukmanović, M. (1998), *Vajuga-Pesak: Nekropola starijeg gvozdenog doba* (Beograd, Arheološki Institut).

Prien, R. (2005), *Archäologie und Migration: Vergleichende Studien zur archäologischen Nachweisbarkeit von Wanderungsbewegungen* (Bonn, Habelt).

Rasmussen, S., Allentoft, M.E., Nielsen, K., Orlando, L., Sikora, M., *et al.* (2015), 'Early divergent strains of *Yersinia pestis* in Eurasia 5,000 years ago', *Cell*, 163: 571–82.

Reinecke, P. (1925), 'Ein neuer Goldfund aus Bulgarien', *Germania*, 9: 50–54.

Reinhold, S. (2003), 'Traditions in transition: some thoughts on the Late Bronze Age and Early Iron Age burial costumes from the Northern Caucasus', *European Journal of Archaeology*, 6(1): 25–54.

Reinhold, S. (2007), *Die Spätbronze- und frühe Eisenzeit im Kaukasus: Materielle Kultur, Chronologie und überregionale Beziehungen* (Bonn, Habelt).

Reuß, S. and Metzner-Nebelsick, C. (2017), 'Mobility and social dynamics in Bavaria and North Tyrol in the Urnfield culture', in S. Scharl and B. Gehlen (eds), *Mobility in Prehistoric Sedentary Societies* (Rahden/Westf., Verlag Marie Leidorf), 181–214.

Romsauer, P. (1999), 'Zur Westgrenze der Mezőcsát-Gruppe', in E. Jerem and I. Poroszlai (eds), *Archaeology of the Bronze and Iron Age: Experimental Archaeology, Environmental Archaeology, Archaeological Parks* (Budapest, Archaeolingua), 167–76.

Sauter, H. (2000), *Studien zum Kimmerierproblem* (Bonn, Habelt).

Sava, V. (2020), 'The Late Bronze Age pottery in the South-Eastern Carpathian Basin', *Slovenská Archeológia*, 68: 253–96.

Sava, V., Gogâltan, F. and Krause, R. (2019), 'First steps in the dating of the Bronze Age mega-fort in Sântana-Cetatea Veche (southwestern Romania)', in S. Hansen and R. Krause (eds), *Bronze Age Fortresses in Europe* (Bonn, Habelt), 161–76.

Schellerer, P. (2020), *Untersuchung transalpiner Mobilität anhand von Blei- und Strontium-Isotopenanalysen menschlicher Leichenbrände der Urnenfelderzeit*, Unpublished Masters thesis (Munich, LMU, Faculty of Biology).

Schmidt, H. (1902), 'Treren und Kimmerier in Troja: Nachtrag zur Buckelkeramik der VII. Ansiedlung', in W. Dörpfeld (ed), *Troja und Ilion: Ergebnisse der Ausgrabungen in den vorhistorischen und historischen Schichten von Ilion 1870–94* (Athen, Beck & Barth), 594–600.

Schopper, F. (1995), *Das urnenfelder- und hallstattzeitliche Gräberfeld von Künzing, Lkr. Deggendorf (Niederbayern)* (Regensburg, Universitätsverlag).

Snoeck, C., Lee-Thorp, J., Schulting, R., de Jong, J., Debouge, W., *et al.* (2015), 'Calcined bone provides a reliable substrate for strontium isotope ratios as shown by an enrichment experiment', *Rapid Communications in Mass Spectrometry*, 29: 107–14.

Sperber, L. (1997), 'Zur Demographie des spätbronzezeitlichen Gräberfeldes von Volders in Nordtirol', in K.F. Rittershofer (ed), *Demographie der Bronzezeit: Paläodemographie, Möglichkeiten und Grenzen* (Espelkamp, Verlag Marie Leidorf), 105–24.

Sperber, L. (2003), 'Siedlungen als Kontroll- und Organisationspunkte für Wirtschaft und Verkehr im spätbronzezeitlichen Nordtirol', *Bayerische Vorgeschichtsblätter*, 68: 19–51.

Sperber, L. (2004), 'Zur Bedeutung des nördlichen Alpenraumes für die spätbronzezeitliche Kupferversorgung in Mitteleuropa mit besonderer Berücksichtigung Nordtirols', in G. Weisgerber and G. Goldenberg (eds), *Alpenkupfer / Rame delle Alpi* (Bochum, Deutsches Bergbau-Museum), 1–43.

Stöllner, T. (2015), 'Die alpinen Kupfererzreviere: Aspekte ihrer zeitlichen, technologischen und wirtschaftlichen Entwicklung im zweiten Jahrtausend vor Christus', in T. Stöllner and K. Oeggl (eds), *Bergauf, Bergab: 10.000 Jahre Bergbau in den Ostalpen* (Bochum and Rahden/Westf., Deutsches Bergbau-Museum and Verlag Marie Leidorf), 99–105.

Stöllner, T. and Oeggl, K. (eds) (2015), *Bergauf, Bergab: 10.000 Jahre Bergbau in den Ostalpen* (Bochum and Rahden/Westf., Deutsches Bergbau-Museum and Verlag Marie Leidorf).

MIGRATION IN ARCHAEOLOGICAL DISCOURSE

Toncala, A., Söllner, F., Mayr, C., Hölzl, S., Heck, K., *et al.* (2017), 'Isotopic map of the Inn-Eisack-Adige-Brenner passage and its application to prehistoric human cremations', in G. Grupe, A. Grigat, and G. McGlynn (eds), *Across the Alps in Prehistory: Isotopic Mapping of the Brenner Passage by Bioarchaeology* (Cham, Springer Nature), 127–227.

Tschetsch, L., Mussauer, A., Mauder, M., Lohrer, J., Kröger, P., *et al.* (2020), 'Multi-isotope fingerprints (O, Sr, Pb) in archaeological animal bone bioapatite: similarity search and the suitability for provenance analysis in a geologically complex Alpine region', *Archaeometry*, 62(Suppl. 1): 35–52.

Ursuțiu, A. (2002), *Etapa mijlocie a primei vârste a fierului în Transilvania (cercetările de la Barnadea, com. Bahnea, jud. Mureș)* (Cluj-Napoca, Editura Nereamia Napocae).

Vinski-Gasparini, K. (1973), *Kultura polja sa žarama u sjevernoj Hrvatskoj/Die Urnenfelderkultur in Nordkroatien* (Zadar, Filozofski Fakultet).

Vulpe, A. (1986), 'Zur Entstehung der geto-dakischen Zivilisation: Die Basarabi-Kultur', *Dacia*, 30: 49–89.

Wiedmann, F., Hofmann, K.P., and Gehrke, H.-J. (eds) (2017), *Vom Wandern der Völker: Migrationserzählungen in den Altertumswissenschaften* (Berlin, Edition Topoi).

11

The Scale of Population Movements: A Model for Later Prehistory

PETER S. WELLS

Movement: mobility and migration

People and mobility

FROM THE EARLIEST times for which we have evidence, humans have been moving about. For later prehistoric Europe, the context with which this chapter is concerned, there are two main categories of evidence bearing on the movement of people. One is the recovery of objects far from their places of origin, the other is bioarchaeological evidence derived from isotopes and aDNA. Both of these approaches show that there has been a great deal of movement of people in the past.

A few examples will serve to make the point. Special kinds of flint were transported over long distances in the Upper Palaeolithic (Delvigne *et al.* 2019). During the Mesolithic and subsequent periods, amber was brought from the shores of the Baltic Sea to points throughout the Continent (Ramstad *et al.* 2013). In the Neolithic, spondylus shells from the Mediterranean Sea were carried to regions throughout Central Europe (Chapman and Gaydarska 2013). In the Bronze Age, copper and tin, mined in limited regions where the ores occurred, were brought together and the resultant bronze moved all over Europe (Harding 2013). In the Iron Age, a vast range of goods was transported across the Continent, including luxury imports from Greece and Italy and weapons and personal ornaments from all parts of Europe (Gosden 2018). For every individual case, we need to consider a wide range of possible mechanisms of transmission (Helms 1988: 129–30). Direct trade can be carried out by long-distance travellers, suppliers and receivers can meet at central points to exchange goods, and down-the-line trade can move objects from place to place along a series of transit nodes. These are just three examples of possible mechanisms for the movement of goods; each implies a

Proceedings of the British Academy, **254**, 234–257, © The British Academy 2023.

THE SCALE OF POPULATION MOVEMENTS

different kind of movement of people and thus different means of transmitting ideas between them.

As the techniques of isotope analysis and aDNA have been developed, they are providing direct evidence from human bodies about how the living individuals had moved from one place to another. Among the important results emerging from these analyses is the realisation that in most of Europe during later prehistoric and early historic times, people throughout the Continent were sharing common genetic inheritance (Schiffels *et al.* 2016). This close relatedness can make ascertaining specific movements difficult for modern investigators.

In this chapter, I argue that small-scale mobility was common, while mass migration would have occurred only occasionally. How many people were moving? Mobility and the resultant transmission of information and goods between communities have important implications for our understanding of later European prehistory.

Nature and scope of mobility

How can we model the scale of movements? In the early part of the 20th century, migration was often suggested as a way of understanding changes represented in the archaeological record (e.g. Childe 1950). In the New Archaeology of the 1960s, migration became less popular as an explanatory device, as emphases shifted to the study of internal processes for explaining change (Clarke 1968; Adams *et al.* 1978). Since the 1990s, migration has re-emerged as a way of understanding change, especially with the results of aDNA analyses of skeletal populations (Burmeister 2000; Scheeres *et al.* 2014; Reich 2018).

As David Anthony (1990; 1997) demonstrated three decades ago, viewed from the perspective of world anthropology and history, the character of migrations is enormously varied. The reasons for migrations also vary widely, some apparently motivated mainly by 'push' factors, others by 'pull' factors, most, perhaps, by both. Migrations can involve thousands or even millions of people, such as those occurring in the past decade, or they can involve a handful of people. Anthony makes the important point that many (most, perhaps) migrations are accompanied by return migrations (see also Fernández-Götz *et al.*, Chapter 1). These can take many different forms and happen for different reasons. If a village community, or part of one, migrates in search of better farmland or of more favourable economic opportunities, some or all members might decide to return to the point of departure after finding that the opportunities were not as attractive as they had hoped they would be. Individuals or families might decide that the benefits of living in the homeland outweighed the advantages of the newly settled place. In many cases, both past and present, people migrate to earn a better living than they could at home; after a time, perhaps months, perhaps years, they return. However, the migrations recorded in early texts ordinarily do not mention the phenomenon of return migrations.

Working towards a model: texts, critiques, archaeology

In an effort to develop a model to apply to prehistoric movements of people, it will be useful to consider a few cases of movement that are attested in written sources and for which we have archaeological evidence as well. Critical questions need to be posed in each case. Why were these texts written when they were? In whose interests were they written? Do they attest to events that were truly different from what was happening earlier and later, or are we misled by the fact that someone chose to write about them, and the texts have survived? To address these questions, I examine – very briefly – three cases of movement for which we have both textual and archaeological evidence. We should bear in mind James Scott's (2017) advice that we understand texts as cultural constructs, not as statements of fact. I am not suggesting that these three cases are in any way similar to any situation in prehistoric Europe, only that from them we can learn what to look for in the archaeological evidence of the Bronze and Iron Ages (Figure 11.1).

Figure 11.1 Map showing locations of places mentioned in the text (image: author)

Caesar and the *Helvetii*

In his account of the war that he conducted in Gaul, Julius Caesar (*De Bello Gallico*) provides numbers of migrants that some modern investigators regard as exaggerated. In Book 1,29, he suggests that 263,000 persons whom he identified as *Helvetii* migrated from their homeland to another location, together with other groups, with a total of 368,000 people on the move. Modern scholars are generally sceptical of Caesar's numbers (Henige 1998; Burmeister and Gebühr 2018), understanding them largely as his political assertions to gain personal glory and to bolster his requests for support from the Roman Senate (Welch and Powell 1998). Caesar provides very little context for his numbers. He says nothing about population density of the peoples he describes, nor anything about the sizes of the major settlements – the *oppida* – although he (*BG* 1,5) gives the numbers of Helvetian *oppida* ('about 12'), villages ('about 400'), and farms. The supposed migration of the *Helvetii* is a major point in Caesar's account, but there is no archaeological evidence to support migrations on the scale that Caesar alleges (Kaenel 2019). Werner Zanier (2016: 529–30) notes that recent research is increasingly showing continuity of settlement in the region during the final century BC (see also Wieland 1996: 184).

Caesar's account depends upon his use of group designations, such as *Helvetii*, *Sugambri*, and *Eburones*, but as is generally the case in the Greek and Roman world, does not tell the reader upon what criteria he recognises these groups. The archaeological evidence does not distinguish those groups or the territorial boundaries that Caesar asserts (Wells 2014; Hornung 2016). It may well be that Caesar describes the geopolitical situation in final-century BC Gaul in the way that he as a Roman general understood it, without knowing much about, or taking into account, how the local peoples thought about themselves and their neighbours. The final century BC was a time of intense cultural change in temperate Europe, with considerable movement of people, but not necessarily mass migrations (Hornung 2016: 236–40). People were surely moving, and new kinds of objects and styles were circulating, but evidence for large-scale migrations is scarce. Gaul and surrounding areas might be understood in terms of Ferguson and Whitehead's (1992) concept of a tribal zone (Wells 1999: 99–121), a region of disruption and dislocation resulting from the actions of a powerful outside force, in this case Rome. Elites may have been moving and troops under their command may have been affected, but there also seems to have been strong continuity (Hornung 2016: 239–40).

Bede and Anglo-Saxon migrations

One of the most familiar and most debated cases of migration in early historic times is that of the Anglo-Saxons. Until the 1950s AD, traditional understanding, based largely on the writings of Gildas, Bede, and the *Anglo-Saxon Chronicle*, was that large numbers of people from Continental Europe whom Bede (1907) referred to as Angles, Saxons, and Jutes migrated from what are now northern Germany and

Denmark across the North Sea and English Channel to Britain (recent summary in Crabtree 2018: 50–4). Bede (1,15) states that the Angles and Saxons arrived first in three ships at the request of a local king to help him defeat local enemies. Later, larger numbers arrived. There ensued a period of destructive warfare. Bede indicates that these new arrivals became the ancestors of the people of Britain of his time.

Bede's account indicates that the first arrivals were a military force that engaged in warfare in Britain. As Crabtree (2018: 52–4) explains, current debate, now based on archaeology and genetic data, as well as on the early texts, is whether the Anglo-Saxon migrations were mainly those of military bands or of mass movements of whole communities, or whether we can speak of an Anglo-Saxon migration at all.

Most researchers now agree that, whatever took place, there was no single mass migration from the Continent to Britain (Oosthuizen 2019). But at various times during the 5th and 6th centuries AD, some people and some groups did move this way (Hines 1984). As Härke (2003: 21) suggests, it is likely that different kinds of migration took place – groups of adult males, family groups, and, perhaps most significantly, small groups of elites with their retinues who had the where-withal to take over where they landed and impose some new traditions and new languages on the native inhabitants. It was probably elites and their followers who were responsible for the introduction and eventual wide acceptance of the language that became the English that we use today. Together with the language, these elites gave new names to places in Britain, a great many of which survive in the 21st century. Härke (2003: 21) believes that some 200,000 immigrants may have made this move. Hodges (2019: 982) posits the same number – 200,000 – but that the migrations happened more gradually, over the course of some 200 years after the end of Roman political control at the start of the 5th century AD. Härke (2003: 24) argues for major cultural change resulting from the immigration, whereas Hodges suggests that the number of new arrivals was too small to have a major effect on local cultural development.

It is now apparent that a great deal of movement was taking place during the 5th and 6th centuries AD in North-West Europe, and this movement involved not only groups that could be identified as Angles from what came to be called Anglia and Saxons from Saxony, but rather a wide range of different groups from different places (Hines 1984; Harland 2019). There had always been movement across the Channel and the North Sea, in both directions, clearly represented by the introduc-tion of the Neolithic economy and the circulation of a wide range of goods through that period and during the Bronze and Iron Ages (Anderson-Whymark *et al*. 2015). It is quite possible that such movement increased at this time in part because of the decline of Roman power both in Britain and on the Continent. What had been pol-itical control over peoples weakened or disappeared altogether, and this situation made it much easier to move and to carry out commerce. And, it so happened that early Christian authors in Britain – Gildas and Bede – began writing about what they thought was going on. Some of the movement was from the Continent to

Britain; movement in the opposite direction did not attract such attention from any writer whose text has survived.

It remains the case that there have not been settlements or cemeteries found in Britain that seem to replicate closely what migrants left behind in their homelands, what Alice Yao (2020: 62–5) would call evidence of 'settler communities'. There are similarities between some of the early architecture in Britain and on the Continent, but no exact replicas of continental buildings (Hamerow 2012). But a lot of objects of apparently continental origin have been recovered, and British material has been found on the Continent. To view this situation in the widest context, we need to recall that the 5th and 6th centuries AD were times of intensified interaction and movement all over Europe, in the wake of the political and economic changes that came about, gradually, with the decline of Roman political, military, and economic power.

Recent isotopic and aDNA studies on skeletal material from Anglo-Saxon cemeteries indicate a predominance of local – that is, indigenous before the supposed migration – ancestry in samples from the Anglo-Saxon period (Martiniano *et al.* 2016). In isotopic analyses of teeth from the Anglo-Saxon cemetery at Berinsfield, south Oxfordshire, where grave goods of continental character were common, 15 of the 19 teeth studied were determined to be of local individuals, and only one that of a European immigrant (Hughes *et al.* 2014; 2018; Oosthuizen 2019: 40).

Thus, present evidence suggests that the migrations mentioned by Bede and the other early writers are best seen as parts of much larger interactions of the 5th and 6th centuries AD, with some groups of people moving at this time but most importantly small warrior bands, merchants, and other travellers moving from place to place, including between the Continent and Britain (Oosthuizen 2019). Some would interpret the lack of what look like transplanted continental settlements and cemeteries in Britain to suggest that direct mass migration across the English Channel and the North Sea was unlikely. But the character of the pottery, metal ornaments, and other objects, together with architectural similarities, make clear that a great deal of mobility across the sea was occurring.

Puritan English to New England

Between 1620 and 1640 AD people known to us as Puritans migrated from England to North America (for a recent account see Hall 2019). This case is well documented both historically and archaeologically. James Deetz (1974) and David H. Fischer (1989) provide rich contextual information that guides us to what we need to look for in cases of potential migration when texts are not available.

Estimates based on historical records suggest that around 20,000 people migrated from England to New England between 1620 and 1640 AD. Although there were various reasons for people to decide to migrate, the principal reason seems to have been religion (Fischer 1989: 16–22; Hall 2019). The people were feeling oppressed

240   *Peter S. Wells*

by conditions at home in England, and they sought freedom to practise religion as they wished. After the two decades of active migrations, the pace slowed after 1640 AD, with a portion of the migrants – Moore (2010) estimates between 7 and 11 per cent – deciding to migrate back to England (see also Fischer 1989: 25).

The migrants did not constitute a cross-section of their home society (Deetz 1974: 21; Horn 1996). Some were wealthy elites, some were prosperous members of what we would call the middle classes today – craftspeople and merchants; only a few belonged to the more modest groups (Fischer 1989: 14, 27). The literacy rate among the migrants was higher than that in England as a whole (Fischer 1989: 30).

Both Deetz and Fischer have studied how the migrants adapted to life in their new environment, giving us important clues of what to look for in the archaeology of prehistoric migrations. Upon arrival, the migrants sought to recreate cultural conditions that they had known at home, a situation that persisted for about two generations, from 1620 to 1660 (Deetz 1974; Fischer 1989: 57). As their towns grew, they named them after the towns they had left in England. They maintained the language and the dialects of their homeland (Fischer 1989: 58) and built their houses as they had in East Anglia and Kent (Fischer 1989: 62).

After the first several decades of migration, around 1660, Deetz recognises in the material culture the emergence of an 'Anglo-American' culture, different from what the Puritans had left behind in England. By this time, many people had been born in New England and knew about the homeland across the sea only through stories told by elders. But – and this point is of special importance in this chapter – for the first 40 years, the new arrivals struggled to recreate in their new land the way of life they had left in England. These efforts would be expected to show up in the archaeology in the form of objects such as pottery, tools, and personal ornaments manufactured in the style of, and using techniques from, the homelands. Especially in design, ornamentation, and representations, we would expect to see evidence for adherence to ideas brought with the immigrants. As Deetz argues, after two decades and the increase in the proportion of locally born members of the communities, we would see the attempts to replicate the styles of the homeland decline, and material culture of the new Anglo-American fashions increase (Figure 11.2).

Migration studies in earlier prehistory

In the recent surge of studies applying aDNA techniques to prehistoric migrations, the case of the Yamnaya, Corded Ware, and Bell Beakers has received the most attention (Reich 2018). It is not my purpose to discuss in any detail the results of the myriad studies related to these issues, but to make a couple of salient points.

The argument is that because aDNA analyses show relatedness between individuals in the area around the northern shores of the Black Sea, known as the Yamnaya group (3500–3000 BC), and individuals in North-East and Northern Europe of what is known as the Corded Ware group, there must have been migration from the former region to the latter (see discussions in Nehlich *et al.* 2009; Allentoft *et al.*

Figure 11.2 Scene in Jackson Heights, Queens, New York. In this modern example of the integration of peoples from different places, the signs indicate the recreation of aspects of the cultures of the homelands of some of the residents in this diverse neighbourhood (image: author)

2015; Haak *et al.* 2015; Müller 2015; Heyd 2017; Kristiansen *et al.* 2017; Furholt 2018; 2019; Anthony 2019; Malmström *et al.* 2019; see also Heyd, Chapter 3). These studies are providing exciting new information about the peoples of Neolithic Europe, but some caution is still necessary when interpreting the results.

So far, the aDNA studies have been carried out on relatively few individuals. As Heyd (2017: 351) points out, the samples analysed are relatively very small, and they often come from individuals widely separated in time. Interactions between groups in the steppes of Eastern Europe and other parts of the Continent have been shown to have been significant from at least the 5th millennium BC (Anthony 2007). In the conclusions to their studies, authors rarely take into account the archaeological evidence associated with the populations whose aDNA is being analysed. As Heyd (2017; 2019) and Furholt (2018) note, aDNA results need to be considered within the broader context of archaeological and other anthropological evidence, including that for the wide range of variability among named cultural groups and the evidence for extensive movements throughout Europe during these times (for further discussion see Gori and Abar, Chapter 2; Metzner-Nebelsick, Chapter 10). In some cases, the movements seem to have been between regions (Price *et al.* 2004; Olalde *et al.* 2018; Brace *et al.* 2019), in others within limited

242   *Peter S. Wells*

regions (Parker Pearson *et al.* 2016). Any attempts to reckon with possible population movements need to consider them in the much broader context of evidence for the variety of kinds of interactions over space, including family visits, trade expeditions, and military incursions. This is not to minimise the significance of the recent aDNA studies, only to urge that they be understood in the context of wider mobility and extensive change that are evident during the 4th and 3rd millennia BC.

Modelling the scale of movement in later prehistory

On the basis of the cases briefly reviewed above, I want to argue that a working model for an approach to prehistoric migrations can be developed on the basis of five principal conditions: population, reasons, portion of communities, abandoned settlements, and new settlements (although, as Anthony [1990] notes, the number of possible factors is infinite).

Population

For a large migration to take place, there must be large numbers of people to take part. In recent years, the large-scale migrations of people from Central America towards North America, and from Syria and parts of Africa to Europe, have been based on large modern populations in those regions.

For movements of people before the enormous increase in population sizes following the Industrial Revolution, much smaller numbers need to be considered. For Gaul around the time of Caesar, McEvedy and Jones (1978: 57, 59) estimate around eight million as the total population of what are now France and Germany, a number that matches roughly other estimates. As explained above, the numbers that Caesar attributes to migrants may be exaggerated. In the case of the Anglo-Saxons, numbers estimated by McEvedy and Jones (1978: 43, 53, 69) for England and Wales, Denmark, and Germany – a total of 4,600,000 – would certainly provide enough individuals for any pattern of mobility between the Continent and Britain. Härke's and Hodges's suggestions of a total of 200,000 for the Anglo-Saxon migrations, whether within a shorter or longer period of time, would represent about 5 per cent of the population of the lands from which the people emigrated. In the case of England in the 17th century AD, the number 20,000 is a reasonable working estimate for migrants to New England between 1620 and 1640 AD; they would represent a much smaller fraction of the population of the mother country, which Horn (1996) estimates at around four million.

Reasons

Caesar suggests that the movements he mentions had to do with political and military machinations in large measure associated with the Roman invasion of Gaul. In

THE SCALE OF POPULATION MOVEMENTS

the Anglo-Saxon case, Bede suggests at first, three boatloads of military personnel, later large numbers of people arriving by boat from the Continent into Britain. Bede suggests that a local king invited the first groups to help him deal with local enemies. In the 17th century AD emigration from England, the texts suggest primarily religious reasons, but economic and political considerations are likely to have played a part as well (Horn 1996: 48–77). In the decades following the successful establishment of the English-speaking communities in New England, it was more attractive for new migrants from England to cross the ocean to find new homes than it would have been if those firmly established communities had not existed there.

Portion of communities

As Anthony (1990: 905) notes, under some conditions, migrations involve only portions of communities. Caesar indicates movement of entire peoples, though the evidence is scant or non-existent, perhaps in part because the movement was so short-lived. In the Anglo-Saxon case, the archaeological evidence and, increasingly, the genetic data suggest small immigrant groups, perhaps in some cases bands of warriors, as suggested by Bede, in others families and groups of families. In the better-documented 17th century AD case, Horn (1996) shows the wide range of individuals who moved, in some cases elite persons, entrepreneurs, and indentured servants, in other cases whole families.

Of special importance in archaeological studies of mobility are craftworkers such as blacksmiths, other metalworkers, and potters, since the archaeological evidence for mobility relies heavily on the occurrence of manufactured goods on archaeological sites (e.g. Rustoiu and Berecki 2014), a point also raised by Hornung (2016: 240).

Abandoned settlements

In the case of Caesar, there is no substantial evidence for the abandonment of landscapes (Hornung 2016: 236–40) in the regions that he mentions, perhaps because such brief movements would be archaeologically invisible. In the Anglo-Saxon case, much has been made by some investigators of the fact that Feddersen Wierde (distr. Cuxhaven) and other settlements on the German and Dutch coasts seem to have been abandoned during the 5th century AD and connected this phenomenon with migrations to Britain. But recently, Oosthuizen (2019: 30, 34) has argued that the landscapes on the Continent along the North Sea coast remained largely occupied. In the 17th century AD, the number of emigrants from East Anglia and other parts of England were so small and constituted such a small portion of the population of individual villages that evidence for abandonment is largely lacking (Johnson, Evanston, pers. comm.; Wrigley and Schofield 1981: 219–21).

It is worth mentioning that many areas in Europe that have been interpreted in the past as 'empty landscapes' and brought into arguments about abandonment

244 Peter S. Wells

have recently begun to be filled in with new discoveries as research progresses, especially as results of rescue archaeology and the expanding use of metal detectors (e.g. Zanier 2016).

New settlements

In the Anglo-Saxon case, evidence for movement between the Continent and Britain is abundant, but neither new settlements replicating those on the Continent nor the new DNA evidence point to large-scale migration. In the case of English Puritans moving to New England in the 17th century AD, both Deetz (1974) and Fischer (1989) emphasise the strong continuity of cultural tradition brought from England and established in New England. The archaeology of domestic architecture, imported material culture, and dietary practices all indicate transplantation of the English ways of doing things directly into North America. After a couple of generations, things began to change, as the colonists began to create new ways (Deetz 1974). Given the less precise chronology of the prehistoric Iron Age, it could be difficult, but not impossible, to recognise the gradual adaptations to newly settled places after two or three generations.

Applying the model

To demonstrate the application of this model to later prehistory, I examine the case of Livy's remarks about migrations of Gauls into Italy. The following is a largely hypothetical example. It makes very rough estimates of possible numbers to demonstrate how the model might apply to specific archaeological situations.

Background

Textual evidence: Livy, Gauls, and Italy

Livy recounts (5,34–9) a series of migrations of Gauls from north of the Alps across the mountains into what is now northern Italy. He describes invaders pouring through the Alpine passes, attacking Etruscans, and founding a city that they named *Mediolanum* (modern Milan). Other groups followed, and later some swept down the peninsula to attack Rome (Figure 11.3). Livy names the Alpine passes through which the first groups of Gauls travelled and names some of the leaders of the Gallic forces (for discussion see especially Pare 1991: 192–8; Vitali and Kaenel 2000: 117–9; Colonna 2017; Roncaglia 2018: 16–7).

Livy was writing in the Augustan period some 400 years after the events that he describes, and some investigators question aspects of his presentation (Roncaglia 2018: 16–7). But most accept his account at least in its outlines, though many

Figure 11.3 View of the site of Marzabotto on the Reno River in the Apennine Mountains of Italy. Excavations at the site have yielded evidence for the presence of people known as Etruscans and Europeans from north of the Alps during the 5th century BC (image: author)

question some details. There is some debate about chronology, concerning possible early 6th century BC movements and the apparently larger movements around 400 BC. Vitali and Kaenel (2000: 118) and Sims-Williams (2020: 523) see reasons to accept the earlier date for movements of people designated as Gauls from north of the Alps into northern Italy; others prefer the later date alone (Pare 1991: 198).

There is also considerable debate as to whether the migrations that Livy describes should be understood as mass movements that took place within a limited period of time, or rather as a series of migrations that occurred over an extended period (on this issue see Lejars 2020; cf. also Pare 1991: 196; Roncaglia 2018: 16–7). Roncaglia (2018: 17) argues that we need to understand Livy's descriptions in the larger context of mobility in Europe at the time (see also Fernández-Götz and Ralston 2017: 273, 275). Livy's portrayal of the arrival and settlement in the Po Plain of groups from north of the Alps is consistent with Polybius's (*Hist.* 2,17) 2nd-century BC account of Celts and other peoples living in the region during the 4th and 3rd centuries BC (Vitali 2004a).

Archaeological evidence

There exists a rich body of literature about the archaeology of the Celts, or Gauls, in Italy, especially in the north, much more than can be summarised here

246   *Peter S. Wells*

(see especially Vitali 2004b; 2010; Colonna 2017; Lejars 2020). A useful map locating the major named tribes of Celtic groups in northern Italy is in Vitali and Kaenel (2000: 117, Figure 1). The most important categories of archaeological material for assessing the migrations and their impact on the cultural landscape of northern Italy are cemeteries (Fitzpatrick 2018 and sources cited above), Celtic-style weapons (Frey 1995; Lejars and Bernardet 2015), and La Tène-style art (Vitali 2010).

A substantial amount of material culture – especially metalwork – in Italy is very similar stylistically to that north of the Alps, as was detailed by Paul Jacobsthal (1944), notably gold ring jewellery, especially that of the 'Waldalgesheim style' (Müller 2009: 85). Many important pieces of Celtic art have been recovered in Italy (e.g. Müller 2009: 90, 106), as well as swords of types similar to those made north of the Alps (Lejars and Bernardet 2015). At the same time, imports from Italy are common in well-outfitted graves north of the Alps. The bronze-beaked jugs (*Schnabelkannen*), believed to have been made mostly at the Etruscan city of Vulci, are common in wealthy Early La Tène graves in France and Germany (Wells 1980: 119–21). These imported jugs stimulated local craft industries to produce vessels similar in shape, but with distinctive northern details, such as those from Basse-Yutz, the Dürrnberg, and the Glauberg (Megaw and Megaw 1990). At the site of Forcello on the Po Plain, 15 fibulae of Late Hallstatt/Early La Tène character attest to interaction between north and south (De Marinis 2012: 179). It is not clear at present whether these represent persons who brought them, lived at the site, and left them there, or some form of trade.

In the regions from which Celtic migrants are likely to have come, there is some evidence for changes that resulted in the abandonment of sites and even of landscapes around the time of the later migrations described by Livy – the end of the 5th and start of the 4th century BC. Fernández-Götz (2019: 184) cites evidence in the Eifel region of western Germany, as well as in other places, for people moving out of landscapes at this time. Settlement and burial activity decreased, and pollen evidence suggests a decline in cultivation although not a complete abandonment. Some major settlement sites, such as the Heuneburg in south-west Germany or Mont Lassois and Bourges in France, declined in activity and seem to have been largely abandoned between the middle and the end of the 5th century BC (Fernández-Götz and Ralston 2017: 272–3). Settlements that replicate the sites north of the Alps from which migrants might have come have not been identified in Italy as yet, but as Lejars (2020) suggests, the migrants may have adapted quickly to their new surroundings and thus 'disappeared' archaeologically as new arrivals.

Isotopic evidence

Recent analyses of evidence provided by strontium isotopes of individuals in the cemeteries of Nebringen in south-west Germany and Monte Bibele in northern Italy, both dating to around the time about which Livy wrote, show that the majority of people at both sites were local in origin, not immigrants from elsewhere (Hauschild

THE SCALE OF POPULATION MOVEMENTS 247

et al. 2013; Scheeres *et al.* 2013; see also Bondini *et al.* 2005). The results from this very limited set of analyses suggest that some individuals and perhaps small groups were mobile, but there is no evidence suggestive of mass migrations. In these studies, males seem to have been slightly more mobile than females overall. However, some caution is needed due to the still small number of analysed samples and the fact that isotopic studies would only identify, in the best of cases, first-generation migrants.

The five conditions

Population

Population estimates for prehistoric times are notoriously difficult to make. Yet the exercise is important, because even the very roughest estimates provide demographic information that helps us to predict social and cultural patterns of behaviour. For my estimates I rely on the following and on extrapolations from them: McEvedy and Jones (1978), Zimmermann *et al.* (2009), Müller (2016), and Burmeister and Gebühr (2018), with their extensive bibliographies of relevant works. Müller (2016: 110) also provides a useful list of 10 different methods for estimating prehistoric populations.

Let us assume that Livy's remarks concern peoples north of the Alps in the general areas of central and eastern France and southern Germany (Pare 1991; Fernández-Götz 2019: 185). On the basis of tumulus numbers, houses in settlements, and calculations of activity areas, Zimmermann *et al.* (2009: 377, Figure 8) suggest a density of three–eight persons per km^2 in Iron Age Central Europe. Burmeister and Gebühr (2018) suggest three–four persons per km^2 for Hallstatt D. If we take an area of 500,000 km^2 for the land of the uplands from central France into southern Germany (map in Hauschild 2012: 259) and work with an average of 3.5 persons per km^2, that would yield a population of around 145,000 for this region. Settlements of this period varied in size from a single farmstead occupied by an extended family (15 persons) to the few major centres such as Bourges, the Heuneburg, the Hohenasperg, and Mont Lassois, with populations in the thousands (Fernández-Götz and Krausse 2016: 322–3).

To arrive at hypothetical figures, I work with these rough estimates for numbers of communities and individuals around the middle of the 5th century BC (Table 11.1).

It is unlikely that many people would leave the farmsteads and villages to travel to Italy because of requirements of tending fields and livestock, as well as looking after families and houses. But at the major and smaller centres, the division of labour would have freed some to engage in other activities, such as administration, crafts, and trade, which is well represented by the imported objects from the Mediterranean world and elsewhere. Some of these persons, along with perhaps a small number of farmers from the hamlets and farmsteads, would have been the likely travellers.

248   *Peter S. Wells*

Table 11.1 Estimate of population figures (table: author)

Bourges, Heuneburg, Hohenasperg, Mont Lassois @ 5,000 people=	20,000
20 smaller centres (Britzgyberg, Ipf…) @ 2,500=	50,000
300 villages @ 200=	60,000
1000 hamlets and farmsteads @ 15=	15,000
Total estimated population of the 500,000 km² area=	145,000

If, from each of the four major centres, an average of 200 persons travelled to Italy each year, that would total 800 persons. If, from the smaller centres, 100 per community made the trip, that would be another 2000. If we allow a total of 1000 from the villages, hamlets, and farmsteads, then we would have a grand total of 3800 persons making the trip each year, on average, in the decades around 400 BC (I emphasise that these are all hypothetical numbers). While some travel may have been consistent year after year (Cicolani 2012), some was probably episodic. Travel by merchants, craftworkers, raiders, and some farmers could account both for the Mediterranean imports in the rich Early La Tène burials north of the Alps and a significant part of the Celtic-style swords, neckrings, fibulae, and other items found in Italy (Figure 11.4). If all of Italy had a population of around four million at this time (McEvedy and Jones 1978: 107), then northern Italy, into which the migrants described by Livy arrived, might have had around one million.

Reasons

Why would people have travelled from north of the Alps into Italy? In Livy's account, named actors (kings, sons) were behind the moves across the Alps. But Livy was writing four centuries after the events he describes. Would the names have been remembered in the oral histories, or perhaps even in Etruscan sources? Livy's personalising of the event is characteristic of early historic accounts – to provide a good story understandable by the people of his time. Archaeology provides a different, more nuanced, picture.

A variety of proxies, including tree rings, Greenland ice cores, and tree pollen indicate an end to warmer and drier climatic conditions and the onset of colder and wetter ones around the middle of the 5th century BC (Tinner *et al.* 2003: 1455–6). Livy suggests that overpopulation and disputes between groups led to the migration of Gauls into Italy. He also suggests that the migrants were lured to Italy by wine and luxurious living. This latter suggestion may reflect elite Romans' knowledge that the interactions taking place during Livy's day had precedents going back centuries.

Figure 11.4 Etruscan bronze jug and basin, together with an Attic Greek cup, from the rich burial at Vix in eastern France. Jugs of this type are well represented in Iron Age graves in West-Central Europe (photo: Erich Lessing/Art Resource, New York)

Portions of communities

There is no clear evidence to suggest that whole communities migrated across the Alps into Italy; this situation would correspond with Livy's indication that only parts of tribes migrated. The evidence suggests instead small numbers of people, many of them with special interests and skills. Some of the mobile groups may have

250 *Peter S. Wells*

been raiding parties intent on seizing valuables and fleeing back across the Alps. The quantity of swords studied by Frey (1995) and by Lejars and Bernardet (2015) would support the idea that small-scale military violence may have played a part, lending some support to Livy's account. Craftworkers may have been another category of persons who travelled across the Alps into Italy (Vitali and Kaenel 2000). The efforts by metal smiths specialising in iron weapons, bronze ornaments, and gold jewellery who travelled to Italy, perhaps lured by a demand for the new La Tène-style products, could account for a substantial portion of such objects there.

Abandoned settlements

Evidence for abandonment of landscapes in temperate Europe around this time is increasing with ongoing archaeological research. Fernández-Götz (2019: 190–3) notes evidence, both in cemeteries and in pollen types, in the Eifel region of western Germany that may indicate a decline in population, and cemeteries in Champagne show decline in use during the 4th century BC. Fernández-Götz and Ralston (2017: 272–3) also note that many of the major Early Iron Age centres declined and apparently were abandoned in the latter half of the 5th century BC. Many other profound changes were taking place around this time (Echt 2016; Wells 2016), and these may have been linked to the abandonment of different settled places.

New settlements

No substantial Central European-style settlements or cemeteries have been found as yet in Italy, and when graves have been identified that contain some Central European objects, they are parts of assemblages that are mixed with local Italic products (Frey 1995: 525, 527; Lejars and Bernardet 2015; Lejars 2020). If entire communities were migrating across the Alps, we would expect to find settlements with houses and domestic debris similar to those north of the Alps, and cemeteries arranged and outfitted in the way that cemeteries north of the Alps were – 'settler communities' in Yao's (2020: 62) sense. On the other hand, since it is likely that only portions of tribes migrated, and the new arrivals may have quickly adapted to their new surroundings, perhaps it is unlikely that such evidence will be identified.

Assessment

Rather than mass migrations from north of the Alps into Italy around 400 BC, all of the archaeological evidence, both south of the Alps and to the north, suggests an intensification of interactions that had been going on for centuries (Cicolani 2012; Metzner-Nebelsick and Grupe 2020). Current evidence suggests extensive cross-Alpine movements of groups of persons, some moving back and forth, some trading, some visiting families, some raiding, and some settling permanently, all giving rise to the oral traditions upon which Livy's account is based. That said, the extensive distribution in northern Italy of material culture and styles derived from communities originating north of the Alps attests to the strong influence of the contacts between north and south. These contacts included individuals and groups that migrated into northern Italy to settle, as well as traders, craftworkers, and probably raiders who also had substantial effects on the material culture and practices in the Po Plain.

Conclusion

From the model suggested here, based on the five conditions, and its application to the case of Livy's account of migrations into Italy, I draw the following conclusions:

1) Population – most communities north of the Alps at this time were made up of much smaller numbers of people than those behind the mass migrations of the 19th, 20th, and 21st centuries AD.
2) Reasons – increasing evidence suggests that climate change may have been a significant push factor. Surely the pull factor of attractive wealth may have motivated groups of traders and raiders, and settlers may have sought both the good farmland of the Po Plain and other advantages in the new lands.
3) Portions of communities – there is currently no evidence to suggest 'settler communities' in Yao's sense – whole village communities intent on establishing new settlements in Italy. The evidence suggests instead largely specialised travellers such as craftworkers, traders, and perhaps raiders, but accompanied by some farming groups seeking new lands to cultivate.
4) Abandoned settlements – recent research indicates decline, and at least partial abandonment, of major settlements in the regions from which the migrants are likely to have come.
5) New settlements – future fine-tuned archaeological investigations may be able to identify new settlements established by the immigrants, though because they are likely to have adopted local practices relatively quickly, it would be challenging to recognise this initial phase of settlement.

The model proposed here, based on the five conditions, can be applied to any situation to assess the likely scale of migration. I hope it will stimulate other researchers to test, refine, or reject this model in favour of others, especially as the archaeological and genetic databases grow, in order to develop an ever-richer picture of human mobility in the past.

Acknowledgements

For helpful advice and for important publications, I thank Bettina Arnold, Bernard Bachrach, Peter Bogucki, John Broad, John Chapman, Pam Crabtree, Craig Cipolla, Manuel Fernández-Götz, Volker Heyd, James Horn, Mark Horton, Matthew Johnson, Oliver Nicholson, Susan Oosthuizen, Günther Wieland, and

252 *Peter S. Wells*

Werner Zanier. And I thank the three anonymous reviewers for their suggestions of ways to improve the chapter.

References

Adams, W.Y., Van Gerven, D.P., and Levy, R.S. (1978), 'The retreat from migrationism', *Annual Review of Anthropology*, 7: 483–532.

Allentoft, M.E., Sikora, M., Sjogren, K.-G., Rasmussen, S., Rasmussen, M., *et al.* (2015), 'Population genomics of Bronze Age Eurasia', *Nature*, 522: 167–72.

Anderson-Whymark, H., Garrow, D., and Sturt, F. (eds) (2015), *Continental Connections: Exploring Cross-Channel Relationships* (Oxford, Oxbow).

Anthony, D.W. (1990), 'Migration in archeology: the baby and the bathwater', *American Anthropologist*, 92(4): 895–914.

Anthony, D.W. (1997), 'Prehistoric migration as social process', in J. Chapman and H. Hamerow (eds), *Migrations and Invasions in Archaeological Explanation* (Oxford, British Archaeological Reports), 21–32.

Anthony, D.W. (2007), *The Horse, the Wheel, and Language: How Bronze-Age Riders from the Eurasian Steppes Shaped the Modern World* (Princeton, Princeton University Press).

Anthony, D.W. (2019), 'Archaeology, genetics, and language in the steppes: a comment on Bomhard', *Journal of Indo-European Studies*, 47: 1–23.

Bede (1907), *Ecclesiastical History of England*, translated by A.M. Seller (London, George Bell & Sons).

Bondini, A., Charlier, P., Lejars, T., Naldi, V., Verger, S., *et al.* (2005), 'Monterenzio (Prov. de Bologne): La nécropole celto-étrusque de Monterenzio Vecchio', *Mélanges de l'école francaise de Rome*, 117(1): 269–82.

Brace, S., Diekmann, Y., Booth, T.J., Van Dorp, L., Faltyskova, Z., *et al.* (2019), 'Ancient genomes indicate population replacement in Early Neolithic Britain', *Nature Ecology and Evolution*, 3: 765–71.

Burmeister, S. (2000), 'Archaeology and migration: approaches to an archaeological proof of migration', *Current Anthropology*, 41(4): 539–67.

Burmeister, S. and Gebühr, M. (2018), 'Demographic aspects of Iron Age societies', in C. Haselgrove, K. Rebay-Salisbury, and P.S. Wells, (eds), *Oxford Handbook of the European Iron Age* (Oxford, Oxford University Press), DOI: 10.1093/oxfordhb/9780199696826.013.9.

Chapman, J. and Gaydarska, B. (2013), '*Spondylus Gaederopus/Glycymeris* exchange networks in the European Neolithic and Chalcolithic', in C. Fowler, J. Harding, and D. Hofmann (eds), *The Oxford Handbook of Neolithic Europe* (Oxford, Oxford University Press), DOI: 10.1093/oxfordhb/9780199545841.013.014.

Childe, V.G. (1950), *Prehistoric Migrations in Europe* (Oslo, Instituttet for Sammenlignende Kulturforskning).

Cicolani, V. (2012), 'Offene Handelsplätze, offener Warenaustausch: Weite Wege für die Waren', in *Die Welt der Kelten: Zentren der Macht – Kostbarkeiten der Kunst* (Ostfildern, Jan Thorbecke Verlag), 180–2.

Clarke, D.L. (1968), *Analytical Archaeology* (London, Methuen).

Colonna, G. (2017), 'I Celti in Italia nel VI e V secolo a.C.: Dati storici, epigrafici e onosmatici', in P. Piana Agostinetti (ed), *Celti d'Italia. I Celti dell'eta di La Tène a sud delle Alpi* (Rome, Giorgio Bretschneider Editore), 3–12.

Crabtree, P.J. (2018), *Early Medieval Britain: The Rebirth of Towns in the Post-Roman West* (Cambridge, Cambridge University Press).

Deetz, J. (1974), 'A cognitive model for American material culture: 1620–1835', in C.B. Moore (ed), *Reconstructing Complex Societies* (Cambridge MA, American Schools of Oriental Research), 21–4.

Delvigne, V., Fernandes, P., Piboule, M., Bindon, P., Chomette, D., *et al.* (2019), 'Barremian-Bedoulian flint humanly transported from the west bank of the Rhône to the Massif-Central Highlands: a diachronic perspective', *ScienceDirect*, 18(1): 90–112.

De Marinis, R. (2012), 'Handelsknotenpunkt in der Poebene: Forcello', in *Die Welt der Kelten: Zentren der Macht – Kostbarkeiten der Kunst* (Ostfildern, Jan Thorbecke Verlag), 178–9.

Echt, R. (2016), 'Phase transition, Axial Age, and axis displacement: from the Hallstatt to the La Tène culture in the regions northwest of the Alps', in M. Fernández-Götz and D. Krausse (eds), *Eurasia at the Dawn of History: Urbanization and Social Change* (New York, Cambridge University Press), 353–69.

Ferguson, R.B. and Whitehead, N.L. (eds) (1992), *War in the Tribal Zone: Expanding States and Indigenous Warfare* (Santa Fe, School of American Research).

Fernández-Götz, M. (2019), 'Migrations in Iron Age Europe: a comparative view', in P. Halkon (ed), *The Arras Culture of Eastern Yorkshire: Celebrating the Iron Age* (Oxford, Oxbow), 179–99.

Fernández-Götz, M. and Krausse, D. (2016), 'Urbanization processes and cultural change in the Early Iron Age of Central Europe', in M. Fernández-Götz and D. Krausse (eds), *Eurasia at the Dawn of History: Urbanization and Social Change* (New York, Cambridge University Press), 319–35.

Fernández-Götz, M. and Ralston, I. (2017), 'The complexity and fragility of Early Iron Age urbanism in West-Central temperate Europe', *Journal of World Prehistory*, 30: 259–79.

Fischer, D.H. (1989), *Albion's Seed: Four British Folkways in America* (New York, Oxford University Press).

Fitzpatrick, A.P. (2018), 'Migration', in C. Haselgrove, K. Rebay-Salisbury, and P.S. Wells, (eds), *Oxford Handbook of the European Iron Age* (Oxford, Oxford University Press), DOI: 10.1093/oxfordhb/9780199696826.013.14.

Frey, O.-H. (1995), 'The Celts in Italy', in M.J. Green (ed), *The Celtic World* (London and New York, Routledge), 515–32.

Furholt, M. (2018), 'Massive migrations? The impact of recent aDNA studies on our view of third millennium Europe', *European Journal of Archaeology*, 21(2): 159–91.

Furholt, M. (2019), 'Re-integrating archaeology: a contribution to aDNA studies and the migration discourse on the 3rd millennium BC in Europe', *Proceedings of the Prehistoric Society*, 85: 115–29.

Gosden, C. (2018), 'Trade and exchange', in C. Haselgrove, K. Rebay-Salisbury, and P.S. Wells, (eds), *Oxford Handbook of the European Iron Age* (Oxford, Oxford University Press), DOI: 10.1093/oxfordhb/9780199696826.013.18.

Haak, W., Lazaridis, I., Patterson, N., Rohland, N., Mallick, S., *et al.* (2015), 'Massive migration from the steppe was a source for Indo-European languages in Europe', *Nature*, 522: 207–11.

Härke, H. (2003), 'Population replacement or acculturation? An archaeological perspective on population and migration in post-Roman Britain', in H.L.C. Tristram (ed), *The Celtic Englishes III* (Heidelberg, Universitätsverlag Winter), 13–28.

Hall, D.D. (2019), *The Puritans: A Transatlantic History* (Princeton, Princeton University Press).

Hamerow, H. (2012), 'Anglo-Saxon timber buildings and their social context', in D.A. Hinton, S. Crawford, and H. Hamerow (eds), *The Oxford Handbook of Anglo-Saxon Archaeology* (Oxford, Oxford University Press), DOI: 10.1093/oxfordhb/9780199212149.013.0009.

Harding, A. (2013), 'Trade and exchange', in H. Fokkens and A. Harding (eds), *The Oxford Handbook of the European Bronze Age* (Oxford, Oxford University Press), DOI: 10.1093/oxfordhb/9780199572861.013.0020.

Harland, J.M. (2019), 'Memories of migration? The "Anglo-Saxon" burial costume of the fifth century AD', *Antiquity*, 93(370): 954–69.

Haselgrove, C., Rebay-Salisbury, K., and Wells, P.S. (eds) (2018), *Oxford Handbook of the European Iron Age* (Oxford, Oxford University Press), DOI: 10.1093/oxfordhb/9780199696826.001.0001.

Hauschild, M. (2012), 'Quer durch Europa: Die keltischen Wanderungen', in *Die Welt der Kelten: Zentren der Macht – Kostbarkeiten der Kunst* (Ostfildern, Jan Thorbecke Verlag), 257–63.

Hauschild, M., Schönfelder, M., Scheeres, M., Knipper, C., Alt, K.W., *et al.* (2013), 'Nebringen, Münsingen und Monte Bibele: Zum archäologischen und bioarchäologischen Nachweis von Mobilität im 4./3. Jahrhundert v. Chr.', *Archäologisches Korrespondenzblatt*, 43(3): 345–64.

Helms, M.W. (1988), *Ulysses' Sail: An Ethnogaphic Odyssey of Power, Knowledge, and Geographical Distance* (Princeton, Princeton University Press).

Henige, D. (1998), 'He came, he saw, we counted: the historiography and demography of Caesar's Gallic numbers', *Annales de Démographie Historique*: 215–42.

Heyd, V. (2017), 'Kossinna's smile', *Antiquity*, 91(356): 348–59.

Heyd, V. (2019), 'Yamnaya – Corded Wares – Bell Beakers, or how to conceptualize events of 5000 years ago that shaped modern Europe', in T. Vulchev (ed), *Studia in Honorem Iliae Iliev* (Yambol, Regional Historical Museum), 125–36.

Hines, J. (1984), *The Scandinavian Character of Anglian England in the Pre-Viking Period* (Oxford, British Archaeological Reports).

Hodges, R. (2019), 'A "processual-plus" corrective to the origins of Anglo-Saxon England', *Journal of Roman Archaeology*, 32: 980–7.

Horn, J. (1996), *Adapting to a New World: English Society in the Seventeenth-Century Chesapeake* (Chapel Hill, University of North Carolina Press).

Hornung, S. (2016), *Siedlung und Bevölkerung in Ostgallien zwischen Gallischem Krieg und der Festigung der römischen Herrschaft* (Mainz, Verlag Philipp von Zabern).

Hughes, S.S., Millard, A.R., Lucy, S.J., Chenery, C.A., Evans, J.A., *et al.* (2014), 'Anglo-Saxon origins investigated by isotopic analysis of burials from Berinsfield, Oxfordshire, UK', *Journal of Archaeological Science*, 42: 81–92.

Hughes, S.S., Millard, A.R., Chenery, C.A., Nowell, G., and Pearson, D.G. (2018), 'Isotopic analysis of burials from the early Anglo-Saxon cemetery at Eastbourne, Sussex, UK', *Journal of Archaeological Science: Reports*, 19: 513–25.

Jacobsthal, P. (1944), *Early Celtic Art* (Oxford, Clarendon Press).

Kaenel, G. (2019), '58 BC: the *Helvetii*, from the Swiss Plateau to Bibracte … and back', in A.P. Fitzpatrick and C. Haselgrove (eds), *Julius Caesar's Battle for Gaul: New Archaeological Perspectives* (Oxford, Oxbow), 73–90.

Kristiansen, K. Allentoft, M.E., Frei, K.M., Iversen, R., Johannsen, N.N., *et al.* (2017), 'Re-theorising mobility and the formation of culture and language among the Corded Ware in Europe', *Antiquity*, 91(356): 334–47.

Lejars, T. (2020), 'Les Celtes et les populations étrusques et italiques entre les VIe et IIIe siècles av. J.-C.', *Mélanges de l'École Francaise de Rome: Antiquité*, 132(1): 67–80.

Lejars, T. and Bernardet, R. (2015), 'L'épée laténienne du sanctuaire de Junon à Gabies. Les Témoignages archéologiques d'une présence celtique dans le Latium', *Archeologia Classica*, 66: 121–88.

Malmström, H., Günther, T., Svensson, E.M., Juras, A., Fraser, M., *et al.* (2019), 'The genomic ancestry of the Scandinavian Battle Axe culture people and their relation to the broader Corded Ware', *Proceedings of the Royal Society B*, 286(1912): 1528.

Martiniano, R., Caffell, A., Holst, M., Hunter-Mann, K., Montgomery, J., *et al.* (2016), 'Genomic signals of migration and continuity in Britain before the Anglo-Saxons', *Nature Communications*, 7: 10326, DOI: 10.1038/ncomms10326.

McEvedy, C. and Jones, R. (1978), *Atlas of World Population History* (Harmondsworth, Penguin Books).

Megaw, R. and Megaw, V. (1990), *The Basse-Yutz Find: Masterpieces of Celtic Art* (London, Society of Antiquaries of London).

Metzner-Nebelsick, C. and Grupe, G. (2020), 'Transalpine migration', *Archäologie in Deutschland*, 1: 18–21.

Moore, S.H. (2010), *Pilgrims: New World Settlers and the Call of Home* (New Haven, Yale University Press).

Müller, F. (2009), *Art of the Celts 700 BC to AD 700* (Bern, Historisches Museum).

Müller, J. (2015), 'Eight million Neolithic Europeans – social demography and social archaeology on the scope of change: from the Near East to Scandinavia', in K. Kristiansen, L. Smejda, and J. Turek (eds), *Paradigm Found: Archaeological Theory Present, Past and Future* (Oxford, Oxbow), 200–14.

Müller, J. (2016), 'From the Neolithic to the Iron Age – demography and social agglomeration: The development of centralized control', in M. Fernández-Götz and D. Krausse (eds), *Eurasia at the Dawn of History: Urbanization and Social Change* (New York, Cambridge University Press), 106–24.

Nehlich, O., Montgomery, J., Evans, J., Schade-Lindig, S., Pichler, S.L., *et al.* (2009), 'Mobility or migration: a case study from the Neolithic settlement of Nieder-Mörlen (Hessen, Germany)', *Journal of Archaeological Science*, 36(8): 1791–9.

Olalde, I., Brace, S., Allentoft, M.E., Armit, I., Kristiansen, K., *et al.* (2018), 'The Beaker phenomenon and the genomic transformation of northwest Europe', *Nature*, 555(7695): 190–6.

Oosthuizen, S. (2019), *The Emergence of the English* (Leeds, Arc Humanities Press).

Pare, C. (1991), '*Fürstensitze*, Celts and the Mediterranean world: developments in the West Hallstatt culture in the 6th and 5th centuries BC', *Proceedings of the Prehistoric Society*, 57(2): 183–202.

Parker Pearson, M., Chamberlain, A., Jay, M., Sheridan, A., Curtis, N., *et al.* (2016), 'Beaker people in Britain: migration, mobility and diet', *Antiquity*, 90: 620–37.

Price, T.D., Knipper, C., Grupe, G., and Smrcka, V. (2004), 'Strontium isotopes and prehistoric migration: the Bell Beaker period in Central Europe', *European Journal of Archaeology*, 7(1): 9–40.

Ramstad, M., Axelsson, T., and Strinnholm, A. (2013), 'Amber', in C. Fowler, J. Harding, and D. Hofmann (eds), *The Oxford Handbook of Neolithic Europe* (Oxford, Oxford University Press), DOI: 10.1093/oxfordhb/9780199545841.013.001.

Reich, D. (2018), *Who We Are and How We Got Here: Ancient DNA and the New Science of the Human Past* (New York, Vintage).

Roncaglia, C.E. (2018), *Northern Italy in the Roman World: From the Bronze Age to Late Antiquity* (Baltimore, Johns Hopkins University Press).

Rustoiu, A. and Berecki, S. (2014), 'Celtic elites and craftsmen: mobility and technological transfer during the Late Iron Age in the Eastern and South-Eastern Carpathian Basin', in S. Berecki (ed), *Iron Age Crafts and Craftsmen in the Carpathian Basin* (Târgu Mureş, Mega), 249–78.

Scheeres, M., Knipper, C., Hauschild, M., Schönfelder, M., Siebel, W., *et al.* (2013), 'Evidence for "Celtic migrations"? Strontium isotope analysis at the Early La Tène (LT B) cemeteries of Nebringen (Germany) and Monte Bibele (Italy)', *Journal of Archaeological Science*, 40: 3614–25.

Scheeres, M., Knipper, C., Hauschild, M., Schönfelder, M., Siebel, W., *et al.* (2014), '"Celtic migration": fact or fiction? Strontium and oxygen isotope analysis of the Czech cemeteries of Radovesice and Kutná Hora in Bohemia', *American Journal of Physical Anthropology*, 155: 496–512.

Schiffels, S., Haak, W., Paajanen, P., Llamas, B., Popescu, E., *et al.* (2016), 'Iron Age and Anglo-Saxon genomes from East England reveal British migration history', *Nature Communications*, 7: 1–9.

Scott, J.C. (2017), *Against the Grain: A Deep History of the Earliest States* (New Haven, Yale University Press).

Sims-Williams, P. (2020), 'An alternative to "Celtic from the east" and "Celtic from the west"', *Cambridge Archaeological Journal*, 30(3): 511–29.

Tinner, W., Lotter, A.F., Ammann, B., Conedera, M., Hubschmid, P., *et al.* (2003), 'Climate change and contemporaneous land-use phases north and south of the Alps 2300 BC to 800 AD', *Quaternary Science Reviews*, 22: 1447–60.

Vitali, D. (2004a), 'La Cispadana tra IV e II secolo a.C.', in S. Agusta-Boularot and X. Lafon (eds), *Des Ibères aux Vénètes* (Rome, École française de Rome), 278–92.

Vitali, D. (2004b), 'I Celti in Italia', in F. Marzatico and P. Gleirscher (eds), *Guerrieri, principi ed eroi: Fra il Danubio e il Po dalla preistoria all'alto Medioevo* (Trento, Provincia autonoma de Trento), 315–29.

Vitali, D. (2010), 'Die keltische Kunst und die Boier in Italien', in M. Schönberger (ed), *Kelten! Kelten? Keltische Spuren in Italien* (Mainz, Römisch-Germanisches Zentralmuseum), 34–7.

Vitali, D. and Kaenel, G. (2000), 'Un Helvète chez les Etrusques vers 300 av. J.-C.', *Archäologie der Schweiz*, 23(3): 115–22.

Welch, K. and Powell, A. (1998), *Julius Caesar as Artful Reporter: The War Commentaries as Political Instruments* (London, Duckworth).

Wells, P.S. (1980), *Culture Contact and Culture Change: Early Iron Age Central Europe and the Mediterranean World* (Cambridge, Cambridge University Press).

Wells, P.S. (1999), *The Barbarians Speak: How the Conquered Peoples Shaped Roman Europe* (Princeton, Princeton University Press).

Wells, P.S. (2014), 'Material culture and identity: the problem of identifying Celts, Germans and Romans in Late Iron Age Europe', in C.N. Popa and S. Stoddart (eds), *Fingerprinting the Iron Age: Approaches to Identity in the European Iron Age* (Oxford, Oxbow), 306–22.

Wells, P.S. (2016), 'Images, ornament, and cognition in Early La Tène Europe: a new style for a changing world', in M. Fernández-Götz and D. Krausse (eds), *Eurasia at the Dawn of History: Urbanization and Social Change* (New York, Cambridge University Press), 380–91.

Wieland, G. (1996), *Die Spätlatènezeit in Württemberg. Forschungen zur jüngeren Latènekultur zwischen Schwarzwald und Nördlinger Ries* (Stuttgart, Konrad Theiss Verlag).

Wrigley, E.A. and Schofield, R.S. (1981), *The Population History of England 1541–1871: A Reconstruction* (Cambridge, Harvard University Press).

Yao, A. (2020), 'The Great Wall as destination? Archaeology of migration and settlers under the Han Empire', in A.L. Boozer, B.S. Düring and B.J. Parker (eds), *Archaeologies of Empire: Local Participants and Imperial Trajectories* (Santa Fe, School for Advanced Research Press), 57–87.

Zanier, W. (2016), *Der spätlatène- und frühkaiserzeitiche Opferplatz auf dem Döttenbichl südlich von Oberammergau* (Munich, C.H. Beck Verlag).

Zimmermann, A., Hilpert, J., and Wendt, K.P. (2009), 'Estimations of population density for selected periods between the Neolithic and AD 1800', *Human Biology*, 81(2–3): 356–80.

12

Alpine Connections: Iron Age Mobility in the Po Valley and the Circum-Alpine Regions

VERONICA CICOLANI AND LORENZO ZAMBONI

Introduction

HUMAN INTERACTION, GROUP or individual mobility, and migration are once again becoming some of the most challenging and debated topics in prehistoric and protohistoric archaeology (Van Dommelen 2014; Bistáková *et al*. 2020; Fernández-Götz *et al*., Chapter 1). The regions between the Mediterranean and Central Europe in the 1st millennium BC represent promising case studies, given the quantity and variability of archaeological, environmental, and historical sources (Fernández-Götz 2019; Zamboni *et al*. 2020).

However, mainstream protohistoric studies in south Central Europe during the last decades, albeit generally avoiding the old-fashioned 'migrationism' (Van Dommelen 2014: 478), have frequently addressed regional interactions at a macro-regional scale by highlighting luxurious and lavish finds, or stressing the presence of imported goods from the Mediterranean and Italy found in 'princely seats' and elite burials. The framework is that of a 'gift-economy' (as outlined by Frankenstein and Rowlands 1978), especially regarding the Early Iron Age. Even after the trade explosion of the 6th and 5th centuries BC, with the opening of new 'globalised' markets and the adoption of new means of exchange (Sherratt 2016; Zamboni 2021), previous narratives have often been narrowed towards exotic goods and high-status artefacts, such as Etruscan bronzes or Greek pottery. Among the variety of objects found far from their places of origin, foreign goods are more easily recognisable and thus commonly utilised for tracing and studying ancient mobility and social status in non-literate societies (Pauli 1978; 1991; Brun and Chaume 1997; Kimming 2000; Lüscher *et al*. 2002; Hurlet *et al*. 2014). The narratives regarding interactions between Central Europe and Italy in the Circum-Alpine regions during the Early Iron Age are mostly focused on the elites, reducing the nature of their relationships to a prestige discourse among aristocrats and a control of power for

Proceedings of the British Academy, **254**, 258–279, © The British Academy 2023.

supra-regional trade (Tarditi 2007; Bonomi and Guggisberg 2015). Another recurring narrative, influenced by a text-based and culture-historical approach, revolves around a connection between exotic and imported objects and individuals of supposed foreign origin (see below).

However, an archaeology of interaction should not be solely focused on more visible objects or social classes, or a conflation of an object's mobility with an individual's mobility and ethnicity. To overcome these imbalances, in this chapter we reassess how different social groups interacted by focusing on north Italian craft productions, makers, and distribution from a wider perspective, testing alternative approaches towards an up-to-date understanding of mobility, both of objects and individuals.

The present study mainly addresses the relationships between the Golasecca culture's core area and the neighbouring regions in the western Alps and the western and central Po Valley during the Early Iron Age, between the 7th and the 5th centuries BC (Golasecca period IC to IIIA1, corresponding to Hallstatt C2–D3 in Central Europe). Our dataset includes a comprehensive distribution of Golasecca-type objects north of the Alps (Cicolani 2017), as well as the current datasets from *Liguria interna* (Cicolani 2021) and western Emilia (Zamboni 2018).

In this chapter, we critically review the archaeological background of northwest Italy and previous interpretations of material remains, especially metal ornaments, as evidence of individual and group mobility. We then suggest the application of quantitative, contextual, spatial, and technological analyses, with the aim of approaching material agency and social complexity within the region and period under investigation.

Archaeological setting and background: material agency, mobility, and interaction across the Alps

Studies on the Iron Age in Central Europe have long been embedded within a 'Mediterranean imports paradigm' due to the appearance of imported artefacts across Europe, which have been discovered since the late 19th century. This has led to the identification of human and material mobility through the tracing of specific, easily recognisable indicators of distinction, namely elites, hierarchical sites, and imported luxury artefacts, or, unusually, finely crafted products from the Mediterranean or Etruscan worlds. This traditional account has too often kept working classes, commoners, and their productions out of the picture, despite their deep involvement in the organisation and maintenance of trade and daily activities. More recent protohistoric studies are gradually overcoming these assumptions (Dietler 2005; Adam 2006; Bats 2006; Verger 2013; Verger and Pernet 2013; Cicolani *et al.* 2015; Cicolani 2017; Guilaine *et al.* 2017; Zamboni 2018) by looking beyond the mere dissemination of objects or their typological features (Angelini *et al.* 2009; Cicolani and Berruto 2017; Brysbaert and Vetters 2020; Van der Vaart-Verschoof and Schumann 2020). Thus, more attention must be paid to comparative and contextual analysis of artefacts, workshops, tools, processing activities, production waste, and their agency as a means of better understanding social practices (Nakoinz 2014; Schumann and Van der Vaart-Verschoof 2017).

Moreover, the interaction between makers, users or consumers, and the material world is now approached in order to explain the creation, maintenance, and negotiation of social distinctions inside dynamic community networks (Roux *et al.* 2012; Brysbaert and Gorgues 2017; Cicolani and Huet 2019; Dubreucq *et al.* 2020). This perspective leads us to question how material culture has been created, used, appropriated, and (re)contextualised in different areas and how it might reveal the nature of social relationships. However, even within this renewed approach, research trajectories still seem focused on investigating the behaviours of consumer and user rather than the producer's activities and their interaction with other social classes.

Regarding north-western Italy, recent archaeological discoveries and theoretical advances are confirming the complexity and long-term continuity of the interaction between the two sides of the Alps starting in the protohistoric period (Zamboni *et al.* 2020). During the Late Bronze Age, for instance, the local cultures were characterised by funerary rituals, styles in pottery, and bronze ornaments closely linked to the western groups of the Urnfield culture north of the Alps (de Marinis 2014a). In the Early Iron Age, it is worth emphasising the supra-regional diffusion of different types of ornaments, including bronze pins and fibulae (such as the ribbed Mörigen types; see Casini 2011; Casini and Chaume 2014: 232–4), testifying that the Alpine arch was not a major obstacle to ancient mobility, trade, and cultural interactions in the *longue durée* (Cicolani and Tribouillard 2018; Cicolani and Huet 2019; Trémblay-Cormier and Isoardi 2019; Trémblay-Cormier *et al.* 2019; Nebelsick and Metzner-Nebelsick 2020; Zamboni 2021).

During the 6th and 5th centuries BC, Europe saw the widening of an elaborate and dynamic system of long-distance connections, a 'globalised' economy (Sherratt 2016), which was reflected in the material culture, social practices, and the dissemination of foreign artefacts, especially bronze items. This scenario is closely connected with the growth of Mediterranean, Greek, and Etruscan trade, involving different social actors and products. Within this framework, the cultures of north-western Italy have been assigned the role of 'intermediary actors' at the crossroads of different spheres of interaction.

North-western Italy in the Early Iron Age

The north-western sector of Italy (in present-day Piedmont, Lombardy, Liguria, and the western Po Valley) represents a large region that was characterised during the Iron Age by three main archaeological aspects, namely the so-called Golasecca culture, *Liguria interna* ('southern Piedmont'), and western Emilia ('western

Po Valley'), connected by different levels of interaction and interdependence (Figure 12.1).

After the Final Bronze Age occupation (Proto-Golasecca period) in western Lombardy, eastern Piedmont, and the Ticino region of southern Switzerland, the dominant Early Iron Age phenomenon corresponds to the archaeologically defined Golasecca culture (de Marinis and Biaggio Simona 2000; Lorre and Cicolani 2009; Cicolani 2017; Teržan and de Marinis 2018; de Marinis and Casini 2020). Since the discovery of the eponymous necropolis of Golasecca south of Lago Maggiore by Giani in 1824 (Lorre and Cicolani 2009), the Golasecca area has benefited from a long tradition of thorough chrono-typological studies. While there are two major urban sites – Sesto Calende-Golasecca-Castelletto Ticino (de Marinis and Casini 2020) and Como (Welc et al. 2020) – the material culture is known primarily from funerary evidence (cremations), as few settlements have been extensively excavated and comprehensively published.

The Golasecca area appears to be actively involved in Mediterranean trade, especially after the 6th century BC when a growth in merchant and craftspeople activity becomes archaeologically visible. In fact, during the same phase, in Castelletto

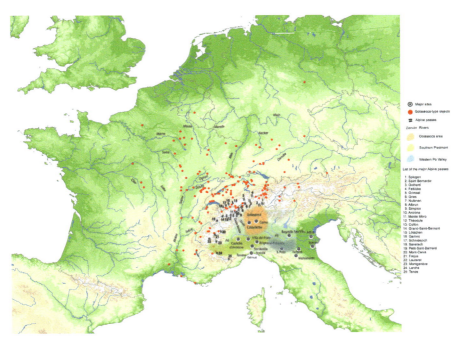

Figure 12.1 Map of Iron Age north-western Italy (major sites and the three cultural regions addressed), with main Alpine passes and distribution of Golasecca-type objects north of the Alps (image: V. Cicolani)

Ticino several craft workshops are documented, including the production of small bronze objects and distinctive ceramics. Some of these products were also traded outside the region, reaching both the transalpine domain and the exchange networks among neighbouring Ligurian, Etruscan, and Venetic populations (Cicolani 2017).

From a cultural point of view, Golasecca is traditionally assigned to the highly problematic (*sensu* Collis 2003) 'Celtic' ethnos based on etic sources, primarily Greek and Roman writings, and the presence of *c.* 140 inscriptions in so-called Lepontic language, written in an alphabet derived from Etruscan (Piana Agostinetti and Morandi 2004). It should be stressed that the suggestion of a supra-regional 'Celtic' ethnos is merely derived from a linguistic view, without any direct correlation in the different material cultures. From a social perspective, while the practice of writing is typically associated with local elites and priests, the practice of writing in Castelletto Ticino was primarily associated with non-elite graves from the 7th and 6th centuries BC, ostensibly belonging to craftspeople and merchants (Cicolani and Gambari 2021).

In the southern part of the region, between the Golasecca area and Liguria after the foundation of Genoa in the 6th century BC (de Marinis 2014b; Melli 2017), a pathway in north-western Italy became the main north–south route connecting the Ligurian Sea to the Alps along the Polcevera, Scrivia, and Ticino Rivers. This led to the development of a local culture called *Liguria interna* in present-day Southern Piedmont. This was characterised by funeral practices and ceramic production connected to the core Ligurian area, adopting locally produced metal equipment, which appears profoundly influenced by Golasecca and Ligurian styles (Cicolani 2021). Several settlements, including the production site of Villa del Foro (Venturino *et al.* 2017; Venturino and Giaretti 2021), were active in Southern Piedmont during the 6th and early 5th centuries BC. Their locations near major tributaries of the Po River and mountain passes emphasise their role as major nodes within a supra-regional trade network (Nebelsick and Metzner-Nebelsick 2020).

The valley south of the Po River, in present-day Emilia, has also been recently re-examined (Zamboni 2018; 2022). Here, the picture is that of a rural region, without clear evidence of centralised and hierarchical settlements, characterised by clusters of farmsteads and villages with small cemeteries likely belonging to kin or social class groups. There is a complete absence of pottery among the grave goods for the entire region, while the typical female funerary costume is a mixture of Golasecca-influenced, as well as Veneto and Eastern Hallstatt-style fashions, including bronze belt plates, fibulae, spoked-wheel pendants, and arm-rings (Zamboni 2018). Overall, comparative analysis of different archaeological settings and categories of objects from north-western Italy suggests the existence of close links between the three areas and their communities, with mutual influences and a high degree of permeability of cultural borders. In what follows, we shall highlight how previous approaches have interpreted a rigid definition for these cultures, primarily based on the distribution of artefacts, even suggesting questionable practices of individual and group mobility.

Previous studies and criticism

The presence of ornaments and artefacts typical of north Italian cultures across the Circum-Alpine area has been highlighted by several scholars (Krämer 1961; Kaenel 1990; Pauli 1991; Adam 1992; Brun and Chaume 1997; Casini and Chaume 2014). Their works, mainly based on spatial distribution and stylistic (chrono-typological) studies, suggested that the diffusion of Golasecca-type artefacts could be seen as an indicator of mobility, especially of women, outside their area of origin. Their assumption was that fibulae and other small finds, as well as ceramics, had no intrinsic value as a means of exchange (Casini 2000: 76; Casini and Chaume 2014: 232), and should instead be interpreted as evidence of personal identity and, thus, of mobility (Casini 2012; Casini and Chaume 2014: 232; Barbieri 2019: 54–5; see also Stöllner 2014: 213; Tori 2019; Trémblay-Cormier and Isoardi 2019).

In the specific case of female ornaments and fashion items, this means that female Golasecca-type fibulae or pendants found outside the area of production should be correlated with the presence of a female individual, who was born in the Golasecca region and died elsewhere, likely after a social bond with the local community. The assumed theoretical model is that of (patrilocal) exogamous strategies, a social norm described by ethnographic and cultural anthropological accounts of marrying outside one's social group, with the intent of enforcing social, political, and economic ties, especially during periods of economic, political, or territorial expansion. The importance of exogamic practices in late prehistory has been proved by increasing contextual and groundbreaking bioarchaeological evidence (see Stockhammer and Massy, Chapter 8; see also Kristiansen 1998; Knipper *et al.* 2017; Fischer *et al.* 2018).

According to this framework, a mutual exchange of 'brides' between the two sides of the Alps during periods of intense trade, for instance the second half of the 6th century and the 5th century BC, has also been proposed. The intention was to explain the presence of a number of Hallstatt fibulae in the Po Valley which, coupled with belt hooks, weapons, and other functional and iconographic items, have been linked to hypothetical early 'Celtic migration' movements, raids, or scout incursions (Casini 2000, 85; Casini and Chaume 2014: 242–7; Stöllner 2014). In fact, the mobility of male individuals has also been suggested, again looking to (less numerous) male-type objects. In this case, however, in addition to warriors, the presence of tradespeople and merchants has been suggested, referring to low-/middle-class people who travelled from northern Italy across Central Europe (Casini 2000: 86; Schmid-Sikimić 2000).[1]

---

[1] A typical example of this approach is the following statement by Schmid-Sikimić (2000: 241): 'Drago fibulae, pertaining exclusively to men, are found outside the territory of origin exclusively in settlement contexts, while fibulae and belt plates typical of women's clothing have been found in burials [...]. These data suggest a temporary presence of men in foreign territories, while women were involved in relationships of patrilocal exogamy aimed at strengthening fruitful alliances with communities along the same trade routes'.

Sometimes, a quantitative approach – the contextual concentration of Golasecca-type ornaments in grave goods – is taken as a reinforcement for the hypothesis of the north Italic provenance of the deceased (Casini 2000: 80). Following the same theoretical assumptions, the presence of sherds of Golasecca-type pottery outside the core area, e.g. in settlements like Tamins (Grisons, Switzerland), is seen as a sign of permanent residency of north Italian families or groups (Casini and Chaume 2014: 235, Figure 3). A more uncertain role has been assigned to metal or composite pendants, including the typical Golaseccan 'basket-shaped' ones, with their interpretation as amulets with apotropaic or other symbolic meanings that could have led to frequent interpersonal exchanges (Casini 2000: 79; Tessmann 2007; Casini and Chaume 2014: 237; Barbieri 2019; Tori 2019).

We believe, however, that the mobility of individuals of both genders, including the practice of exogamy (which itself played a crucial role in history), should not be assessed on the sole basis of the distribution of foreign objects, as in the case of the female Golasecca-type ornaments. Whenever possible, interpretations should be supported by additional evidence, especially bioarchaeological data (Oelze *et al.* 2012; see also Kristiansen, Chapter 5; Stockhammer and Massy, Chapter 8). We also argue that, while relatively probable for this chronological and territorial context, the exogamic model is only one of the possible social strategies demonstrable for the complex network of interactions across Iron Age Europe. The role of artisans and merchants should be highlighted as one such alternative (see below). In other words, in the absence of strong bioarchaeological evidence (such as in the north Italian cultures), the traditional explanation of brides' mobility, if based only on material evidence, appears reductive compared with the complexity and diversity of social dynamics in Iron Age Europe. More importantly, previous approaches to individual mobility are likely to appear flawed by the rough equation – typical of the culture-historical approach[2] (Reher Díez 2012; Johnson 2020: 11–25) – 'object/ornament=individual and ethnic identity', but also by the underestimation of the social role of women (Busoni 2001; David-Elbiali 2009; Bolger 2013).

On the contrary, according to up-to-date cultural anthropological and archaeological theoretical approaches, there are more nuanced relationships between objects, personal or individual self, or external perception. Objects are characterised by agencies and articulated biographies (Knappett and Malafouris 2008; Van Oyen 2018), and they could have been active or passive markers of self-expression (Reher Díez 2012).[3]

---

[2] In this view, the given ornament (or personal equipment) is considered an element of individual clothing, and thus a clue for detecting personal identity, personhood, and ethnicity. The same paradigm has been widely applied to neighbouring areas in northern Italy, e.g. as a means to explain the presence of imported objects in Bologna-Felsina and the Po Valley (Sassatelli 2014; see further comments in Zamboni 2018: 232–8).

[3] For a summary of some of the problems associated with the concept of ethnicity in archaeology, cf. Jones 1997; Reher Díez and Fernández-Götz 2015. The theoretically broader concept of 'recognition', as already suggested by Pierre Bourdieu and Francesco Remotti, appears as a more open, relational, and inclusive research tool (Zamboni 2022 for further discussion and references).

Reassessing the theoretical framework: new approaches

The approach we adopt in this chapter aims to go beyond mere typological analysis, which appeared crucial in earlier stages of archaeological research in order to build solid and useful chronological and typological grids, but is insufficient for addressing the whole spectrum of social and cultural aspects. Adopting a contextual and comparative approach, using quantitative and qualitative analysis combined with technological and experimental studies, we can study the manufacturing process, highlighting different skills and techniques, addressing the main sources of raw materials, and identifying the places and modes of production. Finally, we want to investigate the anthropological and economic implications, evaluating different degrees of inclusion, exclusion, and adaptation of external features within societal networks.

Spatial approach to Iron Age mobility

In sites showing both local and foreign products, it is possible to better understand the different levels of integration, transformation, and adaptation of external traits, as well as aesthetic tastes and artisan practices that could suggest mobility. The presence of hundreds of Golasecca-type objects across Central Europe and northern Italy has traditionally been explained with the 'intermediary role' played by the Golasecca culture in transalpine trade, especially during the 5th century BC (Pauli 1991; Brun and Chaume 1997). However, the involvement of north-western Italian communities in long-distance trade networks appeared in the mid-7th century BC, diversified during the 6th century BC, and gradually decreased towards the end of the 5th century BC (Casini and Chaume 2014; Cicolani 2017). This is reflected in the diffusion of typical clothing elements, primarily fibulae and pendants, but also to a lesser extent arm-rings and belts (Figure 12.2).

Their spread in northern Italy, Alpine, and transalpine areas can be seen not only in cemeteries or single graves (Kaenel 1990; Casini 2000; Casini and Chaume 2014), but also in settlements and hoards, e.g. Source de la Douix near Vix, linked to natural springs (Cicolani *et al.* 2015; Cicolani 2017). This contextual and spatial variability is probably linked to the diverse forms and stages of mobility of humans and objects across Alpine passes and waterway networks (Trémblay-Cormier *et al.* 2019). Thus, in the transalpine area fibulae and pendants, especially the basket-type ones, are found in different categories of settlements, from hillforts (such as Chassey, Bourguignon-lès-Morey, or Souvance in eastern France) and urban sites (such as Vix and the related graves and hoard, or Salins-les-Bains) to productive sites, workshops, or districts (such as in Bourges or Bragny-sur-Saône). They are also encountered in Alpine settlements located near natural paths, including mountain passes leading to the Valais and Grisons regions, waterways to the lake stations of Baar or Zug, or natural crossroads like Estavayer-Bussy in the Fribourg canton (Cicolani 2017: 201–22).

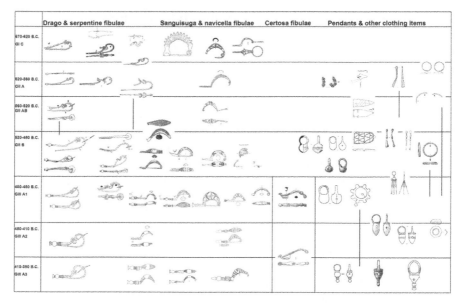

Figure 12.2 Chrono-typological scheme of the main Golasecca-type clothing items (after Cicolani 2017)

The occurrence of Golasecca-type clothing in transalpine settlements, such as in Bragny-sur-Saône, could be linked to cultural contacts, not excluding individual or small group mobility (including women), seen as actors within the supra-regional trade or as members of mixed communities. The presence of Golasecca-type ornaments during all phases of occupation suggests regular or recurrent movements based on different temporal and spatial stages. In this framework, the mixed population established (permanently or seasonally) in the Alpine settlements of Gamsen, Bussy, and Chur, as shown by the high concentration of north Italian ornaments in the whole stratigraphic context, could be interpreted as the first stopover point during longer transalpine journeys (Figure 12.3).

In northern Italy, the end of the 6th century BC marks a moment of increasing exchange between Central Europe and the Mediterranean, as demonstrated by the foundations of trading hubs in the Po Valley and Delta (cf. Figure 12.1), including San Polo-Servirola (Reggio Emilia, Emilia-Romagna), Forcello-Bagnolo San Vito (Mantua, Lombardy), Adria, and Spina (Zamboni 2021). This also affects the wider distribution of specific Golasecca-type ornaments, such as the Cerinasca drago- and Gajaccio-type fibulae associated with male clothing, as well as Sanguisuga fibulae decorated with coral inlays and belts for female clothing. These have been found in settlements or single burials in Southern Piedmont and the Po Valley.

In contrast, arm-rings and bronze belt plates, currently associated with female-type burials, seem to have a shorter range of diffusion. Thus, the Chiavari-type

ALPINE CONNECTIONS: IRON AGE MOBILITY

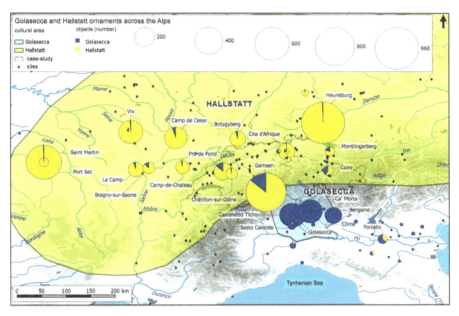

Figure 12.3 Spatial analysis, quantitative and percentage distribution of Golasecca and Hallstatt ornaments across the Alps, showing the ratios of both local and foreign materials within each site (after Cicolani and Huet 2019)

arm-ring or the bottoms with conical knobs typical of the Ligurian tradition show a narrower distribution during the 6th century BC in the Po Valley (de Marinis 2016; Zamboni 2018), the eastern Golasecca group (Castelletto Ticino), and the productive settlement of Villa del Foro, with several new examples produced locally (Cicolani 2021). The circulation of bronze belt plates points to a similar pattern. These clothing elements are known from several sites in the Po Valley and neighbouring Alpine regions, mostly from funerary contexts, suggesting similar short-range diffusion (Cicolani 2017; Zamboni 2018). This distribution attests to a short- to medium-range mobility, probably linked with long-lasting contacts between neighbouring groups sharing common fashion styles, especially in the female sphere (Trémblay-Cormier and Isoardi 2019; Trémblay-Cormier et al. 2019).

To sum up, an ongoing review of the north-western Italian dataset and context shows a pattern of social and cultural interaction and human mobility in the Circum-Alpine regions of increasing complexity, avoiding the previous paradigms of gift exchange or exogamous marriages. The close similarities between stylistic features of fibulae and pendants found on both sides of the Alps, as well as the presence of semi-finished Golasecca-type objects (e.g. drago fibulae from the Ipf (southern Germany), Souvance, and Estavayer-Bussy; basket pendants from Southern Piedmont), and local variants or stylistic adaptations (e.g. the drago and serpentine fibulae from Haguenau cemeteries) are highlighting a deeper implication of the Golasecca communities in short-, medium-, and long-distance relations. We can also envisage a more active role of north Italic craftspeople or tradespeople involved in trade, raw material procurement, mining, and perhaps pastoral activities (Trémblay-Cormier *et al.* 2019: 159–61). An effective role of women in trade and production activities could also be suggested. In order to test this scenario, ongoing projects (e.g. *Programme Collectif de Recherche* on Bragny-sur-Saône; Venturino and Giaretti 2021) are evaluating different contexts of production, assessing the presence of local versus foreign elements, or the coexistence of female- and male-associated imported ornaments inside settlements characterised by intense metal-working activity.

Mapping Iron Age mobility

Furthermore, a modelling of contextual quantitative and qualitative data regarding the distribution of north Italic productions can be addressed to highlight underlying timing, strategies, and logics of medium- and long-range commerce (Cicolani and Huet 2019). During the Early Iron Age, there is evidence of exchange networks between north Alpine and south Alpine domains in the Central Alps (modern Switzerland), where products of various origins arrived or travelled through different intermediaries.

In order to study the formation and functioning of these networks, two classes of objects have been compared: north-western common and individual items, belonging to short- and medium-range interactions, and Mediterranean imports of valuable objects linked to long-distance and cooperative networks. The corpus has been studied in the framework of theoretical displacements, by using a 'shorter-paths' algorithm, and by modelling relations between archaeological sites, cultural domains, and classes of artefacts. This approach tests and stresses the variability of site integration and exclusion within the networks of object distribution. A sample of 289 settlements and 2187 objects has been collected, including Golasecca and Hallstatt bronze ornaments, Etruscan and Greek vessels, and amphorae. By using these variables, multivariate patterns of connections across the Alps can be highlighted through the coexistence of both Hallstatt and Italic objects within the same archaeological sites (settlements, graves, hoards).

The application of the shortest-path algorithm to the Alpine diffusion of Golasecca-type ornaments has allowed for the evaluation of the diachronic organisation and exploitation of pathways and mountain passes, taking into account altimetry and gradients of difficulty (Figure 12.4). Thanks to a specific algorithm aimed at simulating different scenarios, based on the quantity and quality of data, it is possible to identify alternative routes and passes, such as the Nufenen and Grimsel passes, not previously emphasised (Cicolani and Huet 2019: 48–50). The evolution and density of locations are connected to changing networks and subnetworks, which are closely linked. Thus, after the opening of new trade paths,

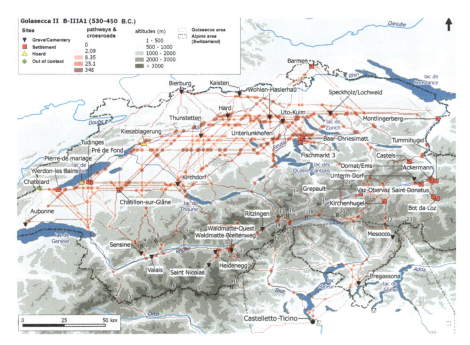

Figure 12.4 Shortest-path model of connectivity networks in the north-west Alpine area, including alternative connections, as shown by the quantitative analysis of contexts and distribution of Golasecca objects (after Cicolani and Huet 2019)

they would have promoted the foundation or growth of new sites in the Po Valley, as well as in the Alpine and transalpine area.

Finally, a mapping approach also further elaborates on the data already processed in the network analysis, focusing, for example, on metal production. Applying mathematical and spatial data modelling (R programme and graph theory), the heterogeneous dataset has been analysed to visualise and identify the connected networks and subnetworks highlighted thanks to the previous contextual and quantitative approaches. On a large scale, the Golasecca network appears to be a major node in the protohistoric Greek and Etruscan trade. The organisation of inter-site networks through time suggests that the Golasecca groups were able to stimulate their own exchange networks, especially in the Alpine area, as is also hinted at by stratigraphic and quantitative evidence.

Towards a technological approach to Iron Age mobility

In order to overcome certain inconsistencies related to some culture-history assumptions previously outlined, another promising approach is the utilisation of technological studies. These include archaeometrical and statistical analyses applied to closed and highly informative contexts. Ongoing research is focused on the comparative and contextual analysis of the dissemination and agency of artefacts, so as to gain a better knowledge of social practices (Verger and Pernet 2013; Cicolani *et al.* 2015; Schumann and Van der Vaart-Verschoof 2017). The interaction between makers, users or consumers, and the material world and culture are also understood to be key to explaining the creation, maintenance, and negotiation of social distinctions in a dynamic community network (Brysbaert and Gorgues 2017; Brysbaert and Vetters 2020; Dubreucq *et al.* 2020). Within this framework, technological studies on craft activities clearly show a high level of creativity and ability, as well as the specificity and diversity of their productions. Bronze ornaments are especially useful in distinguishing between different areas of production and consumption. Unfortunately, few technological studies on bronze ornaments are available for northern Italy. After studies carried out on groups of objects by Schindler (1998) (on the Arbedo hoard), Giumlia-Mair (2003) (on the fibulae of Slovenian cemeteries), and Northover (Nagy 2012) (on the Castaneda grave goods), no other comprehensive and supra-regional studies have been published.

To overcome this major gap, an ongoing research project focuses on copper alloy objects, especially fibulae, from six sites in three different areas: the Golasecca core area, southern Piedmont, and western Emilia (Cicolani and Berruto 2017; Cicolani 2020; 2021) (Figure 12.5). Preliminary results on metrical, stylistic, and

Figure 12.5 Main settlements in Southern Piedmont and distribution of decorated coral fibulae: an example of local production and variants of Golasecca-type objects (image: Cicolani; base map: GoogleEarth)

typological traits show some differences between the three areas. The decorations, for instance, can be divided into two main groups, incised and inlaid. The most common are composed of arrangements of fine transverse and parallel lines. In the case studies they are neither very regular nor sharply outlined, suggesting work that took place after finishing the object. On the other hand, more regular decorations made by a deeper V-shaped outline and subsequent polishing could suggest the preparation of the decoration during the original shaping of the object. Behind an apparent stylistic homogeneity, metrical and pattern studies highlighted the adoption of different models, probably linked to local aesthetic taste and textile wearing. For example, in Southern Piedmont the fibulae are smaller with a slightly curved and swollen arch, and irregularly incised decoration. Semi-finished or failed objects, as well as trash fragments from Villa del Foro and San Polo demonstrate their local production, suggesting different stages of casting experimentation and/ or learning (Cicolani 2021).

From a technological perspective, fibulae and pendants appear to be locally crafted using the same techniques usually applied in the Golasecca workshops, according to the analysis carried out on the Arbedo hoard (Schindler 1998). Thus, female ornaments and fibulae are either cast in a mould or made using lost wax and then poured on to a clay core which can either remain in place or be removed after casting. Male ornaments, on the other hand, seem to be most often cast in a mould and then shaped by stretching and hammering.

Furthermore, X-ray analysis has revealed two technical solutions that were invisible to the naked eye: the overflow fixing of the barb to the body of the fibula and the holding of the clay core by means of rivets and/or sheet metal fragments cut into triangles, arranged transversely and horizontally to the body of the fibula. These technical solutions have been also partly verified by experimentation. The replication of ancient craftsmen's copper alloy techniques is able to confirm the use of overcasting as an efficient technique to fix separate functional parts of fibulae, as suggested by both optical observation and X-ray analysis.

From an archaeometric point of view, analysis of the elemental composition and alloy trace elements was carried out in French and Italian laboratories, with the assistance of the Centre De Restauration des Musées de France, on 50 ornaments from Golasecca and San Polo-Servirola, which were stored at the National Museum of Saint-Germain-en-Laye. Preliminary results indicate the use of a standard alloy, but with differences in the concentrations of trace elements and alloyed lead, which are still being studied in order to identify the work of different craftspeople or workshops.

Finally, Raman and FTIR analyses have also been applied to a particular type of decoration found on Sanguisuga fibulae, which are commonly associated with female individuals in north-western Italy. The decoration appears in the form of circular cells filled with a substance having colour variations ranging from white to very light pink. Often considered to be deteriorated coral, these residues have rarely been analytically studied. Preliminary analyses carried out by Turin University on

272   *Veronica Cicolani and Lorenzo Zamboni*

13 fibulae revealed that at least three fibulae from Brignano Frascata and one from Villa del Foro were indeed decorated with red coral, which has a recognisable signature (beta-carotene). For the other specimens, the analyses still need to be completed to determine the organic or mineral nature of different kinds of pastes which also recorded the presence of talc or hydroxyapatite (indicators of the possible presence of white pigments).

Bioarchaeological approach to Iron Age mobility

A substantial lack of published bioarchaeological data from Iron Age northern Italy hampers a thorough discussion on mobility of individuals and groups in this region. However, the availability of comparable and contemporary evidence from the other side of the Alpine arch (Oelze *et al.* 2012; Knipper *et al.* 2013; Koch 2017) clearly suggests, on the one hand, a heterogeneous and multifaceted composition of European Iron Age societies. This includes the presence of immigrants from neighbouring areas, who lived and died in central and southern Germany and were assimilated or integrated into different roles within the local communities (Oelze *et al.* 2012; Knipper *et al.* 2013). On the other hand, available bioarchaeological evidence proves that there is no correlation between the isotopic signature of individuals who were born and grew up south of the Alps or elsewhere, and the contextual presence of imported grave goods coming from the Golasecca area or other Alpine regions.

In other words, there are bioarchaeological signatures for mobility of individuals and small groups across the Alps during the Iron Age. These involved both female and male individuals, especially in their earlier life stages, thus suggesting relocation practices, perhaps correlated to the fosterage of children (Knipper *et al.* 2013; see also Stockhammer and Massy, Chapter 8; Rebay-Salisbury, Chapter 9). This mobility, though, cannot be demonstrated by looking only at the presence of imported materials. On the contrary, the German case studies suggest that foreign individuals from Alpine or Italian regions were buried in local costume and socially assimilated into the host community – at least those who received 'formal' burials. Conversely, imported goods (from the Golasecca area or elsewhere) were commonly buried in graves belonging to people who had been born and grew up locally or in the immediate surroundings (Koch 2017: 222–3).[4] The picture formed is that of a heterogeneous society that adopted highly mixed funerary assemblages, and

---

[4] An explanatory example is grave 96 of the Magdalenenberg, belonging to a mature woman buried with a mixed assemblage of goods. According to Koch (2017: 222, Figure 8), her 'belt hook is a typical object of the south alpine Golasecca culture, but the isotope values show that most likely the female individual of grave 96 spent her childhood in the direct surroundings of the Magdalenenberg. The foreign belt hook thus symbolised a *cultural* contact to south alpine landscapes' (emphasis added).

whose individual identities, if any, appear to have been dissolved into the community with few or no visible links with the cultures of origin.[5]

Since no isotopic data are known to date from north Italian Iron Age burial sites between the 7th and the 5th centuries BC, we lack corresponding scenarios south of the Alps. However, it is possible to hypothesise a certain incidence of mobility, exchange, and relocation between Golasecca, Ligurian, and Emilian communities, leading to mixed and heterogeneous societies (Cicolani 2017). Yet personal objects and ornaments alone do not necessarily indicate mobility or descent, since integration, assimilation, and the negotiation of social status are much more complex phenomena involving different layers of recognition instances and an active and selective adoption of materiality (Zamboni 2018).

Concluding thoughts

Metal objects and ornaments manufactured in north-western Italy, or influenced by north Italic models, are widespread and highly informative items across the Alpine regions during the Iron Age. Thanks to their morphological and stylistic variability, these findings are valuable cultural markers to address different areas of production and consumption. However, previous studies have been mainly focused on high-standard productions and looking at south and north Alpine distribution patterns, thus overlooking how such objects were produced, received, imitated, or adapted by local societies. More importantly, previous interpretations were directed towards a mere identification, or juxtaposition, between non-local objects and (supposedly) foreign individuals. Based on culture-historical assumptions, the discovery of a Golasecca-type fibula or belt hook, for example, would have been enough to hypothesise the presence of an individual of north Italic origin.

While the latter scenario might have sometimes been the case (i.e. a foreign object occasionally marking the presence of a non-local individual), in this chapter we suggest a more complex approach towards Iron Age mobility and interaction. This should be based, firstly, on a reevaluation of small finds and common elements of daily life and clothing, beyond luxury items and high-standard Mediterranean imports, leading to a renewed interest in less visible social classes, including craftspeople, tradespeople, and commoners. Secondly, a rejection of the culture-historical paradigm (the simplistic 'objects=people' equation), since objects and ideas seem to have been exchanged in more complex ways across Iron Age Europe, regardless of supposed (and often built a posteriori) ethnic boundaries, as suggested

---

[5] It is worth remembering that within Hallstatt burial sites, such as the Glauberg (Knipper *et al.* 2013), the variability in funerary practice and in multiple isotopic values, indicating different access to resources and diets, point to class and hierarchical status, rather than kin, ethnic, or origin differences. A class of 'princes' and elite wealthy companions show isotopic ratios of higher shares of meat/dairy products, while workmen or slaves buried in 'non-normative' contexts bear signs of poorer, millet-based diets and lower lifestyle conditions and health (Knipper *et al.* 2013: 831–2).

by an evaluation of comparative bioarchaeological data from neighbouring regions. Thirdly, in the absence of and, when available, in addition to bioarchaeological evidence we looked at detailed spatial and technological analyses based on contexts of discoveries, their networks of interaction, modes of production, technological transfer, and local adaptation.

The overall outcome of this approach is a tentative reconstruction of the social complexity of Iron Age societies, characterised in our view by more heterogeneous and mixed cultural traits, with an emphasis on social differences, as well as mutual technological influences. In this scenario, it is possible to better comprehend a diffuse and multifaceted mobility of objects, models, and even of individuals and groups. In the case studies briefly outlined, we showed how technological and typological analyses could highlight the role, for example, of local metal craftspeople in reinventing amalgamated styles (Villa del Foro). We also saw how contextual studies on both settlements and cemeteries could suggest the presence of mixed and hybridised societies (Gamsen; Emilian Po Valley). Regarding mobility, network and geostatistical analyses seem valuable tools for identifying and defining ancient paths and connectivity between different groups and cultural areas. At the same time, a reevaluation of the roles of women and children inside the social sphere should also be addressed in future research (Rebay-Salisbury and Pany-Kucera 2020; see also Stockhammer and Massy, Chapter 8; Rebay-Salisbury, Chapter 9) in closer connection to manufacturing processes and supra-regional exchange.

In conclusion, this chapter, focused on the diffusion of north Italian artefacts across the Alps and the Italic Peninsula, represents a starting point for rethinking empirically and theoretically the complexity of European connections and mobility, within the ongoing debate on human and cultural mobility, integration, resilience, or rejection.

Acknowledgements

The authors are grateful to the editors of this volume and the organisers of the Edinburgh conference for their hospitality and fruitful support.

References

Adam, A.-M. (2006), 'L'Europe tempérée dans ses contacts avec le monde méditerranéen (Ve–IIe s. av. J.-C.)', in M. Szabó (ed), *Les Civilisés et les Barbares du Ve au IIe s. av. J.-C.* (Glux-en-Glenne, Bibracte), 193–204.

Adam, R. (1992), 'L'apport d'objets italiques dans le Jura: voie unique ou voies alternatives?', in G. Kaenel and P. Curdy (eds), *L'âge du fer dans le Jura* (Lausanne, Bibliothèque historique vaudoise), 181–87.

Angelini, I., Molin, G., and Artioli, G. (2009), 'L'atelier metallurgico di Monte Cavanero: indagini chimiche e metallografiche', in M. Venturino (ed), *Il ripostiglio del Monte Cavanero di Chiusa Pesio* (Alessandria, Linelab), 107–66.

Barbieri, E. (2019), 'Pendagli a secchiello golasecchiani in un contesto di abitato etrusco-padano', *Lanx*, 27: 38–62.

Bats, M. (2006), 'L'acculturation et autres modèles de contacts en archéologie protohistorique', in M. Szabó (ed), *Les Civilisés et les Barbares du Ve au IIe s. av. J.-C.* (Glux-en-Glenne, Bibracte), 29–41.

Bistáková, A., Březinová, B., and Ramsl, P.C. (eds) (2020), *Multiple Identities in Prehistory, Early History and Presence* (Nitra, Archeologický ústav Slovenskej akadémie vied).

Bolger. D. (2013), 'Gender, labor, and pottery production in prehistory', in D. Bolger (ed), *A Companion to Gender Prehistory* (Hoboken, John Wiley & Sons), 161–79.

Bonomi, S. and Guggisberg, M. (eds) (2015), *Griechische Keramik nördlich von Etrurien: Mediterrane Importe und archäologischer Kontext* (Wiesbaden, Reichert Verlag).

Brun, P. and Chaume, B. (eds) (1997), *Vix et les éphémères principautés celtiques: les VIe–Ve siècles av. J.-C. en Europe centre-occidentale* (Paris, Errance).

Brysbaert, A. and Gorgues, A. (eds) (2017), *Nobility versus Artisans? The Multiple Identities of Elites and 'Commoners' Viewed through the Lens of Materials and Technologies during the European Bronze and the Iron Ages* (Leiden, Sidestone Press).

Brysbaert, A. and Vetters, M. (2020), 'Practicing identity: a crafty ideal?', *Mediterranean Archaeology and Archaeometry*, 10(2): 25–43.

Busoni, M. (2001), *Il valore delle spose: beni e persone in antropologia economica* (Milano, Meltemi).

Casini, S. (2000), 'Il ruolo delle donne golasecchiane nei commerci del VI–V sec. a.C.', in R.C. de Marinis and S. Biaggio Simona (eds), *I Leponti tra mito e realtà* (Locarno, Dadò Editore), 75–100.

Casini, S. (2011), 'Le fibule a coste rinvenute a Bologna: nuovi spunti di riflessione', *Notizie Archeologiche Bergomensi*, 19: 257–70.

Casini, S. (2012), 'La pratica dell'esogamia nella cultura di Golasecca', in S. Marchesini (ed), *Matrimoni Misti: una via per l'integrazione tra i popoli* (Verona, Alteritas), 65–76.

Casini, S. and Chaume, B. (2014), 'Indices de mobilité au Premier Âge du fer entre le sud et le nord des Alpes', in P. Barral, J.-P. Guillaumet, M.-J. Roulière-Lambert, M. Saracino, and D. Vitali (eds), *Les Celtes et le Nord de l'Italie (Premier et Second Âges du fer)* (Dijon, SAE & AFEAF), 231–50.

Cicolani, V. (2017), *Passeurs des Alpes: la culture de Golasecca entre Méditerranée et Europe continentale à l'âge du Fer* (Paris, Hermann).

Cicolani, V. (2020), 'Interactions techno-culturelles en Italie nord-occidentale aux VIe–Ve siècles av. J.-C.: Nouvelles recherches', *Mélanges de l'École française de Rome, Antiquité*, 132: 115–24.

Cicolani, V. (2021), 'Piccoli bronzi e metallurgia', in M. Venturino and M. Giaretti (eds), *Villa del Foro: un emporio ligure tra Etruschi e Celti* (Genova, De Ferrari), 527–50.

Cicolani, V. and Berruto, G. (2017), 'L'ornementation des fibules de Ligurie interne: approches typologiques et archéometriques pour l'étude des faciès d'Italie nord-occidentale', in S. Marion, S. Deffressigne, J. Kaurin, and G. Battaille (eds), *Production et proto-industrialisation aux âges du fer: perspectives sociales et environnementales* (Bordeaux, Ausonius), 411–18.

Cicolani, V. and Gambari, F.M. (2021), 'Des chefs guerriers aux seigneurs des terres et du commerce: les "princes" de la zone occidentale de la culture de Golasecca entre VIIe et Ve a.C.', in P. Brun, B. Chaume, and F. Sacchetti (eds), *Vix et le phénomène princier* (Pessac, Ausonius éditions), 191–206.

Cicolani, V. and Huet, T. (2019), 'Essai de modélisation des échanges et des réseaux de circulation dans les Alpes centrales au premier Âge du Fer', in M. Deschamps,

S. Costamagno, P.-Y. Milcent, J.-M. Pétillon, C. Renard, *et al.* (eds), *La conquête de la montagne: des premières occupations humaines à l'anthropisation du milieu* (Paris, Éditions du Comité des Travaux Historiques et Scientifiques), DOI: 10.4000/books. cths.7827.

Cicolani, V. and Tribouillard, E. (2018), 'Analyse exploratoire des relations transalpines au premier âge du Fer: les cartes de chaleur et la BaseFer', in E. Hiriart, J. Genechesi, V. Cicolani, S. Martin, S. Nieto-Pelletier, *et al.* (eds), *Monnaies et archéologie en Europe celtique: mélanges en l'honneur de Katherine Gruel* (Glux-en-Glenne, Bibracte), 81–6.

Cicolani, V., Dubreucq, E., Milcent, P.-Y., and Mélin, M. (2015), 'Aux sources de la Douix: objets et dépôts métalliques en milieu humide au Premier âge du Fer à partir de l'exemple d'un site remarquable', in R. Roure and F. Olmer (eds), *Les Gaulois au fil de l'eau* (Bordeaux, Ausonius), 719–56.

Collis. J. (2003), *The Celts: Origins, Myths and Inventions* (Strout, Tempus).

David-Elbiali, M. (2009), 'Des femmes et des hommes dans l'arc alpin occidental entre le XIIe et le VIIe siècle av. J.-C.', in M.-J. Roulière-Lambert, A. Daubigney, P.-Y. Milcent, M. Talon, and J. Vital (eds), *De l'âge du Bronze à l'âge du Fer en France et en Europe occidentale (Xe–VIIe siècles av. J.-C.): la moyenne vallée du Rhône aux âges du Fer* (Dijon, SAE, APRAB & AFEAF), 343–60.

de Marinis, R.C. (2014a), 'Correlazioni cronologiche tra Italia nord-occidentale (aree della cultura di Golasecca) e ambiti culturali transalpini e cisalpini dal Bronzo Recente alla fine del VII secolo a.C.', in P. Barral, J.-P. Guillaumet, M.-J. Roulière-Lambert, M. Saracino, and D. Vitali (eds), *Les Celtes et le Nord de l'Italie (Premier et Second Âges du fer)* (Dijon, SAE & AFEAF), 17–36.

de Marinis, R.C. (2014b), 'I rapporti di Chiavari con la cultura di Golasecca', *Notizie Archeologiche Bergomensi*, 22: 95–122.

de Marinis, R.C. and Biaggio Simona, S. (eds) (2000), *I Leponti tra mito e realtà* (Locarno, Dadò Editore).

de Marinis, R.C. and Casini, S. (2020), 'The Early Iron Age protourbanisation along the Ticino River and around Como', in L. Zamboni, M. Fernández-Götz, and C. Metzner-Nebelsick (eds), *Crossing the Alps: Early Urbanism between Northern Italy and Central Europe (900–400 BC)* (Leiden, Sidestone Press), 243–56.

Dietler, M. (2005), *Consumption and Colonial Encounters in the Rhône Basin of France: A Study of Early Iron Age Political Economy* (Lattes, CNRS).

Dubreucq, E., Cicolani, V., and Filippini A. (2020), 'Productions métalliques au premier et au début du second âge du fer dans le domaine nord-alpin centre-occidental (7e–5e siècles av. J.-C.): quand créativité et spécialisation caractérisent les artisans', in R. Peake, S. Bauvais, C. Hamon, and C. Mordant (eds), *Specialised Productions and Specialists, Proceedings of the session no. XXXIV-2 of the XVIIIth UISPP World Congress* (Paris, Séances de la Société Préhistorique Française), 63–84.

Fernández-Götz, M. (2019), 'Migrations in Iron Age Europe: a comparative view', in P. Halkon (ed), *The Arras Culture of Eastern Yorkshire: Celebrating the Iron Age* (Oxford, Oxbow), 179–99.

Fischer, C.-E., Lefort, A., Pemonge, M.-H., Couture-Veschambre, C., Rottier, S., *et al.* (2018), 'The multiple maternal legacy of the Late Iron Age group of Urville-Nacqueville (France, Normandy) documents a long-standing genetic contact zone in northwestern France', *PLoS ONE*, 13(12): e0207459, DOI: 10.1371/journal.pone.0207459.

Frankenstein, S. and Rowlands, M.J. (1978), 'The internal structure and regional context of early Iron Age society in south-western Germany', *Bulletin of the Institute of Archaeology*, 15: 73–112.

Giumlia-Mair, A. (2003), 'Evoluzione tecnica e formale nella produzione di fibule e spilloni tra il IX ed il IV sec. a.C. nell'area alpino-orientale', in E. Formigli (ed), *Fibulae: dall'età del Bronzo all'alto Medioevo, tecnica e tipologia* (Firenze, Polistampa), 49–58.

Guilaine, J., Carozza, L., Garcia, D., Gascó, J., Janin, T., *et al.* (2017), *Launac et le Launacien: dépôts de bronzes protohistoriques du sud de la Gaule* (Montpellier, Presses Universitaires de la Méditerranée).

Hurlet, F., Rivoal, I., and Sidera, I. (2014), *Le prestige: autour des formes de la différenciation sociale* (Paris, Éditions de la MAE).

Johnson, M. (2020), *Archaeological Theory: An Introduction* (Hoboken, Wiley-Blackwell).

Jones, S. (1997), *The Archaeology of Ethnicity: Constructing Identities in the Past and Present* (London, Routledge).

Kaenel, G. (1990), *Recherches sur la période de La Tène en Suisse occidentale: analyse des sépultures* (Lausanne, Bibliothèque historique vaudoise).

Kimmig, W. (2000), *Importe und mediterrane Einflüsse auf der Heuneburg* (Mainz, Verlag Philipp von Zabern).

Knappett, C. and Malafouris, L. (eds) (2008), *Material Agency: Towards a Non-Anthropocentric Approach* (New York, Springer Science & Business Media).

Knipper, C., Meyer, C., Jacobi, F., Roth, C., Fecher, M., *et al.* (2013), 'Social differentiation and land use at an Early Iron Age "princely seat": bioarchaeological investigations at the Glauberg (Germany)', *Journal of Archaeological Science*, 41: 818–35.

Knipper, C., Mittnik, A., Massy, K., Kociumaka, C., Kucukkalipci, I., *et al.* (2017), 'Female exogamy and gene pool diversification at the transition from the Final Neolithic to the Early Bronze Age in Central Europe', *Proceedings of the National Academy of Sciences of the United States of America*, 114(38): 10083–8.

Krämer, W. (1961), 'Fremder Frauenschmuck aus Manching', *Germania*, 39: 305–22.

Kristiansen, K. (1998), *Europe before History* (Cambridge, Cambridge University Press).

Koch, J.K. (2017), 'Between the Black Forest and the Mediterranean Sea: individual mobility in the Early Iron Age', in S. Scharl and B. Gehlen (eds), *Mobility in Prehistoric Sedentary Societies* (Rahden/Westf., Verlag Marie Leidorf), 215–28.

Lorre, C. and Cicolani, V. (eds) (2009), *Golasecca (VIIIe–Ve siècle avant J.-C.): Du commerce et des hommes à l'Age du Fer* (Paris, Réunion des Musées Nationaux).

Lüscher, G., Rebsamen, S. and Zimmermann, K. (2002), *Die Hydria von Grächwil, ein griechisches Prunkgefäss aus Tarent* (Zürich, Chronos Verlag).

Marion, S., Deffressigne, S., Kaurin, J., and Battaille, G. (eds) (2017), *Production et proto-industrialisation aux âges du fer: Perspectives sociales et environnementales* (Bordeaux, Ausonius).

Melli, P. (2017), *Genaua Kainua Genua Ianua: Genova. Le molte vite di una città portuale dal Neolitico al VII secolo d.C.* (Genova, Oltre Edizioni).

Nagy, P. (2012), *Castaneda GR. Die Eisenzeit im Misox* (Bonn, Habelt).

Nakoinz, O. (2014), 'Fingerprinting Iron Age communities in south-west Germany and an integrative theory of culture', in C.N. Popa and S. Stoddart (eds), *Fingerprinting the Iron Age: Approaches to Identity in the European Iron Age* (Oxford, Oxbow), 187–200.

Nebelsick, L. and Metzner-Nebelsick, C. (2020), 'From Genoa to Günzburg: new trajectories of urbanisation and acculturation between the Mediterranean and South-Central Europe', in L. Zamboni, M. Fernández-Götz, and C. Metzner-Nebelsick (eds), *Crossing the Alps: Early Urbanism between Northern Italy and Central Europe (900–400 BC)* (Leiden, Sidestone Press), 43–68.

Oelze, V.M., Koch, J.K., Kupke, K., Nehlich, O., Zäuner, S., *et al.* (2012), 'Multi-isotopic analysis reveals individual mobility and diet at the Early Iron Age monumental tumulus of Magdalenenberg, Germany', *American Journal of Physical Anthropology*, 148: 406–21.

Pauli, L. (1978), 'Fremdformen im Frauengrab 44', in J. Waldhauser (ed), *Das keltische Gräberfeld bei Jenišův Újezd in Böhmen/Keltské pohřebiště u Jenišova Újez da v Čechách* (Teplice, Krajské Muzeum), 93–102.

Pauli, L. (1991), 'Les Alpes centrales et orientales à l'âge du Fer', in A. Duval (ed), *Les Alpes à l'âge du Fer* (Paris, CNRS éditions), 291–311.

Piana Agostinetti, P. and Morandi, A. (2004), *Celti d'Italia: archeologia, lingua, scrittura* (Roma, SpazioTre).

Rebay-Salisbury, K. and Pany-Kucera, D. (eds) (2020), *Ages and Abilities: The Stages of Childhood and Their Social Recognition in Prehistoric Europe and Beyond* (Oxford, Archaeopress).

Reher Díez, G.S. (2012), 'The "introduction to ethnicity syndrome" in proto-historical archaeology', in T. Moore and A. Xosé-Lois (eds), *Atlantic Europe in the First Millennium BC: Crossing the Divide* (Oxford, Oxford University Press), 656–67.

Reher Díez, G.S. and Fernández-Götz, M. (2015), 'Archaeological narratives in ethnicity studies', *Archeologické rozhledy*, 67: 400–16.

Roux, V., Mille, B., and Pelegrin, J. (2012), 'Innovations céramiques, métallurgiques et lithiques au Chalcolithique: mutations sociales, mutations techniques', in J. Jaubert (ed), *Transitions, ruptures et continuité en préhistoire* (Paris, Société Préhistorique Française), 61–73.

Sassatelli, G. (2014), 'Etruschi, Greci, Veneti e Celti in area padana: contatti commerciali, relazioni culturali e mobilità individuale', in R. Macellari (ed), *Gli Etruschi e gli altri. Reggio Emilia terra di incontri* (Ginevra and Milano, Skira), 14–33.

Schindler, M.P. (1998), *Der Depotfund von Arbedo TI und die Bronzedepotfunde des Alpenraums vom 6. bis zum Beginn des 4. Jh. v. Chr.* (Basel, Schweizerische Gesellschaft für Ur- und Frühgeschichte).

Schmid-Sikimić, B. (2000), 'An den Wegen über die Alpen. Minusio und Mesocco: Referenzorte der älteren Eisenzeit in der Südschweiz', in R.C. de Marinis and S. Biaggio Simona (eds), *I Leponti tra mito e realtà* (Locarno, Dadò Editore), 215–43.

Schumann, R. and Van der Vaart-Verschoof, S. (eds) (2017), *Connecting Elites and Regions: Perspectives on Contacts, Relations and Differentiation during the Early Iron Age Hallstatt C Period in Northwest and Central Europe* (Leiden, Sidestone Press).

Sherratt, S. (2016), 'A globalizing Bronze and Iron Age Mediterranean', in T. Hodos (ed), *The Routledge Handbook of Archaeology and Globalization* (London, Routledge), 602–17.

Stöllner, T. (2014), 'Mobility and cultural change of the early Celts: la Tène openwork belt-hooks north and south of the Alps', in P. Barral, J.-P. Guillaumet, M.-J. Roulière-Lambert, M. Saracino, and D. Vitali (eds), *Les Celtes et le Nord de l'Italie (Premier et Second Âges du fer)* (Dijon, SAE & AFEAF), 211–29.

Tarditi, C. (ed) (2007), *Dalla Grecia all'Europa: la circolazione di beni di lusso e di modelli culturali nel VI e V secolo a.C.* (Milano, Vita e Pensiero).

Teržan, B. and de Marinis, R.C. (2018), 'The Northern Adriatic', in C. Haselgrove, K. Rebay-Salisbury and P.S. Wells (eds), *The Oxford Handbook of the European Iron Age* (Oxford, Oxford University Press), DOI: 10.1093/oxfordhb/9780199696826.013.32.

Tessmann, B. (2007), 'Körbchenanhänger im Süden – Göritzer Bommeln im Norden', in M. Blečić, M. Črešnar, B. Hänsel, A. Helmut, E. Kaiser, and C. Metzner-Nebelsick (eds), *Scripta Praehistorica in Honorem Biba Terzan* (Ljubljana, Narodni Muzej Slovenie), 667–94.

Tori, L. (2019), *Costumi femminili nell'arco sud-alpino nel I millennio a.C.: tra archeologia sociale e antropologia* (Zürich, Chronos Verlag).

Trémblay-Cormier, L. and Isoardi, D. (2019), 'Mobilité des individus et des biens dans la vallée de l'Ubaye (Alpes-de-Haute-Provence) et le Guillestrois (Hautes-Alpes) à l'âge du Fer', in M. Deschamps, S. Costamagno, P.-Y. Milcent, J.-M. Pétillon, C. Renard, *et al.* (eds), *La conquête de la montagne: des premières occupations humaines à l'anthropisation du milieu* (Paris, Éditions du Comité des Travaux Historiques et Scientifiques), DOI: 10.4000/books.cths.7902.

Trémblay-Cormier, L., Isoardi, D., and Cicolani, V. (2019), 'Voisins ou cousins? Comparaison de deux régions alpines à la frontière franco-italienne à l'âge du Fer', in J. Serralongue (ed), *La notion de territoire dans les Alpes de la Préhistoire au Moyen Âge* (Aoste, SVPA), 147–68.

Van der Vaart-Verschoof, S. and Schumann R. (2020), 'Connected by more than exceptional imports: performance and identity in Hallstatt C/D elite burials of the Low Countries', *European Journal of Archaeology*, 23(1): 22–42.

Van Dommelen, P. (2014), 'Moving on: archaeological perspectives on mobility and migration', *World Archaeology*, 46(4): 477–83.

Van Oyen, A. (2018), 'Material agency', in S.L. López Varela (ed), *The Encyclopedia of Archaeological Sciences* (Oxford, Wiley-Blackwell), DOI: 10.1002/9781119188230.saseas0363.

Venturino, M. and Giaretti, M. (eds) (2021), *Villa del Foro: un emporio ligure tra Etruschi e Celti* (Genova, De Ferrari).

Venturino Gambari, M., Giaretti, M., Peinetti, A., and Quercia, A. (2017), 'L'artisanat dans le Piémont méridional et le cas emblématique de la Villa del Foro (Alessandria, Italie)', in S. Marion, S. Deffressigne, J. Kaurin, and G. Battaille (eds), *Production et proto-industrialisation aux âges du fer: perspectives sociales et environnementales* (Bordeaux, Ausonius), 675–92.

Verger, S. (2013), 'Partager la viande, distribuer l'hydromel: Consommation collective et pratique du pouvoir dans la tombe de Hochdorf', in S. Krausz, A. Colin, K. Gruel, I. Ralston, and T. Dechezleprêtre (eds), *L'âge du fer en Europe: Mélanges offertes à Olivier Buchsenschutz* (Pessac, Ausonius), 511–20.

Verger, S. and Pernet, L. (2013), *Une Odyssée gauloise: Parures de femmes à l'origine des premiers échanges entre la Grèce et la Gaule* (Montpellier and Paris, Errance).

Welc, F., Nebelsick, L., Metzner-Nebelsick, C., Balzer, I., Vanzetti, A., *et al.* (2020), 'The first results of geophysical prospections using the ADC method on the proto-urban settlement site of Como, Spina Verde', in L. Zamboni, M. Fernández-Götz, and C. Metzner-Nebelsick (eds), *Crossing the Alps: Early Urbanism between Northern Italy and Central Europe (900–400 BC)* (Leiden, Sidestone Press), 257–74.

Zamboni, L. (2018), *Sepolture arcaiche della pianura emiliana: il riconoscimento di una società di frontiera* (Rome, Quasar).

Zamboni, L. (2021), 'The urbanization of northern Italy: contextualizing early settlement nucleation in the Po Valley', *Journal of Archaeological Research*, 29: 387–430.

Zamboni, L. (2022), 'Do you think we are Etruscans? Recognition issues in the 6th century BCE Po Valley', in F. Saccoccio and E. Vecchi (eds), *Who Do You Think You Are? Ethnicity in the Iron Age Mediterranean* (London, Accordia Studies), 77–96.

Zamboni, L., Fernández-Götz, M., and Metzner-Nebelsick, C. (eds) (2020), *Crossing the Alps: Early Urbanism between Northern Italy and Central Europe (900–400 BC)* (Leiden, Sidestone Press).

13

Mobility and Migration in Bronze and Iron Age Britain: The COMMIOS Project

IAN ARMIT

Introduction

CURRENT SCIENTIFIC ADVANCES are transforming our ability to understand the nature and complexity of past human societies. Major breakthroughs in recent years have come through advances in ancient DNA (aDNA) analysis, which have increasingly opened up new vistas for understanding the diversity, mobility, structure, and social dynamics of past communities. For European prehistorians, the most important developments have been in our knowledge of earlier periods, from the introduction of farming (e.g. Brace *et al.* 2019), through the steppe migrations of the 3rd millennium BC (e.g. Haak *et al.* 2015), to the population dynamics associated with the spread of the Beaker phenomenon (e.g. Olalde *et al.* 2018; Armit and Reich 2021). Much of the focus has been on population movement, usually seen in terms of large-scale migration, an area of emerging concern for the discipline of archaeology as a whole (e.g. Altschul *et al.* 2020).

Beyond delineating these continent-wide phenomena, aDNA studies have also begun to shed light on period-specific regional population dynamics (e.g. Knipper *et al.* 2017; Cassidy *et al.* 2020) and kinship relations (e.g. Fowler *et al.* 2022; Armit *et al.* in press), as well as to provide time transects through the *long durée* of particular regions (e.g. Olalde *et al.* 2019). The pace of these discoveries has been astounding, as are their scope and potential. Once again, however, these advances have so far had relatively little impact on the later parts of European prehistory and protohistory: the Late Bronze and Iron Ages.

The COMMIOS Project

The COMMIOS project (Communities and Connectivities: Iron Age Britons and their Continental Neighbours) has been established to address this apparent

Proceedings of the British Academy, **254**, 280–291, © The British Academy 2023.

imbalance and to take forward aDNA studies of Bronze and Iron Age populations in tandem with other scientific approaches, including isotope analysis and osteoarchaeology. Although led by the present author, the project is a collaboration with a range of partners including the Reich Laboratory at Harvard Medical School, the British Geological Survey, and the Scottish Universities Environmental Research Centre (SUERC; see COMMIOS 2020 for full details). The project takes its name from the historical Commios, a Gaulish noble who, according to Caesar (*De Bello Gallico* 4–6), had lands and kin on both sides of the English Channel during the Late Iron Age, making him emblematic of our themes of mobility and interregional connectivity. The project, supported through an ERC-Advanced Grant (Grant agreement ID: 834087), began in late 2019 and is planned for completion in late 2025, so it is too early to provide a detailed overview of results (particularly given the delays introduced from 2020 through the global COVID-19 pandemic). This chapter instead sets out the research context and aims of the project, with some indication of where we see the most promising avenues for advances in our understanding.

Integrating ancient DNA

Given the high profile and substantial impact of aDNA studies over recent years, it is hardly surprising that they have attracted criticism (e.g. Brück 2021). In particular, there have been justified concerns that the hard-won subtleties in our analyses of past societies are at risk of being ignored or overwhelmed by broad-brush interpretations that draw on simplistic or outdated understandings of the prehistoric past to provide frameworks for new scientific data.

A major issue, for example, has been the tendency for continent-wide studies, of the kind mentioned above, to be formulated in terms that appear to equate archaeological cultures with biological populations (e.g. Vander Linden 2016). This seems often to reflect an outmoded form of archaeological practice rooted in the early 20th century (e.g. Furholt 2019). As well as potentially skewing our archaeological writings, there is a significant danger that such simplistic equations of ethnicity and genetics will be used to underpin racist narratives (Frieman and Hofmann 2019).

It is patently unwarranted to conflate ethnic with genetic identities and it is critical not to lose sight of the major theoretical advances made within archaeology in relation to the understanding of identity construction in the past (e.g. Jones 1997). We cannot assume that genetic shifts will correlate with changes in language, material culture, or various forms of social ordering. They undoubtedly reflect mobility, but the scale, duration, and form of that mobility must be problematised and analysed in depth; it must never be assumed. Migration is a complex and highly variable phenomenon, as is discussed elsewhere in this volume. Evidence for genetic change gives us valuable, perhaps unparalleled insights, but it does not provide an explanation in itself. If we are fully to grasp the dynamism, subtlety, and complexity of the human past, we must integrate the emerging potential of aDNA

282   *Ian Armit*

analyses with cultural archaeological analyses, drawing on approaches rooted in the humanities.

Moving forward for the Bronze and Iron Ages

It is with these issues in mind that we established COMMIOS, which set out with the initial aim to apply a combination of scientific and humanities approaches to the analysis of Iron Age communities in Britain, between *c.* 800 BC and AD 100 (though this chronological core has expanded to accommodate Middle/Late Bronze Age developments, as I will explain below), situated within their north-west European context (COMMIOS 2020). Combining the study of aDNA with multi-isotope analysis, osteoarchaeology, and approaches drawn from funerary archaeology, COMMIOS is designed to operate at a range of scales to provide both breadth and depth of new knowledge. At the broad scale, we will examine patterns of genetic diversity of Iron Age populations in Britain and neighbouring parts of Continental Europe, to generate insights into mobility patterns and interregional contacts (Figure 13.1). With a focus on key regions where larger site assemblages of human remains are available for analysis, including East Yorkshire, Atlantic Scotland, southern Scotland, Wessex, and northern France, we will also examine biological relationships within cemeteries which can potentially shed light on kin group structure, issues of patrilocality versus matrilocality, and the degree and nature of social inequalities within Iron Age communities. While the project builds on previous collaboration between the author and the Reich Laboratory at Harvard Medical School, which examined the spread of the Beaker phenomenon across Europe using a continent-wide sample of *c.* 400 individuals (Olalde *et al.* 2018), COMMIOS will provide a greatly increased sample size and density which, together with the interdisciplinary context of the work, marks a step change from previous research.

The communities of Iron Age Britain are generally regarded as having evolved in relative isolation from Continental Europe (e.g. Haselgrove and Pope 2007, though see also Webley 2015 for an alternative view), at least until the last two centuries BC. Certain cultural features, such as the dominance of the roundhouse as the basic unit of domestic settlement (Harding 2009), occur across the British Isles and form a marked contrast with continental practice throughout the Early and Middle Iron Age. Within Britain, the Iron Age is highly regional in character (Haselgrove *et al.* 2001): some areas have dense distributions of hillforts (e.g. Wessex; southern Scotland), while others do not (e.g. Yorkshire; Atlantic Scotland). Mortuary practices are highly variable, ranging from large cemeteries containing hundreds of individuals in East Yorkshire (e.g. Stead 1991; Halkon 2013) to fragmentary disarticulated human remains on settlements across Atlantic Scotland (Armit 2012; 2017). Nonetheless, and despite this apparent regionality, certain features of Iron Age culture are shared across the English Channel. Aside from

THE COMMIOS PROJECT

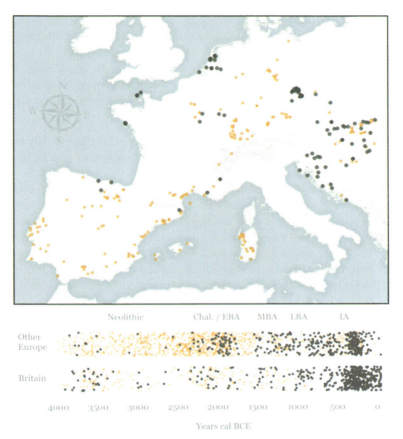

Figure 13.1 The map shows the distribution of sites in mainland Europe from which samples were obtained for the Patterson *et al.* 2022 study. The timeline shows the density of sampling through time for both Britain and mainland Europe. Black dots indicate new samples obtained through the present project (drawn by Helen Goodchild: map made with Natural Earth; elevation data Copernicus, European Digital Elevation Model version 1.1; data from Patterson *et al.* 2022)

technological innovations such as the adoption of iron itself, and rotary technology (e.g. the potter's wheel and the rotary quern), for example, the appearance of La Tène art shows Iron Age Britons sharing a common visual culture with their continental contemporaries (Garrow and Gosden 2012); the rich and distinctive archaeology of East Yorkshire shares many aspects of its material culture, and its use of chariot burials, with continental La Tène communities (Stead *et al.* 2006; Anthoons 2007). Indeed, earlier generations of archaeologists argued that the British Iron Age was a period of 'folk' movements, during which the islands were overrun by successive waves of Celtic invaders bringing new forms of culture and introducing Celtic languages (e.g. Hawkes 1959). This apparent tension between long-distance contacts and highly regionalised expressions of cultural difference makes Iron Age Britain an ideal context within which to examine the relationships between genetic and cultural identities.

With COMMIOS, we aim to take a step forward in analysing a larger, denser sample of complete genome data than has been attempted before, to examine fine-grained genetic differences in a large and culturally diverse prehistoric population. Our major research questions include:

1) Does the perceived regionality of Iron Age Britain reflect locally isolated populations with limited mobility and a high degree of genetic diversity between groups in different areas?

2) How far does the transmission of ideas, inherent in the appearance of new technologies, languages, and art forms, reflect cross-Channel movement of people? If people were moving in significant numbers between Britain and Continental Europe, which areas were most closely connected?

3) To what degree does population mobility and interregional connectivity of Iron Age populations change through time, for example in the 2nd/1st centuries BC, when Roman expansionism displaced populations across Gaul?

4) How homogenous or otherwise were Iron Age communities in Britain? Were marriage partners drawn from a small local pool, or did individuals move long distances, perhaps cementing socioeconomic or political alliances?

5) Did communities in Iron Age Britain practise patrilocality, matrilocality, or a mixture of both? What inequalities existed in diet, health, and status, and how were these inequalities materialised through mortuary practice?

6) How does the distribution of genetic clusters in Iron Age Britain compare with that created on the basis of modern DNA (e.g. in the 'People of the British Isles' project; Leslie *et al.* 2015), and what inferences do the similarities and differences allow us to make about population movement, admixture, and genetic drift in the intervening millennia?

Underpinning our work is the genome-wide analysis of *c.* 1000 individuals in order to address questions about demographic history and genetic substructure within the British and European Iron Age, and the relationship between Iron Age and present-day populations. Analysis of aDNA is being undertaken by COMMIOS project partner David Reich at Harvard Medical School, whose team have already pioneered significant advances in the understanding of genetic change in prehistoric Europe (e.g. Haak *et al.* 2015; Olalde *et al.* 2018; 2019). Our proposed sample size broadly matches that of the Leslie *et al.* 2015 study of present-day British populations and will potentially allow us to make similarly fine-scaled inferences. Critical to this is a substantial programme of AMS dating and Bayesian analysis led by COMMIOS project partner Derek Hamilton at SUERC, which will provide the appropriate chronological resolution.

In selecting sample populations for aDNA analysis, our primary concern is to establish as complete a geographical and chronological coverage as possible. Substantial burial populations exist in a number of regions, including East Yorkshire, southern Scotland, Wessex, and Cornwall, and sample selection in such areas is relatively straightforward, focusing on the larger cemeteries (Figure 13.2). In northern France, too, we are sampling large cemetery populations, notably at the site of Urville-Naqueville, where our current work builds on previous aDNA analysis led by COMMIOS team member Claire-Elise Fischer (Fischer *et al*. 2018; 2019). In the many regions of Britain where Iron Age cemeteries are few (or even absent), however, it is necessary to collect samples from individual burials and, in certain cases, human remains from non-funerary contexts, such as caves, settlement sites, and middens. This introduces additional complexities into interpretations regarding the origins and status of such individuals and underlines the necessity of conducting a broader suite of analyses than aDNA alone.

Figure 13.2 This map shows the distribution of sites in Britain from which samples were obtained for the Patterson *et al*. 2022 study. Black dots indicate new samples obtained through the present project (drawn by Helen Goodchild: map made with Natural Earth; elevation data Copernicus, European Digital Elevation Model version 1.1; data from Patterson *et al*. 2022)

In order both to contextualise the results of aDNA analysis and to deepen our understanding of population dynamics, we are also undertaking multi-isotope analysis of a significant proportion of the sampled individuals. This work, led by COMMIOS project partner Jane Evans, at the British Geological Survey, will investigate key features of Iron Age communities including diet, nutrition, health, mobility, and population homogeneity/heterogeneity. Although it is intended that isotope analysis will focus on the larger site assemblages, where we can examine a representative sample based on age, sex, and funerary treatment, we are also, wherever possible, conducting detailed isotopic analysis of individuals identified as local outliers on the basis of aDNA, and individuals subject to distinctive mortuary rites or with unusual pathological conditions or trauma. The primary techniques comprise isotopic analysis of strontium, oxygen (on tooth enamel), and sulphur (on dentine) to determine childhood origin relative to geography (Evans *et al.* 2012), climate and proximity to the coast, and the analysis of rib bone collagen for carbon and nitrogen, to assess diet. The application of this suite of isotopic techniques is critical given the relatively local scale and subtlety of changes in diet and location expected during this period; as previous studies have demonstrated (e.g. Jay and Richards 2007), bulk carbon and nitrogen analyses (now commonly employed in archaeology) are often insufficient for detailed interpretation of changes across the individual lifecourse. Where reliable modern osteoarchaeological data are unavailable, individuals selected for aDNA and isotope analysis will, wherever possible, also be subject to osteoarchaeological examination.

Taken together, osteoarchaeological, aDNA, and multi-isotope analysis can be used to build detailed osteobiographies of individuals. A core aim of COMMIOS, however, is to understand the relationship between biological and cultural identities, which requires us to draw on perspectives from the humanities. Within COMMIOS, we are conducting analyses of mortuary practices at the cemeteries from which our Iron Age populations derive, as well as those associated with the many individuals recovered from less overtly funerary contexts (e.g. human remains on settlements). As well as highlighting social inequalities within Iron Age communities, this work will provide insights into community structure, ideology, and cosmology, contextualising the detailed genetic, isotope, and osteoarchaeological data. Analysis of funerary treatments in COMMIOS is guided to a large extent by the data provided through the various bioarchaeological analyses. For example, aDNA evidence for the presence of related individuals can be combined with the analysis of spatial patterning within cemeteries in order to assess whether the distribution of burials is structured by biological relatedness. It is also important to pay particular attention to the mortuary treatments and grave goods associated with closely related individuals, and individuals originating from different geographical areas, as well as individuals of different ages and those with unusual pathologies or signs of peri-mortem trauma, all informed by our bioarchaeological analyses.

Ultimately, it is the layering of all these datasets that is of the greatest significance. Ancient DNA provides us with definitive sexing of individuals and information on biological relationships. Isotope analysis and osteoarchaeology can tell us much about the differential life histories of individuals within communities, between sexes and now, in certain cases, within families, while critical examination of mortuary treatments can extend that biography beyond the death of the individual.

Preliminary results and current directions

While work remains at an early stage, a good deal of aDNA analysis has already been undertaken and some preliminary observations can be made. One important factor that was built into the project from the start was that our aDNA analysis would include a number of individuals dating to the periods before and after the Iron Age, in order to better contextualise our results. The analysis of Middle/Late Bronze Age (*c.* 1500–800 BC) individuals has already emerged as a particularly important element in our work. Indeed, it appears that this period saw a significant movement of people into southern Britain from Continental Europe, peaking in the period from 1000–875 BC (Patterson *et al.* 2022), which cumulatively represented a genetic turnover of the order of 50 per cent. This had the effect of significantly reducing the amount of steppe ancestry (i.e. the amount of ancestry ultimately derived from Yamnaya or related populations who inhabited the steppe during the early 3rd millennium BC) present in southern British communities (cf. Olalde *et al.* 2018; Armit and Reich 2021). The population movements into Britain seem to be paralleled by similar movements into other parts of Central Europe and Iberia, suggesting a period of considerable interregional contact and mobility across much of the Continent, as we might expect from the widespread networks evident from material culture at that time.

Potential first-generation migrants have been identified from two sites in Kent, hinting at a possible entry route into Britain for at least some of the Bronze Age incomers (Patterson *et al.* 2022), although the geographical location of the source population(s) remains to be securely identified. One of these locations, the site of Cliffs End Farm, had already been identified through previous isotopic analysis as containing a number of non-indigenous individuals (McKinley *et al.* 2014), although the earlier suggestion that these were of likely North European origin does not accord with the new genetic data, which is more suggestive of an Alpine origin. This was a site where extremely unusual mortuary rites were conducted, and it will be important to examine how these relate (or not) to the differing genetic profiles of particular individuals.

The population movements of the Middle/Late Bronze Age contrast in several ways with those previously identified at the start of the Bronze Age (Olalde *et al.* 2018). Firstly, although significant in terms of genetic turnover, they were smaller in scale than those associated with the Beaker phenomenon, where in excess of 90 per cent of the genetic signature of the population changed (Olalde *et al.* 2018; Armit and Reich 2021). Secondly, they have a distinct regional distribution within Britain: the genetic changes seen in the south are not evident in Scotland (current gaps in our sampling in northern England prevent a more refined analysis of the nature of any cline between the two), where proportions of steppe ancestry persist at broadly the same levels as they had following their first appearance in the Beaker period (Patterson *et al.* 2022). Thirdly, they manifestly occurred over several centuries, since potential first-generation migrants have been identified in both Middle and Late Bronze Age contexts (Patterson *et al.* 2022). Finally, the nature of this genetic shift was considerably more subtle, between populations who already shared much of their genetic make-up; this not only requires more sophisticated statistical analysis on the part of the geneticists, but it also carries the implication that the shift may have been less obvious to individuals living through it than previous migrations had been.

The current genetic data show no indication of substantial population movement into Britain during the Iron Age, which has conventionally been regarded as the period when Celtic languages were introduced. Thus, we can already say with some confidence that, if large-scale population change was the principal vector by which Celtic languages were introduced into Britain, then that introduction is unlikely to have occurred during the Iron Age. As Celtic languages were undoubtedly spoken in Britain by the end of the Iron Age, the Middle/Late Bronze Age now emerges as one of the principal candidates for the period of their introduction. There are, of course, other mechanisms by which languages can spread that may be unrelated to the large-scale, interregional movement of people, but we would anticipate that a degree of mobility must be invoked. Here, as elsewhere, our isotope analysis of lifetime mobility will be critical.

At the smaller scale, we can already begin to identify genetic outliers among Iron Age populations (Patterson *et al.* 2022). The life histories of these individuals appear unrelated to the wider processes of population movement that characterise the Middle and Late Bronze Age and must reflect smaller-scale mobility among individuals or small groups. Whether the identified individuals were themselves migrants (using the term broadly to include, potentially, traders, mercenaries, slaves, or marriage partners), or whether they were recent descendants of small migrant communities is something that can potentially be investigated through isotope analysis. In certain cases – a young girl buried in articulated segments within a pit in the eastern settlement area at Thame, in Oxfordshire, for example – such individuals appear to have been subject to unusual mortuary rites (Patterson *et al.* 2022; Ellis *et al.* in prep). By focusing isotope analysis, osteological analysis, and detailed evaluation of mortuary practices on such individuals, in relation to the wider communities within which they lived and died, it should be possible to approach an understanding of the degree to which biological unrelatedness was recognised, acknowledged, and marked within Iron Age communities.

Prospect

Although we are still very much at the start of the COMMIOS project, it has already made significant strides. At the broad scale, we have identified significant population movement into southern Britain during the Middle to Late Bronze Age, followed by a lack of perceptible change through the Iron Age. This, of course, is an initial, broad-scale reading of a situation that may be significantly nuanced through future work. For example, we currently lack an adequate coverage of samples from much of France (a potential source region for migration into southern Britain) that might enable us to gauge whether these movements of people were unidirectional or reciprocal. Isotope analysis is now being directed at potential first-generation migrants, holding out the possibility of assessing more precisely the source regions involved in population movement into southern Britain. The genetic substructure of the ensuing Iron Age regional populations of Britain is also under study as more samples are assembled with a greater density of geographical coverage. At the more local scale, we have also begun to identify individual genetic outliers in Iron Age communities, and site populations with unusually heterogeneous genetic composition. Future work will explore the degree to which the distinctive genetic heritage of these individuals and groups affected their broader life course and social identities.

Acknowledgements

This project has received funding from the ERC under the European Union's 'Horizon 2020' research and innovation programme under grant agreement no. 834087. The author would like to thank all members of the COMMIOS team, whose work informs this contribution, and especially Dr Lindsey Büster for her comments on a preliminary draft.

References

Altschul, J.H., Kintigh, K.W., Aldenderfer, M., Alonzi, E., Armit, I., *et al.* (2020), 'Opinion: to understand how migrations affect human securities, look to the past', *Proceedings of the National Academy of Sciences of the United States of America*, 117(34): 20342–5.

Anthoons, G. (2007), 'The origins of the Arras culture: migration or elite networks?', in R. Karl and J. Leskovar (eds), *Interpretierte Eisenzeiten 2: Fallstudien, Methoden, Theorie* (Linz, Landesmuseum), 141–51.

Armit, I. (2012), *Headhunting and the Body in Iron Age Europe* (Cambridge, Cambridge University Press).

Armit, I. (2017), 'The visible dead: ethnographic perspectives on the curation, display and circulation of human remains in Iron Age Britain', in J. Bradbury and C. Scarre (eds), *Engaging with the Dead: Exploring Changing Human Beliefs about Death, Mortality and the Human Body* (Oxford, Oxbow), 163–73.

Armit, I., Fischer, C., Koon, H., Nicholls, R., Olalde, I., *et al.* (in press), 'Kinship practices in Early Iron Age southeast Europe: genetic and isotopic analysis of burials from the Dolge njive barrow cemetery, Dolenjska, Slovenia', *Antiquity*.

Armit, I. and Reich, D. (2021), 'The return of the Beaker Folk? Rethinking migration and population change in British Prehistory', *Antiquity*, 95: 1–14.

Brace, S., Diekmann, Y., Booth, T., Van Dorp, L., Faltyskova, Z., *et al.* (2019), 'Ancient genomes indicate population replacement in Early Neolithic Britain', *Nature Ecology and Evolution*, 3: 765–71.

Brück, J. (2021), 'Ancient DNA, kinship and relational identities in Bronze Age Britain', *Antiquity*, 95: 228–37.

Cassidy, L.M., Maoldúin, R.Ó., Kador, T., Lynch, A., Jones, C., *et al.* (2020), 'A dynastic elite in Monumental Neolithic society', *Nature*, 582: 384–88.

COMMIOS (2020), Project website, https://commiosarchaeology.com/.

Ellis, C., Boothroyd, J., and Davies, A. (in prep), *Early Thame: Archaeological Investigations at Site F1, Thame, Oxfordshire, 2015* (Kemble and Oxford, Cotswold Archaeology).

Evans, J., Chenery, C.A., and Montgomery, J. (2012), 'A summary of strontium and oxygen isotope variation in archaeological human tooth enamel excavated from Britain', *Journal of Analytical Atomic Spectrometry*, 27: 754–64.

Fischer, C.-E., Lefort, A., Pemonge, M.-H., Couture-Veschambre, C., Rottier, S., *et al.* (2018), 'The multiple maternal legacy of the Late Iron Age group of Urville-Nacqueville (France, Normandy) documents a long-standing genetic contact zone in Northwestern France', *PLoS ONE*, 13(12): e0207459, DOI: 10.1371/journal.pone.0207459.

Fischer, C., Pemonge, M.H., Santos, F.J., Houzelot, H., Couture-Veschambre, C., *et al.* (2019), 'Multi-scale archaeogenetic study of two French Iron Age communities: from internal social- to broad-scale population dynamics', *Journal of Archaeological Science: Reports*, 27: 101942, DOI: 10.1016/j.jasrep.2019.101942.

Fowler, C., Olalde, I., Cummings, V., Armit, I., Büster, L., *et al.* (2022), 'A high-resolution picture of kinship practices in an Early Neolithic tomb', *Nature*, 601: 584–7.

Frieman, C.J. and Hofmann, D. (2019), 'Present pasts in the archaeology of genetics, identity, and migration in Europe: a critical essay', *World Archaeology*, 51: 528–45.

Furholt, M. (2019), 'Re-integrating archaeology: a contribution to aDNA studies and the migration discourse on the 3rd millennium BC in Europe', *Proceedings of the Prehistoric Society*, 85: 115–29.

Garrow, D. and Gosden, C. (2012), *Technologies of Enchantment? Exploring Celtic Art: 400 BC to AD 100* (Oxford, Oxford University Press).

Haak, W., Lazaridis, I., Patterson, N., Rohland, N., Mallick, S., *et al.* (2015), 'Massive migration from the steppe was a source for Indo-European languages in Europe', *Nature*, 522: 207–11.

Halkon, P. (2013), *The Parisi: Britons and Romans in Eastern Yorkshire* (Stroud, History Press).

Harding, D.W. (2009), *The Iron Age Round-House* (Oxford, Oxford University Press).

Haselgrove, C. and Pope, R. (eds) (2007), *The Earlier Iron Age in Britain and Beyond* (Oxford, Oxbow).

Haselgrove, C., Armit, I., Champion, T., Creighton, J., Gwilt, A., *et al.* (2001), *Understanding the British Iron Age: An Agenda for Action* (Salisbury, Trust for Wessex Archaeology).

Hawkes, C. (1959), 'The ABC of the British Iron Age', *Antiquity*, 33: 170–82.

Jay, M. and Richards, M.P. (2007), 'British Iron Age diet: stable isotopes and other evidence', *Proceedings of the Prehistoric Society*, 73: 169–90.

Jones, S. (1997), *The Archaeology of Ethnicity* (London, Routledge).

Knipper, C., Mittnik, A., Massy, K., Kociumaka, C., Kucukkalipci, I., *et al.* (2017), 'Female exogamy and gene pool diversification at the transition from the Final Neolithic to the Early Bronze Age in Central Europe', *Proceedings of the National Academy of Sciences of the United States of America*, 114(38): 10083–8.

Leslie, S., Winney, B., Hellenthal, G., Davison, D., Boumertit, A., *et al.* (2015), 'The fine-scale genetic structure of the British population', *Nature*, 519: 309–14.

McKinley, J.L., Leivers, M., Schuster, J., Marshall, P., Barclay, A.J., *et al.* (2014), *Cliffs End Farm, Isle of Thanet, Kent. A Mortuary and Ritual Site of the Bronze Age, Iron Age and Anglo-Saxon Period* (Salisbury, Wessex Archaeology).

Olalde, I., Brace, S., Allentoft, M.E., Armit, I., Kristiansen, K., *et al.* (2018), 'The Beaker phenomenon and the genomic transformation of northwest Europe', *Nature*, 555: 190–6.

Olalde, I., Mallick, S., Patterson, N., Rohland, N., Villalba-Mouco, V., *et al.* (2019), 'The genomic history of the Iberian Peninsula over the past 8000 years', *Science*, 363: 1230–4.

Patterson, N., Isakov, M., Booth, T., Büster, L., Fischer, C.-E., *et al.* (2022), 'Large-scale migration into Britain during the Middle to Late Bronze Age', *Nature*, 601: 588–94.

Stead, I.M. (1991), *Iron Age Cemeteries in East Yorkshire* (London, English Heritage).

Stead, I.M., Flouest, J., and Rigby, V. (2006), *Iron Age and Roman Burials in Champagne* (Oxford, Oxbow).

Vander Linden, M. (2016), 'Population history in 3rd millennium BC Europe: assessing the contribution of genetics', *World Archaeology*, 48(5): 714–28.

Webley, L. (2015), 'Rethinking Iron Age connections across the Channel and North Sea', in H. Anderson-Whymark, D. Garrow, and F. Sturt (eds), *Continental Connections: Exploring Cross-Channel Relationships from the Mesolithic to the Iron Age* (Oxford, Oxbow), 122–44.

14

Migration and Ethnic Dynamics in the Lower Rhine Frontier Zone of the Expanding Roman Empire (60 BC–AD 20): A Historical-Anthropological Perspective

NICO ROYMANS AND DIEDERICK HABERMEHL

Studying group migration in the tribal frontier of an expanding empire

PREHISTORIC ARCHAEOLOGY HAS made great progress in the past two decades in the study of migration, and the chapters in this volume bear witness to this. After a period of being more or less discredited in scholarship under the impact of the processual research agenda, human mobility has again become a serious factor in the explanation of social change and is increasingly regarded as a study object in itself. This success of prehistoric archaeology is, to a great extent, the result of theoretical and methodological innovations and the contributions of new science-based analyses (isotopic and genetic research).[1] However, for the prehistoric periods we remain confronted with some fundamental problems when investigating migration. Archaeological research and isotopic and ancient DNA studies hardly allow us to draw conclusions on the scale of migratory movements; are we dealing with small-scale reallocations of only a limited number of individuals, or with a case of mass migration? Furthermore, we have hardly any insight into the process of migration due to the low chronological resolution of archaeological data, making it often impossible to distinguish between event-based group migrations and small-scale migrations spread over an extended period of time. Moreover, in the case of group migrations we are missing contextual information on the impact of asymmetrical power structures and major conflicts which may have been the cause, as well as

---

[1] See the excellent overviews of Burmeister (2017), and for genetic studies Krause and Trappe (2019).

Proceedings of the British Academy, **254**, 292–312, © The British Academy 2023.

the effect, of migration movements. Archaeology, certainly for prehistoric periods, should not overestimate its potential for studying the social dynamics of migration. Manuel Fernández-Götz (2019: 182) warns us of 'the temptation to provide quick, big answers to complex questions'.

The problems mentioned above can partly be tackled by using ethnographic and historical analogies when modelling late prehistoric migrations. Of great heuristic value are a series of general classification schemes of different forms of migration related to geographical distance (long-distance versus short-distance reallocations), temporality (seasonal, temporary, and permanent migration), demographic scale and social composition of the group (sex and age profiles), motivations (coerced migration, career migration, population pressure), or to the different phases in migration trajectories (migration as a process) (Tilly 1978; Anthony 1997; Manning 2005: 2; Prien 2005). Human mobility seems to have been a characteristic of every society; the basic issue is not whether migration existed, but what are the forms of migration with which we are dealing.

For north-west Europe, archaeology is in the fortunate position that it can also make use of historical data on group migrations in the transition period between late prehistory and the Early Roman era. This evidence is related to the phase of territorial expansion of the Roman Empire into the Celto-Germanic frontier zone. The earliest written sources inform us about conflict-related group migrations, the size of the moving groups, the temporal framework, the regions of origin and settlement of migrant groups, and the crucial role of asymmetrical power relations between groups. We also observe that in the written sources group migrations are often connected to ethnically defined actors or tribes which have their own name and agency. It is clear that Roman military expansion often triggered processes of human mobility in frontier regions. Moreover, the written evidence provides many examples of the formation of new tribal groups through processes of migration, fusion, and fission, often in the context of a reordering of power relations by the Roman authorities.

We are aware that the scholarly use of historical data for migration studies has been criticised for being based on outdated theoretical assumptions and for making simplistic equations between group mobility, culture, ethnicity, and even language (Alt and Schönfelder 2017; Burmeister 2019: 231; Fernández-Götz 2019: 180–2). However, it is important for archaeology to restart the dialogue with historical research. The starting position for archaeology now fundamentally differs from that of a few decades ago. Equipped with a strongly increased dataset, with new methods and techniques for getting to grips with human mobility, and with renewed theoretical insights originating from the social sciences, archaeology is in a much better position now to contextualise and critically assess written information. It is obvious that the historical sources on group migrations in the Roman frontier have their own problems. They all represent a Roman perspective that is embedded in a broader 'colonialist' narrative (Woolf 2011; Burmeister 2019: 231). The fragmentary, biased, and strongly simplified information tells us little about the social dynamics at local and regional levels. Furthermore, we are poorly informed about the complex social realities behind the use of ethnic labels for migrating groups. However, the written sources invite us to investigate a special category of migration that has received little serious attention so far in archaeology: conflict-induced forced migration.[2] This category seems especially relevant for understanding group mobility on Rome's tribal frontiers in periods of expansion. The key question is whether this category of migration can be tracked in the archaeological record.

We advocate an interdisciplinary historical-anthropological approach for migration studies in the late prehistoric and earliest historic periods in Europe. Its basic characteristics are:

1) Attention to historical contexts
2) Critical use of historical data
3) Integral use of a broad range of archaeological data and methods (including both conventional material culture studies and new science-based methods)
4) Use of concepts and insights from the social sciences

The aim of this chapter is to demonstrate the potential of such an integrated approach. Our contribution focuses on the Late Iron Age/Early Roman transition period, when we can study the complexity of crisis-induced group migrations in the context of Roman military expansion, and where the challenge is to use both historical and archaeological sources.

Migration of groups in the Lower Germanic frontier: the historical evidence

Our study area is the Lower Rhine region, which covers the area on both sides of the Rhine River downstream from Bonn and roughly corresponds to modern-day Belgium, the German Lower Rhineland, and the Netherlands. At the time of Caesar's conquest, both sides of the Rhine were inhabited by tribal groups collectively indicated as *Germani*. In the 50s BC, the region – and in particular the part on the west bank of the Rhine – was confronted with Roman military expansion. According to Caesar's war narrative, the process of conquest developed extremely violently here and sometimes adopted genocidal proportions. The final result was a substantially depopulated landscape marked by trauma and terror – a picture that is being increasingly confirmed through archaeological study of regional habitation trajectories (Roymans 2019). In the decades following Caesar's conquest, Rome consolidated its control over Northern Gaul by suppressing local revolts and by

---

[2] For the concept of forced migration see Driessen (2018).

acting against Germanic warbands that crossed the Rhine. In the second decade BC, the repeated Germanic threat prompted the emperor Augustus to start offensive campaigns against trans-Rhenish tribes with the aim of controlling the wide area between the Rhine and the Elbe Rivers. After the annihilation of three legions in AD 9 and the campaigns of revenge by Germanicus (AD 14–16), Rome ended its offensive acts in *Germania* and withdrew its troops to the Rhine, where a linear network of forts appeared in the mid-1st century AD (for recent overviews see Polak and Kooistra 2013; Burmeister and Rottmann 2015).

In the post-conquest period and during the reign of Augustus we observe a profound change in the tribal map of our study area (Figure 14.1). Old tribal names had disappeared and were replaced by new ones. The dynamics behind this process is strongly determined by the Roman policy of allowing or enforcing friendly or defeated Germanic groups to settle in the underpopulated Lower Rhine border zone. For the period between 60 BC and AD 60, the historical sources describe a series of group migrations that are summarised below (Table 14.1).

We are dealing here with a specific category of migrations for which the following characteristics can be given:

1) They all refer to migrations of tribal groups of substantial size, including women and children.

2) All migrating groups bear ethnic names, but this does not imply that complete ethnic groups were involved. In several cases we are clearly dealing with subgroups that had split off.

3) The migrations should be understood in the specific context of Roman military expansion in the Lower Germanic frontier zone, with Rome being the superior party.

4) All cases of migration are connected with war and crisis. Roman involvement could vary from forced deportation of groups (*Sugambri/Suebi*, *Frisii*) or even mass-enslavement of defeated enemies (*Aduatuci*), to grants of land to pro-Roman allies (*Ubii*, *Batavi*). Requests by Germanic groups for permission to settle in the Lower Rhine frontier zone could also be rejected by Rome, and in several cases ended in a massacre (*Tencteri* and *Usipetes*, *Ampsivarii*).

5) The migrations are to a considerable extent coordinated by tribal leaders (war leaders, kings, senates) on the one side, and imperial agents (the emperor, Roman governors) on the other.

6) The direct motive for groups to migrate is internal conflict (*Batavi*), military pressure by rival Germanic groups (*Suebi*, *Chauci*), and above all Roman military pressure.

7) In most cases we are dealing with reallocations over relatively short distances (less than 400 km). Most migratory moves went to areas inhabited by culturally more or less related (Germanic) groups; this may limit the visibility of the moves in the archaeological record (cf. Anthony 1997: 26).

The political core of Germanic immigrant groups transferred by Rome to the west bank of the Rhine usually consisted of a warband and its leader. Germanic groups which had accepted the authority of Rome were often directly exploited as suppliers of auxiliary troops. These troops consisted of irregular warbands led by native commanders, which participated in Roman military campaigns in

Table 14.1 List of historically documented migrations of tribal (sub)groups in the Lower Germanic frontier

---

57 BC. Mass enslavement and deportation of the **Aduatuci** after Caesar had conquered their oppidum. 53,000 persons were sold to Roman slave traders. Caesar, *BG* 2.33.

56-55 BC. Rhine crossing and settlement of the **Tencteri** and **Usipetes** in the Dutch river area where they were massacred by Caesar's army. The group – including women and children – would have consisted of 430,000 persons (sic!). In the preceding years, both tribes had yielded to the pressure of the Suebian tribes and had given up their homelands. After three years of wandering in Germania they decided to look for a new place in the extreme north of Gaul. Caesar, *BG* 4.4–15.

50–12 BC. Migration of the **Batavi**, a group that had separated from the Chatti, from the east bank of the Rhine (probably northern Hesse) to uninhabited land in the Dutch river delta. Tacitus, *Hist.* 4.12; *Germ.* 29.1.

39–38 or 20/19 BC. Transfer of the **Ubii** to the west bank of the Rhine, organised by Agrippa during his first or second governorship. They were settled on the Gallic bank of the Rhine as a reward for their loyalty. Tacitus, *Germ.* 28; Strabo 4.3.4.

---

8 BC. Transfer of 40,000 defeated **Sugambri** and **Suebi** to the left bank of the Rhine by Tiberius. Where they were settled remains unclear. It is often assumed that smaller peoples, like the Cugerni, Baetasii, and Sunuci, may have been their descendants. Suetonius, *Tiberius* 9; idem, *Augustus* 21.

AD 47. A group of **Frisians** who had been hostile before offered hostages to the Romans and were resettled on lands appointed by the governor Corbulo, probably on the south bank of the Lower Rhine where they are known as Frisiavones. Tacitus, *Annales* 11.19: Pliny, *NH* 4.101. Cf. Polak and Kooistra (2013: 439); Galestin (2007/2008).

AD 55–58. Settlement of a group of pro-Roman **Frisians** under their petty kings Verritus and Malorix on the north bank of the Lower Rhine in lands that had been confiscated by Rome as grazing grounds for the army. The group – including children and older persons – erected houses, sowed fields, and tilled the land. However, the emperor Nero refused to give his consent to this initiative, after which the Frisians were forced to evacuate the land and return to their former home area. Tacitus, *Annales* 13.54.

AD 58. After the departure of the Frisii, the pro-Roman **Ampsivarii**, led by Boiocalus, occupied the confiscated 'empty' land on the north bank of the Lower Rhine that had formerly belonged to the Chamavi, Tubantes, and Usipii. The Ampsivarii had been expelled from their homeland by the Chauci and were looking for new lands under the protection of Rome. However, Rome refused to give permission and treated the Ampsivarii as enemies. The latter moved back to neighbouring tribes, which – fearing Roman punishment – exterminated the fighting men of the Ampsivarii and distributed their young and old as booty. Tacitus, *Annales* 13.55–56.

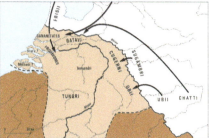

Figure 14.1 Tribal map of the Lower Germanic frontier zone in the conquest (left) and post-conquest period (right), showing considerable discontinuity. Light brown shading: military district and later province of *Germania inferior* (image: Roymans)

Germania.[3] This practice of ethnic recruitment guaranteed an effective control of the indigenous groups by creaming off their military potential, while at the same time strengthening Roman military power.

The reality of migration in the Lower Rhine frontier during the Germanic Wars was no doubt more diverse than the written sources suggest. We focus here on movements of (parts of) ethnic groups, but in the chaos of the Germanic Wars there will also have been more small-scale and individual forms of mobility (fugitives, merchants) which are almost unmentioned in the written sources.

In this contribution we want to focus on the case of the *Batavi*. According to Tacitus, they had broken away from the Germanic *Chatti* after an internal conflict and then moved to the Rhine Delta where they settled in an uninhabited area (*vacua cultoribus*).[4] Their move can be dated in the period between Caesar's departure from Gaul (51 BC) and the year in which Drusus started using the Batavian region as a base for his operations in *Germania* (12 BC). Their reported descent from the *Chatti* points to an origin in the area east of the Rhine in northern Hesse. It is generally assumed that the settlement of the *Batavi* occurred with Roman consent and was based on a formal treaty. This treaty, described by Tacitus as an *antiqua societas*, defined the relationship of the *Batavi* with Rome and specified their obligations as a client tribe.[5] The *Batavi* were intensively exploited by Rome as a breeding ground for auxiliary soldiers.[6] Nothing is said about the demographic

---

[3] Irregular Germanic auxiliary formations or their leaders are known for the *Batavi* under Chariovalda (Tacitus, *Ann.* 2,11), the *Cherusci* under Arminius (*Ann.* 2,10), the *Cananefates* (*Ann.* 4,73) and the *Frisii* (Cassius Dio 54,32). The *Chauci* served in AD 15 and 16 as auxiliaries in Germanicus' army (Tacitus, *Ann.* 1,60,1; 2,17).

[4] Tacitus, *Germ.* 29,1; *Hist.* 4,12.

[5] Tacitus, *Germ.* 29; *Hist.* 4,12; Roymans (2004: Chapter 5).

[6] Tacitus, *Germ.* 29: 'Immune from burdens and contributions, and set apart for fighting purposes only, they [the Batavians] are reserved for war, to be, as it were, arms and weapons'.

size or social composition of the Batavian immigrants, but we may assume that the group consisted of complete households, including women and children. Calculations proceeding from the number of Batavian soldiers in Roman service and the estimated number of rural settlements in their area suggest a population size in the mid-1st century AD between 15,000 and 40,000 persons (Willems 1984; Vossen 2003).

Migration and the archaeological evidence: the case of the *Batavi*

What can archaeology contribute to this historical picture? Archaeology can provide an important contribution by contextualising and evaluating historical information on group migration. Basic questions are: what was the material culture of the immigrants, and can we specify their region of origin? In this section, we want to explore this potential by presenting a case study on the *Batavi* in the Dutch river area. Our project employs a combination of conventional material culture studies and science-based methods and is carried out by a team of specialists. The results of the diverse investigations are briefly presented here.[7] The key evidence comes from recent excavations of a number of rural settlements in the study area.[8] Many sites appear to have been newly founded in the Augustan period. We focused on the earliest phases of settlements, especially so-called first-generation farmsteads. Study of their material culture can help us to identify the region of origin of the settlers.[9] We investigated house architecture, handmade pottery, Early Roman military equipment, Late Iron Age coins, Roman bronze coins from the Augustan period, and isotope signals in the dental material of domestic animals.

We are well informed on house architecture in the Batavian area. Most are longhouses combining a living area and a byre under a single roof. Within this general tradition, specific developments can be reconstructed. While during the later Iron Age a long-standing tradition of rather lightly constructed two-aisled byre houses existed (Figure 14.2 A), significant and rather swift developments in house building can be reconstructed from the transition period between the Late Iron Age and Early Roman period. These entail the introduction of new house types and new building techniques, including the development of hybrid forms. Remarkably, in settlements from the Early Roman period, different house types occur alongside each other.

---

[7] Definitive results will be published in *Germania*.

[8] Wijk bij Duurstede-De Horden, prov. Utrecht (Vos 2009), Tiel-Passewaay, prov. Gelderland (Heeren 2009), Geldermalsen-Hondsgemet, prov. Gelderland (Van Renswoude and Van Kerckhove 2009), Houten-Castellum, prov. Utrecht (Van Renswoude and Habermehl 2017), Tiel-Medel, prov. Gelderland (Habermehl *et al.* 2019).

[9] Cf. also the broader methodological discussion in Burmeister (2000: 559–60).

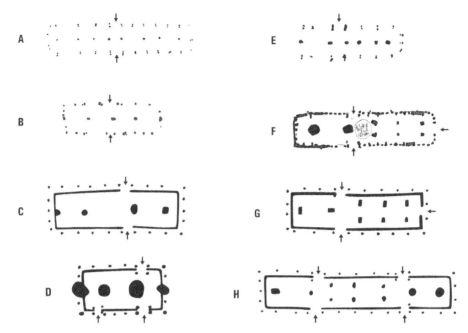

Figure 14.2 Different variants of long houses encountered in the Batavian river area in the Early Roman period. House A is a Late Iron Age type (images: A) after Schinkel 1998: 123–4; B) after Hiddink 2005: 87; E) after Hiddink 2014: 188; F) after Vos 2009: 78; C–D, G–H) after Wesselingh 2000: 18)

More specifically, during the late 1st century BC, new, sturdier houses started being built. These so-called Alphen-Ekeren type houses are characterised by their deeply set central posts (Figure 14.2 B–D). Another new introduction, the combined two- and three-aisled house, is of particular interest here (Figure 14.2 F–H). These often (very) long buildings are unknown from the pre-Roman period and should probably be understood as a hybrid creation, combining elements from the two-aisled and three-aisled house-building traditions associated with the Lower Rhine area and the regions north of the Rhine respectively. Recently, other new house types have been recognised in the Batavian area: so-called wall-ditch houses, (partly) constructed with sods, or houses constructed on platforms. One of the earliest farmsteads in Tiel-Medel-De Reth (prov. Gelderland) should probably be interpreted as such a construction (Figure 14.3). Again, these house types can be associated with the areas north of the Rhine. A specific new element in many houses from the Augustan period onwards is the use of wall ditches, especially in the Alphen-Ekeren type houses and the houses with a combined two- and three-aisled structure (Figure 14.2 C–D, G–H). It remains difficult to definitively interpret the appearance of these wall ditches, but we are possibly dealing here with

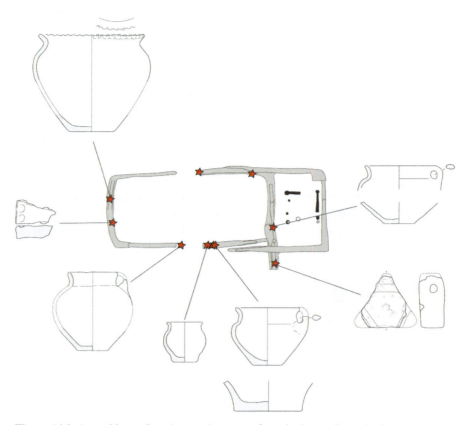

Figure 14.3 Assemblage of northern-style pottery from the house ditch of a first-generation farmhouse at Tiel-Medel (c. 30–1 BC). Several pots appear to be imports from the northern coastal region (after Habermehl *et al.* 2019: 744)

influences from further north or east.[10] Finally, houses in local Late Iron Age style have been found within settlements from the Early Roman period (Figure 14.2 E) (Hiddink 2014: 187–90).[11] These could be understood as indications for a continuation of an existing local or regional tradition.

Overlooking the developments described above, it remains a challenge to interpret these developments in any detail. However, we clearly see the introduction of new forms, the development of hybrid forms, as well as the continued use of pre-existing traditions. Moreover, it can be established that different types of houses

---

[10] In the German Rhineland, the introduction of wall ditches is often associated with (Elbe)-Germanic influences (Heimberg 2002/3).
[11] Examples are known from Tiel-Medel-De Reth, dated to the first decades AD (Habermehl *et al.* 2019: 858–9), and Geldermalsen-Hondsgemet, prov. Gelderland (Van Renswoude and Van Kerckhove 2009: 505, 513).

coexisted within a single settlement. These circumstances clearly illustrate the highly heterogeneous and dynamic nature of the society in this region during this specific period in time. In this light, studies of domestic architecture in polyethnic colonial settings (such as the early colonisation of the Americas) are interesting (Jordan 1985; Burmeister 2017; Maxwell and Oliver 2017). From these studies, it appears that architectural variation can be related to complex social realities and relationships, and should not be explained in simple ethnic terms. Building in a new land may imply different forms of sharing of skills and knowledge, the mediation of traditions, and the formation of new communities (Maxwell and Oliver 2017: 27–8).

Recent excavations of rural settlements have also substantially increased our knowledge of handmade domestic pottery in the Batavian region. Most striking is the remarkable variation in the pottery assemblages. For the Augustan period, a break with pre-existing Late Iron Age pottery traditions can be observed. During this period, new pottery assemblages with previously unknown characteristics emerge within the region. Even within individual settlements there is often a considerable variation in the relative proportions of the various pottery styles. Definitive conclusions cannot be drawn yet, but some main trends can be sketched on the basis of research carried out by Julie van Kerckhove.

Combining stylistic and provenance analysis (including chemical and petrographic analyses), Van Kerckhove arrives at a number of preliminary conclusions. Firstly, in several rural settlements within the Batavian region a pottery style associated with the coastal regions of the northern Netherlands and north-west Germany can be recognised ('ear pots', pots with 'striped band'/*streepband* decoration) (Figure 14.3). Provenance analyses show that part of this pottery was indeed produced in the northern coastal region, while another group of pots in 'northern style' was made in the Batavian region. The biggest pottery group, however, can be traced back to the area east of the Lower Rhine, in particular the Lippe region, on the basis of provenance analysis. Remarkably, part of this pottery is executed in the 'northern style' described above, while another part can be associated with the earliest development of the so-called Rhine-Weser-Germanic pottery style (Meyer 2013a; 2013b; Rasbach 2013). Finally, there is a small group of pottery in the Batavian region that seems to continue the local Late Iron Age stylistic tradition and may point to the presence of remnants of a Late Iron Age population in the area. However, provenance analysis has in some cases shown that these pots were in fact imports from areas east of the Lower Rhine where similar form types were in use. Further research is required here. That the region was not totally deserted between *c.* 50–25 BC is suggested by the coin evidence from the sanctuary at Empel (prov. Noord-Brabant), which covers the entire second half of the 1st century BC (Roymans and Aarts 2005), and by the evidence of house architecture summarised above.

The above results illustrate the complex social dynamics behind the pottery assemblages we encounter within the settlements of the earliest Roman period.

They indicate the presence of newcomers bringing in pottery and continuing their pottery traditions in their new homesteads. Similar to the patterns observed in the study of house building, the heterogeneity of the pottery assemblages within a single settlement points to a heterogeneous origin of first-generation settlers, coming not only from areas east of the Lower Rhine, but also from the northern coastal regions. Also interesting is the temporal development in the earliest pottery assemblages. The heterogeneity of pottery styles is characteristic of the period until *c.* AD 40; over the next 30 years the handmade pottery tradition was gradually replaced by wheel-thrown pottery.

Thanks to a systematic registration of metal detector finds in the past decades, we are well informed about the circulation of small metal objects in the Netherlands. The Dutch river area has produced extensive evidence for Late Iron Age coin use. 'Celtic' coinage was adopted here in the mid-1st century BC with the appearance of gold coins of Scheers 31 type and silver 'rainbow cup' coins of the triquetrum type, both probably minted by (subgroups of) the *Eburones* (Roymans 2004: Chapters 4 and 6; Roymans and Scheers 2012). In the early post-conquest period coin circulation, and probably also production, further intensified with the mass appearance of bronze 'rainbow cup' coins of the Bochum type and silver *quinarii* of Scheers 57 type. Both coinages started as emissions of groups living on the east bank of the Lower Rhine. The dense concentration of Bochum-type coins in the Batavian river area suggests that several variants were minted here between *c.* 40 and 20 BC. It is an attractive hypothesis to connect the shifting distribution pattern of both coinages from the east to the west bank of the Rhine with the historically documented migration of the *Batavi* and the *Ubii* (cf. Roymans 2004: Chapter 6; Heinrichs 2005; Schulze-Forster 2005).

To date, isotopic research of human remains has been of limited importance for the earliest Roman period in the Batavian region, the main problem being the absence of rural cemeteries, probably due to mortuary practices that remain archaeologically elusive. As an alternative, we initiated a programme of strontium isotope analysis of animal remains carried out by Lisette Kootker, in order to gain insights into animal mobility in the Late Iron Age and earliest Roman period. Were all the animals born and raised locally, or were some of them brought in from outside the region? For this pilot study, 31 samples from 31 animals were analysed. The samples are from five different rural settlements in the Dutch river area; 10 are from Late Iron Age contexts (*c.* 150–50 BC) and 21 from Early Roman contexts (later 1st century BC–first decades AD). Of these animals, 21 are identified as cattle, six as sheep/goats, two as pigs, one as a dog, and one as a horse. For nine animals – seven cows and two pigs (*c.* 29 per cent of the assemblage) – the strontium isotope ratios do not correspond with the expected local isotopic signature, suggesting a non-local provenance. Remarkably, eight of these non-local animals are dated to the Late Iron Age, and only one to the Early Roman period.

The interpretation of these first results is challenging, in particular the extreme difference of the ratios between animals with a local and a non-local signature,

2:8 for the Late Iron Age and 20:1 for the Early Roman period respectively. Theoretically, non-local animals may have been brought in by new settlers from outside the region. However, the relatively short life cycle of domestic animals seriously reduces the chance to identify cattle that were brought in by first-generation immigrants. Historical and recent archaeological studies point out that cattle mobility (as attested here for the Late Iron Age) can better be interpreted in alternative ways as related to various forms of gift exchange, tribute payment, raiding, or transhumance practices (Groot *et al.* 2020: 1, 7–9). Accepting such an alternative interpretation would imply a major break in social networks related to animal husbandry between the Late Iron Age and Early Roman period.

A key issue for the Lower Rhine region is the large-scale exploitation of Germanic immigrant groups for the recruitment of auxiliaries for the Roman army. What is the earliest archaeological evidence for auxiliary service? The first material category to discuss in this context are Roman *militaria*. Nicolay (2007) has shown that every excavated rural settlement in the Batavian area has produced bronze fragments of Early Roman military equipment (Table 14.2), probably related to returning soldiers or veterans, e.g. fragments of helmets, of *gladii* or *gladius* scabbards, of shields, of plate armour, and of buckles and fittings of military belts. Most of this material cannot be dated more narrowly than '1st century AD'; however, this does not mean that military service started relatively late in this region. We have to take into account that iron objects, like spearheads and swords, are heavily underrepresented in the archaeological record. The most plausible interpretation is that the earliest generation of Batavian auxiliary soldiers served in irregular warbands which still used their traditional equipment. In the course of the early 1st century AD this native-style equipment was gradually replaced by Roman-style equipment, which included many more bronze elements, thus increasing their archaeological visibility.

The question of the start of Batavian auxiliary service can also be addressed by studying the earliest influx of Roman coinage into the Batavian area. Silver coins are unsuitable for this, since we know that Republican and Augustan *denarii* remained in circulation during the entire 1st century AD. More suitable as a chronological marker are the Augustan bronze issues, especially the so-called Nemausus I coins struck by Augustus in the colony at Nîmes, probably between 16 and 10 BC. The Nemausus I coins were widely used in the Rhineland for the payment of soldiers during the Germanic campaigns of Drusus (12–9 BC), as appears from their dominant proportion in the coin assemblages of the camps of the 'Oberaden Horizon'. However, Nemausus bronzes had almost disappeared in the camps of the 'Haltern Horizon' of the later Augustan period (Van Heesch 1998: 57, 64; Kemmers 2005: 28–30). Given this chronological framework, it is significant that Nemausus coins are surprisingly well represented in rural contexts in the Dutch Lower Rhine region, with some 45 sites (Figure 14.4). The most plausible interpretation is that the coins reflect payments to members of irregular Batavian units that participated in Drusus' campaigns. The numismatic evidence confirms the intensive military exploitation of the *Batavi* by

Table 14.2 Overview of metal parts of 1st-century AD Roman military equipment and horse gear from (partially) excavated rural settlements in the Batavian river area (after Nicolay 2007: 194, Table 5.4, with additions)

	Helmet	Armour	Shield	Sword	Sword belt	Horse gear
Houten-Hofstad, Diepriool	>4	2	-	-	1	-
Oosterhout-Van Boetzelaerstraat	2	1	-	2	3	40
Tiel-Passewaaijse Hogeweg	1	1	-	1	3	39
Tiel-Oude Tielseweg	1	-	-	-	1	9
Geldermalsen-Hondsgemet	-	4	-	-	2	5
Beneden Leeuwen-De Ret	-	3	2	1	2	11
Wijk bij Duurstede-De Horden	-	2	-	1	9	44
Kesteren-De Woerd	-	2	-	1	3	17
Wijk bij Duurstede-De Geer	-	1	-	-	-	7
Wijchen-Tienakker	-	1	1	-	1	7
Houten-Castellum	-	1	-	2	2	11
Tiel-Medel, Hazenkamp/ De Reth	-	3	1	2	-	32
Houten-Zuid 8A	-	-	1	-	1	2
Utrecht-Terweide	-	-	2	2	1	13
Arnhem-De Laar 6/7	-	-	-	1	1	9
Tiel-Medel, Rotonde	-	-	-	1	-	10
Lent-Dijkterugelegging	-	-	-	1	1	1
Lent-Steltsestraat	-	-	-	1?	-	12
Geldermalsen-Rijs en Ooyen	-	-	-	-	1	13
Groesbeek-Klein Amerika	-	-	-	-	1	18
Oss-Westerveld	-	-	-	-	1	4
Arnhem-De Laar 4	-	-	-	-	-	8

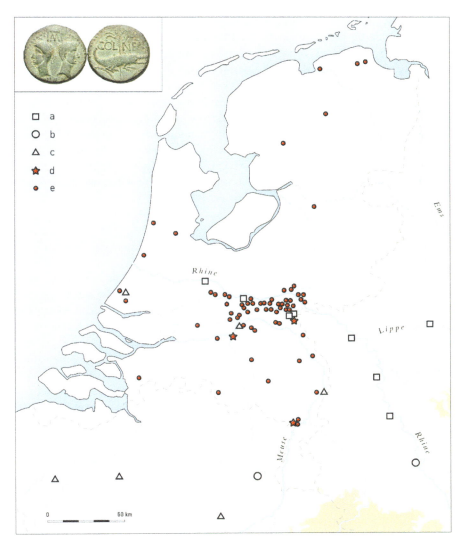

Figure 14.4 Distribution of bronze Nemausus I coins, widely used by the Roman army for payment of soldiers during the Germanic campaigns of Drusus (12–9 BC). Only the coins from the Netherlands have been systematically mapped: a = Roman army camp; b = urban settlement; c = nucleated settlement; d = (probable) native cult site; e = (probable) rural settlement (image: Roymans)

Rome from at least the middle-Augustan period onwards. Older coinages – though in smaller numbers – are also present in the Batavian countryside, in particular so-called Vienna/Copia bronzes and Gallic silver *quinarii* of Central-East Gaul, which may reflect payments by the Roman army in the early Augustan period.[12]

---

[12] The first author is working on a full publication of this early numismatic material from the second half of the 1st century BC. Finds of Republican *denarii* are less relevant in this context since their circulation continued into the first centuries AD, thus seriously reducing their role as a chronological marker.

It is difficult to overestimate the great social and cultural impact of large-scale military service by Batavians in the Roman army in this early period. Firstly, it introduced a form of cyclical return migration among adult males, based on part-time army service during the campaigning season followed by a return to their farmsteads until the start of the next year's cycle. Secondly, the monetary payments to the soldiers enabled them to buy and take home a wide range of objects from the Roman military market, like cups of Italian *terra sigillata*, new types of bronze fibulae, and (somewhat later) pieces of Roman military equipment (Roymans 2009). These first imports marked the start of a process of profound transformation of the material culture of the Batavian rural community in the 1st century AD. Thirdly, military service triggered and cultivated a new self-consciousness and shared identity of the *Batavi* as a soldier people.

The formation of a Batavian identity group

It is generally accepted that group migration involves intensive social, economic, political, and cultural changes. Important are the relations between the diverse groups of newcomers, and between newcomers and descendants of the original inhabitants. The archaeological evidence shows that the *Batavi* started as a heterogeneous ensemble of groups of diverse origin, be it with a more or less related material culture and also value system, as indicated by a common tradition of building byre houses and the prominent societal role of cattle husbandry (Roymans 1996). However, in the course of the 1st century AD, the *Batavi* underwent a process of increasing internal integration, culminating in a community with a strong sense of shared ethnic identity. Crucial for this process was the interaction between the *Batavi* and Rome, characterised by a highly asymmetrical, colonialist power relation aimed at optimal control and exploitation of the Batavian polity. Historical and epigraphic evidence (see below) shows us that it was through interaction with the Roman Empire and above all the Roman army that Batavian ethnicity was moulded. It was not only propagated by the *Batavi* themselves, but also consciously cultivated by the Roman authorities by assigning ethnic labels to the cohorts and having them operate in closed ethnic units led by their own commanders.[13]

The earliest Batavian society can be conceptualised as a polyethnic colonial melting pot characterised by processes of hybridisation and adaptation to the new social and political reality. In this context we should not underestimate the role of return migration of soldiers and veterans. They cultivated the identity of the *Batavi*

---

[13] Roymans (2004: 221–34). See also the classic anthropological study by Ferguson and Whitehead (2000) on the impact of ethnic recruiting on the ethnogenesis of groups on tribal frontiers of states and empires.

MIGRATION AND ETHNIC DYNAMICS 307

as a soldier people and were the driving force behind a rapid diffusion of the Latin language and the creative appropriation of new forms of material culture, ideas, and values. In the public or outside sphere, Batavian rural groups increasingly emphasised their shared identity within the context of the Roman Empire. There is no trend towards the formation of spatially segregated sub-communities. It is only in the private domestic sphere of individual farmhouses that we observe some continuity of traditions in handmade pottery and house architecture.[14]

The above model of the Batavian ethnogenesis starting from a polyethnic background and leading within a few decades to a community with a strong sense of collective identity is confirmed by the epigraphic data on the self-identification of *c.* 60 individuals coming from the Batavian region. According to the epigraphic evidence, this process of ethnogenesis was more or less completed around the mid-1st century AD. From this period onwards we have a rich assemblage of inscriptions (Table 14.3) in which Batavian individuals identify themselves with the tribal affiliation *Batavus* and above all *natione Batavus* (=Batavian by birth). The archaeological evidence, however, suggests that in the late 1st century BC such a notion of common ethnic belonging did not exist yet among the subgroups coming from the North Sea coastal region and the local Late Iron Age residual population.

Table 14.3 Specification of origin in inscriptions by Batavian individuals (after Derks 2009: Table 1). The number of people who possessed Roman citizenship (judging by their name) is given in brackets. IA=first half 1st century; IB=second half 1st century; II=2nd century; III=3rd century

	I A	I B	II	III	Totals
Natione Batavus	1 (0)	11 (1)	8 (7)	9 (9)	29 (17)
Domo Batavus		3 (0)	10 (5)		3 (0)
Batavus		3 (0)			13 (5)
Natione Batavus Ulpia Noviomago			3 (3)		3 (3)
Ulpia Noviomagi Batavus			1 (1)		1 (1)
Ulpia Noviomagi Batavorum			1 (1)	1 (1)	1 (1)
Ulpia Noviomago			6 (6)	3 (3)	7 (7)
Noviomago					3 (3)
Civis Batavus				2 (2?)	2 (2)
Totals	1 (0)	17 (1)	29 (23)	15 (15)	62 (39)

[14] On the distinction between a public and private sphere of the world of immigrant groups see Burmeister (2017: 61).

Conclusions

What are the new insights presented in this chapter on tribal migrations in the Late Iron Age/Early Roman transition period? We want to mention three, partly overlapping, points. Firstly, this chapter shows the potential of a historical-anthropological approach to migration, based on the use of a broad range of methods and data about first-generation migrants in the northern frontier zone of the Roman Empire. The integrated use of historical and archaeological evidence gives us a more balanced and nuanced picture of migration processes of groups. The written sources allow us to place the archaeological data in the context of the dramatic military confrontation of the Roman Empire with Germanic groups that had a huge impact on the situation in the Lower Rhine region for almost a century. The written sources also inform us about the role of imperial agency in understanding major population movements. Archaeological data from the Dutch river area confirm the historical picture of a substantial influx of immigrant groups from the east bank of the Rhine River in the later 1st century BC. However, archaeology also shows that the origins of the new settlers were more heterogeneous than the historical sources suggest, and it informs us about the complex social dynamics in the newly formed indigenous communities.

Secondly, the Batavian case study shows that tribal groups – certainly in a context of migration and conflict – can be of a more heterogeneous composition than the single ethnic name suggests. The *Batavi* started in the post-Caesarian frontier as a fusion of groups of different origin under the supervision of Rome. The traditional picture of a simple move by a culturally more or less homogeneous group to an empty land is replaced by a picture of a gradual ethnogenesis of a group from a complex, polyethnic background (Figure 14.5). Archaeology is able to analyse this social transformation on a local and regional scale during a longer period of time. This phenomenon of newly formed polyethnic groups in a context of war, societal stress, and highly asymmetric power relations confronts us with an extreme variant of 'creolised' societies which has received little scholarly attention until now.

Thirdly, military exploitation of immigrant groups by the Roman army generated new types of migration. The season-based, irregular auxiliary formations of the earliest period introduced a pattern of cyclical return migration, comparable with the movements of seasonal labourers in modern periods (Tilly 1978; Anthony 1997: 26). The later regular auxiliary units corresponded with a migration for a much longer period of time, but here, too, we see a considerable component of return migration of veterans who brought back new ideas, knowledge, and material culture. This impact of veterans as return migrants and transcultural mediators can be investigated archaeologically.

Finally, the evidence from the Lower Rhine frontier draws our attention to the much-understudied category of conflict-induced group migrations in the past. This category is evidently important when Rome started manifesting itself as a new superpower in the tribal zone of north-west Europe. But hierarchical power relations and conflicts between tribal polities already existed here long before Rome appeared

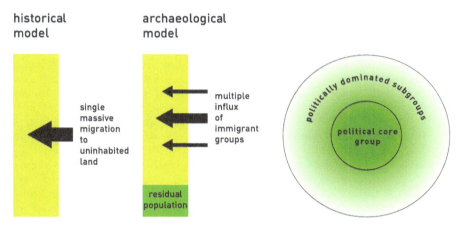

Figure 14.5 Model of the formation of the *Batavi* in the Lower Rhine frontier zone according to historical data (left) and archaeological evidence (centre). Internal political structure of the Batavian client tribe in the Augustan period (right) (image: Roymans)

on the scene (Roymans and Fernández-Götz 2018). We can point to the period of Celtic migrations of the 4th and 3rd centuries BC, and to the wanderings of the *Cimbri* and *Teutones* who experienced military confrontations with northern groups well before they met Roman armies in the late 2nd century BC (Luginbühl 2014). This is consistent with the conceptualisation of tribal societies as flexible political constructs integrated and kept together by power relations. Overpopulation, ecological crisis, or military threat from rival groups may have motivated (sub)groups to leave their homeland and to look for new living areas, but such moves by larger groups inevitably generated tensions and often violent confrontations with other groups. In most cases hard military power directly or indirectly played a decisive role in rearrangements of the social order.[15]

Acknowledgements

This research is part of the project 'Tiel-Medel as a Key Site for Innovative Research into Migration and Ethnogenesis in the Roman Frontier' that is funded by the Netherlands Organisation for Scientific Research (NWO). We thank Julie van Kerckhove, Lisette Kootker, Henk van de Velde, and Stijn Heeren for their information and stimulating discussions. Bert Brouwenstijn helped us with the illustrations and Sasja van der Vaart-Verschoof corrected the English text. Furthermore, we want to thank the two anonymous reviewers for their useful comments on an earlier draft of this chapter.

---

[15] Cf. the anthropological perspective of *War in the Tribal Zone*, developed by Ferguson and Whitehead (2000).

References

Alt, K.W. and Schönfelder, M. (2017), 'Keltenwanderungen und Ausbreitung der Latènekultur – Fakt oder Fiktion? Historische und naturwissenschaftliche Konzepte auf dem Prüfstand', in H. Meller, F. Daim, J. Krause, and R. Risch (eds), *Migration und Integration von der Urgeschichte bis zum Mittelalter* (Halle/Saale, Landesamt für Denkmalpflege und Archäologie Sachsen-Anhalt), 169–82.

Anthony, D.W. (1997), 'Prehistoric migration as social process', in J. Chapman and H. Hamerow (eds), *Migrations and Invasions in Archaeological Explanation* (Oxford, Archaeopress), 21–32.

Burmeister, S. (2000), 'Archaeology and migration: approaches to an archaeological proof of migration', *Current Anthropology*, 41(4): 539–67.

Burmeister, S. (2017), 'The archaeology of migration: what can and should it accomplish?', in H. Meller, F. Daim, J. Krause, and R. Risch (eds), *Migration und Integration von der Urgeschichte bis zum Mittelalter* (Halle/Saale, Landesamt für Denkmalpflege und Archäologie Sachsen-Anhalt), 57–68.

Burmeister, S. (2019), 'Archaeological migration research is interdisciplinary or it is nothing', in V.I. Molodin and L.N. Mylnikova (eds), *Mobility and Migration: Concepts, Methods, Results* (Nowosibirsk, IAET SB RAS Publishing), 229–37.

Burmeister, S. and Rottmann, J. (eds) (2015), *Ich Germanicus, Feldherr, Priester, Superstar: Internationale Sonderausstellung vom 20. Juni bis 1. November 2015 in Museum und Park Kalkriese* (Darmstadt, Theiss Verlag).

Derks, T. (2009), 'Ethnic identity in the Roman frontier: the epigraphy of Batavi and other Lower Rhine tribes', in T. Derks and N. Roymans (eds), *Ethnic Constructs in Antiquity: The Role of Power and Tradition* (Amsterdam, Amsterdam University Press), 239–82.

Driessen, J. (2018), 'An archaeology of forced migration: introduction', in J. Driessen (ed), *An Archaeology of Forced Migration: Crisis-Induced Mobility and the Collapse of the 13th c. BCE Eastern Mediterranean* (Louvain-la-Neuve, Presses Universitaires de Louvain), 19–23.

Ferguson, R.B and Whitehead, N.L. (2000), 'The violent edge of empire', in R.B. Ferguson and N.L. Whitehead (eds), *War in the Tribal Zone: Expanding States and Indigenous Warfare* (Santa Fe and Oxford, SAR Press), 1–30.

Fernández-Götz, M. (2019), 'Migrations in Iron Age Europe: a comparative view', in P. Halkon (ed), *The Arras Culture of Eastern Yorkshire: Celebrating the Iron Age* (Oxford, Oxbow), 179–99.

Groot, M., Evans, J., and Albarella, U. (2020), 'Mobility of cattle in the Iron Age and Roman Netherlands', *Journal of Archaeological Science: Reports*, 32: 1–10.

Habermehl, D., van Kampen, J., and Van Renswoude, J. (eds) (2019), *Opgravingen te Tiel-Medel-Hazenkamp en -De Reth: Twee grafvelden uit de Romeinse tijd en nederzettingssporen uit de Late IJzertijd, vroeg-Romeinse tijd en laat-Romeinse tijd* (Amsterdam, VUhbs archeologie).

Heeren, S. (2009), *Romanisering van rurale gemeenschappen in de civitas Batavorum: De casus Tiel-Passewaaij* (Amersfoort, Rijksdienst voor het Cultureel Erfgoed).

Heimberg, U. (2002/3), 'Römische Villen an Rhein und Maas', *Bonner Jahrbücher*, 202/3: 57–148.

Heinrichs, J. (2005), 'Ubische Quinare im Lippegebiet: Ein Modell', in J. Metzler and D. Wigg-Wolf (eds), *Die Kelten und Rom: Neue numismatische Forschungen* (Mainz, Verlag Philipp von Zabern), 183–228.

MIGRATION AND ETHNIC DYNAMICS

Hiddink, H.A. (2005), *Opgravingen op het Rosveld bij Nederweert 1: Landschap en bewoning in de IJzertijd, Romeinse tijd en Middeleeuwen* (Amsterdam, VUhbs archeologie).

Hiddink, H.A. (2014), 'Huisplattegronden uit de late prehistorie in Zuid-Nederland', in A.G. Lange, E.M. Theunissen, J.H.C. Deeben, J. van Doesburg, and J. Bouwmeester (eds), *Huisplattegronden in Nederland: Archeologische sporen van het huis* (Amersfoort, Rijksdienst voor het Cultureel Erfgoed), 169–207.

Jordan, T.G. (1985), *American Log Buildings: An Old World Heritage* (Chapel Hill, University of North Carolina Press).

Kemmers, F. (2005), *Coins for a Legion: An Analysis of the Coin Finds of the Augustan Legionary Fortress and Flavian* canabae legionis *at Nijmegen*, Unpublished PhD thesis (Nijmegen, University of Nijmegen).

Krause, J. and Trappe, T. (2019): *Die Reise unserer Gene: Eine Geschichte über uns und unsere Vorfahrern* (Berlin, Propyläen Verlag).

Luginbühl, T. (2014), 'La "migration des Cimbres et des Teutons": Une histoire sans archéologie?', in C. Gaeng (ed), *Hommage à Jeannot Metzler* (Luxembourg, Centre National de Recherche Archéologique, Luxembourg Musée National d'Histoire et d'Art, Luxembourg Service Régional de l'Archéologie de Lorraine & Landesdenkmalamt des Saarlandes), 343–60.

Manning, P. (2005), *Migration in World History* (New York and London, Routledge).

Maxwell, A.E. and Oliver, J. (2017), 'On decentring ethnicity in buildings research: the settler homestead as assemblage', *Journal of Social Archaeology*, 17(1): 27–48.

Meyer, M. (2013a), 'Frühe "Germanen" in Hessen', *Berichte der Kommission für Archäologische Landesforschung in Hessen*, 12: 57–78.

Meyer, M. (2013b), 'Rhein-Weser-Germanen: Bemerkungen zur Genese und Interpretation', in G. Rasbach (ed), *Westgermanische Bodenfunde: Akten des Kolloquiums anlässlich des 100. Geburtstages von Rafael von Uslar am 5. und 6. Dezember 2008* (Bonn, Habelt), 31–8.

Nicolay, J. (2007), *Armed Batavians: Use and Significance of Weaponry and Horse Gear from Non-Military Contexts in the Rhine Delta (50 BC–AD 450)* (Amsterdam, Amsterdam University Press).

Polak, M. and Kooistra, L. (2013), 'A sustainable frontier? The establishment of the Roman frontier in the Rhine Delta, Part 1: from the end of the Iron Age to the death of Tiberius (*c.* 50 BC–AD 37)', *Jahrbuch des Römisch-Germanischen Zentralmuseums*, 60: 355–457.

Prien, R. (2005), *Archäologie und Migration: Vergleichende Studien zur archäologischen Nachweisbarkeit von Wanderungsbewegungen* (Bonn, Habelt).

Rasbach, G. (2013), 'Der Beginn der rhein-weser-germanischen Kultur: Die handgemachte Keramik aus Waldgirmes', in G. Rasbach (ed), *Westgermanische Bodenfunde: Akten des Kolloquiums anlässlich des 100. Geburtstages von Rafael von Uslar am 5. und 6. Dezember 2008* (Bonn, Habelt), 137–46.

Roymans, N. (1996), 'The sword or the plough. Regional dynamics in the romanisation of Belgic Gaul and the Rhineland area', in N. Roymans (ed), *From the Sword to the Plough. Three Studies on the Earliest Romanisation of Northern Gaul* (Amsterdam, Amsterdam University Press), 9–126.

Roymans, N. (2004), *Ethnic Identity and Imperial Power: The Batavians in the Early Roman Empire* (Amsterdam, Amsterdam University Press).

Roymans, N. (2009), 'Becoming Roman in the Rhineland frontier zone', in O. Dräger (ed), *Kelten am Rhein: Akten des dreizehnten Internationalen Keltologiekongresses, Vol. 1: Ethnizität und Romanisierung* (Mainz, Verlag Philipp von Zabern), 25–46.

Roymans, N. (2019), 'Conquest, mass violence and ethnic stereotyping. Investigating Caesar's actions in the Germanic frontier zone', *Journal of Roman Archaeology*, 32: 439–58.

Roymans, N. and Aarts, J. (2005), 'Coins, soldiers and the Batavian Hercules cult: coin deposition at the sanctuary of Empel in the Lower Rhine region', in C. Haselgrove and D. Wigg-Wolf (eds), *Iron Age Coinage and Ritual Practices* (Mainz, Verlag Philipp von Zabern), 337–59.

Roymans, N. and Fernández-Götz, M. (2018), 'The archaeology of warfare and mass violence in ancient Europe: an introduction', in M. Fernández-Götz and N. Roymans (eds), *Conflict Archaeology: Materialities of Collective Violence from Prehistory to Late Antiquity* (New York and Abingdon, Routledge), 1–10.

Roymans, N. and Scheers, S. (2012), 'Eight gold hoards from the Low Countries: a synthesis', in N. Roymans, G. Creemers, and S. Scheers (eds), *Late Iron Age Gold Hoards from the Low Countries and the Caesarian Conquest of Northern Gaul* (Amsterdam, Amsterdam University Press), 1–46.

Schinkel, K. (1998), 'Unsettled settlement: occupation remains from the Bronze Age and the Iron Age at Oss-Ussen. The 1976–86 excavations', in H. Fokkens (ed), *The Ussen Project: The First Decade of Excavations at Oss* (Leiden, Faculty of Archaeology, University of Leiden), 5–305.

Schulze-Forster, J. (2005), 'Der Dünsberg und die jüngsten keltischen Münzen in Hessen', in J. Metzler and D. Wigg-Wolf (eds), *Die Kelten und Rom: Neue numismatische Forschungen* (Mainz, Verlag Philipp von Zabern), 159–81.

Tilly, C. (1978), 'Migration in modern European history', in W. McNeill and R. Adams (eds), *Human Migration: Patterns and Policies* (Bloomington, American Academy of Arts & Sciences), 48–74.

Van Heesch, J. (1998), *De muntcirculatie tijdens de Romeinse tijd in het noordwesten van Gallia Belgica* (Brussel, Koninklijke Musea voor Kunst en Geschiedenis).

Van Renswoude, J. and Habermehl, D. (eds) (2017), *Opgravingen te Houten-Castellum: Bewoning langs een restgeul in de IJzertijd, Romeinse tijd en Vroege Middeleeuwen* (Amsterdam, VUhbs archeologie).

Van Renswoude, J. and Van Kerckhove, J. (eds) (2009), *Opgravingen in Geldermalsen-Hondsgemet: Een inheemse nederzetting uit de Late IJzertijd en Romeinse tijd* (Amsterdam, VUhbs archeologie).

Vos, W.K. (2009), *Bataafs platteland: Het Romeinse nederzettingslandschap in het Nederlandse Kromme-Rijngebied* (Amersfoort, Rijksdienst voor het Cultureel Erfgoed).

Vossen, I. (2003), 'The possibilities and limitations of demographic calculations in the Batavian area', in T. Grünewald and S. Seibel (eds), *Kontinuität und Diskontinuität: Germania inferior am Beginn und am Ende der römischen Herrschaft* (Berlin and New York, Walter de Gruyter), 414–35.

Wesselingh, D.A. (2000), *Native Neighbours: Local Settlement System and Social Structure in the Roman Period at Oss (The Netherlands)* (Leiden, Faculty of Archaeology, University of Leiden).

Willems, W.J.H. (1984), 'Romans and Batavians: a regional study in the Dutch Eastern River Area II', *Berichten van de Rijksdienst voor het Oudheidkundig Bodemonderzoek*, 34: 39–331.

Woolf, G. (2011), *Tales of the Barbarians: Ethnography and Empire in the Roman West* (Chichester and Malden, Wiley-Blackwell).

15

On the Move:
Relating Past and Present Human Mobility

COURTNEY NIMURA, RACHEL CARTWRIGHT, PHILIPP W.
STOCKHAMMER, AND MANUEL FERNÁNDEZ-GÖTZ

Engaging with the complex

AS REITERATED THROUGHOUT the volume, migration is a complex phenomenon. To some extent, it might appear banal to emphasise this; at the same time, the contributions in this volume demonstrate the importance of being aware of this complexity in order to overcome simplistic interpretations of the past (and present). As demonstrated by the chapters, new approaches and methods are allowing us to radically rethink mobility in the prehistoric past. By integrating archaeological, anthropological, and occasionally also historical evidence, the chapters in this volume comprise one of the first large-scale archaeological reactions to the new lines of evidence deriving from the so-called 'Third Science Revolution' (cf. Kristiansen 2014; 2022), with all the possibilities but also potential pitfalls of the latter (a summary of which is presented in Metzner-Nebelsick, Chapter 10). In this concluding chapter, we will offer some further reflections about how archaeologists can recognise complexity and engage with some of the more 'invisible' aspects of migrations.

The case studies from late prehistoric Eurasia presented in the volume leave no doubt that humans have always been mobile. Even travel to foreign lands in order to stay there for a longer period of time (a more permanent migration) has been part of human existence over the millennia. However, the scales, rhythms, motivations, and characteristics of these migrations can take very different forms. Where bioarchaeological approaches have been applied, they have contributed to identifying previously unimagined scales of mobility, but sometimes also to uncover subtle nuances at a local, even individual level. In Chapter 6, for example, Stöllner and colleagues redefine not only the extent of Bronze Age Andronovan mobility in Central Asia, but also draw a more detailed picture of the nature of

Proceedings of the British Academy, **254**, 313–329, © The British Academy 2023.

this mobility and the activities associated with it. However, while archaeologists are becoming increasingly aware of the importance and scale of migrations in the past, the *act of migrating* itself has not (yet) found much reflection. To some extent, the reason is simple: the subjective experiences of the migrants, their emotions, hopes, and expectations, are usually beyond the reach of archaeologists, particularly when working in prehistoric contexts – many authors in this volume have recognised this shortcoming of our collective thinking. We cannot trace the tears shed when a beloved daughter left forever in order to move to her new partner's home hundreds of kilometres away (a scene which would have taken place in the case study presented by Stockhammer and Massy, Chapter 8); we cannot feel the aches resulting from weeks of walking, the feeling of moss and earth under the feet, the uncertainty of if and when the destination will be reached; but we can also not grasp the excitement and hopes that some migrants would have experienced about their new destinations, the opportunities for new lives lying ahead, or the feeling of relief after moving away from problems in the homeland.

Our scholarly approaches are always from a bird's-eye view, an etic perspective, a look from above on maps and landscapes that prehistoric people would have perceived in different ways than we do. In this sense, we need to acknowledge the 'otherness' of the past, which largely remains a 'foreign country', to use the expression popularised by Lowenthal (1985). Moreover, influenced by functional and structural thoughts, we often reflect on prehistoric migrations looking for the shortest way, the easiest path, the fewest metres of altitude to overcome. But while approaches such as least-cost pathways analysis can have their value, we always should keep in mind that other factors (e.g. of a social or political nature) might sometimes have played an even larger role for prehistoric migrants, as they often also do in present-day migrations. This was arguably the case in Bronze Age Denmark, as Kristiansen (Chapter 5) reminds us, where travellers' routes would have been influenced by the established social and political institutions.

Archaeology, as stated in the introductory chapter, can and should contribute to current debates on migrations (Altschul *et al.* 2020), particularly thanks to its long-term perspective and engagement with the materiality of migratory processes. At the same time, archaeologists can also greatly benefit from engaging with literature from the wider field of migration studies (Martiniello 2013; Brettell and Hollifield 2015). Thus, historically documented migrations can provide some avenues for reflection that hold value, at least inspirationally, for approaching the more distant past. Human mobility over long distances in the present and more recent past leaves no doubt about the diversity of experiences. It often shows illogical action (from the perspective of a 'rational' worldview), as well as experiences of violence, displacement, and danger. Present-day migrations are frequently associated with images of refugee camps, fences, and conflicts, but also with creative solutions, multicultural encounters, and processes of hybridisation.

Migration is work, is practice, is perception, and is a permanent effort of translation – in a verbal, but also a very cultural dimension (Latour 1986; Hofmann and

Stockhammer 2017). We too rarely ask ourselves how migrants communicated with the people they met along the way. There have been hypotheses about the spread of languages in the context of large-scale migrations (Haak *et al.* 2015), but the role of languages and the possibilities and creativity of communication have hardly been discussed so far. Too seldom do we ask about the creative translations of languages, practices, and worldviews along these routes. In many cases, we focus solely on evidence of the potentially violent side of migration (Olalde *et al.* 2019; Schroeder *et al.* 2019), which can easily lead to big, but often misleading, headlines in the media. The dangers of this tendency have rightly been pointed out, particularly in relation to the political misuse of genetic studies (Frieman and Hofmann 2019; Burmeister 2021).

While many of the issues previously raised cannot be answered by this volume, we want to reiterate here our call for a truly interdisciplinary approach. The future of archaeological research into migrations cannot rely solely on the biological sciences in tandem with archaeology; it must also include approaches that have been utilised by other disciplines in studying modern-day migrations. The fields of anthropology, sociology, migration studies, and many of the other social sciences are all important in building an understanding of migrations, both past and present. As Gori and Abar argue in their contribution (Chapter 2), social and natural scientific approaches are perfectly compatible for better understanding past migrations. An example is given in Rebay-Salisbury's Chapter 9, which explores marriage and motherhood through bioarchaeology, as well as in terms of social conventions and traditions. Interdisciplinarity is also highlighted in Metzner-Nebelsick's Chapter 10, which showcases a project that tackled transalpine mobility in the Late Bronze Age Urnfield period. It is clear from some of the chapters in this volume that truly interdisciplinary research on migration is within our reach. As migration is a phenomenon that can be seen from the very beginnings of human existence, it represents an exceedingly important aspect of life. Therefore, the reduction of migrant humans to genes, objects, and practices spread over large geographical distances also risks reducing human existence to a very biological, technical, and structural history. As stated by Burmeister (2016: 57): 'Scientific results alone provide no historical knowledge, but have to be interpreted within the context of cultural studies … Future archaeological migration research will only develop further in conjunction with the natural sciences; but the explanations that have to be given lie mainly in the field of the humanities'.

Some historians have recognised that micro-histories can sometimes inform us about the past in a much more immediate and meaningful way than an abstract, and to some extent fictitious, history built on top of individual stories (Ginzburg 1979; Zemon Davis 1983; Revel 1998; Kroll 2013). Prehistoric research is often still dominated by the verdict that its task, and ultimately also its potential, is structural history and not event history (cf. Brather 2004; Müller-Scheeßel 2011). Such an approach focusing on structural aspects can be very useful and important in order to reconstruct institutions of mobility (patrilocality, transhumance, etc.), but at the same time does not do sufficient justice to the individuals whose large numbers are hidden by terms like 'migrant groups' or 'patrilocal societies'. Doing justice to the remains of prehistoric people and the narration of their histories presents an increasing challenge with the growing corpus of scientific data informing us in much detail about past individual lifeworlds (Hofmann *et al.* in press). We are, of course, aware that micro and macro perspectives are not in opposition to each other, but rather both ends of a continuum. However, our aim should be neither an in-between nor an extreme position. We need to build a bridge, continuously trying to zoom in and out, integrating structural and individual perspectives in order to see the overall historical context and individual biographies. As case studies, the latter often have a very powerful character in the narration of the past.

In our view, it is important to widen our thinking and our narrations of past migrations in a creative way in order to do justice to aspects like emotions, senses, and detours. In Chapter 3, for example, Heyd agrees that some topographical/geographical features such as rivers presented versatile/volatile boundary situations for potential Corded Ware and Bell Beaker migrations, but he also argues that these would have presented a chance for people, cultures, and practices of different backgrounds to meet, mix, and to create something innovative out of it. As we have seen with published aDNA and isotopic studies, mobility in late prehistoric Eurasia was far more common than most archaeologists had acknowledged since 'the retreat from migrationism' (Adams *et al.* 1978) that took place in the decades following World War II. In looking at these episodes of past migration, it is increasingly important to take into account migrations occurring in the modern day in order to better understand motives and outcomes, thoughts and emotions, detours, and pauses of migratory processes. Simultaneously, in gaining a better understanding of past migrations we can also develop further insights into the factors leading to and outcomes of population movements today. When performing this task, we should, however, always be aware of the differences that could have existed between migratory processes occurring in various periods and parts of the world, as well as to varied social classes, as Cicolani and Zamboni remind us in their Chapter 12. This difference refers not only to matters of technology (a good example of which is described in the discussion of Bronze Age mining and metallurgy by Stöllner *et al.*, Chapter 6), push and pull factors, and scale (e.g. the model proposed by Wells, Chapter 11), but also to variations in mentalities and, more broadly, ways of 'being-in-the-world'. Recognising the usefulness of analogies and comparative approaches should not obscure the richness and diversity of human experience across time and space.

Emotivational perspectives

From a psychological perspective, we must recognise the frequency with which emotions underpin fundamental human motivation, including in processes of migration (Eimontaite *et al.* 2016; Beall and Tracy 2017). These 'emotivations' (emotions behind human motivations) may be nearly impossible to grasp as archaeologists, particularly in contexts without written sources, but nevertheless they must be recognised as playing a vital role in people's decision-making. In the study of modern migrations, social research has revealed the complex emotional dimension of migratory processes (Boccagni and Baldassar 2015; Campos-Delgado 2019). In moving forward, we propose that archaeologists attempt to take this into account in their portrayal of the archaeological evidence.

In attempting to relate this dimension within archaeological interpretations, one possible solution is the integration of artists and artworks in publications. This is something that we have tried with the cover image of our book, which shows a young woman leaving behind her home in order to join a caravan that will bring her to her new marriage partner. The artist, Tom Björklund (www.tombjorklund. fi/), created this image in order to illustrate an article in the magazine *Phox Pop* (Freeborn 2018), which reports on new archaeological insights into female mobility in the Early Bronze Age (Knipper *et al.* 2017; see also Stockhammer and Massy, Chapter 8; Rebay-Salisbury, Chapter 9). With their aim to reach a broader audience, such press reports and magazine contributions add emotions to the otherwise very technical style of academic publications. At the same time, they can produce strong narratives. And so, we must ask whether scientific writings or literary narrations do more justice to past actors and their worldviews. Or is the incorporation of both, while drawing on modern examples of migrations, able to create a more holistic and encompassing understanding of past mobility? The integration of scientific information with artistic representations, as well as ethnographic, sociological, and psychological research on migrants, can be used to bridge the past, the present, and the emotions associated with migrations in both – albeit while still being aware of the necessary criticism towards the attempts to recreate scenes of past lives (Röder 2019).

A sense of belonging

For the last decade, archaeologists have become more and more interested in an archaeology of the senses or sensory archaeology (Hamilakis 2011; 2014; 2017; Day 2013). This holds significant potential for the study of migrations. For example, how do immigrants make themselves feel at home within their new setting? Or have they settled in a place because it has some familiar or reassuring aspects? One's senses likely played a significant role in why migrants settled where they did. Perhaps the soil from the new settlement felt or looked very similar to that of the homeland. Not only would the way of working the land be similar, but the level of fertility could then also be a 'known' factor. If after travelling hundreds or thousands of kilometres the landscape started to look similar to home, could this not have been an enticement to settle there? While these obviously are not the only aspects that play a role in migrations, they should be acknowledged for the possibility of their presence in the decision-making process.

In examining historically recorded migrations, we can start to see some of the features that might have enticed people to settle in a certain area. A good example is provided by the Swedish migrations to Minnesota in the 19th and 20th centuries AD (Figure 15.1). Minnesota received the most Swedish immigrants of any state in the United States, over 250,000 out of nearly 1.3 million between 1850 and 1930 (Anderson and Blanck 2001), and undoubtedly, several factors played a key role in this mass migration to the area. The Swedish immigrant Bremer (1853: 313–4) wrote the following on the suitability of Minnesota for 'northern emigrants':

> What a glorious new Scandinavia might not Minnesota become! Here would the Swede find again his clear, romantic lakes, the plains of Scania rich in corn, and the vallies of Norrland; here would the Norwegian find his rapid rivers, his lofty mountains, for I include the Rocky Mountains and Oregon in the new kingdom; and both nations, their hunting-fields and their fisheries. The Danes might here pasture their flocks and herds, and lay out their farms on richer and less misty coasts than those of Denmark.

(Bremer 1853: 314)

From this description and the comparisons with her homeland and the rest of Scandinavia, it is clear that Bremer felt a sense of belonging within the landscape that made up the Minnesota territory (which encompassed the modern states of Minnesota as well as parts of North and South Dakota, and comprised extensive woodlands and thousands of lakes). As one of the first Swedish settlers in this area,

Figure 15.1 Swedish immigrants in Rush City, Minnesota, in 1887 (public domain, Nordiska Museet, Stockholm)

the visual similarities to Scandinavia might have helped her to situate herself within this new landscape.

Later Scandinavian settlers to the Minnesota Territory, while influenced by the similar climate and landscape to their homelands, also felt a communal connection. There are several examples of communities moving from the Old World to the New World and establishing new settlements with a similar social structure, but with greater economic opportunities. Continuing with the example of Swedish migration to Minnesota, there are numerous historical examples of chain migrations from one parish in Sweden to a county in Minnesota, with neighbours from the homeland often continuing to be neighbours in the New World. The parish of Rättvik in Dalarna County (Sweden), saw 85 households move to Isanti County in Minnesota throughout the late 1800s (Ostergren 1979). Furthermore, the other families who had left Rättvik for the New World generally passed through Isanti County before taking up residence in other Dalarna settlements or further west. The communities established throughout Dalarna-based settlements tended to be divided into the same groupings as seen in the homeland down to the parish level (Ostergren 1979).

The example of Scandinavian settlement in Minnesota is just one historically based migration that can be shown to be influenced not only by a similarity in the actual sensory experience of the settlers, but also by a sense of community and belonging (e.g. Geschiere 2009). There are many factors that contribute to the choice to settle in a place following a migration; however, these may not always be as obvious in a prehistoric context. In trying to incorporate an archaeology of the senses into our understanding of migrations, we are not suggesting that we can actually have an empathetic grasp of what migrants were feeling (Hamilakis 2011). Rather, we are proposing that the embodied experience of migrations and how these experiences influenced the identities, perceptions, and overall lives of peoples moving around should be a subject of consideration when looking to population movements in the past and present.

Detours

Detours are an undesirable, often unintended routing that means a longer and usually circuitous route to the destination. While we usually associate detours with delay and waiting, research has demonstrated that detours are an inherent characteristic of migrations. On these detours, the migrants' horizon of experience changes, which again has the potential to shape their future actions (Dogramaci 2017). In modern migrations, we can see that detours and stopovers, whether for a short period of time or several years, unintentional or intentional, are a typical element of the migratory process.

Looking to modern transit migrations from Sub-Saharan Africa to Europe illustrates this point quite clearly. In the journey across Africa to the Mediterranean, migratory itineraries are based on paths already trodden by previous migrants (Alioua 2007), incorporating the same stopover points and similar stages throughout the process. However, as new rules are imposed by the states that they must pass through, alternative pathways are formed in order to circumvent the barriers (Bredeloup and Pliez 2005). Since the 1990s, the Maghreb has seen the establishment of staging posts for newcomers to the area, from which trans-Mediterranean migration is further planned (Alioua 2017). The social relationships that are formed both within these migrant communities and between them and the local population transcend ethnic and national backgrounds, reorganising and gathering people based on shared migratory goals and modes of movement (Alioua and Heller 2013). The interaction of groups at stopover points with local peoples can create new communities, organising their diversity around common social values. The migrants thus fill the gaps within society that the state has left undisturbed and which the local populations negotiate locally (Alioua 2014). However, we need to be careful not to draw a too idealistic picture of these encounters, as they are frequently accompanied by various sorts of social tensions. The migrants themselves are often forced into places and situations that fall short of their initial hopes and expectations when starting their journeys from the homeland.

The lessons learned from modern migrations such as these can be applied to the past when we consider detours and stopovers that might have occurred. One of the key points to take away from the above example is that people will not have always taken a 'least-cost pathway'. There are different variables that determine the path of a migration, not just the terrain. While undoubtedly mountain passes are preferable to going over a mountain, which pass a group chooses to go through will be determined by the social networks of migrants and the availability of resources along the way. As discussed above, the migration of Swedes into the Minnesota Territory also included stopovers, with people from Rättvik parish stopping in Isanti County before going on to permanently settle elsewhere.

In trying to examine similar events in prehistoric migrations, island journeys are likely the easiest in which to see this phenomenon. While taking a straight line across water might be easier and take a shorter amount of time, theoretically, it would be more typical to have stopover points at islands along the way. The Mediterranean provides a prime example of the use of stopping points and purposeful detours within a prehistoric context (Broodbank 2013). The earliest sites on the island of Cyprus illustrate this point. While they had been thought of as sites of colonisation, they are now often understood to be stopping points for seafaring foragers or hunters (Ammerman and Noller 2005; Ammerman et al. 2006). The pre-Neolithic site of Aetokremnos (c. 9500 BC), as well as many other coastal sites in Cyprus show evidence of having been frequented by those who occasionally visited the island by boat in order to travel to the mainland (Ammerman and Noller 2005: 541). Given the intervisibility of many islands in the Eastern Mediterranean, most would likely have been used as 'stepping stones', or short stopover points, in order to reach an end destination (Knapp 2008).

However, even within an island context, this level of connectivity and mobility is not always recognised. When looking at trade in the Late Bronze Age and Early Iron Ages between Cyprus and Sardinia, a direct trade route has often been assumed. However, more recent research points to the existence of a maritime network composed of various nodes that served to connect the Eastern Mediterranean to the Western (Knapp *et al.* 2022). This level of connectivity for trade can be extrapolated out to other forms of mobility and communication. While the use of detours to various stopping points may at first glance seem undesirable, they serve the purpose of allowing an easier journey. This can also apply to terrestrial mobility, and migrations more specifically. While it may not be necessary to take on the same number of supplies as a maritime venture, land journeys also require that supplies and shelter be acquired along the way. In fact, historical sources often cite that communities and individuals established agreements prior to their departure with at least some of the groups they would encounter during their intended migratory routes. Some examples are the cases of 'negotiated migration' compiled by Fichtl (2003) for the Iron Age, including Caesar's quote about the preparations made by the *Helvetii* prior to their departure: 'they determined to collect what they needed for taking the field, to buy up as large a number as they could of draught cattle and carts, to sow as much corn as possible so as to have a sufficient supply thereof on the march, and to establish peace and amity with the nearest communities' (Caesar, *BG* 1,3,1–2). That agreements between distant communities also existed in purely prehistoric contexts is suggested by the models proposed by Kristiansen (Chapter 5) and Stockhammer and Massy (Chapter 8).

While it may seem more reliable to use quantitative methods, such as least-cost or shortest-path algorithms, often these do not take into account the social and cultural aspects that migrations in the past almost certainly entailed. The journeys may not have always been straightforward; rather, the paths followed were likely originally established by trade or a group/individual in the explorer phase of migration (cf. Prien's [2005] 'contact/exploration phase', mentioned by Fernández-Götz *et al.*, Chapter 1). Finding a safe harbour or place to camp is not only about climate and terrain, but also the human element. Are you in hostile or friendly, known or unknown territory? Was one mountain pass known to be safer than another? These are aspects of a migration that may not necessarily be visible to archaeologists now, unless sporadic finds or campsites are found, but should still be considered as possibilities in our interpretations of past migrations.

Past and present mobilities

In the previous sections, we discussed aspects of migrations, such as emotions, that are often left ignored, arguing for the human element to be given a greater role in future research. In this section, we want to add some thoughts on what can connect the study of past and present migrations. This is an increasingly important question for archaeologists working on these themes, as migration is a highly contested political issue in our current world. The public dialogue on assumed impacts of present-day human mobilities – especially migrations into Europe and the United States – is dominated by the idea that such dimensions and scales of human mobility are an outcome of modern globalised societies. Archaeology has the capacity to confront this assumption with the insight that migration is a key element of human existence, rather than a particular outcome of modernity (Demoule 1989; Hahn 2015), as archaeologists investigate 'processes in a much longer temporal perspective than any other discipline of human sciences' (Przybyła 2020: 17).

We can begin to think thematically about what the archaeological study of prehistoric migrations and present-day migration studies can contribute to each other. Archaeology has, for a long time, depended on human mobility to form many of our basic understandings. Modern-day humans evolved and migrated out of Africa, and the spread of farming in the Neolithic or the new metal technologies of the Bronze and Iron Ages would have involved the movement of people with this new knowledge. Despite the decline of uncritical diffusionist theory, we still grapple with these processes and our work is intertwined with the discourses of modern migration studies.

Migration is not usually accidental; it is not always by choice (as mentioned by Fernández-Götz *et al.*, Chapter 1 when discussing 'forced migrations'), but it is the result of a decision made by a person or group. In Chapter 1 we introduced some of the 'push' and 'pull' factors for migration that archaeologists have identified (e.g. Anthony 2006), as well as the archaeological evidence that we have (or lack) for these factors. These included opportunistic motivations (promise of wealth, work) or the opposite (threat of war, famine), natural disasters (e.g. the volcanic eruption of Thera in 1600 BC), slavery/indentured servitude, and patrilocal customs. Migration can also be a way of 'escaping' state powers (Scott 2009) or preventing their development (Clastres 1989). Many of these push and pull factors are discussed in the chapters in this volume. Fitzpatrick (Chapter 4), for example, draws attention to the many reasons that could have spurred the Bell Beaker expansion, from primogeniture to population pressure and worsening climatic conditions. Molloy and colleagues (Chapter 7) show that, although mobility between the Po Valley and the Pannonian Plain in the Bronze Age was systematic and long-standing, it was interrupted by crisis-driven factors at two distinct moments in time. In this volume, we recognise that many of these push and pull factors would have been intertwined and migrations were usually not the result of a single cause or desire.

These factors can also be identified in more recent periods, from Ireland's 19th century potato famine to the early 21st century Syrian refugee crisis. Wells' (Chapter 11) use of three different, historically documented migrations ('Celtic' migrations to Italy, Anglo-Saxon to Britain, and Puritan to New England) shows several factors quite succinctly, while also discussing the potential causes for return migrations. The analysis of push and pull factors and their potential consequences can provide a starting point for comparison with modern migration studies.

Identifying the motivations behind migrations is important, but we must equally focus on what happens after embarking. There is much work to be done exploring the social and physical mechanisms for the journeys: what type of transport was used, what was their carrying capacity, and how did people travel safely from one location to another?

We also need to theorise the consequences of migration on the receiving end and its relationship to social change (Van Hear 2010). As McSparron and colleagues (2020: 219) argue, 'Unlike other social sciences, the archaeological discipline has been lacking a theoretical framework to discuss the mechanism of migration'. Did incomers experience discrimination, social exclusion, or inclusion (Kristiansen 2022)? How did migration affect people's former status/class (Van Hear 2014)? We must challenge ourselves to address the social interactions that took place upon arrival. Cohen (2020) summarises these as conflict, cohabitation, and creolisation/hybridisation. For example, the concept of place and the identities attached to it, which were once thought to be static and tended to promote sedentarism, territorial nationalism, and 'authenticity', are now being increasingly understood as fluid and created through performance and repetition (Sheller and Urry 2006). Thus, incoming and outgoing people would undoubtedly change and be changed by them. This social fluidity and heterogeneity is explored in Roymans and Habermehl's Chapter 14 in the context of Roman military expansion, where 'fusion' and 'fission' spurred a change in power relations.

The 'new mobilities paradigm' (Sheller and Urry 2006), which developed out of multidisciplinary work, continues to challenge dominant 'a-mobile', sedentarist theories in social science research. It 'attempts to account for ... the concomitant patterns of concentration that create zones of connectivity, centrality, and empowerment in some cases, and of disconnection, social exclusion, and inaudibility in other cases' (Sheller and Urry 2006: 210). This is a moment when the ideas, theories, and methods presented in this volume have much to offer.

Science and mobilities

Many of the contributions to this volume base their insights on one, or several, more or less recent bioarchaeological approaches that have enabled a novel way of tracing mobility in the past (Figure 15.2). This is not the place to explain again in detail the two most prominent approaches, which are strontium isotope analysis and archaeogenetics. Both methods have their potentials, limitations, and challenges, of which the community of archaeologists has increasingly become aware. Strontium isotope analyses crucially depend on knowledge and variability of bioavailable strontium in the region of study and are only able to inform us about longer periods of absence and/or foreign places of staying during childhood (i.e. until the third molar is finally mineralised at about 17 years of age). It provides us with only a minimal number of non-local individuals, indicating only those who spent their

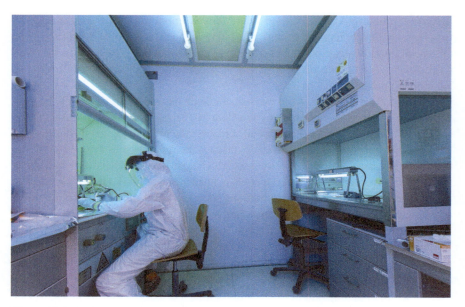

Figure 15.2 Archaeogenetic analysis in the clean room (© Max Planck Institute for Evolutionary Anthropology)

childhood at a place in which strontium isotope signatures differ significantly from the local bioavailable signatures. Thus, most mobilities during adulthood remain unseen. In addition, even in the best case scenario, strontium isotope analyses would generally only identify 'first-generation' migrants, but not their immediate descendants born in the new land. Archaeogenetic approaches have so far enabled us to understand if the genetic signature of an individual can be explained as continuity from previous local signatures or if an individual requires additional, non-local genetic components in order to explain his or her genetic make-up. Again, this method very much depends on the understanding of regional variabilities of genetic signatures within populations and their transformation over time. Moreover, a non-local genetic signature indicates either the foreign origin of the respective individual or that of his/her more or less recent ancestors.

The use of these natural science techniques can be found throughout the contributions to the present volume. In their discussion of the Lech Valley, Stockhammer and Massy (Chapter 8) were able to identify several females of non-local origin, as well as determine the biological relatedness of the people buried in the cemeteries examined in their study. Likewise, Armit's (Chapter 13) ongoing ERC project seeks to integrate isotopic analysis and archaeogenetics with more traditional archaeological approaches in the study of mobility and migration in Bronze and Iron Age Britain. Stöllner and colleagues (Chapter 6), in addition to using these biological approaches, also incorporate archaeometallurgical analyses, investigating the various isotopic signatures found in metal objects in order to determine their potential origins. These and other examples illustrate the importance of an interdisciplinary approach to studying the movement of people and objects in the past.

Current bioarchaeological approaches enable us to trace only a small portion of past mobility, depending on a complex intermixture of variabilities in strontium isotope ratios and population genetics. These methods are likely to be revolutionised in the near future. Just now, another method of tracing human mobility in the past is being developed based on the so-called IBD (Identity By Descent) method. This method depends on the detection of runs of homozygosity in ancient DNA (Ringbauer *et al*. 2020). The potential of this novel method is twofold. First, it enables us to trace in an individual genome if the parents of an individual were already biologically related. Therefore, we are now able to see if an individual was the offspring of, for example, siblings, first, second, or even third cousins. Secondly, this method widens our ability to trace biological relatedness between two individuals. Previous approaches (e.g. lcMLkin software; Lipatov *et al*. 2015) were only able to trace biological relatedness up to the 3rd or 4th degree (cf. Monroy Kuhn *et al*. 2018; Mittnik *et al*. 2019). Now, the novel IBD method allows us to detect biological relatedness up to the 8th to 10th degree. It goes without saying that these degrees of relatedness are usually far beyond the individuals who know each other personally. Moreover, a biological relatedness of, for example, 6th degree can either be a grandparent who lived six generations (and thus probably 100–200 years) in the past, but it can also be the second-degree cousins living at the same time and knowing each other. However, radiocarbon or other dating methods of both related individuals might indicate if the degree of relatedness has a deeper temporal dimension or not.

This novel method is able to create completely new networks of biological relatedness across regions and times, meaning that our ability to interpret first related datasets is still in its infancy. In the future, there will be maps with lines between individuals indicating their relatedness over larger geographical distances. While this is an amazing new development, we should not forget that, even with these enhanced maps, we might not know if the individuals ever knew each other, if their biological relationship was also meaningful and relevant from a cultural point of view, and how related individuals ended up in different places. In line with all previously developed and established bioarchaeological methods, there is the need for a cultural and anthropological correlation and contextualisation. This is now the time to continue and enhance our dialogue with colleagues from different disciplines and areas of specialisation.

Conclusion

While some of the points raised throughout the chapters, and in this conclusion in particular, might provide more questions than answers, we hope that the volume as a whole can help in the ongoing task of refining our understanding of migrations in late prehistoric Eurasia and beyond. As one of the most defining characteristics of the human journey, studying migrations allows us to connect the past with the present, contributing to address some of our most pressing global challenges. Although this, in itself, does not necessarily guarantee the right answers to current and future challenges, looking at the 'deep history' of human mobility at the very least allows us to put debates into perspective, and to counteract simplistic approaches and modern political misuses.

The present volume has been written during the years 2020–21, at a time when lives across the globe were seriously impacted by the dangers and restrictions imposed by the COVID-19 pandemic. This has been a time of severe limitations to our mobility. And while many of us have spent most of this time coming in and out of lockdowns, the fact is that people have continued to migrate, even over very long distances. It might appear as a surprise, but the growth of international migration slowed by only 27 per cent according to the United Nations (www.un.org/en/desa/growth-international-migration-slowed-27-or-2-million-migrants-due-covid-19-says-un). Humans continue to be, very much, *on the move*.

References

Adams, W.Y., Van Gerven, D.P., and Levy, R.S. (1978), 'The retreat from migrationism', *Annual Review of Anthropology*, 7: 483–532.

Alioua, M. (2007), 'Nouveaux et anciens espaces de circulation internationale au Maroc: Les grandes villes Marocaines, relais migratoires émergents de la migration transnationale des Africains subsahariens au Maghreb', *Migrations Sud-Sud*, 119–20: 39–58.

Alioua, M. (2014), 'Transnational migration: the case of Sub-Saharan transmigrants stopping over in Morocco', in F. Düvell, I. Molodikova, and M. Collyer (eds), *Transit Migration in Europe* (Amsterdam, Amsterdam University Press), 79–98.

Alioua, M. (2017), 'Transnational migration is always a migration in stages: the Moroccan stopover of Sub-Saharan migration', in L.-A. Bernes, H. Bousetta, and C. Zickgraf (eds), *Migration in the Western Mediterranean: Space, Mobility and Borders* (London, Routledge), 139–60.

Alioua, M. and Heller, C. (2013), 'Transnational migration, clandestinity, and globalization: Sub-Saharan transmigrants in Morocco', in S. Witzgall, G. Vogl, and S. Kesselring (eds), *New Mobilities Regimes in Art and Social Sciences* (London, Routledge), 175–84.

Altschul, J.H., Kintigh, K.W., Aldenderfer, M., Alonzi, E., Armit, I., *et al.* (2020), 'Opinion: to understand how migrations affect human securities, look to the past', *Proceedings of the National Academy of Sciences of the United States of America*, 117(34): 20342–5.

Ammerman, A. and Noller, J. (2005), 'New light on Aetokremnos', *World Archaeology*, 37: 533–43.

Ammerman, A., Flourentzos, P., McCartney, C., Noller, J., and Sorabji, D. (2006), 'Two new early sites on Cyprus', *Report of the Department of Antiquities, Cyprus*: 1–22.

Anderson, P.J. and Blanck, D. (2001), 'Introduction: being Swedish American in the twin cities', in P.J. Anderson and D. Blanck (eds), *Swedes in the Twin Cities: Immigrant Life and Minnesota's Urban Frontier* (St. Paul, Minnesota Historical Society), 3–13.

Anthony, D.W. (2006), 'Three deadly sins in steppe archaeology: culture, migration and Aryans', in D.L. Peterson, L.M. Popova, and A.T. Smith (eds), *Beyond the Steppe and the Sown: Proceedings of the 2002 University of Chicago Conference on Eurasian Archaeology* (Leiden and Boston, Brill), 40–62.

Beall, A.T. and Tracy, J.L. (2017), 'Emotivational psychology: how distinct emotions facilitate fundamental motives', *Social and Personality Psychology Compass*, 11(2): e12303, DOI: 10.1111/spc3.12303.

Boccagni, P. and Baldassar, L. (2015), 'Emotions on the move: mapping the emergent field of emotion and migration', *Emotion, Space and Society*, 16: 73–80.

Brather, S. (2004), *Ethnische Interpretationen in der frühgeschichtlichen Archäologie: Geschichte, Grundlagen und Alternativen* (Berlin and New York, Walter de Gruyter).

Bredeloup, S. and Pliez, O. (2005), 'Migrations entre les deux rives du Sahara', *Autrepart*, 4(36): 3–20.

Bremer, F. (1853), *The Homes of the New World: Impressions of America, Vol. 2* (New York, Harper & Brothers).

Brettell, C.B. and Hollifield, J.H. (eds) (2015), *Migration Theory: Talking Across Disciplines* (New York and London, Routledge).

Broodbank, C. (2013), *The Making of the Middle Sea: A History of the Mediterranean from the Beginning to the Emergence of the Classical World* (London, Thames & Hudson).

Burmeister, S. (2016), 'Archaeological research on migration as a multidisciplinary challenge', *Medieval Worlds*, 4: 42–64.

Burmeister, S. (2021), 'Does the concept of genetic ancestry reinforce racism? A commentary on the discourse practice of archaeogenetics', *Zeitschrift für Technologiefolgenabschätzung in Theorie und Praxis*, 30(2): 41–6.

Campos-Delgado, A. (2019), 'Emotional geographies of irregular transmigrants' journey', *Migration Studies*, 9(2): 179–95.

Clastres, P. (1989), *Society against the State: Essays in Political Anthropology* (New York, Zone Books).

Cohen, R. (2020), *Migration: The Movement of Humankind from Prehistory to the Present* (London, Welbeck Publishing).

Day, J. (ed) (2013), *Making Senses of the Past: Toward a Sensory Archaeology* (Carbondale, Southern Illinois University Press).

Demoule, J.-P. (1989), 'Trois millions d'années d'immigration', *Le Genre Humain*, 19: 19–37.

Dogramaci, B. (2017), 'Schiffspassagen: Die Kunst der Flucht übers Wasser', in B. Dogramaci and E. Otto (eds), *Passagen des Exils / Passages of Exil* (Munich, Edition Text + Kritik), 334–52.

Eimontaite, I., Nicolle, A., Schindler, I., and Goel, V. (2016), 'The effect of partner-directed emotion in social exchange decision-making', in C. Corradi-Dell'Acqua, L. Koban, S. Leiberg, and P. Vuilleumier (eds), *What Determines Social Behavior? Investigating the Role of Emotions, Self-Centered Motives, and Social Norms* (Lausanne, Frontiers Media SA), 189–99.

Fichtl, S. (2003), 'Cité et territoire celtique à travers l'exemple du Belgium', *Archivo Español de Arqueología*, 76: 97–110.

Freeborn, A. (2018), 'Queens of the Stone Age', *Phox Pop Magazine*, 5: 56–61.

Frieman, C.J. and Hofmann, D. (2019), 'Present pasts in the archaeology of genetics, identity, and migration in Europe: a critical essay', *World Archaeology*, 51(4): 528–45.

Geschiere, P. (2009), *Perils of Belonging: Autochthony, Citizenship, and Exclusion in Africa and Europe* (Chicago, University of Chicago Press).

Ginzburg, C. (1979), *Der Käse und die Würmer: Die Welt eines Müllers um 1600* (Frankfurt, Syndikat).

Haak, W., Lazaridis, I., Patterson, N., Rohland, N., Mallick, S., *et al.* (2015), 'Massive migration from the steppe was a source for Indo-European languages in Europe', *Nature*, 522: 207–11.

Hahn, H.-P. (2015), 'Migration, Mobilität und kultureller Wandel als Grundlage menschlicher Gesellschaften', in T. Otten, J. Kunow, M.M. Rind, and M. Trier (eds), *Revolution Jungsteinzeit: Archäologische Landesausstellung Nordrhein-Westfalen* (Darmstadt, Theiss Verlag), 103–9.

Hamilakis, Y. (2011). 'Archaeologies of the senses', in T. Insoll (ed), *The Oxford Handbook of the Archaeology of Ritual and Religion* (Oxford, Oxford University Press), DOI: 10.1093/oxfordhb/9780199232444.013.0016.

Hamilakis, Y. (2014), *Archaeology and the Senses: Human Experience, Memory, and Affect* (Cambridge, Cambridge University Press).

Hamilakis, Y. (2017), 'Sensorial assemblages: affect, memory and temporality in assemblage thinking', *Cambridge Archaeological Journal*, 27(1): 169–82.

Hofmann, K. and Stockhammer, P.W. (2017), 'Materialisierte Übersetzungen in der Prähistorie', *Saeculum. Jahrbuch für Universalgeschichte*, 67(1): 45–66.

Hofmann, K., Sanchez-Stockhammer, C., and Stockhammer, P.W. (in press), 'Sollen wir den Knochen einen Namen geben? (De-)Personalisierung und Objektifizierung prähistorischer Menschen', in M. Renger, S. M. Rotermund, S. Schreiber, and A. Veling (eds) *Theorie | Archäologie | Reflexion: Kontroversen und Ansätze im deutschsprachigen Diskurs* (Berlin, H-Soz-Kult).

Knapp, A.B. (2008), *Prehistoric and Protohistoric Cyprus: Identity, Insularity, and Connectivity* (Oxford, Oxford University Press).

Knapp, A.B., Russell, A., and Van Dommelen, P. (2022), 'Cyprus, Sardinia and Sicily: a maritime perspective on interaction, connectivity and imagination in Mediterranean prehistory', *Cambridge Archaeological Journal*, 32(1), 79–97.

Knipper, C., Mittnik, A., Massy, K., Kociumaka, C., Kucukkalipci, I., *et al.* (2017), 'Female exogamy and gene pool diversification at the transition from the Final Neolithic to the Early Bronze Age in Central Europe', *Proceedings of the National Academy of Sciences of the United States of America*, 114(38): 10083–8.

Kristiansen, K. (2014), 'Towards a new paradigm: the Third Science Revolution and its possible consequences in archaeology', *Current Swedish Archaeology*, 22: 11–34.

Kristiansen, K. (2022), 'Towards a new prehistory: re-theorizing genes, culture, and migratory expansions', in M. Daniels (ed), *Homo Migrans: Modeling Mobility and Migration in Human History* (Albany, SUNY Press), 1–33.

Kroll, T. (2013), 'Die Anfänge der *microstoria*', in J. Granda and J. Schreiber (eds), *Perspektiven durch Retrospektiven: Wirtschaftsgeschichtliche Beiträge, Festschrift für Rolf Walter zum 60. Geburtstag* (Köln, Böhlau Verlag), 267–87.

Latour, B. (1986), 'The powers of association', in J. Law (ed), *Power, Action and Belief: A New Sociology of Knowledge?* (London, Routledge and Kegan Paul), 264–80.

Lipatov, M., Sanjeev, K., Patro, R., and Veeramah, K. (2015), 'Maximum likelihood estimation of biological relatedness from low coverage sequencing data', *bioRxiv*: 1–20, DOI: 10.1101/023374.

Lowenthal, D. (1985), *The Past is a Foreign Country* (Cambridge, Cambridge University Press).

Martiniello, M. (2013), 'Comparisons in migration studies', *Comparative Migration Studies*, 1: 7–22.

McSparron, C., Donnelly, C., Murphy, E., and Geber, J. (2020), 'Migration, group agency, and archaeology: a new theoretical model', *International Journal of Historical Archaeology*, 24: 219–32.

Mittnik, A., Massy, K., Knipper, C., Wittenborn, F., Friedrich, R., *et al.* (2019), 'Kinship-based social inequality in Bronze Age Europe', *Science*, 366(6466): 731–4.

Monroy Kuhn, J.M., Jakobsson, M., and Günther, T. (2018), 'Estimating genetic kin relationships in prehistoric populations', *PLoS ONE*, 13(4): e0195491, DOI: 10.1371/ journal.pone.0195491.

Müller-Scheeßel, N. (2011), 'Ereignis- versus Strukturgeschichte: Zum Verhältnis von Archäologie und Geschichtswissenschaft am Beispiel der frühprinzipatszeitlichen Fundplätze Kalkriese und Waldgirmes', in S. Burmeister and N. Müller-Scheeßel (eds), *Fluchtpunkt Geschichte: Archäologie und Geschichtswissenschaft im Dialog* (Münster, Waxmann Verlag), 131–50.

Olalde, I., Mallick, S., Patterson, N., Rohland, N., Villalba-Mouco, V., *et al.* (2019), 'The genomic history of the Iberian Peninsula over the past 8000 years', *Science*, 363(6432): 1230–34.

Ostergren, R. (1979), 'A community transplanted: the formative experience of a Swedish immigrant community in the upper Middle West', *Journal of Historical Geography*, 5(2): 189–212.

Prien, R. (2005), *Archäologie und Migration: Vergleichende Studien zur archäologischen Nachweisbarkeit von Wanderungsbewegungen* (Bonn, Habelt).

Przybyła, M.J. (2020), 'Migration studies in archaeology: building a circumstantial case', in A. Bursche, J. Hines, and A. Zapolska (eds), *The Migration Period between the Oder and the Vistula, Vol. 1* (Leiden and Boston, Brill), 15–64.

Revel, J. (1998), 'Microanalysis and the construction of the social', in J. Revel and L. Hunt (eds), *Histories – French Constructions of the Past: Postwar French Thought 1* (New York, The New Press), 492–502.

Ringbauer, H., Novembre, J., and Steinrücken, M. (2020), 'Human parental related-ness through time: detecting runs of homozygosity in ancient DNA', *bioRxiv*: 1–32, DOI: 10.1101/2020.05.31.126912.

Röder, B. (2019), 'Zweierlei Maß – nicht nur beim Alkohol: Geschlechterklischees bei der Interpretation eisenzeitlicher Prunkgräber', in P. Stockhammer and J. Fries-Knoblach (eds), *In die Töpfe geschaut: Biochemische und kulturgeschichtliche Studien zum früheisenzeitlichen Essen und Trinken* (Leiden, Sidestone Press), 365–87.

Schroeder, H., Margaryan, A., Szmyt, M., Theulot, B., Włodarczak, P., *et al.* (2019), 'Unraveling ancestry, kinship, and violence in a Late Neolithic mass grave', *Proceedings of the National Academy of Sciences of the United States of America*, 116(22): 10705–10.

Scott, J.C. (2009), *The Art of Not Being Governed: An Anarchist History of Upland Southeast Asia* (New Haven, Yale University Press).

Sheller, M. and Urry, J. (2006), 'The new mobilities paradigm', *Environment and Planning A: Economy and Space*, 38(2): 207–26.

Van Hear, N. (2010), 'Theories of migration and social change', *Journal of Ethnic and Migration Studies*, 36(10): 1531–6.

Van Hear, N. (2014), 'Reconsidering migration and class', *International Migration Review*, 48: S100–21, DOI: 10.1111/imre.12139.

Zemon Davis, N. (1983), *The Return of Martin Guerre* (Cambridge, Harvard University).

Index

Page numbers in *italics* indicate figures, those in **bold** indicate tables.

abandoned settlements 243–4, 250, 251
aDNA *see* ancient DNA (aDNA) studies
adolescents 70, 189
agriculture 124, 317–18; Dniester–Dnieper
  River 45; Lech Valley 173
Albania, Yamnaya expansion 43
alliance building, marriage 200
alliance theory 193
Alpine region *see* circum-Alpine region
  mobility
Alps, mobility *see* Urnfield period
Altertunswissenschaften 22
amber transport 234
Amesbury Archer 77, 79, 81
ancient DNA (aDNA) studies 211;
  Anglo-Saxon Britain 239; Bell Beaker
  burials 69–70; Bell Beaker east–west
  dichotomy 50; Bell Beaker family
  groups 71, 74; Corded Ware culture 44;
  distrust of 26; French longitudinal
  studies 81; large-scale movements 24–5;
  migration studies 241–2; population
  replacement studies 55; pre-Scythian
  pastoralists 221; publications of 35–6; 3rd
  Millennium BC migrations 42
Andronovo culture 110–41, *111*, 115n1;
  consequences of 132–4; formation of
  110–11; *see also* Askaraly community;
  Bochum Kazakhstan project; Nurataldy
Anglo-Saxon Chronicle 237–8
Anglo-Saxons, new settlements 244
animals, local *vs* non-local 302–3
Anthony, David 11, 209–10, 235, 243
archaeogenetics *see* genetic analysis
aridisation, Central Asia 114–15
arm rings, Iron Age Po Valley 266–7
artisans, circum-Alpine region mobility 264
Askaraly community 118–19, 121–6, *125*
Augustus (Emperor), Lower Rhine Frontier
  Zone 295, *297*
autochthonism, colonisation *vs* 8

bacterial DNA studies, Lech Valley 182–3
Barsarabi group 220–1

Batavi group 297, 298–303, 305–7, 308, *309*
Battle of the Tollense Valley 95–6, 102
Bavaria: Early Corded Ware culture 48;
  Lech Valley *see* Lech Valley (Augsburg,
  Bavaria)
Beaker peoples: All Over Cord Beakers
  80, 82; Bronze Age Britain 287–8; cord-
  decorated Beaker vessels 44, *45*
Bede 237–9
Bell Beaker network 12, 63–88;
  archaeological history 63–6; arrowheads
  68; Britain, migration to 81; Britain *vs*
  Continent 80–1; burials 68–70, 173–4;
  Early to Middle Bronze Age 175–6; end
  of 184–5; expansion of 322; family groups
  71, 74–7; Lech Valle; burials 173–4;
  migrations 77, 79–83, 240; mobility
  199–200; regions covered 65, *66*; social
  status 67–71
belonging, sense of 317–19
belt plates, Bronze Age 91
biconical urns, Pannonian Plain *156*, 158
bioarchaeological data 7; circum-Alpine
  region mobility 264, 272
biodeterministic models 75
BMAC (Bactria-Margiana-Archaeological
  Complex) 111–12
bone *see* hydroxyapatite isotope studies
Boscome Bowmen 77, *78*, 79, 81
bowls, Pannonian Plain 156, 158, *159*
brides: bride price 97
Bronze Age 97–9; circum-Alpine region
  mobility 263; *see also* marriage
Britain *see* Great Britain (GB)
Bronze Age 89–101; archaeometallurgy 90–1;
  British mobility *see* COMMIOS project;
  career strategies 99–100; Early *see*
  Early Bronze Age; goods and people
  mobility 90–6; Late *see* Late Bronze Age;
  Pannonian Plain (Late Bronze Age); Po
  Valley, late/middle Bronze Age; metal
  working 91–3; Middle *see* Middle Bronze
  Age; Po Valley, late/middle Bronze Age;
  migrations 22, 97–9; strontium isotope

Index

331

studies 93–6; trade and political economy 92, 100–2
bronze-beaked jugs *(Schnabelkannen) 245*
bronze belt plates 266–7
bronze figurative art, Scandinavia 98
bronze pins, Bronze Age Po Valley 152
Budapest, Bell Beaker network 64
Budzhak group 43, 44; *see also* Yamnaya expansion (3100–3050 BC)
Bulgaria, Yamnaya expansion 43
burial rites, Bell Beaker network 63
burials: circum-Alpine region mobility 272; females *see* female burials; Humanejos collective tombs 70–1; Iron Age Britain 285, *285*; males *see* male burials; Scandinavia 98; *see also* cemeteries; graves
Burmeister, Stefan 10, 209, 210

C4 plant consumption 123, *124*
career strategies, Bronze Age 99–100
Carpathian Basin 146; pre-Scythian pastoralists 213–21; *see also* Mezöcsát group tell cultures, trade networks 91; *see also* Pannonian Plain (Late Bronze Age); Po Valley, late/middle Bronze Age;cattle, bone/tooth hydroxyapatite studies 121–2, *122*
cemeteries: Bell Beaker family groups 71; Bell Beaker network 65; Bronze Age Po Valley 149–50, 157; Corded Ware culture 48; Iron Age Po Valley 265; Lech Valley 173; Mezöcsát group *216*; *see also* burials; graves
Central Asia, desert area aridisation 114–15
central Kazakh, east Kazakh *vs* 129, 132
ceramics *see* pottery
chain migration 6, 145, 158, 319
Chatti group 297
Chiavari-type arm-rings 266–7
Childe, V. G. 8, 10
child legitimacy, marriage and 193–4
children: Bell Beaker burials 68–70, *69*, 75–6; foster children 97–9; Lech Valley 180
chronological coverage, COMMIOS project 284–5
Ciempozuellos-style pots 65
Cimmerian migrants 213–14; Danube Bend finds 221
circular plots, migration flows 34
circum-Alpine region mobility 258–79; archaeological setting 259–62; previous studies 263–4; spatial analysis *267*; *see also* Po Valley, Iron Age
climate change, 11, 25–6, 28, 43, 83, 201, 248, 251, 322
coerced migration 145

coinage, Batavi group 303, *305*, 305–6
colonisation: autochthonism *vs* 8; Urnfield period mobility 223
COMMIOS project 280–91; aDNA data integration 281–2; British sites *285*; European sites *283*
community portions: Gaulish migrations (Livy) 249–50, 251; population movement models 243
composite pendants, circum-Alpine region mobility 264
contact/exploration phase, migration 12
copper alloy objects, Iron Age Po Valley 270–1
copper awls, Bell Beaker burials 68, 70
copper imports, Bronze Age 100
cord-decorated Beaker vessels 44, *45*
Corded Ware culture 26, 44–5, *47*, 47–8; emergence (2950–2750 BC) 55; Esperstedt cemeteries 49; grave goods 47, *46*; group mobility 199–200; Lech Valley complex burials 173; Małopolska aDNA study 49; migrations 240; mobility even; (2700.2600 BC) 48–50; single and bounded culture as 31; Yamnaya expansion and 44
Cord Zone Maritime Beaker 80
craftworkers: Iron Age Po Valley 270; migration 243; mobility in Bronze Age 161
cremations: Pannonian Plain 154–5, 157; Urnfield period mobility 222
culture-historical approach 8, 10, 13, 23, 25, 145, 211, 214, 259, 264, 273
cultures, migration and 241, 314–15
Cyprus, migration sites 320–1

daggers *see* knives/daggers
data visualisations 33–4
De Bello Gallico (Julius Caesar) 237
demic flow 145
demographics: Bronze Age migration 99; migration and 10–11
Denmark: Bronze Age archaeometallurgy 90; Bronze Age male migration 95; Bronze Age trade routes *92*; foster children 97; octagonally hilted swords 96
Depopulation: Pannonian Plain 161–2; Roman Empire 294
destinations, migration and 212
detours 319–21
dietary isotope values 121
diffusion, migration *vs* 8, 10
directional migration drivers 144
direct trade 234–5
distance measurement 4
diversity of migration 3–4, 6–8
Dniester–Dnieper River 44–5, 47–8

Index

Early Bronze Age: central Germany 94; marriage and motherhood 195, *196*; mobility 170–88; *see also* Lech Valley (Augsburg, Bavaria); steppe cultures 114

Early Corded Ware culture 48

Early Iron Age, Cyprus migration sites 320–1

Early Neolithic farmers, Corded Ware culture 45

ear pots, Batavi group 301

east Kazakh, central Kazakh *vs* 129, 132

ecological perspective, migration 23–4

economics: Bronze Age 89; Early Bronze Age steppe cultures 114; networks 144

Elbe River, Corded Ware culture 47–8

emotivational perspectives 316–17

Encrusted Pottery traditions, Pannonian Plain 154–5

epigraphic data, Batavi group 307, **307**

establishment phase, migration 12

ethics in research 34

ethnicity concept 264n3

ethnicity, Lower Rhine Frontier Zone migration 295

ethnographic anthropological research, palaeogenetic research *vs* 21

ethnology, Lower Rhine Frontier Zone 293

exogamy 264; patrilocal residences 201

family groups, Bell Beaker network 71, 74–7

family pedigrees, Lech Valley 179, *179*

farming *see* agriculture

female burials; Bell Beaker burials 68, 70, *72*, 75–6; funerary costume, Golasecca culture 262; Lech Valley 176, *177*

female identity, motherhood and marriage 194–5

female migration: Bronze Age 94–5, 150; motivation for 146; Po Valley 150

female mobility; Lech Valley 180, 181, 184; marriage and 189, 198–201

female ornamentation; Bronze Age 91; circum-Alpine region mobility 263

fibulae, Iron Age Po Valley 265, 271

first-generation migrants, Bronze Age Britain 287, 288

flange-hilted swords 96

flint transport 234

forced migration 4; definition 3

foreign dress elements, marriage 200

foreign-type swords, Bronze Age 95–6, 101

foster children 97–9

Frattesina 149–50

Füzesabony-Mezösát group 215

Gaulish migrations (Livy) 244–51; abandoned settlements 250; archaeological evidence 245–6; assessments 250–1; community portions 249–50; isotopic

evidence 246–7; new settlements 250; population 247–8, **248**; reasons 248; textural evidence 244–5

gender: biodeterministic model projection 75; Corded Ware culture 44; inequality 192

gendered migration 189, 198–201

genetic analysis 7, 12, 324–5; advances in 24; Bronze Age Po Valley 160; ethnographic anthropological research *vs* 21; Lech Valley 200; pre-Scythian pastoralists 221; *see also* ancient DNA (aDNA) studies

genetic shifts, archaeological evidence *vs* 281

genome-wide analysis, COMMIOS project 284

geography: COMMIOS project 284–5; migration and 316

geology, Askaraly 119

Germani 294

Germanicus, Lower Rhine Frontier Zone 295

German-Kazakh project 116, 118

Germany, octagonally hilted swords 96

Gildas 237–8

Gimbutas, M. 32, *33*

Global North–South modern migration 25, 28–9

Globular Amphora culture 43; Dniester–Dnieper River 45

Golasecca culture 259, 260–1; clothing 266, *266*; female funerary costume 262; Lepontic language 262; Mediterranean trade 261–2; ornament distribution *267*; transalpine trade role 265–6

grave goods: Bell Beaker network 64, 68; Golasecca culture 264; Maritime Beakers 52, *53*, 54; Pannonian Plain 155; Urnfield period mobility 225, *225*

graves: Askaraly community 126; Gaulish migrations (Livy) 250; Urnfield period mobility 223–4; *see also* burials; cemeteries

great apes 191–2

Great Britain (GB): Bell Beaker network isotope studies 64; Bronze Age migration 287; Iron Age communities 282–3; mobility in *see* COMMIOS project; Neolithic individuals 80; steppe ancestry 83

guest friendship, Bronze Age 98

habitation, Lech Valley 173

Hallstatt culture: burial sites 273n5; ornament distribution *267*

Helvetii (Julius Caesar) 237, 321

herd animals, isotope studies 119

hillforts, Iron Age Britain 282–3

historical data: Lower Rhine Frontier Zone 293–4; migrations 314

hoards, Iron Age Po Valley 265

Index

Holocene migrations 22
homogenous communities, Iron Age Britain 284
homophily 145, 146, 160
horse gear and rein ornaments, Mezőcsát group 217
housing: Andronovo culture 133; Batavi group 298–301, *299*; density in Bronze Age Po Valley 147; Lech Valley 178
Hulín-'Pravčice' 2 cemetery 71
Humanejos collective tombs, social status 70–1
humans; bone/tooth hydroxyapatite studies 122–3; non-human interactions 36
Hungary, Yamnaya expansion 43
hunter-gatherer culture, Corded Ware culture 45
hydroxyapatite isotope studies 119, 122–3

IBD (Identity By Descent) 325
identity, biodeterministic model projection 75
infectious diseases, Lech Valley 182–3
Inn–Isarco–Adige corridor 222–3
intermarriage, Mezőcsát group 217
interregional connectivity, Iron Age Britain 284
invasion 9, 23, 32–3, 142–3, 210, 213–15, 217, 242
Iron Age: British mobility *see* COMMIOS project; horses 215n7; Po Valley *see* Po Valley, Iron Age
iron objects, Batavi group 303, **304**
island journeys 320
isolated populations, Iron Age Britain 284
isotope studies 7, 211, 324–5; advances in 24; Anglo-Saxon Britain 239; Askaraly 118–19; Batavi group cemeteries 302; Bell Beaker groups 64, 74–5, 80; Bronze Age 90; COMMIOS project 282, 285; dietary isotope values 121; Gaulish migrations (Livy) 246–7; hydroxyapatite isotope studies 119, 122–3; Lead Isotope Analysis *see* LIA (Lead Isotope Analysis); Lech Valley 200; nitrogen isotope studies 121, 123, *124*; oxygen isotope analysis 121, 126; strontium isotope studies *see* strontium isotope studies; Urnfield period mobility 222

Julius Caesar 237, 242

kin groups, Bronze Age migration **96**
kinship 14, 22, 71, 77, 79, 81, 83, 90, 94, 98, 148, 181, 189, 191–3, 197, 200, 202, 226, 280
Kleinaitingen 176, 184

knives/daggers: Bell Beaker female burials 70, *72*; Hulín-'Pravčice' 2 cemetery 71; Nurataldy 128, **130**, **131**
Kosovo, Yamnaya expansion 43
Kossinna 8, *9*
Kurgan invasion model 32, *33*

language changes, genetic shifts *vs* 281
language spread, migration and 315
large-scale migrations 10; Bell Beaker network 77, 79–83
Late Bronze Age; Cyprus migration sites 320–1; *see also* Pannonian Plain (Late Bronze Age); Po Valley, late/middle Bronze Age; Urnfield period
late Budzhak group 49
La Tène art 283
Late Neolithic, Lech Valley 173–4
late post-Stog groups 45
Late Urnfield period pottery 217
Lead Isotope Analysis *see* LIA (Lead Isotope Analysis)
least-cost algorithms 321
Lech Valley (Augsburg, Bavaria) 170–88, *172*, 200; geography 171–3; health 182–3; settlement structure 171–3; societal organization 175–6, 178–82; temporal frame 173–5, *174*
Lepontic language, Golasecca culture 262
LIA (Lead Isotope Analysis) 128, **130**, **131**, *131*; Nurataldy 126; tin bronzes 113; Urnfield period mobility 222
Liguria interna (southern Piedmont) 260–1, 262
Linearbandkeramik 35
local migrations 6
local-scale site clusters, Pannonian Plain 154
long-distance migrations 6, 32; Andronovo culture 133
Lower Rhine Frontier Zone (60BC - AD20) 292–312; archaeological evidence 298–303; 305, 6 *see also* Batavi group; documented migrations **296;** geography *297*; group migration 292–8; written sources 308
Lower Rhine region 54

Madrid, Bell Beaker network 66, *67*
male burials: Bell Beaker network 68; Lech Valley 176, 178; lineage emphasis in Bell Beaker culture 76
male migration: Bronze Age 95; Bronze Age Po Valley 150; circum-Alpine region mobility 263; motivation for 146
Maritime Beaker culture 50, 52, 54
maritime economies, Middle Bronze Age 103

334 *Index*

maritime journeys 103
marriage 190–2: age 195; age differences 197; alliance building 200; cultural universal as 192–4; Early Bronze Age cemeteries 195, *196*; female identity 194–5; female mobility 198–201; foreign dress elements 200; group bonds 193; motherhood and 194–5, 197–8; traditional definitions 192–3; wealth and property 195; *see also* brides
Marzabotto *245*
Mastau/Chernogorka burials 116, **117**, *117*, **118**
material culture: Batavi group 306; genetic shifts *vs* 281; mobility markers 142–69; *see also* Pannonian Plain (Late Bronze Age); Po Valley, late/middle Bronze Age
matrilocality 198–9; Iron Age Britain 284
meat consumption, Askaraly studies 123
Mediolanum (Milan) 244
Mediterranean trade: Golasecca culture 261–2; imports paradigm 259–60; Iron Age Po Valley 268
medium-sized groups, Bronze Age migration 101
mega-forts, Western Romania 216
merchants: circum-Alpine region mobility 264; *see also* trade/traders
Mesolithic–Neolithic transition 24
metallurgy (metal working): Andronovo culture 112, 133; Bronze Age 91–3, *92*; Bronze Age Po Valley 150, 152; Central Asia *see* Andronovo culture; Únětice culture 181; metal pendants, circum-Alpine region mobility 264
Mezöcsát group 213–17, *216*, 219
micro-histories 315–16
Middle Bronze Age 103; *see also* Po Valley, late/middle Bronze Age
middle-range theory 10
migrants, travellers *vs* 55–6
migration: Anglo-Saxon Britain 238; chain migration 145; characteristics of 313–14; coerced migration 145; consequences of 323; definition 3; destination and 212; diffusion *vs* 8, 10; diversity of 3–4, 6–8; evidence of 7; factors of *11*; females *see* female migration; forced *see* forced migration; Gauls *see* Gaulish migrations (Livy); gendered migration 189, 198–201; Global North–South modern migration 25, 28–9; Holocene migrations 22; intention of 4; large-scale *see* large-scale migrations; local migrations 6; long-distance *see* long-distance migrations; Lower Rhine Frontier Zone 295;

males *see* male migration; mobility form as 27; mobility *vs* 143, **144**, 212; modern *see* present-day migration; moving boundaries 83; non-uniformity of 4; phases of 12; present day *see* present-day migration; return migration 3; small-scale migrations 10; small-sized migrations 101; short-distance migrations 6; studies of 239–42; systematisation of *6*, 6–7; 3rd Millennium BC migrations 41–62, *42*
migrationism 146, 258, 316
Migration Period (AD 375–568) 55
military service, Batavi group 306, 308
mining: Andronovo culture 112; Central Asia *see* Andronovo culture; Nurataldy 127
Minnesota, Swedish migrations *318*, 318–19
mitochondrial DNA analysis: Bell Beaker burials 76–7; Lech Valley burials 178
mobility 234–5; definition 3, 212; Early Bronze Age 170–88; *see also* Lech Valley (Augsburg, Bavaria); forms of 27; Iron Age Britain 284; Iron Age Po Valley *see* Po Valley, Iron Age; migration *vs* 143, **144**, 212; nature and scope of 235; networks in 144–5; reasons behind 10; science and 323–5
Moravia: Corded Ware culture 47; Hulín-'Pravčice' 2 cemetery 71
Motherhood: age 195; Early Bronze Age cemeteries 195, *196*; female identity 194–5; marriage and 194–5, 197–8
motivation, migration 313–14
movement: migration boundaries 83; population models *see* population movement models
multi-family groups 192
multiple contacts, pre-Scythian pastoralists 219–21

nationalism 8, 24–5, 226, 323
Nazi regime 8, 210
neck collars, Bronze Age 91
neo-evolutionary paradigm 24
Neolithic migrations 22
Netherlands: Early Corded Ware culture 48; Maritime Beaker culture 54
networks: Bronze Age migration 100; Bronze Age Po Valley 160; mobility in 144–5; Pannonian Plain 160; Pannonian Plain collapse 152–3
new bronze bridle types 214–15
New England, Puritan migrations 239–40
NGS (next-generation sequencing) 211
nitrogen isotope studies 121, 123, *124*
NMP (New Mobilisation Paradigm) 27–8

non-local individuals, Urnfield period mobility 224, 225–6
North-West England, Bell Beaker society 80
Nurataldy 126–9, *127*, 132; Sejma-Turbino phenomenon 127–12

Oberottmatrshausen 176, 184
octagonally hilted swords 96
ontological approaches 211–13
open landscapes, Carpathian Basin 216
overpopulation, migration 10–11
oxygen isotope analysis 121, 126

palaeogenetic research *see* genetic analysis
Pannonian Plain (Late Bronze Age) 152–7; material culture 155–7; mortuary 154–5; prevailing model 146–7; settlement 152–4; system collapse 160; *see also* Po Valley, late/middle Bronze Age
pastoral systems, Early Bronze Age steppe cultures 114
patrilocality 198–9; exogamy and 201; Iron Age Britain 284; Lech Valley 178–9
Pécs-Jakabhegy cemetery (Hungary) 219–20
pendants: composite pendants 264; Iron Age Po Valley 265, 271
perceived regionality, Iron Age Britain 284
personal mobility 145–6
phases of migration 12
plague *(Yersinia pestis)* 55; Lech Valley 182–3
Poland, Corded Ware culture 47
political alliances 89
political economy 100–2
political systems, Pannonian Plain 153–4
polygynous groups 192
population: Gaulish migrations (Livy) 247–8, **248**, 251; growth in Bronze Age 99
population movement models 234–57; abandoned settlements 243–4; application 24, 51;*see also* Gaulish migrations (Livy); community portions 243; Iron Age Britain 288; new settlements 244; reasons 242–3; texts, critiques and archaeology 236, *236*
pottery: Batavi group *300*, 301; Bronze Age Po Valley 150, *151*, 157; Ciempozuellos-style pots 65; cord-decorated Beaker vessels 44, *45*; Cord Zone Maritime Beaker 80; Encrusted Pottery traditions 154–5; Late Urnfield period 217; Mezöcsát group imports 217, *218*, 219, *219*; Pannonian Plain 155, *156*; *see also* Bell Beaker network; Corded Ware culture

Po Valley, Iron Age 258–79; bioarchaeological approach 272–3; maps of *261*, 268–9; settlements *270*; spatial approach 264–8; technological approach 269–72; *see also* circum-Alpine region mobility
Po Valley, late/middle Bronze Age 147–52, 260; material culture 150, 152; mortuary 149–50; settlements in 147–9, *148*; 12 century BC 148; *see also* Pannonian Plain (Late Bronze Age)
preferential relationships 145
pre-Scythian pastoralists 213–21
present-day migration 2–3, 319–20, 321–3; Global North–South modern migration 25, 28–9; human securities as 28; misunderstanding of 26–7
processual archaeology 210–11
processual perspectives, migration 23–4
property, marriage 195
provenance analysis, Batavi group 301
pull factors: human mobility 10, *11*; migration 235
Puritans, migration to New England 239–40
push factors: migration 235; mobility 10, 11, *11*

querns, Iron Age Britain 283
quinarii, Batavi group 302

radiocarbon dating 95n2; Bell Beaker culture 54, 65, *67*, 174–5; Bell Beaker East Group 54; Mezöcsát group 216–17; Steppe Bell Beaker culture 52
reallocations, Lower Rhine Frontier Zone migration 295
refugee crisis (2015–16) 28–9
regional forms, Andronovo culture 112
resources: access to 197; lack and migration 10–11
return migration 3–4, 9, 235, 306, 308, 322
Rhône–Saône River system 54
rhythms, migration 313–14
rock art, Scandinavia 90–1, 98
Roman Empire: history of 294–8; Lower Rhine *see* Lower Rhine Frontier Zone (60BC - AD20); *militaria* 5
Romania, Yamnaya expansion 43
rotary technology, Iron Age Britain 283

Sauerbrunn-Boiu swords 150, 152, 156, *156*
Sava River 160
scale adoption 31–2
scale, migration 313–14
Scandinavia, Bronze Age 98
Schnabelkannen (bronze-beaked jugs) *245*
science, mobility and 323–5

336 *Index*

Sejma-Turbino phenomenon 112–13, *113*, 115, 127–12
semi-professional warriors, Bronze Age 101
sense of belonging 317–19
Serbia, Yamnaya expansion 43
settlements: Bronze Age Po Valley 157; density in Pannonian Plain 152, *153*; Gaulish migrations (Livy) 250, 251; Iron Age Po Valley 265; Pannonian Plain 157; population movement models 244
settler communities, Anglo-Saxon Britain 239
sex, biodeterministic model projection 75
shared metalwork, Bronze Age Po Valley 152
short-distance migrations 6
shortest-path algorithms 321; Iron Age Po Valley 268, *269*
Silesia, Corded Ware culture 47
single-handed carinated cups, Pannonian Plain 156
situlae, movement depiction 198, *198*
slim Maritime Beakers 52
small-scale migrations 10
small-sized migrations 101
smiths, Bronze Age trade routes 92–3
social differentiation, Middle Bronze Age 103
social impact, personal mobility 145–6
social institutions, Bronze Age migration 96, **96**
social ordering, genetic shifts *vs* 281
social practices, Early Bronze Age steppe cultures 114
social rankings, Bell Beaker network 67–8
social realities, Nurataldy 132
social science techniques, natural science techniques *vs* 21
social status, Bell Beaker network 67–71
social venues 160–1
socioeconomics, Yamnaya expansion 43
soil fertility 317–18; Lech Valley 171, 173
southern Piedmont *(Liguria interna)* 260–1, 262
south German Tumulus culture 91
Spain: Bell Beaker network 65; steppe ancestry 83
spatial distribution, circum-Alpine region mobility 263
statistical analysis, Iron Age Po Valley 270
Steppe Bell Beaker emergence (2600–2540 BC) 50, *51*, 52, 54
steppe cultures 114; Bell Beaker network 82–3; Corded Ware culture 45; Lech Valley burials 178; Spain 83
Stonehenge (UK) 74–5

striped band decorations, Batavi group *300*, 301
strontium isotope studies 323–4; Askaraly 118–19, *120*; bone/tooth hydroxyapatite 119, 122–3; Bronze Age 93–6; Bronze Age Po Valley cemeteries 149–50; Denmark Bronze Age 94; Gaulish migrations (Livy) 246–7; Lech Valley burials 176, *177*, 178; Pannonian Plain 155; patriarchy and matrilocality 199; Urnfield period mobility 222
stylistic studies: Batavi group 301; circum-Alpine region mobility 263
Sub-Saharan Africa, modern migrations 319–20
Swedish migrations (Minnesota) *318*, 318–19
Switzerland, Bell Beaker network 64
swords: flange-hilted swords 96; foreign-type swords 96–6, 101; Gaulish migrations (Livy) 250; octagonally hilted swords 96; Sauerbrunn-Boiu swords 150, 152, 156, *156*
synoikismos 184
systematic wetland-oriented strategy, Bronze Age Po Valley 147
systematisation of migrations *6*, 6–7

technological development, Andronovo culture 133–4
Terramare 146–50, 152, 154, 158
textiles, Bronze Age 100
texts: Gaulish migrations (Livy) 244–5; Lower Rhine Frontier Zone 293; population movement models 236; Po Valley (Iron Age) mobility 259
3rd Millennium BC migrations 41–62, *42*
Third Science Revolution 2, 10, 146, 211, 213, 313
tin bronzes 112–13
Tisza River (Serbia) 43, 153–4
Tisza Site Group (TSG) 154
topography, migration and 316
trade/traders: Bronze Age *92*, **96**, 97–9, 100–2; Bronze Age migration 100, *101*; *see also* merchants
transition zone, Askaraly community 124–5, *125*
travellers, migrants *vs* 55–6
tribal migrations, Lower Rhine Frontier Zone 295
triggers, Yamnaya expansion 43
Tyroll cemeteries, Urnfield period mobility 223